RENEWALS 458-4574
DATE DUE

METROPOLIS
. . . and BEYOND

HANS BLUMENFELD

METROPOLIS ... and BEYOND

Selected Essays

By
HANS BLUMENFELD

Edited by
Paul D. Spreiregen FAIA

A Wiley-Interscience Publication
JOHN WILEY & SONS
New York • Chichester • Brisbane • Toronto

Copyright © 1979 by John Wiley & Sons, Inc.

All rights reserved. Published simultaneously in Canada.

Reproduction or translation of any part of this work beyond that permitted by Sections 107 or 108 of the 1976 United States Copyright Act without the permission of the copyright owner is unlawful. Requests for permission or further information should be addressed to the Permissions Department, John Wiley & Sons, Inc.

Library of Congress Cataloging in Publication Data

Blumenfeld, Hans.
  Metropolis and beyond.

  "A Wiley-Interscience publication."
  1. Cities and towns—Addresses, essays, lectures.
I. Spreiregen, Paul D.   II. Title.
HT151.B56   301.36'2   78-17955
ISBN 0-471-04281-1

Printed in the United States of America

10 9 8 7 6 5 4 3 2 1

A NOTE FROM THE AUTHOR

When I published my book, *The Modern Metropolis*, in 1967, a friendly reviewer hailed it as my legacy. This well-intentioned remark was, to quote Mark Twain, slightly premature.

To continue to live beyond the biblical threescore years and ten certainly has its rewards. Many heresies that I have been preaching for decades have now become accepted dogma. That is, of course, very comforting to my ego; but it has the drawback that I now feel compelled to combat these new dogmas and myths.

For half a century I have warned against excessive use of the automobile in cities and tried to promote public transportation, in particular rail transit. Now I find it necessary to question the new religion that expects to find salvation by building a few rapid transit lines and regards any urban freeway as a straight road to hell.

For a quarter century I have been critical of low-density suburbs and concerned with the problem of the scale of skyscrapers. Now I have to point out that "high-density low-rise" is not a universal formula for urban living.

I have opposed any form of rigid isolationist planning, be it an "enclosed" neighborhood or a "pure" zone. Now I fear that the newfound enthusiasm for mixing all uses, household types, income groups, and building forms may produce chaos rather than the hoped-for vitality.

The attentive reader will notice that I seem to be bent on burning my idols. While in one place I criticize our treatment of land as a commodity, I subsequently dismiss the now standard formula "land is a resource, not a commodity" as vacuous. While 12 years ago I wrote that "the gods of the sacred soil will not tolerate forever the violation of their laws," in a recent piece I ridicule the "true believers of the sacred soil."

The most significant change, however, occurred in my view of the role of the planner. I have proudly proclaimed myself a universal dilettante and often annoyed my colleagues who strive for recognition as professionals by saying, "there ain't no such animal as a planner; man is a planning animal." I do not retract that statement but I have to admit that while all men (and women) are planners, some are more planners than others. Like any other human ability, the ability to plan is developed by study and practice.

I am less worried by these contradictions than by the repetitions which abound in this volume. This is an unavoidable result of putting together under one cover articles written for different readers at different times. Another consequence is the fact that some of the data are no longer valid. In some cases, but not consistently, they have been brought up to date.

I am entitling this book *Metropolis and Beyond* for two reasons. First, I have become increasingly aware of the close interdependence between the metropolis and the entire ecosphere beyond its boundaries. Second, metropolitan phenomena are spreading far beyond the "metropolitan area," as it has been correctly conceived by the census, into a much vaster region. It is here that the greatest challenge lies.

I have not found it possible to present a list of books that have influenced me. To a greater or lesser extent everything I have read in the 70 years since I taught myself the alphabet has gone into my thinking, starting with those unsurpassed images of archetypal humanity, old fairy tales.

HANS BLUMENFELD

Toronto, Canada
August 1978

A NOTE FROM THE EDITOR

About twenty five years ago I began a conscientious inquiry into the nature of cities. Like many forays into new territory it was not too systematic. In retrospect I know that there is a considerable and even ancient literature of cities that would have helped me, indeed a literature of human settlements, rural and urban. But I did not know that then.

Inevitably I found my way to the work of Hans Blumenfeld, whose illuminating perspective was like multiple beams of sunlight. I searched for more of his work and eventually found my way to the man himself. That was in 1962. I went to visit him in Toronto and experienced firsthand, even in the first hours together, his ability to see large phenomena in incidental minutia, the whole in a detail. That ability is reserved for the keenest thinkers and most penetrating observers and is, I believe, characteristic of a mind capable of the highest intellectual grasp. Never, in the many (and still too few) hours that I have spent with Dr. Blumenfeld have his observations been other than enlightening, lucid, and concise. I have never known him to have to labor a point, in speaking or in writing. His perception is the soul of comprehension.

Not long after I had started collecting his essays an obvious thought occurred. Why had it been necessary to search for his work at all? Why had it not been gathered in a book? I had several contacts in publishing and proposed the idea to Dr. Blumenfeld. He accepted. In 1967 a collection of 33 essays appeared under the title *The Modern Metropolis: Its Origins, Growth, Characteristics, and Planning.* It was published by the MIT Press, and reissued in 1971 as a paperback. More than once I thought another subtitle would be in order: *A Guide for the Perplexed.*

The book was, and continues to be, well received. It is a standard if not major reference. Needless to say, I do not hesitate to recommend it to others whom I find wandering a route that I well remember and that I continue to travel myself. Then, about two years ago, I suggested to Dr. Blumenfeld that we do a second edition, with added essays. I knew that he continued to write and was still quite active as consultant, teacher, and speaker. He was not enthusiastic, explaining that he thought the first book should stand as it was. However, he said he would be interested in doing an entirely new book.

The 33 essays which comprised *The Modern Metropolis* were selected from about 70. I questioned whether there was enough material to warrant a second book. He answered by mailing me assortments of article reprints, carbon copies of drafts, and tear sheets. Before long I had 50 or more new essays. Most of them had been written after those in the first book. Forty-five of them comprise this volume. The magnitude of Dr. Blumenfeld's creative contribution cannot be made more graphic.

Like others who know his work, who love it, and who have been so well informed by it, my outlook will never be able to rest assured. Once, while working on the essays with him over the dining room table, I remarked, with a laugh, "You know, Hans, you have a way of presenting a sequence of arguments that leads your readers down a path until they're confronted squarely with the point you want to get across!" "Yes," he replied, a characteristic twinkle in his eye, "I lead them right into my trap." I suppose his "trap," as he calls it, is the only trap in history which liberates.

As this enriching task comes to a close I am left with the feeling that a treasure has passed through my hands. I hope the reader will find that it has been properly transmitted.

PAUL D. SPREIREGEN, FAIA

Washington, DC
August 1978

CONTENTS

PART I PERSPECTIVE

1. **Settlement Problems in North America**   3
   Habitat, Vol. 19, No. 3/4 Central Mortgage and Housing Corporation (CMHC) Ottowa, Ont., 1976.

2. **The Urban Physical Environment**   9
   Lecture presented at a Gannett Urban Journalism Center Seminar, Northwestern University, Evanston, Ill., March 28, 1968.

3. **Continuity and Change in Urban Form**   16
   Journal of Urban History, Vol. 1, No. 2 (Sage Publications, Inc., Beverly Hills, Calif.), February 1975.

4. **The Old City and the New Metropolis**   26
   Unpublished lecture.

5. **Criteria for Judging the Quality of the Urban Environment**   33
   The Quality of Urban Life, Urban Affairs Review, Vol. 3 Henry J. Schmandt and Warner Bloomberg, Eds. (Sage Publications, Inc., Beverly Hills, Calif.), 1969, and *Contact,* Bulletin of Urban and Environmental Affairs, (Occasional Paper Vol. 6, No. 4/5 No. 14), October 1974.

6. **Europe's Reborn Cities**   53
   By Leo Grebler (Urban Land Institute, Washington, D.C., 1956). A review published by Urban Land Institute, 1956.

7. **Cities to Live in**   57
   By M. V. Posokhin (Novosti Press, Moscow, U.S.S.R., 1974). A review in *Contact* (University of Waterloo), February 1976.

8. **Review of the New York Metropolitan Region Study**   59
   By various authors, 9 vols. and technical supplements (Harvard University Press, Cambridge, Mass., 1959–1960). A review in *Journal of the American Institute of Planners,* February 1961.

9. **Cities of Canada, Vol. 1: Theoretical, Historical and Planning Perspectives**   62
   By George A Nader (Macmillan of Canada, Toronto, Ont., 1975). A review in *Urban Forum,* Vol. 1, No. 3, Fall 1975.

10. **Metropolis and Beyond** 65
    Originally published as "Au delà de la métropole," *Revue Critère,* no. 19 (Société de Publications Critère, Inc., College Ahuntsic) Automne 1977; also in *Papers on Planning and Design,* No. 12 (Department of Urban and Regional Planning, University of Toronto, Toronto, Ont.), July 1977.

PART II RECONSIDERATIONS

11. **Glories and Miseries of a Master Plan** 73
    Architecture Canada (Journal of the Royal Architectural Institute of Canada, Ottowa, Ont.), May 1967.

12. **Canadian Planning Issues** 79
    Report prepared for The United Nations Conference on Human Settlements, Vancouver, Canada, 1976, and published by The Canadian Institute of Planners, Ottawa, Ont., January 1976.

13. **Trend to The Metropolis** 89
    The Canadian Council on Urban and Regional Research, Ottawa, Ont., 1969.

14. **Hamburg and Toronto: A Comparison** 94
    Plan (The Canadian Institute of Planners, Ottawa, Ont.), Vol. 11, No. 1, 1970.

15. **Planning in a Human Way** 110
    Review of Harry Lash, Ministry of State for Urban Affairs (Macmillan, 1976). A review, under the title "The Planner: City Builder or Ombudsman?" in *Contact* (University of Waterloo).

16. **Megalopolis: Fact or Fiction?** 116
    Lambda Alpha (International Fraternity) Yearbook and Roster, 1976.

PART III GOVERNMENT

17. **The Effects of Public Policy on Urban Development** 129
    (Under the title "The Effects of Public Policy on the Future Urban System") *Urban Futures for Central Canada,* University of Toronto Press, Toronto, Ont., 1974

18. **The Role of the Federal Government in Urban Affairs** 139
    The Journal of Liberal Thought (Liberal Federation of Canada Ottawa, Ont.), Spring 1966.

19. **The Impact of Urban Renewal on Family Life** 148
    Lecture presented at the Trendsetter Convention, Panel Conference on Family Life, 1966, and published in *The Canadian Home Economics Journal,* December 1966.

20. **The Role of the Technocrat** 153
    The City: Attacking Modern Myths (University League for Social Reform), edited by Alan Powell, McClelland and Stewart, Toronto, Ont., 1971.

PART IV ECONOMICS

21. Some Vexing Questions in Urban and Regional Economics   159
XXIX World Congress, World Congress of the International Federation for Housing and Planning, Philadelphia, 1968.

22. On Land Taxes and Land Banking   162
Plan, Vol. 14, No. 1 (The Canadian Institute of Planners, Ottawa, Ont.), October 1974.

23. Land Control and Land Prices   169
Lecture presented to The Community Planning Association of Canada, June 1973, and reproduced by The School of Economic Science, University of Toronto, Toronto, Ont., June 1976.

24. Growth Rate Comparisons: The Soviet Union and German Democratic Republic   177
Land Economics (University of Wisconsin, Madison, Wis.), May 1973.

25. Competition Between Urban and Agricultural Land Use   189
Review of Charles Beaubien and Ruth Tabacnik, *Perceptions 4: People and Agricultural Land* (Science Council of Canada, 1977).
A review in *Urban Forum/Collogue Urbain,* Vol. 3, No. 5 [Canadian Council on Urban and Regional Research (CCURR), Ottawa, Ont.], January-February 1978.

PART V HOUSING

26. Good Housing for Everyone?   197
Paper prepared, under the title "Est-ce qu'il est Possible de Loger Convenablement Tout le Monde?" for The Conference of the Canadian Institute of Public Affairs, Montreal, 1968.

27. Swiss Housing Estates, 1940–1950   205
By Julius Maurizio (Verlag für Architektur, Erlenbach-Zurich, 1952).

28. Housing and Employment International Labor Office Geneva, Switzerland, 1948   207
By International Labor Office (Geneva, Switzerland, 1948).

29. Housing of Low-Income Persons in Ontario   209
Report presented to the Ontario Advisory Task Force on Housing Policy Ottowa, Ont., March 7, 1973.

30. Programs in Search of a Policy: Low Income Housing in Canada   227
Review of Michael Dennis and Susan Fish (Hakkert, Toronto, Ont., 1972).
A review, under the title "The Policy C.M.H.C. Never Wanted," in *City Magazine* (Toronto, Ont.), Vol. 1, No. 4, May-June 1975.

31. The Role of Conservation and Rehabilitation in Urban Renewal   231
Report to the Metropolitan Toronto Planning Board, 1963.

32. The Upper Limits of Residential Density   264
Report to the Montreal City Planning Department, January 1968.

33. **Housing Form in the Metropolis** 271
Unpublished essay, December 1977.

PART VI TRANSPORTATION

34. **Transportation** 279
Published as the introduction to a special issue of *Architecture Canada* (Journal of the Royal Architectural Institute of Canada, Ottowa, Ont.), August 1966.

35. **Planning for the City in Motion** 282
Habitat, Vol. X, No. 1, Central Mortgage and Housing Corporation (CMCH) Ottawa, Ont.), 1967.

36. **Environmental Aspects of Transport and Urban Development** 288
Report prepared for the Privy Council of Canada, November 25, 1969.

37. **Myths and Realities of the Urban Transit Problem** 305
Published in "Mass Transit: The Urban Crisis of North America," J. Alex Murray, Ed. *Proceedings of the 17th Annual Seminar,* Canadian-American Seminar, University of Windsor Press, Windsor, Ont., 1975.

38. **Urban Freeways** 311
Canadian Architect, April 1970.

39. **Airports and Cities** 318
Report to the Civil Aviation Division, Department of Transport, Ottowa, Ont., July 1968.

40. **Cities and Transport in Evolution** 332
Report to Urban Transportation Research Branch of the Canadian Surface Transportation Administration as part of Transport Canada's study of the role of the automobile, Montreal, Que., June 1977.

41. **Transportation and Land Use** 353
Discussion paper for the National Capital Transportation Agency Conference, Annapolis, Md., sponsored by the Washington Center for Metropolitan Studies, October 1961.

PART VII PROSPECTS

42. **The Changing Urban Environment of North America** 361
Energy Resources and Development Administration Yearbook, University of Kansas, Lawrence, 1974.

43. **The Future of Canadian Cities** 369
Review of Boyce Richardson (New Press, Toronto, Ont.). A review in *Last Post,* Vol. 3, No. 5, September 1973.

44. **The Social and Economic Implications of the Physical Characteristics of Urban Development**	372
Paper prepared for The United Nations Seminar in Copenhagen, U.N. Committee on Housing, Building, and Planning, May-June 1970.	
45. **The Role of Design**	393
Journal of the American Institute of Planners, September 1967.	
Appendix A The Career of Hans Blumenfeld	401
Appendix B Contents of the Modern Metropolis	404
Appendix C Additional Essays	407
SUBJECT INDEX	411
GEOGRAPHICAL INDEX	419

METROPOLIS
. . . and BEYOND

Part One
Perspective

Chapter 1

SETTLEMENT PROBLEMS IN NORTH AMERICA

THE SPIRIT OF OUR RURAL PAST

The United States and Canada developed during the first two centuries of white settlement as predominantly rural societies.

In the early years of the nineteenth century, the level of living for the mass of the population probably was higher than on other continents. Yet the percentage of the population living in cities was lower than it was in Europe, Latin America, or east Asia, and the size of the largest cities was much smaller. After these early years, however, urbanization proceeded very rapidly, and at present more than three out of four North Americans live in urban or metropolitan areas.

The bulk of the rural population lived not in compact villages or hamlets, but in scattered settlements. And, although only a minority of the present rural population consists of farmers, the isolated and independent farmstead set the pattern. For the European peasant, escaping from feudal fetters, North America was "the land of the free" because the land was free. The immigrant was free to do on and with his land whatever he pleased—to improve or destroy it, to buy and sell and mortgage it. This "fee simple" form of landed property has been enshrined in North American ideology as a "natural" right, as the basis of human freedom and dignity.

Just as the spirit of the pioneer farm has largely dominated the spirit of urban development, so has the form of rural land division generally determined the urban street pattern, which, with few exceptions, was established as an undifferentiated grid. The public contribution to city building was limited almost exclusively to the maintenance of the street system and its gradual improvement by engineering services. What happened beyond the street line was for the owner to decide.

When railroads developed, every city wanted them to come as close to its center as possible; tracks and yards ruthlessly disrupted the street system and occupied the waterfronts. The railroads attracted commercial and industrial enterprises which, in turn, attracted people. The city developed with "mining camp" mentality concentrated on immediate gain, with a ruthless disregard for ultimate consequences. As such, as a place for making a living, the North American city has been, and still is,

---

Source: Habitat [Central Mortgage and Housing Corporation (CMHC), Ottawa, Ont.], Vol. 19, No. 3/4, 1976.

highly attractive. But as a place for living, the city, with its increased noise and pollution, has become increasingly unattractive.

The railroads, however, were seen by some early reformers, such as Robert Gourley in Boston in 1840, as the instrument which would give every urban dweller access to land for a house and garden of his or her own. In fact, railroad companies commissioned landscape architects, such as Frederick Law Olmsted, to design suburbs around their stations. They were designed as places for living. Replacing the grid with curved streets, they attempted to create a "natural" healthy and pleasant environment for their inhabitants. The detached single-family house surrounded by lawns and trees on a quiet residential street, which they provided, has set the standard of aspiration for the typical North American family and for most government actions.

The railroad suburb was generally accessible only to the upper-income groups, but subsequent developments in transportation and communication (electric traction, the bicycle, and the telephone, followed by automobiles, trucks, and buses) enabled an increasing percentage of the population to satisfy its desire for more space in the form of the suburban single-family house. Industrial, commercial, and recreational land uses, accompanying or following the outward spread, also absorbed more extensive areas. The total amount of land absorbed by each urban dweller for all urban purposes is now at least five times as great as it was around 1850.

Thus the North American city has been transformed into a new, much vaster and looser form of settlement, containing "rural" as well as "urban" elements, which the census recognizes as a "metropolitan area." Like the city which preceded it, the metropolitan area is defined as a common labor and common housing market.

THE INCONGRUENCE OF OUR URBAN PRESENT

The political/administrative structure has not been adjusted to this new reality, and still largely perpetuates the forms inherited from our rural past. In Canada, where sovereignty is vested in the Crown, provincial legislation has established various forms of metropolitan government, though their effectiveness is circumscribed by the limited extent of their territories as well as of their powers. In the United States the constitutional right to "local autonomy" has largely frustrated attempts to establish metropolitan governments. This is ironic, because the autonomy does not extend to financial matters. Consequently, municipalities are totally dependent on grants tied to prescribed programs from higher levels of government and have lost the power to determine their own priorities.

In both the United States and Canada the main source of revenue available to municipalities is the real property tax. Thus, while their obligations are proportional to people, their revenues are proportional to property. This has driven them to use their regulatory powers, in particular zoning, to prevent housing for low-income families. Zoning has been the main North American response to the problems created by the impact of the landowner's right to develop his property as he pleases on the value of the properties of his neighbors. It has been, and is, a measure of property protection more than one of planning. The provision of public works, the other major contribution of public authorities to the shaping of settlements, has largely followed private development rather than leading it. In the main, North American cities have been designed by the invisible hand of the market.

This design is not devoid of logic. The regular decrease in density from the center to the periphery, the preponderance of residences for adults in the inner and for children in the outer areas, and the concentration at the center of establishments dependent on the entire area and/or on each other, and of manufacturing and warehousing along major transportation corridors, are functional and rational. However, market factors, reinforced by restrictive policies of suburban municipalities, have led to increasing segregation. In the United States, where class distinctions are expressed and reinforced in terms of race, this has led to an abandonment of the central cities by middle- and upper-income groups, with consequent deterioration of their financial situation. In the 1950s and 1960s, the central cities attempted to counteract this trend by "urban redevelopment," financed by the federal government, which enabled them to tear down low-income housing and replace it by housing for people of substantial purchasing power. The inevitable resistance of those displaced by this policy, as well as the simultaneous construction of radial freeways, has been a major factor in the social disintegration of the United States.

In Canada there has been no exodus of the upper-income groups from the central city. To the contrary, the center is becoming the preserve of the wealthy; working-class housing is disappearing not only from displacement by multistory apartment houses, but even more from rehabilitation to luxury standards. The net result has been the same on both sides of the border: a shrinking of the housing supply available to low- and moderate-income groups, with the dream of owning a single-family house farther from reality now than it was 20 years ago.

THE CRISIS OF HOUSE PRICES

More than ever there is talk of the "housing crisis." This crisis has existed ever since the industrial revolution, and the main reaction of governments has been the establishment and enforcement of rising standards of housing quality. Census data indicate that the overwhelming majority of urban dwellings in North America actually do conform to fairly high standards in terms of structure, equipment, and occupancy, although not necessarily in terms of environment. These data show an average of 1.5 rooms per person (about 1.2 without kitchens). As well, the average number of gross square feet per person appears to be no less than 350, more than five times the average found in most developing countries. The North American housing problem seems to be predominantly one neither of quality nor of quantity, but of cost, that is, price or rent.

One of the elements of housing costs which has risen very steeply in recent years is the cost of land available for urban development. With an increase in the number and wealth of the members of a given community, their effective demand for land is bound to increase its price. To the extent that the resultant "rationing by price" allocates land in response to different demands and counteracts wasteful use, it is desirable. However, it can be, and is being, claimed that the increment in land value, being created not by its owners, but by the growth of the community, should be appropriated by the latter by means such as a site-value tax.

Such a change in appropriation would, by itself, not change the cost to the user. As a result of restrictive public policies, the cost of residential lots in many urban areas, such as Toronto, has risen far above the level determined by community growth to an oligopolistic level. The declared purpose of these policies is to prevent the scattering of development, which involves high financial, social, and environmental costs. It may well be that the only way out of the dilemma of accepting either scatteration or oligopolistic land prices is public ownership of the bulk of potential urban development land. Such ownership could allocate rationally suitable areas of land to be developed for various urban purposes, and other areas to be preserved for nonurban uses, such as agriculture or recreation. These concerns, popularly expressed in the negative form of "preventing land speculation," are leading to increased interest in public ownership of land.

One of the concerns frequently expressed is absorption of agricultural land by metropolitan growth. While waste certainly should be avoided, the concern appears to be excessive, considering that land occupied by all urban uses equals, at most, 3% of all agricultural land in North America. It should also be noted that 5 million people living in a metropolitan area absorb far less land than do the same number living in 1000 villages, each of 5000 population.

THE LEGACY OF THE CAR

A far better reason against excessive urban land absorption is the cost involved in overcoming the resultant distances, in particular the excessive movement of motor vehicles. Even if those aspects presently causing alarm—energy consumption and air pollution—should someday be overcome by technology, the accident toll would remain. Year after year, motor vehicles kill 50,000 and hurt over 0.5 million human beings in North America.

In the first quarter of this century, persons in large North American cities traveled largely by collective transportation which used highly efficient electric traction, while individual transportation relied exclusively on inefficient human or animal muscle. Once individual movement was also supplied with a mechanical motor, it became greatly superior to transit in terms of door-to-door travel time. The only way to at least partly compensate for this advantage in time is to provide transit with a right-of-way free from the congestion which impedes automobile movement, that is, to offer rapid transit. However, the capital cost of such facilities is so high that they can be justified only by the high volumes of riders which can be attracted to a limited number of lines in the largest cities. In general, the wide dispersal not only of residences, but also of places of work and other destinations (in part a result of the motor vehicle), makes it extremely difficult for transit to compete with the private car. Even partial success can be achieved only by long-term, systematic coordination of the means of land use control—compact shapes, higher densities, and balanced mix of functions—with preference for transit in terms of financing and of the right to the use of street space.

As the evil consequences of the long-standing exclusive reliance on the private automobile have been realized, public opinion has, in the manner characteristic of societies manipulated by mass media, elected the freeway as its scapegoat. This too is ironic, considering that the freeway is the most effective means to radically reduce (per vehicle-mile) the number of accidents and also substantially reduce energy consumption and pollution. In fact, the antifreeway crusade can be understood only as part of the sudden reversal of the attitude toward growth.

SLOWING THE GROWTH

With a high rate of growth of both population and of real income per head and with increasing concentration of both population and wealth in metropolitan areas, their expansion was exceedingly rapid during the century from 1860 to 1960. In the last 15 years all three of these trends have slowed down; indeed, the latest data supplied by the U.S. Census indicate a net migration loss in the largest metropolitan areas. Nevertheless, while the rate of expansion will be much lower than in the past, the absolute amount will remain substantial.

As noted earlier, North American cities developed as places to "make a living." From this point of view, bigger was always better. Growth meant more customers for the businessman, more jobs for the worker, more buyers or renters for the owner of real estate. Public opinion and public policy were dominated by a "growth ethic."

In recent years, however, the pendulum has swung to the other extreme. Now small is beautiful; "progress" and "development" have become dirty words. The role of persons as participants in the economy has become less important to them than their role as residents, interested in their settlements as "places for living." In this role they are interested in protecting their environment against more people who will spoil it with more concrete, more cars, more noise and pollution. In the suburbs this concern neatly dovetails with the traditional fiscal concerns, surrounding them with the halo of preservation of the environment.

While this antigrowth ethic has become predominant in many metropolitan areas, most small settlements continue to clamor loudly for more growth in order to provide employment for their young people. Given this constellation, it is inevitable that politicians advocate decentralization and that governments promote it. In some cases success is achieved at the "positive" end of accelerating small settlement growth. However, large settlements can be prevented from attracting more people only by making them less attractive as places for making a living (e.g., by higher unemployment) and/or as places for living (e.g., by poor housing and more pollution). It is not likely that their residents will vote for such policies.

THE SOCIAL DILEMMA

The growing concern of middle- and upper-income neighborhoods for the preservation of their environmental amenities has merged with the struggle of low-income residents against displacement by public and private redevelopment to produce a vigorous movement for direct citizen participation in urban government, based on informal local groups. This movement has mobilized much creative energy and detailed local knowledge for improving the environment, but its demands frequently conflict with the aspirations of people who want to, and probably will, live in that locality in the future, as well as of those living in other localities.

The popular demands raised by citizen participation have made it evident that the problems of human settlements are social rather than physical. Unemployment, poverty, unsatisfactory housing, alienation of the worker from both the process and the product of his work, poor physical and mental health, and crime and delinquency certainly are problems *in* the city, but not *of* the city. They are not correlated with either the size or the form of the human settlement. Instead, they are products of basic structure of North American society.

The lesson to be learned from the North American experience is that the single-minded pursuit of higher monetary income, regardless of the kind of goods and services reflected in money and their distribution, is insufficient to create satisfactory human settlements.

Chapter 2

THE URBAN PHYSICAL ENVIRONMENT

"God made the country, but man made the city" is a popular old saying. It is not entirely true. Man is also, and increasingly, making and remaking the country, not always for the better; and God still has a hand in making the city—if we accept the view of the great Renaissance architect and humanist Leone Battista Alberti, who wrote, "Nature, that is God." Not the least of the problems of our urban environment stem from our reckless abuse of its God-given elements: air, water, and soil.

But why did and does man make the city? Aristotle said, "Men come together in the city for security, and they stay together for the good life." As for security in American cities, the less said the better. Is it then the good life that attracts the swelling flood of humanity that has poured into the city in all corners of the globe, ever since the beginning of the industrial revolution? I think that the answer must be: yes and no. It is not the good life all around, but one very important aspect of it: the hope of earning money to buy the goods and services without which life cannot be good. The city is regarded primarily not as a place for living, but as a place for making a living. In North America in particular, we have treated the city as an economic machine rather than as an environment for the good life.

People can make a living in the city and enjoy more goods and services because the concentration of many people in close proximity makes possible an ever-growing division and specialization of labor, with ever more complex cooperation between all these specialized activities, resulting in an unprecedented and continuing increase in the productivity of labor. For the first time in the history of mankind, the great majority of the population in all "developed" countries lives in cities. Growth feeds on growth, and there appears to be no "natural" limit to the size of the urban area in the foreseeable future, as there was for the preindustrial city. In fact, the modern "city" has in common with the city as we have known it through history hardly more than the name. I prefer to call this new phenomenon, in conformity with the U.S. Census, a "metropolitan area" or, for short, a "metropolis." The gradual, evolutionary change in quantity has resulted in a revolutionary mutation, a new and different quality of urban life.

Because metropolitan areas exist as concentrations of economic functions, their

---

Source: Lecture presented at a Gannett Urban Journalism Center Seminar, Northwestern University, Evanston, Ill., March 28, 1968.

structures and forms have been determined by the links between these functions—the lines and terminals for the movement of goods, persons, and messages—rather than by the desires of their inhabitants for a healthy and pleasant environment. Most of our cities owe their origins to the terminals of water transportation. Around the harbor gathered the places for business, manufacturing, and storage, as well as dwellings and services. When the railroads developed, they were welcomed with enthusiasm and invited to the front door. The rails were located in the streets and the terminals in the squares, and the yards were established wherever they could insert themselves into the growing urban tissue. We are still today, after a hundred years, struggling to overcome, at great cost, the consequences of this blind enthusiasm, by providing grade separation, rebuilding terminals, and relocating freight and classification yards.

This experience, however, has not kept us from repeating the same mistake over and over again. Every new means of transportation is greeted enthusiastically and brought as close to the center of urban life as possible, regardless of its impact on the urban fabric. We are doing the same thing for the airplane, though we know that flight paths blight far larger areas than do railroad lines and that airports create far stronger barriers than railroad yards ever did. We are doing the same for electricity, with high-tension lines cutting large swaths through the landscape and the poles of the wirescape cluttering up our streets. But most of all we are doing the same for the motor vehicle, moving and standing.

The concentration of population and activity resulting from efficient long-distance transportation and communication would long ago have become intolerable if it had not been supplemented, with a time lag of about half a century, by equally efficient means of short-distance transportation and communication: electric traction, the telephone, and the motor vehicle (all three now also used over long distances). This meant that speed and the distance required for functional proximity increased by a factor of 10; consequently the area in which urban life could function increased by a factor of 100. People avail themselves of this greatly increased space, first and foremost, for their homes. The homes are soon followed by institutions and commercial establishments serving their residents. Industry and warehousing, freed from the necessity to be close to water and rail terminals and to the central city labor force, find it even more advantageous to spread out in large sites at the periphery.

As a result of this sorting out of the various activities and "land uses," the modern metropolis tends to develop a fairly typical pattern. There is a highly concentrated central business district (C.B.D.), usually still close to the original terminal of the water and/or rail transportation. From the center, population and urban activities spread farther and farther in all directions—*all*, not only residences, decreasing quite regularly in density toward the periphery. Within this concentric density pattern heavy industries concentrate on water- and railways, less heavy ones increasingly along freeways. Within the perimeter reached by urban development there remain extensive areas of "open" land, much of it used for outdoor recreation, but some in farms or forests, often abandoned and neglected.

No planner invented this pattern. It has been designed by the "invisible hand" of competitive forces operating in the real estate market. It is a basically logical and functional pattern, beautifully readable from the air at night. What, then, is wrong with it?

Five aspects of our urban development can be defined which prevent it from being a good environment for living.

1. There is a conflict between moving and living. In our eagerness to go places, we are in danger of destroying any place worth going to.

2. As we increase production and consumption, their wastes increasingly pollute air, water, and soil.

3. As urban activities spread, central functions become too scattered to form attractive centers, and open land too much cut up to form attractive recreation areas.

4. The entire area becomes formless; both urban and rural beauty are lost.

5. With increasing difference and distance between the old central, densely developed and the new low-density, peripheral residential areas, segregation by class and race increases.

Probably no aspect of urban life and city planning is more widely discussed (usually with more heat than light) than transportation. It is discussed in terms of wasting or saving time. Traffic engineers provide economic justification for a proposed freeway by elaborate calculations showing the number of hours saved by its users and assigning a dollar value to an hour.

There is plenty of evidence indicating that in the long term the increased speed and mobility provided by transportation improvements is consumed not in the form of less time, but in the form of more space, as well as of wider choice. More space is certainly desirable, and wider choice—of places to live, to work, to shop, to learn, to visit—is the very essence of the city. In fact, it is identical with freedom; the medieval saying "city air makes free" is still true.

However, to use pseudo-scientific gobbledygook, the correlation between mobility and the marginal utility of space and of choice appears to be nonlineal. I cannot formulate a "law of diminishing returns" or define a "threshold"; but is there not a point where enough is enough? How much land does man need? You may recall that Leo Tolstoi wrote a marvelous short story under that title. It deals with a peasant who comes to his death in his frantic search for more land—and finds all he needs, 2 by 6 feet.

How much choice does man need? There are in the Chicago area some 2 million jobs to choose from, but a person can hold only one at a time—give or take some moonlighting. There are certainly in this area hundreds of thousands of attractive men and women, but a person can be married to only one at a time—give or take some moonlighting.

I will leave with you this question of the possible limits of man's desire for space and for choice. Certainly within very wide limits greater mobility is desirable. We have obtained an unprecedented degree of mobility by the use of the private automobile, but we are beginning to discover that its unlimited use destroys the livability of the city. The famous British Buchanan Report, entitled "Traffic in Towns," calls for standards defining the amount of traffic that any area can absorb without destroying its amenity. All traffic in excess of these norms should be channeled on arteries at the boundaries of these defined "amenity areas." The basic concept is, of course, not new. Even before the advent of the automobile, city planners insisted on separation of traffic arteries and residential streets. In most parts of the urban area such horizontal separation is adequate, and in new residential developments it is becoming fairly general. However, in the area of highest concentration, notably the C.B.D., it can be applied to only a limited area. Two other methods are available: separation in time, and vertical separation. Neither is new. Imperial Rome banished vehicular traffic during daytime. Vertical separation is even older; it was used by the lake dwellers. One of these lake dweller towns still exists; it is called Venice.

It may well be that it was the example of Venice that inspired Leonardo da Vinci to apply the same principle on land, proposing different levels for the movement of pedestrians, of horsemen, and of carts. I have no doubt that we would apply such separation if we built the center of a big city from scratch. This does not happen, and none of the big European cities has used the opportunity of rebuilding its war-destroyed center on this principle. Nor has any big American city used for this purpose the many millions extracted from other people's pockets by means of "urban renewal." It was left to the city of Stockholm to create the first example in its highly successful Hoegtorget project.

In existing cities it is generally easier, though less desirable, to create a new pedestrian level below rather than above the existing one. This has been done in Philadelphia and in Montreal, and is planned in Toronto and likely to be done in other cities.

Even if this type of grade separation were extended to the entire city center—and this is not likely to happen—it would not be possible to accommodate all the cars which would like to drive downtown. This number must be restricted. In my opinion the best way to do this is rationing by price: all-day parking must be made so expensive that most people will prefer to park their cars at the downtown fringe or, preferably, leave them at home and use public transportation.

In recent years there has been renewed interest in public transportation in the United States. However, it is a mistake to expect salvation from the building of rapid transit lines alone. These are indispensable as the backbone of the system, but they cannot do the entire job. Given the money, any fool can build a subway; the tough problem is to bring people to and from its stations. Required are both an effective feeder system and intermediate means, faster than the conventional street bus and less costly than a subway line.

Because public transportation benefits not only its user but also the nonuser, who can drive his or her car on a less congested street, it is perfectly justified to operate it as a free public service, financed out of public revenues rather than out of the fare box. I have not been able to make an exact estimate of the consequences of such a change, but a moderately informed guess is an improvement of the cost-benefit ratio by about one third.

Disturbance of the amenity of the environment and interference with pedestrian movement are not the only drawbacks to mass use of the private automobile. Rapid movement of a multiplicity of heavy, hard bodies is inherently dangerous. When 150 persons travel in two buses, there is a risk of one clash between these two vehicles. When 150 persons travel in 100 cars, each car can crash into each of 99 others; the risk is $(100 \times 99)/2 = 4950$. Considering that each bus carries 50 times as many people as each car, the risk for the car traveler is still 99 times greater than for the bus traveler.

When the car is not moving, but standing, it does not create danger, but it absorbs space. Before the end of this century, the United States will use about 100 billion square feet for parking. That is over 35,000 square miles, three times the size of Belgium. We could, of course, provide all parking in multistory garages, at a construction cost of about $500 billion. Maybe the United States is big enough and rich enough to afford either the land or the buildings. But maybe it would be preferable to use some of that money to clean up the urban environment.

Pollution is the presence of waste materials in air, water, and soil. I believe that the concept of "waste material" may and should become obsolete. Progress in chemical technology is approaching a stage where we can make anything out of anything and something out of everything. This would mean the replacement of "waste disposal" by waste utilization. The wastes of the animal body are the natural nutrients of plant life, and plants are the nutrients of animal life. The Chinese have become the most populous nation on earth by careful utilization of this natural circular process. Why can't we do the same on a higher technical level? It seems a profound irony that, on the one hand, nutritionists tell us that the world's best hope to provide its growing population with proteins is chlorella algae; and, on the other, we are wringing our hands because our rivers and lakes are being clogged by an overgrowth of algae due to an overdose of nutrients.

Too many of our present methods of waste disposal merely shift the burden from one element to another. If trash is dumped, it pollutes the soil; so we burn it, and pollute the air. It is, of course, not possible to maintain in a populated area the same ecological balance that exists in a wilderness, but this does not mean that there can be none. The ecological balance of the Netherlands today is radically different from what it was a thousand years ago, but this new balance sustains the densest population on earth, and sustains it at a higher life expectancy and a far lower rate of infant deaths than are enjoyed by the people of the United States.

The best way to eliminate dirt is, of course, not to produce it. We could eliminate air pollution from automobile exhaust fumes by replacing the internal combustion engine with a different power plant, such as an electric battery or a thermoelectric cell. We could eliminate smoke from factories and homes by replacing fossil fuels as sources of heat and energy with solar, tidal, or geothermic energy. I am convinced that the long-term solution to our pollution problem lies in these directions rather than in the frequently advocated expedient of shifting it to other places, such as the proposal of dispersing metropolitan populations into a number of smaller towns.

This is not to say that there is no place for "satellite towns." Generally speaking, however, I think it is a sounder approach to build "satellite boroughs," such as Vällingby in Stockholm, which are an integral part of the metropolitan area, within easy commuting distance from its center, rather than to attempt to isolate the new urban areas from the mother city by a greenbelt. The green, of course, is right, but the belt is wrong. What matters is that the large amount of open land which is to be found within every metropolitan area not be scattered in useless parcels as it too often is at present, but rather be held together in areas of usable size and shape; and that, inversely, the developed land be held together in compact areas around vital outlying centers (I like to call them "secondary downtowns"), each serving a population of 0.25–0.5 million people.

As noted earlier, most of the activities characteristic of downtown are increasingly to be found also in the peripheral areas. But they are all scattered: centers for shopping in one place; offices and welfare, health, educational, cultural, and recreational services in others. If they were all concentrated in one location, this would not only eliminate a lot of automobile traffic, but also give identity to the surrounding district. I am convinced that identity is created far more by a common center than by a boundary. However, if it is considered desirable to keep these communities physically separated, it would be much cheaper and more effective to surround them with walls than to surround them with greenbelts. Many medieval cities consisted of two or more adjacent walled towns. In most cases the burghers had the good sense to tear down these separating walls; in my own hometown of Hamburg they did that more than 700 years ago. After all, you want your citizens to identify not only with Evanston or Cicero, but with the Chicago metropolis as well.

The scatteration and formlessness of our urban areas are the result of scattered, uncoordinated decision-making. Each private and public agent decides without full knowledge of the impact on all others. The beautiful cities of the preindustrial age were built under the guidance of a three-dimensional image of the environment which was shared by all those engaged in creating or changing it. With the increasing complexity and specialization of the modern world this unified image has disappeared. Surveyors lay out the streets and lots; the roads department determines the street profile and paving; the traffic department puts up its signs and lights; the power and telephone companies erect their poles; contractors erect the buildings; landscape gardeners plant the trees and shrubs; and so on. No wonder that the result is chaos.

City planners are supposed to coordinate all these activities, but they do not control them. Their chief instrument has been zoning. Insofar as the zoning ordinance controls not only use but also such physical aspects as bulk, height, and setbacks of buildings, it has become the main public designer of our cities. But zoning is not a design tool, but a legal tool for the protection of property. As such it must give equal protection to all property owners and impose equal restrictions on all of them. The inevitable result is monotony. Generally speaking, our buildings are too close together and too similar to register as individual structures, and too far apart and too dissimilar to register as a unit, as do, for instance, the crescents of Bath or the squares of London.

Only when a large piece of land is in one ownership, private or public, has it been possible to coordinate all elements into a harmonious three-dimensional image. The number of large-scale developments is increasing, and there is some hope that those in charge will avail themselves of their opportunities.

However, while such large developments may create order within their own boundaries, they do not overcome, and may even increase, the chaos within the metropolitan area as a whole. This chaos is institutionalized and increased by the splitting up of the area into a number of separate municipalities, each relying on the real property tax as its main source of income.

Inevitably, municipal policy is guided by the desire to gain assessment and to rid itself of inhabitants who cause expenses. From the point of view of the municipal treasurer, the only desirable inhabitants are industry, commerce, and wealthy bachelors. Poor people, in particular those with school-age children, must be shunted into another municipality. Most of the piously proclaimed "high standards" of suburban building, housing, and zoning codes serve this purpose.

This has greatly increased the segregation by income which would exist in any case because of the price difference between old and new housing. As old housing is generally to be found only near the center of the metropolis, this means that "the other side of the tracks," the environment of the poor, is now miles away from the upper- and middle-class areas. In the United States the rift is immeasurably deepened by the freezing of the class distinction of master and slave into the "race" distinction of white and black. This has now become the most burning aspect of the so-called urban crisis. I say "so-called" because the crisis is *in* the cities, but not *of* the cities. It is a crisis of the entire socioeconomic system. It is in the cities because that is where the people are and because their concentration makes the problems more visible.

There is clearly only one way to overcome the growing segregation by class and race. We must use the public purse to close the gap between the incomes of a large section of our population and the cost of decent housing, and see to it that such housing is available to all persons in all parts of the metropolis. It is absurd and futile to talk about "bringing the middle-class families back into the city" as long as there is not enough room in the city for those who live there now. This fashionable slogan has served as a rationalization for the attempt of the central cities to beat the suburbs at their own game by bulldozing out the poor in the name of "slum clearance," "redevelopment," or, now, "urban renewal." We need more houses, not fewer. The ways to renew blighted areas are better management, rehabilitation of dwellings, and addition of the many public facilities which are now lacking in these areas.

There is no doubt that the wealth and productive capacity of the United States are sufficient to make a reality out of the promise of the Housing Act to provide "a decent home in a good environment for every American family." Even we in poorer Canada can afford this; and we can also afford all the other things which I have mentioned: clean air, water, and soil, good public transportation, separation of vehicular and pedestrian movement, lively subcenters, ample outdoor recreation—and, yes, even beauty. The question is: do we want them? Do we want a good environment badly enough to pay for it? Are we willing to change our priorities, to shift a substantial part of our gross national product from private consumption, largely of useless junk, but all sold at a profit, to public consumption?

We will have to choose whether we want to place priority on private wealth or on common wealth, on res privatae or on the res publica. If we choose the former, we may well end up losing both.

Chapter 3

CONTINUITY AND CHANGE IN URBAN FORM

THE CITY'S IDENTITY PROBLEM

Sixty years ago, in his perceptive introduction to the catalogue of the International City Planning Exhibition in Berlin, Werner Hegemann remarked that the modern city has little more in common with the historical city than the name. This prophetic insight has been confirmed by subsequent developments. In fact, it can be said that we no longer live in cities, but in a new, much vaster, and more dispersed form of human settlement which, for lack of a better word, we call a "metropolitan area." It partakes of characteristics of both country and city; but as it is essentially urban, I will identify it with and by the city which is its core.

This is in conformity with common usage. When a person is in Detroit or Toronto, he or she may say, "I live in Grosse Point" or "in Richmond Hill." But the same person, when far from home, will say, "I am from Detroit" or "from Toronto." But what has today's London really in common with medieval London? What constitutes its identity?

For the first time in history these contemporary, vast urban areas contain the majority of the population and are the places where most of the work is done. The historical city was the seat of a small minority, substantially composed of the politicomilitary, ecclesiastical, and economic elite, and of those who immediately served them. The mass of the population lived in villages, in "urban" as well as in "preurban" cultures. In the latter also the elite lived not in the village, but in a different form of settlement, the castle or manor; or, in Buddhist and Christian countries they lived in a significant variant of the manor, the monastery. The city is a synthesis of the village and manor.

In the farming village there are a number of basically identical decision-making units, the farm households. They may and do cooperate by addition of identical forces, but they do not interact, do not interchange different goods or services. (This is, of course, a heroic oversimplification.) On the other hand, in the manor there is a differentiation and specialization of functions, interacting and interdependent; but all its members are subject to a single decision-maker, the lord of the manor.

Source: Journal of Urban History, Vol. 1, No. 2 (Sage Publications, Inc., Beverly Hills, Calif.), February 1975.

The city combines the characteristics of the village and of the manor into something uniquely new and different. It is one big unit with a decision-making government (however constituted) that is composed of a number of independent decision-makers—households, corporations, and the like—which perform different functions and are therefore interdependent by an exchange of goods and services.

It is the interplay between the decisions of the community and the decisions of its individual or corporate constituents which creates and recreates the form of the city. Many writers have made a rigid distinction between "planned" and "grown" cities, often identified with "geometric" versus "organic" urban form. But the distinction is not absolute. No living city is built entirely according to plan. Only if and when rigor mortis sets in right after birth, as in Aigues Mortes, may it come close to it. And nothing in any city is ever built that has not been planned by somebody. The real question is: who planned what, and why?

The one big unit, the city government, sees the city primarily as a container. In most historical urban cultures the wall of the city was its primary concern, and even contemporary planners want to "contain" their city by a greenbelt. The wall contains and protects the citizens, their sanctuaries, and, last but not least, their goods. As did the manor and the royal palace—as we know from the biblical story of Joseph—so does the city assemble and distribute the goods of the region. It contains and conserves the inventory. It was from keeping record of the inventory that writing developed. All urban cultures are literate; no nonurban culture is. So a second and more important inventory is added: the city becomes the container and transmitter of the accumulated knowledge and wisdom of the culture, the preserver of its continuity.

Continuity there is, of course, also in the village, as well as in the manor. Indeed, both are essentially static; generation after generation follows the same way of life. They are static because they are self-contained. No city is self-contained; it depends on interchange and interaction with other regions and cities, and this interaction is typically, though not exclusively, carried out by many independent decision-makers, individual and corporate citizens. Jane Jacobs is right in defining Catal Hüyük as a "city" because its specialized merchants and craftsmen used materials from afar and presumably sent their products to other places.

As interaction with the outside world expands or contracts, the city grows or shrinks. Moreover, these exogenous forces have their impact on the structure of the city, its internal relation of forces, its functions, and its mores. Change is as much of the essence for the city as is continuity. The city is never the same as it was in the "good old days"; not for it the stability of the village.

This instability of the city has disturbed many observers. Plato wanted to prevent it by literally isolating his polis, which, not accidentally, was modeled on rural Lakedaimon. Plato was, of course, a son of the city. So were the mandarins of the Ming dynasty who dismantled China's great merchant fleet, because the impact of foreign trade undermined the stability of the established Confucian order. They, like Plato, regarded identity and change as mutually exclusive.

This appears to be an evident truth by Cartesian logic. How can an entity at one and the same time change and be the same? Yet we know that such entities do exist. Every organism changes constantly, but preserves its identity. Moreover, it preserves its life and identity by change, by metabolism.

A city is not an organism. It is, strictly speaking, not even an organization.

Certainly there are organizations in and of the city. But, in contemporary North American cities at least, there is not even an organization of the real city, the socioeconomic system of the metropolis. The city is, or can be defined as, a system. But while every organism is a system, not every system is an organism. The city is a social system and, as such, is not preprogramed by genetic endowment, as is an organism. An organism can develop only within certain fairly narrow limits of space and time. The organismic view, as represented by Lewis Mumford, postulates that a city must degenerate once it grows beyond a certain size, that being the size of the modern metropolis. But all the evidence is to the contrary.

Dixi et animam meam salvavi. (Having said that my spirit is free.) Having stated that the city is not an organism, I feel free to resort to analogy with a most highly developed organism, the human person. An adult person looks and acts completely different from an infant. Yet we say without hesitation "when I was 5 years old" or "I knew her as a child." We do not doubt our own identity or that of another person.

Indeed, it may well be said that normally developed adults are more themselves, more their own specific personalities, than they were as infants. Similarly, we speak of "medieval London" or of "Kublai Khan's Peking." But what makes it the same London, the same Peking? What constitutes the identity of a city? And can a city, like a person, become more itself as it develops? Is there, to use a term of medieval philosophy, a *logos spermatikos* in cities, a germinal idea? Does a city have "genes"? And if so, what are they?

I cannot answer this question. I can only attempt to look at it from several sides, to touch it here and there with my fingertips, to try to get the feel of it. But, after all these speculative generalities, I will at least try to be a bit more specific.

DETERMINANTS OF URBAN FORM

The form of the city results from the interaction of situation, function, and site; from the concepts in the minds of its citizens and from the types of structure they build, both derived from preurban roots; and from the reaction of these on situation, function, and site, and on subsequent human activity. None of these factors is absolutely fixed; all are subject to change. The city is a historical process; its image at any given time is merely a cross section through a continuous stream. It is not a work of plastic art, not "architecture on a large scale," as a manor or monastery may well be. It may have some similarity to a work of the temporal arts, of poetry or music. There may be a recurrent leitmotif, or at least a basso ostinato.

The situation determines whether there will be a city at all. Cities do not have one common origin. A city may develop from the growth of a village, the area around a castle or monastery, or from a temporary camp- or fairground; or it may be consciously established as a "new town." But whether it becomes a city or withers on the vine depends on its situation. Geographers define three such situations: the central place, the transfer point, and the specialized city, usually deriving its specialty from a localized natural resource.

The central place as the sanctuary, refuge, and meeting place of the tribe dominates the surrounding tribal territory. A hill rises in the center of the fertile plain known as the Beauce, and a cave at its top became a sanctuary of the great Celtic mother-goddess, venerated far beyond the boundaries of the Beauce. With the Roman Conquest the mother-goddess became Venus Genetrix, and with Christianity she became Notre Dame. Directly over the sacred cave stands the high altar, the center of the great cathedral, which crowns the hill, which is the core of the city of Chartres, which is the center of the Beauce. Here the interaction of situation, function, and site, unchanged over millennia, has been made more and more visible by the changing works of man. Chartres has become more itself: a great sacred center.

Similarly, the rock on which the mythical king Erechteus built his house became the dominant central place of the surrounding plain of Attica, its *polis*. In Homeric Greece *polis* means the "royal castle." At its foot spreads the *asty*, the settlement of the common people. The inherent duality of the city, being both manor and village, is still separated in space as well as in language. In Athens, where the natural resource of fine clay gave rise to pottery, the *asty* developed mainly around the *kerameikos*, the potter's market. But when the craftsmen and merchants assumed power and constituted themselves as the *polis* with the *kerameikos* as their central *agora*, the former polis became the *akropolis;* deserted by men, the acropolis remained the seat of the gods. The city has become the center of all of Greece as well as Attica, but it is still the glorious rock which proclaims to the world: "This is Athens."

In Athens, as in Chartres, it is a decisive element of the natural site, enhanced by unique works of man, which is the main element of continuing identity. Sometimes it is the natural element alone, as in Montreal, where the mountain has given its name to both the city and the island. It may even be a distant mountain which becomes identified with the city, such as Fujiyama with Tokyo and Mount Hood with Portland, Oregon.

But landmarks, natural and/or man-made, are not the only elements of identity and continuity in cities. Toronto is located at the mouth of the small river Humber, from which a short portage was used by the Indians to carry their canoes to the Holland River, where they continued through several smaller lakes to the Upper Great Lakes. This situation at the junction of the east-west route along Lake Ontario and the St. Lawrence River with the shortest south-north route to the Upper Lakes continued to influence the growth of the city. When wheeled carts and carriages superseded canoes, the roads to Kingston and Dundas, located at the eastern and western ends of Lake Ontario, respectively, were soon supplemented by a road named Yonge Street, leading north to Holland Landing and becoming the "main street" of Toronto. Urban development followed these three main streets, giving the city the form of an inverted T. All subsequent means of urban transit—horse-drawn trolleys, later electric streetcars, and finally subways—were first and foremost established on Yonge Street. At present, after the Yonge line was supplemented by an east-west line, it is being extended further, thus strengthening and extending the "finger" to the north, while areas to the northwest and northeast remain underserved and underdeveloped. Thus all changes in transportation and development have reproduced the original inverted-T form on a larger and larger scale.

This is not the only element that has continuously shaped Toronto. The land of Upper Canada, like that of the United States, was divided by governmental fiat into geometric squares. Here these were "concessions" of 1000 acres each, separated by road allowances. These "concession roads" still form the main arterial road system. The area of each concession has been subdivided largely into blocks approaching a square shape.

In Quebec the original land division followed a different system. Starting from the river bank, each settler was allotted a narrow strip which he extended inland as far as he could clear the land. Starting from this basis, Montreal has developed a pattern of long, narrow blocks. The original street and block pattern, far more permanent than buildings, continues to identify the city. It has its roots in the systems of measuring and allotting agricultural land. In Mediterranean countries the parcels were square, and so are the city blocks. In medieval northern Europe, with a different technique of plowing and correspondingly different methods of land measurement (by the chain rather than by the gromma), fields were oblong, and so are the city blocks. The connection, illustrated by the use of the plow to delineate the perimeter of the city, is found in India, Thailand, and medieval Bohemia, as well as in ancient Rome. In Rome, as in India and China, the rectangular pattern was tied to the cosmological notion of the four cardinal points which determine the direction of the main streets. Secularized as a principle of order, the cross of main streets dominates the plans of William Penn's Philadelphia as well as Le Corbusier's Ville Radieuse. In Philadelphia the *logos spermatikos* of the basic cross has generated the cross of the city's two subway lines, and their crossing point is City Hall. The changes made by generation after generation have repeated the basso ostinato with stronger and stronger instruments.

Where the cosmological notion of the axial cross and its correlate, the rectangular pomerium, is absent and the grid is adopted as a purely utilitarian lot and block plan, as in most North American cities, there is no predetermined boundary or a predetermined center. The cells of the blocks may proliferate in any direction, and the center of the city may shift. The classical case is Manhattan, which is still moving to the north. It is, however, remarkable that the wall of the original core, pregrid Nieuw Amsterdam, has remained the locus of the financial center. "Wall Street" still stands for New York as the center of a worldwide financial empire.

Similarly, the other superpower is referred to as "the Kremlin." In medieval Russia, as in ancient Greece, the duality of the city existed spatially, as *Kreml* (fortress) and *posad* (settlement). In Novgorod, as in Athens, the Kreml is now a museum of religious monuments. In Moscow, in addition to being a museum, it has again become the seat of power. The original reason for its location was the character of the site. The selection of the site is the first and most important decision of city planning. When defense is the predominant objective, very frequently a "cape" is chosen. In Moscow it was formed by the acute angle between the Moskva River and the swampy mouth of a small tributary, the Neglinaya Creek. The swamp was long ago transformed into a park, and the creek buried in an underground sewer. Few Moscovites even know that it exists; for them Neglinaya is just a street name.

On the land side of the Kreml triangle, a marketplace developed known as Red Square. Along the three roads leading to the Kreml, a town developed, called, for unknown reasons, Kitai Gorod (Chinatown). It was enclosed by a wall, which describes a third of a circle from the northeast corner of the Kreml. The city expanded along the roads radiating from Kitai Gorod and the Kreml. This second layer was enclosed in the late Middle Ages by a wall of white stones, describing two thirds of a circle; it is still known as the "White City." Growth continued along the radial arteries and on a maze of small alleys between them, extending also to the opposite bank of the Moskva. In the seventeenth century this third layer was enclosed by an earthen fortification which, for the first time, describes a full circle, defining what is still called the "Earthen City." The "radiocentric" pattern, which existed only in embryonic form in Chinatown, was now fully developed and has continued ever since. The places outside the gates of both the White and the Earthen City have been developed as the main squares of Moscow. When railroads were built, their terminals, new forms of the gateway, were located close to the gates of the former earthen wall; and their radial lines were soon connected by a circular railroad. The three concentric walls have all been replaced by broad ringroads. Farther out another ringroad and finally a circumferential expressway were added. In the 1930s the radial arteries were all widened to 200 feet, and the subway lines located under them were supplemented by a circular subway line. Thus, through all the changes of 700 years of history, the radiocentric pattern has become stronger and stronger. Today, Moscow is its classical example.

It is, of course, not the only one. Wherever a city rose as the central place of a relatively uniform plain, its containing wall assumed the form of a circle, the shortest line for enclosing a given area; the roads connecting it with its region radiated in all directions, converging on the marketplace. The market was the real center of the medieval city—not the cathedral, which often, as in Pisa, Salisbury, and Luebeck, is located at the city's periphery.

Where and when the city grew into an important trading center, specialized markets for space-consuming goods, such as wood, hay, horses, or cattle, were located outside the gates. People settled outside these gates, and sooner or later these "suburbs" were taken into the city and protected by a second and sometimes a third circular wall. Later, when these walls were torn down, they were replaced by ringroads. When they consisted of extensive earthworks and moats of the "Vauban" type, they sometimes also became greenbelts, separating the older city from its later extensions, as in Vienna. It has been said that the walls became more significant for the form of the city after they were torn down than while they were standing.

As cities of this type tend to expand in all directions more or less equally, the center of gravity remains at the original center. As the city grows, its centrality increases; the center becomes stronger. The situation is different in the most typical form of the transfer point, the harbor city, where a large body of water limits expansion to one side. As such "half-cities" grow, the point of gravity moves further and further away from the original center. The resulting pull weakens the center, as in St. Louis and Detroit. In Toronto, where the downtown center is still very strong and growing, about a mile further inland a new uptown is in the process of formation. The most extreme example of the "moving center," Manhattan's uptown, has already been referred to.

Not all cities are monocentric. In London the financial center in the city is separate from the government center of Westminster, and over the years the specialization of each has become more pronounced. The street system resulting from this bipolarity, as well as from the autonomous development of the large feudal estates, is rather complex and not easily identified. Probably the strongest element giving continuing identity to this unique city are the tree-planted squares which each of these estates created as focal points of their well-designed residential developments: a leitmotif played with many variations.

Medieval Rome was primarily a center of pilgrimage. The processions went from one shrine to another. The reconstruction of Rome, carried out under Sixtus V by Domenico Fontana, transformed these winding pilgrim paths into impressive straight streets between these focal points, and between them and the two main gates. This system of diagonals still dominates Rome; there is no single center. It is, however, worthy of note that the city hall is the Campidoglio, rebuilt by Michelangelo on a substructure dating back to the days of the Roman Republic.

The embryo of Paris, the Gallic Lutetia Parisiorum, was located on an island in the Seine. The Romans built their town on the left bank, on the "Mountain of Paris" now crowned by the Pantheon. After the Romans had left, the cathedral and the royal palace were built on the island, which thus again became the center, now known as the "Cité." On the right bank merchants settled. This part, governed by the "Provost des Marchands," became known as the "Ville." On the left bank were several monasteries; from their schools developed the "Université." Around 1200 this tripartite city was enclosed by a new wall. Outside its western gate, on the right bank of the Seine, the king built a hunting castle, the Louvre. It became the seed of a fourth district, the Paris of aristocratic splendor.

All changes during the succeeding seven centuries have maintained and reinforced the specific character of these four districts. The Cité, while no longer the seat of the government of France, still houses the real government of Paris, the Préfecture, in addition to the courts, the cathedral, and the archbishop. The Ville houses the stock exchange, the banks, and the leading department stores. The Université has become the fabled "Left Bank," the Paris of the intellectuals and artists. From the Louvre, via the Tuileries and the Champs Elysées, has developed the Paris of wealth and luxury.

The Renaissance intoned the second theme of the symphony. At the beginning of the fifteenth century a Parisian said of a proposed new street, which would open up a long vista toward Porte St. Antoine, "ce que sera très triomphant." This theme of the triumphant, wide, and straight street leading to an impressive building or monument as *point de vue*, has been played again and again, moderato under the monarchy, forte by Napoleon, fortissimo by Haussmann. It merges with the subtheme of the axial, geometrically shaped square formed by uniform buildings, which appears first with Henri IV's Place des Vosges.

The same king also gave to Paris the Pont Neuf, of which a writer said, "It is in the city what the heart is in the human body." It is indeed the focal point of Paris, connecting the lower end of the Cité with the Ville and the Université, just above the Louvre. The Pont Neuf also was the first open bridge. The previous bridges were lined with buildings, as were the banks of the river. In the following centuries these were gradually displaced by broad quais. Only then did the Seine with its bridges and quais become an integral part of the image of the city to which it had given birth. Now the mature "person" of Paris has fully developed all the characteristics which, one after another, emerged during her childhood and adolescence.

Cities other than Paris also ignored for a long time the inherent characteristics of the site, and sometimes of the situation as well. Peter the Great founded St. Petersburg as a "window to the west" on the river Neva at the point where it branches out into a delta, its two arms enclosing an island. Inherent in this situation were two directions: westward to the sea, and southeast to the Great Russian heartland, to Novgorod and Moscow. Initially only the first direction was recognized. Peter adopted the plan of the French architect Le Blond, which provided for urban development of the entire island by a rectangular grid of canals and streets.

The oval fortification also enclosed a part of the north bank with the Peter-Paul fortress, but only a narrow sliver on the south bank. Development on the south bank outside the fortifications was expressly forbidden. But on the south bank was the city's biggest employer, the Navy Yard, called the "Admiralty," as well as Peter's modest "winter house." From the southeast came the migrants who were attracted by the new capital city—and they stayed there at its gates. From the southeast also came the country's highest ecclesiastical dignitary, the Metropolit of Novgorod. On his visits to the Imperial Court he stayed at the Alexander Nevsky Monastery, some two miles from the Winter Palace which soon replaced Peter's little house. For his convenience this road was paved; as the "Nevsky Prospect" it became and remained the main street of the city.

Not until two generations after the city's foundation did a new plan recognize the preeminence of the south bank. The Nevsky Prospect was supplemented by two other main arteries, radiating at equal angles from the tower of the Admiralty. This fan-shaped pattern, greatly extended and enlarged, remains the basic arterial system of modern Leningrad.

The island remained a quiet residential district, with its canals filled in and transformed into broad, tree-lined avenues. Its eastern tip, the apex of the delta, remained vacant for a long time. Only in the early nineteenth century did this focal point receive its architectural form. Meanwhile, St. Petersburg had also become an important commercial center, and, appropriately, the stock exchange was chosen to occupy this most conspicuous site. It was built in the form of an enormous Doric temple, flanked by two even more enormous columns, with broad granite stairs leading down to the river; the whole on the majestic scale set by the broad river. Only now, with this articulation of its focal point, was the inherent character of the site fully spelled out; only now had the city fully become its unique self.

The site is generally the most permanent element establishing the continuing identity of a city. Where the site is primarily characterized by hills or mountains, it is not substantially changed by man; but human activity may obscure or articulate it. Where water is the characteristic element, modification by man may be substantial. This is evident where water appears mainly in the form of canals, as in Venice, Bruges, or Amsterdam. But it may also happen with natural watercourses, as in Hamburg.

Hamburg was founded by Charlemagne as an outpost on the north bank of the Elbe, which here consisted of a shifting maze of watercourses between tidal flats. The site was a typical "cape" site, a slight rise of land protected on both sides by two small tributaries of the Elbe. Charlemagne's son established an archbishopric in the town, and a cathedral was built with a parish church next to it. The main street followed the ridge of the height. For a long time the only paved street, it still retains the name "Stone Street." Similarly, the Horse and Fish Markets, established outside the land and water gates, respectively, still retain their names.

In the twelfth century the counts of Holstein built a rival town directly adjacent to the bishop's town, by surrounding some mud flats with a dyke and situating a parish church at its center. With both towns growing rapidly because of expanding trade, each soon added a second parish. In the thirteenth century the burghers of the two towns united and obtained the privileges of a "Free and Hanseatic City." They built their city hall on the bridge connecting the two towns. Later, in the sixteenth century, the bourse and the bank were built next to it, a fitting ruling trinity. The four parishes were protected by a common wall, with one of the tributaries, the Alster, serving as its moat on the west side of the city.

Ever since it became a free city Hamburg has controlled the Elbe River. By progressively deepening and widening its northernmost course, Hamburg transformed it into the main channel. Now, with the harbor and shipyards relocated to the opposite side of this wide channel and visible from a broad promenade on the city side, the Elbe has become a much stronger and more integrated part of the city's image than it was in the Middle Ages.

Even more interesting is the gradual and consistent transformation of the Alster River. In the thirteenth century a mill dam was built just outside the bishop's town. This transformed the tidal swamps upstream into a lake with a stable water level—fairly large, but still rather formless. During the sixteenth century development spread to the right bank of the Alster. In the beginning of the following century an area slightly larger than that of the old town was organized as a new town on a grid scheme, with its parish church at its highest elevation. Its main street, extending the main street of the bishop's town, is still called the "New Stoneway." This enlarged town of five parishes was enclosed by an extensive fortification of earthworks, just in time to protect the city from the ravages of the Thirty Years' War. For three centuries the city remained confined by this egg-shaped boundary. At the beginning of the nineteenth century this fortification was replaced by a broad ringroad, accompanied by a greenbelt. This line still clearly defines the "City" as distinct from the vast area of former suburbs, villages, and towns now included in Hamburg.

The fortification was carried across the Alster by a causeway and bridge, dividing the lake into two basins, a trapezoid "Inner Alster" of about 45 acres and an "Outer Alster" of some 400 acres defined by a large sweeping curve. The contrast between the geometric form of the smaller inner basin and the free form of the outer basin has been increasingly articulated over the years. Most of the shoreline of the Outer Alster is now a public park, generally just a narrow strip, but quite wide in its newest section created out of the gardens of patrician manors after World War II. The Outer Alster presents itself essentially as a landscaped lake.

The Inner Alster has become increasingly "urban." In the seventeenth and eighteenth centuries its southern and western banks, respectively, were transformed into tree-lined streets with granite embankments. However, the east bank (the longest) was still, in the medieval manner, occupied by structures. In 1842 a huge conflagration destroyed 250 acres which comprised the core of the old city. This area was rebuilt according to a radically different plan, basically a rectangular grid. Only then was the shaping of the Inner Alster completed by the transformation of the third side into a tree-lined street. But, in addition, the plan added a third basin to the Alster. The dam which had created Alster Lake was moved 450 feet downstream, creating a third basin, only 150 feet wide, called the "Little Alster." Thus there is now a tripartite Alster: a small, intensely urban basin without any vegetation, and a larger one, still urban, but lined with trees and opening up across the landscaped causeway and the bridge on its outer side to the third part—the again larger and completely landscaped Outer Alster. The short sides of the Little Alster are formed by bridges; along its western side runs an arcade. After World War II this arcade was extended along the narrow canal which connects the Alster to the Elbe. The eastern side opens up to the newly created City Hall Square. Its spatial relation to the Little Alster is a probably conscious replica of the relation of the Venetian Piazza and Piazetta. Characteristically, the wings of the City Hall are joined to those of the Stock Exchange, and across the street is the State Bank. This not-so-holy trinity survives in a new location. The square, as the junction point of three subway lines, is more than ever the center of the city. It is only a stone's throw from the spot on which, almost 12 centuries ago, the first cathedral was built.

As the difference between the various sections of the Alster have gradually become more and more articulated, so has also the contrast between the Elbe as the working river and the Alster as the playground of the city. In the eighteenth century a local poet could sing, "The Elbe makes us richer by shipping; the Alster teaches sociability." This is even truer today; but it was not yet true in the Middle Ages, when both rivers carried freight and their banks looked very much alike.

The broad expanses of these two bodies of water are dominated by the silhouette of the "City." It is still determined by the spires of the five parish churches, rising over the solid mass of its buildings, which are fairly uniform in height as a result of a legal limit. The physical structure of none of the spires antedates the middle of the last century. They are all still in exactly the same location at which they were founded. Altogether, in this millennial city there are very few structures built before 1800, far fewer than there are in Boston or Philadelphia. But there can be no doubt of the city's continuing identity. The interaction of the inherent element of the site, the two rivers, the outline of the inner city shaped by the wall, and the silhouette has created a strong and unique image. Nobody planned that image. But each generation, as it changed the city to suit its needs, continued and developed the themes played by its predecessors. It is still the same Hamburg, only more so.

SUMMARY

American cities are rightly concerned about losing their identities through the ruthless destruction of their landmarks. Certainly we should increase our efforts for the preservation of buildings of historical and architectural value. However, it is important to realize that elements other than buildings may be equally or even more important factors in the continuity of city form. The natural site is fairly permanent, and it can and should be articulated—made more visible by human action. The astonishing longevity of the street pattern is grounded not only in its increasingly important infrastructure, but even more so in legal notions of property lines in the heads of men; gray matter is harder to move than concrete. The city center remains in most, though not in all cases, in its original location, strengthened by one transportation system after another. Many districts continue, in ever-changing ways, their characteristic functions.

The words with which Goethe characterizes the human person in the first of his "Orphic Primal Words," entitled "Daimon," may be true of cities as well:

No time, no power ever can dissolve
Created form that living will evolve.

Chapter 4

THE OLD CITY AND THE NEW METROPOLIS

You have asked me to talk about "older cities." That is, of course, a relative concept. The oldest known city, Jericho, is 7000 years old. Athens and Jerusalem are only half that age, and mere youngsters like Paris and London again not much more than half as old as these. But I shall confine myself to my experience in still younger cities, such as Philadelphia, age 295, and Toronto, age 184.

However, it is quite true that all these cities, over the centuries, were in some decisive respects of a common type, different from the cities whose problems we face today. For 5000 years and more mankind has lived primarily in two forms of settlements—the town and the rural village. The vast majority of the world's population everywhere lived in the "country," and it was there that most of the world's work was done. Only a small ruling and guiding elite and those immediately serving them lived in the "city."

Not until 200 years ago did this pattern begin to change under the impact of the process known as the industrial revolution, that is, the application of the scientific method to material production, resulting in rapidly growing productivity, ever-increasing division and specialization of labor, and, as a corollary, ever-increasing interdependence and exchange of goods and services.

Transportation played and continues to play a key role in this process. By the middle of the nineteenth century the new means of long-distance, interurban transportation and communication—the steamboat, the railroad, and the electric telegraph—made possible the concentration of industrial production in big cities, which grew rapidly by a vast migration from the countryside. But within these great agglomerations, movement of persons, goods, and messages continued to proceed on foot or on hoof, limiting their size generally to a radius of 3–4 miles. The result was the densely built up "big city," where factories, residences, and all other uses were crowded close together.

Only toward the end of the nineteenth century did new means of short-distance, intraurban transportation and communication become general—electric traction, applied to street cars and to trains traveling on their own grade-separated rights-of-way, and the telephone, soon to be followed by the internal combustion engine, applied to passenger cars, trucks, and buses, as well as by radio and television. The

---

Source: Unpublished lecture.

boundary set by the distance which could be daily traveled on foot or on hoof was broken, and the concentrated "big city" proved to be a transitory phenomenon, due only to the half-century time lag between the impacts of the industrial revolution on interurban and on intraurban communications.

The country-to-city movement of population continues, all over the world, and stronger than ever. But this centripetal wave is now being met by a second, centrifugal city-to-suburb wave. The combined result of these two movements is the modern metropolitan area. It differs radically from the city as we have known it throughout history. As did its precursor, the nineteenth century "big city," it combines the traditional "central" ruling and organizing function of the town with the function of being the major seat of material production. Not only are the populations of the modern metropolitan areas several times greater than those of even the largest preindustrial cities, but also their daily activities are spread out over a far wider territory; and this territory includes not only "urban" but also extensive "open" areas—parks, golf courses, airfields, even farms and forests. The modern metropolis is "neither city nor country." Finally, it is characterized by separation of places of residence from place of work.

DISTRIBUTION OF FUNCTIONS IN THE MODERN METROPOLIS

The basic raison d'être of the modern metropolis is the need for cooperation and communication resulting from the division of labor. Only the large metropolis offers to the highly specialized worker, in particular in the professional and managerial groups, a wide choice of employment, and to the employer a wide choice of highly specialized workers. Primarily the metropolis is a labor market, a place for making a living. This role also sets its limits. It is a commuting area, extending as far as daily commuting is possible and no farther. Under present North American conditions this means a radius up to 30–40 miles or an area 100 times as large as that of the nineteenth century "big city." Within this area the land use pattern and the transportation system should maximize mutual choice of place of employment and of persons employed by maximizing the possibility of commuting, but should also, in order to minimize travel time and cost, minimize the need for commuting.

This makes it desirable to provide, within every major section of a metropolitan area, an approximate equilibrium between resident labor force and places of employment. Analysis of available data shows clearly that the percentage of residents of an area who work in different employment areas, and vice versa, decreases regularly with increasing distance between places of work and places of employment. It is therefore evident that by coordination of their locations commuting can be minimized; it is, however, an illusion to believe that it can be eliminated, that planning can create a pattern in which everybody walks to work. In the free choice of place of work (and of residence) many other motives are far stronger than the desire to minimize the journey to work. In Hudson County, New Jersey, for instance, an urbanized area of 44 square miles within the New York Metropolitan Area, there were, in 1960, 244,000 jobs and 233,000 employed residents, as close to a "balance" as one can ever hope to achieve. But over 35% of those employed in Hudson County commuted "in" from other counties, and 32% of the residents commuted "out." Similar patterns were shown by a survey made in 1954 in Metropolitan Toronto.

CENTER AND PERIPHERY

This increasing pattern of cross-commuting indicates that the role of the center of the city and of the metropolitan community is changing. In the nineteenth century, with its limited facilities of intraurban transportation, the center was the preferred location for all activities.

Since that time there has been an increasing and still-continuing shift from activities dealing with goods—manufacturing, warehousing, and, to a lesser extent, retailing—to those dealing primarily with persons, the wide and growing array of business services and, to a lesser extent, of consumer services. These "tertiary" industries, typically carried on in offices, proliferating with increasing specialization, serving a wide region, and dependent on contact with each other as well as with their widely dispersed customers, are even more characteristic of the modern metropolis than is manufacturing. In view of their rapid growth it is surprising to find that in the largest metropolitan areas in the United States employment in the central business district (C.B.D.) and traffic into and out of that area have not increased during the last five decades. In Canada this leveling off occurred later. However, since 1948 the number of persons counted between 6:30 and 10 A.M. as crossing a cordon line encircling the C.B.D. of Toronto has also remained constant.

From the C.B.D. outward the density decreases with amazing regularity in subsequent concentric zones. Over time there is a gradual decrease in residential population density in the inner and a fairly rapid increase in the outer zone. The outgoing wave of population growth has a definite crest, a concentric zone with the highest rate of growth, which moves regularly outward. The lines describing the change in population (or density) of all concentric zones follow, one after another, a logistic curve, gradually leveling off after a period of most rapid growth. But (and this is of decisive importance) in each subsequent zone the leveling off occurs at a lower overall density. This regular falling off of densities toward the periphery holds true not only for residential but also for all land uses. Industry and commerce also require increasing land areas per employed person, the farther from the center they locate. Employment density in new outlying industrial districts may be as much as 20 times lower than in old industrial areas near the center. This pattern of distribution of land use, population, and employment, the result of transportation, in turn determines the pattern of movement of goods and persons.

While the metropolitan area has inherited the bane of the big city of the nineteenth century—too many people in too little space, resulting in congestion of people—it has, paradoxically, compounded this problem by its opposite—dispersion of more and more people and establishments over too much space. The resulting distances are far too great to be overcome by walking, and densities in the outer reaches of the expanding area are too low to be served efficiently by public transportation. A rapidly increasing number of persons rely on the private automobile for their trips, and an increasing volume of goods is moved by trucks. It is this demand for space by the motor vehicle, both moving and standing, which is popularly referred to as "the traffic problem."

PERSON MOVEMENTS WITHIN A METROPOLITAN AREA

Traffic surveys made during the past few years in Metropolitan Toronto indicate that the inhabitants of that area made an average of 2.0 trips per capita on an average workday, with an average trip length of close to 5 miles, or a total of about 10 miles per person, within the boundaries of the metropolitan municipality. Thus the 2 million inhabitants of that area traveled, by mechanical means, a total of about 20 million miles daily, an average of over 80,000 miles per square mile. By far the most, and also the longest, of these trips were made to or from work. About one sixth were made for social or recreational purposes, only one tenth were shopping trips, one out of 20 was made for business, and other purposes, primarily education, accounted for the remaining one tenth. The great majority of these trips were made from or to the home, but about one fifth were made between two points other than home. Almost half of these were for the purpose of work, indicating the great number of persons—presumably businessmen, salesmen, repairmen—who had to travel in performance of their work. Their total number exceeded the commonly overrated number of trips from home to shopping. Surveys in the United States reveal generally similar patterns.

PRIVATE AND PUBLIC TRANSPORTATION

All these trips are made either by public transit or by private car, and their optimal distribution between these two modes of transportation is the most vexing problem of the modern metropolis.

It is not too difficult to define the role which various means of transportation are best suited to play. The decisive factor is the density in the zones of origin and of destination of the trips.

The private automobile must serve all movements within low-density areas, including travel to work in outlying factories, and travel to rapid transit and railroad stations. In addition, it must serve movements in medium-density areas in unusual directions and/or at unusual times. Finally, those people who use their cars to move about during business hours have to bring them to the downtown concentration during the day.

Public surface transportation serves most movements in medium-density areas, including feeder movements to rapid transit and surburban railroad stations, short- and medium-length movements from medium-density areas to the high-density downtown area, and very short movements within the downtown area.

Rapid transit serves long- and some medium-distance movements within medium-density areas, most movements from medium-density areas and some from low-density areas to the downtown area, and very short movements within the downtown area.

Suburban railroad lines mostly serve the movement from the more distant low-density areas to the downtown area. These may travel directly to the downtown area or to transfer points for rapid transit lines.

If, where, and when major outlying concentrations are developed, these may also be connected with the downtown area by rapid transit or suburban railroads.

The distinction made here between "rapid transit" and "suburban railroad lines" refers not necessarily to the operating agencies, but rather to the type of service. The former operates on headways of 90 seconds to 5 minutes; the latter, generally on headways of 10 minutes to 1 hour.

"Medium" densities are here defined as residential densities of 7000–25,000 persons per square mile.

Public transportation requires concentration of trips not only in space, but also in time. If 1000 persons want to travel from point A to point B during the same 5-minute period, it is obviously more rational to transport them in one train than in 700 cars, each carrying one or two persons. However, if the same 1000 persons make their trips between the same two points during 200 different time periods, they will have to use their cars.

The main concentrations in time occur, of course, during the morning and evening rush hours, as a result of the journey to and from work. It is therefore not surprising to find that transit loads are increasingly concentrated at these hours, while the private car has become more and more predominant for trips at other hours and on weekends. While generally not more than 20% of all person-miles in private cars are made during the two morning and two evening rush hours of the five weekly workdays, about 50–60% of all transit rides are concentrated during these periods. This means that structures (very expensive in case of rapid transit), vehicles, and personnel are fully used only during 20 out of the 168 weekly hours during which they have to be maintained.

In Metropolitan Toronto in 1976 over three fourths of all trips were made by private car. However, while only few trips for social and recreational purposes were made by transit, one third of the trips from home to work were transit trips. Of the trips most highly concentrated in space and time, the rush-hour trips to and from the C.B.D. transit still accounted for about 70%, the same percentage as in 1929.

It is evident that private and public transportation fulfill different purposes. Movement into and out of the center is best served by transit; that within the center, by walking. However, private cars cannot be completely barred from the center, because many of the people working there need them for their work. Probably the only feasible way to limit their number is rationing by price, by raising fees for parking, in particular all-day parking, in the C.B.D. well above the price for parking at outlying stations of rapid transit and suburban railroad lines. The remaining road traffic should interfere as little as possible with pedestrian movement. This can be achieved to some extent by creating "pedestrian islands," as has been done in Ottawa and in a number of American and European cities. Complete elimination of the conflict between vehicular and pedestrian traffic by creation of a second level has been proposed for Fort Worth, Texas, but so far has not been implemented. However, in a small part of the center such a scheme has been successfully carried out in Stockholm and in Montreal.

Decisive for the potential of public transit to attract riders is, in addition to speed (including headways), comfort, and price, the connection between the stations or stops and the points of ultimate origin and destination of its passengers. The great attraction of the private car is its ability to provide door-to-door service. Public transportation must always rely on some second means to assemble and distribute its riders. These means are walking, driving a private car to and from a parking facility at a station, and riding other transit vehicles and transferring. In the C.B.D.s of big cities large numbers of passengers, sufficient to support rapid transit trains at frequent headways, can be assembled and distributed by a combination of walking and the use of elevators, a means of public transportation which is usually not considered as such. In areas of medium densities a sufficient number of passengers can be assembled by walking to support surface transportation by streetcar or bus; and by combination of transfer from surface lines and walking, rapid transit stations can be fed. However, this necessitates relatively close spacing of transit stations, resulting in a relatively low traveling speed. It is therefore hardly feasible to extend rapid transit lines of this type far out into the peripheral low-density areas, because total traveling time will become too long to be competitive with the private automobile. Also, the loads that can be assembled in these outer areas are too small to justify use of the long and frequent trains which are required on the inner sections of a rapid transit system. These outer areas can be better served by a different system with widely spaced stations, relying for the assembling of its passengers largely on the private automobile, the "park-and-ride" or "kiss-and-ride" method.

Such "combined" trips, using private and public transportation for different parts of the way, are possible when the destinations are concentrated so that they can be reached either by walking (destinations in the C.B.D.) or by transferring to the transit system (destinations in the inner, medium-density area). However, when the destinations are dispersed, private cars appear to be the only feasible means of transportation.

As stated, traffic to and from the center has leveled off and traffic within the inner ring of medium density is also not increasing. As places of employment disperse, a greater proportion of work trips from these areas is bound to go to dispersed destinations. All future growth of residential population will necessarily occur in the outer rings. If it continues to take place, as it has during the past 10 years, at densities averaging about four to five households per acre of residential neighborhood, it will be impossible to provide the residents with public transportation, even in the main direction toward the center. However, this type of development is by no means mainly the result of consumer preference, but largely reflects public policy. The Central Mortgage and Housing Corporation has encouraged homeownership of detached houses on large lots; municipalities have excluded more intensive development by zoning. As the effects of these policies are becoming evident, the policies are beginning to change and some increase in residential densities in the outer zones may be expected. Even so, it is inevitable that the proportion of all trips which are made by private automobile will continue to increase because of the increasing dispersal of destinations for employment, shopping, and recreation. Peripheral, "ring" or "bypass" expressways are required to handle the increasing number of trips to these destinations. While these movements originate and terminate in a multitude of thin streams, they collect for a major part of their way in a mighty flow.

It is questionable whether radial expressways are desirable because they tend to pour more cars into the overloaded streets and parking facilities of the center. On the other hand, they serve a very useful purpose for trucks, for the considerable number of cars which are needed for use during the working day by persons employed in the C.B.D., and for trips outside of rush hours. However, they should terminate, not in the C.B.D., but in an inner ring which also serves to bypass the center, and this ring should be fairly large to permit the location of a sufficient number of interchanges, spaced widely enough apart to allow for weaving, acceleration, and deceleration.

COST AND BENEFITS OF PUBLIC AND PRIVATE TRANSPORTATION

Both private and public transportation require substantial investments and large operating costs, and these have to be weighed in assessing the respective roles of the two types.

The total cost of an urban passenger-car-mile may average 25 cents. If a transit fare of 40 cents is assumed, this indicates that driving a car without passengers is cheaper for distances up to 1.6 miles, and with one, two, or three passengers, up to 3, 4.5, and 6 miles, respectively. It is therefore evident that in a considerable number of cases it is cheaper for the individual to drive than to ride, even if the total cost is figured. However, about three fourths of the cost of operating an automobile consists of more or less fixed costs; and in practice the driver counts only the "out-of-pocket" costs of operation, which average about 6 cents per mile. So, except when it is necessary to pay for parking, from the point of view of the individual car owner it is always cheaper to drive.

However, the cost to the public and to the economy of the metropolitan area is a different matter. If all movements in a large metropolitan area were to be made by car, so much space would be required for the moving and standing vehicles that little would be left—particularly in the center—for the other land uses which are the destinations of all these movements.

It is evident that today the market does not allocate resources in the most rational way to private and public transportation, respectively. As indicated, the greater part of the cost of operating an automobile consists of fixed costs. If public transportation is to compete with the private car, a substantial portion of its cost will also have to be transformed into fixed costs. The only practical way of doing this is by covering these costs out of general tax revenues. The objection may be raised that it is unfair to ask the automobile driver to pay for a service which he or she does not use. However, the driver benefits from the fact that the transit rider, by leaving his or her car at home, frees the street for those using their automobiles.

Generally, support of public transit out of tax revenues underwrites a deficit, obviously an undesirable procedure; or it assumes responsibilities for all or part of the capital cost, in particular of rapid transit lines, while the operating agency must cover the operating cost out of user charges. This militates against a rational weighing of capital versus operating costs and may lead to a curtailment of surface feeder lines, which frequently can be run only at an operating loss, and to subsequent underutilization of the rapid transit lines and of the capital invested in them. The only sound procedure is for the municipality to pay in accordance with the service performed, that is, per passenger-mile or seat-mile. This method has been adopted by the state of New Jersey for subsidizing suburban railroad service.

A strong case could be made for operating public transit as a public service free of charge. This would permit considerably faster loading of buses, resulting in greater speed and consequent economies of operation. There is a precedent for this in vertical public transportation. The entire cost of elevator service in office and apartment buildings is always assessed, as a "fixed cost," as part of the rent, regardless of the amount of use of the service by the various tenants.

Chapter 5

CRITERIA FOR JUDGING THE QUALITY OF THE URBAN ENVIRONMENT

A sudden and general awakening of interest in the "urban problem" has taken place in America during the past decade. Some critics have said that the greatest threat to the future of mankind, next to nuclear war, lies in "the problems of the cities." Statements of this kind, however, mistake social problems *in* the cities for those *of* the cities. They happen to have their locus in the cities because that is where people are. Since these problems are more visible in the cities, because of their concentrated populations, they force themselves on the consciousness and the conscience of society. Were the same problems scattered in many small pockets, public attention would not be so forcefully directed to them; they could even be swept under the rug more easily.

While most so-called urban problems are, in fact, problems of the larger society, there are some which refer to a smaller unit within the total urban environment: the "city" as a political entity in contradistinction to the "suburbs." A good deal of semantic confusion has arisen from the widening gap between socioeconomic fact and legal fiction. Until the turn of the present century, the legal boundaries of the city followed its socioeconomic boundaries fairly closely. Philadelphia, for example, expanded its corporate limits in 1854 from 2 to 130 square miles; and half a century later five counties united to form the city of New York. Since then, the local body politic in the United States has suffered a hardening of the arteries. Canada, as well as several European countries, has, on the other hand, given recognition to the transformation of the city into a much larger and looser metropolitan area.

The expansion of cities into metropolitan areas, usually seen merely in quantitative terms, has resulted in a profound qualitative change, in the emergence of an entirely new form of human settlement which is indeed, as it is frequently accused of being, "neither city nor country." It differs profoundly from the city as it has been known throughout history. Although its peripheral sections show some of the aspects tra-

---

Source: "Criteria for Judging the Quality of the Urban Environment" by Hans Blumenfeld is reprinted from *The Quality of Urban Life*, Urban Affairs Reviews, Vol. 3, Henry J. Schmandt and Warner Bloomberg, Jr., Editors, © 1969, pp. 137–164 by permission of the publisher, Sage Publications, Inc. (Beverly Hills/ London).

ditionally associated with a "rural" environment—low densities and extensive open areas—it is nonetheless "urban" in its totality. The entire area forms a single functional unit, a single labor market, and a single housing market. The division into "city" and "suburbs" is obsolete and obscures the reality.

URBAN GROWTH

There has been, and continues to be, considerable hostility toward urban growth. "The intellectual versus the city" has become a fashionable theme of scholarly studies in contemporary America. This hostility, however, is by no means exclusively American, nor is it new. It appeared in the Western world with the first appearance of the big city: in Anakreon's shepherd poetry in Alexandria and in Cicero's praise of "rustic" Tusculum in Rome. It disappeared temporarily with the dissolution of urban life in the Dark Ages, only to surface again during the Renaissance. Both Elizabeth I and Cromwell tried to stop the growth of London by establishing a "greenbelt." The French kings left Paris for Versailles, and the kings of Prussia left Berlin for Potsdam.

At the other end of the political spectrum, socialists like Karl Marx and anarchists like Peter Kropotkin were even more emphatic in their condemnation of the big city and in their call for dispersal of industry over the countryside. Both they and later critics advocating "decentralization" were alarmed by the increasing centralization of decision-making and the consequent alienation of the individual from participation in the determination of his or her own fate and that of fellow beings. However, given a complex economy, integrated and interdependent on a national and even international scale, it is inevitable that many decisions vitally affecting the local community will be made elsewhere—and the smaller the community, the more this will be the case. Moreover, it is evident that spatial decentralization can be brought about only by a powerful central decision-making body. Only such a center can decide to locate the many various elements of economic and cultural activities simultaneously in one place, be it a "new" or an "enlarged" town. When decision-making is decentralized, as it largely is in the United States, each individual decision-maker of necessity locates where the supplementary facilities and institutions which he or she needs are available, that is, in existing large urban areas.

Louder than the warnings of the decentralizers that "bigger is worse"—and more typically American—have been the "bigger and better" barkings of chambers of commerce and other spokesmen of the business class. What both groups have in common is an emphasis on quantity. What ultimately matters, however, is the quality of life in urban areas, be they large or small.

THE "GOOD LIFE"

Few writers on urban affairs fail to quote Aristotle's dictum that "men come together in cities for security; they stay together for the good life." Considering that many people in American cities fear to walk on the streets and few dare to walk in a park at night, one might feel that we have come full circle and that our cities fail by the most basic and elementary criterion. The modern city is far better protected than its predecessors against "acts of God" (fires, floods, earthquakes, and hurricanes), but not against acts of man or woman.

Do people remain in the city because of the good life? It is not too difficult to define the good life in general terms: health, happiness, wisdom, and virtue. An environment may be defined as "good" if it produces healthy, happy, wise, and virtuous men and women. But it is difficult to measure these general qualities. Perhaps life expectancy can serve as a yardstick of health, but what are the indices of happiness, wisdom, and virtue?

Mortality is no higher in our cities than in the countryside. This is in itself a quite remarkable achievement, because for centuries the cities have been the breeding places of deadly epidemic diseases, in particular of waterborne diseases. Indeed, the universal provision of an ample and safe supply of water—also decisive for the control of fires—is an essential precondition for the very existence of the modern city. However, as Frederic L. Osborn, the head of the British Town and Country Planning Society, remarked, after having been treated to many glasses of chlorinated water on the occasion of his visit to the United States, "The American engineers seem to be more concerned that I should live as long as possible than that I should enjoy the time that I am alive." "Increased life expectancy" means an increased quantity of life; the term tells us nothing about its quality and the quality of the environment.

Social and Physical Environment

The old school of environmental geographers attempted to explain human characteristics and human behavior as direct effects of the physical environment, of climate, soil, and nurture. To some extent this notion still persists. The crumbling buildings of slums are supposed to "breed" crime and vice. But serious study leaves no doubt that a far stronger influence is exercised by the social environment, by the totality of human relations into which an individual enters in his or her lifetime—in the family, in work and business, in school and church and neighborhood—formal and informal, from person to person, and mediated by various modes of communication. This all-pervasive human environment is determined by the structure of the total society, by its "culture." The man-made or man-modified physical environment is the effect rather than the cause of the quality of the life of human society. But the physical environment reacts on the social, indirectly influencing it by limiting or facilitating human relations. In addition, it has a direct influence on health and may have, through its aesthetic aspects, an influence on happiness.

THE CITY AS AN ECONOMIC MACHINE

Of all the social relations into which people enter, one with another, probably none is more basic and more variable than the economic, the arrangements for the production and distribution of wealth. "Wealth" was not mentioned among the four aspects by which we tried to define the good life. This is at variance with the predominant American attitude, which tends to regard the gross national product (G.N.P.) as the be-all and end-all of the life of society, by which all other aspects are measured. Many products forming part of the G.N.P. may be useless and even positively harmful to health, happiness, wisdom, and virtue—as is the strain of accumulating them. Yet it remains true that there can be no life without the material means of life. There can be no living without "making a living."

The millions of people who have been, and are still, pouring into American cities from the countryside and from all over the world have been primarily attracted not by the prospect of "living" in the city, but by the hope of "making a living." In the context of a fully developed money economy this means "making money." Essentially American cities developed as money-mining camps, with the mentality characteristic of such camps: a sense of impermanence and an indifference to the despoiling of the environment by the waste products of the mining process.

The negative aspects of the industrial city should not obscure the profound significance of the fact that for the first time in history the urban areas have become the main producers of the wealth of society. Preindustrial cities were largely, sometimes exclusively, consumer cities, places in which the ruling elite consumed the wealth which it extracted from the countryside. It is, therefore, hardly realistic to expect in the working cities of today the kind of urbanity which graced the life of the Kaloi-k-Agathoi in classical Athens, of the princes of the Church and their retinue in papal Rome, or of the gentry in Georgian Bath.

Before discussing the quality of the urban environment as a place for living, it may therefore be appropriate to consider its qualities as a place for making a living, to evaluate the contemporary American urban area on its own terms as an economic machine.

Urbanization is the product of the interacting processes of rising productivity and increasing division and specialization of labor. As productivity increased in "primary" production (agriculture and mining), and as more and more goods and services previously produced on the farm were supplied from the outside by specialized factories and institutions, an increasing portion of the total labor force was shifted to "secondary" production (manufacturing and construction). And as productivity in the secondary sector increased, as more and more functions previously carried out by the manufacturer (research and development, selling, accounting) were performed by outside specialists, and as many other services were similarly transferred from the household to other specialized enterprises, an increasing portion of the labor force was shifted to the "tertiary" or "service" sector.

The highly advanced specialization and division of labor characteristic of modern society requires a complex and many-sided cooperation between an ever-growing number of specialized establishments, as well as a growing number of specialists within each establishment. Moreover, changes both of product and of production process become more frequent as technical progress accelerates and as a rising level of living leads to more differentiated and variable demand for consumer goods and services. These changes can proceed effectively only if the enterprise can draw on a broad and deep assortment of specialized goods, services, and skilled workers—resources usually found only in the larger urban areas.

From the point of view of the urban worker, these developments mean a wide range of job opportunities. In a small community an employee who leaves a job because of a change in product or process is generally faced with a choice of pulling up stakes and seeking employment elsewhere, or of accepting the role of "a square peg in a round hole," working at a job which does not utilize his or her best skills and talents. For the total economy, this means a loss of productivity; for the individual, a loss of income.

There is considerable evidence that productivity and income per person do indeed increase with population size. As census data show, per capita income tends to be highest in the largest urban areas. This relationship is based in part on the concentration of high-income occupations in these areas. However, wages and salaries for the same occupations also tend to be higher. A study of the Stockholm Region[1] concluded that the size factor alone accounted for 15–20% difference in incomes between Stockholm and the rest of Sweden. This variance must be ascribed to higher productivity resulting from the wider range of choice.

A wide range of mutual choice between employer and employee and between buyer and seller is certainly the decisive criterion for the urban area as an economic machine, as a place for making a living. But it is hardly less important for the city as a place for living: a wide range of choice of location and type of residence, of shopping and consumer facilities, of educational, cultural, and recreational opportunities, of medical services, of voluntary associations, and, last but not least, of personal contacts.

ACCESSIBILITY AND TRANSPORTATION

Without accessibility, however, the mere existence of a wide range of choice within an urban area is only an empty promise. This was dramatically illustrated by the fact that the unskilled workers of Watts who did not own a car could not avail themselves of those jobs in the Los Angeles area which might have been open to them.

Accessibility can be brought about in two ways (which are not mutually exclusive): by locating points of potential origin and destination close together, and by decreasing the friction of space between them. It is possible to reduce the need for commuting to work by providing within each section of an urban area an approximate balance between the number of residents in the labor force and the number of jobs. A purely quantitative balance, however, is not sufficient; a combination of residences in a price range accessible only to white-collar workers and of an equal number of blue-collar jobs in manufacturing plants (a situation found in some large real estate developments misnamed "new towns") will be of little value. A fairly broad range of types of jobs, as well as of types of residence, is required. Similarly, a distribution of a broad range of shopping and public and private service facilities in balance with the demands of the surrounding residential population can substantially increase accessibility. Minimizing the need for travel is a valid criterion for the arrangement of the physical environment.

Ample data on travel in urban areas confirm that the percentage of residents of a given area traveling to a given number of potential destinations for work or other purposes decreases with increasing travel distance. Other things being equal, people prefer to locate their residences as close as possible to their places of work. But other things are not equal, and are becoming less so. The more work becomes specialized,

---

[1]Folke Kristensson, People, firms, and regions, Economic Research Institute, Stockholm School of Economics, September 1967, pp. 1–10.

the more some jobs become more attractive than others. The more the level of living rises, the more some types of residences and of neighborhoods become more attractive than others. In other words, people avail themselves increasingly of the wide range of choice which is the very hallmark and raison d'être of the large urban area.

For these reasons the second method of improving accessibility, decreasing the friction of space, is of growing significance. Even more important than minimizing the need for travel is the criterion of maximizing the possibility of travel, or, expressed differently, increasing mobility. It is, therefore, quite natural that in the public mind demands for improving transportation outweigh all others.

Criteria for Urban Transportation: Mobility

Mobility or mutual accessibility is as important for goods and for messages as for persons. The problem is less severe with messages since for the most part they are equally accessible throughout the urban area. Goods transportation, however, deserves more attention than it is usually accorded. To a greater extent than is generally realized, it has been relieved by substituting movement by pipeline and, for fossil fuels in the form of electricity, by wire for surface movement. Minimization of surface transportation by wider use of such substitution, as well as by proximate location of establishments which generate substantial interchanges of goods, is an important, if secondary, criterion for the arrangement of the urban physical environment.

The main problem, however, remains the reduction of the friction of space for the movement of persons. Friction of space can be adequately measured not in terms of miles, but only in terms of time, money, and inconvenience. It is possible, though difficult, to express these three aspects by a common denominator—time or money—by a systematic analysis of the trade-offs between these different aspects, in which people actually engage. Although quantification of inconvenience has not yet been achieved, translation of time into terms of money—at present, usually $1.55 per person-hour—is common practice. It is on this basis that proposals for investment in road and transit facilities are considered justified. Saving time is generally regarded as the goal and product of a good transportation system.

There is considerable evidence that, in the long run, the benefits of increased mobility are taken out not so much in terms of less time, as in terms of more space and of wider choice. It seems that the time people are willing to spend on a trip for a given purpose is fairly constant. Even in large urban areas the median duration of the journey to work has been found to be no more than 0.5 hour. If walking at a speed of 3 mph is the predominant mode of movement, about half of all people will live within 1.5 miles of their places of work; if streetcars at 9 mph are universally used, within 4.5 miles; if car driving at 18 mph is predominant, within 9 miles. The area within which destinations can be reached within a given time is enlarged 36 times. If the density of potential destinations were the same, the range of choice would also be increased 36 times. In fact, the overall density of American urban areas is about one fifth to one sixth of the density prevailing a century ago, when walking was the predominant mode of transportation. It seems that the benefit of increased mobility is being taken out about equally in terms of more space and in terms of wider choice, each being increased more than fivefold.

The direct result of increased mobility is an enormous increase in the number of person-miles (and ton-miles). Once this new pattern is established, many trips require more time, money, and inconvenience than are acceptable. In particular, any unusual circumstances lead to congestion and delays. At many places and times movement is far slower than "normal." Thus the "traffic problem" constantly reproduces itself; it is never solved. It might appear from this that all improvements in transportation are futile; the expected saving of time does not materialize. However, if people take out the benefits of increased mobility in terms of more space and wider choice, it means that they value these higher than they value savings in travel time, cost, and inconvenience. The benefits of mobility are real, both for living and for making a living.

It may, however, well be asked: How much space? How much choice? Is there not a point where "enough is enough"? Even if there are millions of jobs in an area, a worker can occupy only one at a time, and can have social contacts with only an infinitesimal fraction of the persons living in the area. The New York Regional Plan Association raised exactly this question: "Isn't there a maximum beyond which it becomes more of the same?" Its answer was: "Apparently not."[2] The appearance may not be entirely conclusive; there may well be a diminishing return. Certainly many people come to the New York Region, but many others live happily in smaller cities. Yet whatever the population size of the urban area, broadening the range of choice by increased mobility remains a valid criterion.

The value of more space is not so easily resolved. Its desirability insofar as manufacturing and warehousing are concerned raises little doubt. The modern landscaped, one-story plant with ample space for loading, parking, and expansion is superior to the multistory loft building, in terms both of productivity and of environment for the life of the workers. Nor is there much doubt as to the desirability of more space for schools and playgrounds, parks, and sport facilities. Somewhat more questionable is the rapidly increased land absorption by residences. Some of this increase is forced by zoning requirements which many municipalities enact in order to keep taxes low by making it impossible for low-income families to live within their boundaries. Some is due to the fact that each individual, in making his or her own decision, does not consider the combined effect of similar decisions made by all other individuals. People move to the "suburbs," in the expectation of being close to both the "city" and the "country." But the more people make this choice, the further they have to move away from the city and the further the country moves away from them. Viewed in this light, the general move to the low-density urban periphery is self-defeating.

The "city-country" location is not the main reason for low-density suburban development. The desire for ample private outdoor space is deep-seated, and the satisfactions derived from its various uses are real, as surveys all over the world have shown time and again. Thus, making an ample and growing supply of land per capita accessible, not only by road and rail, but also by pipeline and wire, is an important criterion for a good urban environment. However, with the presently prevailing methods of ownership, control, and development, much of the land made accessible is not used. The "overall density" previously referred to relates population to all land within a given area. This includes not only that actually used for any urban purposes (including parks), called "developed" in the planners' language, but also "unde-

---

[2] New York Regional Plan Association, *Regional Plan News*, No. 86, October 1967.

veloped" or "open" land. Much could be gained if both types were held together instead of being scattered haphazardly. The cost of accessibility, of all types, within the developed areas would be reduced, and the open spaces would be far better suited for recreation as well as for agriculture and forestry. The criterion of more accessible land must, therefore, be supplemented by that of compact and continuous urban development, at whatever density.

Criteria for Urban Transportation: Safety

Overcoming the friction of space not only incurs costs in terms of time, money, and inconvenience, but also exacts its price in accidents. The toll in human life and personal injury on the streets and highways of America is rightly a cause for alarm. It is important to realize that, whatever may be achieved in reducing this toll by improvement of the road, the vehicle, and the driver, the individually directed fast movement of many heavy bodies is inherently dangerous. If 60 persons travel in two buses, the probability of a collision is 1. If the same 60 persons travel in 40 cars, the probability is 40×39, or 1560. Considering that buses have been assumed to carry 20 times as many persons as cars, the danger to persons is still 78 times greater in cars than in buses.

For reasons of safety alone—aside from many other considerations which will be discussed later—minimizing automobile and maximizing transit usage is an important criterion. Collisions between vehicles, as well as delays, occur almost exclusively because of two kinds of friction, cross-friction and side-friction (weaving). Provision of a grade-separated rights-of-way eliminates both types of friction completely in public transportation; for vehicular movement, freeways eliminate the former completely and greatly reduce the latter. Hence, minimizing the movement of all types of vehicles on surface streets and maximizing the use of grade-separated facilities—subways for transit, and especially freeways for cars and trucks, as well as buses—are an additional criterion for a safe environment.

Criteria for Urban Traffic: Indirect Effects

So far this discussion has dealt only with the benefits and costs to the user of transportation, that is, with the bargain between seller and buyer which, according to classical economics, is supposed to result in maximizing the benefits of both. However, in an urban environment any "deal" affects not only seller and buyer, but also third persons on whom it confers benefits—and "malefits."

Third-person benefits of vehicular traffic are few; third-person malefits are many and overwhelming. The latter may be divided into two groups: interference with other movements, and dangers to pedestrians. The first includes the interference of private cars with the movement of transit vehicles and of trucks, and in particular the interference of all vehicular movements with those of pedestrians. Pedestrian movement suffers considerable delay by being forced to make detours and to wait for traffic lights. But delay is not the only or the most serious malefit inflicted on the pedestrian. He is in almost constant danger. Noise and vibration, as well as the glare of headlights, disturb rest and sleep in adjacent houses. Exhaust fumes pollute the air. These factors, together, increase nervous tension. It has been rightly said that in our eagerness to go places we are in danger of destroying places worth going to.

The fact that traffic interferes with a good living environment has long been recognized. Even before the advent of the automobile, separation of residential streets and traffic arteries was an accepted principle of city planning, a principle which has developed further into the concept of the "superblock" or "precinct." The most complete and systematic statement of this concept was developed in the famous Buchanan Report,[3] which proposed to establish standards of amenity for each built-up precinct. These standards, designed to preserve a "civilized" living environment, would determine the number of cars which would be permitted to move within the boundaries of each precinct.

Protection of the Pedestrian Realm

Traditionally the public domain of streets and squares has been a communal outdoor living room. It served for the play of children, for informal chats and meetings, for assemblies, demonstrations, and processions, and simply for sitting, standing, and walking around to enjoy the sun or the shade, to see and be seen. More and more the upper- and middle-income groups have transferred most of these activities to off-street enclosed and open spaces, at some loss of contact among neighbors. The lower income groups, however, still rely on the street as their outdoor living room.

Large volumes of speeding automobiles have destroyed the age-old amenities of this pedestrian realm. It should be noted (and was recognized in the Buchanan Report) that a limited volume of cars moving at moderate speed is quite compatible with street life. Indeed, it may enhance it, as one can appreciate by watching the use made of cars by boys and girls on Saturday night on any small-town main street. In many cases, however, complete separation of cars and pedestrians is desirable. This separation can be achieved in three ways: temporally (in time), horizontally, and vertically.

Separation in time was practiced in imperial Rome and is now being successfully applied to Copenhagen's main shopping street, Strøget, but its applicability is limited.

The first systematic attempt at complete horizontal separation of vehicular and pedestrian movement was the Radburn Plan, developed around 1930. Radburn also uses vertical separation in the form of pedestrian underpasses under arterial streets. However, the most discussed and copied feature is the horizontal separation between cul-de-sacs for vehicular "service" access and walkways leading to the front door on the other side of the houses. Ironically, separation has here been applied where it is definitely not needed, because the number of cars serving the dozen or so houses on each cul-de-sac is minimal. As a consequence, the pathways and front doors are little used and most pedestrian life, including the play of children, occurs on the "service" roads.

Separation is needed where traffic volumes are high, particularly in city centers and shopping districts and in concentrations of high-density apartments. Shopping centers owe their success largely to this separation. Strangely, the example they provide has been followed more widely in Europe than in America, by transforming parts of the city center into pedestrian malls, sometimes extended to whole pedestrian precincts.

---

[3] Colin Buchanan, Traffic in towns, Her Majesty's Stationery Office (HMSO), London, England, 1963.

Horizontal separation can cover only a limited area, because access from the rear must be provided and because the network of streets cannot be interrupted for too long a distance. Over a large area complete separation can be achieved only by establishing separate levels. Ideally, pedestrians should move on arcaded sidewalks above the vehicular levels. In built-up areas it is, however, generally easier to accommodate them on a lower level, as has been done in Philadelphia's Penn Center and in Montreal's Place Ville Marie.

A combination of horizontal and vertical separation is also possible by a system of walkways in the interior of blocks, with overpasses or underpasses crossing the streets. Whatever the method, protection of the pedestrian realm by total or partial segregation of vehicular traffic is an increasingly important criterion of the quality of the urban environment as a place for living.

While separation eliminates most of the malefits inflicted on the environment by the motor vehicle, it cannot overcome what may be the most serious one: pollution of the air by the waste products of the internal combustion engine. This by-product of the motor age affects not only the immediate environment, but also entire urban areas extending over hundreds of square miles.

WASTE AND POLLUTION

The mentality of the money-mining camp led its inhabitants to dispose of waste by dumping it in the easiest and cheapest way, whether on the soil, in the water, or into the air. But production and consumption have increased and are daily augmenting the volume of wastes of all kinds, to such a degree that life itself is endangered. The situation has been aptly described by a West German scholar[4] in the following words:

No satisfactory solution has yet been found for disposal of the accumulated waste resulting from living standards brought by industrialization. Despite purification systems, rivers and canals can no longer eliminate the pollution; they are becoming biologically dead—sluggishly flowing cesspools. . . . The atmosphere all over the world is contaminated by certain technical robots that are part of the equipment of all civilized states and are regarded as indispensable.

And he continues:

While on the one hand the findings of a number of research groups in the field of biology and geophysics have given us an added insight into this liaison between human existence and natural preconditions, on the other we are using technical means to abuse nature in a horrifying way. But, by destroying vital biological systems we are contriving our own destruction.

Too many attempts to dispose of waste merely shift its incidence from one element of the environment to another. If garbage is dumped, it pollutes the earth; if it is incinerated, it pollutes the air; if it is run through grinders and flushed down the drain, it pollutes the water.

[4]Bodo Manstein, Shaping the future in a rational manner, *Perspectives*, 6, World Federation of Scientific Workers, London, England, June 1963.

Water pollution may be the most immediate problem. Great concern is caused by the proliferation of algae. This is ironic when it is considered that many nutritionists see in the growing of chlorella algae the best hope to supply mankind with an adequate protein diet. The algae in our sewage effluent are, unfortunately, not chlorellae. But their exuberant growth testifies to the wealth of plant nutrients contained in sewage. Plants are the ultimate source of food for all animals, including human beings, and the excrements—and ultimately the bodies—of animals are food for plants. The Chinese have become the most numerous nation on earth by carefully husbanding this natural cycle, although at the risk of the spread of waterborne diseases. Modern technology should be able to reestablish this natural cycle without this risk and on a larger scale.

With a chemical technology able to make almost anything out of anything and something out of everything, the entire concept of waste is becoming obsolete and should be replaced by the concept of recycling. Rather than thinking in terms of disposal of waste, we must learn to think in terms of reuse of by-products. The by-products of industry and transportation which pollute the water and interfere with its natural biological cleaning process, and also those which pollute the air, such as particles of fossil fuels resulting from incomplete combustion, consist of usable materials. However, the cost of recapturing them generally exceeds their market price, and their reuse is, therefore, not worthwhile for the enterprises which dump them. But such action may be very much worthwhile for the community as a whole. A difficult problem of cost allocation arises here.

Although water pollution may be the most immediate problem, in the long run air pollution may be even more serious. Here, too, a natural ecological balance is involved. Plants absorb carbon dioxide and produce oxygen; animals absorb oxygen and produce carbon dioxide. But so does combustion of fossil fuels, and in vastly greater amounts. Concern has been expressed that continuation of the rapidly rising trend of combustion may reach a point where the volume produced may adversely affect the earth's climate.

A more immediate danger lies in pollution of the atmosphere by the poisonous exhaust fumes of motor vehicles. Some reduction can be achieved by measures to encourage a shift from private to public transportation and from surface streets to freeways (which minimize exhaust-producing starts and accelerations) and by the installation of afterburners. But the only complete and satisfactory solution lies in the replacement of the internal combustion engine by a different type of power plant. Electric batteries with a greatly improved power-to-weight ratio or thermoelectric cells hold some promise. Some research and development in these fields is going on, but far too slowly. If an effort comparable to that of putting one man on the moon were made to allow all people to breathe freely on earth, results would quickly be produced.

The list of human actions endangering the biosphere could be extended indefinitely. They all are expressions of the mentality of the money-mining camp, which in its pragmatic, single-purpose pursuit of immediate gains brings about unforeseen and often catastrophic results. The floods which for the first time in seven centuries reached and heavily damaged the priceless art treasures of Florence certainly were the combined result of many such single-purpose actions in the watershed of the Arno River. What is needed is replacement of the single-purpose approach by ecological thinking. Preservation of the biosphere by maintaining and restoring the ecological balance of nature is the most basic criterion of the urban environment, as indeed of any environment for human life.

MICROCLIMATE

While the climate in urban areas, as a whole, generally differs from that of the surrounding countryside by having higher temperature and humidity and a severe deficiency of ultraviolet rays, there are very great climatic differences within each urban area. Ancient Greek and Chinese city planning was far ahead of contemporary practice in paying attention to sunshine, wind, and humidity in the selection of sites. In our cities the wealthy, who have a choice, generally have occupied the west end, where, thanks to the predominance of western winds, air pollution is less. They have also preempted the higher altitudes, where the air is cleaner and the heat of summer nights less oppressive. Less favorable climatic conditions obtain in most areas occupied by the non-air-conditioned dwellings of the mass of the population.

In addition to judicious selection of sites, many other means are available to improve the microclimate. Water and plants, in particular trees and shrubs, mitigate extremes of temperature and absorb dust and soot, as well as noise. The placing and the shape of buildings greatly influence the movement of air and can create or prevent both violent gusts and complete stagnation. Much of our present built environment adversely affects the microclimate by shutting out sunshine and air and by radiating until deep into the night the heat stored in walls and pavements during a hot day. In narrow street canyons this may even produce local inversion. Replacement of moisture-absorbing soils by the hard surfaces of pavements and roofs often leads to a harmful lowering of the water table in the immediate area and to flash floods downstream. Creation of the best possible microclimate in all parts of the urban area, but especially in its residential sections, is an important criterion for a physical environment conducive to health and happiness.

Recreational Facilities

Health and happiness require not only passive freedom from disturbing effects of the environment, but, even more importantly, opportunities for active exercise of the body and mind. Although many American cities can boast of large parks, there is still a dearth of parks and playgrounds where they are most needed: in the densely populated, low-income areas. Moreover, facilities and programs are often not geared to the real needs and demands of the population. Playgrounds, for instance, generally attract only a small section of the age groups which they are intended to serve. There is also a lack of small outdoor spaces in the immediate vicinity of the dwellings, easily accessible to preschool children and to the aged and the physically handicapped. Few immigrants from European countries, east or west, fail to comment on the lack of swimming pools to cool off in during our long, hot summers, and also of indoor facilities for physical exercise and for cultural activities.

Adequate provision of community facilities, geared to the needs of the surrounding population, is an essential element determining the quality of the urban environment.

IMPACT OF THE PHYSICAL ENVIRONMENT ON THE SOCIAL ENVIRONMENT

The aspects of the physical environments so far discussed certainly have an impact not only on physical health and well-being, but also on mental and moral health. However, in this respect their impact can only be peripheral; the human environment is decisive. Obviously, large sections of America's urban population are spiritually sick, torn between overactive aggression and passive despondency, expressed in a constantly rising rate of violence, crime, and delinquency, race and class hatred and strife, alcoholism, drug addiction, clinically definable mental sickness, and other symptoms of anomie. While the root cause of this state lies in social, economic, and political conditions, these are exacerbated by certain aspects of the physical environment. Before discussing these, a general analysis of the typical structure of our urban areas may be in order.

The Structure of Urban Areas

The structure of urban areas has developed, starting from the original and generally continuing center, in a fairly logical response to market forces. As an area increases in proportion to the square of distance, the increasing supply of land with increasing distance from the center results in a rapid decline in land prices, and consequently in densities for all types of uses, toward the periphery. This density gradient is universal, inevitable, and, in itself, not unhealthy.

As Ebenezer Howard, the father of the "Garden City" idea noted, people are attracted by two "magnets": city and country. Whatever one may think of Howard's therapy, his diagnosis is certainly correct. Hence a basic criterion for the urban area as a place for living is the contradictory pair of requirements of accessibility to both the urban center and the country at its periphery.

While all people to some extent are attracted by both magnets, the relative strengths of the two vary greatly, not only with personal preference, but primarily with the composition of the household. Single persons and childless couples, especially those in which both partners are working in white-collar jobs, are most strongly attracted by the occupational, educational, recreational, and cultural opportunities of the city center. They can satisfy their desire for the country by driving out to it. Preadolescent children do not have this mobility; they need open space right at their doorstep or in their neighborhood, and they have no use for the central city. Nor are their housewife-mothers generally attracted to the center for more than an occasional trip. The concentration of small dwelling units, generally as apartments, at the core of the urban areas, and of larger units, generally as single-family houses at the periphery, is therefore a perfectly logical response to entirely rational and voluntary decisions.

What is not rational and voluntary, but largely the result of arbitrary zoning, is the absence of dwellings suitable for small householders who want to live at the periphery, notably older couples and widows, whose children have left home, and who want, or are forced, to give up their homes, but do not want to give up their neighborhood. At the same time many families with numerous children now live in and immediately around the core of cities, in areas called "slum," "blighted," or "gray." They live there not voluntarily, but because lack of money and lack of mobility leave them no other choice. Just as second-hand cars are cheaper than new ones, second- or twenty-second-hand dwellings are less expensive than new ones. This is the only housing that one third to one half of the American urban population can afford, and it is, with few exceptions, to be found only in the older inner areas of the central cities.

The result is an increasing territorial division by class. Separate residential locations for different income groups are, of course, not new. In the typical American small town the poor lived "on the wrong side of the tracks." However, the scale of the entire community was so small that all its inhabitants inevitably "rubbed shoulders." But the children growing up in the vast peripheral areas of our urban agglomerations never see how the other half lives. In the United States this general class segregation is immeasurably aggravated by race segregation, which confines the rapidly growing urban nonwhite population in overcrowded ghettos.

The remedy is evident: provide in all sections of the area dwelling units of various types accessible to all classes and races. This objective is an important criterion of a good environment. Its achievement would, of course, require the massive use of public funds to bridge the gap between the price or rent of a new dwelling and the amount low-income households could pay. It would also require the massive use of public power to break down the resistance of white prejudice.

The opposite approach, propagated under the fashionable slogan "Bring the middle-income families back to the city," is utterly wrong. First, the often repeated statement that "only the very rich and the very poor" live in the center is simply not true. Even in Manhattan, in 1959, over one third (34.4%) of all families were in the $5000–$10,000 income bracket.[5] Second, and far more important, bringing the middle-income families back to the city means displacing low-income families. Under such a policy more families would be pushed out than brought in, because the middle-income families demand more space, both inside and outside the dwelling. There are, moreover, better reasons for the poor than for anybody else to live close to the center. Their households frequently contain several persons looking for work, much of which is casual, part-time, or done at unusual hours. The employment open to them may be either in the center—which does, and will continue to, contain the greatest concentration of such jobs—or at varying points at the periphery which can be reached by public transportation only from the center.

These observations are not meant to imply that no low-income families would live at the periphery, if dwellings within their means were available. Those with a steady job at a peripherally located establishment could live close to it. Those who owned a car could reach employment in any part of the outlying area (as well as at the center) from any other part of the periphery. The number of families in these categories may increase; but at present, and for a long time to come, very many low-income families will be forced to live in the center because of lack of mobility as well as of income. To force them out by "slum clearance" is, in the words of Patrick Geddes, "a pernicious blunder." Yet the practice continues. Though the verbiage has changed from "slum clearance" to "redevelopment" to "renewal," it is still the same old bulldozer, with rare exceptions, which is expected to "eliminate slum and blight." It is obvious that the demand for low-rent dwellings greatly outruns the supply when rooms are overcrowded and families are forced to share bathrooms, and when

---

[5] New York Regional Plan Association, *Regional Plan News*, No. 86, October 1967.

landlords can find tenants for dwellings in need of major repairs. Slum clearance makes this condition worse by further decreasing the supply of housing. Instead, the supply should be increased both by new low-rent and low-price units at the periphery and by maintenance, improvement, and rehabilitation of old units, without raising their rents or prices. This action should be combined with addition of facilities and services in the "blighted" areas.

"Urban renewal," as it has been and is being practiced in North America, is harmful not only because it decreases the scant supply of low-rent housing, but also because it completely destroys the social fabric of the neighborhood. The displaced persons not only are forced to pay higher rents or prices for dwellings often no better and sometimes worse than those that have been destroyed, but also are deprived of the support of neighborhood friends and families, stores, and institutions on which they rely far more than wealthier people. The time is long overdue to stop this criminal folly. Maintenance and constant improvement of existing houses and neighborhoods is one of the most important and most neglected criteria of a good urban environment.

PRIVACY AND NEIGHBORLINESS

It has already been noted that for lower income groups the street is an indispensable outdoor living room—an extension, indeed an integral part, of their homes. By contrast, the higher the economic, social, and educational level of a group, the more it identifies the home with its own dwelling and yard, and the greater the value it attaches to privacy, that is, protection from sight and sound. At the same time its human contacts are selective over an ever-widening area.

While both privacy and ease of contact are desired by everyone, rising income and education make more unrealistic than ever the dream of reproducing the "community feeling" of the old village by surrounding "neighborhoods" of 5000–10,000 people with green belts. This unlikelihood does not invalidate the desirability of organizing residential areas in units of approximately this size, for which the Russians use the more modest term *mikro-rayon*, with all community facilities of daily use, notably elementary schools, easily and safely accessible to pedestrians. But neighboring, in any meaningful sense, occurs only in much smaller groups of perhaps a dozen or so households. Actually, neighboring depends little on the physical environment. The widespread notion that it can be promoted by increasing densities is not borne out by the facts. A survey in the New York Region[6] showed that far more neighboring occurred among people living at densities of two or three houses per acre than among apartment dwellers and even among inhabitants of two- to three-family houses.

Density

The current obsession with raising density by packing more people on top of each other in higher and higher apartment towers seems to be the result of a Leibnitzian prestabilized harmony between the urge of the landowner to squeeze the last square foot of rentable space out of his property and the compulsion of the architect to erect

[6] New York Regional Plan Association, *Regional Plan News*, No. 86, October 1967.

a steep monument to his prowess. It leads to such strange rationalizations as the following from *Nations Cities:* "We wish more people would face up to the obvious fact that as our population doubles, the only way to bring low density close in is to develop much higher density at the center. . . ."[7] The obvious fact is that at a distance of 3 miles from the city center there is only one ninth as much land as at a distance of 9 miles. Yet we find proposals, such as the one reported in *Nations Cities,* calling for the razing of most buildings inside the present low-density belt, and the accommodation of all uses presently found in the intermediate "gray" belt by piling them up in the inner core. Even if this fantastic proposal were carried out, only a very small proportion of low-density dwellers could live closer in than they do now. It is impossible to believe that all of the very outstanding members of the panel, whose discussions this report purports to summarize, have checked this totally irresponsible statement of their reporter.

A wider variety of densities, between about 8000 and 40,000 persons per square mile of residential area, can and should be achieved by a mixture of housing types of different heights. Beyond these limits excellent accommodation at higher densities can be provided for households of one or two adults who can afford to pay for air-conditioned apartments in tall structures with underground parking, swimming pools, and other amenities. Excellent accommodation at much lower densities can be provided in single-family houses on large lots for people who can afford to pay for two or more cars and for hundreds of feet of streets and utilities.

Some observers believe that with rising incomes the proportion of these two extreme densities will greatly increase. This may well happen if the present extreme inequality in the distribution of the national income continues. However, should we develop sufficient economic rationality to maximize the utility of personal disposable income—which decreases exponentially with increase in volume—by distributing it more evenly, the intermediate densities will accommodate the vast majority of the population during the lifetime of houses presently on the drawing boards.

Lively Centers

While neither higher density nor greenbelts or other boundaries have any noticeable effect on human relations, centers at which people meet and engage in common activities can promote community identification. It is difficult to define the most appropriate population size to be served by such centers; probably a hierarchy is required. The traditional "neighborhood" size appears to be too small in a typically urban environment. Some[8] have advocated groups of 20,000–30,000 persons. Groups of this size will undoubtedly have a role. But at least in large urban areas of millions of people, spread out over hundreds of square miles, there is a need for larger centers, veritable "secondary downtowns," serving populations of 250,000–500,000 and more. The functions traditionally concentrated downtown—public, private, and professional offices, a great variety of retail stores and consumer services, hotels and restaurants, theaters and concert halls, museums and exhibition centers—are more and more to be found also on the periphery, but in scattered locations. By concentrating them in major centers, their attraction and accessibility would be greatly increased; and the infrastructure, notably public transportation, would be more fully utilized and could, therefore, provide a higher level of service.

[7] *Nations Cities,* 1967.
[8] Humphrey Carver, *Cities in the Suburbs,* University of Toronto Press, Toronto, Ont., 1962.

Common use of such subcenters of various sizes and the contacts developed by their use might indeed provide identification with a unit which is closer to the individual citizen, more comprehensible, and more conducive to active participation in public affairs. Yet it should not be overlooked that identification with an in-group implies a certain degree of rejection of out-groups. This may take such extreme forms as gangs of youths defending their "turf" with knives and guns against intruding outsiders, or the less violent, but far more vicious and harmful zoning policies of exclusive suburbs.

Identification with a part of the urban area must, therefore, be supplemented by identification with the whole. Here we have another pair of contradictory criteria. The whole of the urban area is symbolized by its center, visually by the dominance of the silhouette of its skyscrapers and functionally by its uniqueness. Only in the largest center can those "highest-order" functions which need the support of the entire metropolitan market be located. In American cities this requirement is often overshadowed by the second function, that of private and public management and their advisers, to whom easy accessibility to each other is even more important than accessibility to the entire urban area.

Because mutual accessibility is the very essence of the center, it is doubtful whether it should be diluted by residential uses, although a concentration of apartment houses close by certainly is desirable. In large centers the office towers, the seat of top management, tend to concentrate so highly that little space is left in or between them for other functions. The fact that such districts are dead and deserted after office hours has greatly alarmed some observers. Yet in itself this is no more alarming than the fact that a baseball stadium is dead and deserted when no game is on. What is important is that there should be at the center an area with a rich mixture of uses, vertically as well as horizontally, which attracts life and movement in the evening as well as during the day and thereby supports the infrastructure and those uses, such as restaurants, which operate during both periods. As previously mentioned, the center should be as far as possible a pedestrian realm, including plazas as outdoor living rooms, enclosed and shaped by the walls of the surrounding buildings, with the sky as the ceiling and with a sensitively patterned floor, furnished by plants, fountains, and sculpture.

Separation and Integration

Development of the finely grained mixture of uses which gives variety and interest to the urban environment is frequently prevented by zoning. Zoning is essentially a device to protect property values from being impaired by the vicinity of incompatible uses and building types. Such incompatibilities do exist and do require separation. At the same time, integration of complementary functions, such as residence and retail trade, and of different housing types is also required. Separation and integration are another pair of contradictory criteria which call for judicious balance.

All too often the desire for protection, implemented not by an administrative device such as the British "development permit" but by the legal instrument of zoning with its inevitable requirement of "equality before the law," has produced a deadening uniformity and monotony in our residential areas. A well-designed mixture of buildings of different heights, types, and uses could produce far more attractive districts. Certainly the mixture should not be the same in all districts; otherwise, the uniformity now found within each of them would be reproduced on a larger scale by uniformity among all of them. A strong individual character of each district is indispensable for identification.

Continuity and Change

Nobody can identify with an environment which constantly changes its identity. Without a sense of stability and continuity, one cannot feel at home. But incessant change is inherent in modern urban life. Here we identify a final and most profound pair of contradictory criteria: continuity and change.

The realization of continuing and unpredictable change has led to the notion that "planning a product" should be replaced by "planning as process." Plans, it is said, must be flexible. But the artifacts which are the objects of planning and which constitute the physical urban environment just do not flex. They can be modified only in a minor way; the possibilities for "plug-in-cities" are, in fact, quite limited. The only way to leave all possibilities open for future development would be to develop nothing at present.

The most that can be done in this respect is to leave some land open for future development, notably in transportation corridors. Leaving substantial areas open would mean scatteration, which has indeed been advocated[9] as a means of providing flexibility and encouraging efficient adaptation to change. But such a policy would also mean an eternally unfinished environment burdened with severe costs in terms of both money and travel time. It might have the advantage of ultimately producing the mixture of old and new buildings so strongly advocated by Jane Jacobs,[10] but it would completely destroy the compactness which the same author values even more highly, and correctly so.

PERCEPTION OF THE ENVIRONMENT

The newness of an environment built all at one time is certainly one of the reasons for the "inhospitability" (*Unwirtlichkeit*) of which the Germans at present bitterly and passionately accuse the new or rebuilt sections of their cities. Probably a more decisive reason is scale. Not only is the contemporary urban area as a whole of such vast scale that it defies visual comprehension, but also in all of its parts there is a conflict between two different scales.

The preindustrial city could be and was comprehended in two ways: from the outside as a silhouette, and from the inside as a sequence of various enclosed spaces formed by streets and squares, all of them on a human scale, the scale of a person standing or walking on his or her own feet. To some extent the structure of the modern urban community can perhaps still be expressed by the silhouette of the group of skyscrapers at its center and the silhouettes of smaller such groups at its subcenters; but these can hardly ever be seen together. However, the city's streets run on to infinity, and its squares are torn apart by the wide openings required for vehicular movement. Only within islands reserved for the pedestrian realm is the experience of urban space and of expressively detailed structure possible, an experience mediated not only by the eye, but by all the senses as well, in particular by the

---

[9]Lessinger, *Journal of the American Institute of Planners*, 1962.
[10]Jane Jacobs, *The Death and Life of Great American Cities*, Random House, New York, 1961.

vasco-motoric sensation of moving and turning, climbing and descending. Within these islands the rich heritage of the design principles of the historical town—not, of course, their specific formal expression—is still valid.

The vast urban area, however, cannot be experienced in this way. It can be comprehended only as what is is—not a city, but an urbanized landscape, a sequence of built-up and open areas and districts of different characters. And it can be experienced only by using the means that have brought this vast new landscape into being—fast vehicular movement. Driving through it can be a rich and meaningful experience, as described by a sensitive Danish visitor[11] to the United States: "On and on flows the traffic, across bridges and down broad ramps, farther and farther in sweeping curves out into the country, without stop, continuously rising and falling in time with the contours of the earth."

We have paid scarcely any attention to using our freeways and rail lines to make the urban landscape visible and comprehensible. Most of our freeways run in straight lines, and, as the cone of vision of the driver is quite narrow, he or she sees hardly anything but the pavement and the sky.[12] Ideally a freeway should consist exclusively of large sweeping curves. In Germany, Hans Lorenz designed the Nuernberg-Aschaffenburg Autobahn on this principle. It is beautiful to look *at* and to look *from*.

In the urban environment these two requirements tend to conflict. From the point of the driver or rider looking *from* them, it is preferable that roads be above or at least at grade level. But the person looking *at* them (and hearing their noise) would rather have them below level in a cut or a tunnel. Occasionally, an escarpment offers a possibility to locate a freeway so that it will articulate, rather than violate, the natural form of the earth, and at the same time offer the rider a view over the lower part of the urban landscape. Wide transportation corridors would open up further possibilities to reconcile both requirements.

The German term for the verb "to experience" is *erfahren*. *Fahren* means "to drive," and the prefix *er* indicates accomplishment of the purpose of an activity. The urban environment as a whole cannot be "seen"; but it can be *erfahren* and identified and thereby become a meaningful part of the citizen's identity.

CONCLUSION

In recent years, as the realization that urbanization is here to stay has sunk in, the old money-mining camp attitude has begun to give way to the insight that the city is a place not merely for making a living but also for living. Concern for the urban environment is growing rapidly. Freeways destroying the urban landscape are rejected and even literally stopped in midair. Protests are mounting against pollution of air and water, against noise and ugliness.

Kenneth Galbraith hit a responsive chord when he pointed out the glaring disparity between the plethora of (often useless or even harmful) goods and services, which are bought and sold at a profit for private consumption, and the dearth of publicly consumed goods and services, which can only be sold and bought "wholesale" with public funds. A generation ago an American president said, "The business of

---

[11] Steen Eiler Rasmussen, *Towns and Buildings*, M.I.T. Press, Cambridge, Mass., 1969.
[12] Christopher Tunnard and Boris Pushkarev, *Man-Made America: Chaos or Control?*, Yale University Press, New Haven, Connecticut, 1963.

America is business." Strangely enough, this man, who saw the res privatae as the be-all and end-all of society, considered himself a Republican. But the sum of the res privatae does not add up to the res publica; accumulation of private wealth does not create a commonwealth.

Only if the res publica is given priority, can a good urban environment be created. This is not a criterion of its quality, but it is the basic condition, both necessary and sufficient, for the successful application of any criteria by which quality may be measured.

Chapter 6

EUROPE'S REBORN CITIES

The slender publication under review contributes more to the comprehension of city planning problems than many comprehensive fat tomes. The author—not a "registerable" planner, but an economist—has a remarkable grasp of all aspects, including those of civic design. The well-selected illustrations further enhance the value of his contribution.

The report is the fruit of 6 months of travel in western Europe, undertaken by the author in 1954 with the aid of a Guggenheim grant. Grebler studied a selected sample of heavily destroyed cities, both large and small, in England, Holland, France, West Germany, and Italy. He selected these on the sound assumption that they would illustrate more clearly than less damaged towns the nature of the basic problems and the range of alternative solutions.

World War II destroyed far more and bigger cities than any previous catastrophe in history, and their rebuilding is indeed a unique laboratory of urban change. Yet in no country had any systematic study of this experience been undertaken. Grebler's book is the first attempt, and it was undertaken at the right moment: early enough to observe reconstruction still in full process, and late enough to observe results already accomplished.

The author expresses regret that he could not make comparisons with the rebuilding of the destroyed cities of eastern Europe and Asia. This reviewer, while sharing his regret, feels that a comparison with the city planning and building in the west European countries spared by war—Sweden and Switzerland—also might have added perspective to the study.

After an opening chapter on the significance of the experience and on its central lesson of "persistence amidst change," Grebler singles out the three most important urban problems: "traffic, civic centers, and housing." He then discusses the contributions made to their solution by "planning innovations, architects, and the planners," followed by a presentation of the "legal and administrative and the economic and financial" aspects. An "interim appraisal" summarizes the results.

The book's title, *Europe's Reborn Cities,* emphasizes the vitality of the contemporary city. "Contrary to some vocal interpreters of urban life, cities are powerful cohesive elements as well as the seedbeds of social disruption," states Grebler. Not one of the many hundred destroyed towns has been abandoned, and only a very few

---

Review of Leo Grebler, *Europe's Reborn Cities* (Urban Land Institute, Washington, D.C., 1956). *Source:* Review published by Urban Land Institute, 1956.

of the smallest have been relocated. Most have regained or exceeded their prewar populations; moreover, the rates of growth are generally the same as they were before the war. Spiritual as well as economic forces appear to sustain this vitality, as shown by the attachment to symbols such as architectural and historical monuments, an attachment which has been intensified by destruction and is expressed in the high priority generally given to the restoration of these monuments.

Equally remarkable is the persistence of the inner structures of the cities. The central core, generally the most heavily damaged section, has everywhere maintained or regained its place. In no case has its size been reduced; generally it has been enlarged. Only in a very few cities, and against considerable resistance from property owners and businessmen, have shifts within the center occurred.

The changes that have occurred within the center were long-overdue measures to increase its efficiency: traffic improvements by street widenings or by new streets; creation of larger blocks and consolidation of small and irregular parcels into larger and more buildable ones; lower coverage and higher buildings, resulting in more open space, but not in any decrease (generally an increase) in usable floor space; relocation of manufacturing and storage as well as of residences on peripheral sites; and clearer separations of land uses. However, the attempt to separate each central city function into a rigidly defined "precinct," made in some English cities, has been found unworkable.

While some residential developments are included in most central city reconstructions, peripheral residential expansion is proceeding everywhere at a rapid pace, but in all continental countries the new peripheral housing consists almost exclusively of apartments. This is due, however, not to any unpopularity of the single-family house, for which there is everywhere a strong demand, but to the fact that these countries can at present afford the cost neither of extended utilities nor of mass use of the private automobile. The author emphasizes the striking differences in the degree of change found in different cities and investigates their reasons. Often these can be traced to the extent or the concentration of damage or to political and economic factors. But in many cases they must be ascribed to the presence or absence of strong personal leadership. This reviewer feels that our current emphasis on "teamwork," "democratic procedure," and "citizens' participation" is too often an excuse for our failure to exercise such leadership. Grebler found that in most cases the leader was a politician, a businessman, or an engineer, rather than a professional planner. However, it strikes this reviewer that in most of the cities Grebler praises most highly—Coventry, Abbeville, Le Havre, Hannover, Kiel—the leadership was in the hands of an architect-planner.

Traffic improvements have been rather limited. The ringroad was found to be not the cure-all which some British planners had thought it to be. Provision of parking space is still inadequate. Nowhere are urban expressways planned, or notable changes in the transit system. Nor has the proposal for general grade separation of pedestrian and vehicular movement—advanced time and again since Leonardo da Vinci's brilliant sketch—been realized anywhere.

Pedestrian islands for shopping have been created in a number of cities, and some of these, in Rotterdam, Coventry, and Lansbury (in London), are among the best contributions of Europe's reborn cities. The other main "planning innovation" mentioned by the author is the introduction into the central city of "open planning," as opposed to the traditional solid blockfront. Some of Grebler's examples, notably the very excellent one in Abbeville, would be classified by this reviewer, not as open planning, but as flexible and imaginative applications of the planning of enclosed streets and squares, enriched by occasional vistas into large interior courts.

In Abbeville and a number of other cities civic design has benefited greatly from the revival of two old and almost forgotten techniques of city building: arcades, and "bridge building," that is, building in air rights over streets. These would be even more appropriate in American cities: the first to protect us from our climate, which is so intemperate in both directions; and the second to break the spatial monotony of our endless straight streets.

Grebler rightly emphasizes that wherever civic design has been successful this has been due to complete and intimate integration of planning and architecture, which has created a pleasant and harmonious urban environment even where the architecture, as such, may be rather indifferent.

One of the most interesting chapters, entitled "Land Reform: Politics, Law, Administration," contains a very lucid and succinct presentation of the different approaches used in the five countries under study. They range from widespread public landownership in Britain to unrestricted real estate speculation in Italy. In Germany, where many legal controls were eliminated, largely under American influence, rebuilding has been very largely "as was." Despite the fact that physical destruction was greater than in any of the other four countries, substantial physical change has been the exception in West Germany, limited mainly to cases of large-scale land assembly through purchase by public or semipublic agencies.

While in England publicly assembled land is generally retained and redeveloped on the basis of the traditional 99-year lease, in the Netherlands condemned land is replatted and the owners receive equivalent parcels for rebuilding. They may forgo rebuilding and receive cash payments instead, which, however, are less than the full value of the lost property.

Between Britain and Holland, where pride of victory and relative wealth encouraged faith in the future and strong public action, and Germany and Italy, where defeat and economic disruption resulted in *laissez aller,* stands France. But France, differing from all of the other four in its strong central and correspondingly weak local administration, has evolved a unique system of state-chartered compulsory associations of property owners, who are charged with replatting by voluntary agreement. The ministry guides the process by appointing for each city a chief planner and a chief architect, and the ministry, not the municipality, retains the power to order replatting if voluntary agreement fails.

As a result the rebuilt French cities show more unity—and sometimes uniformity—and more "planning" than those in the other countries, but rebuilding has been much slower than anywhere else. It seems to this reviewer that France deserves the title of "the best and the worst," which the author bestows on Italy. He sees "the best" there in the modern architecture, notably in Milan. To one traveler's eyes, however, the postwar Milanese architecture appears stunting rather than stunning, as Grebler describes it. The discrepancy between the excellent work done on paper by Italian planners, and the way the actual building is proceeding, is nothing less than tragic.

Compared with the high hopes with which planners looked forward to reborn cities of Europe, the results of reconstruction are disappointing. But Grebler rightly points out that a much better job has been done than after World War I or after the San Francisco earthquake; and he is also right in emphasizing that the greater the destruction, the greater the need to conserve and utilize whatever is left. Contrary to appearances, it is much easier to change an undestroyed than a destroyed city.

The author tries to find a bright side: "When the contrast between the new housing and the prewar slums is considered, one begins to sense some of the compensatory benefits that have come from war destruction." Comparison with the quantitatively and qualitatively superior achievements of Sweden, Switzerland, and Denmark shows the fallacy of this argument. War destroys; there is no compensation.

In our fortunate country we have a greater opportunity for "reborn cities" than Europe had or has. But the attempts made in Europe—the failures as well as the successes—hold valuable lessons for us. Grebler's summary of the European experience is one of the most important contributions to American planning literature.

Chapter 7

CITIES TO LIVE IN

The author of this book, an architect who designed the Palace of Congresses in the Moscow Kremlin and the Soviet Pavillion at Expo 1967, here presents thoughts on city planning which he developed in his work as head of the new development plan for Moscow and as an observer on travels all over the world.

While he considers his work as "architecture," he defines this term to include "population distribution, utilization of natural resources, the building of communication lines. . . ." Throughout the book there is a strong emphasis on harmony with nature. Posokhin goes so far as to claim that "nature conservation and the rational use of natural resources coincide with the major goals of modern architecture; they are in fact the chief factors determining the direction of its development." While he is acutely conscious of the destructive and dehumanizing tendencies of modern development, he believes that they can be overcome in a socialist society, and advocates full use of new technology.

The language of the book is refreshingly simple and free of jargon. Some statements show considerable sophistication, while others may sound simplistic, for example, a short comparison of the rebuilding of the French cities of Le Havre and Rouen, and an extended discussion of the city as seen. Posokhin's own work on the new Black Sea resort of Pizunda and on the historic town of Suzdal is of high quality—rather different from an earlier huge apartment tower in Moscow which he also presents.

A lively chapter on the historical development of Moscow from its origin to the year 1960, richly illustrated by maps, drawings, photographs, and quotations, leads to the final, longest, and most interesting chapter, which presents the new plan, started in 1962 and officially adopted in 1966, that provides for the development of the Moscow region up to 1985, with a forecast for the year 2000.

Although as late as 1959 planners still upheld the 5 million population limit for Moscow, the new plan provides for 7.5 million by 1985. In order to accommodate this growth, as well as a substantial increase of space per person, the urban territory has been more than doubled to 333 square miles. The resultant overall density averages 22,500 persons per square mile, about the same as in the city of Montreal. This urban area is separated by a new circumferential freeway from about 1000 square miles of greenbelt, also under the city's jurisdiction and containing parks,

---

Review of M. V. Posokhin, *Cities to Live In* (Novosti Press, Moscow, U.S.S.R., 1974). *Source:* From *Contact,* February 1976.

lakes, forests, and farmlands, as well as a number of settlements with a future total population of about 0.5 million. Beyond this lies a "suburban zone," in which only moderate growth is planned. By contrast, 16 existing towns at distances averaging 60 miles from the center are to be expanded to self-contained cities of 150,000–200,000 population. It thus appears that a total of about 12 million people will live and work within a radius of about 80 miles from Red Square. A number of old factories located in residential areas are to be removed, and industries using large quantities of raw materials, energy, or water are to be limited. Moscow will specialize in the manufacture of high-quality producer and consumer goods and in research and teaching institutes related to these products. Institutes related to other types of goods are to be relocated to other parts of the country. Altogether, a slight shift from secondary to tertiary (service) industries is foreseen.

The plan divides the city into a hierarchy of districts with a corresponding hierarchy of service centers. The historical central district is surrounded by seven major districts, each divided into an average of three subdistricts, which are further divided into "residential districts" of 30,000–70,000 inhabitants. The major districts and, to a large extent, also the subdistricts are separated by green wedges. The seven major centers are strongly connected to the city center visually as well as functionally.

Housing space, at a per capita ratio equal to about 80% of the current Canadian average, is to be provided in 9- to 16-story apartment houses. However, the floor space index, calculated on *gross* residential area, is only 0.45–0.55. Public open space, exclusive of the greenbelt, is ample at 6 acres per 1000 population (10 acres including forests).

In an article published in Moscow at the time, this writer criticized the 1935 plan on two counts: the exclusive reliance on a radial-concentric road system, which would overload the streets of the center; and the lack of reconstruction of the railroad system and of its coordination with the subways. Both deficiencies are remedied in the new plan. Two pairs of diagonal freeways, following largely existing railroad and hydro rights-of-way, relieve the street system, in particular in the center, where they form a 7-by-7-mile square. In addition, several streets in the heart of the city are to be put underground, thus enlarging the pedestrian realm. Four railroad lines will be served by a new consolidated passenger terminal, with easy transfer to the subway. Altogether, it is anticipated that in 1985 no less than 65% of all person-miles will be traveled by electric traction.

It is evident that the new Moscow plan presents a vigorous and well-studied approach to the urban problems which also face Canadian planners. In addition, there is great emphasis on the visual "design" aspect of city building. While it is doubtful whether Soviet planners are succeeding better than their Western colleagues in reconciling the huge scale of the modern metropolis with the small scale of the human person, their attempts, as presented in this volume, certainly are bold and thought-provoking.

Chapter 8

REVIEW OF THE NEW YORK METROPOLITAN REGION STUDY

Thirty years ago the New York Regional Plan set an example of comprehensive metropolitan planning which has never been equaled. Like other parts of that monumental piece of work, its section on the economy has become a source from which a great deal of work in this field has been fed right to this day.

Great changes have occurred in the economy in these 30 years, and now the Regional Plan Association has initiated another study which sets a new standard and is likely to have an equally far-reaching influence.

Of the nine volumes written under the direction of Harvard economist Raymond Vernon, this review will deal only with the first two.

Hoover and Vernon's *Anatomy of a Metropolis* is exactly what its title implies and, as such, is required reading for every metropolitan planner. The concepts and insights which it develops are indispensable for the understanding of any metropolitan region. The two main parts of the book, "The Jobs" and "The People," are preceded by an introductory part, "Cities and Suburbs," and are followed by a summary: "The Jobs, The People, and the Future."

The first part investigates the general distribution of jobs and people within the 22 counties of the New York Metropolitan Region, primarily in terms of concentric zones: the "core" (broken down into the central business district (C.B.D.) and "the rest"), the "inner ring," and the "outer ring"; and it also deals with differences within each ring. The results once again show the enormous and consistent decrease in density of population, and, to an even greater degree, of employment, from the center to the periphery. The carefully developed picture gives no support whatever to the current theory which claims that the metropolitan region is being superseded by a newer form of human settlement, described by various fancy terms such as "megalopolis" or "interurbia." Another highly significant result of the investigation is the finding that New York City, outside of the C.B.D., is far more of a "dormitory" than any of the suburban counties.

Part II deals first with manufacturing and then with "white-collar" jobs. The influence of changed space requirements and modes of transportation, the role of

---

Review of *The New York Metropolitan Region Study*, by various authors, 9 vols. and technical supplements (Harvard University Press, Cambridge, Mass., 1959–1960). *Source:* From *Journal of the American Institute of Planners,* February 1961.

labor, and in particular the growing importance of "external economies" are brilliantly analyzed. The bewildering multiplicity of manufacturing industries and of their varying locational trends is made comprehensible by a many-faceted conceptual scheme, which differentiates them by market ("national" or "local," "consumers" or "other producers"), by value, by size, and by orientation (to "communication," to "water transport," etc.). In general, it is found that the region is attractive to unstandardized rather than to standardized products and to designing and merchandising rather than to manufacturing.

Within the white-collar industries New York, particularly its C.B.D., is especially attractive to "elite" functions, while "routine" functions may move out. This, in part, explains the continuing high demand for office space and the resultant "boom in skyscrapers." On the other hand, the authors demonstrate convincingly that industrial redevelopment cannot be anticipated because the new manufacturing and warehousing space could not compete with the available old one, even if land cost were written down to zero.

Part III, "The People," attempts to understand the changing distribution of residences in terms of "spacious living versus easy access"—basically identical with Ebenezer Howard's "two magnets." Factors such as the journey to work, income, and occupation are carefully measured, and their influences on choice of residential location and density are evaluated. The interesting devices of a "job specialization index" and "residence specialization index" are developed.

After presentation of a static picture of the "where and why," a chapter deals with the dynamics of "the spread of the people." In their analysis of the process of concentric growth the authors identify a "second wave" of transition of peripheral zones to higher densities, primarily as a result of apartment construction, and a "thinning out" in the older central areas. On the basis of these observations, they develop the significant concept of a five-stage neighborhood cycle: (1) new single-family subdivisions, (2) apartment development, (3) downgrading generally associated with conversion, (4) thinning out, and (5) renewal. Although it can be objected that apartment development may also occur in stage 1, this is a generally valid and valuable conceptual scheme.

The analysis of anticipated changes in housing supply, access, and population characteristics points to an extensive dilution and dispersion of slums and blighted areas. The authors feel that demand will not keep pace with the rapidly growing supply of old ("second-hand") housing in these spreading "gray areas"; this view may be questioned, as, with a rapidly growing metropolitan population, low-income households are bound to increase absolutely, even though they may decrease relatively.

The concept of vast and growing gray areas, that is, obsolescent residential and industrial areas, has met with strong objections from many planners. To this writer it appears that these objections are based more on wishful thinking than on fact. We would be well advised to take the gray areas very seriously and devote to them a great deal more study and attention than we do at present.

The short concluding Part IV, entitled "The Jobs, The People, and the Future," summarizes the perspective for the core, the inner ring, and the outer ring. The authors are aware that many factors may modify their forecasts. In particular, they recognize that "a projection of future transportation patterns is inseparable from a projection of the location of future jobs and homes." Such a projection went beyond the limits of their assignment, and they limit themselves to some general remarks on the future of transportation. Their evaluation of the future of suburban railroads may be too pessimistic, though it will require considerable effort to make it so.

The sophisticated methods and concepts developed in this volume are far superior to those to be found in other studies of metropolitan regions and can serve as a guide for all work in this vitally important field. The book is extremely well written, in lively, meaty, and clearly formulated English.

The second volume, entitled *Made in New York* and edited and introduced by Max Hall, contains three case studies in metropolitan manufacturing: "Women's and Children's Apparel" by Roy B. Helfgott. "Printing and Publishing" by W. Eric Gustafson, and "Electronics" by James M. Hund. These, as is known, are three industries which show a particularly high concentration in the New York Metropolitan Area, but they are also generally and characteristically important in most major metropolitan areas.

The authors study the factors which have made Metropolitan New York attractive to these industries, their specific locational preferences within the region, and their perspectives. These are studies in depth, dealing thoroughly with all factors affecting the growth and location of these industries.

All three studies find that these factors vary widely for various segments of the industries in question. Although "women's and children's apparel" comprises only part of the apparel industry, it had to be broken down into no less than 12 segments. "Printing and publishing" comprises 13 different segments. In the case of electronics, Mr. Hund found it necessary to devise his own classification system: consumer electronics, with three subclassifications; components, with eight; military electronics, with five; and industrial electronics, with five—and with considerable overlapping.

For each classification and subclassification at least two different steps are required: first, an analysis and forecast of the industry nationally, and, second, an analysis and forecast of the share of the New York Metropolitan Region. This inevitably requires a careful and comprehensive study of the linkages with other industries—which themselves are subject to constant changes in size and location.

Not surprisingly, it is primarily the new, nonstandardized, high-quality, high-wage segments of each industry that prefer location in the New York area. The role of the metropolis as an incubator of new industries—and of new ideas in each industry—stands out clearly.

The three studies make fascinating and highly informative reading. One is impressed with the enormous quantity and high quality of work which the three authors have devoted to their task. Any planner and researcher embarking on a study of the economy of an area can learn much from their methods.

There is no doubt that only this kind of detailed study can yield any valid forecasts and that an attempt to make forecasts on the basis of the "first-digit" classifications of the census of manufacturing—still all too frequent in "economic base" studies—is likely to be grossly misleading. However, if even this study of the world's biggest and richest metropolis had to limit itself to only three—admittedly important—of its many industries, what can smaller metropolitan areas hope to accomplish in this line? If for no other reason than to ponder this question, planners will do well to study this volume carefully.

Chapter 9

CITIES OF CANADA, VOL. 1: THEORETICAL, HISTORICAL AND PLANNING PERSPECTIVES

This work by a Canadian geographer may well be the most ambitious attempt among the rash of publications dealing with Canadian cities. A second volume, presenting case studies of 15 Canadian metropolitan areas, is to follow the present one, which deals with "theoretical, historical and planning perspectives."

Considering that the first part of the book, entitled "Modern Urban Structure," inevitably has to deal with the historical genesis of that structure, it might have better followed, than preceded, Part Two, "Canadian Urban Development," and led more directly into the third part, which deals with the "prospects" of Canadian cities.

The book starts with an excellent discussion of the process of urbanization which has led to the existing national and regional system of cities. The writer correctly emphasizes, as the main driving forces, first, growing interdependence as the result of increasing specialization, and, second, the function of control, leading to a concentration of services. It is, therefore, surprising that he follows this by defining a city's basic activities "as those which produce goods for export," neglecting the income which the city derives from its control functions. (In the Alice-in-Wonderland world of establishment economics, the functions of extracting taxes, rents, and surplus value are defined as "services exported" to the taxpayers, tenants, and workers living outside.) However, he is well aware of the existing "Heartland-periphery relationship." The interaction of communications and metropolitanism, and the increasing importance of rapid access to current information and of agglomeration economics, are very clearly presented as factors resulting in the overwhelming strength of the centralizing tendency on a national scale. Equally well presented is the decentralizing tendency outward from individual cities and the resulting formation of metropolitan regions as the most significant components of the national economic system. These first 24 pages are the meatiest part of the book.

They are followed by 14 pages presenting Christaller's central place theory.

Review of George A. Nader, *Cities of Canada, Vol. 1: Theoretical, Historical and Planning Perspectives* (Macmillan of Canada, Toronto, Ont., 1975). *Source:* From *Urban Forum*, Vol. 1, No. 3, Fall 1975.

Excellent as such, this extended treatment might be more appropriate for a geography textbook than for the present volume. Strangely, no reference to central place theory is made in the following chapter, which deals with "internal city structure." Here the application of von Thuenen's rent-bid theory for urban land uses is developed. The author soberly assesses the limitations of this model, as well as those of the familiar, empirical Burgess, Hoyt, and Harris models, and adds two very informative chapters dealing with observed changes related to changes in transportation—one devoted to the character and citywide distribution of industrial, residential, and commercial land uses, and the other to the specific problems of the city center. The latter pays due attention not only to the core, but also to the usually neglected frame and periphery of the center. Here, again, the author's realism provides welcome relief from the strident prophets of bliss or doom; he notes that "in only a few cities . . . has downtown employment shown any recent increases."

Part Two of the book, in two chapters, deals with Canadian urban history to 1867 and with the following 107 years. Interesting as the facts about the fur and lumber trade, and the impact of the Napoleonic wars and of the canals, may be, the infinitesimal number of persons involved hardly warrants the exceedingly detailed account of these early events. The following story of the evolution since Confederation, under the impact of changing technical, economic, and political forces, accounts well for the formation of the Canadian urban system.

The third part is divided into two chapters, dealing first with "urban planning, municipal finance, and metropolitan government" and then more broadly with "urban problems and public policy." The definition of "city planning [as] concerned with anticipating and regulating change in the physical environment in order to . . . increase the social and economic benefits of urbanization" is valuable both in emphasizing prediction, as much as prescription, and in limiting its action to the physical environment. The author, recognizing that planning cannot be an exact science, wrestles with the relation of planning to politics as well as to the land market but, in particular, with the problem of public participation. After a long and tortuous discussion which attempts to show that representative democracy is adequate at the federal and provincial level but not at the municipal, he is forced to conclude that "citizen participation is better suited to the protection of the status quo than to the task of directing change," that is, the task of city planning.

In addition to calling for better information and for "goal formulation by increased citizen participation," the book advocates amended public control over land use, expanded financial resources for municipalities, and metropolitan government. In the frequently stated opinion of this reviewer, these are, indeed, the three essential preconditions for effective city planning. However, the author does not face the fact that public planning, by shifting values from one piece of land to another, is inherently in conflict with private ownership of land. This limits the relevance of his discussion of land banking as well as of development control. The inadequacy of the real property tax, its regressive character, and the way it prompts municipalities to resort to vicious "fiscal zoning" are all convincingly exposed. However, the difficulties of correct assessment, which so greatly concern the author, might be overcome by the simple device of having each owner assess his own property—with the provision that it may be expropriated on that basis. Also, the author makes no distinction between the opposite effects on urban development, in particular on housing, which this tax has on the two entirely different elements which it lumps together: site and building. Nor is it recognized that local collection of any progressive tax will be frustrated by the threat of the wealthy evading it by moving to another municipality. Metropolitan taxation reduces this danger considerably but cannot eliminate it.

The experiences with metropolitan governments in different Canadian provinces are well presented and lead to the final discussion of urban problems. The book's reasonable recommendation to governments that they concentrate on improving the process of urbanization, rather than attempting to limit it, could have been strengthened by demonstrating that this process is already slowing down quite strongly. Equally reasonable is the distinction between the truly "urban" problems, defined as being caused by the process of urbanization, and those caused by the governmental-institutional system, which appear to be urban merely because the people affected by them happen to live in cities. However, the claim that an urban problem occurs when the rate of change of any one of the three subsystems—social, economic, physical—is out of step with that of the others is questionable. By definition, the physical system is always lagging. The examples given of new types of physical structures—vertical-residential and horizontal-industrial—allegedly "in advance" of social change, are far from convincing. To say that "when a city grows too slowly it invariably experiences problems of unemployment" also seems to put the cart before the horse. The author claims that urban problems exist mainly at the outskirts and in the center. As an answer to the former, defined as "urban shadow" and "sprawl," he advocates "new towns," renouncing, however, the condition of self-sufficiency in employment originally associated with that concept. The discussion of the center deals fairly completely with its familiar problems and with proposed and attempted solutions. It is, however, surprising to read that transportation is "a central city problem." In fact, it is increasingly a problem of movement between different sectors of the periphery.

The book concludes with a short and appropriately sceptical discussion of attempts toward a national urban policy. In sum it does not (probably no book can) provide all the answers to the problems of Canadian cities. But it makes a substantial and often original contribution towards their understanding.

Chapter 10

METROPOLIS AND BEYOND

In current discussions of urban problems, these are sometimes seen as the result of the "postwar phenomenon of suburbanization"—implying that suburbs are something new. In fact, suburbs are as old as cities. The French term *fauxbourg* is medieval; the English term is inherited from ancient Rome. Suburbs have been found even in Ur, long regarded as the oldest of all cities.

What distinguished the inhabitants of suburbs from those living within the city walls? They belonged to two different groups, at opposite ends of the social scale. In the Roman *villa suburbana* lived the rich patricians who enjoyed the amenities of country life while preserving their dominant role in the city. They have had many successors in this role right down to the present day. On the other hand, in the medieval *fauxbourg* lived those who lacked the political and economic power to be accepted as bourgois. These outsiders trying to get in also have had their counterparts throughout the ages, most conspicuously today in the *barriadas* and *favelas* surrounding the cities of Latin America.

Both of these groups are to be found in our North American suburbs, but they are not typical; the majority of the suburban population is "middle class," just as it is in the city. In many cases it is as or more numerous than its counterpart in the city. With this disappearance of both quantitative and qualitative differences, the traditional distinction between "city" and "suburb" has become obsolete and meaningless. What is new is not the presence of suburbs but their disappearance, together with that of the city. Both have merged into a new and much more extended form of human settlement. The census, both in the United States and in Canada, has recognized this fact under the name of the "metropolitan area"; and in Canada it has also been given some political recognition. Whatever the name, the area is basically held together by economic exchange within a common housing and labor market. The census establishes its boundaries as those of the "commuter watershed" of the central city.

There is little doubt that the metropolitan area is becoming the dominant form of settlement all over the world. Moreover, in the developed capitalist countries and even more so in the third world, but not in the Socialist countries, there is growing concentration in the largest "primate" cities. In Canada from 1951 to 1971, the rate

---

Source: Originally published as "Au delà de la métropole," *Revue Critère,* no. 19 (Société de Publications Critère, Inc., College Ahuntsic), Automne 1977; also in *Papers on Planning and Design*, No. 12 (Department of Urban and Regional Planning, University of Toronto, Toronto, Ont.), July 1977.

of population growth of five groups of cities was consistently correlated with size, ranging from 25.2% for those of 5000–10,000 population to 46.6% for those over 0.5 million.

Is this going to continue? Will the entire population of Canada—and of the world—be concentrated in a few gigantic agglomerations? What lies beyond the metropolis?

Some people answer: the megalopolis. The term has gained currency since Jean Gottman selected it as the title of his monumental study of the urbanized northeastern seaboard of the United States. Sometimes it is just used in its literal meaning of "big city." Others use it to denote a cluster or string of metropolitan areas, such as those from Boston to Washington or from Tokyo to Osaka. The late Konstantinos Doxiadis and his followers believed that these constitute a new type of human settlement, as different from the metropolis as the latter is from the "big city" which preceded it. However, no distinguishing characteristics have been identified. Nor is there greater interchange between cities located within "megalopolis" than between them and other cities, as I have found from analysis of the data on long-distance telephone calls used in Gottman's book.

If the metropolis is not likely to be superseded by the megalopolis, are there other changes to be expected? The most conspicuous difference between the metropolis and the preceding big city is its vastly greater extent. It is indeed, as it has often been accused of being, "neither city nor country." Within its perimeter there are rural uses such as farms and forests. Moreover, the land that is "developed" for urban purposes is used at low and decreasing densities. A study by the New York Regional Plan Association of all urban land in the region, which includes scores of small and medium-sized cities in addition to New York, shows an increase in density from some 50,000 persons per square mile in 1820 to 64,000 in 1860, but since that time a consistent drop to about 8000 at present. A study of 11 Canadian cities made by N. D. Lea about ten years ago showed a convergence toward an even lower average of 6500 persons per square mile.

It appears that the transformation of the city into the metropolis has reduced density by about 90% or, expressed positively, has led to a tenfold increase of urban land use per head of population. Swedish studies have shown that this increase is closely correlated with increase in real income. This increase is likely to continue, albeit at a lower rate. It is also important to realize that more land per person is absorbed not only for residence, but also for industry, commerce, institutions, parks, and playgrounds—even for cemeteries.

The prognosis seems to be for more of the same: more people coming from the countryside and small towns to the metropolis, and within the metropolis spreading out further and further, at lower and lower densities—an alarming perspective; one wishes for a reversal. Some people take the wish for reality. They interpret the occurrence of so-called white-painting, the rehabilitation of old city houses by wealthy purchasers, as a "return to the city" from the suburbs. Some doubt is thrown on this interpretation by the results of a small survey of white-painters in three areas of Toronto: out of some 20 respondents, not a single one had come from the suburbs. The sample is, of course, too small to be conclusive, but results of the census of 1976 show, for the first time, substantial population decreases in the cities of Montreal and Toronto by about 80,000 persons since 1971, while suburban populations have continued to grow substantially.

A more serious claim of reversal comes from the United States. The data on changes in net migration between metropolitan and nonmetropolitan areas are impressive. While in the 1965–1970 period the metropolitan areas gained 352,000 internal migrants, from 1970 to 1975 they lost 1.594 million and in 1975–1976 an additional 396,000. As a result the long-term trend to increasing concentration in metropolitan areas has been reversed; indeed, the largest of them, those with populations over 2 million, actually lost 243,200 persons, or 0.4% of their population, between 1970 and 1974.

Where did the people go who left these large metropolitan areas? Not to the 23 smallest metropolitan areas, those with less than 100,000 population. These also lost 1% of their population to internal migration, though their total still grew by 2.7%, as a result of natural increase.

The net loss of 1.6 million migrants from metropolitan to nonmetropolitan areas between 1970 and 1974 represents the difference between 5.1 million in and 6.7 million out. It is known that about five out of eight of these out-migrants, roughly 4.2 million, ended up in counties at the fringe of the metropolitan areas. No doubt there has also been a sizable movement in the opposite direction, from these fringe counties to the metropolitan areas. Its size is apparently not known; it is not unlikely that the net gain of these fringe counties exceeds the net loss of the metropolitan areas. This would mean that the reversal of the trend is a statistical illusion, hiding the reality of metropolitan expansion beyond the boundaries defined by the census.

Population change is, of course, determined not only by internal, but also by international migration, as well as by births and deaths. A recent analysis of the data collected by the Canadian censuses of 1966 and 1971 by Professor J. W. Simmons of the University of Toronto throws some light on these changes.

Simmons divided all of Canada into 124 areas, each centered on a city, and grouped these areas into five classes by the size of their central cities. Total growth during this period (later data are not yet available) shows that the 11 largest areas still were growing four times faster than the 63 smallest ones. These 63 areas lost 2.2% of their population to internal migration. But Montreal (0.6%) and Toronto (1.1%) also suffered losses. It is interesting to note that Toronto lost more than Montreal. But while Toronto lost 24,300 migrants to other parts of Canada, it gained nine times as many immigrants from abroad. No doubt, many of these did not stay in Toronto but after a while moved to other parts of Canada. Thus much of what appears in the statistic as "internal migration" is, in fact, a movement of foreign immigrants from the big city where they landed to the places where they finally settle down. To a lesser extent, this may also account for the U.S. figures.

Another interesting result of Simmons' work is evidence disproving the widespread assumption that the population of small towns is stable, while that of the metropolis is drifting in and out. In fact, of every 100 people living in an area in 1966, in small towns 16 left in the following 5 years, while 13 newcomers arrived. But during the same 5 years in the Montreal area, there were only 6 newcomers to the area and 7 who left it.

The upshot of all these statistics is that there is so far no conclusive evidence for a reversal of the trend to the metropolis. There is a slowing down. In part, this is a function of the slowing down of national population growth. In part, it may be a temporary effect of the downswing in the business cycle. In part, it may be due to some equalization in the availability of services between big and small centers. *But by far the most significant change is the rapid growth of the fringe surrounding the metropolitan area.*

It has long been known that a metropolitan area is surrounded by a much more extensive fringe which is strongly dominated and transformed by its center. John Friedman calls it the "urban field"; I prefer the term "metropolitan region." The influence of the central metropolitan area is felt in two ways. Productive enterprises, primarily manufacturing, settle in the fringe because they can draw on the services of the center. Inhabitants of the center draw on the recreational resources on the fringe, by retiring there temporarily or permanently. This larger region may extend as far as 100 miles from the central city.

As mentioned earlier, the census defines the metropolitan area as a commuting watershed. This definition was fairly clear-cut as long as employment was largely concentrated in the center. But manufacturing employment long ago left the center—in the city of Toronto it has dropped by half in the last 30 years—and "service" employment is following suit. A person living 40 miles from the center is not likely to work there, but he or she may well commute to work to a factory, shopping center, or office, located 20 miles from the center and 20 miles from home. In this way the distinction between the central "metropolitan area" and the "fringe" of the metropolitan region becomes increasingly blurred.

Nevertheless, as long as people commute daily to work, the distinction retains some meaning. However, there are two emerging trends which may eliminate this barrier. The first is the possibility of replacing the movement of the worker to the job by a movement of the job to the worker by means of electronic communication such as closed circuit television and computer consoles.

While this change may affect a minority of office workers, primarily in the professional-managerial group, the second trend, the introduction of a 4-day workweek, may affect all workers. With 4 workdays per week and 48 workweeks per year, a worker would have to sleep only 144 out of 365 nights of the year at a location close to his or her place of work. It is likely that the person would establish there just some *pied-à-terre* and establish a permanent family residence in the countryside. In many cases the transition might be achieved by conversion of a summer cottage to an all-year house.

There is little doubt that most people everywhere, not only in Canada, would make this choice. In a recent French survey of preferences for habitation, 80% of the respondents opted for *une maison à la campagne*. In many ways this would offer an attractive life-style, but it would also involve some serious dangers. It would encroach on farm land and would seriously interfere with agricultural production. It would lead to a proliferation of automobile movements which might well turn the dream into a nightmare. Alarmed governments may decide to oppose the trend, but I doubt that they will do more than channel it, at best.

To sum up, beyond the metropolis I see neither a "megalopolis" nor a "return to the city" nor a "reversal" back to a dispersal into many small towns, but, rather, a further expansion leading to transformation of the metropolis into a very extensive semirural, but still urban-centered region.

But will such huge agglomerations be manageable? It strikes me as strange that national governments that consider themselves competent to manage some 20 or some 200 million people declare urban areas of a few millions to be unmanageable. I know of no evidence that it is easier to manage 10 cities of 1 million each, or 100 with a population of 100,000 each, than one metropolis of 10 million. Governments always seem to manage poorly—on any scale.

Does all the foregoing mean that there is no future for small and medium-sized towns? Not necessarily. The trend to the metropolis is the result of its economies of scale. But there are also diseconomies of scale. The economies are primarily, though by no means exclusively, "economic" in the narrow sense of the term. Productivity of labor tends to increase with scale, and consequently money income tends to be higher. The diseconomies are social and environmental. As people begin to look at the city less as a place for making a living and more as a place for living, a home to feel comfortable in, the weights may be shifting. I mentioned the fact that consumer services are becoming more accessible to small-town dwellers. An interesting case in point is the Danish town of Holste. This small town, somewhat isolated in the west of Jutland, had for many years failed in its attempt to attract industry. Finally, a Copenhagen architect-planner, John Alpass, advised its officials to try the other way around: create good services to attract people. They established an art school and a theater; the town became known as a cultural center. As a consequence it got better doctors for its hospital, and better teachers for its schools, thus further increasing its attractiveness. I have not seen the statistics, but when I visited Holste last summer, it impressed me as a lively and prosperous place.

I also mentioned the fact that in the Socialist countries, although most of their big cities have grown more than planned, they have grown less than those of small and medium size. In an article published some years ago, I showed this in detail for the U.S.S.R. and the German Democratic Republic.* The latter country, East Germany, now has exactly the same population it had in 1939, just under 17 million. There are now, as there were then, six cities with populations over 0.25 million; all of them now have fewer people than they had in 1939. The decrease ranges from 8 to 32% in the capital, East Berlin, which now has just over 1 million population. By contrast, there are far more people in the towns of 20,000–100,000 population than there were before World War II. The East Germans have also published data on internal migration during 1975. The small places, under 10,000, lost 8 per 1000 of their population. But these persons went primarily to cities in the 50,000–100,000 range, which gained 17 in 1000; those over 100,000 gained only 7 in 1000.

One can only speculate about the reasons behind the opposite trends of population distribution in the centrally planned and in the market economies. For one, office employment, which accounts for so much of the growth of our metropolises, is much lower in the Eastern countries, despite their cumbersome bureaucracies. But the decisive reason may be found in the different motivations of both management and workers. In our countries managements prefer the big centers because of their "contacts." They can gain a competitive advantage by being the first to obtain information about impending changes in the prices of their inputs and outputs. In the planned economies this particular type of competition does not exist; managers can compete only in terms of technical performance.

For the worker, whether blue- or white-collar, the metropolis offers a wider choice of jobs. If a person loses one—or cannot stand it any longer—he or she may find

---

*See Chapter 24.

another one. In a small town, however, there are few others, so the worker is forced to move to find one. This is almost certainly the reason for the greater population turnover in our smaller towns, which I cited earlier. In the countries with planned economies, people also have their worries, of course, but difficulty in finding or keeping a job is the least of them.

If this interpretation is correct, the answers to the question: "What lies beyond the metropolis?" may ultimately depend on the socioeconomic structure which Canadians choose for their future.

Part Two
Reconsiderations

Chapter 11

GLORIES AND MISERIES OF A MASTER PLAN

THE CONCEPT OF A MASTER PLAN

The concept of a master plan as the main task of city planning, generally accepted in the first half of this century, is presently being strongly challenged by professional planners. As a static concept is is considered to be incompatible with the dynamic nature of modern urban development. "Process planning," so it is said, is required, rather than an image of an ideal future state. Such an image says nothing about the steps by which it is to be achieved, their timing, or their cost.

Granted that any image of a future state can be only a cross section through the continuous stream of development, and that ideally a whole series of such cross sections should be developed, it is hardly possible to give coherent direction to day-to-day decisions without the guidance of a *Leitbild*, a guiding image, even though it is realized that this image is bound to change and develop over time. The planner of Amsterdam, C. van Eesteren, referring to the analogy of the gradual development of the Gothic cathedral, speaks of the need for "a preconception which urges towards consciousness." A master plan is an attempt at a conscious formulation of a preconception.

All too many master plans have ended up as copiously illustrated weighty tomes gathering dust in the mayor's office. It is therefore of particular interest to follow the successes and failures of Gréber's master plan, which has been used consistently as a guide.

BASIC ASSUMPTIONS OF THE GRÉBER PLAN
Population

Gréber assumed that the area's population would grow to 400,000–500,000 by the end of this century. Population projections made in the first postwar years were strongly influenced by the experience of the 1930s and have therefore generally underestimated future growth. However, Gréber was extremely optimistic about the future of Canada. Calling it "one of the greatest nations of the world," he anticipated

---

Source: Architecture Canada (Journal of the Royal Architectural Institute of Canada, Ottawa, Ont.), May 1967.

a population of 40 million by the end of the century—well above present estimates. Metropolitan regions and, in particular, national capitals tend to grow at a faster rate than does the national population. In fact, the National Capital Region's share of Canada's population increased from 1.7% in 1931 to about 2.0% in 1947. The master plan's estimate implies a future drop to 1%. Presently, the region's probable population at the end of the century is estimated at 1.0–1.2 million, or 3.5 to 4.0% of the nation.

Gréber was, of course, aware of the uncertainty of population projections. He stated that growth beyond 600,000 should be accommodated outside the proposed greenbelt in "completely self-contained new towns" of 20,000–25,000 inhabitants. However, this eventuality was considered so distant as not to merit consideration in the master plan.

Employment

The population of the National Capital Region has always found employment primarily in government service, but also in the lumber and pulp industry, as well as in the local services required by these two "basic industries" and the households supported by them. The plan assumes that these sources of employment will continue to expand, without, however, attempting to quantify the share of each of these three major categories. Specifically, it is assumed that light industries will find suitable locations in residential areas, and heavy industries close to the railroad yards. The original reasons for the location of the lumber industry—proximity to sources of raw material and proximity to falling water as a source of power and cheap transportation to markets by floating rafts down the Ottawa River—have lost much of their importance. The establishments of this industry remain tied to their location for two reasons: the existing investment, and the possibility of using the water of the Ottawa River for processing and waste disposal. If heavy industry is to be relocated away from the river, these plants are not likely to continue to operate in the region.

Transportation

For all transportation of goods and of people, public and private, within the urban area, the plan relies entirely on the motor vehicle—cars, buses, and trucks—and almost entirely so also in the balance of the region. No estimate of the future number of vehicles was attempted. In 1947 there were 40,000 motor vehicles in the National Capital Region; by the end of the century there will probably be over 400,000.

Gréber was confident that movement would be greatly reduced by the planned decentralization of employment and the planned "nucleation" of communities and neighborhoods. He assumed that people would choose to live close to their places of work and to satisfy their other needs at small centers close to their places of residence, overlooking the fact that increased "automobility" greatly reduces the attraction of proximity.

The movement of vehicles was to be made easy by a combination of three means: traffic regulation, street widening, the new arteries, supplemented by provision of off-street parking. The arterial system was conceived as a system of surface roads, with only a few grade separations; interchanges were generally designed as traffic circles. No reserved rights-of-way were provided for public transit, assuming implicitly that transit would remain competitive with the private automobile despite great disadvantages in traveling time.

Summary of Assumptions

Gréber visualized the future National Capital essentially as a conglomeration of relatively self-contained villages, embedded in and encircled by green, grouped around a center devoted to the representative functions of government and culture. He referred to "the old village from which inspiration can always be safely taken." In this, as well as in its underestimate of the explosive growth of population and motor vehicles and of their impact, and its misunderstanding of the locational requirements of industry and commerce, the plan was typical of its time. In its imaginative grasp of the development of the urban and rural landscape, however, it was well ahead of current North American practice.

IMPLEMENTATION OF THE PLAN

The implementation of the plan depended and continues to depend on three agents: the federal government, the various municipal and provincial governments, and private enterprise. Gréber felt that an overriding administrative unit, such as a "federal district," was not needed, but that the plan could be carried out "without deeply changing their [the municipalities'] respective administrations." In fact, relations between the National Capital Commission and the municipalities, notably the city of Ottawa, have been rather strained. By and large the municipalities have disregarded the plan. Ottawa has never adopted an "official plan" incorporating its proposals. The municipalities in and beyond the greenbelt, which were supposed to remain rural, have permitted and, indeed, frequently encouraged industrial, commercial, and residential developments on their territories.

By contrast, the federal government has followed the plan faithfully, using its powers as the major landowner, employer, and source of funds in the National Capital Region. As a result the most salient features of the plan have been or are being carried out: parks and greenbelt, location and siting of federal buildings, relocation of railroads, and major road system. All other elements of urban development are governed, as in all other Canadian cities, mainly by the financial considerations of private enterprise and of municipalities.

THE GREENBELT

The guiding concept of the Gréber plan was the containment of urban development by a greenbelt. The area outside the greenbelt was to retain permanently its "rural character, with the exception of limited and controlled minor developments." The means of control were not spelled out. Indeed, the plan stated that this outer area "requires no planning operations, but merely the application of protective regulations," which were, however, not specified.

The idea of limiting urban growth by a greenbelt is not new. Elizabeth I decreed a greenbelt around London; so did Oliver Cromwell. In the nineteenth century many writers, both in England and on the continent, advocated it; current British legislation has adopted it. In practice, greenbelts have been no more able to contain urban growth than were their predecessors, the medieval city walls.

In the years immediately following adoption of the master plan, 15 subdivisions were developed in the area designated as the greenbelt. In 1956 the federal government decided to step in and acquired, during the following 5 years, about 44,000 acres at a cost of some $20 million. With minor exceptions a greenbelt of a width of 2–5 miles is now public property.

As mentioned, the plan assumed that all urban development would occur within the approximately 70 square miles enclosed by this perimeter. As less than 20 square miles had been absorbed by urban development at the time the plan was developed, this appeared indeed to be ample: the anticipated population of 450,000—which has been approximately reached at present—could live there at a density only half as high as that of the occupants of the 20 square miles in 1947.

It could, but it does not. It is rather strange that Gréber, who was very realistically aware of the impact of land values on planning, appears to have ignored the reverse impact of planning on land values. Any planning measure shifts the "floating" development value from one piece of land to another. The development value which was shifted by government action out of the greenbelt has floated into the enclosed area. The increase in land values within the enclosure exerts a strong pressure to develop there at higher densities than the very moderate ones envisaged in the plan. At the same time the increased difference between values inside and those outside the greenbelt increases the attraction of the outside areas for residential developers and even more so for industries. Consequently, while large tracts of land inside the perimeter are still vacant, new industries establish themselves outside rather than in the planned zone near the railroad yards; and residences multiply there.

Ottawa has been fortunate in that residential development so far has occurred primarily in the well-planned "new town" of Kanata, created by an imaginative private developer, but there is no guarantee against scattered development anywhere. It is evident that, contrary to Gréber's expectations, the main planning problem lies in the outside area.

RELOCATION OF THE RAILROADS

Probably the outstanding achievement of the Gréber plan is the complete relocation of the railroads, which has now been largely completed. For reasons discussed earlier, the related hoped-for relocation of heavy industry from the waterfront to the new yard area is not likely to occur.

While the elimination of freight trains from the urban area is an inestimable gain, the elimination of rail passenger access is a definite disadvantage. As evidenced by his treatment of the plaza and street approaches to the large new passenger station which he proposed to build more than 4 miles from the center, Gréber took it for granted that railroads would retain their dominant role in long-distance passenger transportation, despite the competition of the airplane, the bus, and the private automobile. In the light of subsequent developments the grandiose plan for this section of Ottawa has been abandoned. Instead, a very small passenger station has been built at the inner end of the freight yard, only half as far from the center but losing the operational advantage of through movement. It is evidently being considered as unimportant.

With the fast trains now coming into use, Ottawa could be reached from Montreal in less than 2 hours and from Toronto in less than 4 hours. But such trains are likely to attract the growing number of visitors only if the latter can reach their destinations on foot or by a short convenient transit ride, as they can in Montreal and Toronto.

The elimination of the central railroad station and the tracks leading to it has also made it more difficult to establish rail rapid transit as the backbone of an efficient metropolitan transit system. While the relocation of the freight railroad system is the most remarkable achievement of the master plan, the elimination of the central passenger station may be its greatest mistake.

THE DECENTRALIZATION OF FEDERAL EMPLOYMENT

In conformance with the plan, the federal government has systematically distributed new complexes for its various services throughout the area, at distances from Parliament Hill varying from 2 to 8 miles. It has been expected that employees would establish their residences close to their places of employment, thereby bringing about a decrease of traffic movement. In fact, their residences are dispersed all over the metropolitan area. As only poor bus connections exist to the center and none to other areas, almost all employees travel to work by car. Personal contacts with Cabinet, Parliament, and their staffs and with the public, as well as with other government agencies, also require fairly long automobile trips.

The attraction to employees of pleasant green surroundings is offset by the absence of shopping facilities and restaurants. Some, fed up with queuing for cafeteria food, tend to roar off at lunch time to more fragrant, though not greener, pastures—no self-containment for them.

For all these reasons many voices are now being raised against the continuation of the decentralization policy and for the creation of a strong, lively center. Commercial offices, hardly considered in the plan, are proliferating in the center of Ottawa, as in all major cities, but the shopping area, split between the Sparks-Bank Street section west of the Rideau Canal and Rideau Street east of it, is still strangely provincial for a capital of over 0.5 million population.

NEIGHBORHOODS AND COMMUNITIES

Gréber was well aware of the split between the wealthier Anglo-Saxon west and the poorer French east of Ottawa. However, he hoped to overcome this division not by a strong common city center, but by a mixture of ethnic and economic groups in every neighborhood. There is scant indication that this is happening.

The life of the neighborhood, as conceived by Clarence Perry, was to be centered around the school. But with the children divided among three different school systems, no such common center exists. Nor have neighborhood shopping centers developed. With moderate densities the number of households within easy walking distance is insufficient to sustain them, and car-shoppers prefer to drive to larger centers. Without a center, there is no periphery, and the plan's small greenbelts encircling neighborhoods and communities have generally not been established.

The concept of a hierarchy of neighborhoods and communities does not correspond to contemporary reality. Life in a modern metropolis proceeds not in relatively self-contained circles, but along a complex and widespread network.

THE ROAD SYSTEM

A physical correlate of this network is indeed being provided by the road network. The master plan developed a complete road system for the area and a schedule for its gradual implementation. With some modifications this plan and schedule are being followed. In particular, the backbone of the system, the east-west artery on the former railroad right-of-way, known as the Queensway, has been built. However, instead of the beautiful tree-lined parkway envisioned by Gréber, it is a roaring freeway, not too pleasant to look at, and in most sections not very pleasant to look *from*. Intersections are complex multilevel structures rather than the classic circles shown in the plan. Inevitably, engineering standards have determined design.

The road system also carries the buses, the only available means of transit. The dispersal of potential origins and destinations, a growing number of them separated from the planned urban area by 2–5 miles of greenbelt, combined with the absence of any rail or other grade-separated right-of-way for public transportation, threatens to lead to the same degree of dependence on the private automobile as exists in Los Angeles—in a climate which at times makes driving difficult. The provision of transit looms as an increasingly difficult planning problem.

PARKWAYS AND PARKS

An outstanding feature of the road system is the inclusion of a network of parkways, sensitively designed to provide the best views of the varied and beautiful landscape of the region and of the impressive silhouette of Parliament Hill. The park system, developed since the beginning of the century, has been carried to completion by the master plan. Most of it is already reality, in particular the Gatineau Hills, brought by a green wedge almost to the heart of the city.

The residents of the National Capital Region will have to do a lot of driving; but, unlike those in almost every other city, they will be able to enjoy most of it. Moreover, when—and if—they get out of their cars, they can walk and rest (weather permitting) in beautiful surroundings.

Gréber rightly emphasized that the desire for beauty is not the preserve of upper-class snobs, but a basic and universal human need. As affluence and leisure time increase, the value of the esthetic qualities of the National Capital Region created by the Gréber Master Plan will rise from year to year.

Chapter 12

CANADIAN PLANNING ISSUES

POPULATION TOTAL

Any discussion of population distribution must start from the present and anticipated total to be distributed. At present, Canada is the world's most underpopulated country. This applies not only to the not too meaningful average population density, but also to the amount per head of natural resources, renewable as well as non-renewable. There are about 10 acres of agricultural land for every Canadian, compared to a global average of 1 acre per head.

This disproportion is not likely to be changed by natural increase. The Canadian fertility rate is now well below parity. Under the assumption of continuation of present fertility rate and life expectancy and of zero net immigration, the Canadian population will reach a peak of less than 30 million around the turn of the century and thereafter decrease at an increasing rate. The fertility rate is, of course, notoriously erratic; however, a further decline is more probable than a rise.

If the disproportion is not to increase even further, Canada needs a substantial net immigration averaging not less than 1% annually. This is not entirely a question of planning. There seems to be a widespread illusion that planners—and/or governments—are God. In fact, while government can exercise a strong influence, it cannot exactly determine net immigration by fiat. Net immigration is the difference between gross immigration and emigration. Both our concepts of personal liberty and the extreme length of our land and sea borders preclude any control of emigration. Both factors also may limit the ability of government to enforce a ceiling on immigration. Even more limited is government's capacity to establish a floor for immigration. In western Europe, the traditional source of our immigrants, there is no longer a strong motivation to go to Canada. Communist governments, controlling one third of the world's population, effectively restrict emigration, and the Third World countries, increasingly aware of their losses by the "brain drain," may adopt similar, if less stringent, restrictions.

Tentatively, it is assumed that net immigration will average 1% annually. The resulting population growth rate will still be below world average. For the foreseeable future, Canada will remain the world's most underpopulated country.

Source: Report prepared for the United Nations Conference on Human Settlements, Vancouver, Canada, 1976, and published by The Canadian Institute of Planners, Ottawa, Ont., January 1976.

REGIONAL DISTRIBUTION

Our small population is very unevenly distributed. Nine tenths of our country is practically empty; nine tenths of all Canadians are concentrated on 7% of the land. However, this 7% equals 700,000 square kilometers, 100,000 square kilometers more than the combined area of West Germany, the United Kingdom, the Benelux countries, and Switzerland, which supports a population of about 150 million, under roughly comparable soil and climatic conditions. Evidently, even this 7% of our territory is underpopulated and underdeveloped, and there is no reason to shift population out of it. It may, however, be considered desirable to shift people into the vast empty areas of the North in order to develop their natural resources. The question is moot. As far as agricultural and forestry products are concerned, it may be that increases can be obtained with smaller inputs in the South than in the North. As for the exploitation of mineral resources and of water power, capital rather than labor appears to be the limiting factor.

In addition to the general south-north difference, population is also, and increasingly, unevenly distributed east to west, giving rise to demands of some provinces that the federal government should counteract this trend. There are good reasons for equity to work toward an equalization of real, including nonmonetary, income, and also to stem the selective migration loss of the most productive members of the community, which threatens some localities and regions. However, the often voiced demand for equalization of growth rates amounts to a demand that the distribution of population, which has always changed throughout human history, be frozen forever at the pattern obtaining in 1975 A.D.

DISTRIBUTION BY SIZE OF SETTLEMENT

Interwoven with, but different from, regional distribution is distribution by size of the unit of human settlement.

For well-known reasons, urbanization is progressing rapidly all over the world. Canada has reached the point where this process has almost run its course and is slowing down. While, both in the 1901–1921 and in the 1941–1961 periods, our urban population grew by more than 100%, in the 20 years from 1975 to 1995 it is not likely to grow by more than 50%. Certainly we have the ability to cope with this rate of growth; maybe we are lacking the will to do so.

The relevant unit of urbanization is no longer the town or city, but the metropolitan or urban area. While in the Socialist countries small and medium-sized urban areas have been growing faster than the largest ones, in market-economy countries there has been an increasing concentration, in particular in the primate cities. However, the latest census reports seem to indicate that in the most advanced countries this trend has stopped or even reversed. As yet it is not clear to what extent this is a statistical illusion, due to a failure to adjust the boundaries of the metropolitan area to its factual extension; but certainly in Canada, as elsewhere in the West, the time of the "metropolitan explosion" is over.

To the extent that public opinion and governments still consider the growth of the three Canadian metropolitan areas with populations over 1 million—Montreal, Toronto, and Vancouver—to be excessive, the most promising approach (apart from redistribution within metropolitan regions, which will be discussed later) appears to be the French strategy of creating "countermagnets" with populations averaging 0.5–1 million.

Two options present themselves for this strategy: foundation of new cities, and enlargement of existing ones. New cities are attractive to administrators because of ease and low cost of land acquisition and to designers because they provide a tabula rasa for the exercise of their imagination. But they have two drawbacks. For a long time the age composition of their population is abnormal, with an excess of young parents and small children, few adolescents, and practically no one over 50. For an even longer period there is an imbalance between demand and supply of services, many of which are "lumpy." Either supply lags, or it is provided ahead of time, at considerable cost. Both drawbacks can be avoided by promoting incremental growth of existing metropolitan areas of a size between about 0.25 and 0.5 million, of which there are quite a number in Canada. Smaller towns will, of course, also continue to exist, but it should be kept in mind that vulnerability increases with decreasing size; if one plant closes, there are few other opportunities for employment.

Governments can, of course, use a number of incentives and disincentives to influence population distribution. However, these will induce people to leave big cities, or to abstain from moving to them, only if they succeed in making these cities unattractive, at least in relative terms. It is unlikely that governments will go very far in that direction. It is therefore assumed that larger metropolitan regions will continue to grow, with a moderate relative shift from the three largest ones to those of the following size group.

URBAN-RURAL COMPETITION FOR LAND

This chapter will not deal with utilization of land for agriculture, forestry, large-scale conservation, and recreation, except to note that these uses are not mutually exclusive. It will concentrate on questions related to urban development.

In recent years concern has been expressed that the absorption of agricultural land by the expansion of our large metropolitan areas may endanger our supply of food. This concern is misplaced for at least three reasons.

First, the order of magnitude is different. It has been predicted that the combined population of the metropolitan areas of Montreal, Toronto, and Vancouver will be 15 million in the year 2000. Assuming that these 15 million occupied land at the low density of 10 persons per acre (the corresponding current figure in Metropolitan Toronto is 16), they would occupy a total of 1.5 million acres, less than 1% of all Canadian land suitable for agriculture.

Second, it is not cities that absorb land, but people. The smaller the community, the greater is the absorption of land per person. If the 15 million people lived not in three metropolitan communities, but in 300, averaging 50,000 population each, they would cover much more land with buildings and pavements; and if they lived in 30,000 villages of 500 each, they would cover still more.

Third, the notion that "urban" land use is identical with a "concrete desert" is unfounded. At a density of 10 persons per acre, the greater part consists of public and private open space which can be used for food production whenever the need arises, as shown by the wartime experience of England and other countries. Indeed, even now it is advisable to provide land for allotment gardens in our cities.

The fact that the fear of urban expansion dangerously reducing food production is spurious is no excuse for the waste of prime agricultural land by excessively low densities and by lack of attention to soil quality; but in metropolitan regions its preservation may have a lower priority than that of scenic-recreational, watershed, and water-recharge areas.

THE URBAN PERIMETER

While the amount of land actually occupied by urban uses is relatively minor, a much larger amount is taken out of agricultural use in metropolitan areas in Canada, in contrast to those in Europe. In part this is the result of institutional arrangements such as the tax system, but it is also due to the scatteration of urban uses. This considerably increases the cost and time required to serve the urban uses, and it cuts up the open land into odd-shaped pieces, ill suited for either agriculture or recreation. The first principle of urban-metropolitan land use planning is to clearly separate and hold together developed and open areas, respectively.

Carried to its ultimate conclusion, this principle would lead to a circular city—the form toward which cities have always tended naturally, and which reduces the urban perimeter to a minimum. However, the urban perimeter is, by definition, the urban-rural interface. It is primarily in order to maximize this interface that reformers have proposed to replace the compact city by other forms. Basically, there are only three of these: the "ribbon," the "constellation" or "satellite," and the "finger" or "radiating" plan. The ribbon makes sense only for small and medium-sized cities, up to a population of 100,000 or 200,000. In larger agglomerations, ribbons may take the form of fingers extending from the more or less circular core. These fingers may consist of a string of "satellites," that is, of relatively self-contained units, which may be defined as "new boroughs." In comparison with isolated "new towns" these have the advantages of incremental growth discussed earlier.

To some extent these same advantages are available to satellite towns if they are developed by planned extension of existing towns, situated outside the metropolitan area but within the metropolitan region. The metropolitan area is here defined as a common labor and housing market or a commuter watershed. The commuting radius tends to extend to about 45 minutes of door-to-door travel time, up to 25 miles from the center. The metropolitan region includes a wide surrounding belt, which relies on the central area for "higher-order" business and consumer services, and on which the central area relies for outdoor recreation. Such a region tends to spread up to a travel time of 2 hours, or as far as 100 miles from the center.

Small and medium-sized towns located within a metropolitan region have, in addition to access to services, also the advantage of lesser vulnerability because their inhabitants have access to other employment opportunities within the metropolitan region. Their resulting greater growth potential is empirically confirmed by an analysis of the population growth from 1941 to 1969 of the 17 cities in Ontario which, during this period, passed the 20,000 mark. While the 7 located outside metropolitan regions grew by 117%, the 10 inside such regions grew by 284%.

To sum up, urban growth should generally be confined within "fingers" radiating from metropolitan cities, and within extension areas of selected towns located within metropolitan regions.

INTERACTION OF LAND USE AND TRANSPORTATION

One of the most disturbing phenomena of modern life is the proliferation of motor vehicle movement with its toll of accidents and air pollution. Two strategies are available for its reduction: first, replacement by less damaging means of transportation, and, second, reduction of the need for movement by locating potential origins and destinations closer together.

Replacement of individual by collective transportation is possible only when a sufficient volume of persons or goods can be collected for movement over a given route at a given time. This requires concentration generally at both ends of a trip, but at the very least at one end. In small towns such concentrations can hardly be found. The larger the population of an urban area, the greater the percentage of person-trips that can be made by public transit. Similarly, only between large urban concentrations can frequent and fast train, or even bus, services be operated; and, even more important, efficient means of goods transportation such as unit trains, ships, and pipelines be provided. While dispersal of people and activities over all parts of the country may have its attraction, it implies almost exclusive reliance on the motor vehicle.

The second strategy, reduction of travel distances, may be even more important. Several measures are available. The most obvious one is an increase in densities. This is certainly worth pursuing, but it must be realized that it runs counter to a trend which has been consistent for over a century, before and independent of the motor vehicle. As wealth and leisure increase, more land per person is absorbed for *all* purposes—not only for residence, but also for work, recreation, and so forth.

Another possible measure, a compact form, has already been discussed, as well as the countervailing desire for an increased urban-rural interface.

More promising is the establishment, within each section of an urban and metropolitan area, of an approximate balance between resident labor force and places of employment, qualitatively as well as quantitatively, as well as between demand for and supply of services. It is important to concentrate all kinds of services—public, voluntary, and commercial—in one closely knit center for each section. This allows the customers to move between their residences and the center by public transit, and between the various services within the center on foot. Equally important, such subcenters help to create a sense of community. There is a widespread belief that a community of this type must be identified by a boundary in the form of a greenbelt. However, there is strong evidence that identity is derived from a common center, rather than from a common periphery. A convincing example is the extremely strong neighborhoods (*harat*) of Islamic cities, which have no visible boundaries.

Organization of each section, whether contiguous or isolated, into a balanced community with a strong center may be formulated as a guiding principle for the spatial planning of a metropolitan region. No definite statement can be made about the optimum size of such subcenters; evidently a hierarchy is required. However, a sub-center of the largest class should probably be designed to serve no less than one twelfth of the total population of the metropolitan area.

WHO PLANS?

The foregoing discussion implies that some unspecified power, variously defined as "we" or as "the planners" or as "the government," determines the distribution of people and activities at various scales, together with the corresponding utilization of land. This model does not reflect the real-life situation.

In Canada, land is a commodity, which is bought and sold at prices determined by the market according to the relation between supply and demand. The owner determines its use. Various government bodies own various pieces of land, primarily those required for services which these bodies supply, such as streets, parks, or schools. However, the bulk of land in populated areas is privately owned.

The provinces have jurisdiction over all lands (except those owned by the federal government) within their boundaries. The power derived from this authority is purely negative: it can tell the property owner what he shall *not* do, but not what he or she shall do. The power is exercised primarily by subdivision control and by restricted area ("zoning") bylaws. The primary function of zoning is the protection of property values, a purpose which requires both equality for all properties within a given zone and predictability—hence uniformity and rigidity.

In addition to these means of direct control, governments can and do strongly influence the use to which owners put their land by the supply or withholding of services such as roads, water, sewage, transit, parks, and schools, which make the lands so served more or less attractive to certain users.

The actual development of urban areas is therefore, as it has always been, the result not of "a plan," but of the interaction of the plans of governments with the plans of many private—physical or corporate—persons, in their role as users representing the demand and/or as landowners developing the supply.

THE ROLE OF VARIOUS GOVERNMENT BODIES

For a sovereign city-state, such as Singapore, there is one government level. In Canada, in addition to the federal and the provincial, there is at least one municipal level with delegated powers, and in the largest metropolitan areas there are two. Moreover, there is an insistent demand for further delegation to units of "neighborhood" size. All of these—three, four, or five levels—plan. By what criteria can decision-making power be assigned to one or the other?

There can be no quarrel with the basic principle that people have the right to control their own environment, but this does not justify a claim to neighborhood autonomy. Apart from questions of economy of scale (a water supply system cannot be planned and built on a neighborhood basis), most decisions have "overspill effects" both in space and in time. They affect not only the people presently living in a given neighborhood, but also those living in adjacent neighborhoods, as well as future occupants who may belong to different classes with quite different needs and demands. Who can speak for these people who are not yet there? Probably only a larger unit in which they are already represented, if not in person, at least by a member of a group with identical needs and demands.

Of course, including overspill effects cannot be the only consideration in defining an appropriate area of planning and government, because some interaction with others beyond the boundary will always occur. The decisive criterion is that interaction within an area is significantly more frequent and intense than interaction with outside areas. This is the case within the commuter watershed, which defines the metropolitan area. It is the predominant form of human settlement in contemporary Canada and, as such, the appropriate unit for government and planning below the provincial level; it should therefore be the government unit mainly responsible for the quality of the human settlement.

Actions of the higher levels of governments, of course, also influence that quality. What is most needed here is coordination of the actions of the various departments of the provincial and federal governments, not only at the center, but also in each region. Regional planning organizations, including regional administrators of these departments, together with representatives of the local municipalities and possibly also of nongovernmental organizations, are essential. However, these bodies probably should not be governments; implementation of agreed-on plans would remain a responsibility of the participating organizations.

Not only higher levels of governments, but all large organizations, including metropolitan governments, are faced with the problem that the "sectoral" organizations which they must set up to deal with specific aspects—health, transportation, and so on—of the lives of their constituents develop programs which tend to become ends in themselves, without regard to their actual impact on the people affected by them. As one Swedish student put it, "we are always dealing with dividuals when we should deal with individuals." Planning "from the top down" must therefore be supplemented by planning "from the grass (or concrete) roots up," by input from the individuals who are affected by it.

One step in this direction is the establishment (or preservation) of smaller elected municipal governments within the area under the jurisdiction of a metropolitan government. However, this is effective only if the metropolitan area is divided into a two-digit number of "boroughs" of much smaller and substantially equal size. Units of 0.5 million population, such as the central cities and some boroughs of our largest metropolitan areas, cannot be significantly closer to their constituents than can metropolitan governments.

Even boroughs with populations of about 100,000 are too big as a basis for meaningful participation of a majority of their members. In Canada only the "unicity" of Winnipeg has given official status to smaller units on the "neighborhood" scale. In the main, "citizen participation" is practiced through nongovernmental groups. Many such groups have, of course, always (and effectively) participated in urban government, both areawide groups representing material or ideological interests, and groups speaking for upper- and middle-class neighborhoods. What is new is that in recent years residents of low-income neighborhoods have also begun to speak up. This is a long overdue and most welcome development. It is certainly true that these—and all other—citizen groups tend to concentrate on protests against the immediately perceptible negative impact of public actions, with insufficient evaluation of the possibility of much greater damage resulting from alternatives. However, this does not justify planners in rejecting participation, but obliges them to explain the alternatives immediately, fully, and clearly, in plain words. Participation needs time to mature; but, as Immanuel Kant noted 200 years ago, "freedom can be learned only through freedom."

PUBLIC AND PRIVATE INTEREST IN LAND

While conflicting interests between citizens' groups and their elected governments are inevitable, they are basically nonantagonistic and amenable to compromise. The contradiction between the interest of the community in land as a resource and the interest of the property owner in land as a commodity is of a different character.

Every planning measure, whether regulatory, such as zoning, or involving the creation of public works, such as roads or sewers, makes some pieces of land more desirable than others. It thereby shifts value from the land of some owners to that of others. Inevitably those who lose protest most strongly; and reasons of equity, frequently reinforced by political influence, make such protests effective. This greatly restricts the flexibility of planning. Once a public commitment, however tentative, has been made, it is hard to change, even if altered conditions or insights call for such a change. When the shift of land values occurs within the property of one owner, this restriction does not exist. Experience confirms that urban development planned on the scale of a large estate, whether private or public, produces better results than piecemeal development under conditions of scattered ownership. As ownership of more than a small portion of a metropolitan area would create an unacceptable monopoly, such large-scale landownership can only be public.

Advocates of public landownership generally put more emphasis on two other points: the right of the community to claim the "unearned increment" of land value, and a lowering of the cost of new housing by a reduction of land cost. The latter implies that the community would pass on all or part of the increment to the owners or renters of new housing; as most of these have an above-average ability to pay, this would mean a regressive redistribution of income. Lowering land cost is in the public interest only under conditions of oligopolistic pricing, resulting from artificial restriction of the supply of developable land. Such restriction may be brought about by a conspiracy of landowners, or, more probably, by a withholding by provinces and their municipalities of permits and/or public works indispensable for development.

The public claim to the "unearned income" or rent derived from land is based on the fact that it is created entirely by the community; the landowner can do nothing to raise it. If the land were still owned by the original settler, who generally did not pay for it, there could be no objection to the community claiming this value. However, as land has for centuries been exchanged against commodities, it is, under our institutions, entitled to the same degree of protection against expropriation as other forms of investment.

The value of investment in industrial and commercial properties is, of course, often substantially decreased by government action in areas such as taxation, tariffs, or regulation of freight rates. Investment in land has no claim to immunity from these types of losses. There can therefore be no valid objection to an increase in the tax on land which is now levied by municipalities. Assuming that this tax now amounts to 20% of the rent, then the 80% remaining for the property owner is capitalized as the value of his or her land. If the tax is doubled, only 60% is capitalized; the land value is reduced by one quarter. This does not automatically benefit the home buyer, who will pay in taxes what he or she saves in mortgage payments. But it will make speculative land holding very costly and thereby bring more land onto the market. Both this easing of the market and the reduction of land prices will greatly facilitate extension of public landownership.

Increases in the land tax will have to proceed together with decreases in the tax on buildings, the two being coupled under the name "real property tax." More than half of the tax on buildings falls on residential buildings and is paid by their occupants, tenants or owners. As the percentage of income paid for housing rises steeply as income falls, this is a highly regressive tax. The part of the tax which falls on industrial-commercial buildings constitutes part of their cost of production and is passed on to the consumers of the goods or services which they sell. It acts as a general sales tax. While this is not as regressive as the housing tax, it is certainly not progressive.

In fact, it is not possible for municipalities to raise substantial amounts by any form of progressive taxation, because it is too easy for wealthy taxpayers to evade these measures by moving across the municipal boundary. Such taxes should be levied on a national basis and allocated to municipalities proportionally to their population. This would also be a much simpler, more equitable, and more effective method of regional income equalization than any presently in use.

The proposed tax reform would do more for the improvement of the quality of life in human settlements and for regional equalization than all the busy housing and regional development programs now being operated by huge and proliferating federal and provincial bureaucracies.

TWO KINDS OF PLANNING

The discussion so far has dealt with the task which has traditionally been the responsibility of professionals in the fields of urban and regional planning (*urbanisme et aménagement du territoire*). This task is the adaptation of the physical environment to human needs. It deals primarily with the where and how of capital investments, both public and private.

However, capital investments in public works and control over private investments in "real estate" are only a part, albeit an important one, of the responsibilities of governments; they engage in many continuous activities, carried out day by day through the work of their employees. All these activities, as well as those of private corporations and of individuals, have to be planned before they can be carried out. Such "activity planning" or "management planning" deals primarily with the question of *what* to do, how much, and in what sequence; its time horizon tends to be shorter than that of physical planning.

Such planning is carried out primarily by the professionals who manage a department responsible for a specified sector, such as education, national defence, agriculture, or health. But who plans the planners? As noted earlier, coordination at the top tends to be weak. One attempt to strengthen it at the urban level has been the creation of professional city managers. On all levels there has been a rapid growth of a planning staff advisory to the executive. In Canada it is being recruited largely, though by no means exclusively, from the established planning profession, which attempts to extend its competence beyond the planning of the physical environment to planning the management of a wide range of activities.

It may be questioned whether a single profession can cover so broad a field. In the U.S.S.R., where social-economic planning developed ahead of physical planning, two distinct planning professions have been established. Certainly, planners of the physical environment have to understand the activities which they need to house; and activity planners must understand the physical framework of the activities with which they are concerned. Evidently, there is overlap and a need for cooperation.

But is the answer complete integration? The question is particularly important for planning schools. Should they attempt to develop a "universal" planner, or a "basic" planner who has to add a special field, or two (or more) different types of planners? An international exchange of experiences and views concerning this problem might well be one of the most fruitful exercises of the Habitat conferences.

CITIZENS' PARTICIPATION IN MANAGEMENT

"Citizens' participation," in the sense in which this term is presently being used, refers generally to organized opposition of the residents of a neighborhood to actions and policies which threaten to disrupt their way of life. First and foremost among these is the policy of slum clearance, variously christened "sanitation," "redevelopment," or "renewal." Despite the warnings of Patrick Geddes, the policy of slum clearance claims to improve the quality of life of the affected residents. Certainly they are more than justified in claiming that they know best and should decide what kind of improvements they need.

The situation is quite different when disruption is the result of changes required by structural changes in the urban area. Such changes are intended to benefit other groups, future occupants and/or residents of other parts of the area. Their interests may legitimately outweigh the interest of the present residents in undisturbed occupancy. In such cases, citizens' participation, while it may sometimes modify the extent and timing of the changes, must be concerned primarily with planning for the reestablishment—not merely the "relocation"—of the present occupants.

Whatever the reasons for disruption, citizens' participation has forcefully brought home the fact that people's main problems are not physical, but social, and call for "social planning." It is here, in the field of the "software" rather than of the "hardware" of physical planning, that there is the greatest scope for neighborhood participation and self-determination. The planning and management of current activities in recreation, social welfare, street maintenance, and many other fields has hardly any effect on future residents and little on those outside the neighborhoods involved. Its results are visible in short order and can easily be evaluated by the residents. Such civic activities are both in themselves an enrichment of the "quality of life" of those engaged in them, and a means for their development into citizens able and willing to exercise their rights and duties. But these activities can bring about the required social change only if they extend well beyond the neighborhood. Indeed, our "urban problems," while *in* the city, are not *of* the city. They are problems of society; they can be defined as the trinity of unemployment, maldistribution of income, and the alienation from their labor and its products of practically the entire working population.

These problems lie outside the responsibility of the planner as a professional. But they are not outside his or her responsibility as a citizen and as a human being.

Chapter 13

TREND TO THE METROPOLIS

A NOTE ON SEMANTICS

The research area under review was defined by the Canadian Council on Urban and Regional Research as "drift to the metropolis." Mr. Leroy Stone suggested "shift." The term "drift" is strongly associated with a negative value judgment; the term "shift" may seem to imply some joint deliberation. The term "trend" appears to be the most accurate description of the phenomenon under study.

Any movement is the result of a parallelogram of forces, or of a combination of such parallelograms. Its direction always differs from the direction of any one of its component forces; for example, the trajectory of a bullet follows neither the direction of the gun barrel nor that of gravity. The component forces of social movements are far more numerous and complex than those of mechanical movements; they consist of the actions of individuals. As these actions are directed by conscious, goal-oriented decisions of the heads of households, enterprises, and governments, they cannot be called "drift." However, the trajectory of a social movement resulting from the combination of the sum of these actions is not directed toward any of these goals; it is not a deliberate "shift." The accepted term for the trajectory of social (including economic) movements is "trend."

GENERALITY OF THE TREND TO THE METROPOLIS

Trends differ greatly as to their generality. Some can be observed to be valid only for short periods, or only in one or a few limited areas. If trends can be observed to be continuous and ubiquitous, experience indicates a fair probability that real-life future will be adequately described by their extrapolation, even if their component forces are only incompletely known. (The components of social movements are never completely known.) In fact, both scientific and every-day practices rely on such extrapolations.

A trend to the metropolis has been observed for over a century in all industrial or postindustrial market-economy countries. In countries with centrally planned economies the trend appears to have been reversed, at least to the extent that the growth rate of cities is inversely correlated to their initial size.

Source: Report published by the Canadian Council on Urban and Regional Research, Ottawa, Ont., 1969.

It certainly is desirable to investigate all aspects of this field of study in Canada in the framework of international experience—the factual developments as well as their effects and their causes, including the accelerating or decelerating results of government policies. In particular, Swedish studies deserve the special attention of Canadians, not only because they are of high quality, but also because Sweden is more similar to Canada than is any other country, both in climatic and soil conditions and in level of economic development.

THE TREND IN CANADA

It is hardly necessary to emphasize the strength of the trend in Canada. Suffice it to say that from 1961 to 1966 the population of urban areas of over 100,000 population increased by 19.5%, while that of towns between 2,500 and 100,000 increased by only 11.4%, and rural population actually decreased. In 1966 the population in places with more than 2,500 persons accounted for 7 out of 10 Canadians, and of this "urban" population 68% lived in urban areas over 100,000 and 42% in those over 500,000. There is no doubt that the 1971 census will show at least one half of our population in the former, and one third in the latter, group.

It is evident that no government will be able to ignore the demand for improvement of the living conditions of so large a segment of the population—and will thereby make our metropolitan areas even more attractive. This will create a serious conflict, *if* the answer to the problem defined below should indicate the desirability of reversing the trend.

THE NATURE OF THE PROBLEM

The problem has been defined by one of Europe's leading economists in the following words:

Both large and small centers have a number of advantages and disadvantages, different for different people, and this is why we have a whole range of sizes. Statistically, we even find that the size distribution is fairly regular. No scientific explanation worthy of that name has been advanced so far. Neither do we know whether or not the existing distribution is optimal.[1]

From this definition it becomes evident that several research problems can be distinguished:

A. The process of distribution of population and activities between urban areas of various sizes.

B. Estimation of the costs and benefits to society of life in urban areas of various sizes.

C. Design and testing of models of alternative size distributions, and their comparative evaluation based on the results of B.

[1] J. Tinbergen, "The Hierarchy Model of the Size Distribution of Centers," in Regional Science Association, *Papers*, Vol. XX, p. 65, 1968; Wharton School, University of Pennsylvania, Philadelphia, Pa., 1968.

D. Development of policy proposals designed to modify the urbanization process towards the distribution found to be optimal as a result of C.

While logically each of these steps depends on the results of the preceding one—and step D would become meaningless if C should show the distribution by the observed trend to be optimal—it is possible and desirable to initiate research in all four subareas simultaneously.

It is also important to note that the universe of urban areas of different sizes cannot be treated merely as the sum of its constituent parts, but is profoundly affected by their spatially conditioned interaction. In this respect this problem area overlaps the problem area of regional development.

Subarea A: The Process of Urbanization. Research in this subarea must explore the following:

A1. The objective characteristics of the process.

A2. The subjective motivations of the various decision-makers whose combined actions result in the process.

Some of the studies required under A1 are these:

a. Exact measurement and analysis of gross migration by such characteristics of the migrants as age, sex, family status, education, income, occupation, and industry. This task requires primarily the skills of demographers and statisticians. Some of it is being carried out by the Dominion Bureau of Statistics.

> a1. This task would be greatly facilitated in the future by a system of registration of residents, such as exists in European countries. A team of experts in political science, law, and public administration might study the possibility of such a system, including its implications for relations between the individual and the state.

b. Studies of the economic structure and development of urban areas of various sizes, in particular of their industrial and occupational profiles. These studies would have to deal with questions such as differences in size, ownership (local or external), development of new products, import substitution, and threshold values required for different types of economic activity.

> b1. A particularly promising and neglected aspect is a study of the linkages (including changes over time) between small ("satellite") towns and nearby metropolitan centers, both as to producer and as to consumer services. A series of monographs might be a rewarding approach.

c. Studies of the social structure and development of urban areas of various sizes. This might cover such aspects as social stratification and mobility, family and neighborhood relations, participation in community affairs, education, and culture, as well as the incidence of phenomena of social pathology.

Studies under A2 would include sample studies of the attitudes and motivations of both migrants and nonmigrants among the following:

a. Individuals and households, with particular attention to changes in attitudes over time.

b. Decision-makers of industries and institutions, with particular attention to initiators of new enterprises.

Subarea B: Costs and Benefits. In a closely knit urban area the benefits and costs of any transaction accrue not only to the parties to the transaction but also to third persons ("overspill benefits" and "social costs"). These can be traced only incompletely. However, several important elements can be identified.

B1. Economies and diseconomies of scale of municipal services. This aspect has received more attention than any other but is of relatively minor importance, as total municipal expenditures rarely amount to more than 10% of gross regional product, and many of them are little affected by scale.

B2. Differences (far more significant, but much less explored) in the productivity of labor, resulting from external economies and diseconomies dependent on scale.

B3. Differences in labor force participation in different communities and their causal relation to size and other factors.

B4. Differences in cost—in terms of time, money, and inconvenience—of person movement in communities of different size. This would have to include costs not only of intraurban, but also of interurban, movements, as well as costs due to change of residence.

B5. Differences in cost of achieving the same level of environmental amenity (abatement of noise, traffic danger, and pollution of air, soil, and water).

B6. Costs and benefits of interaction between urban areas as determined by the absolute and relative sizes of the interacting areas and by the distances between them.

Subarea C: Design and Testing of Alternatives

C1. Development of a theoretical model representing correlations between relevant variables. The model could become operative as soon as parameters could be derived from subareas A and B.

C2. A study of developments in other countries.

Subarea D: Policy Proposals

D1. An analysis of the impact of costs and benefits, on urban areas of various sizes, of federal and provincial programs in such fields as transportation, education, health and welfare, housing, and urban renewal.

D2. A study of policies applied in other countries and of their anticipated and unanticipated effects.

CONCLUDING REMARK

The foregoing represents not a research program, but at most an outline for a conceptual framework for such a program. Conceivably it might help to identify gaps and to maintain balance in the development of a research program.

Chapter 14

HAMBURG AND TORONTO: A COMPARISON

URBAN REGIONS IN GERMANY AND IN NORTH AMERICA

North Americans who have seen Germany and Germans who have visited the United States or Canada both have been struck by the great contrasts in the image of the big city. For the German visitor the strongest first impression was the concentration of office skyscrapers in the central business district (C.B.D.) and its sharp distinction, visually as well as functionally, from the life and the buildings surrounding it. After a longer acquaintance this was overshadowed by the view of the endlessly sprawling residential areas of detached single-family houses with their complete dependence on individual transportation by millions of private cars.

North Americans are beginning to have second thoughts concerning the drawbacks of this type of development. A swelling chorus of voices calls for an end to the indefinite absorption of the countryside and to the continuing lengthening of everyday travel: "Stop building single-family houses—we need high-rise apartments; stop building urban freeways—we need subways and commuter railroads! Then the countryside will be country, and the city will be a city—as in Europe."

Much as value judgments may differ, experts and laymen on both sides of the Atlantic agree on the "facts": while in North America workplaces are more strongly concentrated in the C.B.D., overall urban population density is far lower than in Europe. This is the general view.

It therefore came as a great surprise when, about 20 years ago, my friend Olaf Boustedt, working with me in Toronto, noticed that the population density of Metropolitan Toronto was higher than that of most German big cities. Both of us suspected some calculating error, but verification confirmed the fact.

Our first conclusion was painful. We in Toronto had been—and still are—proud that this city had been the first on our continent to adjust its administrative structure to the realities of the modern metropolis. Now we found that most big cities in Germany—and in several other European countries—had long ago achieved the same result by the traditional method of extending the city boundary.

However, this did not explain the reasons for their unexpected low population densities. I took the question up again when the published preliminary population

---

Source: Plan (The Canadian Institute of Planners, Ottawa, Ont.), Vol. 11, No. 1, 1970.

figures for 1966 happened to be identical for Hamburg and Toronto at 1.85 million (the revised figure for Toronto was slightly higher). The fact that these are the two cities which I know best, Hamburg being my hometown and Toronto my present residence, encouraged me to make a comparison.

HAMBURG AND TORONTO

There are certain similarities between these two cities. Both originated on a harbor on the north shore of a large expanse of water—Lake Ontario and a network of branches of the river Elbe, totaling 5 miles in width—and grew in a semicircle around this core on land rising slightly to the north to a height nowhere exceeding 300 feet. True, the city-state of Hamburg comprises also extensive territories south of the river and on its islands. With the exception of the harbor area on the south shore of the northern branch of the Elbe, this area constitutes the district of Harburg. This district, containing 22.3% of the area, but only 11.2% of the population, is to some degree separated from the main urban area. In order to compare the semicircular metropolis of Toronto with an equally semicircular metropolis, some comparisons with "Hamburg north of the Elbe" (excluding the district of Harburg), or "H. n. E.," are also presented in the following discussion.

There is also a similarity of administrative structure, with two levels of self-government. The city-state of Hamburg contains seven "districts" administered by their elected councils; Metropolitan Toronto consists of six "municipalities." However, these structures originated in opposite ways. In Hamburg a unified city was decentralized. In Toronto separate municipalities were "federated" by provincial legislation.

The economic structure is also broadly similar, with over 60% of employment in the tertiary sector.[1] However, this similarity must be evaluated in different national contexts. The share of the secondary sector is considerably lower in Hamburg than in any of the major German urban areas, while in Canada it is higher than average. This is explained by the fact that the secondary sector accounts only for 34% of all employment in Canada, but for 48% in the German Federal Republic, with the primary sector accounting for 12% in both countries.

The historical background differs widely. Hamburg, the oldest German city beyond the Elbe, looks back almost 12 centuries. Toronto came into being in 1794 and became a city only in 1834. More important is the fact that Hamburg suffered heavy damage during World War II and has since been cut off from its hinterland, while Toronto has had a spectacular growth since the war. But the most noticeable difference is to be found in the historical development of housing types and in means of transportation. In Hamburg the predominant dwelling type is the apartment, and most single-family houses are row houses. In Toronto the detached or, more rarely, semidetached single-family house predominates. In Hamburg an electrified city-suburban railroad system with 12 or more trains per hour has been in operation since 1908, and a constantly expanded subway-elevated system since 1912, while the private car has become significant only since about 1954. On the other hand, it was

---

[1]Sectors are as follows: primary = raw materials, agriculture, mining, fishing; secondary = manufacturing, construction; tertiary = administration, services.

only in 1954 that Toronto opened its first 4.6 miles of subway, and only in 1966—after the date chosen for the comparison presented here—that a more extended system was put into operation, as well as a rather modest commuter railroad operation.

By contrast, the private car has had a decisive role in Toronto since the 1920s, but in particular in the postwar period. Long ago, employers felt that they could rely on their workers reaching their places of employment without the aid of public transportation and built new establishments many miles from the city center in open country. No doubt these profound differences lead one to expect a far more concentrated and less extensive form of settlement in Hamburg than in Toronto. This investigation will test this assumption.

THE METHOD OF INVESTIGATION

Essentially this investigation is based on statistics. The data are taken primarily from publications of the Hamburg Statistical Office and of the Dominion Bureau of Statistics, as well as from those of the Hamburg Building Authority and of the Metropolitan Toronto Planning Board. I am deeply obliged to both of these agencies for their generous aid in assembling unpublished material and putting it at my disposal. For the surroundings of Hamburg, I have relied exclusively on the excellent studies undertaken by Dr. Olaf Boustedt. For the surroundings of Toronto, the Metropolitan Toronto and Area Transportation Study (M.T.A.R.T.S.) supplied most of the data.

The two planning offices have utilized different methods of measuring land use areas. The Hamburg data are "net," summations of the areas of the parcels devoted to specific uses. The Toronto data are "gross," including the street surfaces associated with each use. Moreover, the land use definitions are not identical. These differences, as well as some data gaps, required a considerable amount of manipulation. When the manipulation is questionable, this is noted in the text. In no case should the figures be taken as exact; they indicate orders of magnitude and trends. In order to minimize the misleading impression of precision inherent in numerical data, all figures have been rounded.

In the following the term "city" applies to the city-state of Hamburg and to the municipality of Metropolitan Toronto; the term "surroundings" denotes the adjacent area within a radius of 25 miles (40 kilometers) from the city hall of the central city; and the term "urban region" refers to the sum of both units.

DISTRIBUTION OF POPULATION BETWEEN CITY AND SURROUNDINGS

As has already been noted, in 1966 overall population density was lower in Hamburg than in Toronto. Although the area of Toronto is 15.8% smaller than that of Hamburg, the population was slightly (1.9%) larger. Consequently, population density was one-fifth (21.0%) higher. See Table 1.

By itself this difference is not too significant, as density depends on the politically determined location of the city boundary. It might be suspected that Hamburg had included a greater reserve for future expansion. This would have the result that a

Table 1. Persons per Square Mile: 1966

	Hamburg	Toronto	Toronto as Percent of Hamburg
Population (1000)	1847	1882	101.9
Square miles	285	240	84.2
Population per square mile	6481	7842	121.0

greater part of the population and, in particular, a greater portion of the population growth would be accommodated within the city boundaries.

The facts are to the contrary. In 1966 in Hamburg, 29.3% of the total population of the urban region lived outside the city boundaries; in Toronto, only 15.4%. Even more significant is the trend. During the period 1961–1966, the surroundings of Hamburg accounted for almost the total population increase (94.1%); those of Toronto, for less than a quarter (23.8%). See Table 2, rows 2, 3, 8, 14.

Table 2. Population Change, City and Surroundings

	Hamburg			Toronto		
	City	Surroundings	Region	City	Surroundings	Region
Population (1000)						
1. 1939 (Toronto, 1941)	1698	355	2053	910	77	987
2. 1961	1841	671	2512	1619	261	1880
3. 1966	1847	766	2613	1882	343	2225
Increase (1000)						
4. 1939 (41)–1961	143	316	459	709	184	893
5. 1961 –1966	6	95	101	263	82	345
6. 1939 (41)–1966	149	411	560	972	266	1238
Increase (%)						
7. 1939 (41)–1961	8.5	89.2	22.2	77.6	228.0	90.6
8. 1961 –1966	0.3	14.2	4.0	16.3	31.8	18.4
9. 1939 (41)–1966	8.8	105.8	27.2	107.0	358.0	121.5
Distribution of Population (%)						
10. 1939 (41)	82.6	17.4	100.0	92.2	7.8	100.0
11. 1961	73.3	26.7	100.0	86.0	14.0	100.0
12. 1966	70.7	29.3	100.0	84.6	15.4	100.0
Distribution of Increase (%)						
13. 1939 (41)–1961	31.2	68.8	100.0	79.4	20.6	100.0
14. 1961 –1966	5.9	94.1	100.0	76.2	23.8	100.0
15. 1939 (41)–1966	26.7	73.3	100.0	78.5	21.5	100.0
16. Square miles	285	1634	1919	240	798	1038
17. Distribution	14.8	85.2	100.0	23.3	76.7	100.0
18. Population per square mile: 1966	6481	469	1361	7842	429	2144

The trend accelerated in the following 5 years. Since 1966 the population of Hamburg had been actually decreasing at an annual rate of about 12,000, while the rate of increase in the surroundings was well over 20,000. In Toronto the increase continued at a rate of at least 30,000 annually, with a considerably smaller increase in the surroundings.

Thus the population of Hamburg was spilling over into the surroundings, while the increase in Toronto was accommodated mainly within its own, somewhat narrower boundaries. This occurred despite the fact that the population in the urban region of Toronto was growing at a rate (about 2% annually) three times greater than that prevailing in Hamburg (0.67%).

In searching for an explanation for this surprising difference, one turns to history. The older pattern of settlement might lead one to suspect that the growth of the surroundings of Hamburg may be due to the "autonomous" growth of older independent towns. Indeed, in 1900 a somewhat larger percentage of the regional population lived in the surroundings of Hamburg (22.6%) than in those of Toronto (16.8%). Developments during the following 40 years are presented in Table 3.

During this period the population of Toronto increased at about five times the rate for that of Hamburg, both in the city and in the urban region. In both cases the rate of growth was much lower in the surroundings than it was in the city. However, the share of the surroundings dropped in Hamburg only from 22.6 to 17.2%, but in Toronto from 16.8 to 7.8%. Therefore the difference in the share of the surroundings can hardly be ascribed to the original structure of settlement.

World War II brought about a radical change in Hamburg. Hundreds of thousands of city dwellers fled to the surroundings. However, after the war they returned gradually. By 1961 the consequences of war destruction had been overcome, and the population of the city exceeded the prewar figure by 141,000. Thus the de-

Table 3. Population, City and Surroundings: 1900–1940 (Hamburg: 1900 and 1939, Toronto: 1901 and 1941)

	Hamburg			Toronto		
	City	Surroundings	Urban Region	City	Surroundings	Urban Region
1. Square miles	285	1634	1919	240	798	1038
Population (1000)						
2. 1900	1079	315	1394	238	48	286
3. 1940	1698	355	2053	910	77	987
Increase: 1900–1940						
4. 1000	619	40	659	572	29	701
5. Percent of 1900	57	13	47	291	60	245
Percent of Total Population						
6. 1900	77.4	22.6	100.0	83.2	16.8	100.0
7. 1940	82.8	17.2	100.0	92.2	7.8	100.0
Percent of Increase						
8. 1900–1940	93.9	6.1	100.0	95.9	4.1	100.0

velopment since 1961 and its difference from that in Toronto cannot be explained as a result of war damage.

Nor can some kind of "autonomous" development of the surroundings serve as an explanation. In fact, the small towns surrounding Hamburg are no more important than those surrounding Toronto. To the contrary, the fact that there are 88,000 (net) commuters from the surroundings to the city, compared to only 20,000 in Toronto, indicates a greater dependence on the central city. The surroundings are clearly orientated towards the city of Hamburg. Their development can be understood only as a result of the dynamism of the city.

The question remains: why is the overspill so much greater in Hamburg than in Toronto? Perhaps the key may be found in the distribution of workplaces. In Hamburg are more of these located close to the periphery of the city?

THE DISTRIBUTION OF WORKPLACES

Again it turns out that the facts are to the contrary, as shown in Table 4. In Toronto one third (33.6%) of all employment is located in the outer districts of the city; in Hamburg, less than one quarter (24.3%). Concentration in the city center is stronger in Toronto (29.4%) than in Hamburg (22.3%), although the volume of city center employment is lower. The most significant difference is to be found in the inner districts surrounding the center. In a practically equal area of about 36 square miles, more than twice as many persons were employed in Hamburg as in Toronto. Over half (53.4%) of all Hamburg workplaces are to be found in this "inner ring," compared to 37.0% in Toronto. It might be added that from 1956 to 1964, in Toronto, the number of employed decreased by 38,000 in the inner districts, but increased by 120,000 in the outer ones, with an additional sizable increase in the surroundings. In 1964, in Toronto, 20,000 workers commuted "out" and 39,000 commuted "in"; in Hamburg, in 1966, the corresponding figures were 8000 and 96,000! Evidently closeness to place of work is not the reason for the greater share of residents living outside the city boundaries in Hamburg.

It is interesting to note that the number of persons employed was almost 50% higher in Hamburg than in Toronto. For every 100 residents there were 54 employed

Table 4. Distribution of Employment

	Hamburg: 1961				Toronto: 1964			
	Area		Employed		Area		Employed	
	Square Miles	Percent	1000	Percent	Square Miles	Percent	1000	Percent
City center	1.2	0.4	227	22.3	1.2	0.5	198	29.4
Inner districts	35.8	12.6	542	53.4	36.8	15.4	251	37.0
Outer districts	248.0	87.0	247	24.3	202.0	84.1	226	33.6
City total	285.0	100.0	1005	100.0	240.0	100.0	675	100.0
Population (1000)			1841				1775	
Employed as percent of Population			54				38	

in Hamburg against 38 in Toronto. If the excess of in-commuters over out-commuters is deducted, the difference between the employment rates is still 48 to 37%. In part, the difference is explained by differences in age distribution. As a result of the arrival of hundreds of thousands of migrants, most of them young, and of a high fertility rate during the postwar years, Toronto is rich in children. In 1966 almost a third (32.8%) of the population was under 15 years of age, compared to 16.2% in Hamburg in 1961. In the age groups over 15, the employment rate was 55.6% in Toronto, 57.8% in Hamburg. This is still a significant difference in view of the fact that the age group 65 and over accounted for 14.0% in Hamburg and only 7.9% in Toronto. The reasons for the difference are probably slightly higher unemployment and lower female employment in Toronto.

HAMBURG NORTH OF THE ELBE

As has been noted, comparison between a semicircular and a circular urban region may be misleading, because, with the same radius, the former is only half as large in area as the latter. Therefore Table 5 compares the urban region of Toronto with the semicircular "Hamburg north of the Elbe (H. n. E.).

The similarity is striking. The figures on area and population differ only slightly, but in opposite directions. Consequently, overall density is still 8% higher in the region of Toronto. However, population density in the surroundings is one-third lower in Toronto, despite the greater dispersal of workplaces. The figures confirm strongly that the tendency to overspill is stronger in the German than in the Canadian city, contrary to general assumptions. Equally in contradiction to general impressions is the fact that density within the city is 6% higher in Toronto than in Hamburg.

Table 5. Population and Population Density, Urban Regions Hamburg North of the Elbe (H. n. E.) and Toronto: 1966

	H. n. E.			Toronto		
	City	Surroundings	Urban Region	City	Surroundings	Urban Region
Square miles	223	887	1110	240	798	1098
Population: 1966 (1000)	1642	553	2195	1882	343	2225
Population distribution (%)	74.6	25.4	100.0	84.6	15.4	100.0
Population density (persons per square mile)	7363	623	1977	7842	430	2027
Toronto as percent of Hamburg	—	—	—	106	68	108

THE INNER CITY AREA WITHIN THE BOUNDARIES OF 1912

Probably these impressions have been gained primarily in the inner city, which tends to be better known to both residents and visitors than the extended outer area. In both cities this inner area can be clearly defined as "the city of 1912." In Toronto it is identical with the municipal city of Toronto. In Hamburg it is identical with the wards which existed before the extension of the city boundaries in 1913. These two areas are compared in Table 6.

The two areas are of practically equal size. However, in 1912 the population of Toronto was only 37% of that of Hamburg. In the following 54 years, population decreased by one third in Hamburg, while in Toronto, it increased by three quarters. The density was still nominally lower in Toronto, but by 1970 this difference certainly had disappeared or may even have been reversed, because there was a significant difference in the population dynamics of the two areas. In Toronto the population of the inner city had been stable since 1941; in Hamburg it had decreased year by year.

It appears that the dwelling type does not have the decisive influence on population density which is generally ascribed to it. In 1966, in the "city" of Toronto, 55% of all dwellings were in single-family houses, mostly detached or semidetached, only 38% in apartments, and the remaining 17% in duplexes. Corresponding data are not available for Hamburg in its 1912 boundaries, but probably no less than 90% of all dwellings were in multifamily houses.

THE CENTRAL BUSINESS DISTRICT

No less misleading than the impression of lower residential densities in the inner areas of Toronto is the image of higher employment density in its C.B.D. The C.B.D. has been defined by the planning authorities both in Hamburg and in Toronto. Employment in the C.B.D. was practically the same in both cities: 106,000 in Hamburg (1961) and 107,000 in Toronto (1964). The area is also very nearly the same: 192 acres in Hamburg and 210 in Toronto. Consequently employment density

Table 6. The City within the Boundaries of 1912

	Hamburg	Toronto	Toronto as Percent of Hamburg
Square miles	34	35	103
Population: 1912 (1000)	1,010	377	37
Population: 1966 (1000)	672	665	99
Change: 1912–1966 (1000)	−388	+288	—
Change: 1912–1966 (% of 1912)	−33.3	+76.4	—
Population per square mile: 1912	29,412	10,771	37
Population per square mile: 1966	19,765	19,000	96

was actually slightly lower in Toronto than in Hamburg, 510 per acre versus 552 in Hamburg, despite the fact that the C.B.D. of Toronto is dominated by skyscrapers of 20–50 stories, while the Hamburg C.B.D. contained no building of more than 10 floors in 1961.

However, in the surrounding 600 acres of the city center, which, in Hamburg, is still clearly defined by the line of the fortifications of 1620, there were 121,000 employed; in Toronto in the corresponding (not clearly definable) area, about 90,000.

LAND USE

Thus it turns out that in all comparisons—city region, entire city, inner city, city center, C.B.D.—the densities were almost the same in the German and in the North American metropolis, and that deviations occurred in the direction opposite to expectations: in Toronto higher than in Hamburg for residents and lower for city center employment.

However, in all these comparisons the number of persons has been related to an area defined by a boundary line, not to the area actually used by these persons. In the medieval city urban and nonurban land uses were clearly separated by the city wall. In the modern metropolis they are intermingled.

The figures presented in Tables 7 and 8 can be taken only as rough approximations, because of considerable differences in the definitions used in the original data. For Hamburg two sets of data were available, which present, in part, different figures. The first one is directed primarily to the uses of land not covered by buildings, while only one summary figure is given for "building and yard areas." The second one employs the categories presented in Table 7; however, the categories "Transportation" and "Public open space" have been broken down into subcategories taken from the first set. The more detailed Toronto data have been summarized to correspond to those available for Hamburg.

In Hamburg the category "Water" accounts for almost one tenth of the city area. In Toronto the water areas, which probably total less than 1 square mile, have been included in the categories "Industrial and Commercial" and "Parks and Playgrounds." In order to achieve better comparability with Toronto, all percentages for Hamburg have been related to "total land area" only. It should, however, be noted that in Hamburg actually over 1 square mile of water is used for public recreation and several square miles form part of the working harbor area.

In Toronto the category "Rural uses" includes also some open-air recreation and minor scattered other uses. In Hamburg this category includes a sizable amount of allotment gardens—a substantially "urban" use hardly to be found in Toronto.

In Hamburg only the portions of residential properties covered by buildings or used as front yards are listed as "Residential"; the balance is classified as "gardens," "roads," etc. In Toronto the entire area of all urban residential properties is included in the "Residential" category; in doubtful cases a lot size of 1 acre has been adopted to distinguish "urban" from "rural," with some minor exceptions. Also, in Toronto the category "Residential" includes some minor mixed uses. It is likely that application of the Toronto definitions to Hamburg would increase the size of the residential area by 10–20%.

The category "Vacant and other" includes relatively small areas used for airfields, military exercises, and power lines.

Table 7. Land Use

	Hamburg				Toronto			
	Square Miles	Percent of City	Square Miles	Percent of City	Square Miles	Percent of City	Square Miles	Percent of City
1. Residential	52.8	20.4			71.0	29.5		
2. Industrial and commercial	15.5	6.0			21.4	8.9		
3. Public and SemiPublic	8.7	3.3			8.4	3.5		
1–3. Built-up Parcels			77.0	29.7			100.8	42.2
4. Streets	21.0	8.2			28.5	11.9		
5. Freeways	0.8	0.3			5.1	2.1		
6. Railroads	4.4	1.7			4.0	1.7		
7. Other transportation	4.5	1.7			—	—		
4–7. Transportation			30.7	11.9			37.6	15.6
8. Parks and playgrounds	25.0	9.7			28.3	11.8		
9. Public utilities					9.1	3.8		
10. Cemeteries	3.0	1.2			2.2	0.9		
8–10. Public open space			28.0	10.9			39.6	16.5
1–10. All urban uses			135.7	52.5			178.0	74.3
11. Rural uses	88.0	34.2			7.5	3.1		
12. Vacant and other	34.5	13.3			54.5	22.6		
11–12. Nonurban uses			122.5	47.5			62.0	25.7
1–12. Total land uses			258.2	100.0			240.0	100.0
				90.6				
13. Water			26.8	9.4				
1–13. Total city area			285.0	100.0				

As already noted, the urban land uses in Toronto are "gross"; they also include the corresponding street space, amounting to about 22%. The resulting total of 28.5 square miles has been deducted from subcategories 1, 2, and 3 by assuming that streets amount to 22.8% of gross residential area, and to 21.0% of the gross area of the two other subcategories.

With these qualifications Table 7 may be evaluated.

The most striking difference between the two cities is the fact that over one third (34.2%) of the Hamburg area is classified as "rural," but less than one tenth of that amount (3.1%) in Toronto. On the other hand, the amount of vacant land, while quite sizable in Hamburg (13.3%), is even more extensive in Toronto (22.6%). Together, these two "nonurban" land uses absorb slightly over one quarter (25.7%) of all land in Toronto, and close to half (47.5%) in Hamburg.

As a result, all categories and subcategories of "urban" land uses, with the minor exception of "Railroads" and "Cemeteries," account for considerably higher percentages of the entire city in Toronto than in Hamburg. It is not surprising that a considerably larger amount of land is devoted to streets and freeways in the North American city. It is, however, surprising, and quite contrary to impressions gained by living in both cities, to find a considerably smaller area devoted to "parks and playgrounds" in Hamburg than in Toronto. In fact, the figures are deceptive. On the one hand, a sizable portion of this area in Toronto consists of golf courses, which are accessible only to a limited number of users. On the other hand, in Hamburg, cemeteries, water, and, in particular, most rural areas are accessible for outdoor recreation.

As for the basic element of urban development, the "Built-up parcels," the percentage absorbed by the net areas, both for work and for residence, is about 30% lower in Hamburg than in Toronto. It is, however, worth noting that even in Toronto net residential land use accounts for less than 30% of the city territory. The "gross" residential area (including streets) amounts to 92 square miles, or 38.3%. Thus, even if net residential density were doubled (and the amount of street space available to each resident were halved), the city area would be reduced by less than 20% and its radius by less than 10%. Increasing net residential densities would not substantially reduce urban sprawl and excessive travel distances.

A table similar to Table 7 has also been developed for Hamburg north of the Elbe. This is not presented here; however, Table 8 compares various density measures for Toronto with the corresponding figures, both for all of Hamburg and for H. n. E.

Table 8. Population Density, Hamburg, H. n. E., and Toronto
(persons per square mile)

	Hamburg	H. n. E.	Toronto
Total city area	6,481	7,363	7,842
Total land area	7,170	7,980	7,842
Total urban-used land area	13,600	14,800	10,600
Total built-up area	24,000	25,550	18,700
Total residential area	35,100	36,900	26,600
Population: 1966 (1000)	1,847	1,642	1,882
Persons per net residential acre	54.9	56.1	41.6

Again it is striking that the overall densities of the total land areas for H. n. E. and Toronto—the two semicircular urban units—differ by less than 2%. However, for the following three, more narrowly defined areas, the difference is fairly substantial. Net residential density averaged 56.1 persons in H. n. E. In Toronto it averaged 41.6, slightly over one-quarter (25.9%) less. If the Toronto definitions had been used in Hamburg, this difference probably would be only 15–20%. If the Hamburg definitions had been used in Toronto, the difference might be still smaller. In any case it is far less than would be expected as a result of the radical difference in dwelling types.

DWELLING TYPES

Unfortunately, detailed housing data for Hamburg and its surroundings are not yet available. However, it is known that in 1966 all types of single-family houses accounted for only 22.5% of the total in Hamburg, compared to 64% in Toronto. In Hamburg the older single-family houses usually have two or more floors; apartment houses, typically five floors. Since 1950 walk-up apartments have been limited to three or four floors, and are being increasingly supplemented by elevator apartments, generally in buildings of six to twelve floors. The number of detached one-story, single-family houses is also increasing, probably even within the city limits. No doubt the desire to own a detached single-family house with a sizable garden accounts largely for the "overspill" into the surroundings. However, even in these areas a sizable number of apartments are being built.

In Toronto the share of apartments is rapidly increasing. However, at least between 1941 and 1966, this increase was balanced by a decrease in "other" types, primarily row and semidetached houses and dwellings over stores, while detached single-family houses continued to account for almost half of the total, as shown in Table 9.

In absolute figures, during the quarter century 1941–1966, the number of dwellings increased 2.5 times, while the number of two- and multifamily units more than quadrupled.

The trend is continuing. In Metropolitan Toronto the share of dwellings in apart-

Table 9. Distribution of Dwelling Types, Metropolitan Toronto: 1941, 1961, and 1966

	Single-Family Houses				Two-Family and Multifamily Houses		Total	
	Detached		Others					
	1000	Percent	1000	Percent	1000	Percent	1000	Percent
1941	100		64		44		208	
		48		31		21		100.0
1961	224		81		125		430	
		52		19		29		100.0
1966	241		89		187		517	
		47		17		36		100.0

ment houses with six or more dwellings increased from 22% in 1951 to 32% in 1966. Nor is the trend restricted to the inner area (the legal "City of Toronto"). In 1966 no less than 58% of apartments were located in the outer municipalities of Metropolitan Toronto, and their number is also growing in the surroundings, as shown in Table 10.

The "fringe municipalities" account for 60% of the area and for 64% of the population of the "surroundings." In the remaining surrounding municipalities, which are not included in the planning area, developments are similar.

The net density of apartments in Metropolitan Toronto is very high. In 1966 it averaged 61 dwellings and 141 persons per acre. The floor space index averaged 1.2. On the other hand, there was an average of eight single-family detached houses per net acre.

In part, the apartment boom has been the result of municipal policies. As the municipalities have to rely almost exclusively on the real estate tax, and as they have to carry most of the cost of education, they attempt to limit the building of single-family houses by all available means, in particular by turning down subdivision applications. The resulting artificial scarcity of building lots has raised their price more than threefold during the past decade so that single-family houses are out of reach for a much larger percentage of the population than was the case in the first 15 or 20 postwar years. On the other hand, the municipalities favor apartment buildings, because they generally contain far fewer children. In 1966 their occupancy rate averaged 2.4 persons per dwelling as compared to 4.3 in single-family houses.

Unquestionably the desire to own a single-family house is one of the main reasons for the migration to the surroundings, because there land prices tend to be lower than in the city. If people are compelled to live in apartments, as has been the case in the Toronto area in recent years, they may as well stay within the city.

Probably the measures recently initiated by the province of Ontario will increase the share of single-family houses in residential construction. However, their share of

Table 10. Dwellings Started, Metropolitan Toronto Planning Area: 1962–1967

	Single-Family Houses				Houses with Two or More Dwellings		Total	
	Detached		Others					
	1000	Per-cent	1000	Per-cent	1000	Per-cent	1000	Per-cent
Metropolitan Toronto	28		17		82		127	
		22		13		65		100.0
Fringe municipalities	13		5		7		25	
		52		20		28		100.0
Total planning area	41		22		89		152	
		27		14		59		100.0
Fringe municipalities as percent of Planning Area	31		23		8		16	

the total supply is bound to decrease. The growing share of apartments and their high density supply a partial, but certainly not a complete, explanation for the fact that residential density averages only slightly lower in Toronto than it does in Hamburg.

In Hamburg, development is going in the opposite direction, towards a broader availability of single-family houses. But while in Toronto 20- to 30-floor apartment houses contrast sharply with one-story or split-level detached homes, in Hamburg there is much less of a contrast between the predominantly three- or four-story new apartments and the predominantly two-story, single-family row houses. Thus the two different mixtures produce a not greatly divergent average density. A certain convergence in the relative share of housing types, as well as in average density, can be observed. In this context it may be worthwhile to mention that Canadian studies point to a convergence toward an overall density of 6500 persons per square mile of land used for urban purposes in the major metropolitan areas of the country, while German city planners assume that 1 square kilometer is needed for every 2500 of urban population. The two figures are identical (1 square mile equals 2.62 square kilometers).

URBAN TRANSPORTATION

As has been noted, differences in the extent of the urban area and of its population density are considered to be correlated with differences in the means of transportation. For Hamburg and Toronto these data are presented in Table 11.

Table 11. Public and Private Urban Transportation: 1966

	Hamburg	Toronto	Toronto as Percent of Hamburg
Assumed: Trips per person			
1. Daily average	1.77	1.82	103
2. Annual average	6.47	6.64	103
Total annual trips, (millions)			
3. Total	1,198	1,298	104
4. By public transportation	647	308	48
5. By private car	551	940	277
6. Public as percent of total	54	25	46
Annual trips per person			
7. By public transportation	349	162	47
8. By private transportation	298	504	169
Number of private cars (1000)			
9. In 1955	79	333	423
10. In 1966	350	618	177
11. Increase: 1955–1966	342	85	25
Private cars per 1000 population			
12. In 1955	43	255	595
13. In 1966	189	329	173
14. Percent increase: 1955–1966	337	29	9

This table is the product of a considerable amount of manipulation. The only data available for both cities were the numbers of registered cars and of annual passenger fares, in addition to the population figures. Both of these actually overstate the relevant facts. Not all cars registered during a given year are simultaneously in the possession of area residents. Frequently passengers have to pay several fares during one trip.

In addition, in Toronto, data were available on the number of trips made by private cars and on the number of person-trips performed in private cars. However, these referred to workday trips in April 1964 and had to be modified to arrive at annual and daily (including nonwork days) averages for 1966. For Hamburg a slightly (2.4%) higher number of annual trips per car was assumed because of the lower share of second cars. The number of total annual trips per person made by mechanical means was assumed to be slightly (3.0%) lower in Hamburg, because of the greater share of trips made on foot or by bicycle, a difference partly offset by the lower percentage of children. Probably *all* figures in Table 11 are on the high side. However, this does not affect the relations between Toronto and Hamburg, presented in the last column, which are the gist of the present inquiry.

In 1966 the difference between the two cities still was very substantial. In Toronto public transportation accounted for only one quarter of all trips; in Hamburg, for well over half (54%). However, the extremely rapid, more than fourfold increase in the number of cars and car trips from 1955 to 1966 indicates again a strong trend towards convergence. In fact, during these 11 years the number of person-trips by car per 1000 population grew at a rate more than 10 times higher in Hamburg than in Toronto.

However, unlike what has been observed in the distribution of dwelling types, here convergence occurs in only one direction. In Toronto the share of public transportation tends to decrease slowly.

ATTEMPTS AT EXPLANATION

The comparison of Hamburg, the biggest city in the Federal German Republic, with Toronto, a fairly typical North American metropolis, shows that their basic structures are more similar than appearances would lead one to believe, and that the similarity is increasing. In particular, overall population density and C.B.D. employment density are surprisingly similar.

Another surprising similarity is the fact that C.B.D. employment in both cities is stabilizing, again contrary to appearances and widespread belief. In Toronto this stability has been observed since the early 1950s. In Hamburg the number of persons employed in the city center (defined in somewhat broader terms than the C.B.D.) was 191,000 in 1939 and 195,000 in 1961.

Two significant differences still exist. First, decentralization of employment, both in manufacturing and in services, is considerably greater in Toronto than in Hamburg. Second, Hamburg still contains large areas in agricultural use. In part, this is a result of topography. A large part of the Hamburg territory consists of extremely fertile alluvial lands, situated below high water level, against which they are protected by dykes. The most important part of these, the *Vierlande* ("Four Lands"), settled by Dutch immigrants three centuries ago, supplies Hamburg with vegetables and flowers. The high water table of these areas is a serious, but by no means an absolute obstacle to urban development. In fact, ever since the twelfth century, Hamburg has transformed such areas into urban land, first by dyking and later by filling.

Moreover, a sizable portion of agricultural and practically all vacant areas are on higher, dry land. The overspill of the Hamburg population cannot be explained by a shortage of building land. In fact, the number of new dwelling units built annually is not much lower in Hamburg than in Toronto—in 1966 it was even nominally higher—despite the fact that Toronto's population increases by 30,000–40,000 persons annually, while Hamburg's is decreasing. It is quite erroneous to assume that housing demand rises only because of increasing population. Replacement of disused dwellings and, in particular, decreasing size of household are equally significant. Certainly, lack of building activity cannot be the reason for the larger overspill observed in Hamburg.

All reasons would lead one to expect a lesser overspill than in Toronto. The total population of the urban region is growing at a much slower rate. Workplaces are more concentrated. Detached single-family houses are far less frequent, and residential density is somewhat higher. Motorization started only 15 years ago and is still considerably less advanced. Rapid rail lines serve the surroundings only to a relatively minor extent.

Then why is the spillover so much stronger in Hamburg than it is in Toronto? We have to admit that we do not know the reasons. It looks as if the distribution of urban population is governed by unknown laws, independent of choice of housing type and of transportation system. In our large metropolitan areas there are forces at work which we understand only very incompletely, if at all. Of course these are not some kind of mystical "cosmic" forces. They are the result of the actions of our fellow citizens, which are determined by their desires and aspirations.

We, as planners, are all too easily inclined to derive norms from our personal aspirations. This is entirely unjustified and can only lead to failure. Only if our "guiding image" reflects an understanding of the real world, can it be an effective guide to development.

Chapter 15

PLANNING IN A HUMAN WAY

The slender pamphlet under review is an extremely valuable contribution to planning literature. Harry Lash presents his rich experiences as director of planning for the Greater Vancouver Regional District (G.V.R.D.) from 1969 to 1975, in particular the role of citizens' participation, and submits them to profound and searching analysis. He feels that "the more general value of the Vancouver experience lies in what we discovered about the planning process, and in a new understanding that human relations among the actors in the process can make the process succeed or fail."

The first chapter is entitled "Introduction to the Six-Sided Triangle." The three corners of the triangle are politician, planner, and public. The "six" is the sum of the two-way flows of information between these three.

It is worthwhile to compare this model with the officially accepted one, which can be visualized as a vertical straight line with the people at the top, the politicians in the middle, and the planners (and other "technocrats") at the bottom. In the straight-line model there is also two-way flow of information between all three partners. Evidently the planner must get as much information as possible both to and from the public. But the *decision-determining* flows occur only between the politician and his partners above and below.

Any attempt of the planners to extend their interaction with the public beyond information into the sphere of decision inevitably will be strongly resented by the politicians. This was the case in Greater Vancouver, and Harry Lash describes the resultant conflicts in considerable detail. He fully and fairly appreciates the justification of the politicians' resentment and the resultant need for the planners' reticence. Curiously, however, he did not practice and does not advocate this reticence for the planners' relation with the public, but only for their relation with the ultimate political decision-maker, the governing board. He says, "We did it . . . by letting the politician lead and keeping ourselves in the background. . . . At the Board, the Committee Chairman and members . . . carried the debate. The staff always hoped that we would not be called upon to say anything."

It is, of course, no secret that the primary and most important flow of the straight-line model, from the people to the politicians, does not function well. As a Marxist I am acutely conscious of this crucial shortcoming of "bourgeois democracy." But it is

---

Review of Harry Lash, *Planning in a Human Way* (Macmillan, 1976). *Source:* From *Contact* (University of Waterloo).

untrue to say that the people can influence decisions only by marking an X on a ballot every 4 or 5 years. In fact, politicians are extremely sensitive to the opinions of their constituents, and there are many ways to communicate these views to them. Nevertheless it remains true that many people feel powerless to modify in any way the decisions which vitally affect their own lives. They express their will to power as a strong demand for "citizens' participation."

I completely agree with Harry Lash's stance "that effective citizens' participation was itself an objective." At the very least it raises the participants' self-esteem. Beyond that it may widen their contacts with other citizens and broaden their views of public affairs. At its highest level it can mean participation in all phases of the work of the planner or politician: assemble and analyze data, predict probable developments beyond the community's control, identify and foresee problems, develop alternatives for their solution, evaluate these and decide which one is likely to produce the most favorable ratio of desirable to undesirable results. Such participation, of course, requires more time and effort than most people are able and willing to devote.

The Vancouver planning staff included in its efforts at citizens' participation also this intense form. It established nine "citizens' policy committees," each to deal with a specific policy field, by asking, through the newspapers, *anyone* to participate. "About four hundred people turned up . . . , but this unmanageably large number melted away to something under two hundred." This is an arresting statement; it says that citizens' participation can work only if, when, and because 4999 out of 5000 citizens do *not* participate. Harry Lash explained in a private conversation that he merely intended to say that his staff could not have managed a larger number. But this explanation raises two other questions. First, should staffs spend more time and effort on citizens' participation than on all other work? And, second, what is the difference between intensely and continuously managed cooperation and cooptation, which Harry, like most advocates of citizens' participation, strongly rejects? In fact, cooptation of qualified citizens into planning and administrative work can be very useful; it is a universal practice in Socialist countries and far from unknown in the West.

The main effort of the Vancouver group was more ambitious: "to go to the public and simply raise the question of livability." The response were demands "to help the group with their current problems; never mind whether [these problems] had anything to do with livability or G.V.R.D.'s responsibilities." The group found that the public "did not much care about a plan." This should not have come as a surprise. People live in the here and now. A plan tries to provide for other people who live at other places at other times.

A government's responsibility is, of course, not limited to planning for the future; its main activities are ongoing services, which *do* affect the lives of people here and now. Citizens want, and are competent, to make decisions concerning this "software" of government, because they experience and can judge the results of their decisions on the here and now. Once the G.V.R.D. planners had invited people to talk about anything affecting their lives, they could not well dodge the issue by "referring" demands and complaints to the officially responsible agency. They tried to deal with the responses received, inevitably treading on the toes of politicians and other bureaucrats. This attention to complaints is a most necessary function, and many efforts have been made to carry it out. At present the preferred one is the appointment of an ombudsman. None had been appointed in the Vancouver area, and so the vacuum was filled by the planning staff. It went all out, even going beyond the normal role of an ombudsman by lending technical support to organizations opposing the government. This was not the function for which the G.V.R.D. Board had hired planners. "The Board wanted a physical development plan, whose primary use would be to guide municipal development decisions." The ensuing conflict ended after 6 months with the resignation of some senior members of the staff. Harry Lash himself decided to stay, but still feels that the staff had fought for the "public interest" and that "Vancouver needs not a . . . plan, but a set of complementary strategies."

"Planning" is a big word. It encompasses corporate planning, military planning, and so on. People plan election campaigns, sales campaigns, burglaries, and any number of activities. Municipal or regional governments have to plan their many ongoing activities, as noted earlier. This planning is primarily the responsibility of the operating agencies—dealing with education, health, recreation, "welfare," safety, traffic, water supply, and so forth—which have the required specialized knowledge and experience. All these activities interact with each other, as well as with those of official bodies. Somebody has to "plan the planners," to coordinate the "sectoral" plans, including the allocation of slices of the financial pie. This is, of course, the responsibility of the elected government, the "politicians," in particular, the Chief Executive. But it has grown far too big for him or her to handle. Various devices have been developed to assist the politicians in this task. Many American cities have appointed a "city manager." Soviet cities have a department for this activity planning, called *planirovanya*. It is separate and distinct from the department charged with the planning of the physical environment, which is called *planirovka*. The latter is, of course, the traditional field of the professional planner in the West.

In the G.V.R.D. there was (and is) neither a city manager nor an agency for *planirovanya*. By default, therefore, the role fell to Harry Lash and his staff. Impressed by the urgent needs and demands of the citizens, they wanted to give priority, in allocating their time and effort, to attending to this task. As already noted, their political masters disagreed. The latter wanted their plan and instructed the cobblers to stick to their last.

Harry Lash, like any other planner who is "with it," adopts the ritual formula "process, not product" and rejects a detailed, long-term comprehensive plan as a "static end-state" concept. It is certainly true that many other planners, particularly those coming from architecture, have conceived their plans in that way: you design it, it is built over a number of years (usually unspecified), and then the people live happily ever after in your perfect city.

But there is another approach to the function of a comprehensive plan. It views it as a cross section through the unending stream of the historical development of the city at a specific future point in time and/or at a specific future population size. If feasible, one would develop a series of such cross sections, starting with the most distant "broad-brush" one and becoming increasingly specific as one approached the present, each stage being both "livable" in itself and helping rather than hindering development towards the next stage. In fact, the very first time I was charged with developing such a plan (in 1931–1932 for the Russian city of Vladimir) I presented two such cross sections for consecutive stages of growth.

Under this approach one does not expect the city ever to be perfect. Feasibility—

cooperation with the inevitable—is as weighty a criterion as is desirability. Such a plan does present in considerable detail, in the form of text, tables, maps, sketches, or three-dimensional models, a *guiding image* in which all elements are in balance and mutually supportive. It is not expected that this detailed image will ever become reality; it is anticipated that many unforeseen events will occur. If, as is likely, they would upset the balance, either other elements of the plan or, if possible, the new events will be modified. At any given stage the plan provides a framework for the process of evaluating the wide-range and long-term effects of the many proposals which are brought forward day after day. This only the planner can do; the local and immediate effects are generally quite fully presented by proponents and opponents.

If there is no such guiding image, what framework can be used to evaluate proposals? The answer given by the "process, not product" school is, of course, to formulate goals and objectives. Harry Lash, after having, like myself, participated in extended exercises for defining goals, has arrived at the same conclusion: the output derived from the substantial input of time and gray matter consists of no more than "motherhood" goals. This slightly obsolete term means that even in our dissent-ridden society there is universal consent on a number of points. It stands to reason that these points will be present in the mind of anyone making a decision, whether they have been spelled out or not.

The G.V.R.D. staff did, however, make a major effort to develop more specific objectives. It greatly improved on usual practice by realizing that ends cannot be separated from means, because these invariably will affect other objectives, often negatively. The result was a matrix of 60 objectives and 80 means, a total of over 4000 cells, each of which was supposed to be filled by three independent opinions with 1 out of 11 possible scores. The staff wisely decided to keep this megamatrix in its own corner of the triangle.

I doubt that this matrix will ever be of much use to the G.V.R.D. planners. The relation of ends to means is case-specific. Whenever any project (by definition a "means") is proposed, they will have to trace all of its possible impacts, distant as well as immediate, indirect as well as direct, and evaluate their degrees of desirability. The ability to do this better than others is the professional skill of the planner, which he or she has presumably acquired by study and experience. Consultation of a prefabricated matrix is no substitute. The currently fashionable approach refuses to articulate a guiding image, which, in my opinion, can and should be developed. Instead it tries to articulate goals and objectives which are unable to serve as adequate guides for deciding specific cases.

It is interesting to note that Harry Lash finally came to the conclusion that he had to articulate "targets." These are defined as future distribution of population and jobs; size, location, and timing of regional town centers; key transit links and facilities; open space and parks—and, for all of these, the required funding. This sounds very much like a table of contents for a typical "static end-state" plan.

As far as I can gather, the targets were developed without direct public participation. The same appears to be true of another aspect of current conventional wisdom, the notion that planners should submit "alternatives" for choice by politicians and public. The G.V.R.D. planners developed what they call a "trend plan." A trend is of course *not* a plan. What they presented was not an alternative but an image of the evils which would occur without a plan. This was just as well. From my own experience I know that politicians resent nothing as much as being asked to choose between two alternative plans. "We pay these experts to tell us what is best. If they don't know, how are we to know?" So they put it. And they are right.

In his detailed and thoughtful description of his experience with citizens' participation, Harry Lash emphasizes that citizens will be willing to accept and support a plan only if they have been involved in its development from the beginning. This is certainly true, and important. But what it really means is that involvement from start to finish is an effective strategy for cooptation, and "cooptation" is a dirty word in the vocabulary of the true believer. I do not know whether Harry Lash shares responsibility for the "Preliminary Report of the British Columbia Provincial Task Force on Citizen Participation, Man and Resources Project," dated April 1973. Point 6 of that report states, "No one knows better than the people themselves where they want to go in the future," and Point 7, "It is the citizens who must live with the solution." This is demonstrably false. The people who will have to live with the consequences of comprehensive long-term plans or of "targets" are not yet there, most of them still unborn. As President Kennedy once said, "Our children and grandchildren have no vote." The politician who depends on votes cannot afford to speak for those who are not yet there. In previous times the Church or the dynasty might do it. In our society only the "technocrat," safely enshrined in his civil service ivory tower, or the "consultant," less safely enshrined in his "professional reputation," can afford to do it.

Public participation does not necessarily produce good government. Its justifications is self-government. The rationale of majority rule is not that the majority is right, but that it is strong. For the minority the only alternative to accepting majority decisions is recourse to civil war. In war, as Frederic II of Prussia said, "God Almighty is usually with the stronger battalions."

But while it is the duty of the minority to submit to the will of the majority, it does not have to submit silently. It is not only its right, but also its duty to speak up, even if it is only a minority of one. This situation was classically dramatized a hundred years ago by Henrik Ibsen in his play "An Enemy of the People." It is an archetypical situation which will repeat again and again as long as human beings are human—and it is the planner's highest calling to play that role.

Out of the confusing chorus of often strident voices of the public in the Vancouver area one dominant leitmotif resounded loud and strong: "Stop growth." Harry Lash quite correctly ascribes this rejection of the "growth ethic" to a shift from concern with acquiring money to concern with the enjoyment of life. The planners realized of course that the G.V.R.D. government had no power to control growth, and they did a yeoman's job in persuading reluctant municipalities to accept their share of it. But they accepted the notion that growth is a result of the "growth ethic" and can be reversed at will by accepting a "zero-growth ethic."

This seems to me to be a misunderstanding of the "human way." Human beings are driven to produce offspring by motivations much older and stronger than the growth ethic. Nor do they migrate because of it; they do so because they consider the selected place of migration to be more attractive than the one from which they came.

I consider the attainment of zero growth on this small planet to be a moral imperative. But to achieve zero growth in Canada by keeping the overspill of overpopulated regions out of this, the world's most underpopulated country, is the opposite. It is the "lifeboat ethic": "I am on board; pull up the ladder." So proclaimed and practiced Adolf Hitler.

Of course the good people of Vancouver do not want the "foreigners" to starve to death. They just want to keep them off their streets and parking lots, their parks and beaches. Realizing that they did not have the power to do this, they petitioned the Great White Father in Ottawa to restrict foreign immigration. But this still left the threat of trespass by other Canadians. They considered, in the words of Harry Lash, "strictly controlled movements of the population within Canada, policies presently in force in many nations." I do not know of any such nation. They settled for a more humane way: to "see if other urban centers could be made more attractive, to stimulate their growth and reduce Vancouver's". They did not say just how Vancouver could be made less attractive than other centers. Might the methods consist of having higher unemployment, lower earnings, or less livability than these other centers?

Harry Lash tries to justify the acceptance of zero growth as a goal by referring to the deterioration of life in New York. Certainly in the 1920s New York was smaller than it is now, but it was much larger than Detroit or Buffalo is now—and these cities have deteriorated even more than New York. Also, in the 1920s New York was growing fast, while now it is losing population. If coincidence of two phenomena in time is to be accepted as proof of a causal connection, a much stronger case can be made for arrested growth than for size as the cause of urban deterioration. I do not accept this kind of reasoning. Neither size nor rate of growth is decisive for urban health. What is required is a social system that sustains hope.

Chapter 16

MEGALOPOLIS: FACT OR FICTION?

Ever since Jean Gottmann gave the title *Megalopolis* to his monumental study of the Boston-to-Washington area,[1] the term has gained currency. Frequently it is used merely in its literal sense of "big city," for example, "the Chicago megalopolis." It is, of course, a fact that now, as always, some cities are bigger than others. This substitution of Greek for English tends to convey a negative value judgment. And this judgment has been given a precise meaning in the organic model of Patrick Geddes and Lewis Mumford. Here "megalopolis" appears as pathological overgrowth of the mature "metropolis" and leads inexorably to the terminal stage: the "necropolis," the dead city. Such models hardly fit historical experience.

For Gottmann and those following in his footsteps, the term does not carry these sinister implications. "Megalopolis" is defined simply as "a larger concept which describes aggregates of metropolitan areas."[2] The term "aggregate" implies, as a minimum, propinquity; the relevant metropolitan areas must form a group, cluster, or constellation spatially separate from other such areas.

Cities have always tended to cluster in situations favorable to urban development. The most outstanding of these are river valleys; others are lines at the foot of mountain chains, such as the Via Emilia along the northeastern slopes of the Apennines, with its string of cities from Piacenza to Ancona. Another is the "fall line" along the southeastern slopes of the Appalachians, which is the subject of Gottmann's study. Indeed, Gottmann recognizes that for three centuries it has been the "main street of the nation."[3] But he believes that this aggregate has now become integrated to a degree which makes it a new form of human settlement—beyond the metropolitan area and metropolitan region—justifying and requiring the distinctive title "Megalopolis." Since then more megalopolises have been discovered and have been honored with such names as Boswash, Chipitts, and Sansan.

A systematic attempt at defining the concept has been made by C. Doxiadis and

---

[1] Jean Gottmann, *Megalopolis: The Urbanized Northeastern Seaboard of the United States*, M.I.T. Press, Cambridge, Mass., 1961.
[2] Jerome Pickard, *Population in Appalachia and the United States: Year 2000*, Washington, D.C., July-August 1972, p. 11.
[3] J. Gottmann, *op. cit.*, paperback edition, 1964, p. 8.

Source: Lambda Alpha (International Fraternity) Yearbook and Roster, 1976.

F. G. Papaioannou of the Athens Center of Ekistics.[4] The center has developed an "Ekistic Logarithmic Scale" in 15 steps from "man" and "room" to "urbanized continent" and "ecumenopolis." Steps 9–13 are called, respectively, "large city," "metropolis," "conurbation," "megalopolis," and "urban region." This terminology calls for some comments. The term "conurbation" was used by Patrick Geddes to describe clusters of cities which had grown together. Such clusters developed in the nineteenth century primarily on coalfields; their constituent units were usually too small to be called metropolises. When they, singly or jointly, reach metropolitan size, the product is best defined as a polynuclear metropolis. The term "metropolis" is here accepted as a shortcut for "metropolitan area" as it has been defined by the census in the United States and Canada. Essentially it means a city (or several cities) together with its surrounding "commuter watershed." There is a wealth of evidence to prove that the metropolis is indeed a form of human settlement qualitatively different from its predecessor, the compact big city. It is equally evident that a "metropolitan area" normally is surrounded by a much larger "metropolitan region." In Germany, Olaf Boustedt has defined this unit as a *Stadtregion* (city-region) and divided it into a "core" zone (corresponding to our metropolitan area) and an outer "fringe" zone.

Gottmann defines his megalopolis as a "unique cluster of metropolitan areas."[5] However, since it includes much more than the census standard metropolitan area (S.M.A.)s, "cluster of metropolitan regions" would be more appropriate. In fact, a large (and the most original) part of Gottmann's study is devoted to the characteristics of the "fringe" areas.

On the Doxiadis-Papaioannou Ekistic Logarithmic Scale there is not much room for metropolitan areas or regions, because "large clusters with a population of over 5 millions . . . will be called Conurbations."[6] This would make the Chicago S.M.A., for example, a conurbation rather than a metropolis. The boundary between "conurbation" and "megalopolis" is equally questionable. According to the scale, a megalopolis should have a population of about 100 million (with a range from 35 to 250 million). However, Papaioannou prefers to accept a lower limit of 10 million and, in addition, a "pre-megalopolis" down to 3 million.[7] He then defines a megalopolis as two or preferably three or more large centers, forming a chain and strongly interacting with each other.[8] The interaction is not actually measured, but is assumed to exist when centers fulfill certain conditions as to size, distance, and transportation links. On this basis a long and interesting list is presented of groups of centers which, at a given future date, are expected to qualify. In 1960 only two were found to be fully qualified: Gottmann's classical case and the Tokyo-Osaka corridor.

Papaioannou modestly recognizes that his study is only a "first approximation towards . . . a deeper approach [which] would involve an understanding of the functional and behavioral aspects . . . those features that go clearly beyond the metropolitan level."[9] That is indeed the crux of the matter. The question raised in the title of this essay can be reformulated: does the megalopolis have any features which

---

[4]F. G. Papaioannou, *Megalopolises, a First Definition,* Athens Center of Ekistics, Athens, Greece, 1968.
[5]J. Gottmann, *op. cit.,* p. 5.
[6]F. G. Papaioannou, *op. cit.,* p. 13.
[7]*Ibid.,* p. 31.
[8]*Ibid.,* p. 23.
[9]*Ibid.,* p. IV.

are not characteristic either of metropolitan regions, which are its constituent parts, or of the national or supernational urban system of which it is a constituent part? Is the megalopolis an integrated unit *of a new type?*

THE ROLE OF INTERACTION

Integration of previously independent units into a new structure can be brought about only by increased interaction between these units. The development of new features is likely to be both the effect and the cause of such interaction. What does the experience of the classic U.S. megalopolis tell us about interaction?

Interaction is realized by the movement of goods, persons, and messages; it can be quantified by measuring their volumes. Gottmann presents an impressive array of data on both the absolute size and the rate of increase of these volumes. Certainly the interchanges per head of population between Boston and Philadelphia, for example, have increased at an impressive rate since the days of Benjamin Franklin. But those between Boston and Tokyo have increased at an even higher rate. In order to prove integration into a "megalopolis," it is not sufficient to show that volumes of interchanges between the cities within it are high; it must also be shown that they are higher than those between cities within and those outside of the megalopolis, other things being equal. These other things are size, in terms of resident population, and distance, in terms of straight-line miles.

Complete data on the interchange of goods are difficult to assemble. Moreover, there exists no satisfactory unit of measurement; neither tons nor dollars are adequate.

Some data on the interchange of persons have been assembled by "origin and destination" (O. & D.) traffic studies. They show surprisingly low volumes; trips between metropolitan areas in Megalopolis accounted for only a fraction of 1% of all trips within a metropolitan area. Gottmann brushes this aside, saying, "The number of commuters who go daily from one of its metropolitan areas to another may seem too small, to persons who rely only on official statistical data for their judgments, to support the concept of an integrated super-metropolitan growth over all this section of the country." [10] It is rather curious to find this remark in a book which relies very heavily on statistical data, and rightly so.

In contrast to the dearth of good data on the interchange of goods and persons, complete and accurate data are available on the most important form of interchange of messages, long-distance telephone calls. Gottmann deals with them extensively.[11] In particular, he presents results, including 11 maps, from a study by Neil C. Gustafson, which investigated long-distance calls between the 5 big centers of the eastern seaboard (Boston, New York, Philadelphia, Baltimore, Washington) and 56 other centers on a weekday in 1958.[12] Gottmann, referring to this study, says, "Whether one considers the total number of calls or their number per capita, the flow between the great Megalopolitan cities is much more intense than the flow between them and other cities in the United States." [13] The large black circles, which repre-

[10] J. Gottmann, *op. cit.,* p. 213.
[11] *Ibid.,* pp. 582–597.
[12] Neil C. Gustafson, "Metropolitan Linkages of the Eastern Seaboard," Department of Geography, University of Minnesota, 1959.
[13] J. Gottmann, *op. cit.,* p. 588.

sent the number of calls on the maps, are indeed impressive. But closer inspection of the maps raises doubts whether these volumes are bigger than those showing interchanges with centers outside Megalopolis, other things being equal. Unfortunately, Gustafson's excellent study has never been published. However, thanks to the generous help of Mr. Gustafson (now associate director of the Upper Midwest Council, Minneapolis) and of Ms. Arlette R. Lindbergh of the Department of Geography, University of Minnesota, this writer was able to obtain a copy. The following section analyzes the data presented in Gustafson's paper.

ANALYSIS OF LONG-DISTANCE TELEPHONE CALLS

The method used in this section attempts to establish the volume of interchanges to be expected between each of the five big centers of Megalopolis and other centers of a given size and distance, by analyzing the exchanges between the five and the centers outside Megalopolis. These expected or "normal" values are then compared with the actual volumes of interchanges between the five and between them and other centers within Megalopolis. It is reasoned that the actual values must be higher than the normal ones, *if* common location in Megalopolis results in a higher level of integration.

Five of the 56 centers in Gustafson's sample were omitted: Toronto and Montreal because of the intervening boundary; Miami and Atlantic City because their abnormally high values are obviously due to their unique roles; and Pittsfield because its population was less than 100,000. Of the remaining 51 centers, 17 are within Megalopolis; all of these had populations of less than 1 million, and all but two (Providence and Hartford) of less than 0.5 million. Of the 34 centers outside Megalopolis, 16 had populations over, and 18 under, 1 million.

Evidently the volume of interchanges tends to increase with population and to decrease with distance. It was found that the impact of size could be adequately normalized for each of two size groups, those over and those under 1 million. It was also found, somewhat surprisingly, that a straight inverse correlation with distance provided a good fit. The resulting formula reads:

$$\Sigma \text{ (telephone calls)} = K - \frac{\text{population}}{\text{miles}}$$

The K factors were found by trial and error methods, seeking the value which resulted in equal numbers of centers with numbers of telephone calls higher and lower than K. Minor corrections were made for differences in the size of the positive and negative deviations.

For each of the five big centers two K factors were found, for cities of over and under 1 million population, respectively. Table 1 presents these factors in the form in which they were used; it also relates them to the populations of the five centers, and finally compares the per capita volumes of the five centers by relating them to the lowest of the five, Boston, as 100.

Not surprisingly, interchanges with larger centers were in all cases more frequent than those with smaller ones. More surprisingly, each person in Washington made more than 2.5 times, and each person in New York made almost 3 times, as many long-distance calls as did a person in Philadelphia. In comparison with Boston, calls

Table 1. *K* Factors for Five Centers in Megalopolis, in Absolute Numbers, per 1 Million Population of These Centers, and Related to *K* Value for Boston

	K for Interchange with Centers of Population ...		K per 1 Million Population for Five Centers Interchanging with Other Centers ...		Columns 2 and 3 as Percent of Boston with Centers ...	
	1	2	3	4	5	6
Megalopolitan Center	Under 1 Million	Over 1 Million	Under 1 Million	Over 1 Million	Under 1 Million	Over 1 Million
Philadelphia	14	17	322	390	69	78
Baltimore	6	7	380	444	82	89
Boston	14	15	404	501	100	100
Washington	16	199	837	1000	180	200
New York	135	165	940	1155	202	231

to centers of over 1 million population outside Megalopolis were twice as numerous in Washington and 2.31 times as numerous in New York.

As noted, the *K* factors were derived by analyzing the interchanges between the 5 big centers of Megalopolis with 34 centers outside. Of the 170 pairs, none was less than 100 miles distant. At shorter distances the straight inverse ratio of number of calls to distance no longer holds, as calls become increasingly local. Therefore, in the analysis of the interchanges of the big 5 with the 17 smaller centers within Megalopolis, all pairs with distances under 75 miles have been omitted; reference to the number of such omissions will be made at the appropriate places in the text. For the presentation of the interchanges between the big five, all interchanges are included, but the 35 miles between Baltimore and Washington make the interchanges between these two cities largely local and therefore abnormally high.

The figures presented in column 6 of Table 1 thus indicate the deviation from the assumed "normal" of 100 for all interchanges between U.S. centers of over 1 million population found to be characteristic of their interchanges with each of the five big centers in Megalopolis. Thus these figures are considered "normal modified *K* factors" for interchanges between any of the five (e.g., 78 for Philadelphia, 200 for Washington) and any other center over 1 million. (Corresponding figures for interchanges between the big five and smaller centers are given in column 5 of Table 1.) On this basis expected "normal" interchanges between each of the five centers with each of the other four have been calculated. Table 2 presents the observed interchanges compared to the "normal" ones.

The results are difficult to interpret. Only Boston interchanges with the other four centers at a level close to, though slightly above, "normal." Interchange between Philadelphia and Baltimore is far higher than "normal," not too surprising because the distance between them only slightly exceeds 75 miles. Interchanges of Washington with Philadelphia and Boston are modestly below and above "normal," respectively. All interchanges of New York are below "normal," conspicuously so with Philadelphia (46 instead of 78, and 136 instead of 231). This is an inverse expression of New York's role as a national center. As mentioned earlier, distance decay was

Table 2. Actual as Compared to "Normal" Interchanges of Telephone Calls between the Five Big Centers of Megalopolis: 1958

Major Center	Major Center				
	Boston	New York	Philadelphia	Baltimore	Washington
"Normal"	100	231	78	89	200
Boston	—	221	92	109	258
New York	113	—	46	66	128
Philadelphia	117	136	—	182	196
Baltimore	122	185	162	—	520
Washington	130	158	74	246	—

found generally to be proportional to miles; in the case of New York it is proportional to distance raised to a power of less than 1. It was, however, not possible to use different powers for distance decay for each of the five centers, because varying both this factor and the K factor does not yield a unique solution.

The result does not support the thesis of increased interchange because of location within a common megalopolis. However, it can hardly be considered conclusive, primarily because of the smallness of the universe. There are only 10 interchanges, of which one, Baltimore-Washington, has to be discarded as unrepresentative.

More promising is the investigation of the 85 potential interchanges between the 5 big and the 17 smaller centers within Megalopolis. Because of distances of less than 75 miles, a total of 14 interchanges were eliminated—3 each for New York and Philadelphia, and 4 each for Baltimore and Boston—leaving 71 interchanges. The results are presented in Table 3.

Again the results are inconclusive, primarily because of the extreme range, 34–726: almost 1 to 20. The greater weight of the higher figures gives a strong upward bias to the average; the median is more representative.

Closer investigation reveals three factors which, separately or jointly, account for most of the abnormally high figures. State capitals have higher than average interchanges, for obvious reasons. For less obvious reasons, Bridgeport and New Haven

Table 3. Interchanges between Major and Minor Centers in Megalopolis: 1958 (actual as % of "normal": average, range, and median)

Major Center	Number of Minor Centers	Interchanges (actual as % of "normal")		
		Average	Range	Median
Boston	13	235	40–598	77
New York	14	80	34–157	72
Philadelphia	14	269	88–615	200
Baltimore	13	149	73–255	139
Washington	17	302	48–726	281

show very high interchanges, possibly because they function as parts of the New York metropolis. But these two factors do not distort the picture, because the 18 centers outside Megalopolis from which the K factors were derived contain an equal number of state capitals and also two other cities, Norfolk and Richmond, which, for unknown reasons, show extremely high interchanges.

The third factor, short distances, however, has no equivalent among the outside centers. As noted earlier, interchanges with distances under 75 miles have been omitted. However, it has generally been found that a "metropolitan region" has a radius of about 2 hours' driving time, or 120 miles. Only one of the 90 pairs in the control sample is within this orbit of any of the five big centers (Richmond-Washington: 100 miles). On the other hand, of the 71 pairs presented in Table 3, no less than 25 had such short distances. Table 4 omits these.

The median is in two cases substantially below, in two substantially above, and in one slightly above, "normal," that is, characteristic of interchanges between centers which are not in the same megalopolis. This indicates at most a marginally higher level of intramegalopolitan interchange.

A more detailed analysis raises further doubts. Gustafson had already noted that six New England centers are "dominated by Boston"[14] and that New York acts as "a barrier of interchange between the areas north of New York City and those south of it."[15] Whatever the role of the intervening opportunities of New York may be, it is evident that the metropolises of Megalopolis are strongly oriented to their own regions and also, to a surprising degree, to their own states, as shown in Tables 5 and 6.

The results shown in Table 5 are striking. Although distances from the Pennsylvania centers to Baltimore and Washington are the same as, and to New York only slightly greater than, to Philadelphia, interchanges with Philadelphia are relatively about 3–6 times as many. This is admittedly in large part a result of the much lower K factor found for Philadelphia. In absolute terms the number of interchanges per head of the six Pennsylvania cities, which were over 75 miles distant from all major centers, with Washington, New York, and Baltimore is only 23%, 33%, and 38%, respectively, lower than the corresponding number for Philadelphia.

Table 4. Interchanges between Five Major Centers and All Centers More than 120 Miles Distant from Them in Megalopolis: 1958 (actual as % of "normal": average, range, and median)

Major Center	Number of Minor Centers	Interchanges (actual as % of "normal")		
		Average	Range	Median
Boston	10	121	40–500	72
New York	7	82	34–157	59
Philadelphia	8	162	88–310	148
Baltimore	9	154	73–255	160
Washington	12	118	50–243	113

[14]N. C. Gustafson, op. cit., p. 5.
[15]Ibid., p. 7.

Table 5. Interchanges between 5 Major Centers in Megalopolis and 11 Centers[a] in Pennsylvania: 1958 (actual as % of "normal": average, range, and median)

Major Center	Distance (miles)			Interchanges (actual as % of "normal")		
	Average	Range	Median	Average	Range	Median
Boston	325	240–420	325	58	14– 77	62
New York	175	85–320	150	66	34–114	59
Philadelphia	158	79–285	136	333	95–615	297
Baltimore	136	80–262	137	132	68–255	110
Washington	144	75–270	140	72	39–136	58

[a]Three centers less than 75 miles distant from Philadelphia and Baltimore are omitted; 4 centers are outside Megalopolis: Altoona, Erie, Johnstown, Pittsburgh.

Gustafson's study included six cities in New York State, all outside Megalopolis: Albany, Binghamton, Buffalo, Rochester, Syracuse, and Utica. Their interchanges with the five major centers of Megalopolis are presented in Table 6.

Again it is evident that interchanges within the state are far higher, relatively, than those with major centers located in the same megalopolis, but in a different state. It may be noted that Tables 5 and 6 use the same basis to determine values for "normal" interchanges and hence for "actual as % of normal." Thus any error in establishing K factors for New York or Philadelphia would affect the data of these two tables in opposite directions, but both tables strongly confirm the strength of intrastate ties.

An equally impressive table showing interchanges of New England centers with the five major centers has been prepared, but is not presented here because the dominance of Boston in New England has already been documented by Gustafson.

To sum up, certainly the analysis of Gustafson's data, as presented here, is deficient because of the smallness of the universe (56 centers), the extremely wide and largely unexplained differences in the reported number of interchanges, and the crude method used to determine their "normal" levels. Nevertheless, the data show

Table 6. Interchanges between Five Major Centers in Megalopolis and Six Centers in New York State: 1958 (actual as % of "normal": average, range, and median)

Major Center	Distance (miles)			Interchanges (actual as % of "normal")		
	Average	Range	Median	Average	Range	Median
Boston	261	135–385	251	141	111–173	130
New York	215	130–293	222	203	45–472	151
Philadelphia	219	155–275	218	88	71–111	90
Baltimore	257	200–275	270	79	54–101	81
Washington	279	225–300	286	69	42– 98	72

clearly that the five major centers have relatively far more interchanges with centers in their own regions or states than with other centers in Megalopolis.

SOME OTHER APPROACHES TO THE PROBLEM

It may be objected that the approach taken in the previous discussion is a theoretical exercise. By comparing actual with "normal" interchanges, it merely showed what these interchanges would be *if* the centers were *not* located in the dense cluster called "Megalopolis." But they *are in fact* located just there. The finding that these interchanges are relatively no higher than "normal" does not invalidate the statement that they are absolutely very high. All that the preceding analysis proves is that the presumed higher level of integration is not reflected in *additional* interchanges; it does not show conclusively that this higher level does not exist.

Gottmann follows the previously quoted rejection of the importance of commuting statistics with the sentence: "The integration, however, is an indisputable fact."[16] Gottmann is right in rejecting exclusive reliance on statistics; these data must be supplemented by judgment based on experience. The trouble with such judgment is its inevitably subjective character; another observer may make a different judgment. This writer, having lived for a total of 18 years in New York, Philadelphia, and Baltimore, and being quite familiar with Boston and Washington as well, has been impressed time and again with a phenomenon opposite to that which impressed Gottmann: each of the major centers leads its own largely self-contained life; each region is orientated almost exclusively to one or the other of these major centers, with very little overlap. The only possible exception is Washington-Baltimore; these two cities are so close together as to form almost a binuclear metropolitan area; and even here the separateness is far more striking than the interchange. Of course, there are many interchanges in Megalopolis; but they do not appear to be significantly different from those with other parts of the U.S. urban system, qualitatively and, in many cases, even quantitatively.

It is just because subjective judgments may differ so widely that the search for objective quantifiable criteria is important. One of these is, obviously, the spatial distribution of population and of buildings. These show strong concentrations in centers, separated by large areas with low densities. This has been recognized by Gustafson, who states, "There are significant breaks in the physical continuity of this area."[17] It is emphatically confirmed by the maps published in 1967 by the Regional Plan Association of New York.[18]

What other tests could be devised to measure the degree of overlap between neighboring areas? One possibility—rejected as too demanding by Papaioannou in a verbal exchange—would be to look for an overlap of the "crest of the wave of metropolitan expansion" (a concept developed by this writer[19]) of two or more neighboring centers. While this test has not been made, it is safe to say that such an

---

[16] J. Gottmann, *op. cit.*, p. 213.
[17] N. C. Gustafson, *op. cit.*, p. 1.
[18] New York Regional Plan Association, *The Region's Growth*. New York, May 1967.
[19] Hans Blumenfeld, "The Tidal Wave of Metropolitan Expansion," *Journal of the American Institute of Planners.* Winter 1954, pp. 3–14.

overlap has not yet occurred and is not likely to occur in Megalopolis, except perhaps between Washington and Baltimore.

A less demanding test, measuring overlap of metropolitan regions rather than of metropolitan areas, would be to identify areas from which at least 50% as many persons commute to a second major center as commute to the one ranking first as a commuter destination. If the population of such areas exceeded a certain percentage, say 2%, of each of the two neighboring regions, this might be accepted as a criterion of overlap. The data on travel to work by the U.S. Census of 1970 probably could supply the information required for studies of such situations.

We have so far tried to answer our basic question by two approaches, asking:

First: Are there substantially greater movements of goods, persons, and messages within a megalopolis than can be found in nonmegalopolitan areas, or between megapolitan and nonmegapolitan areas? The answer, based on scanty information on movement of persons and more complete information on movement of messages, appears to be in the negative.

Second: Do the centers in a megalopolis merge or overlap strongly? Impressions from maps suggest a negative answer. The two tests described above have not yet been carried out, but available information suggests strongly that the answer would be in the negative.

A *third* and more basic approach would be to ask: Are there, in a megalopolis, institutions or enterprises which are not to be found in centers of similar size outside of it? Are there any that serve substantially all parts of the megalopolis but do not serve significantly areas outside of it?

Such questions are, in principle, researchable, but present formidable problems of assembling and classifying relevant information. Until such research is done, only impressionistic evidence is available and appears to be strongly negative. This writer has asked many knowledgeable persons for pertinent examples. So far he has found only one: Richard Meier mentioned a pumpernickel bakery in Kalamazoo which supplies Chicago and Detroit, but no other center. Pumpernickel bread is an excellent product, but a rather narrow foundation for the grandiose conceptual structure of megalopolis. At this time the evidence relevant to the question: Megalopolis, fact or fiction? permits the following tentative answer:

If the term means merely an "aggregate of metropolitan areas," it denotes a fact.

If it means a new and larger integrated unit of human settlement with "features that go clearly beyond the metropolitan level," it denotes a fiction.

IMPLICATIONS FOR DECISION-MAKING

At first sight this whole discussion may appear to be nothing more than a sterile semantic exercise. However, the assumption that aggregates of metropolitan areas constitute highly integrated units has given rise to at least two potentially harmful conclusions.

First, the assumption has been and is being used as an alibi for our failure to establish effective metropolitan planning and government. Explicitly or implicitly, it is argued that this is no longer a worthwhile goal, because the area covered today will be too small for the conditions that will prevail tomorrow.

Second, because aggregates of metropolitan areas, like aggregates of cities before them, tend, for geographical reasons mentioned earlier, to assume a linear shape, the notion of the megalopolis has given added credence and strength to the fashionable notion of the "development axis." While this is not the place to discuss this notion, it must be pointed out that considerable evidence indicates that development tends to spread outward from major centers rather than to follow a line.

These are important questions which call for thorough studies and discussions. It is hoped that this chapter will help to stimulate them.

Part Three
Government

Chapter 17

THE EFFECTS OF PUBLIC POLICY ON URBAN DEVELOPMENT

INTERNATIONAL EXPERIENCE

In attempting to evaluate the probable effects of the policies on urban growth recently enunciated by the government of Canada, as well as the governments of the provinces of Ontario and Quebec, it may be instructive to study the experience of other countries which have been pursuing similar policies for a number of years.

Such policies relate to two aspects of urban growth:

1. Distribution of growth on a national scale.
2. Distribution of growth within urban-metropolitan regions, or "urban fields," to use John Friedman's term.

Distribution of Growth on a National Scale

In surveying the policies related to the national distribution of urban growth, it is striking to note that all governments concerned with these questions, in "developing" and in "developed" nations, in countries with "free enterprise" and with "centrally planned" economics, without exception proclaim the two closely related goals of regional equalization and of restraining the growth of their largest cities, in particular of their primate city.

The United Kingdom, following the recommendations of the Barlow Report of the 1930s, has attempted to counteract the growing concentration in the Southeast and in the Midlands, centered around London and Birmingham, respectively. However, despite some successes in stimulating other areas, these two regions continue to grow at a faster rate than the balance of the kingdom.

France has long been concerned by the historical overcentralization of national life in Paris, popularized by the slogan "Paris et le désert Français." The government

---

Source: (Under the title "The Effects of Public Policy on the Future Urban System") *Urban Futures for Central Canada,* University of Toronto Press, Toronto, Ont., 1974.

is attempting to build up eight of the largest provincial centers into "countermagnets" to Paris. Again, while some of these centers are developing rapidly, the Paris Region continues to grow at a considerably faster rate than the rest of the country.

The Netherlands government has been concerned with the growing together of its largest cities into a contiguous urban area called the "Randstad," as well as with underdevelopment in the northeastern provinces. A multifaceted policy, consistently pursued over a quarter century, has succeeded in stimulating the Northeast and in reducing the growth of the Randstad to a rate just a shade below the national average. However, the Northeast, as well as the Randstad, shows a modest out-migration, while in-migration is found in the Southwest, which lies on the periphery of Europe's strongest urban field, the Rhine-Ruhr area.

In the developing countries, the primate cities are everywhere growing at an alarming rate, often concentrating the majority of the nation's urban population. Sometimes they account for over a quarter of the entire national population.

In the countries with a centrally planned economy, the situation differs. Despite the fact that their primate cities are also the seats of government and leading industrial centers, they account for less than 10% of the national population, except in Hungary, and grow at a somewhat lower rate than the total urban population. However, the planned limits of city size have been exceeded in practically all cases.

Because of similarities in size of area, location, and climate, the experience of the U.S.S.R. is of particular interest to Canada. The goal of industrializing the entire country has been largely achieved. However, contrary to notions widespread in Canada, the U.S.S.R. has not set an example of "northern development." In fact, during the last intercensus period (1959–1970), population growth in Siberia was even nominally lower than in the European part of the Russian Republic (10.3% versus 10.8%); and practically all of this growth was concentrated in the large cities on the southern edge of Siberia. By contrast, population increased by 42.8% in the Central Asian Republics and by 28.2% in the Caucasus. In the European part of the U.S.S.R. the three southernmost regions, North Caucasus, Southern Ukraine, and Moldavia, increased at twice the average rate of the other regions. This substantial southward shift, only partly due to differences in the birth rate, had been neither planned nor foreseen by the government. It seems that even in a centrally planned economy the locational preferences of individuals have a substantial impact.

As to population distribution by city size, the U.S.S.R. has since its inception pursued the goal of limiting the growth of its largest cities, and for several decades Soviet theory has proclaimed a size of about 0.25 million as optimal. In fact, the population of the 31 cities which in 1927 had populations between 100,000 and 500,000 had almost quadrupled by 1970, while Moscow had grown by 246% and Leningrad by 134%. The total population of towns under 100,000—many of them, of course, new—had grown even faster; their share of total urban population increased from 62.1 to 73.9% during these 43 years, while that of Moscow dropped from 7.7 to 5.2%.

However, this relative success should not obscure the fact that the repeated attempts to fix an upper limit to the size of Moscow, as of a number of other cities, have universally failed. In recent years many voices have been raised advocating abandonment of this policy as unrealistic and harmful. A respected Soviet economist claims that productivity in Moscow is 40% higher than in cities of "optimal" size. While this estimate, like similar ones made in other countries (e.g., 15–20% for

Stockholm), is controversial, there is little doubt that the agglomeration economics of big cities are substantial, and continue to promote the universal "trend to the metropolis."

The reasons for the failure of all governments to give effect to their proclaimed policies are highlighted by the experience of West Germany, where governments and public opinion have been particularly vocal in condemning the large *ballungen* (concentrations). As a result of the phasing out of coal mining, the Ruhr area, by far the biggest of these concentrations, showed a sluggish growth. Far from welcoming this, both the provincial and the federal governments rushed in to promote other industries in order to take up the slack in employment.

It may sound cynical, but it is safe to predict that governments and political parties everywhere will continue to proclaim their devotion to decentralization, but will do little about it. The goal will always be highly popular with everyone in the regions and smaller towns which desperately want growth and with many in the big cities who suffer from congestion. It is not difficult to think of any number of incentives and disincentives to implement such a policy. But substantial migration will come about only if and when living conditions, in particular employment opportunities and earnings, are continuously and substantially less favorable in big metropolitan areas than they are in the rest of the country. So far such a situation has not been acceptable to any government. There is no indication that Canada will be an exception and that government policies will have more than a marginal effect on population distribution on a national or provincial scale.

Distribution of Growth within Metropolitan Regions

In contrast to the universally proclaimed goal of distribution of urban population on a national scale, there is no consensus on its distribution within metropolitan regions. This has generally been determined by market forces, more or less modified by local planning, without national directives. The one major exception is the United Kingdom, which has since the end of World War II consistently pursued a policy of "decanting" the population growth of large urban centers into "satellite towns." The main instrument of this policy is Crown corporations, which assemble and hold large tracts of land at distances averaging about 30 miles from the city center, erect industrial and commercial as well as residential and public buildings, and promote their sale or lease. More than two dozen "new towns" have been successfully launched by this method, with a total population of about 1 million. However, this accounts for less than one sixth of total postwar urban growth.

The experience has led to some significant modifications. Originally these towns were conceived as "self-contained," and commuting was frowned upon. Now they are seen as constituent parts of their metropolitan regions, and commuting, not so much to the central city as to and from other places in the region, is accepted as normal.

Originally great stress was laid on a rigidly fixed upper limit of population; now growth beyond the planned limit is accommodated. The "planned" size itself has continuously been revised upward, from the 30,000 proposed by Ebenezer Howard to 50,000–60,000 in the first government-built "new towns" and to 100,000–250,000 in those presently in process.

Several other governments have also experimented with various types of "new towns," without, however, developing any clear and consistent policies. The frequent assertion that the Scandinavian countries follow such policies is in error. It is based on a misinterpretation of developments such as Vällingby near Stockholm. Thanks to a policy of large-scale assembly of surrounding land areas, initiated by a conservative city government at the beginning of this century, Stockholm has been able to create well-planned settlements for about 50,000–100,000 people at distances of about 10 miles from the city center. These settlements are not "new towns"; they might be called "new boroughs." They are not intended to be self-contained but, on the contrary, are connected as closely as possible to the central city by both rapid transit lines and freeways. They were expected to provide employment locally for about half of their residents; in fact, the percentage is lower, as a result of a great deal of both in- and out-commuting. The easier access to a wide range of employment opportunities, as well as of services, has enabled these "new boroughs" to avoid some of the difficulties experienced in "new towns," particularly in their early years.

SOME OBSERVATIONS ON CANADIAN DEVELOPMENTS

The contrast between the success of decentralization within metropolitan regions and the failure of decentralization on a national scale reflects the fact that the latter runs counter to economically determined "natural" trends, while the former is in conformity with them. There is no need for further documentation of the rapid "suburbanization" of population and activities on the North American continent.

It may, however, be of some interest to study the growth of the 17 towns in Ontario which passed the 20,000 population mark between 1941 and 1969. The population of 10 of these,[1] which are located in metropolitan regions, increased by 284% while the 7 "isolated" towns[2] increased by only 117%. Data from the 1971 census indicate continuation of this trend difference.

Rather surprisingly, towns in the Montreal Region did not share in this growth. From 1966 to 1971 nine towns in the Toronto Region increased their population by 34.0%, more than twice the rate of the Toronto standard metropolitan area (S.M.A.) (16.2%). But nine towns in the Montreal Region, comparable as to size and as to distance from the central city, had a combined growth of only 4.9%, below the growth rate of the Montreal S.M.A. (5.8%).[3] The reasons for this anomaly are unknown; a study currently being carried out by an interdisciplinary team from several universities in Quebec may bring them to light.

[1]Metropolitan Region	Towns
Toronto	Barrie, Oakville, Orillia, Whitby
Hamilton	Burlington
Kitchener	Galt
London	St. Thomas
Niagara Peninsula	Fort Erie, Port Colbourne, Welland

[2]Belleville, Brockville, Chatham, North Bay, Sarnia, Stratford, Woodstock.
[3]The towns are, in the Toronto Region: Acton, Ajax, Aurora, Georgetown, Milton, Newmarket, Oakville, Richmond Hill, Whitby; in the Montreal Region: Granby, Iberville, Joliette, St. Hyacinthe, St. Jean, St. Jerome, Sorel, Valleyfield, Vaudreuil.

FEDERAL POLICIES

The federal government has established two ministries, one for Regional Development and one for Housing and Urban Affairs. In recognition of the fact that Canada is an urban nation and that federal policies, notably in the fields of transportation and housing, as well as in the location of federal facilities, have a far-reaching impact on urban development, the latter ministry has been charged with the development of a national urban policy. While policy objectives have not yet been formulated, the Lithwick Report,[4] commissioned by the ministry, may be taken as indicative of its thinking.

Starting from an excellent analysis of the process of urbanization, the study concludes that the present urban system in Canada is mature and stable. Noting that most so-called urban problems are problems *in* rather than *of* the city, the author attempts to relate their specific urban forms to the two interrelated phenomena of "land scarcity" and "high land values." As prices or rents are transfer payments which do not affect the size of the gross national product, it is hard to understand why they should be a national concern. From the point of view of urban development, differences in land prices serve an important allocative function. Scarcity of urban land is more apparent than real. Improvements in urban communication increase available urban land. The mathematical relation is that linear communication improvements increase land area by a squaring factor. A population of 6.5 million, anticipated by the Metropolitan Toronto and Area Transportation Study (MTARTS) for metropolitan Toronto and its region, would, for example, even at the extremely low density of 6500 persons per square mile (10 per acre), absorb only 35% of the land used for all urban purposes, including parks. The theoretical foundation of the study appears to be on shaky ground.

As to the "preferred urban future," the study considers the option of "completely new cities . . . unrealistic because it fails to account for the interdependencies of the urban system" (p. 232) and states, "The one attempt that comes closest to our concept has been the Vallingby-Stockholm model." However, surprisingly the study then proposes the creation, over the next 30 years, of "three new communities of about 800,000 each" in the Montreal-Toronto corridor (p. 235). This proposal corresponds in no way to the Vallingby-Stockholm model; not only is the population 10 times as big, but the distance to Montreal or Toronto is 10 or 20 times as great as the distance from Vallingby to the center of Stockholm. The assumed availability of trains with a theoretical speed of 250 mph would not eliminate this difference, because it would have no effect on goods transportation and only a marginal effect on the door-to-door travel time and cost of most person-trips.

In fact, the proposal to develop cities of this size in order to deflect growth from the Montreal and Toronto Regions corresponds to the French model. Should the federal government opt for this model, the best way to implement it would be to build up existing fair-sized cities to the level of countermagnets. In central Canada, Ottawa, Quebec, Hamilton, Kitchener, and London are obvious candidates for this role.

---

[4]*Urban Canada: Problems and Prospects*, Government of Canada, December 1970.

POLICIES OF THE ONTARIO GOVERNMENT

The governments of Quebec and Ontario share the federal government's objectives of decentralization. Both profess a desire to channel development away from their primate cities, and both have set up regional development agencies for this purpose. Also, both have established various forms of metropolitan government.

However, only the province of Ontario has produced a plan for its major urban region.[5] Realistically, the plan assumes continued strong growth of the region's population, from 3.6 million in 1966 to 8.0 million in 2000. The assumed growth by 123% is about 50% in excess of the probable growth rate of the Canadian population and therefore appears to be somewhat overstated. The plan accepts, also realistically, that the bulk of the population (71%) will be concentrated in the urbanized area along the lakeshore. It proposes, however, three modifications of the presently discernible trends.

1. In the outer zone, beyond the Toronto commuter watershed, a shift of growth from the west to the north and east.

2. A severe limitation of growth in the part of the commuter watershed immediately to the north of Toronto, in order to preserve it for agriculture and recreation.

3. A "two-tier" arrangement for the urbanization along Lake Ontario.

Some comments may be in order.

In regard to the first proposal, two reasons are presented for favoring the north and east. First, this policy is supposed to stimulate growth in the lagging northern and eastern areas of the province. While this certainly is politically appealing, development of Midland and Cobourg is not likely to promote growth in Timmins and Cornwall, respectively. Second, this policy is supposed to reduce congestion in the west. However, as the area west of the Toronto commuter watershed, consisting of the commuter watersheds of Hamilton and of the Kitchener-Guelph-Galt conurbation, could absorb 0.5 million more people than is proposed in the plan without absorbing more than one fifth of its land, it appears that congestion could more easily be reduced by appropriate planning within that area.

The second proposal, which conforms to an objective of the Metropolitan Toronto Plan of 1964, is encountering strong local objections. Its implementation would require unusually strong provincial intervention.

As for the third proposal, the "two-tier" concept is one of the alternatives presented by MTARTS.[6] This alternative was based on the notion that two tiers of urban development, paralleling the lakeshore, would be separated by a transportation corridor which would also serve as a greenbelt. Each tier was to be served by a high-speed, high-capacity commuter rail line, operating both local and express trains at high frequencies. While the proposal to concentrate all major modes of transportation—by road, rail, pipe, and wire—in one corridor has great merit, the one mode of transportation which *cannot* be located in it is a commuter rail line, because it has to serve the centers of the communities of the "second tier," which are located about 2 miles north of the corridor. The proposal is therefore hardly realistic.

[5]*Design for Development: The Toronto-Centered Region*, Government of Ontario, May 1970.
[6]*Choices for a Growing Region*, Department of Municipal Affairs, November 1967, pp. 43–48.

In view of the weakness of the arguments for the three proposed policies, there is reason to doubt that they will be strongly and consistently pursued by future provincial governments. The present government has based its proposal for the location of a major airport and a "new town" on the recommendation for growth to the east. In fact, however, it does not conform to the "Design for Development" because the "new town" is within easy commuting distance from Toronto; regardless of its municipal status, it will function as a satellite borough of metropolitan Toronto, comparable to the privately sponsored "new town" of Erin Mills to the west. As such, it will serve the useful function of maintaining an east-west balance in the traffic to and from the central city.

MUNICIPAL POLICIES

The task of guiding and controlling urban development has been delegated to the municipalities by the provinces of Ontario and Quebec. Both provinces have enacted planning legislation providing extensive powers, including provisions for planning on a metropolitan or intermunicipal scale. In Ontario the Municipal Board has *nolens volens* developed into a kind of super planning board, a role which the legislation establishing the board did not foresee. Of late, the province of Ontario has also intervened directly in metropolitan planning, in a rather erratic manner. The province first obliged the Metropolitan Toronto municipality to extend the Spadina Freeway beyond its original terminus at Davenport Road—then scrapped it entirely in response to protests aroused by plans for this extension. The province first developed elaborate plans for a "harbor city" for 60,000 people—then casually dismissed the project in a side sentence of a Minister's speech on another subject.

However, far more pervasive and persistent than these occasional forays has been the effect of provincial policies in establishing the boundaries, rights, and obligations of municipalities, in particular the distribution of revenues and expenditures. As the latter depends to a considerable extent on federal-provincial fiscal relations, the relevant federal policies also have a strong, if indirect, effect on urban development. These policies of the higher levels of government have had, and are having, a far greater effect than those specifically conceived to guide urban development, policies which have been nonexistent in the past and are likely to have only marginal impact in the future, as explained above.

Under present legislation the obligations of the municipalities are proportional to the number of residents, in particular of school-age children, while their revenues, derived almost exclusively from the taxation of "real property", are proportional to the value of land and "improvements"—a rather quaint name for a 50-story office tower on a 0.5-acre lot. Hard-pressed to balance their books, many municipal councils are guided by a cost-benefit calculation which clearly shows that low-income families are a heavy liability, while buildings for commerce and industry or for well-to-do bachelors and childless couples are an asset. Inevitably these fiscal considerations take precedence over planning proposals aimed at better living conditions for the inhabitants of the municipality.

Many policies are available to municipal councils in their pursuit of a favorable assessment ratio. Suburban councils use their powers of subdivision control to limit the amount of development. This results in monopoly prices for serviced land. Land cost per house could be reduced by reducing lot size, for example, in the form of row houses. Suburban councils tend to preclude or limit this option by using their zoning powers to require large minimum lot sizes. The high price of these lots precludes the erection of small, relatively cheap houses on them. The municipality becomes and remains the preserve of high- and middle-class families; the poor must live elsewhere.

"Elsewhere" *in praxi* means the older central cities. Their councils attempt to counter by replacing "blighted" housing—the only housing the poor can afford—with apartment houses (the result of public and private redevelopment) for predominantly childless tenants with sufficient income to make their demand effective. The net result of these converging policies of suburban and municipal governments—forced on them by the existing distribution of revenue sources and obligations—was succinctly summarized by the late Hugh Pomeroy, planning director of Westchester County, New York: "The poor are zoned out into the Atlantic Ocean."

This, then, is the most important effect of the public policy of the higher levels of government on urban development. It has not entirely escaped the attention of legislators. The introduction to the Smith Report on Taxation to the Select Committee of the Legislature of Ontario proposes to "lower property taxes, which are unquestionably regressive, with greater reliance on provincial taxes, which are . . . more progressive" (par. 3), and proposes specifically "increased reliance on corporate and personal income taxes" (par. 9). Implementation of this proposal obviously would require the consent of the federal government to a revision of federal-provincial tax-sharing agreements.

There can be no doubt that the tax on "improvements" acts like a heavy sales tax on housing, reducing its availability to the consumer to a far greater degree than the availability is increased by the busy and earnest efforts of all the well-staffed agencies charged with implementing assorted government policies designed to "relieve the housing shortage." Reduction of the tax on improvements certainly would provide a strong stimulus to investment in housing, in particular to rehabilitation. A relative reduction would also result from a shift of expenditures, notably for education, also advocated in the Introduction to the Smith Report, from the municipalities to the province. Some steps in this direction have been taken in recent years, and more may be expected.

It should be noted that the impact of the tax on land differs from that of the tax on improvements, because of the different origins of their respective values. The value of an improvement, like that of any commodity, is created by the labor and capital of its producer. Like the tax on any other commodity, a tax on improvements can be and is being passed on to the consumer. By contrast, the "site value" of a parcel of land is the capitalization of the "differential rent," which that site commands because of its accessibility. As the accessibility is specific to the location of the site and not subject to modification by its owner, he or she cannot pass it on; the owner is forced to cede a greater share of the differential rent to the community.

As the site value is the product of combined individual, as well as of collective, efforts of members of the community other than the landowner, it has been claimed that this value should be fully appropriated by the community as a matter of equity. Considering that, since the coming of the white man to this continent, land has legally been a commodity and has been exchanged against the money equivalent of other commodities, the equity argument is questionable. However, a gradual shift of the "real property" tax from improvements to land may be acceptable. It would have the dual advantage of forcing land into the market and of reducing the cost of building occupancy. The Introduction to the Smith Report approaches the problem of taxing "unearned income" from community-produced increases in land value by advocating a "capital gains tax on land-value appreciaton" (par. 17). without contesting the justification of a tax on these as on other capital gains, it should be noted that such a tax, if collected at sale, would tend to discourage owners from bringing land into the market, opposite to the effect of an annual tax on market value.

In any case, some shift of government policy towards higher taxation of land-value appreciation seems probable. Carried to its logical conclusion, the equity argument leads to the advocacy of public ownership of land, or at least of its "development value." Whatever the philosophical evaluation of this argument, there is a strong practical argument for public land ownership. It is the only available means to assemble large contiguous tracts of land suitable for rationally planned development. Attempts by private developers to assemble such tracts require great amounts of money, time, work, and often devious ingenuity, and are rarely successful. It is therefore not surprising that several leading developers in Ontario advocate public land ownership. It would relieve them not only of the onerous task of land assembly, but also of the burden of carrying the capital during the long period between land purchase and sale (or lease). This burden would be carried by the public in the form of interest payments on government bonds. As governments can borrow money at lower rates than can private developers, this would tend to lower the market value of developed land, to the benefit of its user. Sale or lease of publicly owned land below market value, frequently and rather illogically demanded and expected by advocates of the equity argument, and sometimes practiced in federal-provincial land assembly projects, would transfer part of the differential rent from the community to those individuals who happen to—and can afford to—buy or rent buildings located on publicly owned land. Such a procedure is hardly in the public interest, but it may prove hard to resist political pressure for it.

It is probable that public landownership for urban development, by whatever level or combination of levels, will play an increasing role in North America, as it already does in Europe. It may be significant that it is now being strongly advocated by the senior of American land economists, Homer Hoyt.[7] If and when—and only if and when—it becomes public policy in Canada, the Vällingby-Stockholm model advocated by the Lithwick Report may become (in many and widely modified forms) the model for the development of our urban areas.

A substantial modification of population distribution within urban fields might thus come about. In place of the present "scatteration," the indiscriminate mixture of urban and rural land uses, there would be fairly large contiguous urban areas in planned satellite boroughs and satellite towns, surrounded by even larger contiguous rural areas.

Presumably life in these developments would be more attractive to both households and enterprises than the alternatives now available in urban-metropolitan fields. If the claims of their advocates that they combine the advantages of small-town and of big-city life should be confirmed, this would imply that the relative attractiveness of isolated small towns would be further reduced—contrary to de-

---

[7]Addresses given at Lambda Alpha Biennial Congress, October 1971, pp. 8–9.

clared government policy. The success of redistribution within metropolitan regions would contribute to the failure of redistribution on a national (or provincial) scale, as may have been the case in the United Kingdom.

The potential impact of municipal fiscal land planning on population distribution is complex, and any evaluation is highly speculative. Two points should be noted. First, legally the decision on the restrictive measures, notably subdivision control, is vested in the province. The province of Ontario frequently turns down municipally supported subdivision proposals which conflict with one or another objective of provincial policy; also, in a few cases municipal disapproval has been overruled as arbitrary. However, the provincial government has never approved, and is not likely ever to approve, a subdivision to which a municipality objects on fiscal grounds.

Second, and more significantly, municipal fiscal planning is far from universal. It is consistently practiced by all municipalities surrounding Toronto and apparently also by those surrounding other major cities in southern Ontario. However, rural and small-town municipalities and, surprisingly, also most suburban municipalities in Quebec have not yet adopted policies based on relatively sophisticated cost-benefit calculations, but follow the older and more primitive philosophy that all growth is good.

There is little doubt that the high prices of suburban houses resulting from fiscal planning are inducing a number of households to seek accommodation in the central city, primarily in high-density apartment developments. On the other hand, a certain number buy and rehabilitate city houses which were previously occupied by low-income families, generally at higher densities. Where these displaced families will go is an unanswered question, as mentioned earlier. However, it seems likely that at least some of them will be "immured" (to use a term coined by Jane Jacobs) in high-density, inner-city subsidized housing projects. Finally, some frustrated would-be suburbanites may buy or build homes in unsophisticated rural municipalities beyond the suburban belt.

The net effect of fiscal planning appears to be that fewer people live in the suburban ring and more in the city and, to a lesser extent, in the exurban ring than would be the case in a market not distorted by fiscal planning.

It may be hypothesized that the lower housing cost resulting from the absence of fiscal planning confers a competitive advantage on small towns (also on Montreal versus Toronto). No hard evidence is available to either prove or disprove this hypothesis. Impressionistic evidence, however, does not appear to confirm it.

To sum up, it seems probable that public policy will have some effects, both intended and unintended, on population distribution within urban fields, but that the distribution of the urban population on a national (and provincial) scale will continue to follow well-established, economically determined trends.

Chapter 18

THE ROLE OF THE FEDERAL GOVERNMENT IN URBAN AFFAIRS

URBANIZATION IN CANADA

Canada is rapidly becoming one of the most urbanized countries in the world. From 37.1% in 1901, the share of the urban population rose to 62.9% in 1951 and to 69.6% in 1961 (according to the definition used by the 1956 census of Canada). Equally significant is the shift among the remainder of the population from "rural-farm" to "rural-nonfarm." While in 1951 "rural-farm" accounted for 19.8% and "rural-nonfarm" for 17.3% of Canada's population, in 1961 their shares had changed to 11.4% and 19.0%, respectively. Thus in the short span of a single decade the "nonfarmers" were transformed from a minority to a majority of almost two thirds of the "rural" population. Many of them, no doubt, are engaged in occupations serving the farmers. But a growing number—soon, if not already, a majority—are either working in urban occupations or have retired from them.

These facts indicate that not only our traditional image of Canada as a nation of farmers but also the basic concept of a sharp distinction between "urban" and "rural" have lost their validity. In the modern world people no longer live either in the "city" or in the "country" but in a new form of human settlement which, for lack of a better word, we call a "metropolitan region." Today and increasingly in the foreseeable future, "urban" affairs are really the affairs of metropolitan regions which, well before the end of the century, will contain 9 out of 10 Canadians.

Metropolitan regions develop around a core of a city or a group of cities. Within an area of several hundred square miles the ease of interchange by modern means of transportation and communication creates a common labor and housing market within which people commute. But beyond this "commuting watershed" (which corresponds roughly to the "metropolitan area" as defined by the census) extend the outer sections of the metropolitan region. Their industry and population depend on the metropolitan center for supply of goods and services, while the population of the center depends on them for recreation and for certain agricultural products—fresh vegetables and dairy and poultry products. The fact that there is not only mutual

---

Source: The Journal of Liberal Thought (Liberal Federation of Canada, Ottawa, Ont.), Spring 1966.

support but also mutual interference and competition for land and water between the agricultural and the "urban" uses is not the least of the problems of the metropolitan region, a problem which cannot be dealt with separately from the entire complex of "urban affairs."

Whenever profound and revolutionary changes affect the life of society, a dual time lag can be observed. First, there is an ideological lag: concepts and words, such as those used in the title of this chapter, derived from past experience, are applied to the new phenomenon, to which they are no longer adequate. Second, there is an institutional lag: when the substantive problems created by the new phenomenon are finally understood—and we are still far from that point—existing institutions are found to be inadequate to deal with them, but can only be changed gradually because of their inherent inertia.

SUBSTANTIVE PROBLEMS

The growing concentration of population, first in big cities and now in still bigger metropolitan areas, and the concomitant depopulation of the countryside have been viewed with alarm by many observers and by most governments for over 300 years. The growing difference in levels of productivity and income between different regions of a nation, and in particular the self-perpetuating downward trend of depressed regions due to emigration of their most active and productive inhabitants, have become a matter of concern to most contemporary governments. The universally recommended remedy is "decentralization." However, this slogan is no guide to action without specification of what is to be decentralized and where to. Nor is it likely to lead to wise action without an understanding of the reasons underlying the strong and continuous trend toward concentration.

Certainly the tempting idea of spreading development evenly to all communities—and all voters—has proved unworkable. All nations, Eastern as well as Western, which have tried it have come to the conclusion that development must be concentrated in "growth points." There are, as yet, no firm conclusions concerning either the optimum size of such growth points or their best location in relation to natural and human resources. There is, however, strong evidence of the increasing importance of human versus natural resources, and of the favorable impact on productivity of the increased specialization, freedom of choice, contact, and competition characteristic of large concentrations of population. It seems that growth points have the most favorable prospects if they have easy access to service functions of the highest order, that is, if they are located within the orbit of a metropolitan region. Both in the United Kingdom and in France national planning has largely taken this direction—in the United Kingdom by the development of satellite towns surrounding the metropolitan centers, and in France by strengthening a small number of major cities as counterattractors to Paris.

The distribution of population and industry—the determining basis of urban development—is evidently a matter of national concern. Research into the existing trends in Canada and their consequences, and the development and evaluation of alternative models of distribution, can be carried out adequately only at the federal level.

While prevailing concepts both of provincial autonomy and of the freedom of private enterprise circumscribe the possibilities of national planning in Canada, it should not be overlooked that the federal government actually exercises a strong influence on the distribution of urban activities through its transportation policy, both by the exercise of its regulatory powers and by its role in the development of waterways, ports, airports, and pipelines, as well as by Crown corporations such as Air Canada and the Canadian National Railroad. While Canadian transportation policy has been effectively used to achieve broad national goals in regard to the distribution of urban activities, it has, as in most countries, followed and served urban growth rather than guided it. Once the federal government has clarified its objectives in this respect, it can greatly contribute to their realization by using the tools of transportation policy which are at its disposal.

Even more critical is the same problem on the smaller scale of the cities and metropolitan areas: the allocation of land to various activities and the development of transportation facilities which both determine their location and are determined by it. Peripheral sprawl at excessively low densities, encouraged by the use of the automobile, has led to a shift from public to private transportation, thereby increasing traffic congestion, and to rapid obsolescence of the older central areas. This is primarily a local responsibility. The Canadian government has not been guilty of the high-handed and often destructive intrusion of a federal highway program which has occurred in the United States. However, federal fiscal policies have strong indirect effects on the form of urban development. Research into the many complex interrelations determining this form, an indispensable basis for effective metropolitan planning, requires stronger support from the federal government.

While control of land is logically a local function, water and air, equally vital to urban life, are no respecters of local or even provincial boundaries. Pollution of air and water in urban areas, often affecting other cities and areas, is endangering the health and the amenities of the population in all sections of Canada and has become a national problem. The federal government should take the lead in the research and development of techniques for the measurement, control, and elimination of water and air pollution and in the formulation and propagation of model codes. A particularly heavy responsibility falls on the federal government in relation to the source of water supply of our most important urban areas—the Great Lakes-St. Lawrence system—because of its international character. It might be very wise to make restoration of this prime water resource of the North American continent to its fullest utility a precondition to entering into discussions about the release of other Canadian water resources to our southern neighbors.

INSTITUTIONAL PROBLEMS

The governmental structure of the British colonies which later became the provinces of Canada was based on the needs of areas in the process of agricultural settlement. The villages and towns which gradually emerged received their political existence only as "creatures of the province." The life of the inhabitants was almost entirely circumscribed within their own boundaries, supplemented only once in a while by a day's journey to the county seat. Urban communities were rare exceptions in this system, with their inner sections incorporated as "cities" or "towns" and their rapidly growing outer sections "organized" into a crazy-quilt pattern of "suburbs."

Evidently such a pattern of local government cannot deal adequately with the closely woven interrelations existing in metropolitan areas and with the somewhat looser but rapidly tightening network of relations within metropolitan regions. "Local autonomy" becomes a hollow phrase when all decisions seriously affecting the life of the community are made elsewhere.

In the United States, where the fetishism of federal and state constitutions has led to a complete hardening of the arteries of the body politic, the insistence on local autonomy for each obsolete small municipality has, paradoxically, led to its total erosion. For almost anything they want to do, municipalities have to go hat in hand to Washington for subsidies and have to accept federal dictation on what they can do and how they must do it. Serious American experts on law and local government have even come to the conclusion that the only way metropolitan government can ever be brought about in their country is by application of financial blackmail by the federal government towards the states and municipalities.

This is hardly the way for Canada. Our provinces have retained their power to reshape their municipal structures and are beginning to use it to create larger and more efficient units. While these measures go nowhere far enough, they are steps in the right direction and deserve encouragement by the federal government.

Not only our institutions of local government but also their rights to the land under their jurisdiction are still shaped by our rural past. What a farmer did on his land hardly affected his neighbor. If the value of his land increased, it was generally due to good farm management. Under these conditions unrestricted ownership, sale, and purchase of land was and is highly functional.

On the contrary, in the closely knit net of interaction in urban and metropolitan areas what anyone does on his property strongly affects his neighbors and the entire community. The value of his land—as distinguished from the value of the buildings on it—depends exclusively on the decisions of other private persons and of the community. His natural desire to increase the value of his land stimulates not productive efforts to improve the land, as is the case on the farm, but highly undesirable efforts to influence his councilman to bend public policy in favor of his private interest.

Such efforts are primarily directed to changes in zoning, the main instrument which we have created in order to control the impact of development of one parcel of land on its neighbors. It is a rather crude and inflexible instrument. It cannot be used at all to reserve the open areas which are vital for the health and livability of our vast urban agglomerations.

Centuries of experience have shown beyond question that a far better coordination of urban development can be achieved by unified than by scattered ownership of the land. The achievements of the British "new towns," as well as of those Scandinavian cities which own most of the land within their boundaries, show that this is more true today than ever. In general, there are in Canada no legal obstacles to municipal land ownership. In our most urbanized province, Ontario, the Planning Act explicitly empowers municipalities to acquire land "for planning purposes." However, this power has never been used, primarily because the municipalities lack the financial means for large-scale investment in land.

We are faced with the paradoxical situation that the communities which contain the greatest concentration of wealth and income which the world has ever seen, the large metropolitan areas of the North American continent, cannot find the money to satisfy the most urgent needs of their citizens. Their main source of income is still the tax on "real estate." This was perfectly appropriate in a rural society in which land was the predominant form of wealth and where the demand for municipal services was small. In an urban society, however, it has several pernicious effects. First, by treating the value of "improvements" created by the owner's effort and investment on the same basis as the value of the site, which is created by the community, it discourages construction and penalizes the improvement of existing buildings. Second, as the percentage of income required for housing, owned or rented, increases as income decreases, it is a strongly regressive tax, destructive of social welfare. Third, it pushes municipal governments into a ruthless, competitive scramble for those "assessments" which produce high income and require few expenses—commerce, industry, apartments for wealthy bachelors and childless couples—and into equally ruthless measures to exclude families with small incomes and large numbers of children.

A tax reform which gave the municipalities a share of the income tax commensurate with their growing responsibilities would relieve them from excessive reliance on the real estate tax as well as on handouts from higher levels of government. Both are slowly eroding the essence of local self-government and the responsibility for the allocation of resources. Such a tax reform is the most important responsibility of the federal government in urban affairs.

To sum up, the three basic institutional requirements for sound urban development are as follows:

1. Metropolitan government.

2. Large-scale municipal land ownership.

3. Adequate financial resources.

FEDERAL POLICIES AFFECTING URBAN AFFAIRS

The federal government is of course involved in urban affairs in many ways. Reference has already been made to transportation policies. Such key ministries as commerce and finance deal predominantly with urban affairs. Indeed, with three out of four Canadians living in urban areas, any distinction between national and urban affairs becomes somewhat artificial.

But beyond this close general relation several specific federal policies affect our cities. Federal loans for sewage-disposal facilities, with forgiveness of up to one quarter of the loan, are well justified by the national interest in clean rivers and lakes. Equally, financial support for waterworks is a valuable aid to cities. An extension of federal credit to municipalities for use at their discretion would be desirable. However, as long as the limitation of their incomes narrowly restricts the ability of municipalities to carry and repay such loans, their use will remain limited.

On the other side the exemption of federal properties from local real estate taxation—even if mitigated by payments in lieu of taxes—is a sore point with municipalities. Of course, tax exemption is granted not only to properties of higher levels of government, but also to those of charitable, religious, and educational institutions, because their purposes are considered worthy of support. However, this indirect form of subsidy has several undesirable consequences. First, because the size of the subsidy is proportional to the value of the real estate owned by the institution, it follows the principle of "he who has to him shall be given" and gives least support to those most in need of it. Second, because the subsidy is available only for capital investments, it induces institutions to spend too much on these and too little on operations which could contribute far more effectively to the accomplishment of their purposes. Finally, it leads to a wasteful underuse of scarce urban sites. This last point applies also to federal properties. It not only would be sounder bookkeeping but also would result in far more efficient allocation of resources to subsidize worthy purposes directly and openly and to tax evenly and fully *all* real estate, including even that owned by municipal departments. The federal government could promote this sound approach by setting an example: renouncing its right to exemption from local taxes.

An aspect of federal policy which has a quite unintended and overlooked effect on urban affairs is the provision of the income tax which permits the cost of employee parking as a business expense, exempt from corporate or personal income tax. The cost of the journey to work is not tax-deductible; employees who use public transportation have to pay the fare out of their taxable income. However, their colleagues who drive to work frequently do not have to pay for one of the main elements of the cost of the trip, the fee for parking. This cost is carried by the employer, who in turn subtracts it from the corporation's income. If employers were forced to collect the cost of parking from their employees, many of the latter would switch to public transportation or to the use of car pools, thereby reducing rush-hour street congestion, accidents, and air pollution. One of the worst offenders in supplying free employee parking is the federal government itself. It could set a good example by abolishing this practice. Employees would of course demand a compensating increase in pay. But as this would benefit the users of public transportation or of car pools as much as the person who insists on burdening the streets with 2000 tons of tin and chrome in order to move the 125 to 200 pounds of his or her body, it would not interfere with the beneficial effect of reducing automobile movements.

HOUSING

More important than such indirect effects of federal policies are the direct and conscious efforts of the Central Mortgage and Housing Corporation (C.M.H.C.) to improve urban living conditions. Like all other modern governments, the Canadian government has assumed responsibility for housing. In conformance with the philosophy predominant on the North American continent, it has concentrated its efforts on promoting the building of houses for those who can pay for them, relying on the "filtering down" of vacated older houses to supply those who cannot afford new ones. Equally in conformance with this philosophy, primary support has been given to the detached single-family house, with lesser and later support going to new rental accommodations and still lesser and later support to the maintenance and rehabilitation of old houses. This bias has greatly contributed to low-density sprawl and to decay at the center of urban areas.

This unanticipated side effect does not invalidate the fact that the activities of C.M.H.C. have greatly contributed to the improvement of the housing conditions of millions of Canadians, both directly and by the filtering-down process. However, decent housing never filters down far enough to reach low-income groups. In order to help them the federal government initiated a program of subsidizing locally initiated public housing projects. However, not many dwelling units have been created under this program. Understandably, for reasons explained above, municipalities are not eager to have large families of low income within their boundaries. Recently legislation has been broadened to permit subsidized housing by means other than the construction of public housing projects.

This is a step in the right direction. Substandard housing conditions exist because there is a gap between the incomes of many families, in particular those with several children, and the cost of decent housing. The logical way to bridge this gap is to subsidize the family rather than the housing unit. This would avoid the danger of creating "low-income ghettos" and would make it possible to subsidize homeowners of low income as well as renters.

A rent subsidy to the family, however, involves the danger of driving rents up and, if a sufficient supply of decent housing is not available, of subsidizing slum landlords, as shown by the sad experience of many relief agencies. The suggested policy of bridging the gap between the purchasing power of many families and the cost of decent housing by federal subsidies must be accompanied by a policy of increasing the supply of housing of moderate cost, available equally to those who can afford its market price and to those who receive subsidies. The present policy of providing loans for limited dividend housing is directed towards this aim. However, the limitation of both dividends and rents, in addition to generally limiting the attractiveness of the program to investors, has two specific drawbacks. Limitation of dividends acts as an incentive toward inflating the capital cost, and limitation of rents weakens the incentive to put an attractive product on the market. In a reasonably balanced housing market it should be possible to replace these limitations by a ceiling of, say, 1% of vacancies, in addition to the existing ceilings on the amount of credit available per unit. Under these conditions federal loans might be extended to any housing project—private, cooperative, or public—which conformed to appropriate standards of planning, design, construction, and management.

URBAN RENEWAL

Our unfortunate inclination to copy our southern neighbor has led to the addition to the National Housing Act of "Part III, Urban Renewal," despite the fact that the deterioration of the lower-income groups' housing stock caused by publicly financed urban renewal (first called "urban redevelopment") in the United States has by now been amply documented. It should be self-evident that housing conditions can be improved only by increasing the supply, not by decreasing it as is done by "slum clearance." Tearing down the roof over their heads increases the hardships of those forced to live in substandard housing. This would be true even if the work of relocation agencies succeeded—as it never has—in procuring decent housing at rents no higher than those previously paid by the persons displaced by clearance. The reason is that these housing units are then no longer available to the many other low-income families who are equally in need of them. The net effect of public subsidies for slum clearance is a dual subsidy to slum landlords, by increasing the prices of those houses which are torn down and the rents of those which remain, and a subsequent spreading of slum conditions.

Because these evil effects of the bulldozer approach are being increasingly realized, emphasis is shifting to rehabilitation. This is to be welcomed. However, if aid consists only of a loan to the owner, the increase in rents necessary to carry the loan displaces low-income tenants just as effectively as does clearance. The best use of the many millions now being made available by the federal government for urban renewal would be for public housing projects consisting of areas of rehabilitated housing in the central urban sections, in addition to new housing projects on open land on the outskirts, where a rapidly increasing percentage of all urban jobs is to be found.

Urban renewal, of commercial and industrial as well as of residential areas, is to a considerable degree being carried out by private enterprise. However, where not only the individual structure but also the street and lot pattern or the entire environment has become obsolete, large-scale land assembly is required. Municipalities should, and in most cases do, have the power to do this and to reorganize the land for a new use for which the particular location is more valuable than other potential locations. The new user should be and, as widespread private redevelopment proves, generally is willing and able to pay for the entire cost of both the land and the new structures which he or she erects. It is argued that a "write-down" of the land cost is justified in order to bring back to the city middle-class families and the commercial facilities which they support. As long as the obsolete division of metropolitan areas into several municipalities persists, this may be an advantage to the central city, justifying a subsidy on its part. But it is hardly a legitimate purpose for a higher level of government to finance the competitive struggle of one municipality against its neighbors.

If the federal government wants to subsidize municipal land assembly, it could produce far greater benefits by acquiring land at the rapidly expanding fringes, where land can be bought for $30,000 per acre, instead of buying and clearing land for $300,000 an acre, as has been done in Montreal and Toronto. The existing program of federal-provincial land assembly, originated for the different and questionable purpose of selling land below market value to private house builders, could be used and expanded for the purpose of guiding peripheral growth according to sound planning principles, in close cooperation with the municipalities concerned.

A FEDERAL MINISTRY OF URBAN AFFAIRS?

In the United States the extensive intervention of the federal government in urban renewal led to the establishment of a federal Department of Housing and Urban Development. The advocates of this measure visualized this department as a coordinator of the many other interventions of the U.S. government into urban affairs, such as highways, health, education, and welfare, and the antipoverty program. However, this would leave few federal activities, except those concerned with relations to other nations, outside the new department. Apparently it was this difficulty which led to the long delay in making the new department a reality. Ultimately it is likely to turn out to be the present National Housing Agency under a new name. In Canada there is no reason to assume that the C.M.H.C. could perform its function better in the form of a ministry than as a Crown corporation.

The coordination of the activities of various federal and, even more important, of various provincial departments operating in a given region certainly is urgently required. The way to achieve this is by the creation of regional offices. If regional planning agencies are created, such regional offices would play an important part in their work. Indeed, by establishing such offices, the federal government could give a strong impetus to regional planning.

As metropolitan regions become the home of an overwhelming majority of Canadians, their problems are bound to become more and more identical with those of Canada itself. To modify a famous (or infamous) quotation, "What is good for the nation, is good for its urban areas—and vice versa."

Chapter 19

THE IMPACT OF URBAN RENEWAL ON FAMILY LIFE

Your program committee has done me a great honor by inviting me to address you. It has done less well by you, the captive audience. It could hardly have picked a less qualified speaker on this theme than a man who, as a lifelong bachelor, never had a family and who has no faith whatever in the virtues of "urban renewal," as it has been practiced in the United States for the past quarter century and is now beginning to be practiced in Canada.

Before explaining my maverick attitude on this question, it may be appropriate to survey shortly the profound changes from a rural to an urban way of life. Urbanization, as you all know, is a worldwide process. While in the year 1800 there were fewer than 50 cities in the world with populations over 100,000, now there are far over 1000, and more than 100 with a population of more than 1 million.

Up to the time of the industrial revolution, at least four out of five families lived in the countryside; in North America more than nine out of ten. The typical family was the farm family, based on and held together primarily by common work on the basic economic unit of the family farm. Similarly, the craftsman's and trader's shop was a family enterprise. Typically, three generations lived and worked together in one household. All this has changed.

The contemporary family consists only of parents and children, and its members work as individuals at some place outside of, and often far away from, their household. Moreover, that household frequently changes its location because of changes in location of the place of work, in income, in family composition, or simply in taste.

In Canada this transition has been particularly rapid. To illustrate, in the province of Quebec, which folklore still pictures as an old-world peasant land, the percentage of the male labor force engaged in "primary industries" (farming, fishing, mining, etc.) dropped from over 40% to less than 13% within half a century, from 1911 to 1961. The percentage engaged in manufacturing remained practically unchanged, at about 28%. The entire increase was absorbed by "services" of all kinds, which doubled their share from 30 to 60%. Of the female labor force also, 60% is now employed in services, against less than 30% half a century ago. Here the increase occurred at the expense of the shares of domestic service, which dropped from 36 to

---

Source: Lecture presented at the Trendsetter Convention, Panel Conference on Family Life, 1966, and published in *The Canadian Home Economics Journal,* December 1966.

20% and, surprisingly, of manufacturing, which dropped from one third to one fifth of the total female labor force. The absolute number of women working in manufacturing has, of course, increased, not only because of population growth but also because the percentage of all women who are in the labor force grew from 16% in 1911 to 28% in 1961 in Quebec.

At present, about one third of all Canadian women over 15 years of age work outside the home, and two thirds of these women workers are married. In fact, in every age group the majority of working women are married. In 1961 in Metropolitan Toronto 31% of all married women were gainfully employed.

The profound change from the old rural to the new urban way of life led to a serious disruption of family life in the early stages of the industrial revolution. In many cases the male family head went alone to the city in search of work, leaving his family in the village. Many of the young men and women who migrated to the city remained unmarried. Many people thought the family was doomed.

As the urban way of life became general and stabilized, the picture changed. Today most migrants to our cities, both those from other parts of our country and those from abroad, come from an urban background. They either bring their families with them or soon establish families. In fact, the family, in its new "nuclear," parents-with-children form, is more dominant than ever. The percentage of all residents of Canada, of both sexes, 15 years and over, who were married, rose from 57% in 1941 to fully two thirds in 1951, and has maintained that level. In part this is due to earlier marriage; the average age at marriage dropped 1.5 years from 1951 to 1961, both for men and for women.

While the great wave of country-to-city migration is still continuing, it is being met, for the last 100 years, by a wave moving in the opposite direction; the city-to-suburb migration. The upper and middle classes move to the suburbs. In the older central sections remain only the low-income groups, including the bulk of the new migrants to the city. People change their places of residence easily; on the average one quarter of all households are to be found in a different location from where they were a year before.

This whole process is often referred to as the "metropolitan explosion" and is regarded as the result of the automobile, and as a purely American phenomenon. This is a quite mistaken notion; the trend is far older and more general. In the year in which I was born—which was quite a while ago, 1892—a sociologist made a survey in the old and stable city of Frankfurt, Germany. He found that the established families were moving to the new suburbs, and that their places in the old town were being taken by new migrants to the city. He also found that one third of all households had moved during the year.

It is these older residential areas of our cities, inhabited by the lower income groups who cannot afford to buy or rent new housing, which have become the prime "target areas" for "urban renewal." The military terminology is hardly accidental.

Urban renewal, in the literary and genuine sense of the word, is a continuous process which always goes on in every city. It serves to overcome the obsolescence which affects every part of the physical structure of the city. It is the adjustment of the structure inherited from the past to the needs of the present and the future. In a stable society, where every generation repeats the way of life of its forebears, obsolescence is merely physical; old houses are repaired or replaced by identical new ones. In a growing and progressive society such as ours, functional obsolescence becomes more important and interacts with physical obsolescence. The more rapid the progress, the more widespread the obsolescence, and the greater the need for renewal. Obsolescence affects not only the individual structure, but also the pattern of lots and streets and of land uses. Therefore public powers for land assembly, if necessary by expropriation, are required in order to make the land available for the new use. But the new use should pay for the cost of land acquisition. I completely agree with the statement by the eminent American housing economist, Lou Winnick, that "publicly sponsored urban redevelopment may be more, not less necessary in non-slum growth areas."

In principle, this wider concept is recognized. The official Ontario *Urban Renewal Planning Studies Manual* says, "Urban renewal aid ranges throughout the entire spectrum of community needs."[1] But two pages later the manual defines the task of the studies as "to search out blight." In fact, federal and provincial legislation restricts public urban renewal action to "blighted areas." Thus obsolescence, a normal and inevitable process—indeed, as a reverse of the medal of progress, a sign of health—is interpreted as a pathological phenomenon. Terms like "the cancer of blight" are widely used. A great amount of work and money (over $2.5 million to date) is expended on studies directed toward designating "renewal areas." Such designation invariably leads to deterioration and demoralization of the area, which feels its future to be threatened. The inhabitants of the area deeply resent the designation, interpreting, not without reason, the term "blight" as a polite circumlocation for "slum."

The continued existence of slums in a relatively affluent society such as ours is a shame. But slums and substandard housing are symptoms rather than causes. They are the housing aspect of poverty. They exist because there is a wide gap between the amount which a large proportion of our population can pay for shelter and the cost of decent housing. They can be abolished only by closing this gap, either by raising incomes or by lowering prices or rents. They cannot be abolished by tearing down the only houses which are available to the poor, in the name of slum clearance. To use a homely parallel, if you see a man with torn and worn-out pants and you want to help him, you do not tear off his pants; you buy a new pair or have the old ones repaired. The same applies to housing; if we are serious in our declarations that every Canadian family is entitled to a decent home, we must build new houses and rehabilitate old ones, and make them available at prices and rents which the people now living in "slums" can pay.

It is passing strange that so many intelligent and well-intentioned people still stick to the notion that slum clearance is a good thing. Over half a century ago one of the founding fathers of modern city planning, Patrick Geddes, stated:

The policy of sweeping clearance should be recognized for what I believe it is: one of the most disastrous and pernicious blunders in the chequered history of sanitation. . . . The large population thus expelled would . . . be driven into creating worse congestion in other quarters, to the advantage of the rack-renting interests.

Over a quarter of a century ago I wrote to the New York Citizens Housing Council that the urban redevelopment legislation which it was then recommending would "inevitably worsen the housing situation of the lower income group."

[1]*Urban Renewal Planning Studies Manual,* Department of Municipal Affairs, Community Planning Branch, Toronto, May 1966, p. 3.

In the United States all such warnings have been disregarded. Tens of thousands of families have been ruthlessly bulldozed out of their homes. All surveys of their relocation have shown that they had to pay considerably higher rents for accommodations only very slightly better, and sometimes worse, than those from which they had been displaced. As the results of this kind of "urban renewal" have become evident, protests have multiplied. The succinct comment made in 1961 by Monsignor John J. Egan, director of the Roman Catholic Conservation Council of Chicago, may stand for many others. He called the practice "planned social anarchy."

The closely knit social life which exists in these "target areas" has been well described by the American sociologist Herbert Gans in his study of the "West Side" of Boston.[2] In Canada an excellent description of the Quartier St. Henri here in Montreal—only a few minutes' walk from this hotel—has been published by my young friend Michel Blondin.[3] There are generally two groups in such an area: a minority of people dependent on public welfare, and a majority of workers with low skills and correspondingly low wages, but steadily employed and self-reliant. Among them are recent immigrants from rural areas, sometimes still maintaining the pattern of the three-generation family. Far more important is the fact that family ties beyond members of the nuclear family, particularly between mothers and daughters, are far stronger than in middle-class families; and the maintenance of these ties is dependent on living in the same neighborhood. But beyond this there are strong ties to the neighborhood as such. While for the middle class the home ends at the lot line, and friendships are maintained independently of location, for this group of our population the street is part of their home, and the world outside the neighborhood is largely unknown and deeply mistrusted. To live among "people of our kind"—*du monde comme nous autres*—is a vital element of security.

This entire social fabric is torn apart by the bulldozer approach of slum clearance. Some people are unable to survive this threat to their world. Cases of fatal heart attacks resulting from the strain and of suicides have been reported.

So far, we have, in Canada, at least avoided the worst aspect of American practice, the replacement of low-rent housing by apartments euphemistically called "middle-income," at $40, $50, or $60 per room. In Canada "slum clearance" has generally meant clearance for a public housing project. However, experience has shown that only a minority of the displaced families return to live in the new project and that the old neighborhood ties are not reestablished. Also, the high cost of acquiring the houses which previously covered the site forces the housing authority to build at high densities. The authority rightly gives highest priority to families with many children, but from the tenth floor of an apartment building a mother cannot supervise her children playing in the yard. Moreover, the abnormally high proportion of children to adults, especially male adults, in such projects creates problems of its own.

The growing recognition of the damage done by wholesale clearance has led to increased emphasis on rehabilitation. But if the cost of rehabilitation is to be borne by the occupant, the present population will be just as completely displaced and replaced by a higher income group as under the typical American "clearance and redevelopment" approach. A promising approach is the acquisition and rehabilitation of old houses as public housing. This has been done in Philadelphia and recently with four houses in Hamilton. The average cost of rehabilitation in Hamilton was

---

[2]Herbert Gans, *The Urban Villagers,* Ont., The Free Press, Glencoe, Ill., 1962.
[3]Michel Blondin, "L'animation sociale en milieu urbain: une solution," *Recherches Sociographices* (Les Presses de l'Universite Laval, Quebec), Vol. VI, No. 3, September–December, 1965.

slightly under $4000, with the total averaging less than $15,000 per house. The houses, with three, four, five, or six bedrooms, provide the suitable accommodation for large families which is so urgently needed, and which can be created in new housing only at a much higher cost.

However, while this is a far better as well as cheaper solution for subsidized housing than the creation of massive low-income "ghettos" in projects, it does not answer the need for areawide renewal which the legislation aims to achieve. The chief tool of this legislation is the authorization of substantial federal subsidies for a "write-down" of the land value. The American practice has been to acquire a "blighted" area at a huge cost, sometimes exceeding $1 million per acre, destroy all buildings on the site—including some good ones—and offer the resulting man-made desert to private developers, at a fraction of its cost to the taxpayers, as a building site for "middle-income" housing. It would be much wiser to sell such an area, with all the existing buildings, to a public housing authority or a housing cooperative at a price which would enable it to rehabilitate the houses without raising the rent. The renewal could then be carried out gradually, according to a phased plan. Such a plan would necessarily also include the demolition of some houses which were no longer worth the investment in rehabilitation and, more importantly, the creation of the community facilities—new schools, community centers, parks and playgrounds, as well as parking facilities—which were necessary to bring the area up to contemporary standards. The displaced families could be rehoused in the vacancies which occur in every area in the course of time. The social fabric of the community would remain undisturbed. The framework for family life would be gradually improved instead of being brutally disrupted. Families whose incomes made them eligible for public housing would receive subsidies to bridge the gap between their incomes and the normal rent.

Such a subsidy is based on the assumption that a family can afford to pay 25% of its income for rent. Most families in the low-income group pay more; but many, both in this group and among those above the level eligible for subsidized housing, prefer to allocate a greater part of their budget to other purposes and to accept housing of a lower standard than they presumably can afford. Many of my colleagues claim that "society cannot tolerate substandard housing" and that these people "can" and therefore "should" allocate a greater portion of their incomes for housing. I find this paternalistic attitude inadmissable in a society which claims to be democratic. Who gives us bureaucrats-technocrats the right to make other people's budgets? Is there any evidence that we know better what is good for them than do the families themselves? In fact, there is some evidence to the contrary.

Certainly, before we go blithely ahead destroying all older and cheaper housing on the assumption that families "can" and "should" pay more for better accommodations, we should know a good deal more of the relative importance of the expenses for housing and for other items in the family budget, and of their contribution to a healthy and happy family life. Nobody is better qualified to answer such questions than you, the experts in home economics.

Chapter 20

THE ROLE OF THE TECHNOCRAT

Everybody seems to be agreed that our cities are in a mess, but who is responsible for this?

Our cities have been and are being built, in the main, by private enterprise, "the developer." When he is accused of not giving the people what they need and want, he protests that he is willing and able to give them a better product at a lower price, but that he is hamstrung at every step by red tape, laws, regulations, restrictions, permits, and endless delays, which always increase the cost and often lower the quality of his product. And he is right.

Who makes the laws and regulations, and also decides to provide the infrastructure on which the developer depends? Obviously the legislators at all levels, the elected representatives of the people, "the politicians." When the politician is accused of not giving the people what they need and want, he protests that he is doing his best, but that he has to rely on the best "experts" whom he can find to inform him of the consequences of his decisions on the complex urban system and to implement the many technical details. And he is right.

The expert, civil servant or consultant, is a "technocrat," and the technocrat has become the bête noire of latter-day populism. He is the "faceless" person who, from his hiding place in the depths of a bureaucratic rabbit warren, conspires to frustrate "the will of the people." But if or when a "common person"—desperate or hopeful—succeeds in penetrating the fortress and comes face to face with the monster, the latter, as likely as not, will assure the visitor that he sympathizes with his difficulties, but that his hands are tied by laws and regulations, and that the visitor's problem really is the responsibility of another department. And he is right.

He is right because we have succeeded, to a considerable degree, in implementing one of the most basic and cherished tenets of liberal democracy: "government by law, and not by men." Checks and balances prevent any one person, or group of persons, from doing total evil; but they also prevent the person from doing total good. Government by law is, by definition, faceless government.

This never becomes a complete reality in a small and simple community. The citizens of Athens could meet face to face with Aristides the Just (and throw him out

---

Source: *The City: Attacking Modern Myths* (University League for Social Reform), edited by Alan Powell, McClelland and Stewart, Toronto, Ont., 1971.

when they got fed up with justice). But when one deals with the complex interactions of millions of people, it is inevitable to abstract out of the totality of their individual lives a series of common characteristics such as age, sex, and income, in order to satisfy them in their roles as residents, workers, commuters, shoppers, or recipients of recreational, medical, welfare, or other services. People become statistics.

"We regard the population as made up of 'dividuals' instead of individuals," quotes Torsten Hägerstrand.[1] Hägerstrand further says:

In the main, people are viewed as parts of activities to be performed within each domain in isolation, and not as entities who need to make sense out of their paths between and through domains.... In total, seen from the point of view of the individual, this is an enormous maze about which he personally can do very little.

No wonder that the individual caught in this maze feels alienated. The root cause of alienation, in the words of Karl Marx, is the "enslaving subordination under the division of labor," and he concluded that the necessary condition for emancipation from alienation is for the working people to repropriate the means of production. A necessary, but not a sufficient condition, as the Marxist philosopher Ernst Bloch remarked in a conversation.

The individual, alienated as a cog in the machine of production, and caught in the many wheels within wheels which make the metropolis go around, revolts and demands that "people should control their own lives." No demand could be more legitimate: "Power to the people!"

Which people?

The currently fashionable answer is: the people of the "community," referring to the present residents of a more or less clearly defined territory within the metropolis, numbering usually a few thousand persons. It is claimed that they should determine not only the "software" of municipal government: how schools or playgrounds are to be run, how streets should be cleaned or garbage collected, but also the "hardware": what should be built in the territory—an apartment house, hospital, or shopping center, a school or a park, a road or a subway, a water or sewer main.

Most of these structures are to serve an area well beyond the "community's" territory, and all of them are destined to serve for a long time, 50 or 100 years. Some of them will begin to serve only after 5 or 10 years. But three quarters or more of the people who will constitute the community 15 years from today do not live there now. Who speaks for them?

Hardly the present residents. Hardly the elected representatives, whose time horizon is inevitably dominated by the next election. So the question remains: who speaks for the people who are not yet there?

The late Norbert Wiener once said, before an audience of city planners, that the best investments ever made were the great medieval cathedrals, because they were built by the Church not just for their own day, but *sub specie aeternitatis*. No other body thinks in quite so long a time span. It may, however, be recalled that dynasties, aristocratic or monarchic, were concerned with the fate of their "houses" in centuries to come.

I am not advocating a return to theocracy or monarchy or aristocracy. But the need

---

[1] Torsten Hägerstrand, Presidential Address, *Regional Science Association Papers*, Vol. XXIV, 1970, pp. 7–21.

for a long time horizon continues to exist. Certainly many citizens are concerned about the futures of their cities, but by and large they have no organized voice, and certainly no organized role in government. In some countries political parties, strongly committed to a specific image of society, have been willing to risk a loss of votes for the sake of the ultimate triumph of their principles. This is hardly typical of Canadian parties, and certainly not of municipal officials elected as nonparty individuals.

In fact, there is only one group in government who can afford to take a longer view: the technocrats. Protected by their civil service status and committed to their "professional standards," they can and do think in terms of the long-range and city- (or metro-) wide "public interest"—as they see it.

They see it, as Hägerstrand's student noted, in terms of "dividuals" rather than of individuals. The Roads Department helps "dividuals" to drive around; the Sewage Department helps them to get rid of their excrements. These are certainly important functions of the individual, but they are hardly the whole person. One department is responsible for one "dividual"; another department, for another.

> I just put them up—where they come down
> That's another department—says Wernher von Braun

as Tom Lehrer so aptly put it.

There is, however, one group of technocrats who make the odd claim that it is their specialty to be "generalists": the city planners. They claim that their planning is "comprehensive": comprehensive in space, comprehensive in time, comprehensive in all aspects of the lives of their plannees.

Patently there is a yawning abyss between this exalted self-image and the reality of city planning, in particular in North America. The reality is well described by Raymond Vernon:

> ... Land use planning in any comprehensive sense really does not exist in our larger urban areas. What does exist is a complex game of chess among localities, each attempting to palm off the undesired applicants for space upon their neighboring communities. This is warfare, not planning.[2]

Two types of applicants are undesired.

First, as Vernon states, "Everyone wants the water, but no one wants the reservoir," nor does he want the incinerator, the road, or the subway in his backyard. But second, and even more important, nobody wants the poor. Every municipality wants land uses which pay high taxes and require low expenditures. Poor people can pay only low taxes, and they, and in particular their children, require high expenditures; they are "undesired applicants." Commercial and industrial buildings contain no children and are welcome; apartments contain few children and are acceptable.

Suburban municipalities, in which "the people of the community control their own lives," long ago learned to use their powers of control to keep poor families out. The "urban renewal" legislation, enacted some 30 years ago in the United States,

---

[2]Raymond Vernon, "The Myth and Reality of Our Urban Problems," *Internal Structure of the City*, edited by Larry S. Bourne, Toronto, Ont., 1971.

gave the central cities a weapon to beat the suburbs at their own game. They cannot, like the suburbs, keep the poor people out; they are already there. But they can try to throw them out, by tearing down the houses in which they live and replacing them with structures which yield higher taxes. This criminal policy is rationalized as "slum clearance" for the sake of "higher housing standards." In fact, the war against the slums becomes a war against their victims; the "war on poverty," a war against the poor. And, as I told the 1967 Annual Meeting of the American Society of Planning Officials, "both the suburbs and the central cities are enlisting the planners as mercenaries in this merciless class war of the 'haves' against the 'have-nots.'"

Warfare, not welfare!

It is only fair to note that the municipal governments, in acting as they do, carry out the wishes of their constituents. They all want lower taxes and better services. The people who suffer, in the case of the suburbs, are those who are not there. In the case of the central city, they are there, but are a minority. Rightly, this minority has begun to fight back.

By organizing themselves as a "community," the residents threatened by "renewal" have copied their more affluent fellow citizens, who typically have established "taxpayers (or ratepayers) associations." While these groups do not have the same interest in taxation as their fellows in the suburbs, they pursue the same goal of keeping out "undesirables," and undesirable is not only the reservoir or the incinerator but also any one of lower socioeconomic status, because his or her presence threatens to lower the selling price of their properties. They have been quite successful in pursuit of this goal by bringing pressure to bear on their elected representatives. "Community control" of development would arm them with the formidable weapons which the suburban municipalities in the balkanized metropolitan areas of the United States are using so successfully in their diastrous *bellum omnium contra omnes*. In Metropolitan Toronto this war is at least mitigated by the power of the technocrats to pursue the areawide long-range "public interest"—as they see it.

They see it, of course, in terms of the power structure which they serve. If they are to see it differently, the power structure will have to be changed. This is not a question of the community versus the technocrat. It can be decided only by political struggle and evolution.

Part Four
Economics

Chapter 21

SOME VEXING QUESTIONS IN URBAN AND REGIONAL ECONOMICS

In Canada, as you all know, a very small population, only 20 million, owns an enormous territory, close to 4 million square miles. Probably no other country has as great a per capita wealth of natural resources, and Canadians have always based their hopes for the future on these. To a considerable extent the country has been, and is still, balancing its books by selling its natural resources to foreign owners and by using capital imported by these owners for their development. There is now growing concern about this trend in terms of loss of political and economic independence. Foreign owners tend to import goods and services required for their operations; in particular, research and development and top-level management functions are carried out abroad. This limits the opportunities to develop these talents in Canada. Does development of natural resources by foreign capital imply underdevelopment of human resources?

This leads to the broader question of the relative weight of natural and of human resources for economic development. There can be no doubt that in the modern world the importance of natural resources is decreasing and that of human resources is growing. Empirically this is evident in the rapid development of countries with high population densities and few natural resources, such as the Netherlands, Germany, and Japan. Are these countries perhaps developing so well not despite, but because of, their loss of *Lebensraum*? And is our enormous territory in Canada perhaps a liability rather than an asset? Should we concentrate our development rather than disperse it? Concentration of population makes possible increased specialization and interaction, mutual emulation, stimulation, and education.

This of course runs counter to the policies adopted by practically all governments, Eastern and Western, which pursue the goal of a "balanced" development of all regions of the nation. What does "balance" mean, and by what scale is it to be weighed? Mechanically applied, it would mean that the proportional geographical distribution of the population should be frozen, and that average per capita income should be the same in any and every region. It is hard to understand why govern-

---

Source: XXIX World Congress, World Congress of the International Federation for Housing and Planning, Philadelphia, 1968.

ments should be so much more concerned with income inequalities between regions than with the much greater ones between groups within each region.

We all know, of course, that income differentials between regions set in motion a stream of out-migration from the poorer regions, which results in a vicious cycle. As the most productive people leave, the income of the remaining population becomes insufficient to support existing services, leading to further loss of population and income.

Less attention has been paid to two potentially countervailing trends. The depopulation of rural areas is the result of rapidly increasing productivity of labor in primary production—agriculture, mining, fishing. A much smaller labor force produces an equal or larger amount of goods, thanks to greater capital investment. This investment in turn requires more producer services, notably in construction, and the higher income of the workers in primary production, resulting from increased productivity, requires more consumer services.

More important is the second trend, towards improved transportation and communication. If the time, the cost, and the inconvenience of traveling a person-mile are halved, the market area of a service establishment quadruples. It should therefore be possible to provide a satisfactory level of living, in terms both of monetary income and of services, for a region with a greatly reduced population. The question poses itself in a slightly modified form in our prairie provinces. Here the grain collection points have been disposed along the railroad lines at intervals based on the driving distance of horse-drawn carts. With motorized transport farmers can easily bring their grain to more distant points, and many do so if these offer more services. The railroads want to reduce the number of their stations. Provincial governments are now aiming at concentrating the populations of the many small, no longer viable service centers into a few larger centers. Obviously these cannot accommodate all of the people involved. Moreover, with further increases of productivity both in farming and in services these centers too will lose population. All our city planning methods have been developed to deal with growth. Should we not also develop methods of planning for decrease?

Our overwhelming problem, of course, remains dealing with growth. There is widespread alarm about "excessive" growth of metropolitan centers, and the governments of Canada and of the province of Ontario propose to counteract it by establishing "new" or "satellite" towns. The questions arising here are so numerous that I will merely list four of them:

1. How do we compare the *total* costs of, say, a metropolis of 5 million with those of 100 towns of 50,000? Most attempts to answer this question have been limited to municipal costs and services, but these account for no more than 10% of the gross urban or metropolitan product.

2. Which types of industry do and do not flourish in small towns? We know that industries with frequent changes of product and/or process depend strongly on the external economies of the large metropolis. Does this mean that only routine production can be successfully carried on in "self-contained" small towns? If this is true, does it mean that their jobs, by definition, are most likely to be replaced by automated machinery?

3. Would it be preferable to build not "satellite towns," but what I call "satellite

boroughs," that is, residential districts providing a wide choice of services and of employment opportunities, but forming integral parts of the metropolitan labor and housing markets, such as have been created in Stockholm's Vällingby and Farsta and have been proposed, for instance, by the "Washington 2000" plan?

4. A market economy is based on the proposition that, under conditions of perfect competition, both seller and buyer maximize their benefits and minimize their costs. But what about the effect of their deal on others—of what I like to call "third-person benefits and malefits" and what are more commonly known as "social costs" on one side and as "overspill benefits" on the other, in particular as "nonmonetary" costs and benefits? Is it possible to translate these into monetary terms by sophisticated market research methods, for instance, by comparing prices of houses on a quiet street with those on a noisy one, or prices in an area with clean air with those in one with polluted air?

Chapter 22

ON LAND TAXES AND LAND BANKING

THE PROBLEM OF LAND VALUES

Canadian cities have been and are being designed, in the main, by the "invisible hand" of the market. Different market prices allocate each site to its "highest and best use," the use which gives the highest return to its owner.

A market transaction is, by definition, a deal between two persons, seller and buyer, who, under ideal conditions, both maximize their benefits. It does not and cannot take into account the benefits or "malefits" accruing to third persons. However, in a closely knit urban environment these effects are very substantial—in particular the "third-person malefits," usually called "social costs."

The first and still the most important public intervention in the use of privately owned land, the "restricted area bylaw," generally referred to as "zoning," attempts to protect third persons from malefits resulting from certain developments or uses on land in their neighborhood. It is generally recognized that zoning strongly influences land prices. However, it is not entirely correct to say that zoning can increase the value of a parcel to which it is applied. It can only reduce it from the value resulting from its unrestricted "highest and best use." But by limiting the satisfaction of a given demand for one parcel, zoning shifts this demand to other parcels and increases their value.

Not only zoning and other restrictive planning measures, such as subdivision controls, but also planned public works, notably for transportation and utilities, but for schools or parks as well, inevitably and profoundly affect the distribution of land values. There is an inherent conflict between the public allocation—by planning—of land values and their private appropriation. Landowners who gain from a particular planning decision quietly pocket their increase. Those who lose cry to high heaven and bring all possible political pressures to bear in order to prevent or reverse the decision. This greatly limits the flexibility of planning.

The growing realization of the problems arising from the private appropriation of land values has led to increased interest in eliminating them by complete public land ownership or at least reducing them by "land taxes" or "land banks."

Source: Plan (The Canadian Institute of Planners), October 1974.

LAND TAXES

A land tax is actually levied in all Canadian provinces. However, it is lumped together with a tax on a completely different economic entity, called "improvements," in the "real property" tax. The value of improvements, mainly structures, is determined by their cost of production. Like the tax on any other product, the tax on structures can and indeed must be passed on to the consumer. However, the value of a site ("land") is not produced by its owner; it is the capitalized form of its differential rent, which is determined by its accessibility to all kinds of activities and resources as compared to the accessibility of all other sites. The property owner can do nothing to either raise or lower this value. A tax simply transfers a portion of the differential rent from the owner of the site to the taxing authority. The owner cannot pass it on, because the differential rent already expresses the advantage the site provides to a user compared to another, much cheaper and much less heavily taxed site. Consequently, the market value of the owner's share is reduced proportionally to the reduction of his or her share of the differential rent. This neither reduces nor raises its cost to the user, who pays the same total differential rent. The only change is a shift in the form of payments from mortgage payments to taxes.

The remark that the site-value tax will not reduce the cost to the user may seem disappointing. Advocates of site-value taxation (as of land banks) are prone to promise that we can have our cake and eat it, that the "unearned increment" in land value which now accrues to the owner—or "speculator"—can accrue both to the community in the form of tax or land rent, and to the user, normally a homeowner or tenant, in the form of reduced price or rent. However, its distribution between these two potential claimants is a zero-sum game: what the community gains, the user loses, and vice versa.

As only persons with relatively high incomes can afford new housing, there is no justification for transferring any part of the site value to them rather than to the community which created it, and therefore might claim not just a part, but 100% of this value (or of the differential rent). Such a policy would be tantamount to expropriation. A land tax of expropriatory character would be manifestly unfair and politically unacceptable, given the widespread character of landownership. While the homeowner, as noted, would not be affected by a site-value tax qua land user, he would be adversely affected qua landowner.

Indeed, not surprisingly, an increase in the site-value tax has never been proposed in isolation, but only as part of a reform of the real property tax, as a partial or total shift from improvements to land. There is no doubt that the present real property tax is highly regressive and contributes more to depressing the standard of housing than all governmental housing policies combined do to raise it. As far as industrial and commercial buildings are concerned, the tax is passed on in the prices of their goods or services. As for residential buildings, the real property tax acts like a sales tax on housing, discouraging construction and rehabilitation, reducing supply, and raising prices and rents. The tax on residential buildings accounts, on the average, for about 15% of the annual housing cost. Because the lowest income groups spend more than three times as much of their incomes for housing as do the highest, this amounts to about 2% of income for the latter, but over 6% for the former.

A shift of the real estate tax from improvements to land would affect different types of properties in different ways. Case studies (in Port Credit, for example) indicate that the average homeowner would about break even. Apartment and row houses would pay less; vacant and underused parcels would pay more. Reducing taxes on housing at moderate or high densities encourages construction of this type of housing. Raising taxes on un- or underused land penalizes its speculative withholding. One result is to bring more land at the periphery of the built-up area on the market and thereby reduce the pressure for "leapfrogging," as well as the possibility of monopoly or oligopoly of development land. First, the cost of housing would be reduced. Another result is encouragement of private rehabilitation or redevelopment. Experience with the site-value tax in various countries, such as Australia, New Zealand, and South Africa, confirms that, in fact, it has all these effects.

Some concern has been expressed that the encouragement of redevelopment may lead to accelerated destruction of structures which should be preserved for social or aesthetic reasons. However, when society considers preservation desirable, it can be brought about better by specific regulatory and financial measures than by penalizing by taxation—as is now the case—all investment in rehabilitation and in new construction.

In addition to the aforementioned benefits, a shift of the real estate tax from improvements to site value would also greatly facilitate public land acquisition by substantially reducing land prices.

LAND BANKING

Land taxes and land banking are frequently proposed as alternatives. In fact, both are likely to produce more desirable results if they are used in combination.

Large-scale public acquisition of land, undertaken immediately, would tend to raise the already inflated current land prices even higher. The public would have to pay not only for all of the past, but also for most of the anticipated future "unearned increment."

By contrast, a site-value tax would permit the public to recover some of the past increment from the land which it acquired, as well as from the land which remained in private ownership. On the other hand, the land tax does not remove the contradiction, mentioned earlier, between public allocation, by planning, of land values and their private appropriation; nor does it avoid the resultant difficulties for comprehensive planning. These difficulties disappear with large-scale public landownership. Within such ownership, values can be freely shifted from one parcel to another. If, for example, experience indicates that an original plan, spreading development over two thirds of the area and leaving one third open, should be replaced by a "cluster" plan, concentrating development on one third and leaving two thirds open, nobody gains or loses money.

This advantage is, of course, due to the large-scale rather than to the public characteristic of landownership. It obtains equally with large-scale private ownership. However, a public agency has three substantial advantages in assembling and holding land for development.

1. A private developer has to spend a great deal of time and money to assemble his land, piece by piece, through middlemen. A public agency, having powers of expropriation, can proceed faster.

2. Practically always there will be some "holdouts" who refuse to sell except at exhorbitant prices, sometimes at any price. The private developer has to adjust his plan to these properties. A public agency can deal with holdouts by expropriation.

3. Finally, a public authority can borrow money at lower rates than can the private developer. As there is a long time span between the start of land assembly and the completion of development, the resulting difference in carrying costs is likely to be substantial.

On the other hand, knowledge of the intent of land assembly tends to raise the asking prices of all owners in the affected area. The private developer can largely avoid this by hiding his intent. Public authorities, assembling land for public works, have frequently used the same method. However, the rising demand for public disclosure and participation makes this increasingly difficult. It is possible to impose a "freeze" on land values for a certain period, but the longer the period of public discussion and the broader the range of alternatives discussed, the less this becomes feasible. The financial advantages of land banks may be less than expected.

This would appear to be true under the assumption of a "normal" land market, in which prices would be determined by the differences in advantages of accessibility over all competing sites. It is frequently claimed that such a competitive situation does not exist and that the price of urban development land is really a monopoly price. The claim is generally based on the assertion that the amount of land is fixed. However, while this assertion is roughly valid for the total supply of land on the globe, it does not hold for urban land. Urban land can be, and indeed has been, increased vastly during the last century by making more land accessible to transportation and utilities. As a consequence, urban land values have been spread out more thinly over a much greater area. Contrary to widespread assumptions, a comparison of urban land values in terms of average wages, or in terms of cost of construction of a square foot of floor area, shows that they were much higher 100 or 200 years ago than they are now. There is no natural monopoly.

There may, however, be an artificial monopoly. It is claimed that such a monopoly has been created by land speculators. Much has been made of the finding of the Dennis-Fish Report that six developers have assembled enough land in the Toronto area to satisfy the demand for the next 5 years. However, this would have given them a monopoly only if no other land suitable for development existed in the area. In fact, a great amount of such land does exist. However, most of it, as well as most of the land owned by the "big six," is not available for development because of absence of subdivision approval and of basic municipal services. A monopoly or oligopoly does indeed exist. However, while some speculators and developers derive vast profits from it, it is created not by them, but by restrictive municipal and provincial policies. The Urban Development Institute (U.D.I.) has proposed a vast increase in subdivision approval and basic services as the most effective means to reduce land prices. That their reasoning is basically correct appears to be confirmed by the experience of the Montreal Region, where less restrictive policies prevail and where lot prices are only a fraction of those in Toronto.

However, implementation of the U.D.I. proposal would inevitably result in urban sprawl, with all its attendant financial and social costs. Under conditions of private landownership, public planning policy has only a choice between the Scylla of sprawl and the Charybdis of oligopolistic high land prices. Only public landownership provides a way out of this dilemma.

Considerable experience exists with advance acquisition of land for urban development by public authorities. In Stockholm a conservative city council inaugurated such a policy at the beginning of this century and it has been consistently followed since; land has been bought by the city beyond its boundaries and subsequently annexed. Most cities in Sweden and also in other Scandinavian countries have adopted similar policies. In the Netherlands all cities are required, by law, to acquire enough land to satisfy the anticipated housing demand for several years. In the United Kingdom the government acquires and retains ownership of all land for its "new towns." In all these, and many other cases, the results have been favorable, both from a planning and from a financial point of view.

In Canada "federal-provincial land assembly" has been used to provide veterans' housing and also to attempt to keep land prices low by offering competing lots below market prices. Some cities, notably Saskatoon and more recently Edmonton, have adopted similar policies with some success.

Various policies have been adopted for the disposal of land assembled by public authorities. In Canada, lots were originally sold to buyers who built houses either for their own use or for sale. Predictably, some of these buyers made considerable speculative gains. Restrictions on resale or rent, imposed to prevent this, were only partially successful. A different method for the same purpose was developed by the German city of Ulm, which, at the turn of this century, had built workers' houses on city-owned land. On sale, the city reserved a "repurchase right" at the original price, modified by adjustments for any deterioration or improvement of the structure, as estimated by independent appraisers. Under today's conditions, adjustments for inflation would have to be added.

In any case it is hardly possible to prevent some benefits of increased land value from accruing to an owner in one form or another. If it is desired that the public should retain permanently both its control over development and its claim to increases in land value, permanent public ownership, with periodically revised leases to developers and users, is the logical method. It is generally used in the Scandinavian cities and in the British "new towns." The Netherlands towns originally sold most of their development land, frequently to housing cooperatives, but are increasingly opting for leasing.

Leasing land to developers has been a practice widely used by large private estates in Great Britain, as a modified inheritance from the feudal system. It is evidently due to this peculiar situation that the British government, at the end of World War II, conceived the idea of nationalizing "development rights," while leaving title to the land to its owners. Anyone who wanted to develop land had to buy the development right from the Crown. But he also needed the consent of the owner. The owner, of course, gave this consent only for a price. It is now recognized that the aims pursued by this legislation can be achieved only by acquisition of full ownership of development land.

Acquisition of development rights has also been advocated in the United States as a means for the preservation of open land. With the possible minor exception of land owned by "gentlemen farmers," such preservation can be achieved much more effectively, at no substantially greater cost, by acquisition of full title. This has been done in Canada in the case of the Ottawa greenbelt. The no longer available development potential of the greenbelt land has thereby been shifted to adjacent properties. Values of land both inside and outside the greenbelt are higher than they would be if it did not exist. It is hardly a good policy for the public to acquire only those development rights (with or without acquiring full title) which are *not* to be used and leave to private owners those that *are* to be used profitably. It would be preferable to acquire *all* potential development land and then decide, on the basis of ecological and aesthetic as well as economic considerations, which portions should be and should not be developed.

Public ownership of development land has to face three interrelated problems:

1. How to allocate land to various claimants.
2. How to determine the price or rent of the land.
3. How to control its development and use.

As noted earlier, the market allocates land to the claimant who can make the "highest and best use" of it, within the limits set by public regulation. There is much to be said for allocating parcels of a land bank similarly by competitive bidding for the highest land price or rent. The only alternative is allocation by administrative decision, with all the concomitant dangers and inevitable suspicions of favoritism and corruption.

Allocation to the highest bidder implies charging as much as the market will bear; otherwise, by definition, demand will exceed supply. Consequently, the goal of counteracting excessive land prices—usually high on the list of the benefits expected from land banking—can be achieved only by offering a considerably increased supply. To some extent this may reproduce the dilemma between permitting monopoly prices and encouraging scatteration. However, the available experience with disposal of publicly owned development land seems to indicate that it is not too difficult to "clear the market" at prices not far in excess of costs, without resorting to unacceptable scatteration.

On the question of control, there is some experience from urban redevelopment. If controls are fairly general and loose, undesirable development may occur. If they are very specific, such as, for example, a specific design, they may deter and prevent desirable development. Therefore in some cases competitive bids have been called, to be judged by a combination of financial and design criteria. This evidently again opens the door to subjective and arbitrary decisions. As a general rule, it may be preferable to use financial criteria only, and to rely on improved and more flexible planning controls, such as the British system of development permits.

Land banking is generally being discussed as a policy for vacant land in advance of development. It might, however, also be applicable to presently developed land. This has, in fact, been done, under "urban renewal," but mainly for "clearance of blighted areas." The land assembly provisions of urban renewal legislation might be more constructively used for the preservation or for the gradual transformation of built-up areas which are threatened by undesirable types of change. In such situations the public authority would normally only acquire the land; the buildings would remain in the hands of their present owners, who would receive a leasehold on the land they occupy. The amount of lease payment would correspond to a normal return on the price paid for the land. The owner would be free to rent or sell his building, but demolition or rebuilding would be subject to approval by the landowning authority.

There can be little doubt that public ownership of land could lead to a greatly improved urban environment. However, it certainly runs counter to cherished notions of private ownership. The average homeowner regards his property not only as a home to live in, but also as a good investment. Canadians pursue two conflicting aspirations: to make an honest penny out of any property they own, and to live in a high-quality urban environment. Sooner or later they will have to decide which one is more important to them.

Chapter 23

LAND CONTROL AND LAND PRICES

DETERMINANT OF LAND PRICES

The values and prices of commodities are generally determined by their costs of production. "Raw" land is not "produced," but a "free gift of nature." However, the costs and benefits of an activity differ widely, depending on the location and other characteristics of a piece of land, or "site." Consequently, persons (natural and corporate) who want to engage in any given activity (work, trade, residence, etc.) are willing to pay a "differential rent" for the right to use a given site which permits them to obtain greater net benefits from their activities than they would obtain if they carried out the same activities on a different site. The "value" of a site is the capitalized form of its differential rent. It is determined by the relation between the "effective demand" for a site with given characteristics and the supply of sites with comparable characteristics.

The value of a piece of urban land is determined partly by natural characteristics of soil, climate, and scenery, but primarily by accessibility to other activities. If population and activities in a given urban region increase, the total of urban land values increases because of increase in total demand; and the difference between the values of sites at different locations increases because differences in the amount of accessibility increase. It therefore cannot be expected that land values will increase only at the rate of some index of purchasing power, or even at the rate of real income per head or per household. Their total is bound to increase faster, either in terms of the total number of acres which have "urban" value, or in terms of value per acre, or in some combination of both. A policy of limiting land *prices* by governmental fiat would not change these *values* (or differential rents). It would merely transfer them from the (private or public) owner of land to its user. The economic and social consequences of such reallocation require careful consideration.

THE ALLOCATIVE FUNCTION OF THE LAND MARKET

Under our current institutions land is a commodity, which is bought and sold in the market. The market allocates each piece of land to the highest bidder; in real estate

---

Source: Lecture presented to the Community Planning Association of Canada, June 1973, and reproduced by the School of Economic Science, University of Toronto, Toronto, Ont., June 1976.

terminology, to its "highest and best use." The reasons for possible divergence between the use which is highest and best from the point of view of the owner, and the one which is highest and best from the point of view of the community and the public, and the measures used to correct this, need not be dealt with here; but the question of allocation by the market mechanism and by possible alternative methods will be discussed.

To a large extent the price which persons (physical or corporate) are willing to pay for a given site is determined by their trading-off of time (as well as cost and inconvenience) of travel against space. Those to whom savings in the movement of persons and goods are important are willing to pay a higher price for land and/or to use less of it (e.g., by multistory buildings). Those to whom space is more important (e.g., single-family house residents) buy more land in locations less accessible to many potential destinations. In this important respect the "highest and best use" coincides for owner and community and the market fulfills an important allocative function. It must be noted that this market function does not require private ownership. It would operate in exactly the same way if a public authority sold or leased land by competitive bidding.

There seem to be only two possible alternatives to allocation by the market mechanism: "first come, first served," or administrative decision.

In its extreme form "first come, first served" would mean that land would be "free"—as it was for the first white settlers. Obviously the first-comers would occupy large and accessible sites, even if they were restricted from selling or leasing to other users; and later comers for whom accessibility was much more important and/or who would use the land more intensely would have to locate on less accessible sites. In comparison to allocation by the market, more land would be absorbed for urban purposes and the cost of transportation of persons, goods, water, sewage, power, and so on would be greatly increased.

In this extreme form the "first come, first served" method is, of course, an absurdity. It would, however, also operate in a market in which people were free to sell and buy, but price was limited by a ceiling. The same tendency to increased land absorption and transportation cost would be present to a greater or lesser extent. In addition, as in any case of legally imposed price ceilings, there would be a strong danger of a black market in the form of secret "under-the-counter" payments. This could, of course, be avoided if the seller (or lessor) was a public agency. In this case the third alternative, administrative decision, would have to allocate land among bidders.

Allocation by administrative decision is being practiced in the U.S.S.R. and other Communist-controlled countries. Soviet economists have come to the conclusion that the fact that an enterprise on highly accessible land pays nothing for this advantage has led to a certain distortion of production costs and a misallocation of resources. They demand that the State charge a differential rent to the user of land, in conformance with Marxist theory.

THE IMPACT OF PLANNING ON LAND VALUES

As noted earlier, the differential rent is determined primarily by accessibility. Accessibility by roads, transit, water, sewer and storm water drainage mains, and power lines is provided by public authority. Moreover, public authorities exercise regulatory powers of subdivision control and zoning which limit, respectively, the amount of land available and the intensity of development. Public works and regulatory measures do not *create* land values, but they *shift* them. In this, as in any urban area, there is more land that can *potentially* be developed for urban purposes than will *actually* be so developed in any practically foreseeable future. The value of this potential has been defined as "floating" value; it may "settle" on any piece of land, but cannot settle on all of them. Just where it will settle depends on public policy decisions. If the area of potential land—in relation to the actual development demand—is large, this value is diluted: many acres have "development value" over and above their value for nonurban purposes, but for most of them this value is small. If the area available for development is relatively small, the floating value is concentrated on fewer acres, with more of it "settled" on each of these.

In its original version, the theory of floating value claims that its total always exceeds the total of land values after settlement. This implies that as a class land speculators always lose money—a rather startling conclusion.

It has long been a policy of many governments to dilute development value by extending lines of transportation, thus making land available at prices lower than those prevailing in the areas previously available for urban development. Inversely, if the amount of land potentially available for urban development is decreased by reserving some of it for nonurban purposes, the development value of this land "floats" onto the remainder, increasing its value. This has been the predictable result of the recent decision of the government of British Columbia to reserve large areas in the Vancouver region for agriculture, greenbelt, or parks. (This does not necessarily mean that the benefits of these measures do not justify them.)

THE DILEMMAS OF PUBLIC PLANNING OF PRIVATE LAND

The fact that any planning decision, whether in regard to public works or to regulatory measures, inevitably shifts land values from the property of one owner to that of another creates serious difficulties for public planning (in distinction to planning of land by its owner). First, it greatly restricts flexibility of planning. If a planning authority designates, or even indicates that it considers, a given location for transportation or service facilities, or for one or another land use, it shifts value to that location. If subsequent events or subsequent insights indicate that it would be in the public interest to locate the facility (e.g., a rapid transit line or a freeway) elsewhere, or to designate a given area for a less intensive use and accommodate the one previously intended elsewhere, the value of that land is shifted to the new location. The owners of land in the original location, who bought it at prices based on the assumption of the presence of public works and/or the right to intensive development, regard this, not without justification, as an inequitable deprivation of their property rights, and protest strongly. Those other property owners who receive a "windfall" by the change of plans tend to be less vocal.

This creates a dilemma for planning. If it extends its time horizon far into the future, uncertainty and consequently the need for subsequent change of plans increase exponentially. If it postpones all long-term decisions and plans only for the area to be developed in the near future, it jeopardizes its coordination with the following phases of development; for example, there will be nothing to guide the determination of both the capacity and the location of water, sewer, road, or transit trunk lines, which will have to be extended in the following period.

A second, even more serious dilemma is posed by the question of the amount of land to be made available for development at any given point in time. In the interest of creating a buyer's market with wide choice and low prices, the amount should be far in excess of anticipated demand. However, this inevitably leads to scatteration, which adds greatly to the total capital and operating costs of the community. If, in order to prevent scatteration, the amount is limited to the anticipated demand, the owners of this limited amount of land available for development can and do collect a monopolistic or oligopolistic rent (or price), in addition to the "normal" differential rent which would occur in an unrestricted market.

Most Canadian municipalities have opted for avoidance of scatteration by severe limitation of subdivision approvals and of extension of services. The resultant oligopolistic, high land prices are usually blamed on speculators and large-scale developers who, because they must assemble land well in advance of development, cannot avoid being speculators. While speculators certainly pocket this "unearned increment," they cannot create it. It is created by municipal policies.

The dilemma of choosing between a buyer's market with scatteration and the prevention of scatteration with consequent oligopolistic land prices, and the dilemma of choosing between long-range planning with consequent rigidity and "leaving all options open" with consequent lack of coordination between phases of development, are both expressions of the inherent contradiction between unified planning and divided landownership. A large landowner, who plans the development of his or her own estate, is not faced with them. In the case of an area as large and diversified as an urban region, obviously such an owner could only be the government. Indeed, the potential benefits of planning can be fully realized only under conditions of public ownership of all land.

PUBLIC LANDOWNERSHIP

Universal public landownership is not a practical option at this time. What is presently under consideration is public acquisition of some areas as "land banks" for future urban development.

Two objectives are being pursued by consideration of land banks: recapture for the community of the increase in land values which has been created by the community, and cheaper land for the user. The two are obviously mutually exclusive.

A third and important advantage is the possibility of comprehensive planning of a large land-bank area. Private developers, who succeed in assembling comparable large areas, can and often do develop them according to comprehensive plans, often of high quality. However, a private developer faces considerable difficulties in assembling a suitable contiguous large area.

A public agency, provided it has powers of expropriation, could considerably shorten and simplify the process of land assembly and deal effectively with "holdouts." In any case—with or without powers of expropriation—it would have the advantage of being able to borrow money at a lower interest rate than can the private developer. Also, a public authority would not be faced with the risk that another public authority would refuse or long delay the extension of services and the regularity measures required before development can start (although this has happened in the case of the federal-provinical land assembly at Malvern in the borough of Scarborough, in Metropolitan Toronto).

For the foregoing reasons a public authority should be able to produce a building lot at somewhat lower *cost* than can a private developer. (The question of *price* will be discussed shortly.) However, this might not be the case if the public authority had to purchase land at a higher price than does the private developer. The developer typically assembles his land secretly through middlemen, well before development is considered to be imminent. The same tactic was used recently by the Ontario Housing Corporation to assemble land in Waterloo County which, according to the known intentions of the county, was not to be developed in the near future. In view of the rising demand for public involvement in planning from the very start of studies however, this precedent can hardly be followed. In many cases the decision to acquire a specific area as "land-bank land" will be taken only as a result of years of public discussion. By that time the price will have been raised substantially by speculative purchases made during the period of public discussion. Therefore the final cost of a lot to the authority may be fairly high.

As noted earlier, the price is not necessarily identical with the cost. If the authority, under conditions which limit the total supply in the interest of preventing scatteration, offers its land for sale or lease by competitive bidding, competition is likely to bid the price up to the current oligopolistic level. If the authority offers land at cost, demand is likely to exceed supply and a problem of allocation arises. It might be possible to reduce the demand to the level of supply by imposing on the buyer, or lessor, the obligation to complete building within a short period, say 2 or 3 years. This would exclude developers who use their skills in subdivision development to create attractive sites for sale or lease to builders. The function of subdivision development would have to be taken over entirely by public authority, with grave danger of bureaucratic uniformity and mediocrity.

If lots were sold, the authority would have to retain the right of repurchase in case of sale, at the original price, with adjustment for reduced purchasing power of the dollar. Even so, it should not be overlooked that by selling (or leasing) at cost the authority would pay a very substantial indirect subsidy to the buyer (or lessor) by foregoing the difference between cost and market price (the "opportunity cost"). The beneficiaries would not be people in the lower income group who cannot afford a new house, even at reduced land prices. The benefits would be greatest for the wealthiest, who would buy or lease the lots which, because of size or location, would command the highest prices.

Therefore a good case can be made for selling or leasing public land at market prices. The increment in land values would then fully accrue to the community which created it. The community then could—and should—use this profit to reduce the housing expenses of low-income families. The benefits of the land-bank policy would accrue to those most in need. Admittedly, a policy of disposing of land-bank land at market prices or rents would not accomplish one objective which is usually high on the list of the anticipated benefits of land banks: it would not reduce, by underselling, the prices charged by private sellers of land, would not "squeeze out" their unearned increment. However, there may be other means to achieve this objective. One, which has frequently been proposed, is a capital gains tax on land sales (over and above the general capital gains tax which is now being levied by the government of Canada).

Such a tax will certainly deter speculators from buying. However, experience indicates that it also deters landowners as well as speculators from selling. It is a rather double-edged measure. More promising is a radical reform of the "real property" tax.

THE EFFECT OF THE "REAL PROPERTY" TAX ON HOUSING COST

The "real property" tax is a combination of two taxes on two values of entirely different character and origin. Buildings or "improvements" are man-made commodities. Their value is determined by their cost of production. A tax on their value can and indeed must be passed on to the consumer. In the case of industrial and commercial properties it is passed on in the price of goods and services sold by their owners. In the case of residential properties it is passed on to the occupant as part of the price or rent; it functions as a sales tax on housing, raising its cost.

This tax is very substantial; it accounts, on the average, for about 15% of the cost of housing. It is a well-established fact, known as "Engel's Law," that the proportion of disposable income spent for housing is inversely correlated with the size of household income. In Canada at present the highest income group spends about one tenth of its income on housing; the lowest, about one third. The portion of the real property tax derived from residential structures is the most regressive tax in existence.

Removal of this tax would be of greater benefit to low-income groups than any other measure presently under consideration. It would greatly expand the market for housing and stimulate residential construction. However, as new construction accounts for only a small percentage of the total housing stock—and could not be doubled from one year to the next without inducing a skyrocketing of construction costs—this beneficial effect would be achieved only in the long term. The immediate result would be an enormous windfall to the owners of existing buildings. Removal of the tax on improvements should therefore be undertaken gradually, over a period of 10, 15, or 20 years.

The tax on land is of an entirely different nature. As noted earlier, the value of a piece of land is the capitalization of the rent which it is expected to yield, discounted to the present. The tax on land claims a certain percentage of this rent for the community, which has created it. At present this percentage probably amounts to about 20% of the land rent. The value of the land is the capitalization of the remaining 80% of the rent, which accrues to the landowner.

If the rate of the land tax were doubled, 40% of the rent would accrue to the taxing authority and 60% to the landowner, whose share of the rent and its capitalized form the land value, would be reduced by one quarter. This would reduce the sales price to the buyer, but not his or her annual cost. The buyer would still pay the same land rent, only its form would have changed, *pro tanto*, from mortgage interest to tax. As noted earlier, the "unearned increment" can be transferred from the seller of land either to the community or to the buyer, but not to both; their claims are mutually exclusive. There could, of course, be some compromise division of the spoils.

Theoretically, it would be possible to raise the share of the taxing authority to 100% of the land rent. In this case the owner's title would become purely ceremonial, much in the way that the title "the Queen of Canada" has become ceremonial, as actual sovereignty has been gradually assumed by Parliament.

There could be little objection to this—or, indeed, to outright expropriation without compensation—if land were owned by the persons who originally occupied it "free" or for nominal payment, or their descendants. But, ever since the white man came to Canada, land has been bought and sold as a commodity, being exchanged against values created by the labor or capital of their owners. It would therefore violate basic principles of equity to deny the present owners the rights to compensation to which owners of other forms of property are entitled. However, there can be no such objection against a gradual shift of the property tax from improvements to land. True, such a shift would not affect all owners of "real property" in the same way; some would gain, some would lose—but this is equally true of the impact of many other public policies. Sample studies indicate that, on the average, owners of single-family houses would break even; the main losers would be the owners of vacant or semivacant land. Holding such land for later sale at a higher profit would be very expensive.

This would strongly deter speculators from buying and put increased pressure on them and other landowners to sell, resulting in an increased supply of land, at lower prices, for building. It would eliminate, or at least substantially weaken, the pressure for "leapfrogging" or scatteration. Finally, it would greatly reduce both the cost and the difficulties of public land assembly.

It is sometimes objected that an increase in the tax on land might be passed on to the consumer, as is the tax on products. However, unlike a product, each site is specific and nonreplicable; for example, a factory located on expensive land cannot add its land tax to the price of its own products, because competitors located on cheaper land would undersell it. The same relation exists between the rents of apartments in central and in peripheral locations. Suppose the increase in the land tax per apartment amounts to $200 for the former and $20 for the latter. The owner of the former cannot increase the monthly rent by $15 more than does his or her suburban competitor.

Experience in countries which tax land, but not improvements, such as New Zealand and most Australian provinces, shows that a greater percentage of families can afford to buy new houses there than can in Canada, and that their urban and suburban areas are interspersed with far fewer vacant and underdeveloped lots.

Provided that limitations imposed by zoning are adequate, the pressure for more intensive development exercised by high land taxes is entirely beneficial. When it is considered in the public interest, for social or environmental reasons, to continue some less intensive use, special arrangements can be made. This applies in particular, though not exclusively, to farmland. As long as such land continued to be used for farming, it would pay only a tax on its value as farmland. But if it had a higher market value because of expectations of future urban development, the tax for this "development value" would also be carried on the books and would be collected, with accrued interest, if and when such development occurred.

It is likely that in some cases the amount of these deferred taxes would equal or exceed the price which the land could obtain on the market if it was sold for urban development. In such cases the owner would refuse to sell for conversion to urban use, even if such conversion was deemed to be in the public interest. The answer in such cases would be compulsory purchase of the land as an addition to the land bank.

SUMMARY

It is recommended that land suitable for urban development be acquired by public authority as a "land bank," and that simultaneously a gradual shift of the real property tax from improvements to land be instituted. The first of these measures would permit more effective comprehensive planning, and capture future increases in land value for the community. The second measure would do the following:

1. Capture a substantial part of both past and future increase in land value.
2. Substantially increase the supply and reduce the cost of housing.
3. Substantially reduce the cost and difficulty of assembling land-bank land.

Chapter 24

GROWTH RATE COMPARISONS: THE SOVIET UNION AND GERMAN DEMOCRATIC REPUBLIC[1]

Practically all governments, whether they have a free-market or a centrally planned economy, whether their countries are developed or developing, uniformly proclaim the same goals for the distribution of urban development. All consider it desirable to reduce the differences between their various regions, implying a higher rate of growth in the less developed and urbanized regions than in those which are more highly industrialized. In particular, they all aim at limiting or at least slowing down the growth of their largest urban agglomerations.

Regardless of the validity of these goals, there is no doubt that in practically all Western countries, including the developing ones, actual development tends to go in the opposite direction. In particular, the largest urban areas have an ever larger proportion of the nation's population. It is therefore of interest to look at actual developments in eastern Europe with respect to the achievement of these same goals; in particular, I shall present census data and some analysis for two of them, the Soviet Union (hereinafter referred to as the U.S.S.R.) and the German Democratic Republic (hereinafter referred to as the G.D.R.).

CONTRASTS

These two countries represent opposite poles within the Eastern block. The U.S.S.R. is by far the largest and the least densely populated, the G.D.R. one of the smallest and the most densely populated, country in this group. Even more significant is the difference in the level of development at which they started when they embarked on

---

Source: Land Economics (University of Wisconsin, Madison, Wis.), May 1973.
[1]The following sources were used in developing the research in this study: S. Soulkevich, *Populations U.S.S.R.* (in Russian), State Publishers of Political Literature, OGIS, Moscow, 1939; *National Economy U.S.S.R. 1958 Statistical Yearbook* (in Russian), State Statistical Publishers, Moscow, 1959, also for 1969 and 1970; *Statistical Yearbook of the German Democratic Republic, 1965* (in German), Staatsverlag der Deutschen Demokratischen Republik, East Berlin, 1965, also for 1970.

Table 1. Comparative Data on Union of Socialist Soviet Republics, German Democratic Republic, and German Federal Republic: 1969, except where otherwise indicated

Item	U.S.S.R.	G.D.R.	G.F.R.
Square miles (1000)	8500	41	95
Population (million): 1970	242	17	58
Employed as percent of population	48	48	43
Population per square mile: 1970	28	415	620
Women as percent of labor force	50	47	36
Percent of labor force in agriculture[a]	29	13	11
Percent of labor force in industry[b]	36	49	48
Agricultural land as percent of area	15	61	59
Cropland as percent of area	10	48	36
Persons in agriculture per square mile of agricultural land	36	44	47
Kilowatt-hours per capita	2864	3884	3763

[a]Includes forestry, fishing, and hunting.
[b]Includes construction, mining, and handicraft.

a centrally planned economy based on public ownership of the main means of production. The G.D.R. was in 1949 more highly industrialized than any other country of the group, while the U.S.S.R. in 1927 was less developed than any other eastern European country—with the possible exception of Albania—at the time they established their present system.

I chose the year 1927 rather than 1917 for the U.S.S.R. This is the first year for which census data are available. (Actually the census was held in December 1926 and is officially known as the census of 1926. I refer to it as "1927" in the interests of comparability with the censuses of January 1939, 1959, and 1970.) The years 1921–1927 had in the main been devoted to repairing the devastation of the preceding 7 years of war; 1927 was the first year in which a national plan was in operation.

Comparative data characterizing the U.S.S.R. and G.D.R. in 1969 are presented in Table 1. The territory of the U.S.S.R. is more than 200 times as large as that of the G.D.R., but the population was only 14 times greater in 1970. Consequently, population density in the G.D.R. was almost 15 times that in the U.S.S.R.

CHARACTERISTICS OF THE G.D.R.

At the time of the establishment of the post-World War II occupation zones in Germany, a remark made the rounds in the United States: "The Russians got the agriculture, the British got the industry, and we got the scenery." The mistaken notion of the Russian zone as agricultural rests on its erroneous identification with the six "East Elbian" provinces of the former kingdom of Prussia. However, these six

Table 2. Population Changes (Approximate) in German Democratic Republic: 1939–1970 (millions)

Population: 1939	16.75
Number of these remaining in 1946	15.25
Gross in-migration: 1939–1946	4.00
Population: 1946	19.25
Net out-migration: 1946–1970	−3.25
Natural increase: 1946–1970	1.08
Population: 1970	17.08

provinces now are wholly or partly Polish territory. The territory of the G.D.R. was previously regarded, in the main, as "Mitteldeutschland" (Central Germany). It covers slightly less than one third of postwar Germany. In Germany a historical west-to-east slope in prosperity has given rise to east-west migration that has gone on for over a century and is still continuing within the German Federal Republic. However, at the war's end, the East—if Berlin is included—had practically the same population density as the West. This has since changed as a result of four factors: net out-migration of over 3 million from the G.D.R., net in-migration of about 5 million to the German Federal Republic (hereinafter referred to as the G.F.R.), separation of West Berlin from the East, and a slightly higher rate of natural increase in the West.

As a result of these changes, the G.D.R. now contains less than one quarter of the total population of Germany, at a density 30% lower than exists in the G.F.R. (Table 1). However, the economic structures of the two German states are strikingly similar. In both of them about 60% of the area is agricultural, though in the G.D.R. about one third more is devoted to crops and one third less to pasture. Employment in agriculture is somewhat higher in the G.D.R. as a percentage of the total labor force, but slightly lower in relation to agricultural land; average yields per acre and per unit of livestock also are very similar. The percentage of the labor force employed in industry and the kilowatt-hours per capita are nominally higher in the G.D.R.

The population of the G.D.R. was 2% higher in 1970 than in 1939. However, the enormous out-migration of the first 16 postwar years, consisting predominantly of people of working age, with a preponderance of males, superimposed on the effect of two world wars, resulted in the abnormally low sex ratio of 85; for the age groups 40 and over (corresponding to 15 and over in 1945), it was 65! The U.S.S.R. in 1970 also had a sex ratio of 85. This, as much as the different social structure and ideology, is probably the reason for the extraordinarily high representation of women in the labor force in both these countries.

CHARACTERISTICS OF THE U.S.S.R.

In contrast to the area of the G.D.R. in 1939 as well as in 1949, at the time of the creation of the republic, the area of the U.S.S.R. in 1913, and even more so in 1920 and in 1927, was a vast, underdeveloped peasant country. Its rise since that time to the rank of the world's second industrial power does not require recounting.

Politically, the U.S.S.R. is a union of 15 republics. The Russian Federal Republic, which in itself contains a number of national "autonomous" republics, is by far the largest, with over three quarters of its area, but only 31% of its population, in Asia. The next most populous republics, the Ukraine and Byelorussia, are in Europe; since World War II the three Baltic republics and Moldavia have been added. The remaining eight republics are in Asia. Three of these—Armenia, Gruzia (Georgia), and Azerbeidjan—are in the Transcaucasus; the remaining five, in Central Asia.

REGIONAL POPULATION DISTRIBUTION AND CITY SIZE

Like their predecessors, the utopian Socialists, and their contemporaries, the Victorian reformers, Marx and Engels regarded the separation of city and country as one of the greatest evils of industrial capitalism; socialism was to do away with the slums and the pollution of air, water, and soil characteristic of the big cities. Their writings leave little doubt that they envisioned small agroindustrial towns spread over the entire national territory. The Soviet leadership fully shared this attitude. Shortly after the revolution it established a "Commission for the Unburdening of the Capitals (Petrograd and Moscow)," which was still in existence in the 1930s. Soviet city planning theory has regarded 250,000–350,000 as the optimal city size, and population limits have been established for every city.

The goals of regional planning are formulated in a textbook published by the Soviet Academy of Science as follows: "economy of social labor, comprehensive development of regions, and specialization of their production, elimination of excessive concentration of population in big cities, overcoming basic differences between city and country and equalization of the level of the economic development of the various regions of the country."[2] The West German author of the review from which this quotation has been taken remarked that these goals would be acceptable to any Western government. He also noted that one goal, always mentioned in prewar publications, is missing: the strategic goal of developing industries in the interior, removed from the threatened western boundaries. Equally notable is the omission of another goal of earlier statements: to raise the minority nationalities to the level of the Russians. Actually both of these goals pointed in the same direction as the remaining ones: to a shift from the developed western to the underdeveloped eastern and southern parts of the country.

In the G.D.R. there appears to have been much less ideological discussion of these questions, but the goals have been the same. The city planner of East Berlin told this writer that he neither expects nor plans for any growth beyond the present population level of slightly over 1 million. How far have these goals been realized in these two countries?

DEVELOPMENT IN THE G.D.R.

Regions

The G.D.R. contains the former states of Saxony and Thuringia in the South and Mecklenburg in the North, separated by the former Prussian provinces of Saxony and

[2]Helmut Lehmann, "Notes on Distributions of Locations and Large Regions in Soviet Russia" (in German), *Informationen*, Institut fur Raumordnung, April 16, 1968, pp. 201–214.

Table 3. Populations of Five Major Regions of the German Democratic Republic: 1939, 1970[a]

Region	Area (square kilometers)	Population (1000) 1939	Population (1000) 1970	Change (%) 1939–70	Persons per Square Kilometer 1939	Persons per Square Kilometer 1970
East Berlin	403	1,588	1,084	−31.8	3950	2690
1. Southeast	26,480	7,415	7,362	− 0.7	280	278
2. Southwest	26,740	3,652	3,867	5.9	137	145
3. Center	27,950	2,518	2,668	6.0	90	96
4. North	26,670	1,572	2,094	33.3	59	78
G.D.R.	108,243	16,725	17,075	2.1	155	158

[a] Districts (Bezirke) in four regions: 1. Karl-Marx-Stadt, Leipzig, Dresden, Halle (4); 2. Gera, Erfurt, Suhl, Magdeburg (4); 3. Cottbus, Frankfurt, a.O., Potsdam (3); 4. Rostock, Schwerin, Neubrandenburg (3).

Brandenburg, exclusive of West Berlin and a part of Brandenburg east of the Oder, as well as small areas of the former provinces of Pomerania and Silesia, now in Poland. Subsequently the G.D.R. incorporated the Eastern Sector of Berlin as its capital and reorganized the balance of its territory into 14 districts, each named after its administrative center. As far as I know, the G.D.R. is the only country which thus has given official recognition to the fact that developed countries function as composites of city-centered regions.

The G.D.R. is characterized by a strong south-to-north slope in terms of population density, industrialization, and urbanization. For the purpose of this discussion I have grouped the 14 districts into four regions of almost equal size (Table 3). The Southeast, covering the eastern part of former Saxony Province (District Halle) and all of Saxony State, is the industrial heartland of the G.D.R., accounting in 1969 for 43% of its population and for 51.5% of its gross industrial product. The Southwest, including the western part of Saxony Province (District Magdeburg) and all of Thuringia, is less densely populated, but still contains almost 25% of the republic's population.

In sharp contrast to Saxony, which was the most densely populated state of prewar Germany, Mecklenburg (North Region) was its least populated and most agrarian state. It contained only one city with a population over 100,000, Rostock (122,867 in 1939). Rostock has now grown to about 200,000 as the G.D.R.'s only major port city.

The Central Region, corresponding in the main to the former Prussian province of Brandenburg, is intermediate between North and South in terms of development. Apart from Berlin it contained only one city over 100,000, Potsdam. The republic's eight other cities over 100,000 are all in the South. The two with over 0.5 million, and two of the three with 0.25–0.5 million, are in the Southeast Region.

There was a considerable shift in population distribution between 1939 and 1970 (see Table 3). East Berlin lost almost one third of its prewar population, the Southeast decreased nominally, the Central and Southwest Regions grew moderately, while the North grew by one third. In 1939 its population was nominally lower than that of East

Table 4. Rate of Change of Population and of Gross Industrial Product: 1964–1970, and of Retail Sales, 1955–1969; Square Meters of Housing Built: 1969

Region[a]	Change (%)			Housing per 1000 Population Built during 1969 (square meters)
	1964–69		1955–69	
	Population	Gross Ind. Product	Retail Sales	
East Berlin	1.22	16.5	62	253
1. Southeast	−0.71	31.7	90	183
2. Southwest	0.34	32.5	99	233
3. Center	2.28	75.5	116	291
4. North	1.80	51.5	111	313
G.D.R.	0.37	36.4	95	232

[a]See footnote to Table 3.

Berlin; in 1970 it was almost twice as high. In part, this spectacular shift was certainly due to the influx of war and postwar refugees to rural areas, as well as to higher birth rates, but some of it appeared to be the result of deliberate policy. New industries have been established in the North and, more recently, in the previously least developed section of the Central Region along the Oder River.

As Table 4 indicates, regional equalization is continuing, though at a moderate pace. Between 1964 and 1969 the Southeast actually lost population, the Southwest remained practically stable, and the Central and North Regions increased. There was also a slight increase in Berlin. The amount of housing built in 1969, as well as the changes in gross industrial product and in retail sales in the preceding years, probably is the cause as well as the effect of these population changes. The relatively slow growth of retail sales in Berlin may indicate equalization between capital and provinces, either in purchasing power or in the available assortment of retail goods—probably in both. On the whole, the policy aimed at reducing regional differences appears to have succeeded.

City Size

The changes are even more dramatic when the development of cities of different sizes is compared (Table 5a). As already noted, the principal city, East Berlin, lost 31.4% of its prewar population. The losses of the two cities in the 0.5- to 1-million group and of the three in the following group were progressively smaller. At the other extreme, the population of the smallest municipalities, with less than 5000 population, declined nominally. Growth was entirely concentrated in the 5 (out of 10) intermediate groups, with a peak growth of more than one third in the 20,000–50,000 group, about 15% in the next larger and smaller ones, and about 10% in the two following groups. Indeed, by far the largest proportion of the urban population (in places over 5000) is found in the 20,000–50,000 group. It is interesting to note that this was regarded as the "ideal" size by the original British "new town"

Table 5a. Population of Municipalities in Various Size Groups, German Democratic Republic: 1939, 1964, and 1969

Size Group	Population (1000)			Population as Percent of Total		
	1939	1964	1969	1939	1964	1969
Over 1,000,000	1,588	1,071	1,084	9.5	6.3	6.4
500,000–1,000,000	1,337	1,099	1,087	8.0	6.5	6.4
200,000– 500,000	895	833	857	5.3	4.9	5.0
100,000– 200,000	654	826	854	3.9	4.9	5.0
50,000– 100,000	904	915	998	5.4	5.2	5.8
20,000– 50,000	1,887	2,506	2,583	11.3	14.8	15.1
10,000– 20,000	1,360	1,560	1,580	8.1	9.2	9.3
5,000– 10,000	1,419	1,559	1,508	8.5	9.2	8.8
3,000– 5,000	1,116	1,071	1,094	6.7	6.4	6.3
Under 3,000	5,581	5,549	5,453	33.3	32.6	31.9
Total	16,741	16,989	17,098	100.0	100.0	100.0

advocates. Altogether, the towns with a population between 5000 and 50,000 contain three out of five urban dwellers, one third of the total population.

Perhaps even more remarkable is the fact that well over half (56.3%) of the entire population continues to live in areas of less than 20,000 inhabitants, which in many statistics are classified as rural. With only 13.5% of the labor force employed in agriculture, however, it is evident that these small areas are predominantly industrial. It appears that the G.D.R. has been eminently successful in decentralizing industry.

Comparison between populations found in different size groups at various points in time, while significant in itself, may be misleading as to the growth rates of cities of different size, because cities, as they grow, move from one size group into another; for example, between 1939 and 1969 the number of G.D.R. towns in the 20,000–50,000 group increased from 59 to 81. Therefore Table 5b presents the subsequent population change in municipalities which belonged to a given size group in 1939.

Table 5b. Population of Municipalities Which Were in a Given Size Group in 1939: 1939, 1964 and 1969

Size Group (1000)	Population (1000)			Distribution (%)			Change (%)		
	1939	1964	1969	1939	1964	1969	1939–64	1964–69	1939–69
Over 200[a]	3,820	3,003	3,017	22.8	17.6	17.6	−21.4	0.5	−21.0
100–200	654	697	718	3.9	4.1	4.2	6.6	3.0	9.9
50–100	904	974	1,056	5.4	5.7	6.2	7.7	8.4	16.8
20– 50	1,887	2,200	2,307	11.3	12.9	13.4	16.6	4.9	22.2
Under 20	9,745	10,138	9,977	56.6	59.7	58.6	4.0	−1.6	2.4
Total	17,010	17,012	17,075	100.0	100.0	100.0	0.01	0.37	0.38

[a]Figures for the three groups over 200,000 are identical with those given in Table 5a.

The table confirms the concentration of growth in the 20,000–50,000 group, with a recent slight shift to the next larger group, 50,000–100,000, and the decreased role of the larger cities, those with an initial population of over 200,000. While their total population in 1939 exceeded that of the smaller (20,000–200,000) cities by 10.7%, in 1969 it was 25.8% lower.

DEVELOPMENT IN THE U.S.S.R.

Regions

In the U.S.S.R. there has been a remarkable development in the Asian republics, reflected in a far higher population growth than in the balance of the country (Table 6). In the prewar period the growth was particularly strong in the Transcaucasus, since 1939 in the formerly least developed part of the country, central Asia. For the period 1939–1959 this growth was partly due to wartime relocation. For the later period it is largely, but not entirely, due to differences in the birth rates, which have increasingly diverged in recent years. In 1969 the number of births per 1000 inhabitants averaged 29.3 in central Asia and 24.0 in the Transcaucasus, while in the Russian Federal Republic it was 14.2, almost the lowest in the world.

Siberia (including the Urals), which had developed rapidly during the prewar and war years, during the last 11 years had a growth rate, surprisingly, slightly lower than that of the European part of the Russian Republic, 10.3% versus 10.8%. It is also remarkable that both in European Russia and in the Ukraine the southernmost regions had a growth rate well above the average, as had the southernmost of the five smaller European republics, Moldavia. The net result has been a substantial southward shift of the population of the U.S.S.R. A shift of this magnitude had been neither planned nor foreseen by the government. It seems that even in a centrally planned economy the locational preferences of individuals have a substantial impact.

City Size

The total population of urban areas in the Soviet Union increased from 26.3 million (17.9%) in 1927 to 136.0 million (56.2%) in 1970. A comparison of the number of

Table 6. Percentage Growth of Population of Five Asian Republics, Three Transcaucasian Republics, and Balance of U.S.S.R.: 1927–1939, 1939–1959, and 1959–1970[a]

Region	Population 1970 (millions)	Growth (%)		
		1927–39	1939–59	1959–70
Five Asian republics	32.8	24.0	35.6	42.8
Three Transcaucasian republics	12.3	36.9	18.6	28.2
Balance of U.S.S.R.	196.6	14.1	6.4	11.5
Total U.S.S.R.	241.7	16.1	10.8	15.7

[a] Figures for 1927–1939 refer to the prewar territory, those for 1939–1959 and 1959–1970 to the postwar territory, of the U.S.S.R.

Table 7. Number of Urban Places in Different Population Size Groups, U.S.S.R.: 1927, 1939, 1959, and 1970[a]

Size Group (1000)	Year				
	1927	1939	1939	1959	1970
Over 1000	2	2	2	3	10
500–1000	1	9	9	21	23
200– 500	9	16	19	32	74
100– 200	21	55	59	91	114
50– 100	60	94	99	151	188
20– 50	135	288	315	481	599
10– 20	253	466	501	807	920
5– 10	378	672	757	1285	1430
Under 5	1066	771	998	1733	2146
Total	1925	2373	2759	4608	5504

[a] The first two columns refer to territory of the U.S.S.R. in 1927; the last three, to present territory. Of the 5504 urban places enumerated in 1970 about 65% were listed not as cities, but as urban-type settlements. These places, with populations generally under 20,000, contained 14.5% of the urban population.

urban areas in nine different size groups in 1927, 1939, 1959, and 1970 is presented in Table 7; populations for the same years and size groups are given in Table 8.

In 1927 Moscow had just over 2 million inhabitants, while Leningrad had dropped from its prerevolutionary 2.25 to 1.7 million. Kiev was the only city which had barely passed the 0.5-million mark, and became the only one to pass 1-million mark in 1959. In 1970 there were 10 cities with a population over 1 million. However, their

Table 8. Population of Urban Places in Different Size Groups[a]

Size Group	Population (millions)				Percent of Total Urban Population			
	1927	1939	1959	1970	1927	1939	1959	1970
Over 1000	3.7	7.6	9.0	20.9	14.1	13.5	9.0	15.3
500–1000	0.5	5.2	15.2	16.4	1.9	9.3	15.2	12.0
100– 500	5.3	14.2	24.4	38.3	20.1	25.4	24.4	28.2
50– 100	4.1	6.8	11.0	13.0	15.6	12.2	11.0	9.6
20– 50	4.0	8.7	14.8	18.5	15.2	15.5	14.8	13.6
10– 20	3.5	6.5	11.2	12.7	13.3	11.5	11.2	9.4
5– 10	2.7	4.7	9.2	10.0	10.3	8.3	9.2	7.3
Under 5	2.5	2.4	5.2	6.2	9.5	4.3	5.2	4.6
Total Urban	26.3	56.1	100.0	136.0	100.0	100.0	100.0	100.0

[a] City populations in 1939 are given for postwar territory of the U.S.S.R.; those in 1959, for the 1970 city areas of Moscow and Leningrad.

population accounted for only a slightly larger share of total urban population than did the two cities with over 1 million in 1927. The size group between 100,000 and 500,000, which includes the size group preferred by Soviet planners, emerges strongly as the modal group, with 27.3% of the entire urban population, equal to that of the 33 cities with more than 0.5 million population.

It is remarkable that the towns which in 1927 either had a population under 100,000 or did not yet exist increased faster than did the 33 cities which had populations over 100,000 in 1927. While these 33 large cities accounted for 38% of the urban population in 1927, they contained only 26% of the urban population in 1970. (City boundaries are regularly extended in the U.S.S.R.; the figures therefore correspond roughly to those given by the U.S. Census for metropolitan areas.) The larger the initial city size, the lower the growth rate and consequently the share of total urban population. The process is continuing, but is slowing down. While the share of the 30 cities with over 200,000 population in 1939 dropped from 37.6 to 27.8% in the succeeding 20 years, the share of the 24 cities with over 0.5 million in 1959 dropped in the next 11 years only from 25.3 to 23.9%.

In 1970 Moscow accounted for only 5.2% of urban and 2.9% of national population, much smaller percentages than are to be found in the principal cities of most countries. However, the *relative* size and growth rate of Moscow should not obscure the fact that its *absolute* growth was a very substantial 5 million, or almost 250% in 43 years. The original goal of reducing or at least stabilizing its population has certainly not been achieved. As late as 1930 it was widely believed that its population could be held slightly more than 2 million. Five years later, the Moscow plan of 1935 established a limit of 5 million. In 1959 the chief planner of Moscow told me he still expected not to exceed that limit by more than a nominal amount and gave a detailed, reasoned enumeration of the measures designed to prevent further growth. However, at present the population of Moscow has already exceeded 7 million. Similarly, in 1959 the Kiev planners gave 1.3 million as their limit; in 1970 this limit had already been exceeded by more than one quarter. Even Leningrad, which between 1917 and 1921 lost almost half of its population and practically all components of its economic base, had recovered half of its loss by 1926 and, despite a second loss of almost 1 million people in World War II, had in 1970 far surpassed its prewar size.

The Soviet experience shows once more the extraordinary vitality and momentum of large urban centers. It confirms that any attempt to set a fixed limit to growth is unrealistic and cannot be achieved even by a government which disposes such powerful means of control as does the Soviet government. On the other hand, the goal of decentralizing urban development, consistently pursued for half a century, has been achieved to a surprising degree. However, in recent years this goal is being questioned by Soviet economists who claim that productivity in the cities of over 1 million is over one third higher than in those of 100,000–250,000 population.

COMPARISONS WITH OTHER COUNTRIES

In Moscow, which is both the principal city and the seat of the national government, the small percentages of both the national and the urban population, 2.9% and 5.2%, respectively, contrast sharply with the situation in the United States, where the combined population of the New York and Washington Metropolitan Areas accounts for about 8% and 11%, respectively, of total and of urban population. The same difference is also found in smaller countries. The relatively low (6.4%) concentration of the population of the G.D.R. in East Berlin is characteristic also of the seven other Communist-controlled European countries, in all of which the national capital is also the principal city and the main industrial center. For these countries the unweighted average of the national population living in the capital in 1968 was 7.24%. In comparison, the principal cities of western Europe generally account for 10–20% of the national population. Even greater is the contrast with the developing countries, where the share of the principal city not only of the national, but also of the urban population is constantly increasing, with the latter share sometimes exceeding 50%.

Considering that in eastern European countries (except Yugoslavia) the entire economic and cultural life of the nation is managed by a huge central bureaucracy, the relatively small populations of their capitals are surprising. It seems that the sum total of persons performing the same functions in market-economy countries is even greater. However, investigation of this question would far exceed the limits of this study.

No less remarkable is the success of the G.D.R. and of the U.S.S.R. in achieving greater regional equalization, compared to the rather limited results of similar attempts in market-economy countries. Even the success of the United Kingdom in attracting 1 million people to its government-built new "satellite" towns has not slowed down, and may even have accelerated, the growing concentration of the British population in the Southeast and Midlands.

The fact that the decentralization policies of the G.D.R. and the U.S.S.R. have been successful does not necessarily prove that they were wise. The estimates of higher productivity in the largest metropolitan areas are paralleled by similar estimates in Sweden. It may well be that the Communist countries are paying a high price, in terms of their gross national product, for decentralization.

CONCLUSIONS

Most governments favor decentralization. However, its advocates desire two different types of decentralization—population and decision-making—without clearly distinguishing between the two. Our study indicates that only highly centralized decision-making can bring about spatial decentralization of population and activities. Decentralized decision-making, characteristic of the United States and generally of market economies, inevitably leads to centralization of population in large metropolitan areas, in particular in the principal city. This is not difficult to understand. The individual decision-maker can locate his enterprise only where there is access to the many other enterprises and institutions on which he is dependent in a complex society, characterized by increasing specialization and interdependence. Only a very strong decision-making center, normally a national government, can create simultaneously, or at least in a scheduled sequence, the many different elements, including those of the urban infrastructure, which are required to make a city or a region viable and self-sustaining. Also, in general, only such a strong center is able and willing to carry the required large capital investments over a lengthy period, until the addition of all other elements makes them fully productive.

This conclusion is confirmed by the experience of the few market-economy countries which have achieved a modicum of success in decentralizing their populations. The Netherlands has succeeded in slowing down the growth of the Randstad to slightly below the national growth rate by consistently, over a quarter of a century, using a portion of the national budget to subsidize both infrastructure and private enterprise in the relatively undeveloped northeastern provinces. The government of Israel has channeled its immigrants into new and enlarged small towns, providing them with employment in the production of housing, urban infrastructure, and factories. It has thereby increased the proportion of its population living outside its three large cities. However, many of these towns, especially the smaller ones, have high unemployment, and many of their inhabitants have migrated to larger towns, in particular to the principal city, Tel-Aviv. These experiences confirm the lesson to be learned from the development in the U.S.S.R. and the G.D.R. concerning the dialectical relation between centralization of decision-making and centralization of location.

Despite the relative success of these decentralization policies, the weight of established regions and cities continues to make itself felt. In the G.D.R. its historical industrial heartland still accounts for more than half of its industrial production. In the U.S.S.R. the big cities continue to grow beyond the planned population limits. The population decrease of the big cities in the G.D.R. is probably due to a confluence of unique circumstances: no growth of national population, heavy war destruction, and easy access to the principal city from all parts of the small country. The fact that East Berlin is again showing some growth indicates that the decrease cannot be interpreted as reflecting a permanent trend.

Basic human aspirations are stronger than laws and edicts. Not only does the Soviet government control the location of industries, but also it has decreed that in Moscow, Leningrad, and Kiev no one can become a resident who does not have a job, and no one can get a job who is not a resident. Still, people continue to come, illegally, semilegally, or legally. If an enterprise in Moscow is far more productive than its counterpart elsewhere, the central government will not prevent it from expanding and from providing both the jobs and the housing required for that expansion.

Perhaps even more telling is the unexpected shift in the population of the U.S.S.R. to the South, which can hardly be explained by anything but the strong desire to live in a milder climate. It appears that ultimately people's aspirations decide the success or failure of land politics, as of land economics.

Chapter 25

COMPETITION BETWEEN URBAN AND AGRICULTURAL LAND USE

The study under review was prompted by well-founded concern about wasteful use of our land resources. It attempts to deal with the important question of the competition for land between agriculture and other uses. The title raises the hope that the authors recognize that the competitors are indeed the growing number and expanding activities of *people, rather than cities*, as trendy media talk would have us believe. The hope is soon betrayed.

Part I, entitled, "Food Preservation," is followed by Part II, "The Expanding City—Devouring the Land." A footnote to the Introduction states, "Curiously enough, for more populous cities, the developed area per capita is less than that for smaller cities, but the extent of the urban shadow is proportionally greater." The only thing curious is the fact that the authors should be surprised by one of the most firmly established facts of urban geography—correlation of city size with density.

There is not a shred of evidence for the second part of the statement, if only because investigations of "urban shadow" have so far been undertaken only in the surroundings of large metropolitan areas. The goal of minimizing the absorption of agricultural land by urban development clearly could best be achieved by concentration of the population in a few large metropolitan areas. This has long been known to serious students of the subject. It is emphatically confirmed by Appendix B of this study. Tables B3 and B4, respectively, show that, for each additional 1000 population, towns of 20,000–50,000 inhabitants absorb 3.67 times as much land as do those with populations over 500,000, and that small towns (2000–5000 acres) absorb 4.44 times as much land as do large (500,000+) ones. But the authors blithely ignore their own data.

Of course, reducing the absorption of agricultural land is not the only aspect to be considered in weighing the pros and cons of various city sizes and of various constellations of cities of different sizes. Exploration of this extremely complex question would be of great value, but certainly was well beyond the terms of

---

Review of Charles Beaubien and Ruth Tabacnik, *Perceptions 4: People and Agricultural Land* (Science Council of Canada, 1977). *Source:* Review published in *Urban Forum/Colloque Urbain*, Vol. 3, No. 5 [Canadian Council on Urban and Regional Research (CCURR), Ottawa, Ont.], January-February 1978. (A rebuttal by C. Beaubien and a final comment by H. Blumenfeld were published with the review.)

reference of this study. However, it could have presented a systematic survey of the amount and types of agricultural land absorbed and likely to be absorbed by each of the major types of nonagricultural uses—residential, recreational, industrial, military, transportation, forestry, wildlife conservation, and proceeded from there to proposals for limiting the absorption of agricultural land by modifying the location and mode of each of these competing uses. Instead, the study presents, apart from some very interesting statistical data, mostly a collection of excerpts and quotations from previously published sources. Many of these are well-known, valuable contributions to the field, but all too many represent emotional journalism.

Many statements included in the study are false or misleading. On p. 28 a British study[1] is quoted in support of the contention that "the space needed to transport people grows exponentially as urban population expands," although a wealth of land use data from Canada and other countries shows a consistent decrease in road space per capita with increase in city size. Page 75 calls Sweden a "country with high population density," although its density is less than one tenth of the global average. Page 99 is entitled "A Developer Denounces Government," although the author quoted, A. Derkowski, is a planning consultant who developed his thesis as a graduate student at the University of Toronto. Pages 114–115 reproduce graphs from a study entitled *The Costs of Sprawl*.[2] This very detailed study, which deals with costs both to the occupant and to the community, found that the difference between "low-density sprawl" and "high density planned" amounted to about $250 in "annual operating and maintenance costs," but to over $36,000 in "capital costs." Inspection of the graph shows that over 70% of this difference derives from differences in the cost of the dwelling unit. As construction cost of a square foot of usable floor space is known to be no higher for single-family houses than for apartments, *The Costs of Sprawl* obviously compares apples with oranges—units of different size. But the study accepts the results at face value.

Page 117, entitled "Overgenerous Standards," compares Canada, with 1062 square feet of floor space in new houses, with some other countries.[3] Although the Canadian value is slightly lower than the 1150 and 1160 square feet given for the United States and Denmark, and only modestly higher than the 774 given for notoriously overcrowded Japan, the study states, "Some nations seem to do with less." This seems to refer primarily to the 405 square feet given for West Germany. That this figure must refer to a different unit of measurement is obvious to any informed reader—but not to the editors of the Science Council study.

These are minor points, but they are indicative of the superficiality of the study, which has led to more basic misconceptions. More than once the study takes issue, rightly, with the complacency with which Canadians treat their natural resources as inexhaustible. Probably most Canadians, if asked about the percentage of our land area usable for agriculture, would estimate it to be higher than the actual 13%, less than half of which is well suited for common field crops. On the other hand, their estimate in absolute terms is likely to be lower than the 294 and 123 million acres, respectively, which are actually available.

Presented in isolation, such figures have little meaning. They become meaningful

---

[1] Janice Tait, "Cities Fit to Live In," *Optimum*, Vol. 7, No. 1, 1976.
[2] Real Estate Corporation of Chicago, *The Costs of Sprawl: Executive Summary*, U.S. Government Printing Office, Washington, D.C., April 1974.
[3] B. Bruce-Biggs, Hudson Institute, Unpublished study, July 1971.

only by relating them to other data, in this case to the availability of agricultural land to the population of the globe or of other nations and, on the other hand, to the amount of land used for other purposes, in particular for urban residence, with which most of the study deals.

Canada's 13% of agricultural land is close to the global average, while the world's population density averages about 14 times ours. The accompanying table presents the amount of agricultural land per head of population in 10 countries.[4]

Country	Agricultural Land (hectares per head of population)
Japan	0.13
United Kingdom	0.32
Federal Republic of Germany	0.33
German Democratic Republic	0.62
France	0.95
U.S.S.R.	2.3
Argentina	2.8
Australia	3.5
United States	4.8
Canada (Science Council data)	5.4
Canada (United Nations data)	6.7

Canadians have more agricultural land at their disposal than any other nation. This certainly is not a justification for wasting it. But this fact might have prompted the Science Council to take a closer look at the ways in which other nations manage their land. More significant is the comparison with urban land use. Canadian metropolitan areas tend to absorb about 1 square mile of land for every 6500 of population,[5] or 1 acre for 10 persons. The figure is identical with the one used by West German planners: 1 square kilometer for every 2500 of population. It refers to land used for *all* urban purposes, including airfields and parks. If the population of the metropolitan areas of Canada should rise to 20 million, it would absorb 2 million acres—less than 1% and 2%, respectively, of agricultural and of crop land.

The many contributors to the study who discuss urban land deal almost exclusively with residential land, which, in fact, accounts for less than half of all urban land. The study is replete with criticism of the conventional suburban development of detached single-family houses on lots of 6000 square feet or more. On the extreme and unrealistic assumption that *all* inhabitants of metropolitan areas lived on lots of 7500 square feet with three persons per house, 20 million metropolitanites would occupy a total of 50 billion square feet, or about 1.15 million acres, 0.40% of all agricultural and 0.93% of all cropland. There are many valid reasons against low-density suburban development, in particular the resultant excessive amount of automobile movement; but absorption of agricultural land is not one of them.

Even more inadequate than the diagnosis is the therapy prescribed to cure the

---

[4]Calculated from data given in U.N. publications. Because of data problems, figures are approximate. The U.N. figure for Canada is for 1966.
[5]Norman D. Lea & Associates, *Urban Transportation Developments in Eleven Canadian Metropolitan Areas*, Canadian Good Roads Association, Ottawa, Ont., 1966.

malady of low densities. Some contributors polemicize against high land prices which, under conditions of private landownership, are the only effective weapon against wasteful use of land—however undesirable their own effects may be. Some of the contributors recognize that the amount of land actually absorbed by urban expansion is minor, showing, for example, that it accounts for only 5% of the land relinquished by agriculture in southern Ontario between 1951 and 1971. These and other contributors put their main emphasis on the effects of "urban shadow."

The important concept of "urban shadow," developed and popularized by Alistair Crerar and Leonard Gertler, has remained somewhat shadowy. It attempts to identify and measure the amount of land adversely affected by the proximity of an urban area. (There has been no corresponding attempt to define "urban light," the favorable effect of the proximity of urban markets and services.) The phenomenon seems to be characteristic of North America; in most European cities highly productive agriculture can be observed immediately adjacent to, sometimes even surrounded by, built-up urban areas. The difference appears to be due to different institutional arrangements. Regrettably these have not been explored by the study.

The "shadow" works in several ways. First, there are adverse physical impacts, such as vandalism or pollution—also reactions of urbanites against agricultural sounds and smells. More important are economic impacts. These have usually been measured in terms of nonfarmer landownership and/or nonfarm land prices. This approach may be quite misleading. As detailed studies by Larry Martin and others have shown in such areas most changes in ownership do not result in changes of land use, and most changes in land use occur without change in ownership. The really disturbing phenomenon is the intrusion of actual nonfarm uses both by occupying farmland and, even more by cutting it up in a way which makes it unusable for large-scale, mechanized field crop farming (though not for small-scale vegetable growing). Some of the contributors to the study recognize that the major threat to farmland stems from the growth not of the "urban," but of the "rural nonfarm" population. This group now accounts for almost three out of four rural inhabitants, even under the extremely narrow census definition of "rural," which limits it to places of less than 1000 inhabitants located outside defined urban and metropolitan areas.

Several incipient developments, notably the 4-day workweek and the improvement of telecommunications, point to an explosive growth of the rural nonfarm population. By adding to the support of services of all kinds, this can be of great benefit to the farm population of rural communities. But this benefit can be realized only if nonfarm uses are restricted to suitably defined areas. This implies the imposition, acceptance, and enforcement of land use controls, comparable to those now grudgingly accepted in urban areas, over scores of millions of acres of agricultural land. This is a formidable political task. It is the *real problem* implied by the title *People and Agricultural Land*.

The editors of the study, however, have not concentrated on this. They have preferred to enrich their bouillabaisse with spicy tidbits of proposals for "The City Reformed" (the last and longest chapter of the study). Most of these have merits for improving urban life, but have no relevance whatsoever for the preservation of farmland.

The authors may challenge this statement. They repeatedly emphasize that the land absorbed by cities, while not extensive, consists largely of "prime" agricultural land. They are right in this. They are also right in stating that to replace the production which is lost through the loss of this land by production on land less suitable for agriculture would incur considerable additional cost. This states the problem correctly as economic, not metaphysical. But throughout the study agricultural land is treated in metaphysical terms, as an absolute. The study uses the standard formula: "land is a resource, not a commodity." The statement is true, but vacuous—as most self-evident truths are. In a market economy any good or service can become a resource only by becoming a commodity. In any economy nothing can become a commodity if it is not a resource.

It seems that public opinion is never willing to recognize shades of gray, but always swings between absolutes of black and white. From the white fiction of absolutely unlimited agricultural land we have swung to the black fiction of an impending absolute limit on food production. It is of course true that the amount of biomass that can be produced on this planet by photosynthesis is absolutely limited by three factors: solar radiation, water, and plant nutrients. But on millions of square miles only one of these is missing and can be brought in by human labor—at a cost. The cost varies from competitive at present prices to science-fiction-type fantastic. In addition, only a very small percentage of the biomass produced annually passes as food through human bodies. This percentage also can be increased by human labor—again at a cost varying from the competitive to the fantastic.

As mentioned earlier, the study repeatedly—and correctly—uses the argument of the higher cost of substitution as justifying the preservation of prime soils for agriculture. It fails to apply the same reasoning to urban development, where it is equally valid. It is common knowledge that almost all of the conditions unfavorable for agriculture are also unfavorable for urban development: high water table, shortage of water, steep slope, bedrock or boulders close to the surface, cold climate. The only major exception that comes to mind is sandy soil, and this may be more apparent than real, a result of the unavoidable imprecision of land classification. For a wide range of vegetable crops sandy soils are better suited than heavy "prime" ones.

It should go without saying that urban development should utilize land of low rather than of high quality—other things being equal. The burden of proof that they are not should always be on the proponents of urban development. What, then, are the additional capital and operating costs of locating the proposed development elsewhere? These costs are of two kinds: those of overcoming the unfavorable physical conditions mentioned above, and those required to overcome additional distances to the existing urban activities with which the users of the new development interact. These additional costs can then be compared with the additional capital and operating costs of producing a given amount of crops on the available poorer soils, rather than on the prime soils under consideration.

An enormous mass of data is available to support such estimates of the costs of development and of operation for various agricultural as well as for various urban uses. These data are of necessity specific both as to site and as to type of use. The range of possible combinations and permutations is practically infinite. But it should not be too difficult to specify a limited number of fairly typical cases and make the appropriate calculations.

To the best of my knowledge a systematic study of this kind has not been undertaken anywhere. But it is urgently needed, in Canada and everywhere else. It is the only way to produce a rational base for dealing with the problem of "people and agricultural land." It would not come as a surprise if this very rationality should be rejected as sacrilegious by the Manichaean true believers in the sacred soil. But science is science only to the extent that it is rational, and the Science Council of Canada is not likely to be afraid of heresy. Thanks to its access to competent specialists in the various fields of both life and technical sciences, the council is uniquely qualified to undertake this task. It is to be hoped that it will do so.

Part Five
Housing

Chapter 26

GOOD HOUSING FOR EVERYONE

Can we supply suitable housing for everyone? Why haven't we been able to do so up to now?

To answer the questions which are the subject of this chapter we must first ask two other questions: What do we mean by "suitable"? And who is "everyone"? What is suitable will depend upon the conventions accepted by the society in question. On the other hand, "everyone" means all of humanity, which includes a lot of different societies. What is acceptable to one society is not necessarily acceptable to another. What suits a New Yorker might not suit a farmer from Chad, and even if it did the latter's poverty might make it inaccessible. Housing problems in the so-called underdeveloped countries are quite different from those in affluent countries like Canada, and far more severe. Therefore, instead of discussing "everyone's" housing problem, let us limit ourselves to a very small segment of humanity, us Canadians.

How should we define what is acceptable to Canadians? We establish standards. And how do we establish standards? We take the average. That which is well above the average is considered to be luxurious; that which is well below it is deemed substandard, not suitable.

In this rather generalized way—perhaps a bit cynically—we can answer the first question; no, it is not possible to house all Canadians suitably. It is not possible as long as they are not all housed according to the same standard, that is to say, in a perfectly equalitarian society. Such a society, as you well know, does not exist, either in the so-called free-enterprise or the so-called Socialist countries.

Let us reformulate the question in a different way, a way in which many others, myself included, have seen it for many years. Why does the market which seems to work so well in providing the large majority of the population with the other necessities of life, such as food and clothing, fail to supply suitable housing? How does housing differ from these other commodities? It differs because of its longevity, which reduces the effect of the demand on the quality of the supply. However, this difference affects the supply of middle-class housing; it has little or no influence on the problem which is of major importance to all of us; the problem of housing the low-income groups, or what we have come to call the "problem of slums."

Source: Paper prepared, under the title "Est-ce qu'il est Possible de Loger Convenablement Tout le Monde?" for the Conference of the Canadian Institute of Public Affairs, Montreal, 1968.

I must confess that the more I struggle with this problem, the more convinced I become that the question as we have reformulated it is also false. The presumed difference between housing and the other necessities of life does not exist for the poor. They lack everything.

The experience of Stockton-on-Tees strongly influenced my thinking toward this conclusion. In this industrial city of northern England the municipality had begun to tear down a slum area, rehousing the residents in public housing units, which are called "council housing" in England. This was during the depression, and the city was forced to halt the half-completed project because of lack of funds. The city's public health officer, a Dr. MacGonigle, saw that this situation offered an unusual opportunity to determine the effects of good housing on the health of the inhabitants because the residents of the remaining slum dwellings represented a perfect sampling for a control group. Imagine the good doctor's surprise when he discovered that the health of the residents of the beautiful new housing was worse than that of the slum-dwellers! The difference was noticeable even among those who still had jobs; it was catastrophic among the unemployed. He discovered the cause for this disparity: the rents in the new units were higher than in the old ones. The difference was not great. You and I might even have considered it negligible, as did the city councillors of Stockton. However, what Dr. MacGonigle found out, upon analyzing the budgets of these families, was that the only way to save a few cents was to cut their expenditures for food.

Perhaps you will respond that this occurred in England during the lean years of the 1930s, while today we are living in a period of unprecedented prosperity, a completely different state of affairs. Several months ago, however, I saw the results of a small survey by the Family Service Society of Toronto, describing the living conditions of 23 of its clients. In all but two of these families the father was employed. Yet despite this relatively favorable situation, they found severe cases of malnutrition in 21 of these 23 families. More recently, I read of a large-scale survey carried out by the Conseil des Oeuvres of Montreal, which reported serious housing deficiencies for 50% of the sample, and severe undernourishment in 44% of the cases.

What does it all mean? What conclusions can we draw from these disturbing facts? The conclusion that I draw from them is that the slum problem does not exist as such. What we call the "problem of the slums" is simply the housing aspect of the problem of poverty. We have not yet been able to provide adequate housing for everyone because we have not succeeded in abolishing poverty.

But, you will say, we all know that all people would be adequately housed if they had enough money. However, I feel it necessary to point out the fact that, despite our relative affluence, hundreds of thousands of Canadian families are poorly housed because there is such a wide gap between the cost of a suitable dwelling and what these families are able or willing to pay.

"Able or willing" implies two questions. As for their ability to pay, there has to be, in one form or another, a redistribution of national income in their favor. Part of the incomes of more financially comfortable people such as you and me must be transferred to help poorer people. Obviously, this is a political question or, if you will, one of political morality. Are the voters prepared to make sacrifices to help fellow citizens who are less fortunate than themselves?

And how much will it cost? Several years ago the Philadelphia Housing Association calculated that $2 billion a year would be needed to close the gap for the United

States as a whole. I would say that for Canada it would take about $300 million a year.[1] That is a lot of money. However, it is only 1% of our gross national income. It is only one fifth of what we pay for what is euphemistically called our national defense.

I will come back to the different methods of applying financial aid to housing. Before doing so, however, I would like to touch on another question. Why are many people unwilling to pay the 20–25% of their incomes which, according to the experts, they can and should be willing to pay for their housing? I want to discuss this question because it is one which disturbs me more and more, and because no one seems to talk about it.

The standard of 20–25% which has been established for subsidized public housing is based on the average paid by low-income families for private housing, which is, in general, of rather poor quality. It is hard to quarrel with the principle of this standard. However, by saying that these families *ought* to allocate a certain percentage of their incomes to housing, we take away their right to determine their own budgets. Is this acceptable in a society which calls itself democratic?

Moreover, is it compatible with a respect for the rights of the individual and for human dignity? Are we, the technocrats in the fields of housing, planning, and social welfare, really better judges of their needs than the families themselves? Are households which allocate their incomes to wants other than housing just foolish? Perhaps they are, but don't we all cherish the right to do the foolish things we like to do?

Besides, in many cases the reason for refusing to spend the "normal" proportion of one's income for housing is far from foolish. In an "urban renewal" project called Trefann Court in Toronto—now halted as a result of well-organized resistance by all of the inhabitants—there was a married couple which had contracted a heavy debt. In order to pay it off, both husband and wife worked long hours. In addition, they settled for poor-quality housing to keep expenses down. When they were told that the house in which they were living was to be demolished, they asked if they would qualify for public housing, and how much their rent would be if they qualified. They were assured that they qualified for public housing, and that the rent, computed on the basis of their combined incomes, would be $150 a month. Obviously they declined the offer. Where, then, would they move when their house was demolished? They would have no choice other than another slum, no better and probably more expensive than the one that was cleared.

A number of surveys have been made on the rehousing of families displaced by urban renewal in the United States and Canada. The quality of their new locations is often a little better, sometimes the same, sometimes worse than the old; however, the rent is nearly always higher. This is virtually inevitable. The price of housing, like that of other commodities, is governed by supply and demand. Demolishing slum housing reduces the supply, so that all those who need an inexpensive place to live–not only those who are displaced — suffer as a result. The war against the slums has thus become a war against those who live in slums.

It is truly strange that so many intelligent and well-intentioned people are not willing to recognize this fact. The existence of slums evokes an emotional reaction. We are ashamed to permit this particular aspect of poverty in our city. It is by no means the only sign of poverty, but it is the most visible one. We see what is obvious

---

[1] All cost figures are for 1968.

from the street; we do not see what there is—or is not—cooking in the pots in the kitchen. Thus we attack symptoms rather than causes. Demolishing slums does not abolish them, but rather enlarges them. It is not an act of social progress, but one of criminal folly.

There is a perverse logic in the voluminous reports which the Central Mortgage and Housing Corporation (C.M.H.C.) requires to prove the need for an urban renewal project in a given section of a city. These reports are full of tables showing such things as the number of overcrowded housing units, those in which the number of rooms is less than the number of inhabitants. If there is a shortage of adequate-sized units, we ought to be adding to the stock, not reducing the supply. It is a strange logic indeed which suggests that to help a person who is badly dressed we must take away the clothes he has rather than repairing or replacing them. In sound logic there is no other way to improve the housing situation than to build new units while conserving or repairing those we already have.

The cost of a new dwelling suitable for a family with three or more children is about $18,000, which calls for a monthly rental of $150, well beyond the financial means of the majority of such families. Perhaps it is worth the effort to take a quick look at the elements which determine this cost. There is the cost of the site, of municipal services, and of construction and improvements on the site, taxes, and interest charges.

The value of the site is the capitalization of the differential rent which a given user is willing to pay to build at this location rather than another. Speculation seizes upon this value; it does not create it. The value of the site is created by the community. Whenever urban land belongs to the municipality, as is the case in Stockholm, for example, the city reaps the benefits of the values which it has created. What is more, it exercises an effective control over the development of the land. This is why I believe that the establishment of public ownership of urban land is one of the most urgently needed reforms. However, it is a reform which will take a long time to accomplish. What is even more important is that it will not reduce land costs. To sell or lease such land at reduced prices would encourage sprawl and the wastage of land through low-density development.

Low densities bring about high municipal service costs per unit. Densities which are too high force reductions in the standards for open space. It is thus important to increase densities enough to assure efficient municipal services without sacrificing reasonable open-space standards. For families with children such standards are hard to achieve at densities much higher than 30 units per net acre. Many of our developments, public as well as private, are built at densities above this figure. Thus there is little hope of realizing economies by juggling with this element of housing cost.

The main element of residential development is, of course, the construction cost of the housing itself. There has been a lot of talk about the possibility of cutting construction cost by increasing the efficiency of the building industry, which is admittedly behind in this regard, particularly in the field of prefabrication. New prefabrication techniques are being developed just about everywhere. The most widespread and systematic application of such methods to the construction of housing has occurred in East Germany. Here they have been building four-story walk-ups with few variations and with a very limited choice of apartments. They have told me that this procedure has enabled them to cut construction costs by 18%, corresponding to a reduction of 15% at the most in overall costs. While this is not negligible, it is far from decisive.

What really matters, for renters and homeowners alike, is the annual cost of the housing. A major part of this expense is the operating cost, which includes maintenance, heating, and so on. The developer who builds housing which he hopes to sell as quickly as possible does not bother much about this aspect; the buyer usually does not know much about it. For both, what counts most is the purchase price. Only after the sale does the buyer learn that he has made a bad deal.

More attention has been given to the problem of reducing operating costs in public housing units. This is one of the reasons why their initial cost tends to be higher than that for privately built housing. Nevertheless, operating costs for public housing have proven to be rather high.

A large part, nearly a quarter, of the annual cost of a dwelling is absorbed by municipal "real estate" taxes. This is a truly regressive form of taxation. It is a well-established fact that the percentage of household income allocated to housing is inversely related to total household income. In Toronto, households with annual incomes of less than $4000 pay more than 30% of their income for housing, while those with incomes of $10,000 or more lay out 15% or less for their housing. Thus municipal taxes take two or three times as much from the incomes of the poor, in percentage terms, as from the rich.

A strange policy indeed! While the government, with one hand, spends millions to make it easier for people to obtain adequate housing, the other hand takes hundreds of millions of dollars away from them, thus keeping good housing out of their reach. Nothing could contribute more to the improvement of the housing situation in Canada, as a long-term measure, than supplanting this regressive source of municipal revenue with a progressive tax, preferably the allocation of a part of a general income tax, proportional to the population of the municipality.

Unfortunately the abolition of the real estate tax would have the desired effect only over the long term; the immediate beneficiaries would be the property owners. What can and should be done right away is to eliminate the most pernicious result of this tax; the fact that it discourages investment in existing structures. At the present time a property owner who makes such an investment to improve and modernize his house is penalized by an increase in his taxes. Such a tax on the value of home improvements could easily be abolished within specified limits.

The final important element of annual cost is the interest rate. Mortgage terms also influence interest payments and annual costs. The principal means used by the federal government to encourage housing construction has been and still is to insure mortgages, and to an increasing degree to make direct mortgage loans at interest rates slightly above those which the government pays on its own bonds. As you probably know, this interest rate is now quite high. As a result the annual cost of a house built with such federal aid is so high that only those on the upper half of the economic ladder are benefited.

Certain European governments give loans for housing construction at interest rates well below what they themselves must pay; this means that they subsidize a number of dwelling units. Experience has shown that over the course of time many of the beneficiaries of such subsidies are people whose incomes are higher than the majority of taxpayers who contribute to the subsidies. It is not, generally speaking, good policy to subsidize specific housing units. A better policy is to subsidize specific households, all those for which 20% of their income is inadequate to pay for suitable lodging. With such a policy each household would be free to locate a dwelling which suited its needs and which at least met minimum standards, which should not be too hard to establish. The household could choose the location it wants, and the style of house, old or new. What is more important, the household should be able to utilize the subsidy to pay the interest on a mortgage and to become the owner of the dwelling.

Such a policy would go far toward housing everyone adequately—except those who cannot or will not put 20% of their incomes into housing, for reasons such as were described earlier. To put such a policy into general operation in Canada would cost, as I have said, about $300 million a year.

A sudden jump in effective demand on such a scale would no doubt generate a rise in prices and in rents. Thus it would be necessary to increase the supply at the same time. In fact, even before instituting such a policy, it would be necessary to build a large number of housing units and to build them at the lowest cost possible, that is to say, on open land. Federal legislation contains several provisions to aid projects built by cooperatives and limited dividend corporations. There is good reason to liberalize and broaden these incentives. Cooperatives and municipalities are not, of course, the only ones who can undertake such enterprises. In many European countries, social security agencies, trade unions, churches, fraternal societies, and the like have carried out the construction and management of such projects.

Obviously such groups would have to be willing to accept subsidized families. This would be preferable to the present public housing formula, which we have copied, like so many other follies, from our neighbor to the south. Even the term we use is false. "Public" housing projects are far from public in the sense that our parks or our schools are public, accessible to everyone. On the contrary, the right to live in these projects is strictly limited. In the United States they are known as "ghettos of the poor," and we have a good idea of their negative social impact. It is a tribute to the moral health of the Canadian people or perhaps to the good work of the project managers that the same phenomena have not yet occurred up here. However, these projects are not very popular; many families refuse to live in them. Among the inhabitants of La Petite Bourgogne renewal area in Montreal, one often hears, "We don't want another Jeanne Mance (public housing) project here."

The kind of housing which I am calling for, moderately priced but not directly subsidized units, can be provided through the acquisition, rehabilitation, and management of existing units, as well as through new construction. This is an important point because many households have valid reasons to choose a location close to downtown in preference to a peripheral location. We can use means already at our disposal for urban renewal more effectively than we have. We have already used federal funds to acquire rather large built-up areas, clear them of structures acquired at high cost, and resell the cleared land to private or public enterprise at a fraction of the acquisition cost. The difference is covered out of the public treasury as an outright grant. It is easy to understand why such a procedure might seem so attractive to local officials; it is one of the few opportunities which they get to obtain large sums from federal coffers. But for the residents of these areas, it means the destruction of their community; the fabric of neighborhood ties is torn apart. This threat generates acute anxiety, even hopelessness in many cases.

In the best of cases, public housing will be built on the cleared site. However, the total cost of such an operation is fantastic. The first project in La Petite Bourgogne renewal area (the St. Martin blocks) will cost about $40,000 per housing unit. If this sum were applied to the construction of comparable buildings on open land, it would be enough to pay for two units instead of one.

There is no doubt that decent low-rent housing accommodations should be available in the central city as well as in peripheral areas. However, these should be provided almost exclusively through the conservation, rehabilitation, and modernization of existing structures. This was the original intention in La Petite Bourgogne, but it was decided that relatively few buildings warranted such an investment. The rehabilitation cost for these buildings was estimated at $13,000 per unit, compared to $14,000 for new construction. The comparison is not strictly accurate, however, because the rehabilitated units would be larger than most of the new units. Even so, if we accept these figures, the possibilities of rehabilitation would seem to be limited.

In contrast, the Philadelphia Housing Authority bought 40 row houses of five or six rooms each at an average price of $5960 in 1958–1959. The average rehabilitation cost was $2763 per unit. Why was the estimated rehabilitation cost in Montreal nearby five times as high as in Philadelphia? The answer is that the former required standards corresponding in every detail to those established for new construction, while the latter was satisfied with a dwelling that was adequate rather than perfect. It seems to me that it is much more important to provide 100 habitable units than 20 model dwellings.

What I would suggest is that the renewal agency purchase or acquire through condemnation all of the property in a renewal area—just as it does now—and that the government allocate it a renewal grant—just as it does now. However, the agency, instead of demolishing the existing structures, would carry out a gradual and continuous transformation within the zone, in carefully planned stages. During the first 6 months the agency would limit itself to satisfying the requirements of good management: cleaning up back yards, repairing sidewalks, making current repairs, and so on. During this period two detailed studies should be undertaken. The first would evaluate the structures and the number of additional years of use which they would have with different levels of physical improvement. The second study would evaluate the needs and desires of the residents. In the course of this study we would probably discover many problems which would require the cooperation of other agencies. Thus the renewal agency would initiate what we now call "social renewal."

Only after a detailed analysis of the results of the two studies would we develop a plan to guide the transformation of the area. This plan would have to be modified as time went on. However, it should give priority not to eliminating what is bad, but rather to providing what is lacking: small play areas for preschool children, spots for tree planting, sitting areas, parking areas, perhaps a community center, a clinic, shops. Obviously such a policy would call for some demolition. However, families who would thus be displaced would not have to leave the area. There would always be someone leaving the area whose dwelling could be put into good condition and offered to a family being evicted to make way for community improvement. The rent should be the same as the family had been paying. The same procedure would be followed in rehousing those families who had to be relocated because their dwellings were structurally unsound. No doubt after several years we could also undertake new construction in the area, but all the time community life could proceed without disruption.

Admittedly, this is a complicated process which would call for a great deal of detailed and difficult work. The agency would need a well-trained staff which included sociologists and social workers, as well as administrators, architects, and engineers. The results would not be spectacular; clearing slums and replacing them with big, new building projects are much more photogenic. The proposed new policy is lacking, perhaps, in political sex appeal. However, it is far more humane, and much more economical, then the present policy.

In summary, we need three simultaneous and coordinated programs: the construction of a large number of new, moderately priced housing units on open land; the rehabilitation and refurbishing of older areas; and, finally, rent supplements for those households whose incomes are not high enough to permit them to pay for a suitable dwelling. The program would be costly, and could not be carried out without a significant change in the allocation of national resources. Given the realities of politics, this presupposes a shift of power among those who now allocate such resources. In other words, in order to assure adequate housing for everyone, we need a revolution, either quiet or violent, depending on the circumstances, but a rather deep and radical one.

Chapter 27

SWISS HOUSING ESTATES 1940–1950

The book deals with the planning of housing developments by a thorough analysis of all aspects of current practice, paying as much attention to the questions of housing economics and of construction as to planning and architecture.

The projects dealt with are relatively small. It is all the more remarkable that both their designers and the author discussing them view them as city planning problems, with major attention to their relation to the city and to the landscape as well as to their site plans. The site plans are developed in all cases from modifications of Zeilenbau, the building of parallel rows independent of the street system, applied in a subtle and flexible way by the Swiss. Entrances are generally approached by walkways; little provision is made for automobiles. Unlike all too frequent practice in our country, the design of the site plan and that of the housing types are always treated as interdependent variables.

The predominant dwelling types are the row house and the walk-up apartment, with an occasional high elevator apartment. There is a definite trend away from uniform height zoning toward a variety and intermixture of types. There are characteristic differences from our standard requirements: an entrance hall is considered indispensable, but closets are not, nor is proximity of kitchen to living room and of bath to bedroom.

The book presents the best of all projects actually built during the past decade in scores of beautiful photographs, supplemented by site and dwelling plans and explanatory text in a very attractive format. The basic theme is formulated in the preface as the interacting relation between the person and his or her dwelling and between house and landscape. What strikes the reader and viewer of the illustrations is the "care taken by both architect and craftsman," which the author justly praises as one of the chief characteristics of Swiss work. This is true not only of the individual buildings, but also, and particularly, of the site plans.

The Introduction briefly sketches the background: from 1940 to 1950 the Swiss population increased by 450,000 (over 10%), and 150,000 new dwelling units were built. Industry was spreading into rural areas, absorbing rural surplus population and resulting in the annual withdrawal of about 9 square miles of Switzerland's limited

---

Source: Review of Julius Maurizio, *Swiss Housing Estates, 1940-1950* (Verlag fur Architektur, Erlenbach–Zurich, 1952).

supply of farmland for urban uses. The decentralized pattern of industry is interesting: while 85% of all persons employed in commerce reside in an urban environment, about half of all manufacturing workers, including three quarters of all textile workers, live in rural communities. Consequently the book presents numerous examples of rural as well as of urban and suburban developments.

In Switzerland, as almost everywhere in Europe, the post-World War I period marked the beginning of a new era in housing. Since that time, practically everywhere the traditional enclosed building block has been replaced by "open" development, first in parallel rows and gradually in more varied and flexible arrangements of structures. At the same time the development of cooperative housing estates was initiated by a pioneer venture called "Freidorf" ("free village" or "open village") in Basel, designed in 1919 by Hannes Meyer. From the beginning these cooperative housing projects, influenced by the traditional rural village, attempted to create a "core" for the new community.

One of the most striking characteristics of these Swiss developments is the great regional variety within so small a country, based to a great extent on imaginative use of the local vernacular. Within this variety several common traits may be distinguished:

1. Most of the developments shown are small, between 8 and 70 houses.

2. Despite their smallness most of them contain a variety of housing types, as well as old people's homes, studios, kindergartens, and so on.

3. There is a refreshing absence of any recipe, rectangular or winding streets or cul-de-sac or loop; each plan is developed from the specific conditions of the site and the housing types.

4. Dwelling plan and site plan have been designed as a unit; these plans have evidently not been made by playing with templates on a drawing board. If a house has a different relation to the contours, the sun, or the view, it has a different plan.

5. The contours, often very rugged, are not regarded as an enemy to be eradicated but as an opportunity to create a work of plastic art, working with nature instead of against her. Where the American developer uses bulldozers, the Swiss use brains.

Not all of the developments presented in the book are of equal merit. Perhaps none quite equals the perfection of that remarkable achievement of the 1930s, Neubühl, near Zürich. Nor should it be assumed that the Swiss have no troubles. One of the most interesting site plans, that of Prilly, near Lausanne, was frustrated by antiquated building regulations. The author also complains about the "unequal struggle" against private real estate interests backed by a highly property-conscious supreme court. All this sounds familiar enough. That so much has been achieved despite these difficulties is most remarkable—and food for thought.

Chapter 28

HOUSING AND EMPLOYMENT INTERNATIONAL LABOR OFFICE GENEVA, SWITZERLAND, 1948

The study under review is *not* a survey of housing conditions throughout the world. It is the development of a thesis which is stated as follows:

Most countries accept rising standards of living and a high and stable level of employment as their basic economic and social aims. The purpose of this study is to bring out the important contribution to be made by housing to the achievement of these aims.

Treating this thesis in conjunction with the question of "the extent to which private enterprise will need in the future to be supplemented by public planning," the author analyzes the housing problem in the broader framework of general economic policy.

The book deals adequately with the problems of cost of land, construction, and financing, of population and family size, and of distribution of income and expenditures. The author correctly emphasizes as the distinctive characteristic of housing its extreme durability, which makes the demand for annual additions to the total supply react violently to relatively slight fluctuations in total demand. He shows how this instability of demand is responsible for the organizational and technical backwardness of the industry, which is split into a great number of small units, each of which concentrates on drawing high profits from a limited market, because it can do little to expand the market. The narrowness of the market in turn increases still further the instability of demand and consequently of supply, and the instability of supply increases the fluctuations of the business cycle. The author proposes to break this vicious circle by public underwriting of a permanent high level of housing production. Without minimizing the value of this approach for the improvement of housing conditions, it must be emphasized that in order to achieve stable employment house-building activity would have to be not stable, but fluctuating in a countercyclical sense.

The author clearly defines the difference between housing need and housing demand and the conditions under which the two would coincide. In the absence of these conditions he considers subsidies to be justified by the "indirect benefits" of

---

Source: Review of *Housing and Employment* (International Labor Office, Geneva, Switzerland, 1948).

housing, frankly recognizing that subsidies involve, first, a redistribution of income and, second, a restriction of consumer choice.

This reviewer questions the statement that "an increase in family size will obviously create a strong pressure to increase expenditure on housing." As the National Resources Planning Board studies on family expenditures have shown, the percentage of income spent for housing varies inversely with family size.

Despite this shortcoming and other minor ones the International Labor Office's publication is one of the best—as well as one of the shortest—treatments of the housing problem.

Chapter 29

HOUSING OF LOW-INCOME PERSONS IN ONTARIO

DEFINITION OF THE PROBLEM

The summary introduction to the report of the Ontario Housing Corporation (O.H.C.) of March 1972 states, "The Government of Ontario . . . accepts the responsibility to provide . . . adequate accommodations for its citizens . . . [and] is confident that in reasonable time the housing needs of the province will be met."

The key words are "adequate" and "needs."

Who is to define these terms? In a democratic society that right belongs to the citizens in their role as consumers of housing. Obviously, many Canadians feel that their housing is not adequate to their wants. At the same time this housing is, by definition, adequate to their effective demand. In other words, a gap exists between the cost (price or rent) of the housing they want and the amount of money they are able or willing to spend for it.

The government of Ontario, by defining "adequacy" in its regulations for public housing occupancy, as well as in the housing bylaws of its subdivisions, in terms of both quantity (number and size of rooms) and quality (structure and equipment), and by accepting responsibility for its provision, has legitimatized wants, within the limits so defined, as needs.

The gap between the cost of adequate housing and the effective demand for it can be narrowed from both sides: by increasing the quantity and quality of the housing supply and/or lowering its price, and by making the demand more effective by increasing the ability and willingness to pay for it.

THE SUPPLY OF HOUSING

Quantity of Housing Supply

Adequacy of supply may be measured in terms of number of rooms per dwelling unit. The standard may be set as $n + 1$ or as $n + 2$, n being the number of persons in a household. The "2" will normally be a living room and a kitchen. In many cases this

---

Source: Report presented to The Ontario Advisory Task Force on Housing Policy, Ottawa, Ont., March 7, 1973.

standard is in excess of the wants of consumers; for example, a couple with two boys and two girls will rarely want five bedrooms, in addition to living room, dining room, and kitchen.

A standard of $n + 1$ indicates a not dangerously inadequate, and a standard of $n + 2$ a more than adequate quantity of housing. In 1971, the housing stock in Ontario was practically $n + 2$. Why, then, is there a "housing shortage" in Ontario? Obviously, there must be a great number of "underoccupied" units, defined as units containing more than $n + 2$ rooms, together with many other units which are "overoccupied" (less than $n + 1$) or even "overcrowded" (less than one room per person).

Where are these "excess" rooms, and why? Three factors can be identified:

1. Geographical Distribution. In localities with stable or declining populations, persons occupy houses with more rooms than they want, because they cannot sell them. The total number of such units is probably not very significant in Ontario.

2. Income Distribution. Many persons with relatively high incomes want and can afford to occupy more than $n + 2$ rooms. This certainly accounts for most "excess" rooms.

3. Lack of Mobility. However, as shown by many detailed surveys (e.g., in areas studied for "urban renewal"), a surprisingly great number of cases of underoccupancy are found also in low-income areas. Largely, though not exclusively, these are single-family houses occupied by elderly couples or widows. I will discuss later a special policy for these cases.

Certainly it is worthwhile to consider policies aimed at a more rational distribution of the total housing supply. Rationing housing space by governmental fiat has indeed been adopted by several governments, but only under conditions of war or revolution. It is certainly not acceptable in Ontario. However, a policy of disincentives may be worth considering. It could take the form of a graded tax on occupancy (by tenant or owner) of "excess" rooms, for example, $5 monthly for the first, $10 for the second, and $15 for the third and following rooms.

A person faced with such a tax would have three options: pay the tax and continue to live as before, move to a unit containing fewer rooms, or, share his or her unit with relatives, friends, or roomers. Each of these options produces a benefit for the community.

An obvious and serious objection to such a tax is that it takes no account of quality. A widow living in a ramshackle six-room house would be taxed heavily, while a rich bachelor occupying a three-room luxury apartment would pay nothing. This imbalance could be corrected by exempting a limited number of rooms in low-priced or low-rent units.

Because of the great variety of conditions in Ontario, the suggested tax could be levied only on a municipal or perhaps regional basis. The province would have to pass enabling legislation and to promote its use. Political acceptability might be enhanced by earmarking the proceeds for housing.

The foregoing does *not* suggest that increase in the housing supply is not urgently needed. It does, however, question the emphasis put on channeling a greater proportion of the gross national product into investment in the "housing sector." Emphasis should rather be on redirection of investment within the sector.

Quality of Housing Supply

Aside from special surveys, there are two sources of data on housing quality: census reports and reports by housing inspectors. Census reports cover the universe; but as they are based on observations of persons who have neither the time nor the competence to make a serious evaluation, they are of questionable value. Housing inspectors have adequate time and competence, but cover only a small part of the universe.

As it is the function of housing inspectors to deal with the owners and occupiers of a property, they cannot deal with inadequacies outside the property line, that is, with the physical and social environment. Inadequacies of the environment may well be more widespread and serious than those of the units themselves, at least in the larger cities of Ontario.

It is important to understand the interaction of the three dimensions of housing: quantity, quality, and price. Increase in quantity, by creating a buyer's market, decreases price and increases quality. Increase in price decreases quantity and quality. Increase in quality increases price and, consequently, decreases quantity. Increased price and decreased quantity in turn result in a decrease in the quality available for a given amount of money; increase in quality may be self-defeating.

Ever since modern governments started to intervene in the housing market, with the English bylaws of the mid-nineteenth century, this intervention has primarily been aimed at raising quality. Minimum standards for new housing have been supplemented by controls on existing housing, zoning, and land subdivision. The combined result of all these virtuous efforts has been a progressive reduction of the percentage of the population who can afford a new unit. This has now reached the point that in Metropolitan Toronto, for example, only 10% of households can afford to buy a new house.

It is an open secret that the flaming enthusiasm of municipal governments for "high standards" is fueled by their desire for high revenues from the "real property" tax, their almost exclusive source of revenue. This tax gives them a sizable share, 25–30%, of the money their residents spend for housing; they get nothing if residents spend their money for other goods or services.

Price of Housing Supply

Of the main elements determining the price or rent which the consumer has to pay for housing—"raw" land, land development, the structure, including equipment, interest, maintenance, and operation, and the "real property" tax—only the last-named can be fully determined by the provincial government.

The Real Property Tax. It is important to remember that the real property tax is a combination of two taxes on two radically different economic entities. The value of the house ("improvement") is determined by its cost of production; like the tax on any other product, it can and indeed must be passed on to the consumer. The value of the site ("land") is the capitalized differential rent, which is determined by the accessibility of the site to all other activities, as compared to the accessibility of other sites. The property owner can do nothing either to raise or to lower this value. A tax simply transfers a portion of the differential rent from the owner of the site to the taxing authority. The owner cannot pass it on. The market value of the property is reduced in proportion to the reduction of the owner's share of the differential rent. This neither reduces nor raises its cost to the user, who pays the same total differential rent. The only change is a shift in the form of payments from mortgage payments to taxes.

While the site user qua user is not affected either way by an increase in the site tax, he or she is of course strongly and negatively affected by it qua property owner. Raising the site-value tax would have two highly beneficial effects. First, it would be a strong disincentive to speculative withholding of land, and thereby weaken the tendency toward "leapfrogging" and "sprawl." Second, it would greatly facilitate public land assembly and reduce its cost. An increase in the site-value tax would therefore be beneficial to housing. A special tax on capital gains from land sales might be equally effective in discouraging speculative buying, but would also discourage selling. This might make it more difficult to assemble public land, as well as to avoid leapfrogging.

However, of far greater importance for housing is the other portion of the real property tax, the tax on housing structures. It is well known that the share of personal income allocated to housing is inversely proportional to level of income ("Engel's law"). As a rough estimate, it can be assumed that, on the average, persons in the highest income group (over $20,000) spend about 12%, and the lowest (under $3000) about 40%, of their incomes on housing.

The real property tax amounts on the average to about 25–30% of the cost of housing. Of this, about one third may be accounted for by the tax on the site, which, as explained above, does not affect the cost to the user. However, the 15–20% which is accounted for by the housing structure is fully paid by the user. This major portion of the real property tax is the equivalent of a 15–20% sales tax on housing.

This tax is highly regressive; it transfers income from the poor to the rich. Abolition of the sales tax on housing (camouflaged as real property tax) might do more to provide low-income persons with adequate housing than all the many "housing programs" of the three levels of government.

Obviously, substitutes must be found for the revenue which municipalities (and school boards) now derive from this tax. Raising the site tax is one; indeed it probably could be accepted only in the form of a gradual shift of the property tax from buildings to sites. Similarly, introduction of a tax on excess rooms would be greatly facilitated by combining it with a simultaneous reduction of the real property tax on housing.

However, any tax which is locally collected will, to some degree, have the same pernicious effect as the municipal sales tax: it will motivate the municipal government to prevent, by all possible means, low-income persons from residing within its boundaries and to try to unload them onto its neighbors. The fact that this policy, when practiced by all municipalities, is self-defeating makes it no less real. The only way out of this dilemma is to collect taxes centrally and distribute them to the localities; for example, the provincial and federal governments would allocate to the municipalities, as a matter of right, a certain percentage of the income tax.

Land. Of all the components of housing cost, the cost of land has risen most steeply in recent years. A certain increase in the differential rent must be expected, as with the growth of cities the advantage of occupying a site well accessible to the increasing number of potential destinations makes some users able and willing to pay more for such a site than for a less accessible one. This important allocative function of the differential rent should not be overlooked; it may, indeed, be indispensable for a rational distribution of land uses. Neither should it be overlooked that improvements in transportation and communications, by making more land available for urban uses, can reduce and, in fact, have reduced, since the beginning of this century, the differential rent per unit of area.

However, because of the aforementioned dominant fiscal considerations, municipalities have tried to prevent all but a small fraction of potential urban land from entering the development market. The province of Ontario has assisted them in this endeavor by strictly limiting subdivision approvals, as well as grants or loans for the extension of municipal services. This has resulted in an *artificial* monopoly, or oligopoly, on "serviced" land with corresponding high prices. There is no doubt that a removal of these limitations, proposed by developers, would indeed substantially reduce prices for serviced land. The obvious drawback, encouragement of scatteration, may be a lesser evil, but it remains an evil.

The only way out of this dilemma is large-scale public landownership. It must, however, be noted that in this case the dilemma would reappear in the form of a difficult policy decision. Two options would be open to the land bank. It could charge what the market will bear; in this case it would be advisable to earmark the resultant profits for support of housing. Or it could charge a lower lease or price. This latter policy would have two serious weaknesses. First, it would preclude allocation by competitive bidding, because at below-market prices demand exceeds supply. Allocation would have to be made by political-administrative decision, with all the resultant complications and dangers. Second, it would mean transferring substantial values from the public purse to persons who could afford to build or buy houses on land-bank sites; evidently these persons do not belong to the low-income group. The public agency should collect the full "normal" differential rent for the benefit of the community, but should bring on the market (for sale or rent) an amount of land sufficient to avoid monopoly (or oligopoly) rent.

Land Development. In addition to raising the price of the land itself, municipal policy has been and is adding greatly to the cost of land development. The fiscal motives are camouflaged as concern for high standards, with the support of the higher levels of government. Two techniques are highly effective in raising lot prices out of the reach of moderate-income families:

1. Zoning, in particular requirements for a minimum frontage of 50 feet or more for each property. Narrower lots and, in particular, row houses are approved only rarely and reluctantly. Minimum frontage requirements also preclude "two-tier" development, with access to the second tier provided by driveways, an economical and desirable method of subdivision.

2. Requirements that all streets, even those serving only a few houses, have a wide concrete pavement, curbs, sidewalks, storm sewers, and the like. No doubt

homeowners prefer to have 60-foot lots on a street of this type rather than 30-foot lots on a gravel road with ditches, but they would rather have the latter than none at all. Moreover, many of those who do pay the several thousand dollars required to achieve the prescribed high standards would prefer to spend this sum of money for the satisfaction of other wants, if they were allowed a choice.

While the high price of new houses directly affects only the middle-income and, to a lesser extent, also the higher income group, these groups react to it in two ways which worsen the housing situations of the low-income group. The frustrated would-be homeowners either move into apartments or buy existing houses. The increased demand for apartments is in part satisfied by "redevelopment" which requires the demolition of low-income housing. The resultant displacement of low-income occupants has aroused strong protest action not only by them, but also by vocal reformers. Strangely, the same reformers have nothing but praise for the displacement of low-income occupants by higher income persons, who buy up their houses and rehabilitate them to a substantially higher standard (so-called "white-painters"). "White-painting," even more than redevelopment, decreases the supply of housing available to low-income groups and raises prices and rents. Moreover, while redevelopment, by increasing population concentration, encourages the use of transit and reduces automobile movement, white-painting results in a very substantial decrease in density. It should be discouraged as much as possible; means to do this will be discussed later.

To sum up, the high level of taxes and of prices for land and land development—three elements of housing cost which together account for at least one third of its total—is the direct or indirect result of the allocation of revenues and responsibilities of its municipal subdivisions by the province of Ontario.

The House. The housing structure, including its built-in equipment, is the biggest single element of housing cost and the one toward which most efforts of cost reduction have been directed.

Much has been said about the inefficiencies of the house-building industry. The main reason for these is to be found in the wide and unpredictable ups and downs of its market, which result in recurring underemployment of the material and human resources of the industry. In particular, this situation is an obstacle to prefabrication, which requires a high fixed investment. The obvious remedy, used in many European countries, is the development and underwriting by the government of a plan for housing construction for a number of years.

It should, however, not be overlooked that, despite these obstacles, prefabrication has been quite successful in producing small, detached, fully equipped, transportable single-family houses, known as "mobile homes" or "trailers." Their use has been entirely banned by most urban municipalities, again primarily for fiscal reasons.

It must be recognized, however, that low-income groups have generally obtained shelter by means other than buying or renting new housing. These means are, singly and in combination; "self-help" housing (usually involving mutual help); sharing, by subletting to families or single persons; and use of second- (or twenty-second-) hand housing.

Throughout history most people have built their own houses. However, with our level of technical development it is more efficient to buy a substantial part of the goods and services required to build a house from specialized suppliers. In the construction of urban new housing there is hardly room for self-help. But self-help can, and in fact does, play a significant role in two areas: first, in the building of single-family houses in rural and small-town areas, including those on the metropolitan outskirts; and, second, in the maintenance and improvement of existing housing. In both fields the scope and effectiveness of self-help could be greatly increased by government aid in three forms: technical advice, supply of materials at wholesale prices, and credit at the rate available to governments, possibly with a modest charge for each of these three types of service.

It is hardly necessary to add that any "do-it-yourself" activity offers nonmonetary satisfaction beyond its purely economic results.

Sharing of housing by subletting is generally frowned upon, limited by zoning and housing codes, and completely outlawed in "public" housing. However, "taking in roomers" is often highly advantageous and satisfactory to both parties. It warrants a reevaluation.

The predominant means of accommodating low-income persons in Ontario is second-hand or "old" housing. Just as second-hand clothing, furniture, or cars are cheaper than new ones, so are second-hand houses. However, as housing has a much longer life expectancy than these other consumer goods, old housing is of far greater importance.

It is inevitable, and quite rational, that the market allocates the more expensive new housing to the higher, and the less expensive old housing to the lower income groups. Strangely, with a few minor recent exceptions, we have provided public housing for low-income groups in new housing, while old housing is private. It might make more sense to have public old and private new housing. This will be explored later.

Interest. Housing is largely financed by borrowed capital, normally in the form of a mortgage. Interest is the amount of money which the borrower pays to the lender, in addition to the obligation to return the capital.

When both sides anticipate inflation, they expect that less than the full amount of the capital will be repaid and agree on payment of a sum equal to the anticipated annual decrease in the value of the capital. Technically this anti-inflation premium is included in the interest rate. The current interest rate is a composite of two types of payments, premium and "true" interest rates.

At present the premium probably amounts to at least 8%, indicating a true interest rate of not more than 4%. The much lamented "high cost of money" is more apparent than real.

This, however, is of little help to the homeowner who is faced with high mortgage payments in the early years of occupancy. It may be worthwhile to consider arrangements by which part of these payments could be deferred to later years by "indexing" mortgage payments.

Maintenance and Operation. At present the builders of apartment houses, as well as of single-family houses, normally sell them as soon as possible, and are therefore not inclined to expend money and efforts to reduce the cost of maintenance and operation. Agencies concerned with annual cost, such as public housing agencies and cooperatives, should not uncritically adopt the housing types and methods developed by private enterprise, which concentrates exclusively on reduction of capital cost. In particular, current North American practice completely neglects the possibility, by appropriate site and building design, to use sunshine (or protection from sunshine) and air currents for the control of room climate, relying instead on costly mechanical heating and cooling devices.

Overhead and Profit. Complex legal and bureaucratic procedures add significantly to the cost of housing directly and also indirectly by long delays which result in substantial carrying costs. A public agency should be in a position to avoid most of these complications.

Profits, under conditions of free competition, should not exceed interest rates plus management fees. However, public and other nonprofit agencies can reduce costs by forgoing oligopolistic profits resulting from land and housing shortages.

LONG-TERM AND SHORT-TERM EFFECTS

Before dealing with the demand side, it is necessary to emphasize the difference between long-term and short-term effects. Because housing has a long life span, annual addition generally accounts for no more than 4% of the total housing stock. Thus, while a decrease in taxes or an increase in effective demand certainly leads to an increase in the quantity and quality of housing in the long run, in the short run it can produce only a windfall to the owners of the existing stock. To counteract this, even with a 1-year delay, a 4% decrease in annual cost or increase in effective demand would have to be offset by an additional increase of the housing stock by at least 4%. Such a sudden doubling of the house-building rate is hardly achievable. Even if it were only partly achieved, it would be accompanied by a steep rise in construction costs.

Measures to substantially reduce the cost of housing, such as the previously proposed abolition of the tax on the housing structure, could therefore be implemented only gradually over a period of about 10 years. There is, however, one exception to this: improvements in existing houses. In fact, an exemption, limited in time and in amount of investment, is now granted. It would be preferable to make the exemption permanent and to replace the ceiling on the amount of investment by a ceiling on total unit value after rehabilitation. No valid public purpose would be served by encouraging a $4000 investment in a $50,000 single-family house. On the other hand, investment of $8000 in a $10,000 four-bedroom house would serve the valid and accepted public purpose of providing a large low-income family with reasonably adequate housing not otherwise available.

This exemption should be available only in areas which, in the judgment of competent authorities, are suitable for continuing use for low-income housing at existing densities. In areas deemed to be suited for a different use and/or a higher density, the exemption would not apply.

DEMAND FOR HOUSING

Ability to Pay

As stated earlier, the basic problem is the gap between the cost of adequate housing and the ability and willingness of persons with low incomes to pay for it. According to the fairly generous scale established by the O.H.C., low-income households are able to pay about 20% of their incomes for housing. How wide is the gap between the total of such 20% payments and the cost (or rent) of a corresponding number of units?

In the absence of complete information, a rough estimate is about $200 million annually, probably less, for the province of Ontario. This is a sizable sum, but it is hardly more than 0.5% of the gross provincial product. Economically, it is feasible to close the gap. The political feasibility of closing it depends on the amount of income redistribution deemed acceptable by the voters of Ontario and their government.

Willingness to Pay

If the required amount of income redistribution is acceptable, all low-income persons can be enabled to provide themselves with adequate housing by spending about 20% of their incomes for it. Are they willing to do so?

Most low-income persons spend considerably more than 20% of their incomes on housing. But a considerable minority pay less. They assign higher priorities to other wants; housing rates less than 20% on their preference scale. This is generally considered unreasonable. Is it really?

In the Northend urban renewal area of Hamilton, it was found that many units rented for about $60 and were occupied by households earning $500 or more per month. Evidently they were able to rent or buy better housing, but they preferred to spend their money for other purposes. Unreasonable?

In La Petite Bourgogne urban renewal area of Montreal, it was found that a number of families who occupied housing which, by everyone's standards, including their own, was inadequate, owned a cottage in the Laurentians (and presumably a car to get there). Unreasonable?

In Stockton-on-Tees, in northern England, in the 1930s, the municipality embarked on replacing a "slum" by "council housing." The project was stopped for lack of funds, after only one half of the people had received new housing at slightly higher rents. The city health officer, Dr. MacGonigle, undertook an investigation of the residents in the "slum" and in the council houses. To his amazement the health of the latter was worse. They had to take the rent increase, slight as it was, out of their food budgets.

Had the "slum-dwellers" of Stockton-on-Tees protested against the project of their council to provide them with vastly improved housing and proposed that the capital be put into other investments and the annual yield be paid to them in cash, they would have been condemned by everyone as unreasonable. Yet the latter approach might have contributed more to their welfare than did the council's project.

While food probably absorbs a smaller percentage of the income of the poor in the Ontario of the 1970s than it did in the England of the 1930s, the situation is essentially the same, as can be illustrated by the following example. The full recovery rent for a unit for a family with three children in a public housing project is probably about $200. If the family earns only $192, it pays $28. The remaining $172 is paid by the taxpayers. If this sum were paid directly to the family, it would probably provide itself with a unit for about $100—not "adequate," but tolerable to it—and use $100 ($72 + $28) for the satisfaction of other wants. The amount available for these would be increased from $164 to $264—61%. It is likely that this would do more to improve these people's lives than would the substitution of an "adequate" for a tolerable dwelling unit.

Housing Subsidy or Income Subsidy?

As long as subsidized housing is limited to tokenism, it can be justified as a holy experiment creating demonstration projects. Once it is to be applied seriously as a means of substantial improvement of the living conditions of low-income persons, however, the question cannot be avoided: will it produce equal or greater benefits than would alternative uses of the same resources?

One alternative would be to extend and improve in low-income areas services for health, child care, education, recreation, and the like. Because of the great variety of subalternatives, as well as areas, no general answer is possible. But it is most likely that in many cases the answer would be: yes, a dollar allocated to services will produce greater benefits than a dollar allocated to housing.

Another alternative, already discussed, is cash payments to low-income persons. While there is wide divergence on the appropriate amount and form, some transfer of income from the rich to the poor is generally regarded as a valid function of government. Housing subsidies do transfer income from the rich to the poor. But they also do something else: they determine, in part, the recipient's budget. There is an implicit assumption that the person is not capable of doing this. The government does it for him or her *in loco parentis*. Papa knows what is good for you.

In general, Canadians prefer freedom to paternalism. Freedom includes—indeed, consists of—the right to make one's own mistakes.

It will be objected that nobody is forced to live in subsidized housing; a person is free to forgo the subsidy and live in housing of his or her own choice. As such housing, almost by definition, will be substandard, the goal of providing adequate housing for everyone will, of course, not be achieved.

More important, it is not true that a person is free to choose how much of his or her income to allocate to housing. This freedom is severely curtailed by legally enforceable minimum housing standards, which are being enacted by an increasing number of Ontario municipalities.

The strongest argument for assumption by the government of a role *in loco parentis* can be made for adequate housing of the children of low-income parents. In this case it may be justified to give to the parents a child rent (or housing) certificate instead of, or in addition to, an income subsidy.

Least justified is paternalism towards senior citizens. The Ontario government should pay to all those who are now eligible for senior citizens' housing an amount equivalent to the difference between the actual and the full-recovery rent for such housing, and leave it to them whether they want to use it to live in that type of housing, or use it differently. It is probable that many of them would choose housing next door to "normal" families. The resultant contact between old people and children would be beneficial to both.

In any case, it is sounder to subsidize the person (or family) than to subsidize particular buildings and/or lots. The way to equalize economic opportunity is to equalize the number of dollars. It is not wise to adopt the principle that "all dollars are equal, but some dollars are more equal than others." This is the case when a dollar spent for rent in public housing commands twice as much space as a dollar spent in private housing. Naturally, this is resented by the person who has only "less equal" dollars at his or her disposal.

The only reason which can be adduced for subsidizing dwelling units rather than persons is that it automatically holds the demand down to the level of the supply. As noted earlier, a sudden massive increase in demand, such as would result from issuance of rent certificates to all low-income persons, would bring about only an equally massive increase in the general rent level. Too much of the housing allowance of welfare agencies is already going down this drain.

The obvious conclusion is that the required massive increase in effective demand must be accompanied or, better, preceded by an equally massive increase in effective supply, that is, of housing units at the lowest possible full-recovery cost at which "adequate" housing can be supplied by any and all means.

Factors affecting supply and cost have already been discussed under these headings. However, some important policy questions require further discussion.

SOME POLICY QUESTIONS

Minimum Housing Standards

When housing laws were first enacted to remedy the terrible slum conditions of the early decades of the industrial revolution, these conditions were giving rise to frequent fires and epidemics, which endangered the entire community. The laws were as much a measure of self-protection as of benevolent paternalism. The deficiencies outlawed by present housing codes only rarely and marginally threaten harm to others; in the main these laws are intended to protect occupiers from doing harm to themselves.

If a house is found to be in violation of the code, the owner has the choice of boarding up (or demolishing) it or investing money to correct it. In the first case the tenants lose their home. In the second case the owner normally raises the rent in order to recoup his investment; and many, if not most, of the tenants, unable or unwilling to pay the higher rent, have to give up their home. If the owner is also the occupant, he will more often than not have only one option: to sell the house at a price insufficient to buy another one and to become a tenant, probably in substandard housing.

The officials charged with enforcing housing codes are, of course, aware of these circumstances and, reasonably, do not insist on compliance with the letter of the law. Similarly, magistrates, when cases are brought before them, frequently assess only nominal fines. As Karl Marx noted, "the law can never be higher than the social reality." For better adjustment to social reality, housing legislation might adopt the "85% rule" used by highway engineers to set speed limits. In fact this is a 90% rule; limits are set at a speed which is exceeded by 10% of all vehicles (5% drive below normal speed). This would mean setting housing standards at the level attained by 90% of all units at any given time. Enforcement would concentrate on the remaining 10%. After these units had been brought into compliance, standards could be raised to the new 90% level, and so on.

In addition to establishing more realistic standards, a second modification is proposed. Before receiving a demolition permit, a property owner should be required to offer the property to the Housing Authority for first refusal. The authority would decide whether it wanted to rehabilitate the structure or to replace it by a new one. If yes, it would acquire the property at the fair market value of the lot. If no, the owner would receive the demolition permit and could dispose of the lot as he saw fit.

The combination of these two proposed measures would keep as much as possible of low-cost old housing in use. Additional measures will be discussed later.

Public Housing

After having been hailed as the answer to not only the "housing problem" but to all other "social problems" as well, public housing is now under attack. Some of the criticism is specious. People who complain that families are held in contempt by their neighbors when and because they live in public housing forget that these same families were held in equal or greater contempt when and because they lived in the "slums."

It is nonetheless true that public housing projects are indeed "poor people's ghettos." The consequences have not been nearly as bad in Canada as they have been in the United States. The main reason for the bad American record is certainly racial conflict. But it should not be overlooked that a vicious circle is involved which has had a much longer time to work itself out in the United States than in Canada. Public housing has evolved a carefully considered point system of admission which gives priority to those in greatest need. Need is greatest in families with many children, in particular those without a male head. Consequently, the population of public housing projects contains an abnormally low proportion of adult males and an abnormally high proportion of children and adolescents—in itself an invitation to trouble. To counteract such troubles or at least their visible manifestations, management tightens the rules. This regimentation, in combination with the "bad reputation" of the occupants, deters the most desirable eligible families from applying for admission. Consequently, the percentage of less desirable occupants increases; the vicious circle has started and continues, ending in some cases, as in St. Louis, in complete catastrophe.

The root cause of the problem is that "public housing," as practiced in the United States and in Canada, is not truly public in the sense that public (or "council") housing is in the United Kingdom and in many other countries, that is, accessible to all or at least most of the population. A truer designation for our projects would be "limited access housing."

The obvious remedy is to make "public housing" public. A valiant attempt to do just that was initiated by the province of Ontario in the form of "full-recovery" public housing. It failed, because the urgency of accommodating the families in direst need of housing forced its conversion to subsidized low-income housing. As long as public housing is the *only* adequate housing accessible to subsidized families, it will remain accessible *only* to subsidized families.

The basic change proposed in this chapter is two-pronged. First, public housing must be accessible to *anyone* who chooses to live in it. Second, subsidized families must be enabled to live in *any* housing they choose, provided it conforms to specified minimum levels of adequacy and maximum levels of price or rent.

It is recommended that all future public housing projects be public, that is, open to all persons at full-recovery rents, or slightly higher, but in no case exceeding market rents. Some of the units, probably no more than 30%, would be allocated to subsidized families.

As nonpublic housing became available to subsidized families, units in existing public housing projects which became vacant should be offered to nonsubsidized families. In this way these projects would cease, after a certain time, to be "poor people's ghettos."

The Use of Old Housing

Public housing—or any housing, for that matter—has been supplied in three ways:

1. In units built on vacant land.
2. In units built on land "cleared" of old units.
3. In rehabilitated old housing.

In general, only the first method increases the housing supply. With rapid growth in urban population and an even more rapid growth in the number of households, it must be the first concern of general housing policy. It will be discussed later.

The second has been the "classical" method of public housing: replacement of "slums" by new, safe, and sanitary units. While this method improves the quality of housing, it generally does not increase the quantity. In order to create one unit, two have to be paid for: the new one and the one which is destroyed. This makes the method unduly costly. To reduce the cost per unit, density is frequently increased by erecting multistory structures, served by elevators. While such units are quite adequate for adult and adolescent occupants, they are totally unsuitable for families with small children, who are most in need of subsidized housing. This method has little to recommend it.

The third method also does not increase the quantity, except insofar as it prevents houses from deteriorating to a point at which they have to be demolished. It improves the quality. The total cost of buying and rehabilitating a unit is normally less than that of building a new one. The quality of the unit may be slightly lower, but this is likely to be more than offset by its more central location.

It is therefore proposed that a major part of the activities of the O.H.C. be directed towards preserving the existing stock of old housing for use by low-income persons, including, but not limited to, those receiving subsidies.

Diverse policies are suggested to achieve this objective. O.H.C. should buy suitable units which are offered for sale. It may be advisable to facilitate this by making it obligatory for property owners to offer them to the Housing Authority for first refusal. This would have the primary purpose of preventing the conversion of low-cost housing into housing for higher income groups. Such housing need not be reserved exclusively for subsidized families; it could also be sold or rented at full-recovery cost. In case of sale the Housing Authority should retain title to the site in order to retain control over both occupancy and maintenance. The house could either be leased or sold, subject to the right of repurchase at a price to be determined by an independent committee of appraisal. In the case of the lease or sale of houses wholly or partly occupied by tenants, the authority would also retain the right of controlling the rents.

Reference has been made to underoccupancy of housing by low-income persons, primarily elderly homeowners. The reluctance of such persons to give up houses which are clearly too big for them and which they may find difficult to maintain stems not only from sentimental attachment, but also from the security of tenure which they offer. As mortgages usually have been paid off, only tax payments have to be met. The Housing Authority would have to give these people equal security by offering them as part of the sale price, a suitable apartment at a low rent fixed for the rest of their lives. The rent might well be no higher than their present tax payments or even lower, down to zero. In addition, it would also be necessary for the authority to delegate a suitably trained employee to assist in finding an apartment, in moving, and also in disposing of any furniture for which there is insufficient space in the new apartment.

Finally, use should be made of urban renewal legislation to conserve and rehabilitate areas of low-income housing. As before, such areas would be designated, giving the Housing Authority the right to expropriate any property within the designated boundaries. As before, a "write-down" grant would be given by the various levels of government to cover the difference between the present value and the value of the land after clearance. However, this grant would not be used to destroy the area, but would constitute a fund given to the authority for use in preserving and gradually improving it.

The Housing Authority would initially limit its activity to freezing (or controlling) rents and improving public services, and to taking over units which were or became vacant. Only after familiarizing itself with the needs and desires of the inhabitants, as well as with the characteristics and potentials of the properties, would the authority develop a flexible plan for gradual change and start to implement it, primarily by rehabilitation of existing houses and by creation of missing community facilities. Properties of absentee owners would generally be acquired and managed by the authority. Owner-occupants would have the options outlined above. They would, however, have to covenant to maintain their properties at prescribed standards; the price paid them for the land would enable them to correct existing substandard features.

Some houses certainly would be beyond repair and would have to be demolished. Others would have to be demolished to make room for community facilities. The displaced occupants would be offered relocation in vacancies within the area. Cleared sites not needed for community facilities would be used for new houses. In the course of time, physical change would be substantial; but at no time would the continuing network of neighborhood relations be disrupted.

The measures sketched above should make it possible to accommodate a high percentage, probably a majority, of low-income persons adequately in old housing. Applicants for public housing generally express a strong preference for living in the inner area. There are not only social, but also valid economic reasons for this preference. Low-income families generally depend on the work of several members of the household; moreover, the jobs of the main breadwinner frequently are unsteady. Access to a great number of jobs is therefore essential. Not only is there the highest concentration of jobs in the inner city, but also it is the only location from which jobs at the periphery can be reached by transit. Commuting from one suburb to another is usually possible only by car.

The Filtering Process

The role ascribed to old housing may be questioned because it is a waning asset. As old houses are displaced by other developments and as the total volume of demand increases, old housing will account for a decreasing share of the required supply.

There is not enough of it. Indeed, this writer has often said, "We need more old housing." This remark is not as facetious as it sounds, when it is realized that "old" and "new" are relative terms. The faster new housing enters the market, the faster "middle-aged" housing becomes old.

This process is known as filtering; it is generally said that it does not work. This is not quite true; the substantial improvement in housing conditions found in successive censuses is largely due to its working. However, it certainly is not working adequately, and it is necessary to explore the reasons for this. A grossly oversimplified model of the filtering process might divide the housing market into four quartiles according to the incomes of the occupants. Quartile A can afford "prime" new housing, B middle-aged housing, C old but adequate housing, and D old, inadequate housing. As a new cohort of housing comes into being, the previous cohort occupied by A becomes vacant and is occupied by B, thus making the housing vacated by B available to C, and former C housing available to D. Housing is filled first at the top, and the process gradually trickles down to the bottom.

Two factors interfere with this flow. First, much potential B housing is absorbed by new A households, in particular as a result of the splitting of the traditional three-generation household into three separate households, one for each generation. Second, and more basic, if a sizable amount of A housing becomes vacant, it competes with new housing, leading to a drop in new house construction. The flow slows down; by the time the stream reaches the bottom it is quite polluted.

If the stream is to reach the bottom in usable form, it must be poured in not at level A, as has been the case with most housing now supported by Central Mortgage and Housing Corporation mortgage insurance and direct lending, but at level C, and in large quantities. It is proposed that all promotional and financial support of all levels of government be concentrated on increasing the supply of housing at level C, at the lowest level at which adequate housing can be supplied. The financing of more expensive housing can be provided by unsupported private enterprise.

Support would primarily take the form of credit at or nominally above the rate at which the government can borrow. It would be made available for both new and rehabilitated housing, for ownership or rent, under equal conditions to all types of suppliers: public authorities, cooperatives, condominia, and private nonprofit and profit-oriented enterprise. The conditions would be a ceiling on cost and a floor on standards of location, site and unit planning, construction, maintenance, and operation. Ceilings would vary according to the size of household which could be accommodated by the unit. Both floors and ceilings would vary according to time and place. It would be one of the main functions of the Housing Ministry to set these standards and to supervise their implementation.

Private enterprise has provided some low- or moderate-cost housing through limited dividend companies. But the present formula has not attracted a substantial volume of activity. The combination of three types of ceilings—on income of admissible residents, on rents, and on dividends—apparently acts as a deterrent. It is hard to see any justification for the ceiling on dividends. It certainly invites cheating, which in turn necessitates cumbersome controls. It eliminates the normal useful function of the profit motive: to act as an incentive to the entrepreneur to use skill and ingenuity to offer to the consumer a better product than does his competitor. Indeed, if and when a normal vacancy rate prevailed, limits on rent might also be unnecessary, and could be replaced by a limit on vacancies of, say, 1%. The latter limit would prevent the practice of renting 90 units at $100 rather than 100 units at

$90. It would force the owner to keep the rent at a level which attracted full occupancy.

Subsidized Home Ownership

Traditionally, subsidized housing has been rented housing. Most low-income families prefer to own their homes; and this has advantages also for the community. Once the principle was accepted that subsidies would be paid not to specific buildings, but to specific persons, the recipients could apply them to pay mortgage interest and/or taxes or repairs. Many present homeowners would thereby be enabled to maintain their homes. For persons who want to become owners, equity payment is generally a big obstacle. In principle, this could be overcome simply by granting a 100% mortgage. This might indeed be the appropriate way in the case of cooperative or condominium ownership of multiple housing. In the case of single-family houses, payment of a small equity might be more appropriate. It could be greatly facilitated by a "hire-purchase" arrangement. In this case the occupant would start as a tenant and acquire title by paying a small additional amount over a number of years. This method should, of course, also be made available to nonsubsidized persons of moderate income.

Some Additional Notes on Cost of Supply

Housing Types. As noted earlier, the cheapest type of new houses available is mobile homes. In addition to providing sites for them, the O.H.C. might also acquire mobile homes for rent.

Apart from mobile homes, row houses remain the most economical way to provide housing for families with children. If they are developed on large blocks with the rows at right angles to the street, a further saving of 30–40% in land development cost and of 10–15% in land can be achieved. Additional savings are possible with a three-story type, which can best be described as two two-story row houses on top of one flat, with direct access to the ground from all three units.

Land Banks. The decisive argument for public ownership of large, contiguous pieces of development land is not financial, but the opportunity for comprehensively planned development. This opportunity exists also for large-scale private development, but a public agency has several substantial advantages over the private developer in assembling and holding land for development. It can deal with "hold-outs" by expropriation, and can borrow money at lower rates than can the private developer. As noted earlier, current excessive land prices could and should be reduced by higher taxes on land, as distinct from taxes on buildings. It is therefore most alarming that the province of Ontario, in its present work on reassessment, is abandoning the well-established practice of separate assessments for land and improvements in favor of a "joint" assessment. Separate assessments should be maintained.

The Subsidy Dilemma

Subsidies to low-income earners, in whatever form, require verification of the income of the recipient, a "means test." The demoralizing effects of means tests are too well known to require discussion. If the authority responsible for allocating the subsidy conscientiously tries to establish eligibility, this effort encroaches on the dignity and privacy of the recipient. If it attempts to avoid this, it invites waste, unfairness, and misallocations of resources.

There is no way out of this dilemma. The only thing that can be done to minimize it is to minimize the number of persons caught in it, that is, to minimize the gap between the actual cost of adequate housing and the income of those who need it. The well-known measures to narrow the gap from the demand side are full employment at adequate pay for all those who are able to work and adequate welfare payments to those who are not. From the supply side minimizing the gap means reduction of the actual, or "full-recovery," cost or rent of adequate housing.

IMPLEMENTATION

The concept developed in this chapter calls for complete separation between the function of supplying housing and the functions of allocating subsidies. Indirect and hidden subsidies invariably lead to a misallocation of resources. The full-recovery cost or rent of every housing unit should be clearly visible to both the public and the occupant. Similarly, the amount of the subsidy, in dollars and cents, should be clearly visible to both the public and the recipient.

There is no point in trying to camouflage the fact that allocation of subsidies is not a housing function, but a welfare function. Logically it could be carried out by a welfare agency, which would give to the recipient a housing certificate of specified money value. The recipient would present this certificate to the housing location office, requesting assistance in finding adequate accommodation.

Operation of the location office would be one of the most important functions of the Housing Ministry. This would include maintaining a constantly updated list of all adequate vacancies by location, characteristics, and price or rent. For the demanding task of inspection, the cooperation of the existing housing inspectors would be indispensable, but not sufficient, because they do not deal with environmental and other "livability" aspects. The services of the location office might also be made available to nonsubsidized persons, possibly for the payment of a modest fee.

As housing markets are regional, this function might well be delegated to regional housing authorities. So also might be the building and management of public housing projects.

The central ministry would then concentrate on two tasks: first, planning, including research into both the demand and the supply side of housing; and, second, allocation of resources to the various regions.

RESTATEMENT OF MAIN POINTS

In sum, it is recommended that, first, the supply of adequate housing at the lowest possible cost be maximized in all forms and by all means; and, second, that all persons whose incomes are insufficient to pay for adequate housing receive a subsidy enabling them to provide themselves with housing of their choice.

Throughout this chapter proposals for a lowering of standards have been presented. This will be shocking to most concerned persons. However, analysis of the experience of a century of housing reform makes it evident that the pursuit of unrealistically high standards, for whatever reasons, has contributed to the present, unsatisfactory situation. Barring a revolutionary redistribution of income, the declared goal of providing to all citizens "adequate accommodations . . . in reasonable time" can be achieved only by a more realistic definition of "adequate."

Chapter 30

PROGRAMS IN SEARCH OF A POLICY: LOW INCOME HOUSING IN CANADA

The report under review was commissioned by the Central Mortgage and Housing Corporation (C.M.H.C.). During the first 6 months of 1971 a staff of 23, supported by about a dozen consultants, produced it, at the expense of federal taxpayers. However, after its completion, the C.M.H.C. decided not to publish it, so the chief authors published it on their own.

The C.M.H.C.'s reasons for keeping the report under wraps can be easily understood by reading its title. The authors state that their client never developed a housing policy, but merely created a number of ad hoc programs. This, of course, is not unique to our federal government, but characteristic of the "housing policies" of many governments inside and outside Canada. Programs have been developed in response to specific demands and pressures. Not all of these have come from consumers of housing; concern about employment and the profits of the building and mortgage banking industries has been at least as important. In particular, governments have found residential building a convenient tool to soften the swings of the business cycle.

The authors have analyzed in considerable detail the resultant disparate programs, one by one, carefully noting the failures and shortcomings of each. This probably unavoidable procedure has resulted in criticism from different and sometimes disparate points of view, from which no underlying policy seems to emerge. Only in their introductory summary and in their concluding recommendations do they articulate a basic philosophy. Quoting the Ontario Association of Housing Authorities, they state correctly that federal housing policy has been production-oriented rather than distribution-oriented. More questionable is their assertion that the "rewards go to the producers." This evidently refers not to the actual producers, the building workers—although the authors suggest that their wages be "policed." Probably they mean by "producers" the owners and sellers of housing, who certainly do benefit. However, the policy of insuring home mortgages, the mainstay of C.M.H.C. policy,

---

Review of Michael Dennis and Susan Fish, *Programs in Search of a Policy: Low-Income Housing in Canada*. (Hakkert, Toronto, Ont., 1972). *Source:* (Under the title "The Policy C.M.H.C. Never Wanted") *City Magazine* (Toronto, Ont.), Vol. 1, No. 4, May-June 1975.

has also substantially benefited middle- and upper-middle-class homeowners. To those who expected that the resulting "filtering-down" process would automatically supply everyone with decent housing, the results certainly are disappointing, as the authors state. They do not discuss what the results actually have been, or what might be done to make the process more effective, or the more general basic question of the interrelation between the three dimensions of housing: quality, quantity or production, and price/rent or distribution. They do, however, clearly state two basic and frequently overlooked truths:

1. There exists a substantial gap between the cost of "decent"—as officially defined—housing and the amount which a substantial part of the population can "afford" to pay.

2. "The simple fact that the majority of the poor will live in existing old houses."

The gap can be closed or narrowed from both sides: by increasing income or by decreasing cost.

The authors rightly put the main emphasis on the first method. They state that they "prefer a guaranteed annual income," but accept as an alternative a shelter allowance to low-income earners. They do not come to grips with the unpalatable fact that any redistribution of income which is brought about not at the source by a change of the economic system, that is, by permanent full employment at decent wages, but ex post facto by extracting tax money from the rich and giving it to the poor, requires some form of means test to determine who is poor enough to be entitled to such benefits.

Accepting redistribution via the tax system as the best that can be achieved within the framework of a capitalist economy, it must be recognized that replacement of a guaranteed income by a shelter allowance adds one more undesirable element: government tells the recipients that they must spend the money for housing, not for the needs they themselves consider most urgent. The authors do not seem to be bothered by this paternalistic encroachment on the freedom of low-income earners.

In view of these unpalatable but unavoidable implications of narrowing the gap between income and cost of housing from the income end, it would certainly be desirable to reduce the number of persons requiring a shelter allowance by narrowing the gap from the other end, by reducing the cost of housing. This can be done in three ways:

1. By subsidizing housing units so that they can be sold or rented below actual cost.

2. By reducing the standard which society accepts as "decent."

3. By reducing the actual cost of one or more components required to achieve a given standard.

The first method, subsidizing dwelling units rather than families, has been preferred by most governments, in Canada and abroad. Its great drawback is that inevitably some of the benefits go to people who are wealthier than many of those from whose pockets the subsidy money has been extracted. Dennis and Fish are aware of this, but are willing to accept it.

They also favor the second method, advocating some reduction of the standards now required by the C.M.H.C. for rehabilitation. They do not investigate the potential of lowering standards for new housing. Their major proposal for reducing the actual cost of new housing is a "major land assembly and banking program." Public ownership of development is most desirable both as a tool for effective planning and as a means to recapture for the community the "unearned increment" in land value which is entirely due to actions and investments by the community. The second purpose can also be achieved to a greater or lesser extent by raising the tax on land. This would also make it easier for a public agency to acquire land at reasonable prices. Immediate acquisition of a 10-year supply, as proposed by the report, would tend to raise the land prices that the public agency would have to pay even higher than they are now. Even more questionable is the authors' acceptance of the goal of public landownership as formulated by the Hellyer report: "The aim . . . must be to reduce the cost of serviced land to the ultimate consumer." This aim conflicts with the aim of recapturing the land value for the community which has created it. As the users of new housing, almost by definition, are more affluent than the majority living in old housing, such cost reduction amounts to a reverse income distribution. Moreover, low land cost encourages low-density sprawl. Both objections hold even more strongly in relation to the report's surprising proposal to shift the cost of land development from the developer (who passes it on to the user) to the municipality.

It is of course true that at present in many, though by no means in all, Canadian cities prices of land reflect not just its normal value (i.e., the capitalization of its differential rent), but also an additional monopoly or oligopoly rent (which a public agency would not charge). Much publicity has been given to the report's finding that in several Canadian cities (e.g., Toronto and Calgary) half a dozen big developers own enough land to satisfy the demand anticipated for the next 10 years. However, this would give them a monopoly only if there were no other land suitable for development. In fact there is a good deal of such land. This land, as well as most of the land owned by the big developers, remains idle because the municipalities are unwilling to give subdivision approval and/or to extend trunk services. The authors discuss these municipal policies aimed at keeping low- and moderate-income families out of their territory. They also explain that the municipalities are virtually forced into the vicious policy by their dependence on the "real property" tax. Their proposal to replace this tax by allocating part of the income tax to the municipalities is one of the most important recommendations of the report. Unfortunately, they do not make a distinction between the antisocial effects of a tax on "improvements" and the beneficial effects of a tax on "land," both of which are lumped together as "real property" for tax purposes.

However, they are right in proposing that publicly acquired land be leased rather than sold for development. They want to lease exclusively to publicly owned or "nonprofit" development agencies. While this would be desirable, few such agencies exist at present, and there is no reason to assume that their products necessarily will be either cheaper or better than those of private enterprise. Even less justified is the authors' demand that *all* new housing (except rural and small-town) be for rent. Homeownership has substantial advantages in facilitating and encouraging good maintenance. If a public authority retains ownership of the land on which the privately owned home stands, it can easily prevent speculation or other abuses.

Their rejection of ownership for new houses contrasts strangely with their proposals for old housing, in which provision for rental housing by public or nonprofit agencies plays only a minor role, the main emphasis being on generous subsidies to the present owners, landlords as well as owner-occupiers. They rather easily dismiss the danger that an 80% subsidy on rehabilitation would act as a premium for neglecting current maintenance, because good maintenance would prevent owners from ever becoming eligible for rehabilitation grants. It also seems that the proposed subsidy could and would go to many owners who could well afford to pay for rehabilitation out of their own pockets.

Specifically the authors' program for "stabilizing low-income neighborhoods" proposes the following:

1. Substantial grants and/or low-interest loans for improvements.

2. No tax on improvements.

3. Improvement of municipal housekeeping and infrastructure.

4. Provision of insurance.

5. Prohibition of demolitions.

Certainly in Toronto and probably in most Canadian cities this program would not stabilize low-income neighborhoods, but would encourage the displacement of low-income residents by "white-painters." The authors of the report are perfectly right in insisting that the bulk of low-income families must live in old housing—at least in cities old enough to have permitted old housing to be produced by the only process which can produce it, namely, filtering down. But they fail to see that old housing in sufficient quantity and quality will remain available to low-income families only if a public agency acquires and retains this housing or, in the case of owner occupancy, acquires the land on which the house stands (or at least the right to repurchase at a predetermined price).

To sum up, the authors' "search for a policy" has not been fully successful. But, in addition to presenting a wealth of significant information, their book raises questions that need to be raised. It is indispensable for anyone concerned with housing in Canada.

Chapter 31

THE ROLE OF CONSERVATION AND REHABILITATION IN URBAN RENEWAL

ANALYSIS OF THE PROBLEM

Urban Renewal—A Continuous Process

Discussion of urban renewal has been confused by a limited focus on the "urban renewal" legislation enacted in the United States and by the propaganda used to gain acceptance of its procedures. In this context "urban renewal" has been defined as a "means to correct past mistakes," as "the elimination of blight," or as "stopping the cancer of blight." This emotion-loaded terminology has carried with it an implication that renewal consists of a number of "projects"; once these projects have performed the required "corrections," "eliminations," or "surgical operations," the "renewaled" city, it is implied, will live happily ever after.

The experience with "clearance of blighted areas" in the United States has clearly demonstrated the fallacy of this naive notion: "blight" is spreading as fast in other areas as it is being eliminated in those which have been "cleared"—or even faster. Evidently, a more adequate understanding and definition of "urban renewal" is required.

"Urban renewal" can best be defined as the adjustment of obsolete parts of the urban structure to meet anticipated future demand. Obsolescence is the inevitable concomitant of progress. The more rapidly a community progresses, in terms of quantitative growth and of qualitative changes in its way of life, the faster will existing structures become obsolete, and the more widespread and urgent will be the need for renewal. In fact, such renewal has always been and is always going on. In completely static communities it is limited to the replacement of parts of structures, or of entire structures, which are physically decayed, by identical structures or parts. In dynamic communities functional obsolescence overshadows physical obsolescence and interacts with it.

Source: Report to the Metropolitan Toronto Planning Board, 1963.

Various Types of Obsolescence

Functional obsolescence, as well as physical obsolescence, may affect different aspects and parts of the existing urban structure. These must be clearly distinguished in order to determine the methods of renewal most appropriate in any given situation.

In a technologically progressive society such as ours, the most frequent obsolescence is that of equipment, such as that for lighting, heating, water supply, and waste disposal. Another type of obsolescence is that of the building plan, such as houses designed for large, three-generation families being unsuitable for the presently predominant much smaller two-generation family, or loft buildings being unsuited for industries using conveyor belts.

Where only one or two of these factors of functional obsolescence are present, the required renewal will generally be undertaken by the property owner. If, however, they coincide with physical decay, it may not always be worthwhile to make the investment required to overcome the functional obsolescence, or, inversely, to make the physical repairs which would justify the installation of new equipment and/or the internal rearrangements required to make the building suitable for contemporary use. In such cases the owner will, rationally, exhaust the remaining useful life of the building and then put the parcel up for sale. If there is a demand for the same type of building, or for a different type which can be well developed on a parcel of this size and shape, such a building will replace the old one in the course of the normal operation of market forces.

A different and more complex situation arises when it is not (or not only) the individual building that is obsolete, but the lot and street pattern and/or the economic or social environment. Realignment of the street pattern and provision of public facilities can be accomplished only by public authorities and will generally require use of the power of expropriation. Adaptation of the lot pattern, involving generally a change from small to large lots, *can* be brought about by private enterprise, as shown by numerous examples in Metropolitan Toronto and elsewhere. However, land assembly purely by private enterprise usually involves certain diseconomies not only in time-consuming and costly negotiations and in excessive prices paid to "holdouts," but also, and more importantly, in less than optimal sizes and shapes of the finally assembled properties and, even more so of remnants of the old pattern left over between parcels for the new use—as witnessed by the numerous single-family properties, left between tall new apartments, which are neither attractive for single-family use nor large enough for apartment buildings. It is in these situations, where the pattern of lots and frequently also of streets is not suited for the type of building, that land assembly and clearance by public authorities can greatly assist redevelopment.

Urban renewal would be a relatively simple matter if all aspects of obsolescence occurred at the same time and at the same rate. However, this is not the case in an economy based on dispersed decision-making by a multiplicity of property owners. It is, therefore, the task of public policy to synchronize the multiple aspects of obsolescence and renewal. The basic decision is between areas requiring disinvestment and those requiring reinvestment in existing structures. The former is indicated when present and anticipated future demand differs radically from the past one; the latter, when the type of demand is substantially unchanged.

By definition, conservation and rehabilitation are applicable only in areas calling for reinvestment. Code enforcement, here included as a technique for inducing conservation and rehabilitation, is a double-edged sword. It gives the property owner a choice between disinvestment by demolition, and reinvestment by bringing the building in questions up to the required standard. His or her decision may be in the direction opposite to that indicated for the area as a whole. In this case, code enforcement will be counterproductive. This aspect will be discussed later.

Definitions of "Conservation" and "Rehabilitation"

The journal, *Ontario Planning*, No. 2, 1964, says:

> Rehabilitation is frequently confused with conservation. Rehabilitation is the raising of standards through physical improvement. Conservation is the maintenance of these, and higher standards on a long-range basis. Buildings are rehabilitated by adding space, painting, repairing, and other physical changes.

This distinction is not convincing. No building can be conserved without repairing and painting; and "adding space" and "other physical changes" are neither a necessary ingredient of rehabilitation nor incompatible with conservation. A distinction might be made between maintenance of standards and achieving higher ones. But the definition quoted above explicitly includes higher standards in conservation—and rightly so, because in a progressive society one can stay in the same place only by running pretty fast.

Commendable as the striving for exact definitions is, it serves no useful purpose to make clear-cut distinctions in words where none exist in fact. Therefore in the following discussion no such distinction will be made, and the theme of "conservation, rehabilitation, and code enforcement" is redefined as "investment in existing urban structures in areas of demand of unchanged type." By far the most important of these are the residential "gray areas," fading into "blighted" and "slum" areas, that is, the areas which do now, and will in the foreseeable future, supply residential accommodation to the households on the lower half of the income scale. These will be referred to in the following discussion by the shorter term "low-income groups."

Housing Conditions of the Low-Income Groups

It is well known that new housing, whether for sale or for rent, is generally beyond the reach of families with annual incomes of less than $5000–$6000.[1] Only very few of the houses built with Central Mortgage and Housing Corporation (C.M.H.C.) financing in the Toronto Metropolitan Area in the recent past were sold to families with incomes below this level. Rents for new two-bedroom apartments range from $125 up. On the basis of an expenditure for housing of one quarter of total income, this rent would require an annual family income of $6000.

As Table 1 shows, in 1961 only 44.1% of all "spending units" (families and independent single persons) in this area had incomes of $6000 or more. Over one quarter had incomes under $4000. Incomes have increased since 1961, but the general picture is still valid.

---

[1] All cost figures as of 1966.

Table 1. Percentage Distribution of Incomes of Spending Units, Metropolitan Toronto Census Area: 1961

Income ($)	Percentage	Cumulative	Percentage
Under 1,000	2.9	2.9	100.00
1,000– 1,999	4.4	7.3	97.1
2,000– 2,999	6.9	14.2	92.7
3,000– 3,999	11.9	26.1	85.8
4,000– 4,999	14.9	41.0	73.9
5,000– 5,999	14.9	55.9	59.0
6,000– 6,999	11.9	67.8	44.1
7,000– 7,999	9.4	77.2	32.2
8,000– 9,999	10.8	88.0	22.8
10,000–14,999	8.1	96.1	12.0
15,000 or over	3.9	100.0	3.9

As is also well known, the lower the income, the higher is the proportion for rent. However, as Table 2 shows, the difference is much greater than is usually realized. Moreover, a comparison with 1949 indicates that both the proportion of income spent for housing and the difference in the proportion so spent between the low- and the high-income groups have increased. The two sets of figures are not strictly comparable. The 1949 survey covered only 11 of the municipalities presently included in Metropolitan Toronto, plus the southern half of Etobicoke and the southwestern corner of Scarborough, while the 1961 census area extended slightly beyond the boundaries of the present Metropolitan Toronto Planning Area. The 1949 survey relates to family income, while the 1961 data refer to the wage and salary

Table 2. Housing Cost as Percent of Income
1961: Wage and salary income of head of household, Metropolitan Toronto Census Area.
1949: Family income, "Greater Toronto,"[a] lower, middle, or upper third.

	Annual Income 1961		Annual Cost as Percent of Annual Income			
	Assumed Group Average ($)	Group as Percent of Total	Owners		Renters	
Group ($)			1949	1961	1949	1961
Under 2,000	1,500	7.0		83.6		72.0
2,000–2,999	2,500	10.3	17.0	50.4	21.9	42.5
3,000–3,999	3,500	20.7		35.2		31.8
4,000–4,999	4,500	22.7	12.9	28.0	16.7	25.9
5,000–5,999	5,500	15.5		24.0		23.3
6,000–6,999	6,500	8.4	9.4	21.6	11.9	20.8
7,000–9,999	8,500	9.8		18.2		17.4
10,000 or over	12,000	3.9		17.1		15.7

[a]Economic Research Department, C.M.H.C., "Basic Data for Estimating Housing Need, Greater Toronto, 1950."

income of the head of the household only, which, on the average, accounts for about three quarters of family income. In the lowest income group, under $2000 annually, it certainly accounts for less, so that the figures for this group may be disregarded. There may also be some differences in the methods of measuring housing cost, especially for owner-occupied housing. For 1961 the annual cost to the owner has been assessed as 8% of the value of the house. This is a modest percentage, but it may be that the data on the value of the home which the owner supplied to the census taker were somewhat inflated, leading to an overstatement of the housing costs of owner-occupiers. Even if all these qualifications are given full weight, there remains no doubt that the financial burden of housing has become heavier since 1949, in particular for the lower income groups.

From 1949 to 1961 real incomes have increased substantially, and of this higher income the people of Metropolitan Toronto (as of Canada generally) have to spend a considerably higher proportion for housing. Do they receive correspondingly higher value? A comparison of the results of the censuses of 1951 and 1969 shows a significant decrease in the percentage of dwelling units overcrowded, lacking private bath, and needing major repairs. However, in comparison to the vastly increased cost the improvement is very modest. The least that can be said is that the standard of housing has fallen even farther behind the general rise in productivity and income than it already had in 1949.

Professor James A. Murray, in discussing "Canada's poor record in providing low rent housing," says, "This should indicate that as a nation we are so rich we don't need it, so poor we can't afford it, or so ineffective we can't do it."

The ineffective method on which we have relied so far is, in the main, the "filtering-down" process, supplemented, to a very minor extent, by the building of "public housing projects" and, to a somewhat greater extent, by "slum clearance," which is widely regarded as a main purpose of urban renewal.

The Rationale and Irrationale of Slum Clearance

The continuing existence of slum conditions, endangering the health and happiness of their inhabitants, their human dignity, and their social usefulness, is rightly considered unacceptable in the midst of a relatively affluent society. There is unanimity that "we must get rid of the slums." As slums are highly visible, the first emotional expression of this intention is a demand for "slum clearance," meaning demolition of the structures in the slum; elected and appointed officials, the press, and well-intentioned individuals point with pride to their achievements in slum clearance. It is considered as an end in itself, recognized by the courts as a "public purpose," and justifying considerable expense of effort and of public funds. It has provided the original and still dominant rationale for urban "redevelopment" and "renewal."

Replacement of emotion by sober thought shows slum clearance to be an inadequate, indeed a counterproductive, means to achieve the desired end of eliminating slum conditions. If a road serves poorly, we do not demolish it; we repair it and/or build a parallel road. Everybody understands that demolition of a road, even a poor one, decreases the supply available to road users and worsens conditions on other roads. Exactly the same is true of housing. Demolition of any dwelling units, even of poor ones, inevitably worsens the situation of the consumers of housing.

The ownership and management of slum dwellings is an industry which, like any industry, expands when profits rise and shrinks when profits fall. Profits rise in a seller's market, when demand exceeds supply. When a government agency enters the market to buy substandard houses, it increases the demand; when it demolishes those houses, it decreases the supply. It thereby benefits the suppliers, the slum landlords, and hurts the consumers, the slum tenants. This elementary fact has been confirmed by experience over and over again.

If clearance spreads rather than cures blight, what, then, is the cure?

There is no secret about the reason for the existence of substandard housing, whether it is concentrated in clearly definable districts or, as in Metropolitan Toronto, scattered over wide areas. The reason is the wide gap which exists between the price of standard housing and the effective demand, that is, the amount which numerous families and single persons are able and willing to pay for housing. This amount is effective as demand for substandard housing only. If the definition of "renewal" given above, "adjustment of obsolete parts of the urban structure to meet anticipated future demand," is interpreted in strict economic terms, it would not apply to substandard housing. Such housing is only too well adjusted to the existing and foreseeable effective demand of low-income groups. But it is very ill adjusted to their needs as human beings and to society's need for raising good citizens and productive workers.

This need can be satisfied only by creating an additional supply of good housing in new or rehabilitated structures. The creation of such an additional supply costs money. There are three, and only three, potential sources for this: the tenant, the property owner (who, in the case of owner occupancy, is also the tenant), and the public, that is, the taxpayers of one or more levels of government. These three sources will be explored consecutively in the following discussion.

Higher Rents as a Means of Stimulating Investment in Rehabilitation

Normally the way to translate need into economic demand is to make it effective by offering enough money to buy the needed goods or services. The immediate result of increased effective demand is a rise in price to a point where the return on capital in the industry supplying the particular demand exceeds the returns in other industries. The consequent second result is an increased flow of investment into that particular industry, leading to increased supply and a consequent fall in price down to a point where returns are no higher than in other industries competing for investment capital. This is the well-known working of the market in a competitive free-enterprise economy. It works reasonably well in most areas of demand; why not in housing?

Housing differs from all other consumer goods in that it is consumed much more slowly, over a period measured in decades and centuries, rather than in years, months, or weeks. Additions to the housing stock average about 2–4% annually in Canada, as in most other countries. Consequently the immediate result of a substantial increase in effective demand—a raising of the prices and rents for the existing stock—would certainly last for many years. As explained previously, the part of the stock available to the lower income groups consists almost exclusively of old housing; and it cannot be increased directly by a rise in the return on the investment in new housing. It can be increased only indirectly and very slowly by a speeding up of the "filtering-down" process, which in turn can be brought about only by expanding the construction of new housing. This is exactly the policy which the Canadian government has practiced for the past 20 years by encouraging the flow of mortgage funds into new housing. It has probably speeded up the filtering-down process, but not sufficiently.

It may be objected that this discussion of the probable effect of raising the prices or rents paid by the users of old dwelling units is academic, because nobody proposes it. However, it is being proposed, and to some extent practiced, in two forms. The first form is rent subsidies or rent certificates. While there is no doubt that in the long run raising the effective demand to the level of the need is the only way to get the need supplied, in the short run—and in this case "short" may well mean several decades—it will result in raising rents and prices, benefiting the landlord rather than the tenant. Experience with the housing payments of welfare agencies, insufficient as these are, is eloquent in this respect.

The second, and more important form of proposals and practices to bring about housing rehabilitation by making the user pay a higher rent or price is to force the person to allocate a greater share of his or her budget to housing, by eliminating housing of lowest standard and correspondingly low cost. Sometimes explicitly, and always implicitly, this policy assumes that people "could" and "should" spend more on housing than they are willing to do. This is implied in the widely accepted statement that the community cannot tolerate substandard housing and that its demolition, by purchase and subsequent clearance or by code enforcement, is "an end in itself," independent of the rehousing of the displaced families. As is to be expected, and as has been confirmed by many surveys of the relocation of families displaced by slum clearance in the United States, practically all of them have to pay higher rents for accommodations which in most cases are only slightly better, and sometimes are worse, than the slum dwellings from which they have been evicted. It is silently assumed that they can pay these higher rents without serious impairment of other aspects of their level of living.

This is a highly questionable assumption. The classic example of Stockton-on-Tees should give food for thought. Certainly the experience of welfare agencies shows that here and now malnutrition is still widespread.

The data presented in Table 2 show that low-income families in Metropolitan Toronto spend, on the average, a very high percentage of their incomes on housing, much of which certainly calls for rehabilitation. If they were forced to pay the cost of rehabilitation, this would not only impose undue hardship, but also lead many of them to attempt to reduce their housing cost by doubling up, subletting, or reducing their demands on the landlord for maintenance, thus contributing to a spread of blight which might easily outpace the reduction of blight by the preceding rehabilitation.

An average, of course, covers and tends to hide a considerable spread. Many families pay much more than the average, but many also pay much less. This is illustrated, for instance, by the situation in the urban renewal area known as the "North End" in Hamilton, Ontario, which is presented by M. V. Jones & Associates on pp. 125–126 of their report entitled "The Role of Private Enterprise in Urban Renewal," from which Table 3 is derived. As the rent given does not include heat, a monthly allowance of $15 has been added to make the ratios comparable to the 25% of income charged in public housing.

Certainly persons with incomes of $500–600 monthly, which in a number of cases

Table 3. Monthly Wage and Salary Income of Head of Household, and Average Monthly Rent, in North End Urban Renewal Area, Hamilton, Ontario: 1965

Monthly Income Range ($)	Income ($) Assumed Average	Shelter Rent ($)	Rent as Percentage of Income	
			Shelter	Shelter and Utilities
100–149	120	49	40.7	53.1
150–199	170	53	31.2	39.8
200–249	220	45	20.4	27.2
250–299	270	46	17.0	22.5
300–349	320	53	16.5	21.3
350–399	370	57	16.3	19.5
400–449	420	61	14.5	18.1
450–499	470	62	13.2	16.5
500–600	540	53	10.5	13.4

probably is supplemented by earnings of other family members, can pay more for housing than $68 a month. In the opinion of housing experts in and out of government they should pay more. But evidently these steelworkers have "a different set of values," to use sociologists' jargon. In plain English, they would spend their money for other things.

As no survey of household budgets was made in Hamilton, we do not know what these other things are. An interesting light was thrown on this question, however, by a survey which was recently made in an urban renewal area in Montreal, known as "La Petite Bourgogne." A number of the people who live in extremely substandard housing in this area own summer cottages. Who is to say that they and their families would be healthier and happier people and better and more productive citizens if they sold these cottages—and maybe the cars that take them there—and used the money to buy or rent "standard" housing?

Any government policy which prevented people from allocating their incomes in the way these inhabitants of La Petite Bourgogne have decided to allocate theirs would be a very serious interference with free consumers' choice. In fact, the government would arrogate to itself the power to draw up the family budget, assuming that it knows better what is good for its citizens than they do themselves. Such a paternalistic—not to say totalitarian—attitude is difficult to reconcile with the tenets of a liberal democracy.

It is sometimes claimed that people forced to move into more expensive and presumably better housing would have done so voluntarily if it were not for inertia, that government interference is justified to overcome this inertia, and that the people affected will come to recognize, after the event, that they are really better off. No doubt such cases do occur. But the argument overlooks the fact that the overcoming of inertia always involves a cost. Moving one's residence not only requires considerable expenses of money and time but also means mental strain and a considerable effort for adjustment to a new environment. Particularly for old people the loss of the support of a familiar environment can be catastrophic. In general, poor people have greater difficulty in adaptation to changes of environment. This is one of the reasons why they are poor, though certainly not the only one.

The practice of the Urban Renewal Program has brought home the reality of the cost of relocation and has forced the authorities to establish relocation agencies which assume some of the cost of overcoming inertia, in the form not only of cash contributions to moving expenses, but also of personal assistance by sizable and expensive staffs of people skilled in real estate and social work. It would encourage rehabilitation if the relocation agency extended this aid also to persons who on their own initiative want to move from houses suitable for rehabilitation, whether previously listed as such or not.

This discussion has so far dealt only with the financing of rehabilitation by the lower income groups. While they represent the great majority of the occupants of older housing, there are certainly many who are willing as well as able to invest in the rehabilitation and conservation of old houses; and their number is probably increasing with the general increase in real income. In fact, a great deal of such private rehabilitation is going on; the improvement registered by the census in the decade 1951–1961 is obviously due mainly to this factor.

More private rehabilitation of this kind could be stimulated by certain changes in credit and taxation, which will be discussed below. It has been suggested that a serious impediment to private rehabilitation may be presented by the environment, individual owners being discouraged from improving their property by the poor conditions of neighboring properties, and that public action is required to bring about simultaneous areawide improvement. Some doubt is thrown on this assertion by the fact that areawide rehabilitation *has* occurred without public intervention. Probably the most famous example is Georgetown in Washington, D.C.; others are to be found on the East Side of Manhattan, on the southern edge of the Philadelphia central business district, and, on a small scale, in Toronto on Collier Street.

Desirable as the rehabilitation of run-down houses for the use of middle- and upper-income groups may be, it cannot be gainsaid that it removes dwelling units from the low-income market just as effectively as does demolition. Stimulation of this type of rehabilitation can therefore be recommended only in conjunction with measures which effectively increase the supply of adequate housing for the low-rent market.

This lengthy section has explained that the money needed to bring about this increase cannot be extracted from the consumers of the supply for three reasons:

1. Most of them already pay an excessively high proportion of their incomes for housing.

2. Of those who do not, most have good and sufficient reasons to spend their money for other things, and are wise to do so.

3. Those who spend their money unwisely have, as free citizens, the inalienable right to be foolish in their own way.

The consumers would react by crowding into the cheapest available housing. The net result would be the spreading of blight rather than its elimination.

The Property Owner as a Source of Investment in Rehabilitation

If the tenant, in the majority of cases, cannot, for both economic and social reasons, pay more than he or she pays now and thereby provide an adequate return for new investment by the landlord, how can the landlord be induced to make such an investment? Obviously, either by the carrot or by the stick, or by a combination of both.

The carrot could consist in more favorable financing than is now available and in complete or partial removal of the tax on property improvement. Both methods will be discussed in some detail later. They may be expected to induce investment by those owner-occupiers who are able and willing to restrict their expenses for other items in order to enjoy better housing conditions. These approaches may also tip the scales for some landlords who are concerned about the continuing ability of their rental premises to attract desirable tenants. However, normally landlords, like other investors, will not make an investment that does not promise an additional return. Nor will the many owner-occupiers, primarily old people, who can even now barely make ends meet.

The stick remains. Housing codes establish minimum standards and force the owner either to demolish the house or make the necessary investment to bring it up to standard. This is considered justified because the property owner could and should have made these investments out of current revenue over the years, instead of "milking" the property by putting the money needed for repairs into his or her pocket.

There is no doubt that, with rare exceptions, the houses now requiring investment to bring them up to their original standard, or to a contemporary higher one, have been milked; that is, the original investment has been fully returned, often several times over. If we still lived in a feudal order, where landed property could be held only by the original owner or his heirs, a good case could be made for expropriation without compensation of the fully amortized building (not of the land). However, under our present institutions real estate is a freely marketable commodity, and present owners may be assumed to have acquired it at current market value and to be entitled to full compensation in case of expropriation. This right is recognized by present law, and it would be quite unreasonable either to expect or to advocate any change in this respect.

However, if a property owner is forced to demolish a building, the building is de facto expropriated without compensation. If he is forced to make an investment which gives no return, this investment is de facto expropriated. Of course, there is at present in Ontario no legal impediment to prevent the owner from getting a return by raising rents. But, as explained above, raising rents would defeat the main purpose of rehabilitation: the *general* raising of housing standards.

Housing codes are one of the oldest tools of housing reform. Their enactment has usually been greeted with high hopes, which have been universally disappointed. The blame has usually been put on lax enforcement, frequently ascribed to corrupt practices. Both accusations are well documented, but they are the characteristic effects of any law which attempts to establish a standard substantially higher than social reality. The late, unlamented prohibition laws of the United States are the classic, though unfortunately not the only, example.

It is easy to understand that legislative bodies and magistrates are reluctant to enact and impose stiff penalties when one considers the consequences of enforcement. This is obvious in the case of the low-income homeowner, who cannot raise the money to make the required repairs and therefore would lose his home, with no prospect of buying or leasing even equally substandard accommodation. Here enforcement inevitably breaks down, but a law which is not uniformly enforced loses much of its authority.

In the case of tenant-occupied houses, most landlords are prosperous enough to make the required investment. If they do, they raise the rent. If they prefer to demolish, they evict the occupants. In either case the tenant suffers. But a law which harms those whom it is intended to benefit can hardly expect much cooperation on their part. Without such cooperation it is extremely difficult to keep track of all violations of the code.

These factors surely limit the range within which a housing code can be effective. It can maintain a rock-bottom minimum standard of health and safety. In general this will be about the average standard of the dwelling units in the lowest decile of the rental range. Landlords can be forced to bring their buildings up to this level, and competition with the better units available in this rent range may prevent or at least limit rent increases. If such competition is relatively effective—which it is not with the present low vacancy rate—other landlords in this rent range will gradually improve their properties to a level slightly above the minimum required by law. It will then be possible to raise the legal minimum to this new, slightly higher average. Only by this very slow and uncertain process may housing codes be able to contribute to an actual raising of standards, rather than to the mere maintenance of a rock-bottom minimum.

The conclusion is inescapable that under present conditions rehabilitation by investment of property owners cannot be expected to rise substantially beyond the past and present levels.

Public Investment in Rehabilitation

If, as shown, the money required for rehabilitation can come neither from the tenants nor from the owners, it will have to come from the public. The reallocation of resources implied in this thesis may be analyzed in terms of gross national product (G.N.P.) and in terms of government expenditures.

The combined claims of private and government consumption and of private and government investment considerably exceed the total Canadian G.N.P. and have done so regularly year after year. The gap has been filled by a sizable net inflow of foreign investment, largely equity investment, most of it from the United States. While the effects of this inflow have been highly beneficial, there is growing and justified concern about the ultimate results. "Living high on the hog by mortgaging the farm" may end in foreclosure—the disappearance of Canada as an independent nation.

Regardless of widely divergent opinions about the amount of foreign investment which can be safely absorbed without running this risk, there is certainly every reason to employ our resources as economically and effectively as possible. For this reason the federal government has found it necessary to restrain the amount of resources going into construction by imposing a sales tax on building materials. At the same time our rapidly increasing population requires a growing stock of housing. This means that it is imperative to make maximum use of the existing stock by reducing demolition to an absolute minimum, and to give first priority to the conservation and rehabilitation of existing housing through government support in various forms: mortgage guarantees, direct lending, tax restrictions, grants, or subsidies. The amount of resources required to rehabilitate an existing house is only a fraction of that required to build a new one. The price that has to be paid for the existing structure, even if excessive in terms of its use value before rehabilitation, is a transfer payment which does not affect the G.N.P. A secondary but not negligible advantage of rehabilitation over new construction is the fact that it has a lower material and higher labor content. Some of this labor has to be highly specialized, but much of it requires only simple skills which can be found in Toronto precisely in the areas most in need of rehabilitation. To the extent that it mobilizes an otherwise unemployed resource, rehabilitation is costless in terms of the G.N.P.

In terms of government finances, wage payments to formerly unemployed labor are, of course, as real a cost as any other. Similarly, the greater cost of acquiring a vacant site in a central rather than in a peripheral area, while due to a higher transfer payment only and therefore irrelevant in terms of the G.N.P., is highly relevant in terms of cost to the taxpayers. In praxis, central sites acquired for public housing are not vacant, but covered with a number of structures with prospective lifetimes of varying length. Of all conceivable methods of supplying decent housing to the low-income groups, this is the most expensive one, both in terms of the G.N.P. and in terms of tax dollars. Rehabilitation of existing dwellings is the least expensive one on both counts, with new housing on vacant land in an intermediary position.

The preference shown to date for the most expensive method is obviously due to the emotional appeal of "slum clearance," and to the mistaken notion that it is "a good thing," though both deductive and inductive reasoning clearly show it to be pernicious.

Professor James A. Murray, in the statement quoted earlier, ascribed our poor record in providing low-rent housing to three possible reasons: too rich, too poor, or too ineffective. He might well have added a fourth one: too unwilling. Quite understandably, the citizen with an income just above the limit set for admission to a public housing project is unwilling to pay higher taxes to provide to others housing facilities much more costly than those he or she occupies. These persons' attitudes might be somewhat different if our so-called public housing were in fact "public," like public parks, schools, or transit, rather than being strictly "limited access" housing. This had been envisioned by the Ontario program for "full-recovery housing." However, the undeniable urgency of the need of many families in the lowest income group has forced the conversion of projects built under this program, such as Lawrence Park, to subsidized housing. A vicious circle exists. As long as the public housing program is small, it must give exclusive priority to the need of the lowest income group. But as long as all other groups are excluded from it, they will, as voters, not accept a really large program. The cycle can only be broken by providing public housing at the lowest possible cost. It is therefore pertinent to attempt a comparison of the cost of housing provided by each of the three methods noted above, however rough and tentative such an estimate must be.

Costs of Three Methods of Supplying Standard Housing

Standard housing is here defined as housing which can serve its occupants for several decades without impeding their healthy development. Such a standard is considerably higher than the one which can be effectively enforced by a housing code, but lower than that prevailing in the private market for new housing, probably close to the lower end of the range supplied by that market.

Under these assumptions the cost of construction, including site utilities, of a three-bedroom dwelling unit in Metropolitan Toronto is estimated at about $14,500. The cost of developed land in the outer sections of Metropolitan Toronto is estimated at $45,000–$60,000 per acre. With densities of 30–40 dwelling units this would amount to about $1500 per unit, for a total cost of $16,000 per unit.

The cost of rehabilitation of old houses, as well as of their clearance and replacement by new ones, is more difficult to estimate because of very limited experience. Some experience has been gained by the Philadelphia Housing Authority.[2] The authority bought, in 1958–1959, in the open market 40 three-bedroom houses, scattered among other similar row houses, in a lower middle-class area (not a "slum"), for prices averaging $5960 per house. Court action delayed rehabilitation until 1962. The cost of rehabilitation, including new refrigerators, averaged $2763, so that the total cost for a rehabilitated three-bedroom row house averaged $8723. While the cost of purchase varied from $3500 to $8000, and the cost of rehabilitation from $1027 to $5400, the total cost for no house exceeded $10,700. It is also worth noting that rehabilitation work carried out by the authority's own work force proved considerably cheaper than that done by contractors.

Prices of houses in Toronto in 1966 were considerably higher than they were in Philadelphia in 1958–1959. However, the average price of 29 properties, presumably single-family houses, sold during 1963 and 1964 in the Napier Place area was only $6800. It is therefore somewhat surprising to learn that the urban renewal study[3] estimates the average market value of properties in the Napier Place renewal area as $12,000. The estimate for properties scheduled for clearance averages about $10,500 per house or $9500 per dwelling unit. In the Alexandra Park urban renewal area the assessed value of 57 houses, a few of which may contain more than one unit, on Augusta Avenue and Wolseley Street averaged $2820. On the basis of the rule of thumb that purchase price in redevelopment areas is four times the assessed value, this would indicate a price of $11,280 per property.

The difference between the average of $11,000–$12,000 estimated for public acquisition in designated renewal areas and $6800 in private sales in the same area is striking. The Napier Place report does not give the assessed values of the 29 properties which changed hands in 1963–1964, but there is no reason to assume that private sales affected exclusively the poorest properties. There is no doubt that the fact that the Housing Authority is known to have only the choice of buying at the seller's price or going through the costly and cumbersome process of expropriation drives prices up. Even in the Philadelphia case, where the authority did have a choice of buying only 40 houses in an area containing over 1000, a rise in prices was noted.

---

[2] See "Successful Experiment—the Used-House Program," Philadelphia Housing Association, April 1963.
[3] "Napier Place Urban Renewal Scheme," June 1965.

Selective buying for rehabilitation, especially if not limited to a narrowly defined area, could largely avoid this inflationary effect. This should offset the fact that purchase for clearance includes a certain proportion of buildings below the level capable of rehabilitation. The proportion may be lower than is usually assumed. The numerous surveys made in Metropolitan Toronto have found no blocks in which all buildings were classified as "poor," and few in which some were not classified as "good." Even in Napier Place fewer than 39% were classified as "poor." Moreover, most of the deficiencies which put them into the "poor" category, such as loose bricks, leaning chimneys, or sagging roofs, in no way preclude rehabilitation.

On the basis of these considerations the average price of a three-bedroom house is estimated as $11,000 for rehabilitation and as $10,000 for area clearance. Estimates made by the staff of the Toronto development commissioner for the cost of rehabilitation of 96 houses in the Alexandra Park area range from $321 to $7494, with an average of $1898. This includes only minimum rehabilitation, without improvement of equipment. Rehabilitation to a level comparable with that of new housing is likely to average about $3000, slightly more than in Philadelphia. The Philadelphia experience also indicated that it is prudent to keep a reserve of $500 for the correction of hidden defects which may come to light during occupancy. Operating costs also tend to be higher, possibly by as much as $100 annually; capitalized at 6.66%, this means an additional $1500. Thus a three-bedroom house, rehabilitated to a level comparable with a new one, may cost about the same, $16,000 ($11,000 + $3000 + $500 + $1500).

In wholesale clearance and redevelopment the number of dwelling units destroyed averages in Toronto about 30–40 per acre, the same as the replacement. It is, of course, technically feasible to obtain a higher density by erecting tall, multistory buildings. However, in addition to somewhat higher construction and operating costs, this involves a very substantial social cost when numerous children are accommodated in this manner. Therefore a 1/1 ratio between demolished and new units has been assumed. With a cost of $10,000 for the demolished unit and of $14,500 for the new unit (both explained above), the total cost would average about $24,500, or 50% more than with the two other methods. (The estimate of $24,500 coincides fairly closely with the *actual* unit cost in Regent Park South.) This is not surprising, since under this method the prices of two units—the old and the new one —have to be paid in order to create one unit.

Between the two other methods, cost differences appear to be marginal, and other factors have to be considered. Two of these weigh strongly in favor of rehabilitation. First, over two thirds of the cost consists in transfer payments, and is therefore no cost in terms of the G.N.P. Second, most of the people in need of low-rent housing prefer to live close to the center rather than on the periphery, for good reasons. It is the area in which they have lived and established strong ties. It is equipped with the type of retail and service facilities which they need. Most importantly, it gives them the best access to the concentration of jobs in the center and also relatively good access to jobs at any point near the periphery. This is particularly important, because frequently several members of a household need jobs and because their employment tends to be unstable. However, with the rapid increase in the number of jobs at the periphery, in all kinds of services, as well as in manufacturing, this reason becomes less important, and location at the periphery becomes equally or even more acceptable to an increasing proportion of low-income families. Both rehabilitated housing in the central and new housing in outlying sections of Metropolitan Toronto are needed, whilst there is no warrant for new housing on cleared land in central locations.

New housing on vacant land has one important advantage. For every one housing unit created by the other two methods, it puts two on the market: the new one and an old one which remains and can and does provide shelter for a family, however poorly. The other methods improve only the quality; new housing on vacant land, while it makes an equal contribution to improvement of quality, also increases the quantity. But insufficient supply in the face of a growing demand of low-income families for housing is the root of the evil: inexorably rents and prices rise and quality falls in this seller's market.

The scant existing supply of housing is constantly being depleted by demolitions to make room for public works, such as expressways and schools, and for private residential and commercial uses, and by conversions to nonresidential purposes, as well as by fire and other "acts of God." To deplete it further by deliberate "clearance" can only make matters worse. We need more old housing, not less.

"Old," of course, is a relative concept. In this context it means second-hand (or third-, fourth-, etc., hand) housing. The supply of old housing in this sense is in fact replenished by the filtering-down process, which constantly brings houses into the category suitable for and requiring conservation-rehabilitation. It is frequently said that the filtering-down process does not work. This is not correct. It does work, but far too slowly. It can provide a sufficiently large supply of housing of a quality worth conserving at reasonable prices to the lower income groups only if it is greatly accelerated. Without such acceleration no large-scale, sustained program of conservation and rehabilitation can be effective. This is the crux of the matter. It is therefore necessary to discuss measures designed to bring about such acceleration.

Accelerating the Filtering-Down Process

It has been the policy of the Canadian government to accelerate the rate at which new housing enters the stream by stimulating the flow of mortgage money. The success of this policy is documented by the fact that the number of occupied dwelling units per 100 families increased from 90.6 in 1951 to 103.4 in 1961; the number of vacant units also increased slightly. However, the improvement in this ratio was mainly due to a steep increase in the number of units occupied by nonfamily persons, mostly living singly. The increase in the number of units occupied by families has only slightly exceeded the increase in the number of families. It appears that the increased supply has been mainly absorbed by a spreading out of the upper- and middle-income groups. The amount of housing which has been vacated by these groups and thereby made available for filtering down to the lower income groups has barely kept pace with the increased number of families in this group.

The filtering-down process could be accelerated if the amount of new housing poured into the stream, in addition to being expanded in quantity, was poured in not as close to the top, but as close as possible to the bottom of the funnel—in other words, if encouragement was concentrated on the building of dwelling units at the lowest level at which decent new housing can be built. The main instrument presently used for this purpose is the limited dividend housing company. This program appears well suited to accelerate the filtering-down process and might already have done so—if it were not so limited in volume. It seems that this limitation in volume is due to the combined effect of the program's three limitations: on profits, on rents, and on income of tenants, which make it unattractive to investors. It seems worth considering whether these particular limitations are really necessary and whether the purpose of the program cannot be accomplished by other means.

If adequate standards of site planning, unit planning, construction, and operation are secured and limits are set on the maximum cost per unit—varied, of course, according to size of unit—a limit on profits seems unnecessary. In addition to killing the main motive for investment, it has the additional disadvantage of discouraging attempts to use imagination and inventiveness to improve the product and to encourage attempts to use ingenuity to hide the profits by a variety of tricks (of which kickbacks from contractors are the most familiar), which in turn necessitate cumbersome controls.

Limits on both rents and incomes are unavoidable in an extremely tight market. Such a market would make it possible to rent the units at high rents to high-income families, at very high profits. Such high profits would certainly lead to a great expansion of investment in this type of housing, which, in the long run, would bring profits and rents down to a normal level by the competitive market process. How long this run would be would depend, of course, on how far supply exceeded demand. It appears at least possible that in this sector of the housing market the excess in Metropolitan Toronto is not so great that it could not be brought into balance within 1 or 2 years.

Elimination of these two limitations would not only simplify its administration and greatly expand the program by making it more attractive to investors, but would also be desirable for other reasons. Rent limitations motivate the owner to cut down on maintenance and services. Income limitations motivate the tenants to "chisel" in their declarations and sometimes to forgo additional income and to refuse to do some additional work which they or members of their family might usefully perform, and necessitate odious and cumbersome controls. If the absence of income limitations should induce some high-income families to live in this type of housing, this would be a welcome contribution to social integration.

In place of these three limitations it is proposed to extend the same favorable mortgage terms to housing of a similar type under the following conditions.

First, there would be a limitation on vacancies to a nominal rate, probably 1%. This is considered necessary to counteract the temptation to resort to oligopolistic practices. To exemplify, if the owner of a 100-unit apartment house has a choice between leasing all 100 units at $90 monthly rent, or 90 units at $100, he or she will choose the latter course because it reduces the operation cost. But the public interest requires that the housing, created with the aid of public credit, be fully utilized. The proposed measure would force the owner to set the rent at a level at which demand equals supply.

Second, the owner should be obligated to put at the disposal of the authority in charge of administering housing subsidies, on demand, units up to a certain percentage of the total available in his or her project, probably 20–30%, at a rent to be determined in the same way as rents in limited dividend housing are now determined. The authority might in turn assume the obligation to supply, on demand of the owner, tenants up to the same percentage of units in the project. Such an obligation certainly would make the vacancy limitation far more acceptable to the owner.

The housing of subsidized families in such housing has been made possible by acceptance of the policy that subsidies are related not to specific buildings, but to specific families (and single persons) who without them cannot obtain decent housing, and that they may be used to obtain housing anywhere. This eliminates the need for projects occupied exclusively by subsidized tenants. The negative aspects of such projects have long been recognized. It is, however, an erroneous conclusion to reject large projects as such, which have great potential advantages, exemplified by many successful projects in Great Britain and Europe. The negative aspects are exclusively due to the specific selection of tenants. It is not so much the fact that they formerly lived in "slums" as the abnormally high proportion of children to adults, particularly male adults, which leads to trouble. The attempt to control the trouble leads to excessive regimentation, which in turn leads many eligible self-respecting families, who would make excellent tenants, to reject such projects. None of this occurs in large-scale projects which are genuinely "public," that is, open to anyone.

This leads to the third proposal: a vigorous development of "full-recovery" housing projects on vacant land, which would accept a percentage of subsidized tenants similar to that proposed above for the "limited vacancy" private projects. They would also in all other respects, including taxation, be similar to and competitive with these and thereby effectively keep their rents in line.

Neither the private limited vacancy nor the public full-recovery projects would make any claim on the public purse (subsidies to needy families are not inherent in the project, and have to be paid wherever these families are housed). They would merely take advantage of the willingness of investors to accept a lower rate of interest on government bonds than they are willing to accept on mortgages. They would not put any burden on the taxpayers, and budgetary considerations would set no limits on their expansion. Indeed, it is possible that the proposed measures would be so successful that expansion might be considered too rapid because of the resultant demands on the G.N.P. and on the money market. Should this be the case, the effect could be reduced by discouraging investment in more expensive housing. This would mean diverting the flow of additions to the housing supply from the top to the bottom of the market for new housing, where it would have an immediate effect on the filtering-down process.

Acceleration of the filtering-down process or, expressed differently, a rapid increase in supply in the market for old housing would eliminate or greatly reduce the obstacles to rehabilitation discussed in the preceding sections. The beneficial effects of a buyer's market would make themselves felt in many ways, in addition to the immediate benefit to tenants of a relative fall in rents. In many cases this would make tenants able and willing to pay slightly higher rents and would thereby act as a "carrot" to induce the owner to make the required investment. The inducement would be greatly reinforced by the "stick" of the prospect of not finding tenants for a run-down building in a buyer's market. If the owner felt that the required investment was not economically justified, he would demolish the vacant structure. The two alternatives available to code enforcement thus being in conformance with market trends, the housing code could be effectively enforced and its minimum requirements could gradually be raised to a higher standard. The excessive prices which now have to be paid even for houses which are barely habitable would be considerably reduced. This would reduce the cost of a rehabilitated dwelling to a more normal level, about 15–20% below the cost of a comparable new one, as occurred in Philadelphia. It would also reduce the cost of clearance for public works or private redevelopment.

Acceleration of the filtering-down process must precede large-scale renewal. This does not mean, however, that aid to rehabilitation should be deferred. The assembly and training of staffs and the gathering of experience would in any case require considerable time, so that any new program could only gradually gain momentum. Such programs should therefore be initiated now.

SUGGESTED POLICIES

Survey of the Available Tools

As mentioned earlier, land assembly and the legal provisions facilitating such assembly are basic tools of urban renewal and will be discussed first. But rehabilitation, as also explained before, also requires substantial public financial aid. The tools available for this, enumerated in ascending order of their claim on the public purse, are as follows:

1. Mortgage guarantees.
2. Government mortgages and direct investments.
3. Tax reductions.
4. Loans at interest rates below those paid by the government.
5. Public works, grants, and subsidies in cash or free services.

The role of these tools differs in their application to owner-occupied and to rental properties, respectively, and to various income groups.

Finally, the role of code enforcement in combination with these financial tools will be discussed.

Land Assembly and Area Designation

Land assembly can often be achieved by purchase in the open market. However, the power of expropriation will sometimes be required, whether merely threatened or actually used. Two legal instruments are available in Ontario. The Planning Act, 1955, states, under Part 1, 19:

(1). For the purpose of developing any feature of the official plan, a municipality, with the approval of the Minister, may at any time and from time to time,

    (a) acquire land within the municipality;

    (b) hold land heretofore or hereafter acquired within the municipality; or

    (c) sell, lease or otherwise dispose of land so acquired or held when no longer required.

Apparently the right conferred on municipalities by this section of the Ontario Planning Act has never been used. It is ideally suited for the purposes of rehabilitation because it could be used for the acquisition of individual properties as well as of areas, and in any part of the municipality—and there are few municipalities in which no properties in need of rehabilitation or conservation are to be found.

Urban renewal has, instead, relied on Section 20-(3), which confers the same powers on the municipality, with identical wording of (a), (b), and (c). However, here these powers are made dependent on prior enactment of a bylaw designating an area as "a redevelopment area," and such designation must be "desirable because of age, dilapidation, over-crowding, faulty arrangement, unsuitability of buildings or for any other reason" [20-(1)(b)]. Aids provided under both provincial and federal legislation have also been tied to such prior designation, and much time, effort, and money have been and are being devoted to prove that this rather than that area, with these rather than those boundaries, should have priority for such designation.

Designation of an area as a renewal area has most undesirable effects. Because renewal has up to now meant clearance of all or part of the existing buildings, nobody wants to invest a penny, not even for the most urgent repairs, in such an area. Because "blighted area," not without reason, is widely regarded as a polite term for "slum," the inhabitants of the area protest bitterly and tend to act out their bitterness in negligent, if not in outright destructive behavior. The inevitable result of designation of an area is its demoralization. Instead of the required increased investment, there is rapid disinvestment. Instead of rehabilitation, there is dishabilitation. This has been the universal experience in the United States and also in Toronto, for instance, in Alexandra Park. Many structures which were quite capable of rehabilitation 12 years ago when the area was first designated have now been found to be beyond repair.

The Philadelphia experience is instructive also in this respect. The Pennsylvania Redevelopment Law of 1945, which served as a model for similar laws in many states south of the border, required the designation of "redevelopment areas," to be followed by the establishment of smaller "project areas" within their boundaries. A few years later one of the two men who had devised that law found himself charged with the obligation of certifying such redevelopment areas in Philadelphia. He stated that his certification would not lead to action until project areas were established. But this was of no avail in stemming demoralization. He concluded that the only way to avoid this destructive impact was to dilute it by designating practically the entire city, with the exception of "new growth" areas, as a redevelopment area. Not surprisingly, this proposal was rejected as outrageously absurd. However, after about 6 years of further experience, the city *did* designate a very extensive urban renewal area," which actually contained a majority of all dwelling units within its boundaries.

If rehabilitation is not to be killed before it is born, it is absolutely essential to avoid official designation of selected areas for renewal. The best way to avoid this would be to rely entirely on Part I, 19-(1), of the Ontario Planning Act, quoted above. If this is not considered acceptable, the widest possible portion of Metropolitan Toronto should be designated as a renewal area.

As noted earlier, there is not a single block in Metropolitan Toronto in which there are not some structures capable of rehabilitation. The strong prejudice against this is pyschologically understandable. Elected and appointed officials responsible for urban renewal are expected to show results. But the results of rehabilitation are diffused, inconspicuous, and not particularly photogenic. It is a slow, tedious process, requiring endless detail work. It is also risky. As it is impossible to predict what hidden weaknesses exist in an old structure, unpleasant surprises and mistakes in judgment are unavoidable. By contrast, wholesale clearance and replacement by new structures is simple, predictable, safe, and dramatic. Consciously or unconsciously, these factors weigh heavily when a decision between demolition and rehabilitation has to be made by public officials.

Sometimes this prejudice is carried to the point where mere chronological age is considered as sufficient evidence for a death sentence, on the assumption that after 50 or 60 years a house must be structurally and functionally obsolete. There is no justification for this assumption. Structures of stone or brick have a lifetime of many centuries. Wood is, of course, vulnerable to fire, rot, and some species of insects. However, when they have not been subject to these hazards, many wooden structures, or parts of structures such as joists or rafters, still serve their purpose after centuries of use. Other parts of the structure, such as roofing materials, plaster, and paint, have, of course, shorter life spans and must be replaced from time to time. But this is necessary in relatively new houses as well as in old ones. Functional obsolescence affects most strongly the equipment, but old equipment can be replaced by new. This has been done and is done daily in thousands of dwelling units, including the installation of complete new kitchens and bathrooms. These are the only rooms which have completely changed their character. Change is very rapid in our ways of producing, but much less marked in our way of consuming, which is carried on in the home. Even if, instead of sitting on stiff-backed chairs as did the Victorians, we prefer to stretch our legs in easy chairs or on the floor, we can do this just as well in an old house as in a new one.

Nor is it justified to judge fitness for rehabilitation on the basis of some arbitrarily established ratio of the cost of rehabilitation to the value of the structure, certainly not on a maximum of one quarter of the assessed value, or one sixteenth of the estimated purchase price, as has been proposed for Alexandra Park. Builders who have engaged in rehabilitation of old houses for higher income groups sometimes have even found it profitable to invest more in rehabilitation than in the purchase of the old structure. Rehabilitation almost always is technically feasible and in a vast majority of cases is preferable for both economic and social reasons.

There are, of course, cases where disinvestment is indicated not only for individual structures, but also for areas. Two different situations should here be distinguished clearly. Elimination of the present use may be considered necessary by the community in the general interest, or in the interest of the inhabitants of the area which is to be cleared. The first situation obtains when the land is required for a public or semipublic use, such as a highway, a school, or the extension of a university, or for a more intensive private use, such as office buildings or apartments. In both cases the full price of the properties which served the old use should be borne by the new use, whether public or private. To pay part of this price as an alleged cost of urban renewal, as is done in the United States and is permissible under Canadian legislation, is fraudulent bookkeeping which can lead only to a misallocation of resources.

The second situation may occur when a previously habitable area has been made uninhabitable by environmental nuisances, which may be caused, for instance, by neighboring industries or by heavy trucking. Here the community which has allowed the nuisance to develop, whether for good and sufficient reasons or through lack of foresight, has a clear responsibility for assuming the cost. As there may be no sufficiently profitable alternative use for such areas, in this case the use of public funds to "write down" the value of the land may be appropriate. Here, as always when people are displaced in their presumed own best interest, the principle should be to pull them out by offering them better alternatives rather than to push them out by forced demolition.

In all these situations it is recommended that the areas in question be acquired at the earliest feasible date and the existing uses left undisturbed as long as possible. This is desirable not only because it eases the transition and reduces the cost, but also because unforeseen circumstances may prevent the anticipated change: the highway may not be built in the expected location; the expected demand for more intensive use may not develop; better housing alternatives may not be available; or, least likely, the nuisances may disappear. In all such cases the area will have to return to its previous use and will frequently require rehabilitation.

Public Works and Public Services

A formerly attractive neighborhood may become undesirable not only by the intrusion of disturbing physical elements, but also by lack or insufficiency of the public facilities required for contemporary living. Indeed, this is typically characteristic of so-called blighted areas. Rehabilitation of individual structures is a questionable investment if the environment does not support its value. Obsolete school buildings on small sites, lack of neighborhood playgrounds and parks, inadequate or decayed water and sewer systems, resulting in interruptions of water supply or in flooding of basements, traffic on residential streets, which precludes their traditional use as an extension of the home for social intercourse and play—all these are factors which adversely affect the attractiveness and value of a neighborhood. All of them can be corrected only by very substantial public investments. These will be required whether the neighborhood is modernized by rehabilitation or by "clearance and redevelopment."

One of the main shortcomings of old neighborhoods in comparison with those developed since the inception of the automobile age is the lack of parking space. Its provision, whether on private or on public land, is essential for successful rehabilitation, and the cost of acquisition of land for this purpose frequently will also have to be assumed by the public.

Provision of adequate public facilities and of parking space generally requires acquisition of occupied and usable residential structures for demolition. Thereby it increases the demand for and decreases the supply of old houses. This reinforcement of the seller's market in old housing is a highly unfortunate but unavoidable side effect of public investment for the modernization of old neighborhoods. It makes conservation and rehabilitation of all the houses that remain all the more urgent.

Because of the high cost of land acquisition the total money cost of providing adequate public facilities, including parking, may be not much lower, and conceivably in some cases even higher, in old than in new neighborhoods. However, the cost in terms of the G.N.P. will always be much lower.

Generally in old neighborhoods not only public facilities, but also public services are inferior to those in new ones: pavements and sidewalks are less well maintained, garbage collection is less effective, and so on. Improvements of public services is necessary to maintain and raise the morale of a neighborhood and to encourage investment for maintenance and improvement of private properties. Because the density is much higher than in new single-family house areas, and because the chutes, incinerators, and janitor services which take care of garbage in new high-density apartments are absent, more frequent garbage collections are required in old neighborhoods to maintain equal standards.

It is frequently argued that not only the physical but also the social environment is a deterrent to rehabilitation. This argument has some weight when rehabilitation for a higher income group is intended, though even in that case the examples mentioned earlier appear to call it into question. It has no validity where the rehabilitation for the benefit of the present inhabitants is concerned, and it is this type of rehabilitation towards which public policy must be primarily directed, as explained in the preceding analysis of the problem.

A few areas requiring rehabilitation, however, are adversely affected by a concentration of asocial individuals. Obviously, these persons can be cured not by changes in their physical environment—least of all by driving them into other neighborhoods by demolishing their abodes—but only by methods of social work which lie outside the scope of this discussion.

A far more widespread factor discouraging rehabilitation is poor housekeeping. Violations of the housing code are not always the fault of the landlord; they may also be committed by tenants, and there is no reason why the tenant should not be held responsible in such cases. However, such punitive measures would be rarely required and are of minor importance. The basic need is for an adequately financed and staffed agency, public or voluntary, that would give positive aid by advice and instruction in good housekeeping; and, in cases where physical or mental incapacitation was the reason for poor housekeeping, would undertake the chores normally carried out by the occupants of a dwelling.

While measures of this kind are outside the jurisdiction of a planning agency, it is important to point out that "human rehabilitation" must go hand in hand with physical rehabilitation.

Such services, like all other measures discussed in this section, require money, but they are indispensable to create the conditions under which rehabilitation of individual structures could be successfully stimulated by the various methods available, to which the discussion now turns.

Mortgages Guaranteed by the Central Mortgage and Housing Corporation

It is well known that many people faced with the choice of buying either an old or a newly built house turn to the new one, often against their preference, because they cannot raise the much higher equity required to buy an old house, in addition to assuming the burden of more onerous mortgage terms. The liberal provisions of C.M.H.C.-insured mortgages are available only for new houses. There is good reason for this, because only new houses increase the housing stock. However, as conservation and rehabilitation of old houses contribute to the maintenance of the stock, consideration might well be given to the possibility to extending the same terms under certain conditions:

1. To any property owner for the cost of rehabilitation based on plans, specifications, and cost estimates approved by the C.M.H.C.

2. To persons who want to buy and rehabilitate a house for use as owner-occupants and who obligate themselves to invest in rehabilitation a sum equal to a certain percentage, to be determined by the C.M.H.C. (probably about 10%), subject to approval of both the purchase price and the rehabilitation proposals by the C.M.H.C.

In both cases it would seem advisable to establish an upper limit for the total cost (purchase price plus cost of rehabilitation) of the dwelling unit. It is hardly justified to give public support, even in the form of pledging the public credit to guarantee a mortgage, to the creation of luxury or semiluxury housing.

Direct Mortgage Lending by Public Authorities

While the measures suggested would promote rehabilitation, the cost of the rehabilitated dwelling units would make them available generally only to families with incomes well above the average of those living in housing in need of rehabilitation. The presence of such families in the older areas is socially desirable and might also have a favorable impact on the willingness of the owners of less valuable properties to maintain and improve them. But it would further reduce the amount of housing available to the lower income groups. Hence further measures are required.

Interest rates on guaranteed mortgages are still fairly high; at present they are set at 6.75%, and very few mortgages are offered at this rate. Direct mortgage loans at 5.75%, available from the C.M.H.C. for cooperatives and limited dividend companies, should be available to them for rehabilitation projects as well as for newly constructed ones. The modifications suggested above for new "limited dividend" projects would apply equally, with the quota reserved for subsidized families probably set somewhat higher, maybe 30–40%. However, it seems probable that limited dividend companies as well as cooperatives would generally prefer to build new housing.

A possibly more promising field would be direct mortgage lending for rehabilitation to owner-occupiers. In addition to the conditions enumerated above, two other conditions are considered appropriate for this greater financial support. First, the applicant would have to submit proof that his income and assets were insufficient to carry out the proposed rehabilitation without the loan. Second, he would have to give the C.M.H.C., or a public authority designated by it, first option of purchase in case of intent to sell.

Loans under similar conditions could, of course, also be made by other levels of government.

Publicly Subsidized Old Housing

Direct mortgage lending might help families somewhat lower down on the income scale, but it could not come to grips with the main problem: adequate housing for low-income families and single persons. Government in Canada, as in most other countries, has pledged itself to this goal and has recognized that public funds are required to fill the gap between low incomes and high housing costs. However, up to now only token compliance with the proclaimed goal has been achieved.

It is here suggested that all funds committed by various levels of government to housing and urban renewal in any form be concentrated on this goal and supplemented as required. Some of them will be needed for the creation of new housing on vacant land, as explained in the preceding analysis. The balance should be used for the acquisition of old houses, subject only to the limitation that the rate of purchase did not lead to a noticeable increase in the price of such houses.

Acquisition should proceed simultaneously in two ways. First, suitable houses should be bought in the open market in any location, rehabilitated, and leased to eligible tenants at rents geared to their incomes.

Second, entire areas should be acquired—as far as possible, by negotiation; where necessary, by expropriation. These would be primarily, but not of necessity exclusively, areas now under consideration as "renewal areas." Owner-occupiers would be given an option either to retain their properties—this would not preclude purchase or expropriation at a later date—or sell them with the right to remain as tenants. When the income of the previous owner-occupants exceeded the level established for admission to public housing, the rent would be based on the purchase price; when it was below that level, it would be geared to their incomes. Similarly, tenants with incomes below the public housing level would be entitled to a rent reduction if their rent exceeded the established maximum percentage of their incomes. If their incomes exceeded the public housing level, they would continue to pay the same rents as before. Only when rents were excessively high or—if such cases exist—unreasonably low, would an adjustment to prevailing market levels be made.

The public authority or corporation, after having acquired the area, would *not* immediately make any decision concerning demolition or rehabilitation, but would at first concentrate on its maintenance, management, and housekeeping functions. During this period it would become thoroughly acquainted both with the condition of its properties and with the needs of its tenants, and only then proceed to develop plans for a gradual, staged transformation of the area.

It will be objected that this puts the authority in the role of a "slum landlord," and that a government body could not assume that role. It may well be asked, "Why not?" The usual answer is that government cannot violate its own laws. It does not have to. If the housing code, as was stipulated earlier, requires only a rock-bottom standard, certainly the authority can rehabilitate a house at least up to that standard within a reasonable time. If thorough inspection shows that rehabilitation is practically impossible, the authority should demolish the house and relocate the tenant. If the requirements of a housing code are such that even a public authority, which does not have to make a profit and even can absorb a loss, cannot live up to it, how can a private owner be expected to do so? If the requirements are really of such a nature, they are practically unrealistic and unenforceable and should be changed.

Rather than rejecting public ownership of houses on the specious grounds that a public authority cannot be a slum landlord, it makes far more sense to say that *only* such an authority can be a slum landlord, because it is the only one which can be expected to maintain such properties in habitable condition without gouging the tenants. The "slum" problem is very largely a problem of management, and enforcement of the housing code should be geared to meeting it. If the owner explicitly opts for demolition rather than for rehabilitation, or so opts implicitly by not carrying out the required rehabilitation within the maximum permissible period, he should be legally obliged not to demolish the house but to sell it to the authority for the appraised value which the site would have after demolition. The owner is not entitled to any compensation for a structure which, because it is not habitable, cannot be rented, cannot produce any income, and therefore has no value. The housing code should be amended accordingly. The authority, having taken possession of the house, would then decide whether to demolish or rehabilitate it.

To return to the aforementioned staged plan for an area acquired by an authority, the authority would first have to determine the probable lifetime of each structure. This determination would have to take into account both its structural condition and the time when its site was likely to be required for other uses. Such uses might include public facilities, new housing, or parking or street space required for a revision of the street pattern. Another important element of the plan would be the remodeling of the interior of the block, usually the most abused part in old areas, for "tot lots," small tree-planted "sitting-out" areas, or, where appropriate, parking spaces. The plan would be frequently modified in the light of experience. The need for this is an additional reason for keeping the area in one ownership.

Public land acquisition should not be limited to "blighted" areas; preferably, areas should be acquired before they become blighted. The proposed procedure would have two decided advantages over present practices: first, it would preserve the social fabric of the neighborhood; and, second, it would make maximum use of the existing housing stock and thereby greatly reduce costs.

Evidently, the agency charged with this task would have to be well staffed with people skilled in real estate and property management, as well as in human relations. At present staffs experienced in these fields have been assembled only by public housing authorities. It is, however, highly desirable that private nonprofit organizations also devote themselves to this task. In several European countries churches, trade unions, and other groups have organized such "public service housing companies" with great success. It is hoped that similar efforts will be made in Canada. Among the churches, at least, there is a growing desire to develop activities for the improvement of housing. It would be an ideal field for practical ecumenism. Such semipublic companies would, in most cases, be able to raise only a modest equity. For the balance of the cost they would have to rely on government loans or mortgages, possibly at reduced rates. Government partnership in mixed societies is also a possibility.

Units in such semipublic housing would, of course, also be available to subsidized families. Subsidizing the family rather than the house is, as observed earlier, the most logical and clear-cut way for improving housing conditions. However, legislation has been enacted, administrative units have been set up, and large funds have been authorized for "urban renewal" as a separate activity. Considering the momentum of any existing organization, it may be advisable to charge it with the task of acquiring the areas destined for rehabilitation and selling them to public or semipublic housing agencies at a "written-down" price. This would enable the agency to rent the rehabilitated dwelling units to the previous occupants at rents within their means.

It will be noted that the proposed policy reverses the traditional approach, under which public housing was always new housing, while old housing was always private. Such reversal is considered reasonable, because new housing can very well be managed by private enterprise, while old housing, at least when it reaches the stage approaching blight, can be adequately managed only by non-profit-making public or semipublic agencies—or, under appropriate conditions, by owner-occupants.

The Problem of Owner-Occupants

However questionable may be the folklore that homeowners are better citizens than tenants, there can be no question that they generally maintain their houses better, for the obvious reason that deterioration would hurt their own pocketbooks. In most cases they use their spare time to make minor repairs and improvements which in tenant-occupied houses are made by the landlord, who recovers the cost from the tenant. This not only reduces the monetary housing cost of the owner, but, by mobilizing otherwise unused labor power, reduces the claims on the G.N.P. Promotion of homeownership is therefore clearly in the public interest.

Measures to encourage rehabilitation of houses occupied by owners in the middle- and lower-middle-income groups, respectively, by extension of mortgage lending have already been discussed. However, many owner-occupants are unable to assume the cost of carrying a mortgage, even under these relatively favorable conditions, and even if the mortgage covers the entire cost of rehabilitation. Several additional measures are therefore suggested, applicable to various conditions.

Sometimes, primarily in the case of older homeowners—and sometimes also of owners of rental properties who have no other income or assets—payment of interest on the mortgage might be deferred by the C.M.H.C. (or any other public lender). The deferred interest would be recovered either on sale of the property (from the purchaser) or on the death of the owner (from his or her estate).

Owner-occupants whose incomes were below the level established for admittance to public housing projects should be entitled to the same subsidies as were tenants. The Housing Authority would pay that part of their housing cost which exceeded 25% of their incomes; normally this would be applied to interest on mortgages, including those for approved rehabilitation.

While these measures would assist existing owner-occupants to maintain ownership and to conserve and rehabilitate their houses, they would be of only marginal importance in aiding families of low and moderate incomes to become homeowners, because they do not have the required equity. For this purpose they would need a special credit. Probably the most feasible form for this would be a "hire-purchase" agreement, under which the occupant would acquire title after a number of years by paying a small monthly sum in addition to the rent; he would thereby immediately have an interest in good maintenance of the property. The equity could not be large; monthly payments of $10 would in 5 years acquire only a 5% equity in a $12,000 house. It might be worthwhile to revive a scheme used over 100 years ago in the "Cite Ouvriere" in Mulhouse in Alsace, France, a limited dividend housing project for textile workers. Here the occupant who was in the process of making such payments could, in case of hardship, return to tenant status and reclaim his payments. During the cotton crisis caused by the American Civil War, many workers availed themselves of this right. In subsequent years under more favorable conditions, however, all became homeowners. Today, after more than a century, the 3000 houses in this development are all owner-occupied, and the development is still a good and attractive working-class neighborhood—proof that with reasonable maintenance low-income housing can have a long lifetime. An even more spectacular proof is the 60 houses built in 1520 in Angsburg, Germany, by a foundation established by the famous banker Jacob Fugger. They are still very much in demand, though this may be largely due to the fact that the rents have been frozen at the level of 1520—which in current money amounts to 5 cents per month.

The suggested methods for maintaining home ownership may also be the best solution for dealing with homeowners in areas acquired for renewal. Similarly, properties acquired by the relevant agency might be brought into homeownership. However, in the latter case it might be advisable to sell only the house—with the aforementioned first option for repurchase—and retain title to the land so as to preserve any increase in site value for the community.

The suggested measures should make it possible to preserve most of the existing housing stock by conservation and rehabilitation, and to maintain and enlarge homeownership. There are, however, two conditions, often coinciding, where continuation of occupancy by the present owner is not desirable.

Inspection records in Metropolitan Toronto show that violations of the housing code have been found in as many owner-occupied as rented properties. In a few such cases decay has reached a stage where rehabilitation is no longer possible. More numerous are cases where houses are inhabited by old couples or single people, who are no longer able to maintain them, but stay because they do not see any alternative. Housing statistics show that alongside a number of dwelling units which are overcrowded, or "overused," there are a far greater number of houses which are "underused," that is, units in which the number of rooms exceeds the number of inhabitants by three or more—often many more. Many of these are, of course, occupied by families who want and can afford these rooms. But a surprisingly large number are very modest or even poor old houses with three, four, five, or more bedrooms, which are occupied mostly by old couples or widows. These houses, often with minimal or even no rehabilitation, could house large low-income families who cannot possibly find decent houses in the private market and for whom very few public housing units have been built, or are likely to be built because of cost limitations. On the other hand, the lone old people would be far better off in small units which they could manage. It should be a function of the relocation agency to help them to make this move. This would require, in addition to paying the moving cost, a great deal of time spent by the relocation worker. This person would have to convince the owner that the move was in his interest and that the price offered by the agency was fair; and would have to help him to find a suitable apartment and possibly to introduce him to future neighbors, churches, and other neighborhood organizations; help him to make an inventory of his belongings and to make up his mind which ones to keep and which ones to sell; and help him in selling the latter. Probably the old people would not only be attached emotionally to these belongings, but would also have exaggerated notions of their monetary value. In such cases it might be necessary for the agency to buy them at an exaggerated price and sell them at a loss; the cost of this type of "write-down" would be minimal and its benefits much greater than those of the currently accepted write-down for clearance and redevelopment. Finally the relocation worker would have to assist in moving and installing the "relocatee." After relocation the housing agency would rehabilitate the house and rent or sell it to a large family, normally a subsidized one. In the few cases where the house could not be rehabilitated, but had to be demolished, only the value of the site should be paid, but in hardship cases a welfare payment might be justified.

Code enforcement should be meshed with all these measures. The enforcement officer would notify the housing and relocation agencies in all appropriate cases. It might also be advisable to make it possible for property owners to contract with the housing agency for rehabilitation of their properties. In cases where a property owner, whether an owner-occupant or a landlord of tenements, failed to carry out the repairs required by the code, and did not want to sell to the housing agency, or the agency did not want to acquire the property, the municipality should have—and use—the power to carry out the required works, and to collect the cost either by sequestering the rents or by registering a lien on the property.

As the Philadelphia experience indicates, a housing agency may be able to perform rehabilitation work more economically than can outside contractors. Evidently an agency which continuously carried out a great amount of rehabilitation work would benefit greatly from various economies of scale. Not only could it utilize a highly specialized, skilled, and experienced staff, but also it could maintain an inventory of the great variety of items required for rehabilitation, and buy these wholesale.

In the preceding discussion the term "agency" or "housing agency" has been used somewhat loosely. Some of the functions discussed are traditional "housing"; others, "renewal"; still others, like subsidy payments to families and relocation and housekeeping aid, "welfare" functions. There is not necessarily one "best" administrative form to carry these out; essential would be the cooperation of all involved in the program.

Tax Policies

It has often been pointed out that our present tax system, which forces our municipalities and school boards to rely for their rapidly growing needs almost exclusively on the "real property" tax, is a strong impediment of development. In 1964 in Metropolitan Toronto 62% of all taxable assessment was on residential properties. After deducting the value of their sites, the value of residential structures amounts to about 50% of all assessment; thus, to one half of its extent, the real property tax is the equivalent of a sales tax on housing. Moreover, unlike any other sales tax, this tax on housing is highly regressive. As shown in Table 2, the lowest income groups pay about three times as great a proportion of their incomes for housing as do the highest ones. Consequently they also pay three times as much of their incomes in real property taxes. This goes for tenants as well as for owners; for the landlord this tax is part of the cost of doing business, which he passes on to the tenants, with a mark-up.

It has been proposed from many sides that this situation could and should be corrected by shifting the incidence of the real property tax from "improvements" to "land." It is undeniable that these represent two entirely different economic categories. The value of an improvement is created entirely by the investment of its owner, who will make that investment only if it promises an equal or higher return than do other investment outlets. If the user of the improvement has to pay, in addition to this normal return, a sizable tax, the effective demand for—and consequently the investment in—this particular commodity, housing improvements (including new housing), will be strongly curtailed.

By contrast, the value of the land is merely the capitalization of the "differential rent," that is, the amount which people are prepared to pay for the use of a particular site because of its locational advantages over all other competing sites. The differential rent is shared by the owners and the community, and public policy can merely affect the distribution of the shares. If the share of the community is high and that of the owner low, the capitalization of the owner's share, that is, the market value of the land, is also low. Thus the effect of a property tax on land is opposite to its effect on improvements. The effective supply of land is increased. That this reasoning is correct is exemplified by the experience of New Zealand, where for many years land, but not improvements, has been taxed.

Unfortunately, the short-term effects of a shift to such a policy would be very different from its long-term results. We have always taxed land and improvements on an equal basis. This has established their values in the market, in which investors have brought properties in good faith. A sudden shift of the tax from improvements to land would result in an enormous windfall for all investment in improvements, and in an almost total loss of all investment in land. As the proportions of the value of land and of improvements respectively, vary widely between various properties, the change would completely disrupt the real estate and mortgage markets. Moreover, the owners of "blighted" housing, where the proportion of land is generally above its normal share of the total value of the property, would attempt to maintain their incomes and the value of their properties by an increase in rents, and for quite a number of years would succeed in doing so.

Because these difficulties have been widely recognized, it has been generally proposed that the shift be accomplished very gradually, for instance, by reducing the rate on improvements annually by one thousandth, while increasing the rate on land by the same amount. This is indeed feasible. However, as the total assessed value of land is smaller than that of improvements, it would lead to a steady decline in municipal revenue.

It is therefore suggested that the dividing line be drawn not between "land" and "improvements," but between "amortized" and "nonamortized" investment. The value of land, as well as of all improvements existing at the beginning of the shift, would be treated as amortized. The assessed value of all improvements—new structures or the rehabilitation of old ones—made during the first year after the shift would be treated as nonamortized. In subsequent years that portion of the assessed value of the improvement which exceeded its remaining nonamortized value would be treated as amortized. Amortization schedules for investment in improvements are generally used for purposes of the federal income tax and could be adopted without difficulty for this modification of the real property tax.

For purposes of easier calculation only—not for adoption—the following example has been based on a flat annual amortization rate of 3% annually. The calculation is made for a period after the shift has been completed. As the land is always treated as 100% amortized, it is disregarded in the following discussion.

Assume that the value of an improvement—say, a new apartment house—is assessed at $1 million. In the first year it is entirely nonamortized and consequently tax exempt. After 10 years 30% or a value of $300,000 is amortized; the remaining $700,000 is nonamortized. If the assessed value now is $700,000 (or less), there is no amortized value and no tax. If the assessed value is $800,000, there is an amortized taxable value of $100,000; if the assessment is $1.2 million, the taxable portion is $500,000; and so on. After 33.33 years the entire assessed value of the improvement is taxable.

In such a situation the competitive position of new and rehabilitated versus unimproved old structures would be greatly strengthened in comparison with the present situation. This would, on the one hand, stimulate investment in improvements both in new structures and in the rehabilitation of old ones, and, on the other hand, reduce the value both of vacant land and of unimproved old structures and make it easier to acquire them for new construction and for either rehabilitation or demolition, respectively. It would increase the tax revenue of the municipality and make this increase less erratic and more predictable, because new improvements would enter the tax rolls only gradually. Because of these important beneficial long-range effects, serious consideration of this proposal by the metropolitan government is strongly recommended.

While the long-range effect of such a shift in the incidence of the property tax would be highly significant, its immediate effect would probably be quite small. A tax reduction of one thousandth annually is not much of an incentive. Therefore another measure is suggested, which could be applied either supplementary to or independent of the long-range proposal. Investment in the rehabilitation of residential buildings might well be exempted from the real property tax for a limited period, say 5 or 10 years. The loss in revenue would be negligible, and the effect might be substantial. At present the owner of an old house feels that he is being penalized for improving it. The exemption might be limited to a moderate amount, perhaps $1000 per habitable room.

Rehabilitation of Nonresidential Properties: General Conditions

Obsolescence and consequent need for renewal exist equally in nonresidential structures and areas. However, the relation of public and private interests and responsibilities is different from that in housing (including those neighborhood services which may be regarded as an extension of housing). Consequently, of the measures discussed so far, only improvement of public facilities and services and the suggested shift of the real property tax to amortized investment appear to be applicable. Enforcement of the housing code evidently does not apply; and there appear to be no major problems in the enforcement of other codes for the protection of health and safety.

The many forms of financial support of various types of housing all amount basically to a redistribution of the national income, in part in favor of housing at the expense of other consumer goods and services—and doubts as to the wisdom of this type of redistribution were expressed previously in this discussion—but mainly in favor of the lower income groups at the expense of those receiving higher incomes through the market process. Such an equalizing redistribution has long been accepted as a legitimate function of government. Indeed, in a free-enterprise economy, where the necessary accumulation of capital is primarily the responsibility of private individuals and corporations, the resultant concentration of wealth makes such redistribution increasingly necessary with increasing productivity—not only for sociopolitical reasons, but also for strictly economic ones. Without such redistribution, consumer purchasing power would be insufficient to support the sales and profits on which productive enterprise depends.

But equally basic requirements of a competitive free-enterprise system argue against government action for redistribution of income from more efficient to less efficient economic enterprises. Such efforts may nonetheless be made for social and political reasons, and many nations have developed plans for the redistribution of industry and are attempting to implement them. The governments of Canada and of Ontario have not developed such plans; and so far as embryonic stirrings of such policies can be detected, they are strongly biased towards "decentralization," that is, towards favoring locations other than Metropolitan Toronto. It cannot be expected, therefore, that the higher levels of government will subsidize the rehabilitation of industrial or commercial structures in this area.

Municipalities, of course, have been and are employing a number of means to induce such enterprises to locate within the areas of their tax jurisdiction rather than within those of their neighbors. It is one of the purposes of a metropolitan federation to eliminate or at least mitigate this far from healthy form of competition. Certainly, the Metropolitan Corporation cannot well employ tax revenues derived from all its constituents to strengthen the competitive position of one versus that of the others.

Rehabilitation of individual nonresidential structures will have to remain the exclusive responsibility of their owners. The public contribution, other than guidance through consultation, will have to be limited to improving the environment. When the expense required for such improvement through investment and improved services far exceeds that allocated to other areas, recourse to special local assessments is appropriate.

Industrial Areas

The older industrial areas in the central part of Toronto have the visual appearance associated with "blight." However, a careful study by Drs. Spelt and Kerr revealed that these areas are still very active. Indeed, the presence of "marginal" and relatively cheap space in old industrial buildings, in particular in locations near the center, is necessary for the continued success of any metropolitan area, because only in such space can young and struggling enterprises get started.

The most serious drawback in such old industrial areas is lack of space for motor vehicles, moving and particularly standing for loading and unloading, and also for parking. Any possibility to provide such space should be utilized, when necessary with the aid of public land acquisition. In a few cases such space may become available by demolition of housing which has been made uninhabitable by its environment. But the space that may become available from this source is small, is not always in the right location, and sometimes may be better used to establish a public park, which will help to improve the visual aspect of the area and similar ones. Other means to this end are better maintenance, cleaning, and lighting of streets, elimination of overhead wires, and control of billboards and other advertising signs. Together with some gentle prodding, such improvements may induce property owners to do their share in improving the aspect of the area so as to make sure that it not only is not blighted, but also is seen to be not blighted.

Commercial Areas

Far more than the old industrial areas, the older shopping areas have been adversely affected by the advent of the automobile. This is particularly true of the "strip" commercial areas which have developed along surface transit lines. Here lack of parking space is the most strongly felt deficiency. Establishment of parking areas at the rear of the stores, either by the municipality or by the merchants, or through the cooperation of both, is required.

Far more than in industrial areas, improvement of the visual aspect is important for commerce. In addition to the measures already mentioned, public measures should include tree planting and careful design and placement of all street furniture, such as street, transit, and traffic signs and traffic lights, letter boxes, trash receptacles, and light standards. However, the main visual elements remain the storefronts themselves. Some improvement can be achieved by control. However, a more effective positive approach has been demonstrated in Norwich, England. Here a team of designers developed a carefully studied plan for the rehabilitation of the main shopping street, taking into account the specific characteristics of each building and each store. After lengthy discussion all property owners and merchants agreed to carry out the plan, which required few structural changes—mainly new signs and fresh paint. The experiment was wholly successful in increasing attractiveness and sales volume, and deserves imitation.

A more radical improvement is the elimination of all vehicular traffic from a shopping street and its transformation into a pedestrian mall, as has been done on Sparks Street in Ottawa. Usually this will require some adjustments in the street pattern to provide access to the stores for delivery and possibly also to accommodate diverted traffic.

That this is not always necessary is demonstrated by the example of Copenhagen, Denmark. There the main shopping street, called Stroget, which extends for almost a mile, was transformed into a pedestrian mall by the simple expedient of prohibiting vehicular traffic from 10:30 A.M. to midnight. Deliveries are made during the other hours. The expected traffic congestion on parallel streets did not materialize; apparently motorists switched to routes at the edge of the city center. Thus public action greatly improved the attractiveness of this commercial area, without any cost to the taxpayers.

All such public actions to improve the environment and thereby revitalize old commercial areas can stimulate rehabilitation of private properties by their owners.

City Center

Of all sections of the metropolitan area in Toronto, as elsewhere, the city center, though it certainly cannot be called "blighted," is the most obsolete—the one whose structure is least adjusted to future demand and therefore most in need of renewal. Here, where both pedestrian and vehicular movements are at their peak, they conflict more strongly than anywhere else. Pedestrian movement, the lifeblood of an area of multiple contacts, loses both its efficiency and its amenity because of this conflict. Pedestrians cannot reach a destination on the other side of the street without making a detour to the next corner, and there they have to wait until the lights turn. Because the greater portion of a street's right-of-way is taken up by the pavement, sidewalks are often so congested that they further delay movement. The total time loss to pedestrians due to these three factors may well amount to several thousand hours daily.

The loss of amenity is even more obvious. Streets are full of fumes and noise, without trees or shade; sidewalks are too narrow for people to stand and talk in a group, let alone to sit down and relax on a bench or at a table. All the things that traditionally have made the city centers attractive—and now make suburban shopping centers attractive—to people and consequently to establishments that serve these people are missing. People go downtown only if they have to and leave as soon as they can.

The reverse side of the conflict, the impediment of the movement of cars by people, is almost equally wasteful of time and equally annoying. The way to solve this conflict is well known: grade separation of vehicles and pedestrians. This would be easy if the center of a big city could be built from scratch, which happens only as a result of total destruction, as in Rotterdam. In an existing city it could be achieved only by carrying out, with consistency and at great cost, a plan for gradual transformation. Generally it is easier to create a pedestrian level below than above the existing street level, but pedestrian movement in the open air is more attractive. If protected by a roof against rain, snow, and, in summer, heat from the midday sun, and by radiant heating in the floor and infrared lights above from biting cold, such a level would be pleasant in almost any weather.

Hardly less important for the continued attractiveness and vitality of the city center is variety—variety both of functions and of forms of buildings, high and low, old and new, interspersed by open spaces with trees, flowers, and fountains. In such a revitalized city center many uses would seek accommodation in older buildings and thus stimulate their rehabilitation. Quantitatively the renewal of Toronto's city center is proceeding fast enough, but a decisive qualitative improvement will require a great deal of public as well as private effort and investment.

Rehabilitation—A Permanent Problem

Rehabilitation and conservation are required in all parts of the metropolitan area. The greatest and most urgent problem is presented by old buildings housing low-income families. "Low" is, of course, a relative concept. Our low-income families would be considered well-to-do in India or Africa. If real per capita income continues to rise, what is considered today a middle income will be called "low" 20 years from now. In this sense the poor will always be with us.

In the same sense and for the same reason, substandard housing will always be with us. Today's standard housing will be considered substandard in 20 or 30 years. Rehabilitation will therefore always be required. It is not a problem that we can solve. It is a problem which we must learn to live with, and can learn to deal with by imaginative and flexible use of a variety of means, some of which have been discussed in this chapter.

Chapter 32

THE UPPER LIMITS OF RESIDENTIAL DENSITY

REASONS FOR STUDY

As the numbers of people and of activities increase in metropolitan areas, the demand for land increases at an even faster rate. While improved means of transportation and communication make sufficient amounts of land available to satisfy all needs within the region, there remains a specialized demand for the limited amount of land close to the center. As practically all of this land, apart from public streets and parks, consists of parcels occupied by structures, assembly of land for new development requires the purchase of structures, resulting in a high cost per square foot or acre, on the average. Even in the few cases where land not occupied by structures can be assembled, its market value is determined by this average. The developer of such land is therefore strongly interested in distributing the cost of each square foot of land onto as many square feet of rentable or salable floor space as possible, that is, in building at a high density. Without such a high density, investment is not likely to return a profit comparable to that yielded by alternative fields of investment, and development will not occur.

The question arises of whether there is a public interest in limiting the density of residential developments in centrally located areas and, if so, at which level such limits should be set.

DEFINITION OF TERMS

"Density" denotes the relation between two units of measurement, the first referring to use and the second to land area. Four types of units are commonly employed to measure use:

1. Persons.

2. Habitable rooms.

3. Dwelling units (assumed to be identical with households).

4. Gross area of all floors above ground level.

Source: Report to the Montreal City Planning Department, January 1938.

Three different units of land area are significant for measurements of residential density. They are defined as follows:

1. Net area—the area of a lot used predominantly for residential purposes.

2. Block area—the area of a block used predominantly for residential purposes, including one half of the width of the surrounding streets up to a width of 30 feet.

3. Neighborhood area—an area, or district, used predominantly for residential purposes, but including all streets as well as all facilities, such as elementary schools, parks and playgrounds, churches, and shops customarily found in such an area and serving its residents.

Parcels larger than 6 acres serving nonresidential purposes and major traffic arteries are excluded.

Densities relating to the "net area" are referred to as "net densities"; those relating to "block areas" as "block densities" (in English literature these are called "net densities"); and those relating to the "neighborhood area" as "neighborhood densities."

While all of these units of measurement are relevant, in the following discussion the main emphasis is on two concepts:

1. The ratio of gross floor area to net area, called the "floor space index" (F.S.I.) or "floor area ratio" (F.A.R.).

2. The ratio of persons (and/or dwelling units) to neighborhood area, called "neighborhood density."

Emphasis on these concepts derives from their role in policy. The main instrument for public control of private property is zoning, which is enforced by issuing or refusing a building permit. The only fact which can be unequivocally determined at the time of the issuance of a building permit and which cannot be changed without obtaining another permit is gross floor area. Number of persons may change at any time, and a change in the number of habitable rooms and even in the number of dwelling units may easily escape control.

On the other hand, comprehensive planning, aimed at relating the various needs of people to their number, is based on the number of residents of a given area, which must be derived from, and expressed in terms of, neighborhood density.

REASONS FOR LEGAL LIMITATION OF RESIDENTIAL DENSITIES

There are three reasons for setting upper limits on residential densities:

1. To ensure adequate living conditions for the occupants.

2. To protect neighboring properties from harmful impacts.

3. To prevent the overloading of public facilities.

It could be—and has been—argued that the first reason is not valid, that the law should limit itself to preventing people from doing harm to others, and that it has no business preventing people from doing harm to themselves. This should be left to their own choice in the market. If they are willing to accept the living conditions produced by high density, they should be allowed to do so. If they reject them, the developer will lose his or her investment; self-interest can be relied upon to guarantee that a developer will put an acceptable product on the market.

If residential structures could be discarded as easily as clothing, this might be a valid argument. But they last for generations, and they are anchored to the soil. When they first come onto the market, their modernity may well make tenants overlook or accept disadvantages inherent in high densities, particularly in a period of housing shortage. Thus the investor will be able to recover his or her equity with a good profit within a relatively short period. However, in later years, when the structures have to compete with newer, more modern developments, the inherent shortcomings make themselves felt. The type of tenants for which the structures were designed shun them, and they gradually degenerate into slums. This has been the universal experience with older housing built at excessive densities and has saddled cities with one of their most difficult and costly problems.

The time horizon of a public authority is necessarily wider than that of the private developer, and the authority has the right and the duty to see to it that any dwelling unit built within its jurisdiction will be acceptable in the future as well as in the present.

High density tends to produce two deficiencies: lack of light, air, views, and sunshine, and lack of open outdoor space. In a large project these deficiencies will affect primarily its inhabitants. In an isolated tower the inhabitants may have ample light, air, and the like by "stealing" them from low-density neighboring properties and, in some cases, may also be able to use adjacent public open space for needs which their neighbors supply on their own properties. In particular locations it may even be possible that an isolated high-density building or group of buildings will harm neither its inhabitants nor its neighbors, and it may be argued that density should not be restricted in such a case. However, the basic principle of equality before law makes it impossible to grant a right to one property owner and deny it to his or her neighbors. Density limitations must therefore be formulated in such a way that they will protect light, air, and so on and a minimum of usable open space on every property within the area covered by such an ordinance.

PROTECTION OF LIGHT, AIR, AND SO ON

English common law has developed the doctrine of "ancient lights," which is still followed, to protect the occupant of a property against encroachment on the light, air, view, sunshine, and privacy which he or she enjoys, by a building erected by a neighbor.

Such protection is best afforded by the requirement of setbacks and of angles delimiting the "envelope" within which a structure may be built. Such limitations result automatically in some limitation of density, which, however, may vary greatly according both to the standards adopted and to the specific situation. The impact on density may be illustrated by an example, using Montreal, based on a standard requiring some sunshine to enter every dwelling throughout the year.

The latitude of Montreal being 45°30′, the sun at midwinter noon stands at an angle of roughly 31 degrees above the horizon. The tangent of 31 degrees being about 2.8, a building 100 feet high would have to be at a distance of 280 feet from the next residential building for any sunshine to reach the foot of that building in midwinter. If development took the form of parallel slabs of 70-foot depth, facing north and south, this would result in a coverage of 70 feet/350 feet = 20%; with 10 stories this would mean a F.S.I. of 2.0. Contrary to widespread assumptions, different orientations or different arrangements would result, under the assumed standard, in even lower coverage. An arrangement of 70-foot square towers placed à la quinquonce, for instance, would result in a 17% coverage. Increasing the height of the slabs from 10 to 50 stories, or from 100 to 500 feet, would increase the required distance to 1400 feet, and consequently the F.S.I. would increase only slightly, from 2.0 to 2.375.

There is no scientific evidence that insolation of rooms is required for health. There is, however, little doubt that lack of sunshine both indoors and outdoors is psychologically depressing. Moreover, experience seems to indicate that densities precluding insolation also tend to encroach on other requirements. In particular, visual privacy on lower floors requires considerable distance from windows on upper floors of facing buildings. Most cities which have adopted F.S.I.s for residential areas have set the ceiling below 2.0. Hamburg, Germany, for instance, a city of about 2 million population, has a maximum F.S.I. of 1.1 for residential areas. The notoriously high-density new residential areas of Moscow (population over 6 million) consist largely of five-story buildings at an F.S.I. of 1.0; some higher buildings raise the F.S.I. somewhat, but not beyond 2.0.

It may be noted that also in the older areas of Montreal, which are densely built up with rows of three-story houses, the F.S.I. is somewhat less than 2.0.

OUTDOOR OPEN SPACE ON THE PROPERTY AND PARKING

One of the most vexing problems in older high-density areas is the need to provide parking for the residents and their visitors. There is general agreement that space for parking, as well as for loading and unloading delivery wagons and trucks, must be provided on the premises.

For the following investigation it is assumed that the number of persons per apartment will average 2.8 and the gross floor area 1000 square feet. This implies a gross floor area of 357 square feet per person, comparable to that contained in a two-story five- or six-room house of 20 × 35 feet, occupied by four persons. It is further assumed that one parking space per dwelling unit is provided, at 350 square feet per space. When the space required for driveways and ramps, visitor parking, and loading and unloading is added, the total amounts to about 400 square feet for each dwelling unit of 1000 square feet.

With an F.S.I. of 2.0, fully 80% of the lot would be required for parking. As noted earlier, with 10-story buildings the structures would cover the remaining 20%. It has therefore been assumed that in high-density developments all parking and loading will be underground except for 5000 square feet for every 100,000 square feet of gross floor space, which will be needed for ramps and for access by taxis and other vehicles.

If the parking and loading spaces were accommodated entirely on the lower floors of the apartment buildings, 4 floors would be required for every 10 habitable floors, or 20 floors for a 50-story apartment house. Even if one half of these were accommodated above ground level, this would not be acceptable because the time required to drive up or down 10 floors would be excessive. Also, parking floors above ground would have, of course, the same unfavorable impact on light, air, and so on as inhabited floors. Furthermore, in very tall buildings, of 30 or 50 stories, all basement space is likely to be needed for mechanical equipment and storage. For the following discussion it has therefore been assumed that parking and loading will be accommodated in four floors under the unbuilt section of the property. It will then occupy the equivalent of 10% of the gross floor area. The roof of this underground facility would be available for other uses, including some potted plants, but the planting of full-grown trees would be precluded.

The requirements for outdoor space for use by the tenants are not clearly defined. At present most apartment buildings in the Montreal area provide little or no such space; such open space as is provided serves mainly decorative purposes. In future, however, they will have to compete increasingly with developments which do provide such facilities, including outdoor swimming pools, which are rapidly becoming standard requirements in many American cities.

It is here assumed that 20% of the inhabitants of the development may want to use outdoor space simultaneously, at 200 square feet per person. This results in a requirement of 40 square feet per inhabitant, or 112 square feet for each 1000 square feet of floor area.

In addition, outdoor play space should be provided for children between 2 and 13. Normally, there are about 1.5–2.0 children in each 1-year age group. (A rate of 1.5 children aged 0–1 year, with a life expectancy over 66.7 years at year 1, would result in a stable population.) However, it is here assumed that in apartment developments there will be only 1% per year, or 12% in the age group 2–13. It is further assumed that one third of these children may use this space simultaneously, at a density of 200 square feet per child. This results in a requirement of $40 \times 200 = 8000$ square feet per 1000 persons, or about 23 square feet per 1000 square feet of gross floor area.

Thus the two requirements for usable outdoor space add up to 135 square feet per 1000 square feet of gross floor area. At least half of this, roughly 70 square feet, should be available for tree planting.

On the basis of the foregoing assumptions, we can now calculate the distribution of the entire ground area of a parcel which would be developed at an F.S.I. of 4.0 in 40-story buildings.

Buildings	10%
Garage roofs	40%
Driveways and ramps	5%
Space suitable for tree planting	28%
Total	83%

As there are limiting conditions, such as distance of windows from outdoor play areas, driveways, and streets, it requires considerable skill in site design to accommodate these requirements even with a "surplus" of 17%. An F.S.I. in excess of 4.0 would make the problem insolvable.

COMMUNITY SPACE REQUIREMENTS

Any residential development brings with it a requirement for supplementary public facilities, for which certain standards have been established. The usual standards are, for 1000 residents, as follows:

Playground	1 acre
Neighborhood park	1 acre
Playfield	1.25 acres
Total	3.25 acres

This standard is rarely achieved in older, built-up areas of cities, which are normally the location of high-density developments. They are also based on the assumption of a much higher percentage of children and adolescents than can be anticipated in high-density apartments. It is therefore assumed that the standard here can be reduced by about one half, to 1.65 acres or 71,000 square feet per 1000 persons, equivalent to 20% of gross floor area.

Requirements for school areas can be more definitely specified as 150 square feet per student. With 12% of the apartment population assumed to be of school age, this amounts to 18,000 square feet per 1000 population, or 5% of gross floor area. The total of required community space is therefore equal to at least one quarter of the gross floor area.

Thus with an F.S.I. of 2.0 every acre devoted to high-density apartment development makes it necessary for the municipality to acquire an equal amount of land in the same neighborhood, generally at the same or higher cost. It would therefore seem appropriate that the developer should share at least part of this land cost. This is frequently required of the developers of subdivisions. In the province of Ontario, for instance, the developer is required to dedicate 5% of his land for public purposes, in addition to land dedicated for streets. With an average of about 20–22 persons per acre of development land, this amounts to roughly 2000 square feet per acre, or, under the assumption of 400 square feet of gross floor space per person, to 0.25 square foot of land dedicated for every square foot of gross floor area—the same as the requirement developed above.

It has not been customary to require any such dedication from developers of individual buildings, particularly in areas which are already developed. The tacit assumption has been that any additional requirements resultant from such construction can be absorbed by existing facilities or may be offset by a decrease in population on other properties in the neighborhood. This assumption is certainly not justified in the case of a large new development at a density substantially higher than that prevailing in the neighborhood. Similarly, a sum of small developments would require additional public facilities. For this reason, as well as for reasons of legal equity, resultant requirements should apply equally to all developments, regardless of size.

SUGGESTIONS FOR LEGISLATION

As noted earlier, in most—probably in all—residential neighborhoods the F.S.I. averages no higher than 2.0. It is suggested that an F.S.I. of 2.0 should be established as a basic maximum. A "bonus" of additional floor space, up to a maximum F.S.I. of 4.0, could be given if the developer dedicates to the city 0.25 square foot of land for every additional square foot of gross floor area, or a money equivalent sufficient to acquire the corresponding land area.

This would safeguard the minimum requirement for public open space, including schools. The upper limit of an F.S.I. of 4.0 is needed to safeguard the minimum requirements for private open space. The minimum requirement of privacy from sight and sound can best be guaranteed by standards for setbacks from lot lines and for distances between buildings or wings of a building. Adequate light, air, and sunshine can best be guaranteed by establishment of vertical and horizontal angles.

In addition, it may be necessary to limit the permissible length of tall buildings, which tend to produce excessively strong winds at their corners. Tentatively, I would suggest that "walls" of more than 50-foot height must reduce their length below 500 feet by 1 foot for every additional foot in height, down to a length of 100 feet.

It is, of course, known that a number of apartment developments with an F.S.I. higher than 4.0 have found acceptance in Montreal. Such acceptance may continue for buildings inhabited exclusively by adults, for whom closeness to the city center may be more important than the factors discussed in this chapter. A case can be made for the establishment of a special high-density zone, with an F.S.I. of 6.0, in areas within 0.5 mile of the central business district, the latter being defined as an area with an employment density of at least 32,000 persons per square mile (500 per gross acre). If occupancy by persons less than 15 years of age could be prohibited in such a zone, it might be able to dispense with elementary schools, playgrounds, and neighborhood parks. It is, however, questionable whether such a prohibition would be politically acceptable.

Chapter 33

HOUSING FORM IN THE METROPOLIS

HISTORICAL DEVELOPMENT OF HOUSE TYPES

When cities first came into being, every family built its own free-standing house, following the type developed in its village. As the population increased within the walls, houses moved close together and the family could expand its living space no longer horizontally, but only vertically. Out of this developed the multifamily house, which in imperial Rome already grew to eight or more stories. The European Middle Ages saw a return to the single-family house, but in the seventeenth century the apartment (or tenement) house reappeared to become during the following centuries the predominant dwelling type in most big cities. However, the predominance varies by countries and even by cities, for reasons not fully understood. In the big cities of the European continent, and also in Scotland and in New York, the apartment house of four to seven stories became typical. But in English towns, including London, and also in Philadelphia and Baltimore, most people preferred the row house, two stories high for the masses, up to five for the wealthy. Chicago produced the "three-decker," and Montreal the two- to three-story house with the upper floors accessible only by outside stairs. Nobody knows why outside stairs were adopted in a city climatically ill suited for them.

There have been endless discussions among architects and others about the relative economy of high and of low buildings. It seems that in every place the generally accepted type is the cheapest one: in England the two-story row house, on the European continent the five-story walk-up, in Los Angeles the one-story bungalow, and in New York the apartment tower. This may be the result of adaptation of building practices and of building codes to the established type.

It is also worth noting that another great civilization, the Chinese, has traditionally housed the people, even of cities with a population of 1 million or more, in one-story compounds. When in the eighteenth century the Jesuit fathers showed engravings of European cities to the Emperor Kien-Lung, he shook his head, saying, "Europe must be an awfully small and poor country that the people must live on top of each other." In fact, it is doubtful that people have ever chosen voluntarily to live on top of each other. The rich in imperial Rome lived in houses of one or two floors opening on

---

Source: Unpublished essay, December 1977.

spacious peristyles. In addition they had villas in the hills or on the shore, as did the wealthy merchants of Venice and Florence.

The high density of the nineteenth century city was the result of necessity rather than of choice. The necessity arose from the fact that without mechanical means of transportation the 1-hour radius (i.e., the distance that could be traveled in 1 hour) from the city center extended only about 3 miles. With modern means of transportation the 1-hour radius extends about 30 miles, increasing the amount of land available for urban development by 100 times. At the same time steel and concrete construction, combined with the elevator, has extended space vertically. The result has been a frequently ignored radical change in the price relation between a square foot of urban building land and a square foot of built space, from 100–150% for the brownstones of Manhattan's West Side to 10–50% today.

CHANGING HOUSEHOLD SIZES AND TYPES

Even more important than this changed cost relation is the change in household type. The medieval household averaged at least seven persons. At the end of the last century the average was still above five. Now it is below three in European cities, and American cities are rapidly approaching this level. The decrease in household size continued even in the 1950s when family size was on the increase. The decrease is due to the disappearance of the three-generation family, the sharp decrease in the number of "doubled-up" families and of roomers, and the steep increase in the number of households occupied by single persons, both young and old. If real disposable income continues to increase, a further rapid increase in "nonfamily" households must be anticipated.

These fundamental changes in household composition have led to an enormous increase in the demand for small dwelling units and a corresponding decrease in the demand for big ones. Demand for big houses has also dropped because of the practical disappearance of "live-in" domestic servants and the increase in the number of women working outside the household. The resulting need to reduce household work has multiplied the demand for small, well-equipped units. However, in the older cities there are still many houses built for the needs of earlier generations. Many have been converted to commercial or multifamily use, but there are still many with five, six, or more rooms occupied by only one or two persons, mostly, though not exclusively, old people. On the other hand, large low-income families remain in overcrowded dwellings. Government policy should enable and encourage these old people to find suitable small dwellings and to make the big houses which they have vacated available to large low-income families.

In sum, the fundamental changes which have occurred in this century favor two opposite housing types. The extension of the urban area favors the detached single-family house, and the increase in small households favors small apartments. For adults, easy access to the employment, recreational, and cultural opportunities of the city center is important; for children, open space, both around the house and in the neighborhood, generally available only at the periphery. The market has responded to both demands. But in addition the occupancy of identical units also reflects these different needs, as shown by a 1961 survey of all commercial apartment houses with six or more units in Metropolitan Toronto. In one-bedroom apartments the percentage of "nonfamily" households decreased regularly from 34.5% in the zone within 2 miles from the center to 6.5% in the zone beyond 8 miles, while the percentage of families with children increased from 6.6 to 32.2%. Of apartments with two or more bedrooms only 60% at the center, but almost all (98.6%) at the periphery, contained children.

SINGLE-FAMILY HOUSES

In Canada we are building generally one-story or split-level—more rarely, two-story—houses on lots 50–60 feet wide and 90–130 feet deep. With a street width of 66 feet and 25-foot setbacks, this type is costly in terms of land and of streets and utilities. Nor is the aesthetic result satisfactory. The houses are too close together to be appreciated as separate units, as are country houses, and too far apart to form a bigger unit, as do the streets and squares of London or Paris. In relation to their height the distance between houses on the two sides of the street is too great to create a form enclosing the street. On the other hand, the rear sides of the houses are too close together to give to the gardens a feeling of privacy or of spaciousness. The street space would be more clearly defined and the garden more intimate if we turned the house outside in, in the Greek-Islamic-Hispanic tradition. In a northern climate this has been done successfully in Albertslund near Copenhagen. Radiant floor heating and infrared lamps make outdoor space habitable even in freezing temperatures. In our traditional way of turning houses inside out, it would be an improvement both economic and aesthetic to group houses into rows or quadruplexes. Land area and, in particular, street frontage can also be reduced by building houses in the interior of a block. This has been outlawed for reasons of fire hazard which are no longer valid with modern equipment. A study of a variant of this type of development with semidetached houses along the street and quadruplexes in the interior of the block showed a reduction of gross residential area by 10%, of frontage by 25%, and of number of driveways by 75%. Moreover, the gardens have a more suitable square shape, and all houses face, on one side, a large enclosed green space of 100×160 feet. It is likely that many families would prefer this or a similar type of development to conventional 60×110 foot lots, to which the comparisons refer. Others are likely to insist on a completely detached house, which appears to have an irrational but deep-seated appeal, possibly related to the symbolic role of the house as a body image.

The row house had been discredited by the monotonous row-house streets of the nineteenth century but is coming back, thanks to its verbal escalation into a "town-house." Built in groups around courts, it has been used in such still unsurpassed examples as Neubuehl near Zuerich, Chatham Village in Pittsburgh, and Baldwin Hills in Los Angeles. The search for economy has also led to the resurrection of the "back-to-back" row house, which had rightly been abandoned because of its lack of cross-ventilation. It can be made acceptable by air conditioning or in the form of one-story row houses with alternating vertical skylights in the rear. A curious variant of the back-to-back row house has appeared in the Toronto area under the name of "maisonnette." It is really a two-story horizontal apartment house, with access to the apartments from a central corridor on the first floor. In England the term "maisonettes" is applied to structures containing two, three, or more superimposed rows of two-story houses, with open galleries providing access to the upper rows. Where the climate is not too severe, this is an excellent solution, combining some of the advantages of the single-family house with those of multistory structures.

MULTI-FAMILY HOUSES

Cross-ventilation can easily be provided in walk-up apartments with two units on each staircase. The attempt to provide it also in tall structures has led to ingenious but overcomplex solutions, with access from internal corridors on each third floor and internal stairways in each two-story apartment. The best known, though neither the first nor the last of these, is Le Corbusier's "Unité" in Marseille. A simpler solution consists in combining typical three-story apartments with different fourth, seventh, etc., floors which contain smaller units on corridors, connecting the stairways with elevators. This solution has been condemned because a variant of it was used in the ill-fated Pruitt-Igo public housing project in St. Louis. However, the failure of this project was due entirely to a deliberate concentration of "problem" families, combined with poor management and a complete lack of community facilities. With normal occupancy, somewhat lower densities, and adequate facilities and management, it could have functioned perfectly well.

The St. Louis catastrophe may have contributed to the swing of opinion against tall buildings. Under the name "high-rise"—as opposed to "low-rise"—they have become the bête noire of latter-day populism. "Style is the man," said Buffon. The absurdity of such terms betrays the mushiness of the thinking that coined them. I have never seen a high building that does not rise or a low one that does. There are good reasons to object to the indiscriminate intrusion of massive high buildings into areas of more modest structures. While the latter affect directly only their immediate neighbors, tall structures are visible from afar. They cast long shadows and may, because of their funneling effect, transform otherwise tolerable air currents into intolerable high winds. Above all, their mass is felt to be oppressive. It is evident that their siting and shape requires controls beyond those deemed sufficient for lower buildings.

But they also offer great advantages to their occupants: wide views, greater privacy from sight and sound, protection from insects, services on the ground floor. If built at reasonable densities, they leave between them large, unbroken open spaces which can accommodate groves of full-grown trees and areas for noisy outdoor recreation such as swimming pools and fields for ball games.

One may ask why contemporary high buildings arouse the disgust and hatred of the inhabitants of our cities, while the equally high church towers of medieval towns inspired the love and pride of their people. One reason probably is that they were towers, not slabs. With low buildings trees and the sky are visible above the roofs; with a tower they are visible at its sides. If buildings are both high and wide, they fill the entire field of vision and imprison the viewer. Any structure of indefinite length should be limited in height, probably to no more than 60–70 feet, preferably to 30. Towers are a different story. It makes much more sense to limit their width than to limit their height. This has been done to some extent in the Westend district of Vancouver, British Columbia, with fairly good results. Towers, if not too closely spaced, can be visually very attractive. Experience seems to indicate that informal grouping of towers is preferable to geometric patterns beyond a simple row. If carefully sited, towers can enhance rather than destroy the beauty of areas of low buildings.

We have come to recognize that our traditional isolationist zoning produces monotony, and "mixture" has become fashionable among planners. Developers have responded by adding townhouses to their "high-rise" projects. All too often the privacy of the townhouse dwellers is disturbed because of exposure to observation by their higher-up neighbors. It may be preferable to provide the desirable transition to a street of low buildings by means of one- or two-story structures for commercial or institutional services. If high and low buildings are adequately separated by space and, in particular, by trees, they can supplement each other very well, as shown by Tapiola in Finland.

One objection to apartment towers retains some validity: form does not follow function. The medieval cathedrals, and equally the towers of our multinational and multibillion corporations and banks, unequivocally proclaim the locus of power in their communities. The tenants in tall apartment houses, however, have, if anything, even less power than their single-family-house neighbors. Some sense can be given to the visual predominance of apartment towers by concentrating them at subcenters, around transit stations, as has been done successfully in the Stockholm satellite borough of Vällingby. In addition to its obvious practical advantages this solution results in the towers denoting the location of these centers. Thereby it contributes to achieving the goal of making visible the otherwise hidden structure of the metropolis.

Part Six
Transportation

Chapter 34

TRANSPORTATION

Cities and transportation are inseparable. Cities have developed and grown for one of two reasons: either as "terminals" or "break-of-bulk" points for transportation, or as "central places" of a region, as focal points at which all roads converge. Most cities combine both functions, but the predominance of one or the other profoundly influences their form and structure. Most of our Canadian cities have developed as terminals of water transportation, with the harbor determining the location of the center from which the city spreads outward. Later, central railroad stations sometimes played a similar role, as gateways and focal points.

In the "central place" city the gateways are no less important, but here they are not in the center, but on the periphery. The streets lead not so much out from the gateway into the city and its hinterland, as into the city from the surrounding hinterland. But it is always the gateways and the channels of movement which are the most permanent elements in the city and which determine its basic structure. Only in moving through this network of channels can the city as a whole be experienced and understood. Only in relation to the ways in which people move and to the places where they stop or turn, only in the interaction of mass with the voids, can structures in the city be perceived and integrated into the memory image of the city. In his studies of the "image of the city" Kevin Lynch found that most people organize their impressions of their environment in terms of the "paths" which they travel. It is in relation to the paths and to their nodes that the other elements of the "image"—the focal points and landmarks, the different districts and their edges—are perceived. One of the greatest achievements of urban design, the replanning of Rome by Domenico Fontana, consisted essentially in giving visible form and emphasis to the paths from the city's gates to the sanctuaries and from one sanctuary to the other which the pilgrims had followed since the early Middle Ages.

With the enormous spatial expansion of our metropolitan areas and with the development of various means and modes of transportation, moving at radically different speeds, challenging new problems have arisen of separating and coordinating the channels of movement and of creating a meaningful form for the terminals where changes from one mode to another occur. Movement between buildings and movement within buildings, horizontal and vertical movement, movement of the human body, and movement by mechanical means require increasing integration and articulation.

Source: Published as the introduction to a special issue of *Architecture Canada* (Journal of the Royal Architectural Institute of Canada, Toronto, Ont.), August 1966.

In addition to channels and terminals, every movement system also requires a third element, the vehicle. Considerable attention—not always of the right kind—has been given to the design of airplanes, ships, and automobiles, but few changes have been made in the design of rail vehicles. Some interesting new departures were made in the vehicles for the Montreal subway and for Expo '67. The main emphasis of the Montreal subway, however, is on its relation to the city structure and on the function of the terminals, both as new nodes and focal points for the renewal of their surroundings and, in particular, as complex transfer points from the subway to pedestrian underground passages linking the stations directly to important buildings and, at the transfer points, from one line to another, but primarily to two types of movement on the surface, on foot and by bus. The most interesting aspect of the Montreal subway stations is the attempt to give to the passenger leaving the subterranean world of the subway a visual connection with, and clear orientation to, the world under the open sky, and, similarly, to the person entering the station visual access to the platforms and tracks underground.

An equally complex transfer problem was tackled in the New York Port Authority's bus terminal; here transfer between long-distance buses, which enter the terminal on separate, grade-separated rights-of-way, and local buses, subways, and pedestrian movement on the sidewalks is mediated by escalators connecting the four levels. The technically ingenious solution works well. Unfortunately, the necessity of fitting the structure into the gridiron street pattern has prevented it from playing its role as a focal point and node in the urban structure.

This role—the direct visual relation to the city—is probably always precluded for airports, which must be located in isolation from the city. Inevitably the connection must be mediated by vehicles, mainly private automobiles.

In terminals for rail and air vehicles and in suburban shopping centers we have long practiced the separation, horizontally or vertically, of fast-moving mechanical vehicles and slow-moving, or standing, pedestrians. We are only beginning to seek solutions for the area of most intense concentration and interaction of people, functions, and movements: the city center. The projects for downtown Vancouver and for Market Street East in Philadelphia are interesting attempts not only to separate the movements of vehicles and pedestrians, but at the same time to integrate them and to relate them to each other, as well as with and to the buildings. We are dealing with an entire scale of different speeds, each adding new elements to our total perception of the environment.

To a greater degree than has been possible in any existing city, the planning of the transportation system was integrated with the planning of the entire complex of structures in the plans for Expo '67. The major transportation system connected the focal points of the four sections of Expo, while four different systems of lower speed and capacity distributed the visitors to main points within each for exploration on foot. Daytime and nighttime visitors were equally considered.

This touches on two important points, both inherently containing contradictions: (1) the view *from* the road versus the view *to* (and of) the road, and (2) the integration of the transportation structure with the buildings which they serve versus the flexibility required to change the one without changing the other.

Where in our cities the roads and the vehicles traveling on them are visible, in the form of elevated railroads or of elevated highways, they are usually a disturbing and disrupting element. We try to eliminate this disruption by putting them underground into tunnels, cuts, or depressions, but we thereby deprive their riders totally or partly of any possibility of orientation to and perception of the structure of the city through which they are moving. Only rarely have we succeeded, or even attempted, as the Expo planners did, to use roads as positive elements to emphasize a line or an edge in the city structure, and to reveal a meaningful image of the city to their users.

The difficult choice between designing a structure as a tailor-made, close fit for one specific function and designing it as a looser—and less characteristic—cover in which various, often unforeseen functions may unfold is familiar to architects. It is equally present in the design of transportation facilities and, in particular, their integration with other structures. In the medieval city this integration was close; streets went under, over, and through buildings, and bridges were lined with houses and shops. It was a proud achievement of the Renaissance when the Pont Neuf for the first time enabled Parisians to cross the Seine with a full and unobstructed view of the river, and to see the piers and arches of the bridge as an elevated road, different and distinct from the densely built-up quarters on the river's banks. Similarly, it was the basic ideal of the Renaissance, consistently pursued through several centuries, to clearly separate the volume of streets and squares from that of the adjacent structures by strictly enforced building lines. The rising spiral of historical development has now reached a point where this direction is again reversed and where integration of channels of movement with architectural structures can again be achieved on a higher level, with new techniques and on a larger scale.

Chapter 35

PLANNING FOR THE CITY IN MOTION

ORIGIN OF THE "TRAFFIC PROBLEM"

Cities exist because people interact in cooperation and competition. Interaction leads to greater specialization and differentiation and to increased productivity and wealth; these in turn increase the need and desire for more interaction, as well as for more and more space.

Ever more people, goods, and messages move over ever-increasing distances. Technology is constantly at work, creating faster and more efficient means of movement; and, being human, we at once make use of these new means to move even more and farther. Because we can cover 10 miles faster and more easily by car than we can cover 1 mile on foot, we do so. Cities spread out further and further, and we travel for work, shopping, recreation, education, or social intercourse to places which previously would have been considered completely out of reach. So, in the end, we find that all these costly technical marvels, designed for the improvement of traffic, have resulted not in the hoped-for saving of time, but in the use of more space and in wider opportunities for contact, because that is what we wanted most. But once we have used the benefits of improved transportation for these purposes, we again regret the amount of time required for travel, and we complain about the "traffic problem" and demand more traffic improvements.

We have a traffic problem not because our means of transportation are so bad, but because they are so good—too good not to make use of them. It is therefore unlikely we ever will "solve" this problem. But, in attempting to solve it, we gain more space to use, more opportunities for contact, and more interaction—all made possible by greater mobility.

METROPOLITAN MOBILITY

It is not easy to visualize this metropolitan mobility. The 2 million inhabitants of Metropolitan Toronto travel close to 20 million miles daily—equivalent to circling the globe almost 800 times. Three quarters of these trips are made by automobile; if

---

Source: *Habitat* (Ottawa, Ont.), Vol. X, No. 1 [Central Mortgage and Housing Corporation (C.M.H.C.), Ottawa, Ont.]

trucks are included, at least 12 million vehicle-miles are traveled on the roads within the 240 square miles of Metropolitan Toronto, about 50,000 vehicle-miles on every square mile.

The city is indeed in motion. But vehicles can serve only if they stop to load and unload passengers or goods; and, unlike transit vehicles, private cars and trucks require parking space not only at their home base, but also at their manifold destinations. Whether these vehicles are on- or off-street, under, over or on the ground, some 20 square miles are required for parking, equivalent to half the total territory of the city of Toronto.

CITY STREETS

Our cities were not built for this. The streets and squares of cities have always served as outdoor living rooms for the city dwellers, where children and adults met, played, conversed, fought, or traded. They still do—less so in the areas of the wealthy, who have other spaces at their disposal, but very much so in the quarters of the poor. But it is just here, in centrally located areas of high density, that traffic is most intense.

Yet movement must continue if the city is to live, just as blood must continue to flow to keep the body alive. There is only one method to resolve the conflict between the needs of being and those of moving, and between moving by different means and at different speeds: separation. Separation can be achieved in three ways: temporally (in time) or horizontally or vertically.

None of these is really new. Imperial Rome permitted vehicles to move on its streets only at night. Some Italian towns have traditionally reserved their main streets for pedestrians during the hours of the *passeggiato* in the late afternoon. We attempt to restrict trucking at night to nonresidential streets. When the city of Copenhagen decided to close its main shopping street, Stroget, to traffic between midnight and 10:30 A.M., the dire predictions about traffic jams in parallel streets did not materialize.

Many European cities, such as Rotterdam, Coventry, and Cassel in Germany, used the opportunity provided by war destruction to create large pedestrian shopping areas, with access for parking and loading from the rear or underground, as we do in our shopping centers. The same principle has been applied to residential areas by the Radburn plan. Here access to the houses and garages by cars is provided by short, dead-end, cul-de-sacs branching out from roads enclosing a large "superblock," while the main entrance on the other side of the house is connected by walking paths, both to the outer road and to a park in the interior of the superblock. The Toronto architect Irving Grossman developed this system further in his row houses in Flemingdon Park by putting the driveways and garages underground, thus combining vertical with horizontal separation.

Vertical separation, providing different levels for different activities and movements, is the most complete and efficient form of separation and the only one applicable over a large area, but is also the most expensive and difficult to achieve in an already built-up area. In Philadelphia and in Montreal, fairly extensive underground pedestrian areas have been developed, including shopping areas, cafes, restaurants, and theaters, as well as railroad and subway stations, and may gradually be extended further.

In general, it is more pleasant for pedestrians to be in the open air above, rather than below, the street level; this has been done in the redevelopment of the center of Stockholm.

More general is vertical separation between the street system, used by both vehicles and pedestrians, and the facilities for high-speed, high-volume traffic: railroads, rapid transit lines, and freeways.

INDIVIDUAL AND COLLECTIVE TRANSPORTATION

There is at present in all big cities a battle raging between advocates of a "freeway system" and a "subway (or monorail) system," and figures are bandied about claiming speeds of 100 mph or more for this or that technical innovation. However, freeways or subways do not constitute a system, but are merely the trunk lines of an automobile system for individual movement and of a transit system for collective movement. The question of the top speed that can technically be achieved on a trunk line is quite irrelevant; speeds of over 100 mph have been achieved for over half a century both by automobiles and by trains. What matters is how people get to the trunk line from the places where they are and from it to the places they want to reach. This depends on all the other elements of each system: interchanges and ramps, streets, parking and loading spaces for automobiles, "feeder" buses or streetcars, automobiles and taxis, escalators, elevators, and walkways for transit passengers. The capacity of any flow system is determined by its narrowest point; it serves no useful purpose to enlarge the capacity of the other elements of the system beyond that point. The establishment of balance between the various elements of each system is one of the most important tasks of planning for movement in the city.

A BALANCED SYSTEM

More fundamental, however, is the task of planning the balance between the two main systems of individual and collective transportation. It is a question of balance, not of either-or. The two systems are far more complementary than they are competitive. They serve two different types of movement. Individual transportation is indispensable for all movements dispersed in space and/or in time, and with the spreading out of urban development and with the increase in leisure time and leisure activities their number is growing rapidly. Such movements cannot be served by collective transportation because it is not economically feasible to supply a bus and a driver, let alone a train, for one, two, or three passengers.

Inversely, collective transportation is indispensable for all movements which are concentrated in space and time. If thousands of people want to travel to the same location from the same direction, or from several directions, it is not economically feasible to provide all the required streets and parking spaces. In addition, it should be remembered that there are many who do not have cars, and many more without cars at their disposal when they want to make a trip.

However, transit generally cannot provide transportation from door to door, as can the individual vehicle. In the densely built-up big cities of the nineteenth century, such as Paris, London, and New York, people walked from the subway station to their homes and then climbed up four, five, or six stairs, and many still do. But contemporary North Americans increasingly refuse to live under crowded conditions, or to climb stairs, or to walk any considerable distance, especially if exposed to inclement weather. Thus any rapid transit system must rely on some additional mechanical means of transportation.

In the central business district these means are vertical: elevators and escalators. The great concentration of people in the skyscrapers of the city center, most of whom travel between it and the surrounding residential areas during one or two morning and evening rush hours, is best served by rapid transit lines radiating in several directions from the center. On the outer stations of these lines there is rarely a concentration of office or apartment towers sufficient to "feed" the line. Most people travel to and from these stations by mechanical means moving horizontally, such as buses, trolley-buses, or streetcars. In Toronto, for instance, most subway passengers transfer to it from surface vehicles. Probably 60% use buses or streetcars for one end of their trip, 20% use them for both ends, and only about 20% walk at both ends.

Because the construction of subways is very expensive, it can hardly be justified if peak-hour loads are less than 12,000 passengers per hour on the most heavily traveled section and 4,000 at the outer terminals. Only rarely, with relatively high densities and with a highly efficient feeder system, can these conditions be fulfilled for lines bypassing the center at considerable distances. In general, trips in these directions must be served by surface transit. For this reason, and because of its indispensable role as "feeder" to rapid transit stations, surface transit is the mainstay of any transit system.

Therefore planning the road system, which has to serve surface transit and the movement of goods by truck and delivery wagons as well as by private cars and taxis, remains the crucial task of planning for the city in motion. Ideally, roads should serve only one of their two contradictory functions: either be outdoor living spaces, providing access to the adjacent properties only, but free from any through traffic, as are cul-de-sacs and loop streets; or serve only through traffic, free from any access, as are freeways. In practice, collector-distributor streets and arterial roads must mediate between these two extremes.

DESIGNING THE "BEST" TRANSPORTATION SYSTEM

Once a system of roads and rapid transit lines has been designed for any given city or area, and their operational characteristics, such as speeds, headways, fares, and parking fees, have been specified, it is possible to "simulate" or "model" the choices between possible trips and routes and between individual and collective transportation which people are likely to make. This is done, using electronic computers, by systematic analysis of a vast array of data concerning the choices people have made under varying conditions. By comparing several alternative transportation systems, it is possible to find the "best balanced" system.

The "best" system can be defined as the one which provides the greatest mobility at the least cost in terms of money, time, and inconvenience. While it is hardly possible to express time and inconvenience exactly in money terms (or vice versa), a reasonable approximation can be made by measuring the price people are prepared to pay in order to save time or to avoid inconvenience.

Most transportation plans have, explicitly or implicitly, attempted to evaluate these costs for the users of the system. However, a transportation system inflicts losses in money, time, and inconvenience, in the form of noise, vibration, fumes, glare, ugliness, accidents, and nervous strain, not only on its users, but on other persons as well. In fact, the disruption of the living environment by traffic is the most serious aspect of modern mobility.

In medieval buildings a person had to go through one inhabited room to reach another one. We have learned during the last four centuries to keep through traffic out of the rooms in which we live, sleep, or work, by channeling it past them in corridors. We must now apply the same principle to cities, by channeling traffic in arteries and freeways around the edges of "environment areas." This principle was brilliantly developed in the British report entitled "Traffic in Towns," known as the "Buchanan Report."

THE CITY IN MOTION

It is, however, strange that this report assumes that, after the great increase in mobility which it expects, people will continue to live, work, and shop in the same locations as they did before and will make the same trips which they made in the past, and no others. As mentioned earlier, increased mobility has always induced people to travel farther and spread out over a wider area. Not only do people, goods, and messages move in the city, but also the city itself is in motion. Day in and day out, structures are erected, altered, and demolished.

No fixed plan can cope once and for all with this constant flux. Planning, as planners like to assert, must be "flexible." But concrete and brick, unfortunately, do not flex. "Temporary" and "mobile" structures have been advocated as solutions to this problem of the city in motion. But "rien ne dure que le provisoire," as our French-speaking countrymen say, and mobile structures have to be anchored to foundations and to utility pipes and ducts. It is doubtful that we can do more to provide for flexibility than to reserve some room for the unforeseen. Some planners, notably the famous Japanese architect Kenzo Tange, have proposed that a city should consist of "megaforms," within which all kinds of changes could take place just as partitions are changed at will within the structure of an office building. In a way the system of streets and railways is such a megaform, and probably the only achievable one.

THE IMAGE OF THE CITY IN MOTION

The vast spread of both the urban area and the transportation structures which make this diffusion possible, notably the freeways, has completely changed the traditional image of the city. We now experience the urban environment on two different scales. For the person standing or walking, or looking out of a window, the human scale is still valid, with all the warmth and richness of spatial enclosure and the relation of detail to the whole. But his or her view encompasses only a very small segment of the total urban area. Except from an airplane, it can never be seen as a whole. However, in driving through it, there may be a sequence of impressions of an urban landscape which build up to an image of the urban structure, of the relations of its parts to each other and to its totality. Only occasionally, and then by accident rather than by planning, have we realized this potential as, for instance, with the opening up of the view of the Humber Bay and the Toronto skyline from the eastern end of the Queen Elizabeth Freeway.

To sum up, planning for the city in motion means planning the right balance between the opportunity for "going places" and the preservation and creation of places worth going to.

Chapter 36

ENVIRONMENTAL ASPECTS OF TRANSPORT AND URBAN DEVELOPMENT

THE FRICTION OF SPACE AND THE SETTLEMENT PATTERN

If the age-old dream of the magic carpet were a reality, there would be no cities. People would live, work, and play wherever a place suited their fancy, probably basing their choice of location primarily on climatic and scenic advantages. Technical progress is asymptotically approaching the magic carpet state. As it comes closer to its ideal, Canada, with its not particularly attractive climate, is not likely to attract a large part of the world's population in the long run.

However, as Lord Keynes remarked, in the long run we are all dead. During the rest of this century, technology is not likely to eliminate the friction of space, though it will continue to reduce it. To carry goods, persons, and messages from one point to another will still require incurring costs in terms of time, money, and inconvenience. As far as messages are concerned, differences in time and inconvenience have already been eliminated; it takes no longer and requires no more effort to make a telephone call from Toronto to Paris, France, than to Paris, Ontario. It still takes more money, but this difference is likely to be greatly reduced by the use of communication satellites.

Some people believe that the development of communications, notably closed-circuit television, will soon replace the movement of persons. Recently the head of the Volkswagen Works remarked in a dinner conversation that, for this reason, in 10 or 20 years there would be few cars around, adding that people would work out their restlessness, which now causes them to travel, in some other way, such as cultivating their gardens. Coming from this source, the remark deserves attention.

However, this writer doubts that many Canadians will acquire the wisdom of Voltaire's Candide. It may also be noted that the telephone, which was a more revolutionary change in communication than any future one can be, has not eliminated the desire for face-to-face contacts. While many of these have been replaced by telephone calls it seems that almost as many calls are used to "make a date," arranging for a person-trip which otherwise might not have been made.

Source: Report prepared for the Privy Council of Canada, November 25, 1969.

Certainly, the development of communications, together with the development of the transportation of goods and persons by rail, road, and air, and of power by wire, has already led to the decentralization of some functions which previously were bound to urban centers. An increasing number of meetings and conferences are held in resorts in "rural" surroundings. Research workers in institutions located in "ex-urban" areas no longer visit central libraries, but order, by telephone, microfilm copies of the material which they want to read. In Los Angeles and probably in other areas, too, many investment counselors and stockbrokers work in the suburbs in which they live; they never go downtown, but handle their business by telephone. They stay, however, within the urbanized area in order to be able to meet their clients face to face. Other professionals—writers, artists, and even some planning consultants—find that they can handle their work from their rural residences.

This trend is bound to continue, but it is not likely to result, at least in this century, in the "aspatial community" which some planners envisage. In the foreseeable future, mutual accessibility for persons and goods, provided by transportation, will continue to shape the urban environment.

IMPACT OF INTER- AND INTRAURBAN TRANSPORTATION

Accessibility has been, throughout history, the main determinant of the location, size, and function of cities: access to the surrounding region for "central places," and access to other urban concentrations for "break-of-bulk" (notably harbor) cities and for railroad and crossroad towns.

The industrial revolution has brought about some fundamental changes in the urban pattern. First and foremost, the interacting processes of rising productivity of labor and of increasing specialization, both within and between enterprises, has led to a shift of the labor force from primary to secondary and subsequently to tertiary industries; and these have located in urban areas, primarily in the largest ones, because the interdependence arising from specialization increases the need for mutual accessibility. This concentration and the resultant country-to-city migration were made possible by the development of efficient means of long-distance transportation and communication.

These large-scale means of transportation have a strong centralizing effect, because only a large volume of traffic can support the required costly terminals and channels and a high frequency of sailings, flights, or trains. As terminals and most channels are man-made, the historical relation between situation and city growth tends to be reversed. Rather than cities growing because they are located at a crossroad, "crossroads" of all types are expanded because they serve a big city. Should the federal government desire to influence the distribution of the urban population by region and/or by city size, its control over transportation by water, air, and rail provides it with a powerful tool to do this—at a cost.

The development of techniques of short-distance, intraurban transportation and communication lagged behind that of interurban, long-distance means. Only a generation after steamships and railroads had become dominant, did electric traction, the bicycle, the telephone, and, finally and most powerfully, the internal combustion engine, applied to cars, trucks, and buses, break the narrow confines of the tightly packed nineteenth century city. A vastly greater amount of land has been made available for urban development, and all users—industry, commerce, institutions, and recreational facilities, as well as residences—avail themselves increasingly of this growing opportunity. Land absorption per 1000 of urban population increases, or, expressed inversely, density decreases, and decreases regularly from the center to the periphery.

Thus the continuing centripetal "country-to-city" migration has been supplemented by a centrifugal "city-to-suburb" migration, which started about a century ago and is still accelerating in all developed countries, apparently at the same rate per capita as disposable personal income. The net result of these two waves of migration is the emergence of a new form of human settlement, the metropolitan region. Within such regions a distinction can be made between the central "commuter watershed," generally defined as a "metropolitan area," and an outer "metropolitan fringe." This fringe contains, on the one hand, enterprises and settlements which *are served* by the "higher order" producer and consumer services of the metropolis, and, on the other, areas of summer cottages and other facilities which *serve* the population of the metropolis.

The fringes of neighboring metropolises may overlap. In Canada this is already the case in the "Golden Horseshoe." But there is no evidence to support the fashionable thesis that metropolitan areas are being submerged in a still newer and larger form of settlement, called "megalopolis"; each area remains as strongly as ever oriented to its own center.

Nor is there any evidence to support the widespread belief that a change in housing type or in mode of transportation would reverse the trend of urban areas to spread out. A study by this writer, comparing two urban areas of equal population, Metropolitan Toronto and the city-state of Hamburg, Germany, showed equal overall densities both in the total area and in its core, and a considerably greater "overspill" of population beyond the metropolitan boundary in Hamburg than in Toronto—this despite the facts that in Hamburg apartments accounted for over three quarters, and in Toronto for less than one quarter, of all dwellings and that Hamburg has had extensive rapid rail transit for over half a century and mass use of the private automobile only since 1954, while in Toronto automobile driving has been widespread since the 1920s and the first subway was opened only in 1954.

There is, however, a noticeable difference between the two areas in the spatial distribution of urban land uses. In Toronto they are intermingled with tracts of disused farmland. In Hamburg there are large contiguous areas of productive farmland, and urban development is largely concentrated in corridors following the rapid transit lines.

Considering the vital importance of internal transportation for large urban areas, it is logical to assume that their rates of growth are correlated with the efficiency of their transportation systems. Strangely, this logical correlation cannot be corroborated by any empirical evidence. It seems that now, as throughout history, external transportation influences the location, function, and growth of cities, while internal transportation influences their areal extent, density, form, and internal structure.

Transportation problems in Canada have, at present, assumed a somewhat paradoxical character. On the national scale, our problem is still too few people and activities in too much space, forcing us to spend a greater portion of our gross national product on long-distance transportation than does any other nation. At the core of our urban concentrations, we are faced with the opposite problem: too many people and activities in too little space, resulting in congestion. But in the rapidly expanding outer sections of the same urban areas, the problem of too few people and activities in too much space emerges again, making it impossible to establish effective mass transportation and forcing exclusive reliance on the private motor car.

URBANIZATION IN CANADA

Canada has been an urban country for 50 years; the census of 1921 showed 51% of the population as living in urban places. By 1966 the urban share had increased to 74%, indicating an annual rural-to-urban shift averaging about 0.5%. The rate of growth of the urban population is bound to slow down, because the three sources of increase are declining: first, natural growth will slow down because of a falling fertility rate; second, internal migration will decline because its source, rural population, is rapidly shrinking relatively and even absolutely; and, third, international net immigration, even if it maintains its present absolute size, will contribute a smaller percentage to the expected larger urban population. Consequently, urban population is likely to increase from 1981 to 2001 no more than 50%, at roughly half the rate of increase experienced in the periods 1901–1921 (116%) and 1941–1961 (110%). The problem of urban growth is far from unmanageable.

More significant is the concentration of urban population in the largest places. Between 1961 and 1966 the urban areas with populations of 100,000 or more grew at almost twice the rate of the smaller towns. In the year 2001 at least 60% of the total Canadian population—18 out of 30 million—is likely to live in about 15 metropolitan areas with populations of 300,000 or more. About half of these persons will be in the Montreal and Toronto areas, each with a population of more than 4 million.

At the other extreme, farm population is likely to account for no more than 4–5% of the Canadian total; together with those who serve the farmers locally, perhaps 6–10%. Of the remainder a sizable number occupied in or retired from secondary and especially from tertiary occupations may also live in the country. Probably most of them will be found in the outer fringes of metropolitan regions. It is hard to estimate the size of this relatively recent phenomenon. These "exurbanites" may account for as few as 1–2% or for as many as 10–12% of the 2001 population. This would leave anywhere between 20 and 33% of the total for cities and towns with populations of less than 300,000. Probably most of these persons will also live within the orbits of larger metropolitan areas, in various types of "satellite towns."

In Canada, as in practically all countries, public opinion and governments have viewed with alarm this "trend to the metropolis" and policies to counteract it have been discussed. So far the goals of such policies are only vaguely defined in terms such as a "more balanced" population distribution or, more generally, "decentralization." Some of the more specific reasons given are the internal transportation problems of big urban areas and their municipal costs.

There is some evidence that, beyond a certain level, increasing city size is correlated with an increased number per capita both of car-miles (despite a greater share of transit in big cities) and of truck-miles and of truck-time. However, it is not known to what extent these intraurban movements substitute for interurban movements for the same purposes; generally the latter will be much longer. It is fairly evident that this occurs with truck movements; many goods which are available within a metropolitan region, either because they have been produced there or because they have been brought in by water or rail, have to be trucked into small towns. With person movements the problem is more complex. In some cases, such as a shopping trip to the big city, there is substitution, but in most the corresponding trip is not made. What is the cost, in terms of productivity and of human fulfillment, of trips which are not made? If there is no symphony in the town, no trips to the city will be made by potential listeners. A cellist living in such a town is likely to move to a city where he or she can play and thus substitutes migration for commuting. There is indeed considerable evidence which suggests that limitation of choice of jobs in smaller towns is a frequent cause for movement; contrary to the popular image of the stable small town, population turnover seems to be inversely correlated to city size.

Limitation in the choice of jobs frequently may prevent those who do not move from realizing their full productive potential in their work. This may be an explanation for differences in the productivity of labor, which a Swedish study found to be at least 15% higher in the largest cities than in the others. This is of a much greater order of magnitude than the differences in the cost of municipal services. While this area has been quite extensively studied, no firm conclusions have emerged as to the correlation of service costs with city size; but it is obvious that the differences do not exceed 2–3% of the gross product of an urban community.

The foregoing considerations are speculative rather than conclusive. We simply do not know enough about the economic and social benefits and the costs related to the size and location of cities to be able to develop a national policy for the distribution of the urban population. Only systematic, sustained, and unbiased research can clarify this important question. Only national research organizations are equal to this task. If or when such research showed that a distribution different from the one resulting from present trends was preferable, it would be the task of the federal government to bring the change about by subsidizing the required infrastructure, locating public institutions, and encouraging the location of private enterprise by tax concessions, tariff benefits, or direct subsidy payments.

Pending the results of such research, it is here assumed that the extremely strong and general trends described earlier will continue and that the metropolitan region will be the setting of urban transportation.

GOODS MOVEMENT

In monetary terms, goods transportation accounts for 40–50% of all urban transportation in Canada. Water, sewage, gas, and, to some extent, oil are carried in underground pipelines, with no detrimental impact on the environment. If it should prove feasible to transport solids in containers through pipelines, this would further reduce disturbances arising from surface transportation. Similarly, the visually disturbing and potentially dangerous "wirescape" could be eliminated from the urban environment by carrying electric currents underground. The slightly higher cost to the consumer, resulting from higher capital cost, would almost certainly be less than the cost resulting from interruptions in the power supply because of recurrent damage to exposed overhead wires.

Apart from pipes, which are, and of wires, which could be, located underground where they in no way harm the environment, goods transportation within urban regions is at present handled almost exclusively by trucks. Such intrametropolitan distribution of goods by rail as may still exist is bound to disappear with the universal adoption of piggy-back services by the railroads. This will permit the elimination of many railroad spurs, branch lines, and secondary rail yards; but on the other hand, it will increase the number of trucks on urban roads.

It is hardly necessary to emphasize the disturbance of the environment due to the noise and vibration caused by heavy trucks, in addition to their contribution to congestion and to air pollution. A considerable reduction of heavy truck movement on city streets could be achieved by transferring and consolidating the loads carried by heavy long-distance trucks to smaller delivery trucks assigned to serve defined city districts for distribution and collection. This is done with some success in the truck terminals created by the New York Port Authority, an agency with jurisdiction over an extensive metropolitan region; it can hardly be accomplished by municipal governments, which control only a part of their region.

PERSON MOVEMENT

While the importance of intraurban goods movement is generally underestimated, public attention is strongly focused on the time consumed and on the congestion experienced in person movement. Traffic congestion has always been experienced in large cities; it was worse in imperial Rome, medieval Paris, and Victorian London than it is in any Canadian city. There is also a good deal of circumstantial evidence that the time spent in travel for various purposes—work, shopping, recreation, and so on—has, on the average, been fairly constant. This inelasticity, surprising at first sight, is explained by the easily overlooked fact that travel demand is not fixed, but expands as supply is expanded by the transportation industry.

The product of the transportation industry is mobility, or the reduction of the friction of space. In terms of person movement, this product can be formulated as reduction of per mile cost in terms of money, time, and inconvenience. The buyer of the product has the choice of consuming it in three forms: either by saving time (and money and inconvenience), or by absorbing more space, or by widening his or her range of choice among the increased number of opportunities which have been made physically accessible.

As already noted, on the average, consumers have not chosen the first option: travel time has remained constant. Many, however, have chosen the second option, absorption of more space. In fact, the radius of urban development for cities of the same size has expanded at least five times in the past 120 years. As this has made 25 times as much urban land accessible within a given time, the range of choice within a given time-distance must have been increased at least fivefold. Although there is no way of measuring exactly the increase in the range of opportunity that has been opened up to urban dwellers by improved urban transportation, it appears to be indeed of this order of magnitude.

Greater accessibility could, of course, be provided by locating origins and destinations closer together, that is, by higher densities, rather than by reducing the time-distance between them. The choice between absorbing more space and the other two options has not been entirely free. Suburban municipalities have prescribed large lots by zoning, in order to keep out poor families, in particular those with children, because they cannot pay high taxes and they require high municipal expenses. The federal government shares some responsibility for this pernicious policy; first, because for many years Central Mortgage and Housing Corporation (C.M.H.C.) policies have favored large single-family lots, and, second and more fundamentally, because the preemption of all other tax sources by the higher levels of government has forced the municipalities to rely almost exclusively on the real estate tax and to subordinate all other considerations to the pursuit of a "favorable assessment ratio."

While large-lot zoning is responsible for some avoidable increase in automobile mileage, it cannot be gainsaid that, on the whole, increased land absorption has satisfied real needs for more space, air, light, sunshine, and green. However drab our "strawberry-box" subdivisions, and however picturesque the crowded slums of Paris or Venice, the former do provide a far healthier physical environment. Even greater is the improvement of the social, economic, and cultural environment by the greater freedom of choice provided by increased accessibility.

The gains of automobility are real, but they are being bought at a high price in terms of social costs.

THE SOCIAL COSTS OF THE PRIVATE CAR

The drivers and passengers of private cars derive great benefits from their use. But in the process they inflict substantial "malefits" on other persons, including themselves. These malefits can be divided into four groups: first, land absorption; second, interference with other modes of movement; third, impact on the physical environment; and, fourth, impact on the social environment.

Land Absorption

The total amount of pavement required for moving vehicles depends on so many variables that it is difficult to quantify. Certainly most of the street system consists of access streets of dimensions determined by considerations other than the accommodation of traffic flow. A far greater, and more nearly calculable, amount of land is occupied for standing cars.

By the end of the century, Canadians probably will be close to owning one car for every two persons. Each car requires one parking space at the home base; about one half need one at the place of work; and a total of 0.50 space per car is a conservative estimate for the parking required for shopping, business, schools, recreation, visiting, and so on. Thus each car requires 2.0 spaces, each averaging, with the space required to move in and out, at least 350 square feet, for a total of 700 square feet per car.

The Montreal and Toronto regions, each with over 4 million inhabitants, will each require about 4 million parking spaces, 1.4 billion square feet, or about 55 square miles. This means an addition of nearly 10% to the land required for all other urban uses, and a lengthening of all distances by an average of 5%. The extended hard surface greatly adds to storm water runoff, thereby increasing flood danger and stream pollution. In some cases the decreased recharge of subterranean water horizons may lead to a substantial lowering of the water table, with serious consequences for vegetation.

The figures here presented may be somewhat reduced by parking in driving lanes, underground, or in garages.

Interference with Other Modes of Movement

Passenger cars account for over 80% of all vehicles; on urban streets, for over 90% at peak hours. The resulting congestion slows down the movement of trucks and delivery vehicles, at a cost amounting to hundreds of millions annually. It also delays the movement of surface transit vehicles which, even in the two Canadian cities which have grade-separated rapid transit trunk lines, account for the majority, and in all others for the totality, of all transit trips. This greatly increases the cost and reduces the attractiveness of public transportation. Finally, the presence of a steady stream of vehicles forces pedestrians who have to cross a street to make detours to the next traffic light and to wait there until it turns green. The resulting loss of time has not been measured, but it certainly amounts to many millions of person-hours each year.

Impact on the Physical Environment

Among the impacts of the automobile on the physical environment, air pollution is the most serious one, affecting the entire area. It could be eliminated by replacement of the internal combustion engine by a different power plant. Attempts to develop an effective steam turbine engine appear to have failed. Use of thermoelectric cells has as yet not proved feasible. Electric batteries, quite widely used 60 years ago, have not been able to compete with the internal combustion engine because of an unfavorable weight-to-power ratio. It is, however, highly probable that this problem could be solved by a concentrated scientific-technological effort of much lesser magnitude than the one required to put a man on the moon. Such an effort will not be made by the automobile industry or by the manufacturers of electrical machinery, who are closely tied to the oil industry. It calls for action by a national government. The nation which is first in this field has a chance to attain a strong position in a multibillion dollar world market.

An electric automobile would also reduce, though not eliminate, the nuisance of noise. It would not reduce the relatively minor nuisance of headlight glare or the most serious effect of the mass use of the motor vehicle, danger. Danger is inherent in the rapid movement of a large number of hard, heavy bodies, whatever improvements are made to the road, the vehicle, and the driver. It can be substantially reduced only by a reduction in the number of vehicles. The chance of collision between two buses, each carrying 30 persons, is 1. If the same 60 persons travel in 40 cars, the chance of collision is $(40 \times 39)/2 = 780$. Even if allowance is made for the greater number of persons in the buses, the risk ratio is $1:52$. The risk ratio for collision with pedestrians is $1:20$.

Finally, the combined effect of danger, air pollution, noise, and headlight glare is nervous tension for drivers, pedestrians, and occupants of adjacent buildings.

Impact on the Social Environment

More elusive, but no less important, is the negative impact of the private automobile on the social environment, even if the psychological effect of the isolation of the person ensconced in a mobile steel fortress and his or her temptation by the arrogance of 40 horsepowers are discounted.

While the automobile has greatly increased the mobility of those who have it at their disposal, it has strongly decreased the mobility of all those who have not. Their number is far greater than might be concluded from the fact that in most Canadian cities the number of cars equals or exceeds the number of households. Car ownership is strongly inversely correlated to income; for example, in Metropolitan Toronto in 1961 the percentage of households without a car increased regularly from 3.5% for those with incomes of $15,000 and over to 57.8% for those with incomes under $2000, averaging one tenth for all households with incomes over $6000 and one third for the other half (53.4% of all households). But even in households owning a car there are those unable to drive because they are too young or are handicapped, and those able to drive cannot use the car while it is used by another member of the household.

All these persons have become less mobile: first, because the dispersed pattern of development induced by the car has removed most potential destinations beyond walking distance; and, second, because the diversion of a majority of potential customers to the private car has greatly reduced transit service. Thus the predominance of the automobile militates against equality of opportunity.

The volume and the speed of car movements have also largely destroyed the age-old function of the street as an outdoor living room, in which people move and rest, meet, talk, trade, and play, see and are seen. The result is a weakening of neighborhood relations and of community cohesion. In particular, the role of the street in the socialization of the young has been lost. In the preautomobile age walking to school was an educational experience. The child observed, overheard, and met adults, saw them at work, noticed the buildings, plants, and animals along his way. The child driven in a school bus or in his parents' car learns nothing of this. No wonder that this person feels bewildered and alienated when, as an adolescent, he meets the adult world. It is hardly accidental that alienation is much more pronounced among the children of middle-class suburbs than among those of the city poor, who still spend a good deal of time in the streets.

PUBLIC TRANSPORTATION

Because of the many and very substantial social costs of the use of the private automobile in urban areas, present market decisions based on consumers' choice between private and public transportation lead to a misallocation of resources, which calls for correction by public action. Transit services must fulfill the dual role of serving those who have no other choice and of inducing those who have a choice to leave their cars at home, by providing them with an attractive alternative. To the extent that such service succeeds in achieving the second goal, it provides a very substantial benefit also to those who do not use it, but drive, by relieving street congestion. Urban communities would be fully justified in buying transit service "wholesale" out of tax revenues, rather than having their citizens buy it at retail through fares. This would permit considerable economies of operation, in particular by eliminating bus delays resulting from passengers being forced to queue up at a single entrance door in order to pay their fares.

In fact, market decisions are distorted in several ways in disfavor of transit. Direct cost of a person-mile by transit averages about 10 cents, and that of an urban car-mile probably about 25 cents, or, with an average occupancy of less than 1.5 persons per car, 17 cents per person-mile. However, the individual choosing a mode of travel disregards the fixed costs of his or her car and considers only the out-of-pocket cost, which may be as low as 3 or 4 cents per car-mile. Financing transit out of tax revenues would transform transit costs into fixed costs and thereby eliminate this distortion. Choice could be made to reflect total rather than out-of-pocket cost only if the bulk of transit cost were also transformed into a fixed cost. Theoretically this could be done by an annual subscription; in practice the only feasible way is to use general taxation to carry this cost.

The choice by the user is further distorted if and when he is supplied with free parking by an employer. The employee using transit has to pay the fare out of his taxable income. But the employee who drives and receives free parking service does not include the value of this service in his taxable income. Neither does his employer, for whom it is a business expense. It would be desirable to disallow the provision of parking as a tax-deductible business expense. This would force employers to charge a parking fee to their employees. At the very least such a fee would encourage car pooling. Free employee parking is, of course, also being provided by nonprofit organizations, including governments. Governments might well set an example by discontinuing this harmful practice.

An even greater distortion affects the judgment of municipal governments. They receive only erratic financial support for transit from the higher levels of government. On the other hand, all provincial governments regularly make substantial contributions to roads. The federal government has not engaged in a massive freeway program comparable to that of the United States, but its only contribution to road transportation, its share of the Trans-Canada Highway, has helped to build in several urban areas freeways which benefit and encourage intrametropolitan car movement. The municipalities receiving these bounties from the higher levels of government are not free to allocate them to transit, where they might produce far greater benefits.

It is not claimed here that the suggested corrections of the distortions of cost allocation, even to the extent of supplying "free" transit, would radically reverse the trend toward a growing share of individual transportation by automobile in urban person movement. This trend is deeply rooted in the development of modern urban society.

Collective transportation, the carrying of a number of people between two points in a single vehicle, or a train of vehicles, is possible only when and where a number of desired trips coincide in space and in time. Concentration in time occurs primarily for trips between home and place of work at the beginning and end of the working day. With the reduction in the number of working days to about 240 of the 365 days of the year, with increasing leisure time and increasing real incomes, nonwork trips, widely dispersed in time, account for an increasing number of all trips.

More important than the growing dispersal of trips in time is their dispersal in space. The popular view of the "traffic problem" as concerning only trips between city center and suburban periphery corresponds less and less to reality. In large urban areas central business district (C.B.D.) employment tends to become stable in absolute volume and consequently to decrease in relation to total employment. In Metropolitan Toronto, for example, this has been observed since 1953; C.B.D.

employment now accounts for less than 18% of the metropolitan total. Employment has decreased in the balance of the city and increased rapidly in the outer boroughs. As a consequence, between 1954 and 1964 the percentage of all centripetal "inbound" trips—most of them with origins and destinations intermediate between the metropolitan periphery and the city center—dropped from 55 to 45%. Centrifugal trips, or "reverse commuting," increased moderately, from 11 to 13%, but "crosstown" trips increased from 34 to 42%. In the future they will account for a growing majority of all trips, with an increasing proportion entirely within the outer area, as both work and all other destinations, as well as homes, spread out more and more.

In reaction against the long-continued, one-sided catering to the demands of the private car, there is currently a great emphasis on rail rapid transit on its own, entirely grade-separated right-of-way throughout North America. So far only two Canadian cities, Toronto and Montreal, have put new rapid transit systems into operation, with outstanding success. It must, however, he emphasized that a sufficient number of passengers to justify the high capital cost can be concentrated at stations only with the aid of additional "feeder" means of mechanical transportation. In the city center these means are vertical: elevators and escalators (which, it may be noted, collect their fares not from each individual user, but in "wholesale" form as part of the building rent). It may be possible to concentrate a sufficient number of multistory commercial and residential buildings at a few other stations. But, in the vast majority of cases, feeding has to be by means of horizontal transportation: buses or cars.

Cars can well serve as feeders between homes and the stations of low-volume lines, such as suburban lines and possibly some outlying rapid transit stations. However, at most subway stations the space they require for parking would interfere with intensive development and, consequently, with pedestrian feeding; and the street space which they require for driving to and from the stations would interfere with feeding by buses. More important, they can serve as feeders only for a trunk-line trip between dispersed homes and concentrated destinations, but not where the work or other nonhome destinations are also distant from transit stations or stops, as is increasingly the case.

For a majority of their riders, rapid transit lines depend on bus feeder lines. The fact that buses are subject to all delays which affect cars, and in addition to substantial delays for loading and unloading passengers at intermediate stops, puts them at a time disadvantage as compared to the private car. More important, in low-density areas either frequency is low, resulting in long waiting times, or access ways are long, or both. To provide frequent service on closely spaced routes in such areas would result in buses carrying no or very few passengers on most of their runs.

The handicaps of public transit in its competition with the private car consist not in lack of technical speed of transit vehicles, but in time loss and inconvenience from four sources:

1. Access to and from transit stop or station.

2. Waiting for transit vehicle.

3. Transfer between transit vehicles.

4. Intermediate stops in order to load and unload other passengers.

Here is not the place to discuss the many possible means to minimize or eliminate one or more of these handicaps. Most of them do not require new technology. The obstacles preventing their adoption are dependent on the type of proposed means:

1. Political—resistance on the part of car users who would be inconvenienced.
2. Financial.
3. Institutional—because of divided responsibility and neglect of research and development, partly because of financial stringency.

The only systems now under study which would eliminate all but the first handicap are those for public individual transportation, such as the "Teletrans." In these the passenger would enter a small vehicle and punch the proper destination station, and a computer would guide the vehicle to the destination. While all elements of the required technology are known, a great deal of development work is still required to make such a system operational. The capacity may be much lower—in this writer's estimate not over 3000 persons per hour per line, and 1500 per station—and the capital and operation cost higher than Teletrans advocates anticipate. However, the system might be particularly suitable for cities of the size predominant in Canada in the coming decades, 300,000–1,000,000 population, and deserves attention.

The generally similar "STARR" system would eliminate also the first handicap, by enabling the cars to be alternatively operated by the driver on the general road system, but its feasibility is very questionable.

DESIGN OF URBAN TRAFFIC FACILITIES

The insertion of traffic facilities into the urban pattern creates difficult problems. From the point of view of visual amenity, there is an inherent conflict between the requirements of the view *from* the path and the view *to* the path. For the person traveling on the path it is most desirable, for orientation as well as for visual enjoyment, to be above ground. But to persons in the vicinity, elevated structures and the vehicles moving on them are likely to be an offense not only to their eyes but also to their ears. Experience with elevated railroads has forced rapid transit lines almost everywhere underground, while elevated freeways are tolerated, despite their much greater bulk. This is ironical, because a view is far more valuable to the transit rider than to the car driver, who has to keep his or her eyes on other cars.

Only where it is possible to locate traffic channels in an escarpment is the view both from and to the path fully satisfactory. In this case the path emphasizes the natural land form and serves as a dividing line between neighborhoods, rather than cutting through them. In most other cases it is preferable to locate the path below grade, in a cut or completely underground.

In densely built areas a greater integration is desirable between the structures serving transportation and those serving other functions. This is presently called "traffic architecture." If the transportation facilities are entirely underground, this may mean simply building in their air rights. Integration of elevated facilities is more difficult, but feasible. It should, however, not be overlooked that such close integration limits flexibility; alteration of one element is not possible without substantial alteration of the other.

The disturbing impact of traffic channels on the environment can be greatly reduced by locating them in a common corridor. Ideally, such a transportation corridor should provide room not only for road and rail lines, but also for pipelines, power lines, and any presently unknown future facilities. This will generally not be possible in built-up areas, but deserves most serious consideration in the vast areas which will be urbanized during the next three or more decades, as well as in the open country between cities.

PLANNING AND IMPLEMENTATION OF TRANSPORTATION AND LAND DEVELOPMENT

As noted earlier, the pattern of dispersed development, largely, though by no means entirely, due to motorization, in turn makes effective transit service extremely difficult and induces more motorization, at high social cost. As also noted earlier, the benefits of increased accessibility can be provided by shortening spatial distance as well as by reducing the friction of space.

While the general trend towards greater space absorption and further spreading out of urban land uses is likely to continue within the foreseeable future, distance could be considerably shortened by the clustering of activities, in particular those which are major traffic generators, such as retail and service establishments and offices of private and public management. All of these are to be found in increasing numbers in the outer sections of metropolitan areas, but in different locations based on separate decisions of the various agents. As a result, access both to them and between them is almost exclusively by private automobile. Much could be gained if they were clustered in what might be called "secondary downtowns," centered on rapid transit stations, and reinforced by adjacent elevator apartments as well as by multistory factory buildings for light, labor-intensive industries, some of which will continue to exist. Access to them would be largely by transit and within them on foot.

Such peripheral centers of new, large, planned residential developments have been created, with great success, by the city of Stockholm, Sweden, on city-owned land. It may not be possible to create them under conditions of scattered private land ownership. There is no legal obstacle to designating and zoning a suitable area for this purpose. However, such designation for intensive use would immediately raise land values far above those in the surrounding area; as a consequence private developers would avoid this area, thus making the designation self-defeating.

It appears that the creation of such centers presupposes that the area be publicly owned. However, if the municipality acquires the land *after* it has designated it as a center, it will have to pay a monopoly price; if it acquires the land *before* designation, it lays itself open to the charge of monopolistic practice. Only public ownership of all or most of the land suitable for urban development obviates this dilemma. It is only one example of the inherent contradiction between public land planning and private landownership which results from the fact that any planning decision, whether on land control or on public works, transfers value from some pieces of property to others.

Public ownership of urban development land has been advocated by some of the leading developers in Canada. On a small scale it has been practiced in the form of federal-provincial land assembly for the somewhat questionable purpose of making land available to house builders below market price. Pending the establishment of urban-regional governments with adequate financial resources, extension of this device might serve as an instrument for public ownership and leadership in urban land development.

The close interdependence of transportation and land development has been pointed out throughout this discussion, as has been the fact that the urban-centered metropolitan region is becoming the most important functional territorial unit within all developed countries. In those which do not contain vast nonurban areas as does Canada, division of the entire national territory into such regions would be the most appropriate structure. The recent proposal of the Royal Commission on Local Government in England came close to this solution; it has been consistently applied so far only in the German Democratic Republic.

At present, in Canada, decision-making on urban transportation is divided not only horizontally, between municipalities, and to some degree vertically, between municipalities and provinces, but also functionally, different agencies being responsible for different elements of the transportation system. A metropolitan-regional government must be responsible for all decisions on the planning, development, and operation of the system, if its benefits are to be maximized. Four conditions are necessary to make such a government effective:

1. It must cover the entire territory which functions as a metropolitan region.

2. It must have jurisdiction over all elements of the internal transportation of the region and over the basic structure of land development.

3. It must have financial resources adequate to carry out its tasks.

4. It must own most of the undeveloped land within its territory.

LONG-DISTANCE TERMINALS AND CHANNELS

While transportation within metropolitan regions is logically the exclusive responsibility of their governments, intermetropolitan, long-distance transportation is necessarily under the jurisdiction of the higher levels of government. In Canada the federal government controls transportation by rail, water, and air by a combination of extensive regulatory powers and direct management, mainly through Crown corporations.

The terminals and channels of these means of long-distance transportation have a decisive impact on urban development. The impact is both positive and negative. Positively, the terminals are generators of urban growth; they are also most important points of origin and destination for intrametropolitan movement of both goods and persons. Negatively, terminals and channels withdraw large areas from development for other urban uses, interrupt the street grid, and create severe nuisances for the environment by vibration, noise, smoke, fumes, visual disturbance, and frequently danger.

A certain dialectic develops in the interrelation between city and terminal. Most

Canadian cities owe their origins to harbors; consequently their core is located on the waterfront. As both city and harbor grew, their growing needs for additional land came into conflict. The same process was repeated with the development of rail and now with air transportation. Always the terminals were brought as close as possible to the core of the city in order to maximize their positive impact. Always the negative impacts soon appeared and kept growing at an exponential rate, as both urban development and transportation development expanded. Usually there follows a long period of unsatisfactory compromises, involving uneconomic operation for the transportation agency and increasing financial and social costs for the city. Ultimately the conflict is resolved, if at all, by relocation of the transportation facilities farther away from the city center.

These costs could have been minimized, and can be minimized in the future, if joint planning provides for space for future expansion of both urban development and transportation facilities. There are a few examples of close cooperation between urban and transportation planners, such as in the case of the relocation of the Canadian National classification yard and main freight line in the Toronto area. But this was entirely due to the initiative and goodwill of the officials responsible on both sides. In most cases municipalities are faced with a fait accompli. It is hardly necessary to mention the recent conflicts about airport location in the Montreal and Toronto areas.

The reluctance of the responsible federal agencies to develop their plans in consultation with the vitally affected municipalities is based mainly on the well-founded fear that disclosure of intentions of location may lead to land speculation and consequent increased acquisition cost. There appears to be no answer to this problem short of public ownership of all development land in metropolitan regions.

In any case the federal government is deeply and directly involved in urban affairs, not only through its role in long-distance transportation, but also through the role of the C.M.H.C. in housing and land development, and the many activities of other departments, such as National Defence and Communications. While a clear division of jurisdiction between different levels of government may be possible in fields which have only marginal spatial implications, such as criminal justice, it is impossible where space is affected, because it is the same space within which all of them operate and for which they compete.

Federal, as well as provincial, governments are organized functionally, with coordination of the activities of different departments only at cabinet level. There is, generally speaking, no coordination or even mutual exchange of information between agents of different departments operating in the same region. There is a clear and urgent need for organs providing for continuous close cooperation between all these agents, as well as with those of the lower levels of government.

NATIONWIDE PROBLEMS AND NATIONAL PROBLEMS

As Canada is already overwhelmingly an urban nation and will be even more so in the foreseeable future, the future of the cities is the future of the nation. Any problems affecting the city affect the welfare of the nation.

However, a nationwide problem is not necessarily a national problem in the sense that it requires action by the national government. The citizens of Canada pursue the same goals of increasing productivity and of improving their environment on all levels of government, and the choice of the means to achieve these goals and the priorities assigned to each of them are best left to the level of government closest to the people.

There are, however, two conditions which require action by the higher levels of government:

1. Economies of scale. Many problems, common to many jurisdictions, can be solved only on a larger scale than any one of them can support.

2. Unbalance of benefits and costs, or "malefits," within one jurisdiction, because of "overspill" of one, but not of the other, beyond its boundaries. A widely recognized example is pollution of air and water produced in one municipality "malefiting" its neighbors.

Even more important, though less widely recognized, is the case of jurisdictions incurring high costs in raising and educating members of the labor force, whose labor subsequently benefits other jurisdictions into which they migrate.

It is sometimes affirmed that a third reason justifying action by higher levels of government is the maintenance of uniform minimum standards. Certainly, redistribution of income to the underprivileged—both individuals and regions—is a legitimate function of government. However, disposition of this income should normally be left to the recipients. The obvious exception, a municipality too small to provide itself with adequate information and advice, falls under the category of economies of scale. Certainly the large metropolitan regions in which most Canadians are going to live do not need the paternalistic tutelage of the provinces. The quaint notion that, as creatures of the province, they are its children and that "Papa knows best" is rather out of place in respect to these husky sons.

In the United States the financial plight of the municipalities has led to a situation where they have to go hat in hand to the higher levels of government for almost everything they want to do, making a mockery of their vaunted "self-government." Bluntly speaking, the result is government by blackmail: "We take your money by our taxing power, and you can get it back if you spend it the way we want it spent, not as you may prefer to spend it." The result is only too often a distortion of priorities, not unknown also in Canada. Reference has already been made to the fact that municipalities neglect transit in favor of roads, because provincial subsidies are available only for the latter. This is by no means the only case of such misallocation of resources.

It is, of course, possible that lower levels of government may use poorer judgment in the allocation of priorities than higher ones. Freedom of choice, however, includes the freedom to make a wrong choice. The alternative is authoritarian paternalism.

Central collection of taxes is necessitated by economies of scale, not only or primarily because it affords greater administrative efficiency, but also because the high mobility of persons and capital makes it too easy to avoid paying local taxes by displacement of the tax source into a jurisdiction which is wealthier or less responsive to the needs of its constituents. But it does not follow that the central government must entirely determine the spending of this money; a substantial portion should be allocated to the lower levels of government (probably on a per capita basis), as is done in several European countries. In the Netherlands, for example, municipalities receive 89% of their incomes from the central government, but have effective self-government.

ROLE OF FEDERAL GOVERNMENT

From the foregoing discussion several functions of the federal government in the field of urban transportation and development can be identified:

1. Encouragement of the formation of metropolitan regional governments.
2. Allocation to such governments of a substantial portion of centrally collected taxes.
3. Promotion of public land acquisition for urban development.
4. Research into all aspects of urban transportation and development; development and pilot projects of promising new transportation technologies.
5. Provision of expert advice, including development of guidelines and model codes.
6. Training, including in-service training, of experts in urban transportation and development.
7. Formation of organs to coordinate federal activities within metropolitan regions.
8. Close cooperation with urban-metropolitan governments in the development and operation of long-distance transportation facilities.
9. Amendments to the federal personal and corporate income tax laws, disallowing employee parking as a tax-deductible business expense.
10. Promotion of underground wiring.

Chapter 37

MYTHS AND REALITIES OF THE URBAN TRANSIT PROBLEM

It is easy to understand that there is such a general interest in the urban transportation problem. Urban North Americans spend about 6% of their incomes on urban or metropolitan transportation, rather more than less. What does this expense buy them? They are buying mobility, which is the product of the transportation industry. What are the benefits of this mobility? What good does it do you? Any transportation proposal, whether for a freeway or for a rapid transit line or whatever, is sold on the notion that it will save time. You now need 30 minutes to go from point A to point B, and once this new facility is put in the trip will take only 15 minutes. So this is your benefit.

Strangely, if you look over longer periods of time, it seems that the time that people spend on a trip for a given purpose, be it a trip to work or a trip for shopping or visiting, remains fairly constant. What changes if you increase your mobility—if you can travel 30 miles during an hour by car rather than 3 miles during an hour by walking—you travel a larger distance rather than less time. You trade time for space. One of the major forms in which people take out the benefits of increased mobility is to use more space, for all purposes—not just for residence, but also for working, shopping, recreation, education, anything. We know that the space absorption for all kinds of urban purposes during the last 100 years has increased in the Western developed countries about five to six times. This is one of the forms of benefit, but it is not the only one. In speeding up your movement by increasing your mobility you can within a given time reach more destinations, for whatever purpose. You have a greatly enlarged choice, and there is no doubt that the increased mobility which we have achieved during the last century has enormously increased the choices of people within an urban area—the choice of a place of residence in terms of where they work or of a place of work in terms of where they live, or the choice for any other service, for visiting, social contacts, and so on. But by making this use of our increased mobility we are increasing the demand on the transportation facilities. The demand does increase with the supply, and the corollary of this is that the

---

Source: From "Mass Transit: The Urban Crisis of North America," J. Alex Murray, Ed., *Proceedings of the 17th Annual Seminar,* Canadian-American Seminar, University of Windsor Press, Windsor, Ont., 1975.

"transportation problem," as it is usually called, is never really solved. It reproduces itself. The better transportation you supply, the further people will move—and do move. You might even say that the problem has to get better before it can get worse, and the public notion that there must be some "solution" to this transportation problem is *myth number 1*.

There is no absolute and final solution; there is just the possibility—and I think the obligation—for constant improvement, but you have to run pretty fast to stay where you are. It is not a new problem. In the year of the Lord 1513 the bridge at Notre Dame in Paris was rebuilt, and there was a discussion in the city council about widening the approach to this bridge, which was a 12-foot-wide street. There were different proposals, and finally one councilman said, "It's terrible, it's terrible; each year there are more carts, and in 5 years we will be paralyzed." Now, what this good man did was, in an informal way and without getting special pay for it, to do what we consultants do in a formal way by extrapolating the traffic and predicting that within 7 years, 3 months, and 5 days the city will come to a standstill. Well, it didn't happen in Paris and it generally hasn't happened anywhere. City centers are always choked, but they never choke themselves to death. Supply and demand somehow mutually adjust themselves; but if the adjustment is a downward one, it means that you can use less space or have less choice. The question is: How much space do you really need; how much choice do you really need? Is there a law of diminishing return to enabling us to absorb more space or to have larger choices? This is a very difficult philosophical question.

However, in the public debate there enters a different criterion. It is said, "Now we have spent all these moneys for improvement, and there is still congestion." Well, there has been congestion in Paris ever since 1513 and even before. But is this really a valid criterion? Who is so worried about congestion? Who thinks in terms of congestion? It is the man behind the wheel. The pedestrian or the transit rider doesn't think in terms of congestion; he or she thinks in terms of time and money and the convenience of the trip. Actually in most, though not in all, cases of congestion, the time loss isn't really so great: it is rather a psychological factor. Why are people so upset about congestion? "I have spent all this money—or rather not spent it, but gone into debt—to buy this damn machine which can run 100 miles an hour, and here I am stuck at 5 miles an hour. This is awful, and somebody should do something about it." Evidently the people who have done something about it don't know their business.

The *second myth* is that it should be or could be the aim of transportation improvements to abolish all congestion. I would go even further and say: If planners, engineers or decision-makers should really ever achieve the goal that in no place and at no time in your city is there any congestion, they should be shot for waste of public money.

Let us now look briefly at the history of urban transportation. For a long time there were no effective means for any land transportation. Movement was primarily by walking or riding on a horse, camel, or whatever other mount could be found, and normally this meant just one person at a time, purely individual transportation. It was only when we developed horse-drawn vehicles and smooth roads that one vehicle could carry more than one or maybe two persons, and that collective transportation could develop. But it actually took a man of genius, one of the great geniuses of mankind, to grasp this idea. It was Blaise Pascal, the great French philosopher and mathematician, who at the end of the seventeenth century organized a bus company in Paris. The buses carried six passengers each. He was a bit ahead of his time, and after 5 years the company failed—not an unusual fate for bus companies. It was only at the beginning of the nineteenth century that horse-drawn coaches on smooth roads (buses) became in the bigger cities somewhat more familiar, and played a certain role but still a relatively minor one. The great change came in the forties and fifties of the nineteenth century. First, the invention of steel wheels on steel rails greatly reduced the friction and led to the introduction of horse-drawn streetcars. Almost at the same time came the invention of the steam engine and its application to transportation. Steam-powered trains began to operate, primarily, of course, for long distances and within the largest urban areas. The really great change, however, came about with electric traction in the 1880s. This applied both to streetcars and to railroads in the larger cities. It made it easier to put rail lines underground and led to the first great rush of subway building, in the beginning of the twentieth century. The rail was not available for individual transportation. There were many attempts made to develop both steam power and electric power for the individual, but they were not economically successful, and it was only the internal combustion engine which made any power other than human or animal muscle available for individual transportation. It is important to realize that this great superiority of collective transportation and its predominance, which was obtained in the first quarter of this century, were the result of the time lag in the application of nonmuscular, mechanical energy, first to collective transportation and, only 30 years later, to individual transportation. Once both individual and collective transportation had mechanical power at their disposal, this superiority disappeared. I think that I might call it the *third myth* to believe that this period of the great predominance of collective transportation was a normal state of affairs which sometimes and somehow, only by a fall from grace, we have given up, and that we should and could return to the path of virtue.

Now, the first reaction, of course, to the availability of competitive and more than competitive individual transportation was as usual a wide swing of the pendulum to the belief that the individual car was the one and only solution for urban transportation problems, leading to a complete neglect of collective transportation. We have now learned by experience that the automobile, while it is a producer of great benefits, also produces very great "malefits," which we want to, and try to, reduce. The malefits are of three kinds. In the present public discussion the greatest emphasis is put on air pollution. Now, air pollution certainly is a very serious problem. It is, however, not really inherent in individual transportation; within the next 20 or 30 years we may very well be able to develop a different power plant which would eliminate pollution. But other impacts on the environment are inherent. First is the very great absorption of space, which of course dilutes the urban fabric. Absorption of space is not so great for moving cars, but it is very great for parking cars. If we get a ratio (and in some places we are very close to it) of one car for two persons, the space needed for parking almost equals the gross floor space needed for residents in the city. It is an enormous amount of space. Moving traffic, if it moves well, does not really absorb that much land, but it is of course very seriously disruptive of the urban fabric to push through arteries or freeways. The most serious and the most inherent environmental damage of the automobile, strangely neglected in discussion, is danger. This is inherent in millions of hard, heavy bodies moving around at high speeds under individual direction. If you have 60 people traveling in two buses, the probability of a collision is 1; but if you have 60 people traveling in 40 cars, it is [40 × (40 − 1)]/2, or 780 chances. This is inherent in the fact that people in cars move individually in individually directed vehicles.

The second set of malefits comprises social malefits for a great number of people. Once you have neglected public transit and once your urban area has expanded very greatly because people have been taking advantage of trading space for time, people who do not have cars at their disposal are very heavily handicapped. There are probably close to 20% who are handicapped because they don't have a car. There are another 20%, partly overlapping, who can't use a car because they do not have a driver's license, either because of physical or mental handicaps or because of being too young—which may or may not be a physical or mental handicap. The same goes for those who are old and have physical or mental handicaps. Of the rest, probably something like 50%, who are members of households where there is only one car, do not have the car at their disposal at the time when they want it because another member of the household is using it. Entire reliance on the automobile and the consequences which it has had in American cities, both of spreading out the city and of killing or weakening public transit, is a very serious social problem.

Third, cars traveling on roads interfere with all other forms of movement: with the movement of pedestrians, with the movement of trucks and delivery vehicles, with the movement of service vehicles, which include emergency vehicles, with the movement of transit vehicles, and finally with the movement of other cars. This may be the most important reason to support collective transportation. Anything that increases the modal split in the direction of collective transportation also helps the movement of the private car, while anything which encourages or helps to increase the movement of the private car interferes both with collective transportation and with individual transportation itself. There are very substantial benefits to the non-rider as well as the rider in any replacement of any passenger-mile made by car by the same passenger-mile made by public transportation. I think that this is more than justification for financial support from sources other than the fare box. What the community does when it pays for this out of taxes is really to buy an essential service wholesale rather than retail, with the savings which are always involved in buying something wholesale. It buys passenger-miles. The adequate form of subsidization, if you want to use that term, is for the community to pay for collective transportation by paying for the service performed, for the passenger-miles—rather than in such devious ways as paying only for the capital investment, or picking up the deficit.

In principle, it would be perfectly justified to supply collective transportation within the urban areas free of charge, as a public service. Now this is decried as socialism; I am not sure that it is. After all, we buy our transportation service wholesale in every office building or apartment house. Nobody pays for using an elevator. It is paid for wholesale by the tenants of the building, and I haven't been quite able to understand why it is socialism when the transportation is horizontal and free enterprise when it is vertical. So *myth number 4* is the prejudice against paying collective transportation out of taxes.

What can collective, and what can individual, transportation do better? If you have a lot of persons moving from point *A* to point *B* at the same time, you move them far better by a collective means; but if movements are much dispersed in space, in time, or in both, you can't provide collective transportation for one person when the next person who wants the same trip comes half an hour later. Between these two extreme cases there is a wide range. What has made collective transportation much more difficult is a change in the structure of our metropolitan areas.

In public discussion, transportation questions are usually formulated in the form of travel from the outskirts to the center, from home to work and back again. This may have been the main problem in the nineteenth century. But planners, politicians, and media people who discuss and try to solve the problem in these terms are really like the familiar generals who are fighting the battles of the last war. We have a very rapid and strong decentralization of places of employment. A rapidly decreasing percentage of all places of employment is located in the center. Almost all secondary employment and very much of the tertiary (service) employment are located elsewhere than in the center. Therefore the proportion of work trips directed towards the center is decreasing. But there is another factor. As we get more money and more leisure, we use our money and our leisure to move around a great deal for all kinds of other purposes—for shopping, business, eating, drinking, or recreation, you name it. Trips to work only increase proportionally to the labor force. They decrease as we shorten the workweek. But these other trips increase more rapidly, and their destinations tend to be more dispersed. Therefore the predominant problem is no longer the centripetal but rather the centrifugal movement and, in particular, movement crosstown from any part of the metropolitan area to any other part other than toward or away from the center. The notion that moving people from the outskirts to the center for work and back again is the main problem—and when this is solved, everything is solved—is *myth number 5*.

Given the fact—and I think it is incontestable—that there is a very strong public interest in strengthening collective transportation in its competition with individual transportation, why is it really so difficult to do this? What are the handicaps of collective transportation versus individual transportation? There are four very, very serious handicaps which makes it almost impossible to compete in terms of time and in many cases also in terms of convenience. First, you have to walk to or from the stop or station. Second, you have to wait for the vehicle. Third, in many, though not in all, cases you have to transfer. Fourth, you have to stop for other passengers to get on and get off. So one of the approaches is to try and eliminate one, two, or three—nobody has ever suggested anything that could eliminate all four—of these obstacles. I will not at this point go into the various technologies and proposals that have been tried, such as the "dial-a-bus," which eliminates the walking, or express services, which reduce stopping. But one thing can be said quite clearly: The problem is not primarily a question of hardware.

Now there is, of course, a second method which would make collective transportation a little more competitive, and that is to eliminate all or part of the friction to which the individual automobile is subject by providing for collective transportation a partly or wholly separated right-of-way. This is probably the most important and most promising approach. What I think is a somewhat mistaken approach is what we have conventionally been doing so far. We have used either a bus which runs with all the other traffic and has to put up with *all* the impediments which other traffic has to cope, or we have provided rapid transit, which eliminates *all* kinds of friction on completely owned, separated right-of-way. This then involves extremely high capital investment and thereby limits the possibility of serving all movements. I believe that we should think far more in terms of eliminating part of the friction at part of the cost.

One means to do this is a reserved lane which eliminates some of the friction—what I call "side friction," friction from vehicles which move in the same direction. It is much more effective, of course, if the reservation is in the center of the road, as we have traditionally done with surface rails (i.e., streetcars) and as I think we should do to a much larger degree—having reserved center lanes or tracks for what we now call light rapid transit. We should provide that amount of separation and of investment which is needed in each particular situation. In some places we have done this for a very long time. We called it not light rapid transit, but a subway-surface streetcar. Put it on its own right-of-way where the friction is very high; put it on its own reserved strip, possibly with some regulations of lights to help it where the friction is less but still serious; and let it run with all the traffic where there is not too much traffic interference.

One of the things we need is a much greater flexibility to use a great number of different technologies in different situations in different ways. There is no magical solution for the problem. There are a very great number of possible improvements, both from the financial side and from the technical side, eliminating the impediments in the road paths and reducing one or more of the handicaps which I mentioned. I think that we have to realize, however, that even with the very best that can be achieved, there cannot be a complete reversal, as some people have dreamed of.

In Toronto, where we have a rather successful system of collective transportation, barely 25% of all person-miles are performed by collective transportation, another 25% by car passengers, and 50% by car drivers. I was interested to find in a visit two years ago to the Ruhr area, Germany's biggest metropolitan area, that it also had a level of about 25%. The officials were very ambitious. They planned hundreds of miles of grade-separated rail facilities and had an equally ambitious plan of changing their settlement patterns so as to concentrate their development around the stations of this planned rail system, and restrict it everywhere else. I do not think that they will carry out either of these ambitious plans. But their simulation model showed that, even if they carried it out, they would increase their share of collective transportation only from 25 to 40%, that is, reduce their movement of the private car by 20%, from 75 to 60%. It would, of course, not reduce any movement of goods vehicles.

A *final myth* is that by strengthening collective transportation—and I want to repeat that it is justified and indeed necessary to do everything possible to strengthen it—you would eliminate the need for an effective road system or make any substantial savings in the building and operation of a road system. This is, I think, a fallacious hope. I do not want to discuss here a broader question which frequently is brought into the debate and which is also a *myth*: that collective transportation will lead to higher densities and thereby reduce substantially the absorption of agricultural land. The notion that urban development is absorbing so much agricultural land that we will all starve is a complete *myth*. And the notion that we are running out of energy is equally a *myth*. Energy is becoming more expensive. I think this is a blessing in disguise so that we will not waste as much and not use as much of our fossil fuels as we have been doing. There are other and better, if more expensive, ways of tapping the sun's energy than transforming highly organized carbohydrate molecules into such primitive forms of matter as carbon dioxide and water.

Chapter 38

URBAN FREEWAYS

WHAT PRICE MOBILITY?

Communities exist because of communication. If a person is satisfied to commune only with nature—or with God—he or she can and will live as a hermit. But most of us build our lives on communication with our fellows, on ever-widening contacts and interchanges, requiring a rising flow of persons, goods, and messages. If the age-old dream of the magic carpet were a reality, we could live scattered all over the globe and at the same time have all the contacts we wanted, whenever we wanted them. In harsh reality we have to deal with the friction of space, which can be overcome only at a price in terms of time, money, and inconvenience.

We can decrease this cost in two ways: (1) by decreasing the distances which separate us—that is why we live in cities; and (2) by increasing mobility—that is why we develop means of communication which reduce the cost per unit of distance. However, once it takes no more time, money, and inconvenience to travel 5 miles than it previously took to travel 1 mile, as many people (and goods) will travel 5 miles as previously traveled 1. In other words, the demand for transportation is not fixed; it expands with the supply. In this sense the "traffic problem" will never be solved; it reproduces itself. Movement always increases up to the point where the resulting congestion deters further increase. There was congestion in imperial Rome, in medieval Paris, in Victorian London. The centers of big cities have always been "choked"; but they have never been choked to death, notwithstanding dire predictions to the contrary which have been made in century after century.

Are all our efforts futile? Does mobility, the product of the transportation industry, provide no benefits? The answer is that it provides a wider range of choice of two kinds: more contacts and more space. If space absorption per person—or, expressed inversely, density—remains the same, the benefit consists in more contacts. If the number of potential contacts remains the same, people can absorb more space. In fact, during the last century both space absorption per person and range of choice have increased about fivefold. The benefits of mobility are real. That they are valued highly can be concluded from the fact that the citizens of Toronto, for example, spend about $1 billion annually for the movement of goods and persons within the metropolitan area.

Obviously the users of transportation consider that they receive benefits greater

Source: Canadian Architect, April 1970.

than these costs. But transportation imposes costs not only on its users, but also on nonusers, by its harmful impact on the environment. These "social costs" or "third-persons malefits" have to be weighed against the benefits of any "improvement" of transportation. Are we, in our eagerness to go places, in danger of destroying any place worth going to? The "stop-the-Spadina" movement believes that we are: its adherents claim that the Spadina Freeway will destroy the city of Toronto.

SWING OF THE PENDULUM

The current outcry against freeways has its precedents. Every new means of transportation has been welcomed with open arms and invited right into the heart of the city. This happened with the railroads. Only later, as both urban activities and railroad movements expanded, was the damage realized. Then the tide turned, and the railroads became the villain: "They cut the city into ribbons, pollute the air, create unbearable noise. Rail is obsolete; rip it out. We now have a new technology—the motor vehicle."

Nowhere else did the pendulum swing as far as in the United States. Everywhere streetcar lines were torn up, elevated lines torn down, and suburban lines neglected or abandoned. For over 40 years not a single American city put a new rapid transit system into operation. All emphasis was on road building. The federal government allocated $100 billion to pay for 90% of freeway construction; state road departments pushed freeways through urban areas, following the practices they had developed in building freeways in open country. There were and are no metropolitan governments to control freeway location and design; attempts of local planning organizations to influence them have been weak. Now the pendulum has swung again, and in city after city aroused citizens oppose freeway construction.

As usual, this controversy has generated more heat than light. Also, as usual, much of the hot air generated south of the Canadian border has drifted north. Apparently many Canadians, notably in Toronto, have their eyes and ears so firmly glued to the American mass media that they overlook the minor fact that Canada is not the fifty-first state. In Canada the federal government has limited its interest in roads to subsidies to the Trans-Canada Highway. The Ontario Department of Highways, far from being "hooked on the expressway drug," has initiated the GO rail service and is subsidizing it to the tune of about 65%. The third partner, the municipality of Metropolitan Toronto, has invested over $300 million in rapid transit, and its planning board has developed its transportation plan as part and parcel of its general "official plan."

Now it is claimed that the road proposals of that plan have been made obsolete by "new technology," which allegedly will soon displace the motor vehicle and the road system on which it operates. It is therefore appropriate to analyze the transportation needs of a metropolitan area and the means available to satisfy them.

METROPOLITAN TRANSPORTATION

Goods as well as persons have to move around. In terms of both cost and benefit, goods transportation accounts for at least 40% of the total. Apart from pipelines, goods transportation within the metropolis is handled exclusively by trucks and delivery wagons on the road system. The only new technology proposed is use of individualized transit, such as "Teletrans," for goods transportation. The technical and, in particular, the economic feasibility of these systems is still very much in doubt. Even if successful, they would take no more than 10% of all goods vehicles off the road.

Public attention has been concentrated almost exclusively on the 60% of transportation carrying persons. Apart from walking, person movement is accomplished by two subsystems, private cars and transit. At present, transit (including GO trains) accounts for less than 25% of all person-trips in Metropolitan Toronto, a higher percentage than in comparable North American cities. Less than half of these, no more than 10% of all person-trips, are made by subway and GO trains; the balance is carried by buses, trolley-buses, and streetcars on the road system. At least 80% of all Toronto subway passengers use Toronto Transit Commission (T.T.C.) surface vehicles at one or both ends of their trip. Without a road feeder system, a subway cannot function.

Different means of transportation serve different purposes. When and where trips are highly concentrated in space and in time, as in peak-hour traffic to and from the center, they can be handled effectively only by trains. When and where origins and destinations are dispersed in time and/or in space, they can be adequately served only by the private car. In intermediate situations surface transit can serve best.

With increasing leisure and wealth, nonwork trips account for a growing percentage of all trips, and many of these are too dispersed in space and time to be served even by buses. Moreover, work destinations are also dispersing very rapidly, with employment densities as low as 10 persons or less per acre, again making transit service practically impossible. The widespread notion that peak-hour traffic consists mainly of people living in the suburbs and working in the center has long ago ceased to be true—if it ever was. Central city jobs account for a rapidly decreasing percentage of the metropolitan total. In Metropolitan Toronto the number of "crosstown" work trips exceeds the number of *all* "inbound" trips, which include all trips going from the outskirts to the intermediate ring, in addition to those going to the center. It is this radical shift in traffic patterns, as much as the faster and more convenient door-to-door service of the private car, which has led to the decrease of transit's share.

Any other vehicle operating on the road is affected by road congestion as much as is the private car and requires a driver, resulting in high operating cost. Any vehicle operating off the road (subway, monorail) needs its own completely grade-separated right-of-way, resulting in high capital cost. This applies to all of the ingenious proposals for new technology. If public transportation is to maintain—let alone increase—its share of person movement, it must be treated as a public service and financed out of general revenue. There are several strong reasons for this.

1. Any increase in the use of public transportation helps private transportation by decreasing the number of cars on the road, while any increase in private transportation harms public transportation by interfering with bus movement.

2. Public transportation provides mobility for many people who cannot drive, do not own cars, or do not have one at their disposal when they need it.

3. Public transportation eliminates or greatly reduces the danger of accidents and the resulting nervous tension.

4. Public transportation eliminates or greatly reduces interference both with goods movement and with movement on foot.

5. Public transportation eliminates or greatly reduces air pollution and noise.

6. Public transportation greatly reduces the amount of space required by moving and, in particular, by parking vehicles.

It would therefore be fully justified to provide "free" public transportation. However, even if this were done, and if the most optimistic assumptions are made concerning new technology on its own right-of-way, at least 70% of all person-miles and 90% of all goods-miles still would have to be carried by the road system.

There is no escape: we have to build roads.

WHAT KIND OF ROAD SYSTEM?

Roads have always served two purposes. First, they provide access for persons and goods to residences and other land uses; such "access" or "residential" streets also play an important role as outdoor living rooms. Second, roads serve through traffic, that is, movement, by any means, not going to or coming from properties on a particular street or section of a street.

The two purposes are in conflict. Long before the advent of the motor car, it was recognized that they require separate and different roads. Ideally, all access roads should be cul-de-sacs or short loops, completely free from through traffic. Ideally, all traffic roads should be free-flowing, completely free from direct access to land uses as well as from crossings. Such an "ideal" traffic road is called a "freeway." The term "expressway" technically applies to a road which is largely, but not completely, free from these impediments.

This ideal is unattainable. Access roads cannot be connected directly to freeways; collector-distributor roads must mediate between these two extremes. Ideally, these should also be free from direct access, but would be crossed by both vehicles and pedestrians. It is not difficult to design, for a new city, a system consisting exclusively of pure access roads, access-free collector-distributor roads, and freeways. In existing cities we must make do with the unsatisfactory compromise of many collectors and through-traffic, or "arterial," roads, which also have to give access to adjoining properties. The best we can do is to reduce these unsatisfactory hybrids to a minimum by bringing interchanges between freeways and the surface street system as close as possible to all points of origin and destination.

How close is possible, and how possible is close? The constraints are severe, because our cities have been built on street systems without freeways and these can be inserted only at very great financial and social cost. Therefore we are forced to continue to use—and abuse—much of our surface street system to move through traffic.

That freeways are a better means for moving vehicles than are surface streets should be obvious.

1. Their capacity is about three times as great. It takes four four-lane arterials to move the volume of vehicles that is carried by one six-lane freeway, three times the pavement, and "slicing" the city in four places instead of one.

2. Their speed is two to three times that of an arterial road, and fuel consumption is lower; they reduce the cost of mobility in terms of both time and money.

3. Their accident rate is much lower; there is less danger for other vehicles and none for pedestrians.

4. They can be crossed by both vehicles and pedestrians without stopping.

5. They cause less air pollution, which is produced largely by idling and gear shifting.

It is, of course, true, as noted earlier, that traffic demand is not fixed, but expands with increasing supply of mobility. Thus, while freeways decrease social cost per vehicle-mile very greatly, they tend to increase the total number of vehicle-miles performed. But this is equally true of *any* improvement of traffic flow, such as improved timing of traffic lights. If the goal of the opponents of freeways is the reduction of *total* vehicle-miles, they should advocate unpaved streets.

WHAT KIND OF FREEWAY SYSTEM?

The main function of freeways is to remove as many motor vehicles—trucks as well as private cars—as possible from the surface street system. As vehicles move increasingly "crosstown," that is, in all directions, the necessity for a universal grid arises. From the point of view of shortening travel distances in all directions, a grid consisting of equilateral triangles would be best. However, as it would require extremely complex six-way intersections, a hexagonal grid, resulting in three-way intersections, appears to be the best theoretical system. In practice any freeway system is largely determined by natural and man-made topography. As the latter in North American cities is generally rectangular, the freeway system is likely to be closer to a rectangular than to a hexagonal grid. It is however, desirable to modify this grid in such a way as to replace four-way cross-intersections by simpler and less space-consuming three-way T-intersections.

The spacing of freeways is, in the first instance, determined by the anticipated volume of vehicles. This indicates that the higher the density of the adjacent area, the closer the freeway spacing. However, the higher the density, the greater will be the financial and social cost of inserting a freeway into the urban fabric. Therefore the densification of the freeway grid towards the center has to be much less than proportional to the density of land use. This is quite acceptable because an area of greater density can provide much better public transportation.

The innermost square of the grid, often called the "inner ring," encloses the center of the city. It serves a dual purpose. First, it acts as a bypass for trips which have both their origin and their destination outside of the center. Second, and more important, it induces vehicles destined to (or coming from) points both inside and at some distance outside the ring to drive on the freeway up to the interchange closest to their destination, thus substantially reducing the number of vehicle-miles traveled on city streets. Many American cities have opted for a very tight inner ring—in Kansas City 0.5 by 0.75 mile; in Philadelphia 1 by 2 miles. This has two serious disadvantages. First, it destroys or preempts a great portion of the area of most intense development. Second, it provides an insufficient number of interchanges with the surface street system. The ring should have a diameter of about 3–4 miles.

The desire to bring freeways right into the heart of the city stems from the notion that they should serve for travel to work in the central business district. That movement, the most concentrated in space and in time, can be served only by rapid transit. To accommodate all cars that might want to drive downtown in the morning peak hour on free-flowing freeways in Montreal would require 18–24 lanes on every freeway link within 7 miles of Place Ville Marie! Urban freeways should be designed and dimensioned for off-peak traffic. Only in outlying areas, where dispersal of places of employment precludes travel to work by transit, must they be designed to handle the peak-hour load.

The fact that freeways cannot and should not serve the peak-hour flow of downtown workers has led some people to the conclusion that vehicular access to the center should be made as difficult as possible by keeping freeways many miles away from it. This is throwing the baby out with the bath water. Good vehicular access is absolutely essential for the life of the city center: for trucks bringing in the goods which are sold in its stores, restaurants, and bars, as well as building materials, and carrying out the huge amounts of waste material which accumulate every day; for persons traveling during off-peak hours to shopping, entertainment, and other activities; and also for those 10–15% of downtown workers—salesmen, repairmen, many professionals and businessmen—who need their cars for work during the day. But if good vehicular access to the center is provided, how can the 9 to 5 worker be prevented from using it? The answer is: carrot and stick. The "carrot" is good public transportation. The "stick" is rationing by price: high fees for all-day parking.

The locational requirements for freeways are different from those for transit lines. Transit lines must go through the centers of districts in order to be accessible on foot. Freeways can and should be located at the edges of districts, whenever possible—either at natural edges, such as valleys or escarpments, or at man-made edges, such as railroads. Only rarely is it possible to find a location suitable for a joint road-rail facility. When this is possible, both cost and disruption are considerably reduced.

FREEWAY DESIGN

A moderate number of cars moving at moderate speed is quite acceptable on an urban street. But a great stream of vehicles rushing along at high speed is as incompatible with city life as are railroads, which also originally operated on city streets. The city cannot live with the vehicles and the railroads—and it cannot live without them. The solution to this dilemma is in both cases the same: remove them from the street level at which city life goes on and locate them above or below it. Location above street level provides a fine view *from* the road (or train). But the view *to* the road is generally acceptable only if it is located below street level. Only when a road can be located in an escarpment, as on the Brooklyn Heights waterfront in New York, are views both to and from the road fully satisfactory.

Elevated structures are generally cheaper and faster to build, require no relocation of utilities, do not interrupt the street pattern, and leave the space below the deck free for use for other purposes. They are acceptable in industrial areas, in particular where they run next to an elevated railroad line. They may also be considered in other areas, if any existing or potential buildings are well over 100 feet distant from lanes or tracks.

Location below street level is generally in an open cut, and highway engineers consider a 300-foot right-of-way as required. Using retaining walls instead of natural slopes, as has been done on Montreal's Decarie Freeway, considerably increases construction cost and restricts the view of the driver. But it allows a six-lane freeway with two three-lane service roads and adequate sidewalks to be accommodated within a right-of-way of 200–210 feet.

It is, of course, always possible to build in the air rights over a depressed freeway, but the additional construction cost may, in most cases, exceed the cost of adjacent land. It is also possible to integrate an elevated freeway into structures, as had been done in an interesting example in Tokyo. Such "traffic architecture" offers an exciting challenge for imaginative design. It should, however, not be overlooked that such a synthesis greatly reduces flexibility: no major change can be made in one element without destroying the other. It is a marriage "for better or for worse, until death does us part."

In any case, freeways are here to stay. They can be integrated into the city by disciplined and imaginative design.

Chapter 39

AIRPORTS AND CITIES

LONG-DISTANCE TRANSPORTATION AND URBAN DEVELOPMENT: HISTORICAL EXPERIENCE

Accessibility to other places has always been one of the prime reasons for the birth of cities, and it has been and still is the main reason for their growth. At the same time the lines and terminals of long-distance transportation have a profound influence on the structure of urban areas.

Certain characteristics are common to all modes of long-distance transportation and may, therefore, hold a lesson for the Benjamin of the family: aviation. They may be briefly summarized as follows:

1. Of the three constituent elements of any transportation system, the vehicle is developed first, the path or channel later, and the terminal last. Vehicle development forces the other two elements to follow.

2. Vehicle speed and, even more, vehicle capacity grow continually beyond expectations. To exemplify, around 1800 the largest ships had about 1000 tons; around 1900 about 11,000, an increase by a factor of 11; and at present over 220,000, an increase by a factor of 20. Before the end of the century capacities may exceed 1 million tons, an increase by a factor of 100 in the second century of rapid growth.

3. First vehicles, then terminals, and sometimes paths become specialized—in particular, between persons and freight, and between short and long hauls.

4. Technical progress is more effective in reducing the time and cost of the line haul than of terminal handling; the terminal thus becomes the most critical element.

5. Terminals attract urban growth. As both city population and activities and transportation grow, they conflict increasingly. Finally the transportation terminal has to move further out, wholly or partly. This was and is the case with ports (Marseilles, Rotterdam, New York).

Every new means of transportation is welcomed enthusiastically and brought as close to the center as possible, using existing paths: in the beginning railroad tracks were simply laid in the streets. Sooner or later, at great cost, special, grade-separated paths,

---

Source: Report to the Civil Aviation Division, Department of Transport, Ottawa, Ont., July 1968.

channels, bridges, and tunnels have to be created; the existing investment in terminals has to be scrapped and new terminals built further out. This has happened and is happening with railroad freight—and sometimes passenger—terminals, truck terminals, and food terminals. It is bound to happen, on a vastly greater scale, with air terminals, if the lessons of history are not learned in time.

NATURE OF THE CONFLICT BETWEEN URBAN DEVELOPMENT AND TRANSPORTATION SYSTEMS

Urban development conflicts with both the paths and the terminals of any long-distance transportation system.

Paths

Paths interfere with urban development in two ways:

1. They interrupt the urban tissue, notably the network of streets.

2. They adversely affect the environment by noise, vibration, glare, and pollution.

Aviation is the only form of transportation free from the first form of interference, because of the location of its paths in the open air. But this same location vastly increases the second type of interference, because the environment cannot be shielded from the paths, as is the case with land transportation paths, which can be, and are being, located in cuts or tunnels.

As noted earlier, all transportation systems started by using preexisting paths, such as rivers or streets. In all cases responsibility for the system of paths finally was assumed either by the carrier (railroads) or by a public authority: provincial departments for arterials and freeways, the Department of Transport (in the United States the Army Corps of Engineers) for navigable waterways. Inevitably the Department of Transport will have to assume full responsibility for flight paths.

Terminals

Terminals interfere with urban development in three ways:

1. They occupy land which is in demand for other, more intensive urban use. The resultant loss is probably best expressed in terms of opportunity cost.

In the case of railroad yards it has sometimes been possible to recoup part of this cost by the development of air rights. This is, of course, not possible in the case of airfields.

2. The extent of the terminal area interrupts the urban tissue. In the case of railroad yards this has been overcome, to some extent, by crossing them on viaducts, generally of moderate length. Again, this is not possible with airfields, where extremely long and costly tunnels would be required. In fact, such tunnels are proposed for two major freeways in the variant for development of the Montreal International Airport at the present location at Dorval. The proposal for the extension of the

Toronto International Airport would result in detours up to 3 miles for many thousands of vehicles daily.

3. The terminal may adversely affect the environment in the same way as the paths do.

CONFLICTING LAND REQUIREMENTS

Land for Urban Development

It is commonplace to state that the population of Canada is rapidly concentrating in urban areas, particularly the larger ones. While their rate of growth may decline gradually, on the average the population of all urban areas served by major airports is likely to about double by the end of this century.

However, population growth is not the only reason for the expansion of urban areas. Equally important is increasing land absorption per capita. During this century urbanized land has tended to increase approximately as the square of population increases. If population increases from 100 to 120, urbanized land increases from 100 to 144. If population doubles, land area quadruples.

Hopes have been expressed that this trend, despite its generality in space and time, may be reversed by a combination of apartment living and rapid transit development. This is largely wishful thinking. Net residential land accounts for about one third of all urbanized land—including residential streets, about 40%. Doubling the net residential density would therefore reduce the urban area by only 20%, or the radius of the urban perimeter by 9.1%.

Nor should great hopes be placed on limiting metropolitan growth by "decanting" people into "new towns." The "new town" policy, pursued with great vigor and skill in the United Kingdom, has absorbed barely one tenth of its postwar population growth.

It must, therefore, be assumed that by the end of the century the population of the major urban areas in Canada will have doubled and their area quadrupled. This means that the urban perimeter will be twice as far from the center as it is at present. It would be wise to base the selection of airport sites on this assumption.

Land for Airports

Land requirements for airports, as for terminals of other modes of transportation, have been increasing steadily and rapidly. The plans for the Montreal and Toronto International Airports require 5000–6000 acres; O'Hare in Chicago covers 7200, and Dulles in Washington 10,000 acres.

With rapid technological development, the number, length, and location of future runways are highly unpredictable; so are the land requirements for the many other functions which have to be accommodated at an airport, in particular the cargo terminal. Here the experience of cargo ports may be instructive. Around 1850 a width of 60 feet was sufficient for 1 lineal foot of wharfage ("length of apron" in airport terms); recent ports have provided about 1500 square feet for each lineal foot, and Roberts Bank near Vancouver provides 6000. Thus the ratio has grown by a factor of 100 in little more than a century.

ADVERSE IMPACT ON ENVIRONMENT

Noise

Here the two sides of the equation are the tolerance of the affected population and the frequency and level of noise produced by aircraft.

North Americans have been, in the aftermath of a pioneer tradition of "roughing it," far more tolerant of adverse environmental conditions than Europeans. This is rapidly changing, however, as shown by increasing protests against billboards and other visual disturbances, against destruction of landscape and historic cityscape, and against pollution of air, water, and soil, as well as against noise.

These protests come mainly from people with high levels of income and education. As these levels rise generally, the protests will become far more widespread and will force political action. It is well to remember that the smoke, noise, and danger caused by railroads were, at first, willingly accepted as a cheap price for a new and superior mode of transportation. But soon the original enthusiasm turned into hostility, from which the railroads still suffer. The same has happened to streetcars and is now happening to freeways. For aviation the handwriting is on the wall.

The frequency of aircraft noise is bound to increase with increase in the number of flights. Consequently, the adverse impact of a zone with a given noise level will inevitably increase. It is obvious that in zone 4 only completely enclosed warehouses and factories can operate. It should not be forgotten, however, that cars, trucks, and construction machinery operate in the open air. Aside from the unpleasantness for their operators, the blocking out of oral warning signals by aircraft noise greatly increases the danger of accidents. Therefore locations in zone 4 are less attractive even for completely enclosed buildings.

In zone 3 these drawbacks become negligible for industrial and commercial use, but residential use must be considered unsuitable. It seems to be assumed that no problem exists in zone 2, with a critical noise ratio (C.N.R.) of 90–100. However, schools, hospitals, churches, theaters, and auditoriums should be built in this zone only if needed noise control features are included in the building design. Evidently these institutions—at least schools and churches—are required in every residential area. More important, if aircraft noise interferes with the rest of sick people in hospitals, it interferes just as much with the rest of the sick at home; if it impedes listening to words or music in school or church, it equally impedes listening in the living room. Therefore, while residential development in zone 2 is feasible, its desirability, and consequently site values, are diminished.

With the increase in size and speed of aircraft, their noise level is likely to increase, leading to an enlargement of noise zones 4, 3, and 2. This expectation is derived not only inductively from the experience of 60 years of aircraft development, but also deductively from the nature of powered flight. The power of a moving object increases proportionally to its weight and to the square of its speed. In order to move an object rapidly through air, the power must move the surrounding air—and rapid air movement *is* noise. Therefore the possibilities of reducing aircraft noise by the application of technical ingenuity appear to be quite limited.

Certainly present plans cannot rely on this hope, but must assume that the noise problem will become more critical not only in time, by greater frequency of flights, but also in space, by affecting larger areas, and will meet decreasing tolerance.

Other Adverse Impacts

Noise is by far the most serious, but not the only, environmental problem posed by airports. Air pollution is beginning to cause concern. Some ecologists even worry about the possibility of a shortage of oxygen in the immediately affected area, because of the enormous amount of combustion by large jet engines.

Far more immediate is the danger of accidents on the approaches to the runways. While technical progress should lead to a decrease in the accident rate, a single accident by one of the larger and faster planes of the future may have far more serious consequences than have been experienced so far. Under unfavorable circumstances it might cause the death of hundreds or even thousands of people on the ground. It is not hard to predict that in such a case public reaction could force the permanent closing of a major airport, with the resultant loss of hundreds of millions of investment.

THE OPPORTUNITY COST OF AIRPORT LOCATION IN URBAN AREAS

Sufficient data for a reliable estimate of this opportunity cost are not available. The following "guestimate" is merely illustrative of its order of magnitude.

Most major airports are located in areas which either already are or in 10–20 years will be in demand at residential densities of about 5000 persons per square mile. In metropolitan areas the value of raw land in such locations is about $10,000[1] per acre, and of land provided with streets and utilities about $25,000.

It is assumed that these values are decreased by 50% in zone 4, by 20% in zone 3, and by 4% in zone 2.

Item	Area (acres)	Land Value ($ per acre)	Decrease in Value (%)	Total Decrease ($000)
Airport	5,000	10,000	100	50,000
Zone 4	15,000	20,000	50	150,000
Zone 3	60,000	20,000	20	240,000
Zone 2	150,000	20,000	4	120,000
Total	230,000	—	—	560,000

From the above values about $60 million, which would be required for land acquisition in a rural area, should be deducted. The resultant opportunity cost of $500 million could possibly be reduced by restricting flights to daytime hours and/or to one or two flight paths. But this might reduce the benefits of the airport by 20–30% or more. It seems that the city cannot live with the airport, and it cannot live without it.

[1] Cost figures for 1968.

AN EQUATION WITH THREE VARIABLES

The problem can be summarized as follows:

1. The size of the metropolitan area will quadruple; its radius will double.

2. The area of the airport and of its high-noise-level zones will far more than double.

3. In order to minimize the resultant conflict, the distance between urban area and airport should be maximized; in order to facilitate access, it should be minimized.

The relevant measure of distance is not miles, but minutes. If a high-speed connection between urban area and airport can be established at a cost less than the cost inflicted on the first two variables by their proximity, the equation can be solved. Before this line of thought is pursued further, it is necessary to investigate the problem of the most critical component of the airport itself, the passenger terminal.

THE PROBLEM OF THE AIRPORT PASSENGER TERMINAL

Airport terminals have grown to truly monstrous proportions. This becomes evident upon comparison with the terminals of land transportation, which did and do handle far greater passenger volumes in a much smaller area, such as the great railroad stations or the New York Port Authority's bus terminal. The latter covers one street block, 200 × 600 feet or 120,000 square feet. By contrast, both the Montreal and Toronto airport plans envisage a passenger terminal length of 6000 feet. It seems warranted to investigate why an air terminal should require 10 times the length of a bus terminal to handle a smaller annual, daily, and peak-hour volume of passengers.

The air terminal serves two interchanges between three modes: wheeled land vehicle to pedestrian, and pedestrian to aircraft (and vice versa). The latter is the more critical one. Pedestrians are slow-moving and small; aircraft are fast-moving and big—and getting bigger. In order to concentrate on the relatively (to *their* size) small passenger terminal, aircraft have to taxi long and complicated ways and then turn on the apron—a procedure which usually requires 5–10 minutes, often longer. In order to disperse to the relatively (to *their* size) large apron areas, passengers have to walk long ways, also generally requiring, from the curb to the aircraft stairs or bridge, 5–10 minutes.

The obvious answer appears to be to employ a mode of intermediate size and speed to mediate between the excessively divergent sizes and speeds of pedestrians and airplanes. This is being done at several European airports in the form of very simple buses, and at Dulles Airport in the form of very luxurious "moving lounges." At none of these airports, however, has the rather obvious consequence been drawn: once a relatively fast mode is employed to connect passenger terminal and plane, they no longer necessarily have to be at the same location.

"Downtown air terminals" exist, of course, in a number of cities, for instance, in London, England. Here the passengers and their baggage are checked in at a counter in the lobby of the Cromwell Road Terminal. They then walk to a bus gate, where they check in again. This bus, however, takes them not to the plane, but to another terminal, where they leave the bus and walk to and check in—for the third time—at a waiting room. From there, in due time, a second bus takes them to the plane.

A SUGGESTED NEW CONCEPT

Consideration of the inherent incompatibility of pedestrian and of aircraft movement at the passenger terminal, together with the far more basic incompatibility of airport development and urban development, has led to the development of a new concept consisting of three basic elements:

1. An airport located at about 10–15 miles beyond the urban perimeter anticipated for the end of this century.
2. A passenger terminal—essentially a bus terminal—located on the periphery of the presently solidly built-up urban area, in the direction toward the airport.
3. A grade-separated right-of-way connecting these two by operation of superrapid buses between the terminal and the aprons.

These three elements will be discussed in order.

An Outlying Airport

Location of an airport well outside the anticipated urban area has several very important advantages:

1. Land acquisition is less costly. The price of rural land in Canada is generally below $500 per acre, in some areas well below. The Montreal report estimates that 50,000 acres at the proposed site could be bought for about $20 million. Acquisition of 50,000 acres, 79 square miles, may sound extravagant. However, the area potentially affected by a major airport extends about 15 miles from its center. An area with a radius of 15 miles comprises slightly over 700 square miles.

2. The relatively low cost and ease of land assembly make it possible to assemble for the airport itself a reserve area several times as large as that required for presently planned facilities, maybe 30 or 40 square miles. In view of the unpredictability of future demand—in particular, for air cargo—and of future technology, this is vitally important.

3. Our major urban areas may, in the future, well require more than one big airport. The extreme difficulties experienced by cities such as New York and London of finding locations for several such airports are well known. The report on the "Third London Airport" (Ministry of Aviation, June 1963) states that, if one of the two existing airports were to be omnidirectional, the third airport would have to be located 50 miles from the center of London; if both were omnidirectional, 80 miles. With the proposed outlying location, which may well be 40 miles or more from the center, location of a second or third airport at the same distance from the center would present no problem.

4. The limited size of airports, unavoidable in close-to-city locations, limits runway length. An aircraft which has used a 12,000-foot runway for landing must taxi back 12,000 feet to use the same runway for take-off. This may not make much difference with the present method, under which the aircraft has to taxi to the aprons at the terminal and back again to the runway. However, if, as here proposed, buses

came to the apron, aprons could be arranged between the end of the landing and the start of the take-off runway. Such an arrangement would require a total length of 20,000–30,000 feet.

Where contours or other local conditions precluded construction in a straight line 20,000–30,000 feet long, the arrangement could be modified. Where the demand exceeded the capacity of one long runway (really two runways arranged end to end), one or more parallel runways could be provided. This would also be possible in the minor direction, if required.

An auxiliary passenger terminal would be needed to serve two groups: first, passengers whose origins or destinations were much closer to the airport than to the main passenger terminal; second, passengers transferring between planes with time intervals too short to warrant going to the main terminal. It is not unlikely that in the future, with increased reliability of airplane schedules, airlines will provide buses or limousines for direct plane-to-plane transfer. If this is done, the interval between connecting planes might be reduced to 10–15 minutes, at least for passengers without checked baggage. The roads required for this type of transfer could easily be fitted into the suggested pattern.

This pattern would reduce taxiing time by at least 10 minutes. This would mean not only a significant time saving for the passengers, but also a substantial reduction of operating cost for the airlines, and a saving in construction and maintenance of taxiways for the airport.

The Main Passenger Terminal

Location. Existing "downtown" air terminals are generally located in the densely built-up central area. The obvious advantage is proximity to the greatest concentration of passenger origins and destinations. However, there are two serious disadvantages. First, a great proportion of passengers has to "double-back" to reach the airport via the terminal. Second, establishment of a terminal-to-airport connection on its own grade-separated right-of-way through densely built-up areas is prohibitively costly.

It is therefore proposed to locate the terminal on the periphery of the built-up area, in the direction from the center towards the airport, at a distance where population density averages about 4000–5000 persons per square mile. Depending on the size of the city and on local conditions, such sites will normally be found at distances 3–8 miles from the city center. Then all but a tiny fraction of the travelers in the urban area can reach the airport faster by driving to the main terminal and traveling from there to the airport on the reserved right-of-way at 120 mph than by driving directly to the auxiliary terminal at the airport on the ordinary road system at 60, 40, or 20 mph. In regard to the second disadvantage cited above, a grade-separated road from this peripheral location to the airport can be built at moderate cost.

Good accessibility of this main terminal is, of course, essential, especially from the city center. In cities provided with rapid transit, an outer station of a line in the given direction would be the best location. However, at the terminal of a rapid transit line, its access and parking requirements would be superimposed on those of the air terminal. Location at the next-to-last transit station would avoid this difficulty, but might raise the cost of the connection to the airport. The best solution will require close coordination of the planning of air terminal, transit, and land use.

The Terminal Building. This is essentially a bus terminal and should, like the New York Port Authority's bus terminal, be a multistory building. Because buses can negotiate far steeper grades than trains, it is quite feasible to establish four bus levels. Preferably two of these would be located above the departure and two below the arrival concourse (or vice versa). The departing ticketed passenger would identify his or her bus gate on the board in the departure concourse, proceed to it by taking one or two escalators up (or down), check in, and take a seat in the bus. Only one check-in would be required.

If the number of passengers for one plane exceeded bus capacity, two or more neighboring gates would be assigned. Whenever possible, passengers traveling on the same plane to different destinations would be assigned to different buses; this would automatically separate their baggage. If loads for two planes leaving at only slightly different departure times were very small, passengers for both might be assigned to one bus. Their baggage would then be put into separate compartments or, preferably, separate containers. Baggage of passengers who would transfer en route to another plane would be separated in the same manner. On arrival, baggage would be loaded directly into the bus at the apron, which could easily be covered by a cantilevered roof.

It may be noted that the amount of baggage will certainly be reduced as air travel becomes more a familiar routine and as a greater percentage, not only of business, but also of personal trips will be one-day round trips. It could be much further reduced if the airlines would provide some more baggage space in their cabins. It may be predicted that under these conditions in the near future—10–15 years from now—only about 10% of all passengers on domestic and transborder flights, and possibly no more than 50% on international flights, will check baggage.

Connection between Main Terminal and City. Here two categories of persons are affected: passengers and employees, the number of the latter exceeding that of the former. According to the "Final Report on the Montreal International Airport" (pp. 84–85) 38% of these were employed in "aircraft maintenance and cargo" and 62% in "airport administration and passenger" (service). All of the former and a certain percentage of the latter would be at the airport. Employees would thus be divided about evenly between main terminal and airport, easing the problem at both locations.

Four modes are being used by passengers and employees to travel to and from airports.

1. Driving one's own car, requiring long-term parking.
2. Being driven in another person's car, involving short-term parking for all arrivals and most departures.
3. Using taxis or limousines.
4. Using public transportation.

At present airports the last two modes account for only an insignificant proportion of all trips. The attractiveness of limousine service could be improved by computerized dispatching and by lower fares, combined with higher parking fees, in particular for short-term parking.

Proposals for rapid rail service to airports abound, but closer examination has generally shown that they cannot be justified economically. As far as I know, they exist in only two cities, Tokyo and Brussels. The Tokyo Alweg Monorail, charging high fares, is heavily underused and incurs a large deficit. The Brussels facility, a conventional suburban railroad, apparently operates satisfactorily.

The difficulty of assembling sufficient passenger volumes to support service to existing airport passenger terminals stems not only from their peripheral locations, but even more from their isolation from any other origins and destinations. The proposed terminal not only would be (while still peripheral) considerably closer to the city center, but also, occupying only a very small area (probably not much more than 10 acres), would soon attract to its immediate vicinity intensive development of hotels, offices, stores, and service establishments in exactly the same way as large railway passenger stations did in their heyday. In fact, its location would be analogous to the original location of railroad terminals in big old European capitals, such as Paris, Vienna, and Moscow. In these cities the terminals, built at the urban perimeter at their time of construction, are now surrounded by urban development which has spread further out, and are accessible by transit from all directions.

While no data are available to serve as a basis for predictions, it seems reasonable to expect that about 30% of the passengers and 50% of the employees would use public transit or limousines for trips to and from the terminal. This should reduce requirements for curb space and parking to manageable proportions, of the order of magnitude found at major railroad terminals. In this respect it might be interesting to study the experience in countries which have high rates of both rail travel and car ownership, such as Sweden, France, or West Germany.

While many variants of design are possible, generally an oblong shape appears preferable, providing extensive curb space on both the arrival and the departure level. Parking would have to be provided in multistory garages, with direct access to the concourse. The design must provide for balanced extension of every element of the terminal.

Connection between Main Terminal and Airport

When the need for ground travel at speeds greatly in excess of current ones is mentioned, the answer is usually sought in terms of futuristic technology. It is too easily forgotten that for several decades vehicles, both rail and rubber, have been available which can perform at sustained speeds of 125 mph and more. There is little doubt that a bus could be developed which, on a reserved right-of-way of adequate geometric design, could run at 120 mph. The radii of horizontal curves would have to be large, approaching those used on railroad main lines. Grades are much less critical, but generous vertical transition curves would be required. Various "signaling" systems are available to guarantee adequate vehicle spacing.

At 120 mph a bus would need 15 or 20 minutes to cover a distance of 30 or 40 miles, respectively, between terminal and apron. To this must be added about 2 to 3 minutes for maneuvering at both ends of the trip. The total time loss would probably be no greater, and in many cases smaller, than the combined time gain obtained by elimination of taxiing, shortening of pedestrian distances in the terminal, simplification of passenger and baggage processing, and shortening of the city-to-terminal trip.

Normally, these buses would go directly from main terminal to apron and vice versa, and passengers using the auxiliary terminal would be carried to and from the airport by simpler buses of the type used in European airports. However, in some cases, buses traveling from or to the main terminal might make a slight detour to pick up or deliver passengers at the auxiliary terminal. Sometimes they might serve to carry groups of employees to various other installations at the airport. The need for this flexibility is the main reason for suggesting a bus rather than a rail link. It might, however, prove preferable to develop bus-rail vehicles, which could operate as trains on the main link and as buses for distribution.

As only a two-lane road would be required, construction costs would be much lower than for a four-lane freeway. Clearance would be about 12 feet instead of 16 feet, and the spans of overpassing roads could be 20 feet rather than 40 feet. As the road would be built mainly through undeveloped territory, the future street system could be planned so as to minimize the number of over- and underpasses. A fleet of about 250 buses might be required.

Mail and Cargo

Mail. Mail would continue to be carried by scheduled passenger planes. The mail terminal would ideally be separate from the main passenger terminal, in order to avoid overloading the approach roads, but close to the special road leading from the main terminal to the airport. Special vehicles, basically identical with the special passenger buses but with mail-truck bodies, would use the same road for connection between mail terminal and aprons.

Cargo. Air cargo tonnage is expected to grow at a much faster rate than air passengers. If the experience of other modes of transportation can serve as a guide, ultimately the separate development, first of vehicles and then of terminals and possibly of channels, may be expected. Use of lighter-than-air craft for cargo has been suggested. While this may or may not be feasible, air cargo (with minor exceptions) certainly does not require the very high speeds essential for movement of persons and mail.

The impossibility of predicting future requirements is an additional reason to develop airports only at locations where future expansion is not restricted and where flight paths will not conflict with those from possible future additional airports—well beyond the urban perimeter.

Whatever the future may hold, present planning must assume that a substantial part of air cargo will be carried in passenger planes, and that cargo planes will share the same runways, primarily at off-peak hours.

Cargo would reach the airport in two ways. Some would be processed through the cargo terminal at the airport. This might well be the greater part, as establishments strongly dependent on air cargo would tend to locate close to the airport. Another part, with origins or destinations in the urban area, would be better served by a terminal in a location similar to, but not identical with, the one discussed for the mail terminal. Cargo processed at this terminal would travel over the reserved airport road in special airport-owned and airport-operated vehicles—in this case with container-truck bodies.

Summary of New Concept

In order to avoid a collision between urban expansion and airport expansion, the mile distance between the airport and the urban area must be greatly increased, but the time distance must be decreased. This is possible only by establishing a high-speed ground-transportation link between the two. The increasing volume of passengers and the increasing number, size, and speed of planes, which have raised the conflict between the needs of city and airport to unmanageable proportions and have made their divorce necessary, have also caused a secondary, but still serious conflict between the needs of pedestrian and of aircraft movement at the terminal, both of which must meet at the apron. For both, the way to the apron has become too long and complicated. Here again a mediating link must be supplied by ground transportation. The essence of the suggested new concept consists in supplying these two links by one vehicle.

Continuation of the system of locating passenger terminal and runways on the same site, inevitable and perfectly adequate in the early years of aviation, forces the terminal to be located too far out and the runways too far in. Three elements suffer, each in three ways.

The Airport

1. Land acquisition becomes increasingly costly and difficult.
2. Expansion is stymied, and operations are restricted.
3. Taxiing causes excessive delays, especially for stopovers.

Urban Development

1. An excessive amount of land is denied to development.
2. The internal communications system of the city is disrupted.
3. The livability of the environment is impaired.

The Passenger

1. Access to the terminal is too time-consuming.
2. The way from the curb to the apron is too long, as is taxiing time.
3. Checking-in and baggage handling are too cumbersome.

All nine problems would be solved or substantially alleviated by the suggested new concept.

PROTECTION OF AIRPORT FACILITIES AND APPROACHES

Whatever the location and type of airport, it is absolutely essential to reserve the land required for the airport and its possible future expansion, as well as for access and other connected facilities, and to prevent incompatible development in the zone of impact of any potential flight path. This requires effective cooperation with land use planning and control.

Land use planning has to deal with three aspects of the problem.

1. Allocate the land for airport and connected uses at the right place and in the right amounts.

2. Adjust the system of communications (road, rail, power lines) so as to minimize the interruption by the airport.

3. Allocate land in the sphere of influence of flight paths to uses which are not or are only marginally affected by noise, such as agriculture, industry, transportation, and public utilities.

The method generally used to accomplish the third and most difficult task is zoning. In all Canadian provinces the zoning power lies with the local municipalities. Under our system of taxation these municipalities have to rely almost exclusively on the real property tax. Their prime interest is therefore to obtain as much assessable development as possible, and under the given conditions it would be foolish to expect them to act otherwise.

Theoretically, the provinces could reassume the zoning power and exercise it in the interest of airport protection. It is unlikely, however, that provincial governments will do this in the face of deeply ingrained custom. Even if they did, political pressures from landowners, developers, and municipalities would probably prevent consistent and energetic exercise of these powers.

Clearly, the tools of land use planning and zoning are inadequate for the task at hand. Experience all over the world has shown that the only effective means of land control is landownership. It is therefore necessary that a public authority acquire, at the earliest possible date, all the land that, at some time in the future, may be needed for airports and for their flight corridors. Unforeseeable developments are likely to show later that some parts of this land are not needed. It is probable that these can then be sold without a loss, in many cases at a profit.

As an airport is a major generator of development, and thereby greatly increases land values in the surrounding areas, substantial returns could be achieved by leasing this land. It could also be sold under appropriate deed restrictions, though this method permits less complete control. The control can and should be used to promote industries which are heavy users of air transportation and to exclude others, as well as to provide adequate housing developments for airport employees at locations and densities suitable for bus connection with the airport. Under all circumstances it would be essential to reserve land not only for presently planned facilities and flight corridors, but also for any future requirements of this kind.

Landownership on this scale and of this duration would, of course, mean a deep and extensive involvement in the business of real estate and land development. If it is considered undesirable that the Department of Transport become so involved, an alternative might be to use the specific Canadian invention of federal-provincial land assembly, in which the federal government participates through the Central Mortgage and Housing Corporation. It might provide a core from which the vastly greater activities required for airport purposes could be developed. Of course, such development would have to take place in close and continuous cooperation with the Department of Transport.

There is great and urgent danger that aviation will repeat, on a vastly greater and costlier scale, the mistakes of earlier modes of transportation, notably water and rail.

The story is always the same. The terminal is located as close to the center as possible. Very soon the need to expand the terminal and its approach facilities comes into conflict with the equally urgent need of the city to expand its facilities. Successive compromises are made, while adverse effects on the urban environment increase. Higher and higher investments are required to keep the transportation facilities in operation, at decreasing efficiency. Finally, the decision has to be made to scrap the entire investment and to start afresh farther out. The scars in the urban tissue remain for decades, if not forever.

There is still time for air transportation to avoid a repetition of this sad story, but it is getting short. The situation calls for bold thinking, far-sighted planning, and decisive action.

Chapter 40

CITIES AND TRANSPORT IN EVOLUTION

INTRODUCTION

Accessibility

The terms "community" and "communication" are derived from the same root. People form and maintain a community by communicating with each other. This presupposes mutual accessibility for persons, as well as for goods and for messages. This chapter will concentrate on the movement of persons, or "travel," and will deal with the movement of goods and/or messages only to the extent that they are either substitutes for or supplements to person movement, in particular by sharing the same vehicles and/or infrastructure.

Accessibility is impeded by the friction of distance, which can be overcome only at a cost in terms of time, money (symbolizing labor), and inconvenience. Accessibility between potential points of origin and destination of movement can be increased either by reducing the distance between the points or by reducing the friction, that is, by increasing either density or mobility. Density is a characteristic of the settlement pattern. Mobility is the product of the transportation industry. They can, and always have, substituted for one another.

Cities are distinguished from villages by three closely interrelated characteristics: a concentration of people and of power, a division and interchange of labor between relatively independent units, and the drawing of all or part of their sustenance from outside, by force or by trade. While cities generally developed as centers of a region from which they drew their sustenance, thus minimizing distances, improvement of mobility was still called for to maintain and, in particular, to extend access to goods to be collected and, in the case of trade, also distributed.

Within the city, accessibility was provided by minimizing distances. As people first came together in cities, according to Aristotle, for security, cities generally were walled. Effective fortification required limited size and compact form; the resultant density was even higher than that required for accessibility, and distances could be

---

Source: Report to Urban Transportation Research Branch of the Canadian Surface Transportation Administration as part of Transport Canada's study of the role of the automobile, Montreal, Que., June 1977.

and generally have been covered by walking. Even today, almost certainly, a majority of all intraurban person-trips and possibly even of person-miles are performed by walking. However, movement of goods within the city called for other modes. Generally, though not in all cases, the lead in innovation has been taken by movement of goods rather than of persons, and by long-distance ("interurban") rather than by short-distance ("intraurban") transportation.

The goal of all innovation in transportation and communication is to reduce the friction of distance, ideally to zero, the equivalent of the magic carpet. Evidently, we will never reach that goal, but we are approaching it asymptotically. Messages indeed move at absolute speed; there is no difference in time or inconvenience between a telephone call over 50 feet and one over 5000 miles, although there is still a substantial difference in money. The closer we approach the "magic carpet" goal, the less is the pressure for concentration in specific areas. Distribution of population over the globe is likely to be increasingly determined by climatic and scenic attractiveness. The process may already be well under way, as indicated by the population shifts to the south in a number of countries in the northern hemisphere: the United Kingdom, West Germany, the United States, and the U.S.S.R. For Canada it raises the prospect of a future negative balance of international migration.

Transportation Systems

The goal of a transportation system can be expressed as a function minimizing the cost, in terms of time, money, and inconvenience, for the sum of trip lengths, in terms of distance: $\Sigma (t + m + i)/\Sigma d$. It may be noted that, in case of goods transportation, the time and inconvenience of the operator are translated into his or her money compensation, so that the function is transformed into the familiar "cost-per-mile" expression. Many attempts have been, and more could be made to achieve a similar transformation for person movement. Most of these have dealt exclusively with costs to the user; however, there are also substantial costs to the nonuser, in particular in the closely knit urban environment. This increases the subjective element in any comparative evaluation of different systems or subsystems.

Any transportation subsystem is characterized by three different elements: vehicle, path, and terminal, and by different property relations of the user to these elements, which can be user-owned, be for hire, or be common carriers. The terminal in turn provides different functions: loading and unloading, vehicle storage, and maintenance.

Innovation practically always begins with the vehicle, which generally starts out by using existing natural or man-made facilities as paths and terminals. As the system evolves, increasing efforts are made to improve these facilities and to build new, increasingly specialized and costly ones. Problems tend to shift from vehicles to paths to terminals, which ultimately may become the most critical elements of the system.

In general, new elements are first developed by their users; as they spread, user-owned elements tend to be supplemented and sometimes replaced by for-hire and common-carrier facilities. Subsystems tend to stabilize as specific combinations of elements and ownership relations. Innovation may involve changes in combinations as well as in the elements to be combined.

INTERACTION OF TRANSPORT AND CITIES BEFORE THE MOTOR AGE

Long-Distance Transport

Long-distance transport has a decisive influence on the location and function of a city, and consequently on its size and rate of growth. It has little direct impact on the form of the city. However, it may modify form indirectly, by influencing the selection of the site and the functions, as well as by the impact of its terminals.

Geographers distinguish three functionally different types of city: central places, transportation nodes, and specialized cities. The functions are not mutually exclusive; most important cities combine two or three of them, and their relative weights may shift over time.

Central places are the oldest and most frequent type. Generally they arose on a prominent site in a fertile region, over which they exercised political, religious, and economic dominance. Athens in the Attic plain and Chartres in the Beauce are classic examples. The radius of their realm expands as improvements in transportation overcome the friction of distance. Soon it overlaps the realm of neighboring centers. By military conflict and economic competition, the strongest emerge as centers of a higher order; the weaker ones are reduced to subcenters or may even disappear.

The dependence of transportation nodes on long-distance transportation is even more obvious. The simplest form of this type is the crossroads town. Far more important are the places where transfer from one mode of transportation to another forces a "break of bulk," primarily a transfer between land and water transportation. Harbor cities on sea, rivers, or lakes are the most important cities in Canada, as in many other countries.

Specialized cities are of lesser importance. They arise on the basis of natural resources, such as mineral deposits or healing springs, and also as religious sanctuaries. Their location is not determined by being favorable for long-distance transportation. Santiago de Compostella is located at the western extreme of the European continent. This did not prevent huge streams of visitors from all parts of Christian Europe from visiting its shrine. To the contrary, the streams of pilgrims stimulated growth of cities along the routes which they traveled.

This reverse effect—the impact of cities on the paths of long-distance movement—has gained increasing importance as the means of transportation have developed. Urban guidebooks and monographs rarely fail to tell their readers that the city in question is located where it is because this location is "at a crossroads"; but, in fact, the roads converge at this spot because the city is there. Moscow is a case in point. There are many other cities in central Russia which are as well or better situated for the role of capital of that vast country. But once Moscow, as a result of specific historical events, had become dominant, a system of roads, then of railroads, of airways, and even of waterways, was developed to converge on the capital. Moscow now boasts of being "the port of five seas." But the 15-foot-deep canals and river channels which connect it to these seas are all man-made. Closer to home, Montreal had its raison d'être as the terminal of ocean shipping, because of the obstacle of the rapids. This obstacle was eliminated long ago by the building first of the Lachine Canal and then of the St. Lawrence Seaway, but this has not stopped the growth of Montreal.

Cities have, however, decayed if their long-distance paths have been cut off either by "acts of God," such as the silting of a river mouth, or by human acts, such as the closing of the mouth of the Scheldt by the Dutch, which put an end to the prosperity which Antwerp had enjoyed in the sixteenth century. More frequent is decay because competing cities develop newer and more efficient modes of transportation.

Vigorous cities generally have been able to reverse the relation between city and path. In the seventeenth century Amsterdam had become the leading port of Europe. Its ships sailed through the Zuyder Zee to the farthest corners of the earth. When the new steamships could not navigate the shallow Zuyder Zee, Amsterdam began to stagnate. But in 1872 it built a new, deep canal directly west to the North Sea, and the city resumed its growth as a major seaport. There are many more examples of the interaction between long-distance transportation and city growth. There is, however, no known case of city growth being reversed because of a shortage of motive power to operate transport.

For millennia, water transportation was superior to land transportation. Long before nonmuscular power, falling water and wind were used in industry, they were used in transportation by the great river civilizations of Asia. There are, however, significant differences between the various water transport systems. In Iraq efficient water transportation was possible only one way, north to south, on the swiftly flowing waters of the Euphrates and Tigris. Unification of the country was achieved only late and sporadically. By contrast, in Egypt ships carried north by the current of the Nile sailed south driven by the strong north wind which blows regularly every day—and the country remained united, almost without interruption, from 3000 B.C. on.

As Thor Heyerdahl has demonstrated, the ancient Egyptian sailships were eminently seaworthy, capable of crossing the Atlantic. However, it was their smaller neighbors, the Phoenicians, Cretans, and Greeks, who first developed self-governing city-states, based on seagoing trade, surpassing their teachers in civilization and founding new cities from the Crimea to the Straits of Gibraltar.

Meanwhile, land transportation still relied exclusively on muscle power. Animals were primarily used as mounts and pack animals. Wheels were known to the great river civilizations since the third millennium B.C., but the use of wheeled vehicles was inefficient because paved roads existed only in cities. The Romans were the first to build a system of solid paved roads over the length and breadth of their empire.

The Roman roads served primarily, as did water transportation, for the movement of military forces and of goods; but person travel, by chariot as well as on mounts, developed also. The vehicles, on land and on water, were generally user-owned, occasionally for hire. The first record of common-carrier travel has come down to us in the tale of Jonah, who "paid his fare" on a ship going from Joppa to Tarshish.[1]

While this first recorded experience of common-carrier person travel was hardly encouraging, passenger travel on sea and river water appears to have continued and expanded. Common carriers on land appeared only in sixteenth century Europe, in the form of the "diligence" or "stagecoach." However, in the following centuries the superiority of water over land transportation continued to increase to the point that, even in areas without access to natural waterways, the canal boat superseded the wagon. The opening of the Erie Canal reduced the cost of shipping a ton of wheat from Buffalo to New York from $100 to $6. With the development of the steamship, passenger transportation on water became superior to that on land in speed as well as

[1]Jonah 3.

in comfort. As late as 1841, young Gustave Flaubert made his way from his native Rouen to Paris on a steamer up the meandering Seine River.

This millennial trend toward the growing superiority of water over land transportation was suddenly reversed by the development of the railroad. Within a single generation it achieved a complete monopoly of overland travel. Water transportation remained superior in cost per ton-mile, but the gap has been greatly reduced by the development of unit trains (as well as of pipelines).

The effects have been far reaching and are still at work. Economic and political power has increasingly passed from the far-flung maritime empires of Portugal, Spain, France, Holland, and finally England to huge continental countries, such as the United States and the U.S.S.R. In these and in other countries, including Canada, large new inland cities have sprung up on empty prairies and have grown within one or two generations to top-ranking size; old inland cities have shown new growth. Areas inaccessibile to railroads—mountain regions and, in particular, islands—are experiencing out-migration, and their cities and towns stagnate.

As noted earlier, the impact is not exclusively one-way. The demands of cities have been the driving force in the development and improvement of waterways and railways, as well as of increasingly efficient, highly specialized, and costly terminals. This has greatly increased the competitive superiority of large cities over smaller places. Only the largest cities can maintain highly mechanized terminals with specialized facilities for bulk goods such as oil or grain, and for container ships. Only they can offer frequent sailings. For this reason many Philadelphia industries use New York rather than their own excellent harbor to ship their goods overseas. Equally important is the presence of firms to handle the required paperwork, brokerage, insurance, and other details. The remaining seagoing passenger services—cruise ships—are exclusively based in the largest cities.

A 300-ton seagoing ship may stop in Port Hope to unload a package of a few hundred pounds. A 15,000-ton ship will unload it in Toronto, to be shipped back to Port Hope by truck.

While goods service by rail is available also in small towns, the service is slower. Unit trains cannot serve them. Passenger trains find the volumes too small to offer more than infrequent service, at best, or even to stop on runs between big cities. The afternoon "Rapido" does not stop at Kingston. Any future superfast ground transportation will be able to serve only the largest cities, because of its high capital cost and the relatively high time loss of intermediate stops.

This is even more true for air travel. Small cities can be served only through infrequent flights by small (and less cost-effective) planes. Connection between two small cities in most cases requires a time-consuming transfer at a major airport.

The result of the continuing improvement of long-distance transportation by water, rail, and air—achieved largely by economies of scale of vehicles, paths, and terminals—has been an exponentially growing trend toward the concentration of activities and population in ever-larger metropolitan agglomerations.

Short-Distance Transport

There is no clear evidence that improvements in urban transportation induce city growth. The claim, often made by advocates of major transportation improvements such as freeways or rapid transit lines, that good accessibility for goods and persons will attract enterprises and households is entirely logical, but it cannot be supported by empirical evidence. This may be due to the fact that the provision of infrastructure usually does not keep up with rapid growth; traffic becomes impeded just *because* the city is growing. The question of the impact of internal transport on city growth therefore remains moot.

There is no question, however, that internal transport had and continues to have a decisive impact on the *form* of cities. As noted earlier, for centuries intracity movement was exclusively on foot and, to a minor extent, on mounts, and goods were carried on the backs of human beings or animals. Compared to these modes, water transportation was superior in capacity, speed, and comfort. Cities such as Alexandria, Venice, Bruges, Hangchow, Tenochtitlan, Amsterdam, and Bangkok owed much of their prosperity to their canals.

Cities which rely entirely on movement on foot or on animal back, such as many in Islamic countries, or on these modes combined with water transport, such as Venice, show a street pattern radically different from the one with which we are familiar. Because human and animal bodies can easily turn on the spot, and also can ascend and descend steps, the streets of such cities frequently change both their horizontal and vertical alignment, with many sharp corners and dead ends. The resulting variety, with the added spice of the pleasures of surprise and discovery, gives these cities their "picturesque" attraction. In trying to reestablish a "pedestrian realm" in our cities, we might do better to follow their example, which often can be done in the interior of blocks, as in Vancouver's "Gastown," than to try to convert a street designed for vehicular to pedestrian use, as has been attempted on Granville Street in the same city.

The movement of wheeled vehicles, especially of four-wheeled ones with their limited turning radius, requires a different type of street. The gridiron pattern of wide streets of the old cities of India, China, and the Hellenistic-Roman world was well suited for this purpose. However, despite the separation of pedestrian and vehicular traffic by means of raised sidewalks, the conflict between the two types made itself felt. Julius Caesar prohibited vehicular movement on the streets of Rome during the daytime. However, the rumble of heavy ox-drawn carts all through the night disturbed the sleep of all Romans except the happy few who could afford to live in large mansions with rooms opening on spacious interior courts and gardens. Not surprisingly, the happy few prevailed. The emperor Marcus Aurelius reinforced Caesar's edict and extended it to provincial cities, condemning the movement of wheeled vehicles and horseback riders on city streets as "uncivic."

In post-Roman Europe the absence of paved streets discouraged the use of vehicles. Only toward the end of the Middle Ages did the spread of street paving, together with the improvement of vehicles by the introduction of hub, rim, and spoked wheels, lead, in the growing cities, to a proliferation of wheeled vehicles—and to the protests of alarmed citizens. In 1513, when the City Council of Paris considered the widening of a street giving access to a new bridge, an honorable member complained that the bridge was "congested, particularly because of the constant cart traffic that passes through it and will be more in the future and will *paralyze* said bridge." The good man anticipated the methods of modern traffic engineers, who extrapolate the trend of increase in traffic volume and conclude that on a specified date traffic will come to a dead stop. It never happens: cities always have choked streets, but they never choke themselves to death.

The reason for this is simple: traffic demand is not fixed, but expands and contracts with the supply. This seems to escape the people who complain that a few years after the completion of a new facility congestion is as bad as it was before. The congesting vehicles serve desired movements which could not be made before. Traffic has first to become better before it can become worse. Such considerations are of little comfort, however, to those who suffer from the "malefits" of traffic, while reaping few of its benefits. In 1563 the French parliament asked the King to prohibit vehicles in the streets of Paris.[2] In 1635 in London "horse carriages had become a nuisance in the city, for not only were his Majesty and his much beloved Queen perturbed by the traffic, but the princes and noblemen as well."[3] Even in the much smaller colonial towns of North America the problems of vehicular traffic were felt. In 1652 New Amsterdam enacted an ordinance against speeding because of accidents and congestion; in the eighteenth century, Charleston restricted the parking of churchgoers' coaches.

Horse-drawn vehicles were generally user-owned, occasionally for hire. For-hire use of water vehicles was more widespread. Strabo, in describing Alexandria in the first century, and Marco Polo reporting on Hangchow in the fourteenth, give vivid descriptions of hundreds of parties hiring boats to visit the equivalents of nightclubs located on lake islands in these great cities. Also on water we find some common carriers in the form of ferries. But I know of no record of any intraurban public carriers on land. It took the genius of Blaise Pascal, the great philosopher and mathematician, to develop the notion of a horse-drawn carriage available to all—an "omnibus"—who could pay the fare. In 1662 he organized a bus company in Paris. However, Pascal was ahead of his time. In 1667 the company went bankrupt, the first in a long series of transit companies to do so.

Not until 150 years later, in the 1820s, did horse-drawn buses and also streetcars gain acceptance. Their use generally was limited to the middle classes. For the mass of the population, the small gain in time and convenience was of less value than the relatively high fare. A paradoxical situation developed in the second half of the nineteenth century. New and highly effective means—the steamboat, the steam railroad, and the telegraph—moved goods, persons, and messages all over the globe, enabling and promoting the concentration of urban populations far bigger than had been possible without them. But within these multimillion-population cities all movement relied still on human and animal muscle. A businessman in Montreal communicated with his partners in London or San Francisco by telegraph, but with another businessman in his own city he could communicate only by sending a messenger. This low mobility of goods, persons, and messages limited the horizontal expansion of cities to a maximum radius of about 3 miles, circumscribing an area of less than 30 square miles. "The daily route which the man living on the periphery has to take to his business in the center reaches the limit of the physically impossible," stated the writer August Orth in Berlin in 1871.

Vertical expansion was even more limited, relying exclusively on human muscle to climb stairs. Multistory buildings could not exceed the limit of 8 or maybe 10 stories, which had already been "achieved" in Phoenician Tyre and imperial Rome, and again in eighteenth century Edinburgh.

---

[2]Lewis Mumford, *The City in History*, Harcourt, Brace, New York, 1961, p. 368.
[3]J. T. Jackman, *The Development of Transport in Modern England*.

With both horizontal and vertical growth narrowly circumscribed, growth could proceed only interstitially, by "filling in" every square foot of ground, depriving the occupants of access to light and air. The resulting density, sometimes exceeding 100,000 residents per square mile, together with their workplaces and services, created intolerable congestion. To relieve it, streets were widened and new arteries broken through—in particular, diagonal arteries to reduce the detours inherent in a gridiron system. Even more ruthless than these new arteries, the railroad lines disrupted the traditional city fabric, spreading noise and smoke along their path, and attracting industries. Some industries established themselves outside the built-up area on radial or circumferential railroad lines, followed by suburbs housing their workers. The "red belt" surrounding Paris is the classic example, but smaller developments of a comparable type can also be found in Canadian cities.

Thus the railroad, which had so greatly contributed to the centripetal movement of people and activities from countryside and small town to the big city, also initiated the opposite centrifugal city-to-suburb movement within the urban concentration. In the 1840s the reformer Robert Gourley had already stated his conviction that the railroads would put an end to crowded cities and enable every family to live in its own house surrounded by a garden. The dream became true for wealthy families from the 1850s on. The railroad suburb created a new pattern of urban development, both on the macro- and the microscale. Because acceleration and deceleration of steam trains is time-consuming and costly, they stopped only at a few widely spaced locations. Distances between station and home were traveled on foot and therefore were short. The result was a number of small, isolated spots along railroad lines radiating from the center. Within these suburbs a new pattern of winding streets was developed, derived from "romantic" park design.

The first successful use of steam power for travel within a city area was the London underground railroad, completed in 1863. While it was intended to carry freight as well, it was in fact the first "rapid transit" line, completely on its own grade-separated right-of-way, and greatly superior to any other mode in capacity, speed, and reliability. New York in 1867, and Berlin in 1872, followed with elevated rapid transit lines.

However, the real breakthrough was brought about by three innovations which were developed in the 1880s, and became dominant in the 1890s: electric traction, the bicycle, and the telephone. Without the possibility for practically instantaneous and ubiquitous communication, people hardly would have accepted the spatial separation involved in a decentralized settlement pattern, even with excellent travel facilities. The bicycle, as a highly efficient and fairly inexpensive means of individual travel, was a forerunner of the automobile and pioneered in the campaign for the improvement of long-distance roads, which had been neglected since the triumph of the railroad. However, the application of electric traction to streetcars and to rapid transit trains was decisive in establishing the predominance of collective, common-carrier travel in all but the smallest cities of the developed world. The horse-drawn carriage survived only as a luxury for its owners and as a semiluxury when used for hire. Animal and human muscle were no match for mechanical power, and mechanical power was the monopoly of public transport.

One after another, the biggest cities built electrified rapid transit. All cities, large and small, down to 50,000 population or less, electrified their streetcar lines and extended them out into open country, certain that they would attract development.

As the stops were located much closer together than were the stations of suburban trains, the zones which they served merged into a continuous ribbon. The result was the "tentacular" city, extending "rays" or "fingers" far out into the countryside, with open country left in the interstices between the fingers.

The internal structure of the city was also affected. First the growing separation of residence and place of work had called for better transport; now its availability enabled people to live farther away from their work. First the concentration of commercial activity had increased the volume of commuters which could be served only by high-capacity transit; now the increased ability to attract customers increased the volume of business in the center.

However, the most important result of improved mobility was a great increase in land absorption per head of population, or, expressed negatively, a decrease in density. This reversal of the trend characteristic of the earlier decades of the industrial revolution appears to have started before the triple revolution of the 1890s. The central wards of Philadelphia have lost population since 1860. The inner city of Hamburg, Germany, reached its population peak in 1880. The New York Regional Plan Association found that the number of persons per square mile of land used for any urban purpose, including parks and open spaces, in all urban areas in the region (which, in addition to New York City, comprises scores of medium-sized and small cities), after having increased from 50,000 in 1820 to 64,000 in 1860, dropped to 39,000 in 1900 and to 22,000 in 1925. In other words, in the 65 years before the automobile had a major impact, density dropped by 66%. In the following car-dominated 45 years, it dropped by 63%, not a spectacular acceleration of the trend.

It turned out that the typical big city of the mid-nineteenth century, the tightly packed "stone desert," was only a transitory phenomenon, due to the 40-year time lag between the application of modern technology to long-distance and its application to short-distance transportation and communication. Once the latter had also been modernized, the city began to transform itself into a different form of human settlement, occupying a much larger area and spreading out far into the countryside. As early as 1910, in his preface to the catalogue of the Berlin International City Planning Exhibition, Werner Hegemann had noted that the present city had hardly more than the name in common with the historical one. This new phenomenon, the product of the combined effect of the centripetal country-to-city and the centrifugal city-to-suburb movement carried by long- and by short-distance transport, respectively, we will call "the modern metropolis," for lack of a better name.

INTERACTION OF TRANSPORT AND CITIES IN THE MOTOR AGE

Long-Distance Transport

Less than a century after the railroad had reversed the millennial trend from land to water transport, an equally unexpected reversal of two closely interrelated trends was brought about by the invention of the internal combustion engine and its application to buses, trucks, and, in particular, automobiles, which spread rapidly from the 1920s on.

For a century there had been a consistent shift from individual, user-owned or for-hire to collective common-carrier (or "public") transport, also called "transit." At the turn of the century, transit had become accepted as the normal mode of intracity travel. Equally accepted was the distinction between modes of long- and of short-distance travel. One traveled to another city either by railroad or by steamer; one traveled to the station or pier by transit or by hired horse-drawn vehicle. To be able to travel from one's front door to any door in another city appeared at first as a romantic return to the age of the stagecoach, if not the knight errant.

The availability of a flexible transportation system for the movement of persons and goods was hailed as liberating the settlement pattern from its dependence on the railroad. Many expected that the ubiquity of the motor vehicle, together with the simultaneous ubiquitous availability of energy in the form of electrical current, would reverse the movement toward concentration in large urban agglomerations and lead to a more even distribution of the population over the countryside. This did not happen. The expectation had been based on erroneous assumptions correlating big cities with big factories and big sources of energy such as coal deposits. The real reason for the attraction of big cities, as Adam Smith had noted, is increasing division and specialization of labor, both within enterprises and, even more important, between them. The importance of the latter has been greatly increased by the growth of highly specialized, "higher order" services, both producer and consumer services. These "tertiary" industries tend to concentrate even more than "secondary" ones in the largest centers. To the extent that extraurban motor vehicle movement has modified the settlement pattern, it has been at the opposite end of the scale, at the level of the rural market town. By greatly expanding their service radii, it has led to the absorption of many small horse-and-buggy-based towns by larger neighbors. This impact has been most strongly felt in Canada's Prairie Provinces, where these centers also serve as collection points for the shipment of grain by rail.

While the considerably lower ton-per-mile cost of water, rail, and pipeline transportation limited the motor vehicle's share of all ton-miles performed in Canada in 1970 to one fifth, it accounted in that year for 87% of all long-distance person-miles; air (9%) was increasing its share of the total, but only 4% represented collective ground transportation, bus and rail. A greater share for these last modes would greatly reduce consumption of energy, air pollution, and traffic accidents with their appalling loss of life and limb.

In Europe and Japan, rail and bus carry a far greater share of long-distance travel. The main reason is population density, which, in the United Kingdom and West Germany, is over 100, in Japan 150, and in the Netherlands 200 times as high as in Canada. Canada's most densely populated region, comprising the 40,000 square miles of southern Ontario, has only one seventh the density of the Netherlands.

Given a fertility rate which implies an excess of deaths over births within a few decades, higher overall density can be achieved in Canada only by greatly increased net immigration. However, immigration policy is becoming more restrictive.

Most effective, both by reducing travel distance and increasing the usage of rail and bus, would be concentrating people and activities in the few regions which now contain most of Canada's population. However, public opinion and governments are committed to the notion that regional equality requires equalization not only of personal incomes, but also of population growth rates. Government policy will therefore try to shift population to low-density areas, though the effect is likely to remain insignificant.

As previously noted, only large metropolitan concentrations can generate the passenger volumes which can justify the establishment of a rail service with a speed and frequency which would make it competitive with both automobiles and planes. As also noted, the secular trend toward concentration in metropolitan regions is continuing. Decentralization policies, adopted by most governments, have often succeeded in promoting the growth of selected towns, but have not noticeably slowed metropolitan growth. However, in the most developed countries, the rate of metropolitan increase is strongly decreasing. This is, of course, inevitable, as the national growth rate decreases and as there is a shrinking rural population from which to draw migrants.

Certainly in Canada metropolitan growth is still vigorous and likely to continue, but at a rate less than half of the 1941–1961 rate. In the foreseeable future there will be nowhere in Canada, an urban pattern comparable to that of Europe or Japan, even if government policies were aimed at promoting rather than at impeding it—nothing that could serve as a basis for a Tokaido-type rail service. At most, a moderately attractive rail service might be provided in the Windsor-to-Quebec corridor and possibly between Calgary and Edmonton. The competitive position of the interurban bus could be strengthened, as to cost and comfort, by subsidies, and as to speed, by regulation, for example, a 90-mph speed limit versus 60 mph for automobiles.

However, even under the most wildly optimistic assumptions, collective land transportation will hardly double its share; if the share of air also doubles, this will still leave three quarters of all long-distance person-miles to the automobile. Their absolute numbers will increase with an increase in population. Even with a stable population automobile travel tends to increase steeply with increasing income. Illustrative of this are data for the 1965–1975 period in the German Democratic Republic (East Germany).[4] With a nominal decrease in population and an 80% increase in gross national product, annual automobile trips per person increased by 155%, together with increases in public transportation person-kilometers of 20% and 36% for local and long-distance travel, respectively.

It is therefore safe to predict that, with any conceivable pattern and type of urban development in Canada, long-distance automobile movement will increase substantially.

Short-Distance Transport

While motorization had no demonstrable impact on the location and growth of cities, the introduction of the motor car into the urban-metropolitan environment brought about a radical change in its *form,* which in turn led to decisive changes in short-distance transport.

As noted earlier, the decrease in overall density of the total area used for urban purposes preceded motorization by about half a century, and had reduced it in the New York Region to 22,000 per square mile in 1925, in the incipient stage of the motor age. In the city of Toronto, the corresponding figure was below 20,000. However, as residential areas account for little more than half of the total urbanized area, their density averaged about twice that high. This average hides, of course, very

---

[4]*Statistisches Taschenbuch der Deutschen Demokratischen Republik, 1976*, Staatsverlag der D.D.R., Berlin, 1976, pp. 15, 23, 93, 95.

great differences in density between center and periphery. Nevertheless, in larger urban areas, with populations exceeding 100,000, practically everyone lived within 10 minutes' walking time from a streetcar line providing reasonably frequent service in the direction of the center. Transit service in other directions was usually poor; none crossed the wedges of open land dividing the "fingers" developed along the radiating tram or rapid transit lines. Travel between two points at the periphery required either a long detour through the central area, involving one or more transfers, or the use of individual transportation, generally the bicycle.

Motorization completely changed this pattern. The green wedges between the fingers were now as accessible as the fingers themselves and were quickly filled with new subdivisions. As the automobile, on the average, cut door-to-door travel time in half, it doubled the radius and quadrupled the area within a given time distance from the center. This vast increase in the supply of land "ripe" for development made it much cheaper than the land previously in the urban market and led to greatly increased land absorption per head. The resulting sharp drop in overall density has been offset by "infilling" or redevelopment at higher densities only in a few very new cities, such as those in Canada's Prairie Provinces. A study by N. D. Lea showed that the average density of their urbanized land was increasing, while that of the older and larger cities decreased.[5] Both converged toward an average of 6500 persons per square mile. It is intriguing that this figure is identical with the rule of thumb of 1 square kilometer per 2500 additional population used by German planners. This coincidence does not necessarily mean, however, that this secular trend to lower densities has run its course. Studies of the urban-metropolitan areas of Sweden showed that the rates of increase of land absorption per head and of real disposable income per head had been identical over the 50-year period for which data were available. As real income is expected to increase, so is land absorption, though both are likely to grow at rates considerably lower than those of the last 30 years.

All available evidence points to the conclusion that the benefits of "improvements" in urban transportation, meaning reduction in time (also in money and inconvenience) per mile traveled, have been taken out not in the form of less time, but in the form of more space, as well as of more choice of potential destination. During the past century, urban travel time per mile has been reduced at least fivefold (speed has increased five times). If densities had remained constant, the area—and consequently the number of potential destinations within that area—would have increased 25 times. If the number of potential destinations which can be reached within a given travel time—say, 0.5 hour—had remained constant, land absorption per person would have increased (density decreased) 25 times. The evidence seems to indicate that the benefits of reduced urban travel time per mile have been taken out in roughly equal proportions in terms of more space and of more choice, not in terms of less time spent in travel.

This hypothesis is strongly supported by the concept of the "travel-time budget," developed by Yakov Zahavi.[6] By analyzing a wide array of data, Zahavi found that the total average time spent on travel during a day varies little under widely varying conditions. If people spend most of this fixed travel-time budget on travel to work,

[5] N. D. Lea & Associates, *Urban Transportation Developments in Eleven Canadian Metropolitan Areas*, Canadian Good Roads Association, Ottawa, Ont., 1966
[6] Yakov Zahavi, *Traveltime Budgets and Mobility in Urban Areas*, U.S. Department of Transportation, FHWA PL8183, Washington, D.C., May 1974.

they make few other trips; if their journey to work is short, they make many trips for other purposes.

Because only a small proportion of potential destinations becomes actual, the hypothesis of increased choice is not amenable to quantification. However, increased space is well documented.

Part of the reason for increased land absorption is increased absorption of floor space per person. Between 1920 and 1970 the population of Manhattan decreased by about one third, but the amount of residential floor space remained exactly the same,[7] indicating a growth in floor space per resident by about one half, on the average, despite the well-known massive exodus of the middle class. The increase is not too surprising, considering that 42% of all Manhattan households are now one-person households, a type rarely found in 1920.

Increased absorption of floor space per person has also occurred in factories, offices, and institutions. But beyond this, and more significant, has been the increase of land area per floor area, as represented by the growing proportion of one-story structures for residence, industry, shopping, schools, and so on, each structure surrounded by open space, paved or planted. The hunger for space seems to be insatiable. In North America the response has been the single-family house and the automobile, the one dependent on the other. It is generally believed that European cities, with greater reliance on multifamily housing and on rapid transit, are much more concentrated. However, a comparison of the city-state of Hamburg, Germany, which is highly representative of these housing and transport types, with Metropolitan Toronto[8] showed a surprising similarity in densities; in fact, the centrifugal trend was even stronger in Hamburg than in Toronto. It is evident that our understanding of the forces shaping urban development is still very incomplete.

Be that as it may, there is little doubt that the automobile has brought about not only a quantitative expansion, but also a qualitative change in our urban areas, profoundly changing their structures. Before the motor age, the bulk of both secondary and tertiary employment was concentrated in the center, even though some peripheral industrial districts had sprung up along the railroads, as mentioned earlier, and the outlying residential areas had local services. In the motor age, manufacturing and warehousing plants can enjoy the advantage of cheap land for expansion by establishing themselves anywhere on the periphery, relying on trucks for assembling goods and on their employees' cars for assembling workers. In the past 30 years the number of manufacturing workers employed in the city of Toronto has been halved, while it has steeply increased in the surrounding area.

But the majority of tertiary jobs also are to be found far from the center, as the numbers and the purchasing power of "suburban" residents increase, and as many services, notably food preparation and child rearing, are increasingly shifted from the household to specialized establishments. The huge shopping centers are the most spectacular signs of this shift, but more and more offices find that they can attract both clients and employees to a peripheral location.

Three functions remain in the central business district (C.B.D.): first, those consumer services which can be supported only by the entire metropolitan area, such as specialty stores or theaters, but also the broadest possible selection of consumer

---

[7]Consolidated Edison Co., "Population of New York City by Districts, 1910–1948," and John Stern, unpublished paper, Tri-State Regional Plan Commission, March 4, 1977.
[8]Hans Blumenfeld, Hamburg and Toronto: A Comparison," *Plan Canada*, Vol. 11, No. 1, 1970; this volume, pp. 94–109.

goods; second, private and public management offices that seek the ease of mutual contact, including associated consultants, lawyers, accountants, and brokers; and, third, establishments serving the first two groups—these include, in addition to transportation services, hotels, restaurants, and bars.

Although these functions represent growth industries, C.B.D. employment tends to level off or to decrease slightly in large metropolitan areas. In Manhattan below 59th Street, no more people are working today than in 1929. In the four biggest English cities, decrease in C.B.D. employment from 1961 to 1966 ranged from 6% in London to 15% in Manchester. In Toronto, C.B.D. employment has been stable since the early 1950s; widely publicized statements about an alleged strong growth trend are the result of erroneous interpretation of the data on which they are based. Equally fictitious is the alleged "return to the city" by residents. In fact, results of the 1976 census show that the populations of the cities of Montreal and Toronto have each declined by 80,000 persons since 1971. This also corresponds to trends observed in practically all large Western cities; for example, in Hamburg the population of the inner city, corresponding to the city of Toronto, had in 1966 receded one third from its peak and has since further declined, and the population of its 2-square-mile historic core was 85% below its former peak.

The changes brought about by the automobile—the vast extension of the urban area at low density, and the dispersal of employment and service destinations—required in turn the service of the automobile. A common carrier can work only if it can carry an adequate number of people in common, which is only the case if they are traveling at the same time between the same points. Transit service requires concentration of trips in space and in time. When both are high, as in peak-hour trips to and from work in the C.B.D., it remains superior to the automobile. Transit accounted in recent years for about 68% of peak-hour and 50% of all-day trips in the Toronto C.B.D.; both percentages were slightly higher than those found in 1939.

In low-density residential areas, transit faces a Hobson's choice providing frequent service on a few widely spaced lines (resulting in long walks) and offering infrequent service on more and closer spaced lines (resulting in long waits). If all workers traveled in one direction—e.g. towards the center—some transit service might still be possible. But if their jobs are located in three or four different directions, no line can assemble enough passengers. If only homes were dispersed, with work and service destinations concentrated, people might drive to the next transit station and complete their trips by train. But if destinations are also dispersed, as is increasingly the case, this option is precluded. Para-transit, discussed later, may provide a partial answer.

Finally, while work trips increase only with the number of employed persons, nonwork trips increase steeply with increases in real income and in leisure time. Whereas 30 years ago well over half of all workday trips, other than pedestrian, were work trips, recent surveys in North American cities show that their share has dropped to 40% or less. If weekends and holidays are included, work trips may account for not much more than a third of all annual trips. But nonwork trips, being highly dispersed both in place and in time, are much more difficult to serve by transit than are work trips.

It is therefore not surprising that the "modal split" is increasingly in favor of the automobile. In most cities, transit ridership has decreased not only relatively but also absolutely, in Europe as well as in North America—for example, Paris, 1965–1966: 1.5%, and Hamburg, 1958–1966: 18.0% per head.

In relatively recent years, 1973–1975, only 15.6% of all Canadians traveled to work by transit; 75% used automobiles, 9% walked, and the small rest bicycled. Only 9% of the car drivers took an average of 1.48 passengers, 13% of the total, to work. It is interesting to note that, if one quarter of those driving alone had taken another car driver as a passenger, they would have taken as many cars off the road as did transit.

Transit was significant only in the 10 largest metropolitan areas, in particular Toronto (30.5%), Montreal (28.9%), and Ottawa (25.7%). In all of Canada outside these 10 areas, transit's share averaged only 3.7%. However, a surprisingly large number, 21.1% of all workers in these areas and 15.4% in all of Canada, worked at home; even in Metropolitan Toronto 6.8% were in this category. Walkers and cyclists, as well as car passengers, also were more frequent in nonmetropolitan areas. As a result the share of all non-car-drivers deviated less from the national average of 39.9% than did the share of transit riders; it was 45.0% in Toronto and 30.0% outside the 10 big metropolitan areas. In Montreal and Ottawa it was higher than in Toronto, but everywhere in Canada a majority of work travelers were car drivers.[9]

Travel mode also differs strongly by age and sex. Only 30% of workers aged 14–19, but 65% of those 20 and over, drove to work; 25.4% of all female, but only 9.5% of all male, workers used transit. Thus higher female participation in the labor force will tend to raise the share of transit, but this factor is likely to be outweighed as car ownership and use ceases to be a male privilege.

Contrary to widespread opinions, time spent on travel to work averaged only 21 minutes—probably less than it has ever been since spatial separation between place of residence and place of work became the predominant pattern. It was almost twice as long for transit as for car users, 34 versus 19 minutes. Transit speed averaged less than 45% of automobile speed. Travel time and distance in Montreal and Toronto were only slightly higher than the national average.

As expected, there were many more very short trips, under 10 minutes, in nonmetropolitan areas than in the Toronto area, 46.8% versus 20.1%. But 1.1% of the former workers spent over 2 hours on their journey to work, whereas no one in Toronto spent that much time and only 2.5% spent more than 1 hour.

These facts raise doubt about the claim that time spent on the journey to work has deprived the metropolitan suburban family of its father. Also, the observed high peak-hour driving speed strongly indicates that complaints about "congestion" may be due more to psychological than to transport reasons, more to frustration of the will to power than to excessive loss of time.

In any case such complaints have not prevented the predominance of the automobile in short-distance as in long-distance travel. Like its predecessor, the mid-Victorian tightly packed foot-and-hoof city, the transit-based, tentacular metropolis has turned out to be a transitory phenomenon, again based on a time lag, this time between the applications of mechanical (nonmuscular) power to collective and to individual transportation. Once the wide availability of the automobile had broken transit's monopoly of mechanical power, intraurban travel reverted to its age-old pattern of individual door-to-door movement. As these trips were again performed at fairly uniform speed over their entire length, the dot and the ribbon patterns produced by suburban trains and by streetcar lines, respectively, were obliterated in an

---

[9]Chris Hanlon, Statistics Canada, Tourism and Recreation Section, Survey November 1973, June and November 1974, and June and November 1975, Ottawa, February 9, 1977 (unpublished).

unstructured mass of roughly circular shape, only with a vastly greater radius than that of the pretransit city.

In fact, individual travel had never disappeared, and automobile travel has grown as much by replacing its earlier forms as by replacing transit. This is strikingly evident from the results of surveys made in West Germany in 1961 and 1970.[10] The surveys present the share of various modes of all trips to work which crossed municipal boundaries (intramunicipal trips probably had a higher frequency of pedestrian and bicycle trips). The surveys showed that in these 10 years the share of automobile trips increased from 16.6 to 55.3%, a gain of 39.7% percentage points. However, only slightly more than one fifth of this gain was taken from public transport, with the balance from other means of private transport, which decreased as follows: walking, 15.3 to 1.8%; bicycling, 12.7 to 4.3%; motorcycling, 11.8 to 3.2%. Most European countries have gone through the same sequence of modes of private transportation: feet, bicycle, moped, scooter, motorcycle, automobile.

The same survey also showed, for all work trips in the two biggest German provinces, Rhineland-Westphalia and Bavaria, a substantial reduction in the time spent on the journey to work: the share of trips under 15 minutes doubled from 9.8 to 19.1%, while trips over 60 minutes decreased from 21.5 to 10.2%—still far higher than the 2.7% found in Canada. The difference is almost certainly due to the fact that the car ownership rate, though rapidly rising, was still considerably lower in Germany in 1970 than in Canada in 1973–1975.

The reduction in travel time observed in Germany appears to conflict with the notion of a constant "travel-time budget." However, it is not known whether the German workers used their time to make other trips, as residents of small U.S. cities do, according to Zahavi. This last observation is strongly supported by another U.S. study[11] which showed a strong and consistent decrease per household in both number of trips, from 5.1 to 1.9, and in trip-miles, from 40.2 to 22.5. This phenomenon held through five population size groups from over 1 million down to the smallest range, 5000–25,000. One can only speculate about the reasons for this surprising phenomenon. It may be that in large cities the higher density enables people to make more trips, notably for shopping and visiting, on foot, or the reason may reflect the observation of one Canadian student that "people drive more in small towns, because there is nothing else to do."

All indications point to an increasing shift in the modal split to the automobile, if the split is determined entirely by market forces, despite its much greater use of resources as compared to transit. Under present average load conditions for the two competing modes, the automobile requires per passenger-mile about four times as much energy and about 30 times as much road space as does a bus. Also, a bus performs about 30 times as many person-miles annually as does a car. Economies in terms of space and number of vehicles for rapid transit are even greater than those for buses, by a factor of 2 or more. However, these substantial savings are offset to a considerable extent by the high personnel costs of transit.

The cost of a transit passenger-mile, including a carrying charge for public invest-

---

[10] Guenter Brenken, "Inwieweit sind die Berufspendler ein Problem der Raumordnungspolitik?" *Beitraege zur Raumplanung in Hessen, Rheinland. Pfalz, Saarland,* Part 2, pp. 89–91. Hermann Schroedel Verlag, Hannover, 1975.

[11] Yarir T. Dajuni and Gorman Gilbert, *Energy, Urban Form and Transportation Policy,* U.S. Department of Transportation, Nationwide Personal Transportation Study, Report No. 7, 1972.

ment, amounts to at least 10 cents. The user cost of a car-mile (including cost for construction, maintenance, and policing of roads) cannot be exactly determined, but is probably somewhat over 20 cents per mile. Thus, for a car carrying two persons, the user cost per head is only slightly higher than for transit. But, except when parking has to be paid for, more than three quarters of this cost is fixed. In making a choice, the driver compares his or her out-of-pocket cost for gas and oil with the transit fare. In order to become price competitive, transit cost would also have to be transformed, in whole or in part, into fixed cost. Transit service would have to be bought wholesale, as elevator service is bought. The only practicable way to do this is purchase by the municipality, with the cost included in the tax, just as it is included in the rent in the case of the elevator.

Various modes compete, of course, not only by minimizing the user's cost, but, even more, by minimizing his time and inconvenience. In this competition, transit faces four formidable handicaps:

1. The walk to and from the transit station or stop.
2. The wait for the vehicle.
3. The transfer between vehicles (not on all trips).
4. The stop and wait for other passengers to get on or off (intermediate stops).

As a result, the time per mile for transit trips is more than twice that for car trips. Inconvenience cannot be quantified, but is probably much more than twice as great.

In order to make transit more competitive, two sets of approaches have been applied or proposed. First, eliminate one or more of these four handicaps. Second, compensate for them by eliminating all or some of the handicaps facing other street traffic, namely, interference by various types of vehicles (including pedestrians), usually referred to as "congestion." This can be achieved by providing transit with an entirely or partly reserved right-of-way.

"Dial-a-bus" eliminates walking and reduces the inconvenience, if not the time, of waiting. Waiting time can be reduced by improved, possibly automated bus passenger information. Number of transfers can be reduced by routing, inconvenience by station design, and waiting time by improved scheduling and bus passenger information, with the aid of computer technology. Intermediate stops can be greatly reduced by express buses or trains; the proposed, technically but hardly economically feasible transfer of either passengers or vehicles to and from moving trains would eliminate them entirely. The proposed "individual rapid transit," computer-guided small cabins, would eliminate all handicaps except walking. While the required technologies are known, their application is still problematic; in addition there are unanswered economic and behavioral questions. This is even truer of proposals, such as "STARR," which would allow these same cabins to be operated manually on the street system. Besides, in this role they are in fact automobiles.

More successful has been the second method, reduction of interference by protection of the transit right-of-way. Completely grade-separated or "rapid transit" systems, because of their high capital cost, can be justified only when they can attract high passenger volumes, generally only in cities of 1 million or more. "Commuter railroads," equally grade-separated, carry smaller volumes at lower frequencies between more widely spaced stations. Because of their fairly high speed, they have been better able than surface transit to compete with the automobile. In the United States, where the automobile accounts for about 90% of all urban trips, surface transit decreased by 24% from 1960 to 1970, but rapid transit only by 6%, and commuter railroads held their own.

More impressive is the record of the Toronto Transit Commission, which increased the number of revenue passengers by 54% in the 13 years from 1962 to 1975. This rate of increase was 10% higher than that of the metropolitan population, resulting in an average of 166 trips per head in 1975. This 54% increase was achieved by an increase in vehicle-miles by 96% and of total cost (in current dollars) of 130%. The expansion of the service was made possible by heavy capital investments, as well as operating subsidies from public funds. By the end of this year, the cost for every Metropolitan Toronto resident is likely to amount to about $90, two thirds paid by the users through fares, and one third by the community as a public service.

The public service consists in reduction of the high social costs of the automobile, which may well surpass in value the service to the transit user. These costs—or "malefits"—fall into four groups:

1. To other movements: interference with goods, service, and transit vehicles, and with pedestrians, as well as extension of all distances as a result of large land requirements for parking.

2. To the environment: air pollution, noise, damage to plant life, and ugliness of parking lots, service stations, and garages, as well as of traffic and advertising signs of a size calculated to attract the attention of fast-moving drivers. Disruption of established neighborhoods by increased traffic, new arteries, and, in particular, freeways.

3. To those who permanently or temporarily do not have access to car use, primarily the poor and the infirm: catastrophic reduction of their mobility by the vast extension of distances due to an automobile-dominated settlement pattern, and to the sharp reduction of transit services because of loss of customers to the automobile.

4. To both users and nonusers: danger to life, limb, and property from traffic accidents, as well as resulting nervous tension.

To these has now been added concern about the conservation of energy. As a result there are strong demands for the promotion of transit. Transit probably will be financed increasingly as a public service and also assisted by regulatory measures to protect its right-of-way, in the form of reserved curb lanes for buses and reserved center strips for trains. The latter, continuing in the most congested central areas on a fully protected right-of-way, and in the least congested peripheral ones without special protection as ordinary streetcars, have been operated successfully for many decades under the name of "subway-surface streetcars" both in the United States and more recently in Europe, and are now being promoted as "light rail transit" or "intermediate transit." Regulatory measures may also include metering of road access, entrance tolls to congested areas (in use in Singapore), road pricing, and parking restrictions, as well as high all-day parking fees.

While much can be done to increase transit use, its characteristics of fixed routes and fixed schedules make it unattractive for many types of trips. Some of these might be served by so-called para-transit, various modes intermediate between riding transit and driving one's own car. They range from variants of the automobile mode to the above-mentioned "dial-a-bus."

Closest to the conventional driving of one's own car is driving a hired car. This does not directly reduce the number of automobile-miles, but may reduce car ownership and thereby indirectly also the number of car trips. The same is true of the use of taxis, which might be made cheaper and thereby more attractive by changes in licensing and tax policies. Also worth considering is the use of taxis as "jitneys," picking up and delivering passengers along their routes, which may be fixed or flexible. Jitneys play a great role in "less developed" countries, where they are price competitive with transit, because the labor cost of the driver is low relative to the capital cost of transit equipment. In a capital-rich and high-wage country like Canada, their cost would be closer to taxi than to bus fare. This is the case even with the dial-a-bus, which may be regarded as a big-vehicle jitney.

More promising may be those forms of para-transit in which the drivers do not have to be paid, because they make the trip for their own purposes and take passengers with them, either without charge or in the form of shared-cost car pooling. While car passengers account for a high percentage of social-recreational trips, they account for only 17.8% of those traveling to work by car in Canada. High fuel costs have not led to an increase in car pooling in Canada, nor have they had that effect in West Germany, where they account for only 14.2% of work trips by car.

Attempts to encourage car pooling by a matching service provided by the government of Ontario have had little success. More effective have been initiatives of employers in the form of putting a van at the disposal of an employee who agrees to carry a specified number of passengers (less than a full load) to and from work. The incentive, in addition to the right to use the van in his or her free time, consists in the right to keep the fare of any additional passenger whom the driver may find independently, up to the capacity of the vehicle. Similar initiatives on the part of the community have also succeeded in a few cases.

Para-transit certainly deserves more attention than it has received in the past. It is a useful supplement to transit, but is not likely to lead to a significant decrease in vehicle movement.

CONCLUSION

Our survey of the historical interaction between the development of cities and of transport points to an alarming increase in automobile movement. Are there forces in sight which may modify or reverse this trend?

Obviously the present pattern of cities and transport is a result of our Western way of life, with its emphasis on "success" in terms of making money and pursuing a career. Many, particularly of the younger generation, are turning away from these "values" toward a different life-style, putting more emphasis on personal fulfillment in a healthy and pleasant environment. Certainly, if we all followed the example of Voltaire's Candide, who, after a long and adventurous life, desired nothing better than to "cultivate his garden," we would have no transportation problem. However, few of us are as old and fewer as wise as Candide. Whatever the new life-style may turn out to be, decreased desire for personal mobility is not likely to be part of it.

But even if we do not *want* to restrict our mobility, will we not be *forced* to curtail it by the "energy crisis," by shortages of, and/or high prices for, automobile fuel? A shortage is the result of an imbalance between supply and demand. As the federal government has many means to influence both, a shortage could result only from a lack of foresight and planning. A price rise seems inevitable—if only to dampen demand—at least in the short- and medium-term future. In estimating its possible effect, it is well to remember that the wellhead price of oil accounted for no more than 10% of the cost of owning and operating a car in 1973. A 300% increase in the wellhead price (in constant dollars) thus means only a 30% increase in cost to the driver—if he or she continues to drive the same type of car. By switching to a smaller car with twice as many miles per gallon as the absurdly wasteful ones now predominant in the United States and Canada, a person can reduce the increase to a negligible 5%, with no significant reduction in use value. It is probable that such a switch, rather than a reduction in car-miles, will be the main effect of rising fuel costs.

The only other means which could reduce the increase in automobile travel are changes in the urban pattern which would reduce travel distances and/or lead to a greater use of transit.

The most important factors influencing the modal split between car and transit remain city size and the closely correlated factor of density. As shown earlier, and as confirmed by many other observations, the bigger the city, the smaller is the mileage traveled per head of population and the larger is the percentage of miles traveled which is performed by transit. If governments really assigned highest priority to energy conservation, they would do everything in their power to promote concentration of the population in the biggest city. For well-known reasons, however, they will no doubt continue to pursue the opposite goal of "decentralization." Governments may be more willing to promote higher densities, in particular at rapid transit stations and in subcenters by means such as zoning, subdivision control, and possibly also public landownership. But it is a naive illusion to believe that any conceivable amount of rapid transit building and density promotion can ever restore the pattern of the preautomobile city.

To the contrary, there are at least three emerging trends which point to a spreading out of urban residents far beyond the present metropolitan area, tending to produce regions comprising many thousands of square miles which are neither city nor country, as well as both city and country.

1. The self-sufficient house, equipped with a system for the use of solar and wind energy and the recycling of sewage and garbage. This would enable fully served houses to be built far beyond the reach of piped sanitary services.

2. The replacement of person travel by new means of communication, such as closed television and computer consoles. The worker would not have to move to his or her job, because electronics would move the job to the home. This would drastically reduce commuting, but would enable people to live far away from their jobs in surroundings requiring long automobile travel for every type of trip.

3. The 4-day workweek. While replacement of commuting by communication would probably affect only a relatively small number of people, the 4-day week could affect all workers. In combination with a 48-week work year, this would mean

that the worker would have to sleep only 144 out of 365 nights near his or her workplace. It is likely that the person would prefer to spend the others in the country by establishing a rural family residence.

Such a pattern would respond to deep-seated and widespread desires. In answer to a questionnaire concerning their preferences for a place to live, 80% of all respondents in France opted for "a house in the countryside."

Their dream may come true. But the implied proliferation of automobile trips will be a nightmare.

Chapter 41

TRANSPORTATION AND LAND USE

In attempting to understand, predict, and plan the development of an area, two main approaches may be distinguished. The first relies on the extrapolation of long-term trends for large groups of observable phenomena; it may, as a second step, attempt to break down the resultant overall picture into some of its component elements. The second method attempts to evaluate the motivations and actions of the various individuals and groups which interact in the development of the area and to build up a composite picture from these parts.

In predicting population and employment, for instance, the first approach usually applies one or more variants of the ratio method of projection. The second approach might start by evaluating the prospects of all "basic" industries actually or potentially operating in the area, then proceed by estimating the "multiplier" effect on "service" industries, and finally derive total population by estimating the number of dependents of those employed in each or all of these industries. In projecting land use, the first approach might extrapolate the trends of major land uses as to location and density; the second might delve into the various factors motivating all locators and derive future land distribution as the composite result of their actions.

Britton Harris has characterized the first approach as "static and descriptive," and the second as "dynamic and behavioristic." This characterization should be qualified. A trend describes change over time—a dynamic process, and it describes the net result of the behavior of all agents which have brought about the changes. The reason for denying the dynamic and behavioristic character of the first approach is primarily the fact that it cannot—as does the second approach—explicitly study the effects of *new* forces which are not reflected in the observed trends. It is concluded that the projection of trends is invalid if and when such new factors start to operate. In particular it is assumed that extrapolation of trends must be modified to take into account decisions of public policy.

I consider this line of reasoning faulty. A trend, as a description of the net result of all past behavior, reflects the impact of many factors, including public policy decisions, which have started to operate during the period described by the trend. Therefore, if it is claimed that a new factor, which will be operative in the future, requires a modification of the extrapolation of a trend, it is not sufficient to prove that

---

Source: Discussion paper for the National Capital Transportation Agency Conference, Annapolis, Md., sponsored by the Washington Center for Metropolitan Studies, October 1961.

this particular factor has not operated in the past. It must be demonstrated that its impact will be different from the impacts of all the factors which have shaped the trend in the past.

This problem may be illustrated by an example. The population of the Toronto Metropolitan Area has been projected, by use of the ratio method, to grow from 9.5% of the population of Canada in 1958 to 10.5% in 1980. It was suggested that this figure should be raised because of the anticipated impact of the opening of the St. Lawrence Seaway—the result of a public policy decision. However, it was decided that the impact of the seaway was not likely to be greater than had been the impact of the establishment, generally by public policy decision, of other new transportation facilities by road, rail, air, water, and pipeline during the period from which the trend of relative population growth had been derived.

To sum up this point, the difference between the two approaches can be defined simply: the second approach deals with dynamic and behavioristic factors explicitly, while the first one takes them into account implicitly. The first employs aggregation; the second, disaggregation. The advantage of the second approach—being able to deal explicitly with known new factors, in particular public policy decisions—is obvious. The less obvious advantage of the first method is its ability to account for not only known but also unknown future factors and policy decisions. It is not as simplistic as it looks.

While the aggregative and disaggregative approaches start from opposite ends, there is, of course, no reason why both should not be applied to the same problem, in the hope that they will meet in the middle and produce the same result. If the end results are different, it becomes necessary to reconcile them, and this involves deciding how much confidence is to be placed in one or the other method. It seems to me that the answer depends on the extent—in time and space—of the universe under study. In dealing with a short-term employment forecast for a small community, for instance, it will be preferable to use estimates of future employment in all existing or proposed establishments. In dealing with a long-term population forecast for a large metropolitan area, on the other hand, extrapolation of a long-term trend is more likely to reflect the impact of the many unknown private and public decisions that will be made.

The claim that a projection can account for future public decisions is based on a hypothesis which may be formulated as follows: people pursue the same goals as citizens, through the political process, which they pursue as buyers and sellers, through the market. This statement implies the further hypothesis that the weights of various groups in the political process are proportional to their weights in the market. Both hypotheses warrant exploration and discussion.

It may be worthwhile to review the development of research in the fields of transportation and land use in the light of the foregoing considerations.

TRANSPORTATION RESEARCH

In the development of transportation research four steps may be distinguished, extending the field both in space and in time, with the methods developed at each step retaining their importance and being integrated into the methods developed at later steps.

At the first step research was mainly directed to measuring present traffic at specific points or on specific lines, with the general purpose of eliminating bottlenecks.

As experience showed that the corrective measures undertaken on the basis of such limited research were soon made ineffective by growing traffic, attention shifted to prediction of future traffic volumes by means of extrapolation of growth trends of traffic volumes and/or of such factors as car ownership, population, and employment. Also, observations of changes in traffic behavior resulting from the opening of relief routes led to the development of indifference curves.

Simultaneously it became obvious that study of individual routes or channels had to be extended spatially to cover the total system of traffic movements within a given area. At this (the third) step the technique of the origin and destination survey was developed. On the basis of such a survey, a system of desire lines can be developed, and predictions can be made as to the volumes of traffic which would use various existing and proposed routes if the desired movements from each origin to each destination remained constant.

Thus the need for a fourth step became evident: the development of a system of predicting future origins and destinations, desire lines, and traffic volumes. This required the development of methods simulating traffic behavior on the basis of the analysis of a great volume of observations of behavior, made possible by the use of electronic computers. The observations, derived primarily from origin and destination (O & D) surveys, concern the "trip generation" of various units of land use, population, and so on, and the choices of destinations made by individuals of various characteristics for various purposes. The choices are dependent on the friction of space in terms of route distance, travel time, and cost, as well as the choices of route and mode, dependent on the same and other variables. From the results of these observations, expressed in various mathematical terms, a "model" of travel behavior is built. By feeding into the model various assumptions on land use and transportation facilities, traffic volumes on each link of the system can be predicted.

Transportation research, as seen in this very rough outline of the present state of the art, has developed fairly sophisticated scientific methods. There are, of course, a number of aspects calling for further research. Four may be mentioned here.

1. Truck-trip generation of various land uses.

2. Pedestrian trips, in order to measure the correlation of total trip generation for various purposes with population characteristics, such as income, household composition, age, and sex.

3. Travel behavior of persons by industry, by occupation, and by sex, in particular for length and mode of work trips.

4. Variables determining the modal split between private and public transportation, in particular the impact of levels of fares and of parking fees.

LAND USE RESEARCH

In contrast to the scientific methods employed in traffic research, the basic data which are processed by these methods, that is, the projections of land use, are still mainly derived by "handicraft" methods, by intuition more or less guided by experience. This state of affairs has stimulated attempts to construct land use models.

Land use prediction requires three steps:

1. Estimates of total population and industry in the area.

2. Estimates of the quantity of land requirements of population and industry, based on assumptions of densities and service standards.

3. Knowledge of the location of land uses and of the distribution of population and industry within the area.

Steps 2 and 3 interact and can only be developed together. In the development of estimates for each of the steps both aggregative and disaggregative methods can be used.

Implicit in any prediction concerning the distribution and density of land uses is the assumption that they are correlated with travel time. In other words, it is assumed that all locators strive to minimize time and to maximize space (i.e., minimize land cost), that in this process they are willing to trade time for space and vice versa, and that the resultant competition produces a distribution by which each locator achieves an optimum balance of time and space.

Thus, while transportation research predicts traffic flows and transportation planning designs transportation facilities on the basis of land use distribution, land uses can be distributed only on the basis of travel time, which in turn depends on transportation facilities—the well-known "chicken-and-egg" relation. Therefore a comprehensive plan, dealing with both land uses and transportation facilities, attempts to achieve a "balance" of transportation and land use. The balance can be tested by a process of iteration, alternatively assuming land use and transportation as independent and dependent variables, respectively.

However, while traffic desire lines can be derived with a fair degree of confidence, provided that distribution of land uses and models of travel behavior are given, it is questionable whether land uses can be predicted if only transportation facilities and models of travel behavior are given.

In considering the use of the transportation system as a tool to bring about a desirable distribution of land uses—usually referred to as a "desirable form of metropolitan development"—a question arises: how effective are transportation facilities in determining land use?

IMPACT OF TRANSPORTATION ON LAND USE

We all know that different modes of transportation result in different forms of land development. Specifically, a significant difference should be noted between the effects of individual (private) and collective (public) means of transportation. Individual transportation, whether on foot, on bicycle, or in a private automobile, is "door-to-door" transportation. When it is predominant within a fairly densely populated, or "urban," area, it will always be supplied with a network of paths in all directions, allowing door-to-door movement at fairly uniform speeds. It is, as the Germans call it, "areal"—as opposed to "linear"—transportation. Consequently travel time is roughly proportional to straight-line distance, and growth tends to occur fairly evenly in all directions, without a definite "structure" in the relation of developed and undeveloped land, or in the distribution of densities on the land, except for a gradual decrease in density from the center towards the periphery.

Any trip by public transportation, on the other hand, always involves at least two changes of mode, usually between modes of greatly varying speeds. The transfer points (stations or stops) become points of attraction for locators; a sequence of transfer points becomes a line of attraction. When the technology of transportation favors widely spaced stops and great differences in speeds—as in the combination of walking and riding steam-propelled commuter trains—a "point" or cluster pattern of settlement results. When stops are close together and the difference in speed between the two modes is moderate, as with walking and riding streetcars or buses, linear patterns emerge.

When and where public transportation is the predominant mode of person movement, a definite structure can be created by the location of transportation lines alone. Areas not served by these lines are kept "open" simply by lack of accessibility. However, where, as in contemporary North America, car ownership and paved roads are so nearly universal as to make accessibility merely a function of straight-line distance, the impact of the location of transportation facilities on the structure of land use is much more limited. It may have a modest influence on the distribution of densities; but any substantial modification of the pattern of ubiquitous "sprawl," in particular the preservation of open space, can be brought about only by far-reaching measures of direct public control, which requires a strong consensus of public opinion concerning the goals of metropolitan development.

Part Seven
Prospects

Chapter 42

THE CHANGING URBAN ENVIRONMENT OF NORTH AMERICA

NORTH AMERICA IN A GLOBAL CONTEXT

Urban problems and attempts at their solutions have always been approached in the national context of North America, of the United States and of Canada, respectively. With the growing recognition that there are "Limits of Growth," to quote the title of the well-known study of the Club of Rome, we are beginning to realize the relevance of the fact that the 7% of mankind living in our two countries account for well over a third of all consumption of raw materials on this globe and of all pollution. Certainly, if the growing population of the world adopted the current "American way of life," the limits of growth would indeed be reached in the foreseeable future. While the recent "shortages" of power and of food actually have nothing to do with these limits, they have called attention to their existence. It may therefore be appropriate to review the global context in which our own urban development proceeds.

GLOBAL TRENDS AND PROBLEMS

Growth of Population

In this century both population and production (as well as consumption) of raw materials per head of population have increased at an unprecedented rate, resulting in an even higher rate for their product, global production. But even if only one of them grew indefinitely, it would finally reach the limit.

Many demographers have tried to arouse people by calculating the year in which there would be standing room only on earth. Such calculations are not too meaningful; *any* trend which continues indefinitely at some point reaches infinity (or zero). In the real world, trends tend to follow a logistic curve. What matters are the factors determining the shape of the curve.

Source: Energy Resources and Development Administration Yearbook, University of Kansas, Lawrence, 1974.

Population growth is usually analyzed in terms of birth and death rates. This can be quite misleading, because both rates are strongly dependent on the age-sex composition of the population in a given year. The significant data are life expectancy and fertility rate. Life expectancy in all developed countries is now slightly over 70 years and is not likely to increase dramatically. In underdeveloped countries it is considerably lower, but generally rising. Nobody openly advocates slowing population growth by reducing life expectancy.

The great question mark is the fertility rate. It looks as if the rate has been completely erratic, and some demographers, like Kingsley Davis, simply state that it "goes in cycles." It seems to me that the changes can be understood as the result of the interaction of two trends. "Development" or "modernization," involving industrialization, urbanization, secularization, and the like, leads to a decrease in the fertility rate to a point at or below parity. This long-term trend is overlaid by a short-term trend determined by optimistic or pessimistic expectations, which, in turn, are conditioned by the business cycle, as well as by political successes and failures. In the United States these led to a steep decline during the depression, a steep rise in the postwar era, which the late Dwight Mills called "the great American celebration," and a renewed steep decline in the subsequent great American katzenjammer. At present, the fertility rate is below parity in the United States and Canada as in practically all developed countries, east and west. While data are spotty, the fertility rate is decreasing also in most developing countries; in some, such as Sri Lanka, Singapore, and, most significantly, China, the decrease is dramatic.

The lesson is clear: "We know that one can stop the increase of births with an elevation of life," in the words of Adam Schaff of Poland, one of the members of the Club of Rome; or, as his fellow member Eduard Pestel, former head of the Volkswagen Works, put it, "One does not make children in an ant-heap city as one does in the country, with a traditional way of life."

Those who want to withhold aid from the developing countries until they have slowed their population growth are putting the cart before the horse. The way to slow down population growth is to accelerate development. A necessary, though not sufficient, condition for such acceleration is greatly increased aid from the developed countries in the form of industrial products. This should preclude any attempt to improve the quality of life in North America by simply reducing production. We may have enough products, but the world certainly needs more.

Growth of Production

"If culture develops spontaneously and is not consciously directed, it leaves a desert behind" (Karl Marx).

The exponential growth of production threatens survival. The threats arise from the opposite ends of the process. The growing input takes too many raw materials out of the natural environment, exhausting resources. The growing output puts too many pollutants into the natural environment, exhausting its absorptive capacity. On a finite globe, growth cannot continue indefinitely.

Evidently there are limits, but how can they be defined? Many discussions of these questions deal with them in terms of the "consumption" of "stocks." It is well to recall the remark of Lavoisier: "Nothing is created; nothing is destroyed." Matter (as well as energy) does not disappear; it changes its form.

In some of its forms it becomes a "pollutant." I do not know why we use this Latin term rather than the good Anglo-Saxon, four-letter word "dirt." "Dirt," goes an old English saying, "is something in the wrong place"; or, as Paracelsus phrased it: "Everything is a poison; nothing is a poison." In the right place, at the right time, and in the right quantity anything is beneficial. For instance, we are greatly worried about the eutrophication of our rivers and lakes. But the Greek word eu means "good." The water is too good; it contains too many plant nutrients, primarily phosphates and nitrates. The result is a lush growth of algae which absorb all of the water's oxygen and thereby kill off all other aquatic life. But if the same water is used to irrigate land, it produces rich crops of vegetables; if it is brought in diluted form into fish ponds, it produces a rich crop of carp; or if suitable algae are cultivated, they can be processed into a very nutritious and tasty food, as is now being done in Japan.

We must discard as obsolete the notion of "wastes" that have to be "disposed" of, and think in terms of the reuse and recycling of the by-products of production and consumption. Recycling is also largely the answer to the exhaustion of those of our nonrenewable resources which are recoverable, in particular metals. The limits of growth are, in fact, defined by the limits of recycling.

This is not to say that there are no limits. We are presently recycling, if I am correctly informed, about 40% of the iron which we use. We could certainly increase this percentage by collecting more scrap. An increase to 50% probably would hardly affect the cost of producing steel; but with further increases the cost would rise exponentially, because more and more labor would be required to collect ever smaller and more dispersed pieces of scrap. The cost would far exceed the cost of mining and processing iron ore into the same amount of pig iron. As technological progress is more effective in mining and processing raw materials than in collecting and separating "wastes," the ratio of matter thrown away to that reused has been rapidly shifting towards greater waste, which, in most cases, also means greater pollution. Immediate economic gain is an inadequate guide for man's relation to nature.

One hundred years ago Friedrich Engels warned as follows:

Let us not, however, flatter ourselves overmuch on account of our human conquest over nature. For each such conquest takes its revenge on us. Each of them, it is true, has in the first place the consequences on which we counted, but in the second and third place it has quite different, unforeseen effects which only too often cancel out the first . . . . Thus at every step we are reminded that we by no means rule over nature like a conqueror over a foreign people, like someone standing outside nature—but that we, with flesh, blood, and brain, belong to nature, and exist in its midst, and that all our mastery of it consists in the fact that we have the advantage over all other beings of being able to know and correctly apply its laws.

We do not know nearly enough of these laws and of the most effective ways to apply them. We need not less, but much more, science and technology—and of the right kind. If the scientific-technological capability now absorbed in war preparation were devoted to developing plentiful and less polluting sources of energy and raw materials and more effective methods of recycling, the dangers of exhaustion of raw materials and of disruption of the biosphere by pollution would be greatly reduced. They would not disappear; there is no life without risk. "The criterion for introducing a new technology is not that it should be safe. Nothing is safe. It is that it should be as safe [as] or safer than the technology that it replaces."[1]

[1] J. Fremlin, "The Hazards of Nuclear Power," *Scientific World*, Vol. 3, pp. 7–11, 1973.

Evidently the use of methods which take into account their consequences "in the second and third place" will add to the cost of their "first-place" products. It has been estimated that the elimination of serious pollution would require about 3–4% of the gross national product of the United States. This is no more than the average annual increase in productivity during the last 25 years. However, since last year this trend has stopped and even reversed. Are we at a turning point?

Growth of Productivity

Productivity of labor must be distinguished from the volume of production. The latter may grow without any increase in the former, simply by using more labor. Similarly, increased productivity may mean less labor (and more leisure) for the same volume of production.

In the fifth century B.C. a Chinese scholar, Han-Fei-Tsu, wrote, "There will be more people and less wealth," thus anticipating the familiar Malthusian thesis. In the twentieth century another Chinese, Mao-Tse-Tung, replied, "With each new mouth a new pair of hands is born." What Mao did not say, but possibly implied, is that also a new brain is born.

All "value" and all "utility" are produced by the application of human labor to natural resources. Malthus, looking at the world through the eyes of the landowner, focused on the fact that the production of an additional bushel of wheat would require more labor than did the production of the preceding one, because it would have to be applied to poorer soil; in other words, the productivity of labor was bound to decrease, assuming implicitly that all other things were equal. But other things have not been equal. Those who look at the world through the eyes of the worker, like Marx and Mao, have focused on the fact that the invention and development of new and better ways of working can and do increase the productivity of labor.

These two facts have influenced the productivity of labor in opposite directions all through the history of mankind. We have been forced to shift from the richest and most accessible soils and ores to ever poorer and less accessible ones. But, on the other hand, again and again, the resulting increased activity has been carried out with less human effort, thanks to improved methods of work. There is reason to believe that, contrary to Malthus' assumptions, population increase has contributed to this increase in productivity in several ways:

1. With twice the population, there is a probability of twice as many innovators, other things being equal.

2. Other things are not equal, because a larger and, in particular, denser population leads to greater division and specialization of labor.

3. Higher density, resulting in increased contacts, stimulates emulation, leading to greater development of innovations and to their wider and faster adoption.

Certainly, from the Palaeolithicum to this day, but particularly during the last 200 years since the industrial revolution, the positive impact of innovation on productivity has far outweighed the negative impact of the growing "scarcity" of natural resources. A major element in this "progress"—again most spectacular during the past 200 years—has been the more efficient use of various forms of solar energy, from human to animal muscle to wind and water to fossil fuels. As fossil fuel, and particularly as oil, energy is stored in a form so convenient for preservation, transportation, and transformation into mechanical movement that we have come to rely on it for 90% of our total energy use. Now we are faced with an "energy crisis" in addition to crises in the supply of food and of water.

Energy, Food, and Water

Energy. The energy conveyed to the earth's surface by the sun's rays and radiated back into outer space exceeds, many hundreds of times, the total captured for all human uses. There is no danger of an absolute "shortage" in the foreseeable future. However, we have neglected utilization of many other forms of energy—wind, tidal, and geothermal energy, but, in particular, direct solar radiation—in favor of the cheaper use of fossil fuels. These fuels have stored solar energy in carbohydrates over millions of years, by photosynthesis. As combustion reduces these carbohydrates, highly organized molecules, to carbon and hydrogen, they represent a nonrecoverable resource, which, at present rates of use, will be depleted in the foreseeable future. This, however, is not the only reason which makes it urgent to reduce their use by replacing them as rapidly as possible with other sources of energy and by eliminating waste. First, they are by far the most important source of pollution of both the atmosphere and the oceans. Second, there *may* be dangers of a radical change in the temperature of the earth's surface, upward by increasing the carbon dioxide layer, or possibly downward by the increase in aerosols. Third, burning hydrocarbons means wasting highly organized matter capable of being transformed into many "raw materials" for the chemical and food industries, in particular proteins. These are better reasons than the so-called energy crisis to combat the waste of fossil fuels, of which North American automobility is the most conspicuous example.

Food. The rather sudden disappearance of the mountains of unsalable food which had been piling up in the world's rich countries during the past decade has caused some of their spokesmen to ascribe the acute starvation in some of the poor ones to the "Malthusian law." This is a false alibi; the 10 million tons of grain estimated by the United Nations commission as required to save these countries from starvation amounts to less than 1% of the annual world harvest and much less than 10% of the amount which we in North America feed to our livestock every year.

The fact that starvation is not due to agricultural production having reached some "limits of growth" does not mean that there are no limits. The biosphere maintains itself as an interaction of a number of cyclical processes. The goal of humanistic planning and management must be to maximize the life-sustaining flows through the bodies of human beings and of animals and plants that are useful (in the broadest sense) to human beings.

We are very far from this goal in our attitudes. I have already referred to eutrophication. We also complain about both air pollution and heat pollution from thermal power plants. But their outputs—water, heat, carbon dioxide—are all necessary inputs into plant growth. Could we channel them into hothouses? Animals, including human beings, feed on plants; plants feed on animal excrements. The Chinese would not have become the most numerous nation on earth if they did not carefully feed their crops with their night soil. We prefer to flush everything down the drain and to forget about the second half of the cycle. We also reduce the potential crop area by paving over excessive amounts of land.

Water. Of the inputs into plants—minerals, heat, light, air, and water—lack of water may be the most widespread constraint on agriculture. Certainly, concern about "shortage" and "excessive consumption" of water is widespread.

Evidently, water is not really "consumed"; the same total amount circulates year after year. About 80% evaporates from the oceans and 20% from the continents, but 27% comes down on the continents; the difference of 7% is returned to the oceans by rivers. How much of this 27% is channeled through the bodies of human beings or of plants and animals useful to them? I would guess that the percentage is very small. One way of increasing it is diversion of river flow from the ocean to the irrigation of fields, already occurring to a minor extent.

Recently a full-page ad by an ecology group, published in the Sunday New York Times, claimed that the United States is already overpopulated, primarily because of lack of water. There certainly is more information available on this than I have explored; but my very crude calculation indicates an annual precipitation of 3–4 *million* gallons for every man, woman, or child in the United States. This is certainly a more than adequate quantity. If it seems insufficient, the reason is that its quality has been impaired as a result of the failure to recycle materials which instead have become pollutants. There is in the United States no excess of people, and the shortage is not of water, but of wisdom.

URBAN GROWTH IN NORTH AMERICA

Impact of Urban Concentration on Global Growth Problems

The lack of actual shortage makes the dangers no less real. We are failing to improve our control of the life-sustaining cycles fast enough to keep pace with the threats arising from the growth of population and production. Many of those concerned with this global threat, including such first-rate minds as the French agronomist René Dumont, see the concentration of people in big cities as substantially contributing to the danger.

It seems to me that this attitude is more emotional than rational, conditioned more by the high visibility of masses of people present, of raw materials coming in, and of waste going out, than by comparing the effect of 5 million people living in a metropolis with the effect of the same 5 million living, at the same level, in 100 towns of 50,000 each, or in 1000 towns of 5000 each.

Three of the most frequently emphasized reasons for concern are as follows:

1. Rapid population growth.

2. Loss of arable land.

3. Motor vehicle movement.

First, there is a well-established inverse correlation between fertility rate and size of city. As mentioned earlier, urbanization is the most effective means to reduce population growth.

Second, there is an equally well-established correlation of city size with density. The same number of people living in small towns cover a far greater amount of land with buildings, roads, and parking areas.

Third, only in big cities can a substantial percentage of person movement be performed by transit rather than by car. Also, goods transport between small towns has to rely largely on trucks. By and large, only big cities receive and produce loads large enough to be served by rail, water, and pipeline.

These considerations, while far from negligible, are of course not sufficient to answer the hotly debated question of the "growth ethic" and its counterpart.

The "Growth Ethic"

In recent years the naive and complacent self-image of planners as guardians of the public good has come under challenge. There is no such thing as a uniquely determined "public good." Such a concept can be defined only in relation to a desired image of society, which is inevitably conditioned by the different life experiences of different classes of society.

It may be less generally recognized that there are real conflicts not only between different classes, but also between different roles played by the same members of a community. Every citizen is engaged in three roles: first, "making a living" as a participant in the economy; second, "living" as a resident; and, finally, as a taxpayer.

There is no doubt that the unprecedented and still continuing growth of cities since the industrial revolution has been due to economic reasons. From this angle there can be no question that "bigger is better." Growth means higher values for the owner of real estate (including the homeowner), more sales for the businessman, more jobs for the worker. If growth also means disruption of the environment, that is the price of progress, which has to be paid without batting an eyelash.

In its crudest form, the "growth ethic" simply means bigger and better pockets to be picked. Is this an ethic?

The "No-Growth Ethic"

The "growth ethic," hardly questioned before the 1960s, is now under universal attack. Municipality after municipality seeks means to limit its growth, in the name of "protection of the environment" or "protection of the quality of life."

While the verbalizations of the goal and of the motivations are new, restrictive attitudes by municipalities are not. They were and are conceived in the interest of their citizens as taxpayers. In the United States and Canada the higher levels of government have assigned to the municipalities obligations which grow with the volume of persons, in particular children of school age, and revenues which grow with the volume of real estate. This has forced the municipalities into fiscal planning which keeps out moderately priced family housing, and invites the development of industry, commerce, and apartments for wealthy bachelors.

While the keeping-out side of these policies continues to be enthusiastically supported by the citizens, development, welcome to them as taxpayers, is an unwelcome neighbor to them as residents. In the past the active citizens solved this conflict by locating such developments on open land or in passive low-income neighborhoods. But as open land becomes scarce and low-income neighborhoods become active, this solution becomes increasingly difficult.

What is new is that more and more citizens put their main emphasis on their role as residents, on the city as a place for living rather than for making a living. This is to be welcomed, but it has led to a desire to fence off the place. In responding to questions concerning their desires for the future of Greater Vancouver, various groups proposed a great variety of amenities. But all were unanimous in opposing any further growth. All these good people want an attractive city—but they do not want it to attract other people.

As one councilman in another area characterized this attitude, "I am safely on board; now pull up the ladder." Is this an ethic?

Growth and Ethics

A decade or two ago, when people complained about the effects of the growth of cities, I used to say, "What you are really complaining about is not cities, but people." At that time most of them denied being misanthropes. But now it is fashionable to proclaim that people are a nuisance, that there are too many of them. It is, of course, always the other fellow who is one too many (just as it is the other car that causes the congestion).

You and I, by being alive, prove that we consider human life to be better than nonlife. If life is good, then 2 billion lives are better than 1 billion—other things being equal. I have discussed at length the danger that the limitations of the earth may make things unequal. Nobody knows what the optimum size of the earth's population may be. We do know that it is not likely to level off at less than 7 billion. We know that the most promising way to slow the growth is to reduce the fertility rate by speeding up the transition from a "traditional" to a "modern" way of life. For a small number of people this transition can be accelerated by migration from "developing" to "developed" countries. To advocate restriction on immigration to our countries as a means of slowing global population growth, as is being done, makes sense only on the assumption that the rejected would-be immigrant will starve to death. From this attitude it is only a small step to the gas chambers of Auschwitz.

Whatever the net immigration to North America may be, natural increase will continue for the next 30 years, and all increase from both sources will have to be accommodated by urban areas. To limit the growth of an urban area in order to avoid growing pains means shifting these pains to others. Such policies are unethical.

I have already said that I also consider it unethical to deliberately slow down overall production in the face of the dire lack of all kinds of products in most countries. This does not mean that our own production of waste and waste of production are less unethical. But I cannot help wondering why our no-growth advocates have so little to say about the worst aspect of all: the massive production of means of destruction, the armaments race.

To sum up, yes, there is a growth ethic, a categorical imperative to work for the quantitative and qualitative growth of human life.

Chapter 43

THE FUTURE OF CANADIAN CITIES

Boyce Richardson, a Montreal journalist, has for several years been involved in the problems of Canadian cities. In this book he puts together his observations and attempts to draw conclusions from them. He calls his book "a layman's report for laymen." As a good journalist, he is a good listener and an observer with a sharp eye and ear for detail and, in particular, for the "human interest side." Occasionally this seduces him into overloading his case studies with an excessive mass of detail.

Richardson is aware that what are usually called "problems of the city" are really problems of society. They are *in* the city because the people are there. Right at the beginning of his book he states, "The basic decisions are political ones" and defines as the key decision: "redistribute wealth." But he seems to overlook the interdependence of political and economic power. He sums up the argument of his book as "to restrain the powers of the big corporations by injecting a public-interest dimension into the decisions they make." Corporate capitalism is accepted, but the leopard is expected to change its spots. But the mode of production determines the mode of distribution; attempts to redistribute income, let alone wealth, after the event can have only a marginal effect, as a century of experience with progressive income and estate taxes has shown.

Richardson seems to swallow the slogan of the "consumer society." He refers to "the consumer-oriented economic system . . . whose primary purpose *seems* [to be] to maximize profits made by the capital-owning class." It does not just seem, dear friend; it *is*.

Of course, it makes good sense to assume that corporate capital will continue to own the Canadian economy for quite a while and to explore the possibilities of improving the human condition in cities under this assumption. Richardson is quite right to refer to Sweden and other European countries, and also to our own Canadian experience, to show that much can be done to guide urban developments in other ways than those followed in the United States.

But his awareness that profit is the only objective of capitalist production leads him to assume that it is its only product. This, in turn, leads him to such strange statements as that the new Montreal airport is being built "for no very good reason"; or to

---

Review of Boyce Richardson, *The Future of Canadian Cities* (New Press, Toronto, Ont.). *Source: Last Post,* Vol. 3, No. 5, September 1973.

overlook the fact that the James Bay Project, whatever its damage to the ecology of 60,000 square miles of northern Quebec, would reduce the greatest danger to the ecology of the globe, the burning of fossil fuels; or to decry "the economic pressures that are forcing people out of their homes to make way for concrete, stone and asphalt." They do that, and often ruthlessly; but basically they make way for other people, who also have a right to "a dwelling of their choice." These people are not yet there and consequently have no vote and no voice. In the perverse way in which our economy works, the developer speaks for them. While Richardson in these statements echoes the "no growth" apostles, he shows his good sense in rejecting their pet peeve, their hostility to city growth. He even exclaims, "Mankind hating cities! Could anything be more unnatural and terrible?" Well, it may be unnatural, but condemnation of big cities and its counterpart, the romantic idealization of country life, have been with us for over 2000 years.

This has not kept cities from growing, and Richardson is excellent in explaining the reason. "The development of human talent," he says, "[is] a task that can be best performed in cities. Inherent in this task is specialization, and inherent in specialization is urbanization." It could hardly be said better. It only remains to add that not only the development of talent but also its productive use is maximized in and by cities.

Richardson's love for cities does not blind him to their dangers. He has much to say about the evil effects of the tension and pressure characteristic of our present cities. But to hold "reaction to urban pressure" responsible for warfare in Biafra or Bangladesh, two of the least urbanized countries of the world, is rather far-fetched—and very characteristic of the man. He certainly has his heart in the right place. But every once in a while emotion flows over into the wrong place, the brain, and prevents this acute observer from seeing the facts.

Richardson quite soberly recognizes that the urban "demand for space is a fact that has to be accommodated by anyone planning for the future." But then he joins the chorus of those who condemn the cities for "gobbling up agricultural land." All cities are surrounded by agricultural land. How can they accommodate the demand for space without "gobbling up" land? If the 2 million inhabitants of Metropolitan Toronto lived in 1000 villages of 2000 population each, they would "gobble up" three times as much agricultural land.

Richardson makes the now-belatedly-familiar plea for transit versus the private automobile. Unlike most Canadian critics, he recognizes that in this respect we have done better than the American cities. But then again he falls for the fashionable notion of treating the urban freeway as the cause of automobile movement, rather than as a response to it which, at high monetary and social cost, effectively reduces its evil effects, especially the killing and crippling of both pedestrians and motorists. Rightly praising Stockholm's rapid transit development, he talks of "the sort of railway psychology that operates in Stockholm." He overlooks the fact that Stockholm at the same time has also built many miles of freeways—far more per head of population than has either Toronto or Montreal.

Perhaps the most interesting sections of the book are the detailed descriptions of the struggles of FRAP and controversy over the proposed Concordia development in Montreal. Here, where he has been close to the scene, Richardson clearly sees both sides and honestly expresses his puzzlement in finding the right answer.

I have emphasized the weaknesses of the book. This should not deter readers. Not only is it unusually well written, with much that is pertinent to say about all important aspects of our "urban problem," but also and most important, it tries always to identify the underlying class struggle, "the people against the big boys," as Richardson puts it. "We cannot simply retreat," he says, "each Canadian into his own little community. The battle for change has to be carried on at all levels at the same time." Amen.

Chapter 44

THE SOCIAL AND ECONOMIC IMPLICATIONS OF THE PHYSICAL CHARACTERISTICS OF URBAN DEVELOPMENT

REVIEW OF BACKGROUND

The Concept of Development

The notion that some nations are "developed," while others are "underdeveloped" or, to use the more fashionable optimistic term, "developing," implies that the former have certain characteristics which are so universally desired and desirable that the latter unquestionably want to acquire them. There are two basic characteristics which distinguish developed from underdeveloped nations. First, age-specific mortality, summarized inversely as average life expectancy, is lower; and, second, per capita gross national product (G.N.P.) and its most important determinant, productivity of labor, are higher.

The desirability of raising life expectancy needs little explanation. The fact that people live is prima facie (though not necessarily conclusive) evidence that they desire to continue to do so. Life expectancy admittedly measures only the quantity of life; it says nothing about its quality. In the absence of any general yardstick for the quality of life, the only available, though very incomplete, indicator is a negative one: measurement of the incidence of phenomena of "social pathology," such as disease, crime, or illiteracy.

By contrast, G.N.P. and productivity of labor are measured in precise quantitative terms, but their desirability is not immediately self-evident; they are instrumental values assumed to increase the quantity and quality of life. However, there is no consistent correlation, at least in the developed countries; for example, the Netherlands, with only about half the per capita G.N.P. of the United States, has a consistently higher life expectancy and far lower indicators of all types of social pathology. It seems that G.N.P. is not a meaningful indicator of well-being in

---

Source: Paper prepared for the United Nations Seminar in Copenhagen, U.N. Committee on Housing, Building, and Planning, May-June 1970.

"postindustrial" societies; nor, as has long been recognized, is it meaningful in "subsistence economies." However, in the intermediate stages, characteristic of "developing" countries, increased supply of goods and services is likely to be the decisive instrument for increasing life expectancy and quality. Therefore G.N.P. and labor productivity as the decisive means for its growth will receive attention in the following discussion.

As the utility supplied by goods and services to the consumer is inversely exponentially correlated to his or her disposable income, the economic benefits are the greater, the more evenly they are distributed. Therefore, while a general discussion of income distribution lies outside the scope of this paper, special attention will be paid to the benefits and costs to low-income groups resulting from various alternative policies. Income distribution, as well as aspects of the quantity and quality of life, are usually distinguished, as "social," from aspects such as G.N.P., income, and productivity of labor, which are called "economic." Considering that economic relations are social relations, inextricably intertwined with political and other relations, the distinction may not be too meaningful. However, it will be retained because it helps to clarify the mutual interdependence between "economy" and "level of living." Judgments on various aspects of the quality of life will not be withheld, despite their inevitably subjective character.

Urbanization in Developing and Developed Countries; Differences

In attempting to understand the process of urbanization in developing countries and to foresee and guide its future course, it is relevant to study the course of urbanization in the countries currently classed as "developed," in particular during those periods during which their levels of urbanization and/or industrialization corresponded to those presently reached in developing countries. However, the former countries experienced their "analogous" periods in a different historical setting. First, because a unique confluence of circumstances had given birth to scientific technology in the countries of western Europe and thereby enabled them, and subsequently also the settlements they established on other continents, to dominate the rest of the world, they determined the terms of trade. Second, because the presently universally available measures for the control of epidemic diseases did not exist during their "analogous" periods, their demographic structure was substantially different.

Natural Increase versus In-Migration. During the period of rapid urbanization in western Europe it was widely believed that city populations were unable to reproduce themselves and that cities maintained their vitality only by constantly drawing fresh blood from the countryside. While this appears to be an exaggerated generalization, certainly mortality was higher in the cities than in the countryside; for example, in 1841 life expectancy in Liverpool and Manchester was 26 years, compared to a national average of 41 years.

By contrast, in the presently developing countries, life expectancy tends to be somewhat higher in the cities than in the countryside, varying, according to the degree of development, from slightly under 50 to about 70 years. With a generally high fertility rate, the natural increase in the urban population is very rapid, frequently 3% or more annually, and generally accounts for one half to two thirds of the total growth of the cities. At the same time the rural population is, in most cases, also increasing fairly rapidly, again in contrast to the trend observed in developed countries, especially in their latter stages of development.

Because of these circumstances attempts to alleviate the growth pains of cities by keeping the population on the land hold little promise. Even if it were possible in some way—it is hard to see how—to contain and sustain the growing population in the villages, the cities would still grow at more than half their present rate.

As a result of the different source of population increase, the age composition of the urban population in the presently developing countries is less favorable than it was (and is) in the developed ones, with a higher proportion of children and a lower proportion of young adults. On the other hand, the substantial proportion of the population represented by these children does not require "acculturation" to city life. This potential advantage may, however, be more than offset if their experience or if the frustration of their parents makes them less willing to make the efforts and endure the hardships which rural in-migrants may accept as a hopefully transitional phase.

Tertiary versus Secondary Industry. The driving force of the industrial revolution was the greatly increased productivity of labor in the new big-city-based factories. However, compared to contemporary methods of manufacturing, these factories were still highly labor intensive and provided employment for the bulk of the in-migrants, while a smaller portion was absorbed by tertiary industries. Since that time productivity has increased in all sectors, but less rapidly in the tertiary than in the secondary and primary. As a result, in the cities of the most developed countries the tertiary sector now accounts for 60–70% or more of the labor force.

In the developing countries productivity is lower in all sectors, but it is relatively high in industrial plants established and managed by capital from the developing countries. Consequently they can provide only a very limited amount of employment. Such native, relatively labor intensive industries as may exist are limited in their growth by a limited market. Employment opportunities are to be found primarily in the tertiary sector, which tends to predominate even more than in "postindustrial" cities. Providing only very limited service to the primary and secondary sectors, this overgrown "service" sector is largely parasitic.

Exogenous versus Endogenous Determination. Industrial development in the presently developed countries was, with few exceptions, directed by their own entrepreneurs and governments and oriented to their own needs. Development in the presently developing countries was initiated by foreign investors and governments with the goal of acquiring raw materials, markets, and opportunities for investment for the economies of their home countries. The entire infrastructure was geared to this purpose. Typically, it consists of one or more port cities from which railroads and roads extend to the areas of products of the soil and subsoil. Typically, transportation connections with adjacent countries are lacking; there is very little of the interchange between neighboring countries which has enabled even small countries in Europe, like Belgium and Switzerland, to reach a high level of prosperity. Perhaps even more important, the "software" infrastructure of financial, trading, educational, legal, and administrative institutions has also been geared to foreign requirements rather than to national development. By and large this pattern and the corresponding social structure have continued after the achievement of formal independence.

Dominance of Primate Cities versus Urban Hierarchy. An outstanding characteristic of this pattern in developing countries is the concentration of a very high percentage—sometimes a majority—of the urban population and of "modern" facilities in the primate city, in contrast to the pattern of developed countries, which is characterized by a hierarchy of cities of varying sizes, with the number of cities in each size group inversely correlated with size in a fairly regular distribution. In part, the great number of small and medium-sized cities in older developed countries is due to urban development preceding the development of effective long-distance transportation. In newer developed countries, such as Australia, such cities are of much lesser significance, but there are a number of big cities qualitatively not much different from the largest one.

Attempts of Developed Countries to Decentralize Urban Populations

In view of the overwhelming problems of the mushrooming primate cities of the developing countries, it is of interest to review the experience of those developed countries which have attempted to stop or restrain the growth of their largest cities.

Market Economies. In the United Kingdom, where the size of London has been considered to be excessive since the reign of Elizabeth I, the national government has created, since the last war, over two dozen "new towns" which function satisfactorily. It is, however, relevant to note two points.

First, they have absorbed only about one tenth of the population growth during the past 20 years; the growth of the largest conurbations has been slowed down only marginally.

Second, practically all "new towns" are satellites of the largest cities, primarily of London; they are constituent parts of metropolitan regions. They have not prevented—indeed, they may have accelerated—further concentration of the national population in southeast England, which the government had intended to reverse. No "new towns" have been built in underdeveloped regions of the United Kingdom, such as the Scottish Highlands.

The government of France is attempting a different approach, promoting the development of a small number of its largest cities to enable them to act as "countermagnets" to the attraction of Paris. While considerable quantitative and qualitative development has been achieved in some of these cities, the growth of the Paris Region continues apace.

The Netherlands are attempting to restrain the growth of the Randstaad by using substantial public funds to improve the infrastructure and support the establishment of industries in the northeastern provinces. A moderate success has been achieved, to the extent that the population of the Randstaad has been growing at a rate slightly below the national average for several years.

Israel, where, at the time of the creation of the state, 80% of the Jewish population was concentrated in the three largest cities, has reduced this percentage by settling the huge number of immigrants in small and medium-sized towns. However, most of these, in particular the smaller ones, have not been successful; they not only have attracted practically no voluntary in-migrants, but also have experienced a substantial out-migration to the largest urban areas, in particular to the primate city of Tel-Aviv, which has grown consistently and rapidly.

Centrally Planned Economies. The U.S.S.R., from its inception, pursued a policy of "unburdening" the capitals, Moscow and Leningrad, and of working toward elimination of the division between city and country by ubiquitous industrialization. Ownership of the bulk of all enterprises gives the central government a powerful instrument for guiding the spatial distribution of the population, which, moreover, has been supplemented by strong administrative measures curtailing migration to the largest cities. Nevertheless, the populations of Leningrad and Moscow have increased more than threefold and fourfold, respectively, since the end of the Civil War. However, their share of total urban population has decreased substantially; Soviet policy has been highly successful in promoting the growth of small and medium-sized towns, many of them new.

In the German Democratic Republic the population of the three biggest cities is well below the pre-World War II level, while that of small towns has increased substantially. Several unique circumstances contributed to this one and only exception to a worldwide trend. First, the population of the republic as a whole is slightly below the prewar level. Second, the large cities experienced very severe war destruction, while many of the smaller ones suffered no or only minor damage. Third, the small size, absence of natural barriers, and well-developed transportation system of the republic make the centrally located capital easily accessible to all its cities. The trend has not persisted; since 1963 even the three largest cities show small population increases, due almost exclusively to a net migration gain.

It remains remarkable, however, that the primate cities of all countries with centrally planned economies, with the single exception of Hungary, account for much smaller percentages of both national and total urban population than do those of comparable market-economy countries.

It may also be noted that nations both in eastern Europe (Poland and Hungary) and in western Europe (Netherlands, Federal German Republic) which, in the early postwar years, attempted to implant industries in small towns and villages, have met many failures and have modified their policies toward the promotion of fewer and larger growth points. Better results have been achieved in some cases by modernization and expansion, primarily on a cooperative basis, of rural handicraft industries based on traditional local skills.

In conclusion, two points stand out. First, attempts to restrain the growth of large cities have had little success. Second, such partial successes as have been achieved have been the result of strong and continuous action by central governments. Spatial decentralization requires centralized decision-making; decentralized decision-making, such as prevails, for example, in the United States and Canada, inevitably leads to spatial centralization.

Summary of Problem

It is evident from the foregoing discussion that the problems of the cities in the developing countries are far more formidable than those which exist at present in the developed countries or even than those which existed in the latter countries during their "analogous" period of urban-industrial development—which, as has been shown, was, in fact, not analogous. In the presently developing countries the "push" factor of rural-urban migration, rural overpopulation, and rural misery is stronger, and the "pull" factor of gainful urban industrial employment is weaker.

It is not within the purview of this chapter to discuss the policies which might increase rural production and well-being and thereby reduce the push, except to note that rural and urban-industrial development are interdependent, as suppliers and as markets for each other. Rapid expansion of industrial employment appears as the key to the solution of the "urban problem." Two conclusions follow from this.

First, industry (and long-distance transportation) has a priority claim on the scarce resources of governments and large financial institutions in terms of money and, in particular, of foreign currency; housing and associated urban development must, to the maximum possible extent, mobilize other resources.

Second, as human resources are the most important factor for industrial development, urban development must be geared to increase the health, educational level, and, most of all, the initiative and the capacity for innovation of the urban population.

Obviously there are no short-term solutions. For many years to come, hard choices and unsatisfactory compromises will be unavoidable. Certainly, attempts to copy the models of building or the regulations of developed countries would be self-defeating. In establishing minimum housing standards it might be wise to follow the example of the highway engineer's "85% rule" for setting speed limits. The rule means that the legal limit is set at the speed observed by 85% of the vehicles; normally 5% drive slower and only 10% faster, so the rule really sets the standard at 90% of voluntary compliance. Similarly, it would be appropriate to set the standard of housing and urban equipment at the level actually achieved by 90% of the units at any given time. As, if, and when the remaining 10% were brought up to this standard or replaced, the standard would automatically rise to what had previously been the 81% level.

MEASUREMENTS OF COSTS AND BENEFITS

Costs

Direct Monetary Capital and Operating Costs. The obvious primary method of measuring costs is in terms of national accounts, expressed in units of the national currency. Without a complete and realistic set of national accounts it is not possible to make a rational choice between alternative development policies. It is all too easy for any government to overlook the cost which any given policy imposes on its citizens or other levels of governments.

Any realistic cost accounting must give equal weight to capital and operating costs by reducing them to a common denominator, either by including annual amortization and interest in annual operating cost, or—a more sophisticated method—by discounting future costs (and benefits) to present value. With both methods the results will differ decisively depending on the assumed rate of interest. With stable currencies the practice of using the rate prevalent in the money market is quite satisfactory. However, practically all developing countries operate under conditions of inflation. This is even the case in "hard-currency" developed countries such as the United States. It is evident that the current interest rate in the United States includes, in addition to the "true" rate, a sizable "inflation risk insurance premium."

Only a calculation based on the true interest rate provides an adequate basis for reducing capital and operating cost to a common denominator. A calculation using a market rate which includes a premium against the risk of inflation understates the value of future costs of operation and replacement (as well as that of future benefits). The only alternative to the use of a true interest rate is the highly speculative one of evaluating future costs and benefits at anticipated inflated prices.

Direct Nonmonetary Capital and Operating Costs. If correct accounting of monetary costs is beset with many complexities and pitfalls, it is practically impossible to account for other costs, such as time, risk of accident, or discomfort, in monetary terms. The fact that they cannot be compared in quantitative terms with monetary costs, however, does not justify their disregard and neglect. At least they can be introduced into the accounts in terms of an ordinal scale, such as "more" or "less," or "negligible," "small," "moderate," "significant," "heavy," or "very heavy" costs, and can be weighted, by judgment, together with and in relation to monetary costs.

In many cases it may be equally valid to list the reverse of nonmonetary costs as benefits, such as saving of time, safety, or comfort. It is important not to list the same factor on both sides of the ledger, so as to avoid double counting. Generally, in the comparison between two alternatives, the benefit side receives less consideration and less careful scrutiny than the cost side, because few benefits can be reliably quantified in monetary terms. Therefore decisions tend to be based more on cost comparisons than on benefit comparisons. Consequently, nonmonetary factors are more likely to be given due weight if they are listed on the cost rather than on the benefit side of the ledger.

Indirect Costs. Costs may accrue not only to the producers, operators, and users of housing and other urban facilities, but also to many others. Some of these costs are monetary. Savings achieved by building on cheap peripheral land may be offset by increased costs of urban transportation; or, inversely, economies may be achieved by building at high densities in a central section of the city, but may impose heavy costs of delay and congestion on traffic moving between neighboring sections. On a national scale a dispersed pattern of relatively small cities might produce sizable economies in municipal services, but might put a heavy burden on the national system of transportation and communication. Indirect monetary costs occur also in fields other than transportation.

Equally significant are nonmonetary costs. Pollution of air and water and impairment or destruction of landscape and "cityscape" come to mind. Social pathologies, as well as tensions arising from segregation or from desegregation, tend to spread beyond the areas in which they are produced.

Probably the most important indirect cost of urban development is the cost which it imposes on the countryside. As rural development depends on goods and services from the cities, it is justified to draw natural, capital, and human resources from the countryside in order to develop an adequate supply of these urban goods and services. However, with the "push" from the countryside so strong that far more migrants come to the cities than can be productively employed, up to what point is it wise to accelerate migration by reinforcing the "pull" through the attraction of improved housing and other urban services? There could be a point at which so many human and other resources were drawn from the countryside as to make rural development impossible.

The often proclaimed, but rarely defined, postulate of a rural-urban "balance" can be interpreted meaningfully as that point at which urban and rural development give each other maximum support as suppliers and markets. Certainly this does not define any general or fixed proportion; it will vary with time and place and shift constantly with shifts in productivity in the different sectors of the economy, and also with changing conditions of foreign trade. However elusive this concept of balance may be, it cannot be disregarded when the costs of various alternatives of urban development are considered.

Costs in Terms of Government Expenditures. While the basic evaluation of costs, monetary and nonmonetary, direct and indirect, must be in terms of national accounts, it is inevitable that any government will be strongly concerned with that portion of the costs which has to be included in its budget. Almost by definition, developing countries have not been able to formulate fully effective systems of tax assessment and collection. Budgetary stringencies are the norm, and the resultant difficulties hardly require discussion. It may not be out of place, however, to repeat in this context three previously mentioned points.

1. Capital and operating costs must be considered together, after being brought to a common denominator on the basis of a "true" interest rate.

2. Costs to various levels of government, local and national, and, in the case of federated nations, federal and state (or provincial), must be given equal weight.

3. Preference should be given to policies which can mobilize a maximum amount of nongovernmental resources.

Costs in Terms of Foreign Exchange. Given the historically developed state of international economic relations indicated earlier in this chapter, practically all developing countries are faced with a severe shortage of foreign exchange. As a result it will often be necessary to reject a least-cost alternative if a large portion of this cost is required for the acquisition of imported resources. Alternatives relying on domestic materials, products, tools, and personnel must be preferred, even if they are less efficient than others requiring high imported inputs.

Decisive for increased productivity are human resources, in particular technical and managerial skills. In the field of housing and urban environment, in which local conditions, habits, skills, and traditional ways of life are of decisive importance, the usual methods of sending young people to study abroad and to invite experienced specialists from developed countries for short periods as consultants and/or teachers appear to be particularly inappropriate. The students returning from abroad—if they return—will find that not much of what they have learned is applicable in their home countries; and it is a rare specialist who, in a few months, can acquire a sufficiently profound understanding of the needs, resources, and restraints of a foreign developing country to be able to give sound advice or to teach a relevant course. On the basis of his personal experience of working in the early 1930s in the U.S.S.R.—which, at that time, could still be considered a developing country—this writer would say that it takes about 5 years for a foreign specialist to become fully effective. Every effort should be made, both by the developing and the developed nations, as well as by international institutions, to develop programs which will induce first-rate specialists from developed countries to work for extended periods in the universities, in the planning and project offices, or on the building sites of a developing nation.

Benefits

Economic Benefits for Urban Population. Costs can, of course, always be reduced—theoretically, to zero—if one is willing to forego the benefits which they are intended and expected to produce. Inversely, a high-cost solution may be preferable to a low-cost one, if the benefits are more than proportionally higher. Here the time factor enters into the equation. By and large, the benefits of low-cost solutions will be produced earlier than those of high-cost methods. Thus, for their accurate comparative evaluation, correct choice of the interest (or discount) rate is crucial.

The primary yardstick for measuring the benefits of any policy is its contribution to the production of the urban area and to the real incomes of the urban population. Important factors for this are access of workers to a variety of employment opportunities and of enterprises to workers of a wide variety of skills, including technical, scientific, and managerial skills. No less important are opportunities for self-employment and for starting new, small enterprises. For these, as well as for most other enterprises, the "external economies" arising from access to other manufacturing and service establishments are vital.

Social Benefits to Urban Population. The primary criterion for any development is physical, mental, and spiritual health. A supply of safe water, elimination of wastes, safety from fire, floods, hurricanes, and earthquakes and from structural and traffic accidents, and protection against vermin, rain, cold, and extreme heat are elementary benefits; however, great efforts are still required to make them available to the entire population of the cities, not to mention the countryside, in practically all developing countries. Control of air, water, and soil pollution, planting of trees and other means to improve the microclimate, and provision of easily accessible open space for outdoor recreation are equally basic, but not easily obtainable, benefits.

Healthy mental development in a new environment requires access to education. This does not comprise only formal education; the importance of informal education in the streets, squares, and markets should not be underrated. The process of urbanization of a rural population inevitably involves a painful separation from deeply ingrained habits and values which may lead to complete disorientation, despair, and anomie. It is a difficult task to create an environment which makes the transition as painless as possible while, at the same time, stimulating the will for innovation. Policy should provide maximum scope for initiative, experimentation, voluntary organization and cooperation, and the development of self-reliance and leadership.

Benefits to Nation. To the extent that improvements in housing and in the urban development succeed in improving the health of the population, raising its educational level, developing its initiative, organizational ability, and will to innovation, and, most important, strengthening social cohesion and identification with national goals, they are vitally important inputs to the creation of human resources. Therefore, as human resources are by far the most important factor of production, housing can well claim the high priority which is given to industries producing means of production.

As noted earlier, the sum total of social benefits is maximized by equal distribution. However, the potential contribution to national development is unequally distributed, both "vertically" between occupations and "horizontally" between regions. This creates contradictory demands which are hard to reconcile. The scarcest resource in developing countries tends to be highly qualified personnel for scientific, technical, and managerial work. Such persons have to be attracted and supported by housing and urban services of a quality and at a cost much higher than those that can be provided for the mass of the population. How can this be done without alienating the vast majority of the "underprivileged"?

The problem may be even more serious in its "horizontal" dimension. As mentioned earlier, there is evidence that productivity is positively correlated with city size. This would point to concentrating efforts on the development of the primate cities. However, such a policy can easily become self-defeating. Few, if any, countries, developed or developing, are so homogeneous that their citizens identify exclusively with the nation. Normally there are strong local and regional loyalties, often reinforced by ethnic, linguistic, or religious differences, clamoring for their fair share of development. Their neglect is likely to lead to disaffection, and in extreme cases to secession or civil war.

The best compromise between these contradictory requirements has to be determined by each nation on the basis of its specific geographic and historic characteristics. It may be noted that the former are more amenable to change than the latter. Construction of a road may radically alter the geographic situation of a region in a few years. Shifts of loyalty, on the other hand, usually take several generations, although they may be greatly accelerated by revolutions, those "locomotives of history."

ELEMENTS OF URBAN INFRASTRUCTURE

Housing

It is hardly necessary to elaborate on the great gap which exists everywhere between the need for housing and the ability to supply it. However, it may be noted that the required quantity of housing is determined not only by population growth, but also by need for replacement and by changes in family and household structure.

Replacement is needed for those units destroyed by fire, collapse, or other catastrophes, for those displaced by or converted to nonresidential uses, and for those that are considered to be unfit for human habitation. The number of the last type can be kept to a minimum by maintenance and improvement, which are strongly encouraged by homeownership and secure tenure. In addition to sound original construction, maintenance and improvement also contribute to decrease the risk of destruction by fire or collapse. The danger of catastrophes will generally be more limited if densities are low. In addition, low densities limit the number of houses which may have to make room for the requirements of transportation, industrial, or other nonresidential facilities, and may also make it possible to accommodate some small-scale economic activities within the individual house or compound.

Housing policy in most developed countries has been directed exclusively to the needs of the nuclear family, to the neglect of other types of families and households which also exist there. In most developing countries the extended family still plays an important role, providing significant support for its members. From the point of view of providing housing it has the advantage that fewer, though somewhat larger, houses are required.

At the other end of the scale there are many single people, in particular young migrants from the countryside. In many cases dormitories or hostels will be needed. But probably most of them will seek and find accommodation as boarders or lodgers, in many cases becoming to some degree members of the enlarged family. It will be wise, therefore, to take into account this type of accommodation.

As development proceeds, the enlarged family is likely to give way gradually to the nuclear family; at a later stage there will be a growing demand for dwelling units for single persons. More and more, the pattern of demand will call for housing types comparable to those in the developed countries. For a portion of the population this is already now the case everywhere. As the term "developing countries" covers a wide spectrum, and as there may be in addition wide differences between urban areas within a nation, the size of this portion will vary widely. It is likely, however, that there are few, if any, developing countries which will not require in the foreseeable future a certain amount of housing for extended families, which, with their changing demands in number of persons and in activities, can best be accommodated in largely self-built, flexible houses and compounds.

It is important to find, for this type of housing, locations which will not stand in the way of later developments of a more intensive type and to plan them in a manner which will facilitate renewal at a still later stage.

Public Utilities and Pollution Control

While in all countries people bring from their rural background some skills for building their own houses, they are not prepared to cope with the needs for water supply and waste disposal which arise in an urban environment. The provision of a safe water supply and of a system for the disposal of sanitary sewage must have first claim on the public funds available for urban development, followed very closely by a supply of electric power. Creating storm water drainage ditches and grading and surfacing streets can, in large part, be accomplished by cooperative self-help if neighborhood solidarity and initiative can be raised to a sufficiently high level. Where this is the case, cooperative labor of the population can also carry part of the burden of providing water supply and sewage disposal systems; in 1934 this writer participated in a successful project of this type, digging ditches for sewage pipes in a steelworkers' settlement at Makeyevka in the Soviet Ukraine.

Utility systems involve considerable economics of scale. These result not only from the need for a certain minimum size of installations such as pumping stations and filtration and sewage treatment plants, but even more from the need for a well-qualified staff to operate and maintain the systems. While generalizations are hard to make, it appears that populations of less than 50,000–60,000 can be served only at increased cost and/or lowered standards of health protection.

While all cities in developed countries supply their populations with safe water, few, if any, have succeeded in protecting them from pollution of water, air, and soil. There are essentially two methods for dealing with pollution, disposal and dispersal. The only really satisfactory way is disposal by some form of reuse or recycling; in this perspective we are dealing not with "waste," but with by-products of production and consumption. Technical procedures are known for reusing almost every pollutant, but in most cases their high cost has so far prevented their adoption, even in the wealthiest developed countries. Recourse is had to dispersal of pollutants, which means that a smaller dosage of them affects a larger, but generally much less populated, area.

In the case of water pollution, biological regeneration is possible if sufficient amounts of fresh water are available, and it is hardly necessary to repeat that water-polluting plants should be located downstream of urban areas. It is equally desirable to locate air-polluting factories downwind. However, it is not sufficient to count the percentage of annual hours of wind direction; velocity, temperature, and humidity, as well as modification of wind direction by local topography, must be carefully studied to determine the least harmful location.

One of the main sources of air pollution in developed countries is exhaust fumes from automobiles. In addition to the high demand for foreign currency to buy cars, and the many other economic and social costs of private automobiles, the pollution factor is a strong reason to keep their purchase and use to a minimum. This is an important consideration for many aspects of urban planning.

Another negative aspect of development is the enormous and rapidly increasing amount of all kinds of solid "wastes" from rising production and consumption. High labor costs make it uneconomic to sort out various materials for reuse. From this angle, developing countries may be able to do better. It may be worthwhile to study some of the methods used in Japan, a highly developed but still relatively low-wage country. However, in any case, the need for sites for disposal of solid wastes will keep growing.

It is evident that dispersal of wastes in any form—gaseous, liquid, or solid—is much easier and cheaper in small than in large cities. Against this must be weighed the greater ability of large centers, based on their higher productivity and greater technical and organizational sophistication, to use advanced methods of disposal.

Community Facilities

A decisive role in "acculturation" is played by community facilities—educational, cultural, health-oriented, religious, political, or simply "social" places for meetings, gatherings, discussions, and, last but not least, festivities, as well as for retail trade and commercial services. Spatial concentration of these varied activities at a strongly identifiable focal point can contribute much to a community spirit which gives rise to cooperative organizations and activities.

Inversely, when such a spirit exists, the population can and will contribute much to the development of the required community facilities. In many, probably in most, cases it will not be possible to construct all desirable community service structures simultaneously with the houses, and temporary makeshift arrangements may have to be made. But it is important to reserve adequate spaces in the right locations. Much of community life will occur in the open, in squares which must be attractive, easily accessible, and free from traffic, and also in parks and promenades.

There is no general rule for the size of a group of people which form a community within an urban area. Certainly there is no magic in the textbook "neighborhood" size of 5000 or 10,000 people. Rather, there tends to be a hierarchy of groupings, not always clearly defined, ranging from a group of about nine houses up to a "borough" with a population of 150,000 or 250,000.

In practically all countries there are traditional groupings in villages, towns, and cities, often highly organized around a religious-educational-welfare center. Such traditions will influence group formations also in new urban areas. Whatever the size, it is important to protect community life by providing a "precinct" free from through traffic.

Transportation

Increasing motorization appears to be inevitable everywhere. However, every effort should be made to discourage the use of the private automobile and to promote other means of transportation. Apart from the already mentioned factors of excessive use of foreign exchange and of air pollution, mass use of the automobile inevitably produces many accidents, interferes severely with the movement of goods by trucks and of persons in buses or streetcars, on bicycles, and on foot, and destroys the important function of the street as an outdoor communal living room.

Essentially four other means of person movement deserve support in developing countries: individual transportation on foot and on bicycles, and collective transportation by bus and by railroad. A combination of walking and bus riding, or of bicycling and train riding, should make it possible for the inhabitants to reach all places of work and education from their homes. In particular, bicycle transportation deserves more attention than it usually receives. Provision of smooth, all-weather bicycle paths and establishment of bicycle manufacturing deserve high priority. The use and repair of bicycles can provide a useful introduction to a mechanized urban-industrial world. It may be recalled that the powerful Japanese automobile industry had its origin in bicycle repair shops which went progressively into the manufacture of bicycles and then of motorcycles.

Facilitating movement on foot, on bicycles, by bus, and by railroad should be a guiding consideration in planning urban areas. Among other things, this means that reasonably level land should be made available for all types of development, including self-built "shacktowns." In many cities—Caracas, Rio de Janeiro, Ankara—these have been forced onto steep hillsides as the only available sites. While such developments, where they exist, should be improved as far as possible, in future, steep hillsides should be preserved for recreation or for possible later development with high-cost housing.

Considerable cost saving can be achieved by timely reservation of transportation corridors, wide enough to accommodate future roads or railways, as well as pipelines, power lines, and any presently unforeseeable future transportation facilities.

FACTORS INFLUENCING URBAN PHYSICAL DEVELOPMENT

Physical Factors

Size of Individual Cities. As noted earlier, productivity is higher in big than in small cities, primarily because the former provide easy access to a great variety of goods, services, and, most important, skilled and highly qualified people. These in turn concentrate in the primate cities because there is the greatest choice of opportunities for work, for learning, for meeting other people who share one's interests, for enjoying cultural facilities, and for buying high-quality goods. The well-known circle of growth feeding on growth develops with increasing momentum. The availability of workers attracts enterprises, and they in turn attract workers—under the conditions of an overwhelming push from the countryside, far more workers than can be productively employed. Therefore, while the productivity of those who produce may be higher than elsewhere, the productivity per capita of the total population may remain quite low.

Meanwhile the size of the city causes rising costs. Pollutants can no longer be dispersed to the outside, because the outside is everywhere already part of the urban area. They must either be disposed of by costly methods—or endured. In order to avoid distances so large as to negate the very raison d'etre of the city, mutual accessibility, costly transportation facilities must be provided and densities must be increased. High-density development requires techniques of construction and operation which leave little scope for self-help. To some extent the higher level of services must also be extended to the nonproductive population, if only to provide for the entire city a minimum of security from the danger of epidemics, fire, and crime. Thus the gap between the level of development in the primate city and that in the rest of the country becomes even wider, and the city's attraction to migrants still stronger.

Probably the most promising way to counteract excessive growth of the primate city is to develop some other cities to a level where they can act as countermagnets. No firm knowledge is available to quantify this level, but it is likely that the required "critical mass" is not less than 0.5 million population and may well be 1 million or more. In many developing countries even the primate city is below that size. It is also not known whether the cost of building and operation is lower for five cities of 1 million population each than for one city of 5 million. Conceivably, it may be higher, in particular, if the cost of additional intercity transportation is taken into account. Generally, benefits may be less during the possibly lengthy period which may be required to build up such cities to the level at which they can be effective as countermagnets.

Constellation of Cities. However, even if the benefit–cost ratio (including "social" benefits and costs) was less favorable, it might still be desirable to develop such cities because of their potential as primary growth poles for their region. Costs and benefits must be evaluated not simply for each city in isolation, but for a national system of cities.

There are, of course, in every country smaller towns, primarily market, service, and administrative centers for agricultural regions, and, in most countries, also towns based on the exploitation of mineral or power resources. As natural resources of soil and subsoil are developed, the need for new towns of this type arises.

However, the economic base provided by the exploitation of natural resources generally supports only a relatively small population. It is a question under what conditions such towns can be strengthened by location of other activities, primarily manufacturing. Manufacturing and other enterprises generally need and want good access to inputs of goods and services, available in large urban areas, which in many cases also provide a market for their products. They tend, therefore, to develop more successfully in "satellite" towns. Considering the importance of access to a major city, it would seem desirable to locate them close to it. This has the added advantage of widening the employment opportunities of their inhabitants by the possibility of commuting. On the other hand, the closer together towns are located, the smaller the extent of rural area for which they can act as secondary growth poles. The best balance between these two considerations will vary from case to case and also over time. As development proceeds, routine manufacturing establishments and branch plants will find it increasingly possible to operate successfully also in isolated small towns.

Small towns can, of course, reduce the cost of urban development in several ways. They can disperse pollutants. Distances are short enough not to require costly transportation facilities. Most important, low-density development by self-help housing can easily be accommodated, possibly even in forms allowing part-time agriculture; and inhabitants from the surrounding countryside can commute to work.

In contrast to large cities, small towns *can* be created de novo. This provides the advantage of ease of land assembly as the basis for implementing a desirable physical town plan. However, a considerable capital investment has to be carried for a number of years before it produces returns.

Density. As the reason for the existence of cities is to facilitate cooperation and interchange by increasing mutual accessibility, this basic function is facilitated the closer together people and facilities are located—all other things being equal.

However, they are not equal. Accessibility is determined not by geometric distance, but by the cost in terms of time, money, and inconvenience required to travel that distance. If efficient means of transportation and communication are available, the advantages of high density can be achieved without its disadvantages and costs.

Higher costs tend to arise, as already noted, from the need for more costly construction methods, as well as from the fact that any newly arising requirements for land for traffic or any other purpose necessitate a greater amount of demolition. Dispersal of air pollutants and maintenance of a healthy microclimate, with sufficient light, air, sunshine or tree shade, quiet, and privacy, are more difficult to achieve than with lower densities.

On the other hand, lower densities also involve costs for transportation of all types, including the movement of water and sewage and of power. Perhaps the best solution for larger urban areas is the development of relatively low-density outlying districts or "satellites," connected with the central city by rail. However, these units will have to be of considerable size and of moderate density to support economic and efficient rail service. For medium-sized urban areas this may lead to a linear shape.

In comparing densities with those in developed countries, it should not be overlooked that the number of persons occupying a certain amount of building volume or of floor space, both at home and at work, tends to be considerably higher in developing countries. An equal gross floor area houses, in Hong Kong, almost 10 times as many persons as in North American cities. As development proceeds, the density of an area of a given building type will decrease; but by that time improvement of transportation and extension of utilities will also be within reach.

"Grain." Accessibility depends not only on the size and density, but also on the "grain" of the city, the coarser or finer grouping of different functions. Heavy, nuisance-producing industries must, of necessity, be located in separate zones, away from other land uses. But light, small and medium-size industries, and, in particular,

services—commercial, public, social, educational, and medical—should be as close to residences as possible. However, establishments requiring mutual contact and/or serving the same population group should be clustered; the size and location of such clusters will depend on the previously discussed community structure. In any case uniform zoning of extensive areas, frequently found in the newer sections of North American urban areas, should be avoided.

Social-Political Factors

Land Ownership and Land Tenure. Any public policies concerning urban development can be frustrated by action (or inaction) of landowners. In most developing countries speculation in urban land is rampant, and high land prices force high densities. When it is not politically possible to prevent this situation, it may leave the development of "new towns" as the only feasible alternative, regardless of other considerations.

With the great variety of systems of landownership and land tenure existing in various countries, it is difficult to generalize. However, it can be said that small-scale private ownership usually creates the most difficult conditions both for planned development and for land assembly by public authorities. Large-scale private ownership sometimes, though by no means always, has resulted in fairly well-planned development within the limits of the private estate; it also facilitates public land assembly. Public landownership provides the only satisfactory basis for sound urban development.

Financial stringencies make it very difficult to acquire an adequate amount of land for urban development, particularly under conditions of intense land speculation. A tax on the capital gain, or "unearned increment," obtained from the sale of urban development land certainly would keep land prices down by discouraging speculative land purchases. However, it would also discourage sales and tend to immobilize land. An annual ad valorem tax might be equally effective in recapturing unearned increment and discouraging speculative buying, while strongly encouraging sale for development.

In any case public authorities must have the right to expropriate (or "condemn") land required for urban development. It would be highly desirable to make payment not in cash, but in some form of shares in industrial or housing development.

In most developing countries "squatting," sometimes in highly organized form, that is, settling on land to which they did not hold title, has been the only way by which people with low incomes have been able to find sites to build their own houses. Certainly it would be disastrous economically, socially, and politically to attempt to remove them; existing settlements will have to be legalized and improved. However, for the future, the need should be anticipated and provided for. Suitable land areas should be assembled and planned by the public authorities, and settlers assisted by technical advice and by supply, on favorable terms, of such materials and parts as they cannot procure themselves. (The Ghana "roof scheme" is a successful example of this approach.)

It is important to give security of tenure to the settlers. From the point of view of continuing public control and also for ease of payment for the settlers, long-term renewable leases may be the most desirable arrangements. Where strong traditions and distrust of public authority result in a categorical demand for fee-simple landownership, some provision should be made for repurchase. In many cases it will be feasible to permit the settlers to make payments in the form of labor contributions to the grading of streets and other public works in their community.

Security of tenure is equally important for those—normally the majority of the urban population—who do not build their own houses, but live in structures provided by the building industry. Ownership of the building—though not necessarily of the land—practically always results in better maintenance and consequently lower operating cost. In multifamily structures condominium or cooperative forms of ownership can achieve this same goal to some extent. But even under conditions of tenancy, security of tenure and organized cooperation of the tenants can contribute much to economical operation.

Governmental and Financial Institutions. The appropriateness of one or another form of urban development will strongly depend on the institutional framework in which urbanization occurs. It was emphasized earlier that any intended distribution of the urban population can be brought about only through very strong direction by the central national government. But policy decisions concerning priorities in building and operating the urban infrastructure are more likely to respond to the needs of the local population and to enlist its support, cooperation, and initiative if they are made locally. Indeed, development of effective democratic urban self-government may be one of the most decisive elements in successful urban-industrial development.

In large urban areas participation can be better mobilized in and by smaller communities. A physical structure encouraging the identification of cohesive social units within the larger urban area can facilitate such activities and permit the decentralization of some municipal functions.

Hardly less important than the structure of government administration is the structure of financial institutions. If such institutions, public or private, are not able or willing to channel funds and invest them constructively in smaller cities and towns, such units can hardly develop, except in the rather undesirable form of company towns.

Attitudes of the Population. The decisive factor in development is ultimately the attitude of the population, its desire and ability for innovation, for learning and adopting new ways of working and living, and the awakening and strengthening of self-confidence and initiative, and of solidarity and identification with the national society. Forms and methods of development which strengthen these attitudes may ultimately contribute more to progress than others which may be more profitable in monetary terms but assign an essentially passive role to the population.

Attitudes, determined basically by the political-social-economic structure, condition the feasibility of different settlement patterns. However, to some extent, the pattern also contributes to shaping attitudes. The experiences and contacts of big-city life tend to encourage innovation. But initiative and cooperation may find a more fertile soil in smaller communities. This may indicate that the most favorable pattern is one of large urban areas composed of constellations of clearly identifiable smaller units.

Movement Factors

Intraurban and Interurban Transportation. Such a "constellation" area will, of course, involve relatively high costs for the movement of goods, persons, and messages. A more concentrated type of development reduces distances and enables public transportation to function more effectively and economically. It can thereby substantially reduce the time and money costs of both goods and person transportation. But experience shows that the homeowners in relatively low-density settlements greatly improve and add to the housing stock, while large multifamily rental housing requires large and rising costs for maintenance and repairs, if rapid degeneration to intolerable slum conditions is to be avoided. Thus, to a considerable extent, cost of housing and cost of transportation are mutual substitutes and must be evaluated together.

Distances within the urban area and the cost of intraurban transportation are, of course, very much lower in small towns. It appears that substantial savings could be achieved if urban development were channeled into a large number of self-sufficient small towns rather than into one or a few large centers. The difficulty is that "self-containment" is incompatible with economic progress, which is based on a highly developed division of labor on a national and even an international scale. Time-consuming and costly long-distance interurban transportation has to be substituted for intraurban transportation. No information is available concerning the cost of such substitution. While most developed countries have made extensive studies both of their national long-distance and of many of their urban or metropolitan short-distance systems, this writer is not aware of any study which has explored their mutual interaction and substitution. Such a study is, however, indispensable for any comparison between the costs of different patterns of distribution of the urban population.

In the case of the inputs and outputs of industrial enterprises located in small towns, it is obvious that much substitution of interurban for intraurban transportation actually occurs. In the case of consumer goods, it does not always occur; some goods are simply not available in small towns. Nonsubstitution is predominant for person trips. It is hardly possible to arrive at an exact estimate of the cost of movements—primarily of persons, but also of goods and messages—which are *not* made, but it is probably quite high. It is a reverse expression of the "external economies" which are available in large cities and appear to be the main reason for their higher productivity.

Migration and Commuting. As noted earlier, a far greater portion of the growth of the urban population is due to natural increase in the developing countries than was the case during the "analogous" periods in countries which are presently considered to be developed. Nevertheless, attention has been concentrated on the portion of the increase which is due to migration from the countryside and may be subject to influence by measures of public policy.

Urban employment of the rural population does not always imply migration of the household. Two other patterns can be observed. In czarist Russia many urban workers left their families in the village, to which they returned if they could not find employment in the city and/or when their help was required for farm work. The same pattern is widespread today in some African countries and probably also in countries elsewhere. Most of these single male or female workers find shelter in the households of others, usually relatives and friends, but the provision of adequate hostels for them is certainly desirable. For the individual this pattern normally represents only a transitional stage, followed either by establishment of an urban household or by return to the village. However, as others take his or her place, the general pattern may continue for a considerable period. As development progresses, it tends to disappear.

More important, at least in countries with a dense rural population, is the combination of urban work with rural residence, usually with part-time farming supplementing the wage. This pattern is dependent on cheap transportation for daily commuting; when this is available, it may play a great role. It is doubtful whether the rapid growth of German industry in the quarter century preceding World War I would have been possible without the heavily subsidized railroad service operated for this purpose.

Both of these patterns can considerably reduce the need for financing urban housing and related services; in particular they reduce the presence of unemployed persons in the city. Acculturation to urban ways may proceed less rapidly, but probably also less painfully. Nor should it be overlooked that these part-time urbanites act as pioneers of urban attitudes in their villages.

It is probably true that the housing of the rural-urban commuters is no better than that found in the shacktowns, but it may be more acceptable in a village environment. More significant may be the difference in schools. Hope for a better education for their children, as much as hope for a better job for themselves, motivates rural families to move to the city. The possibility to substitute financing of transportation facilities for commuting and of rural schools for urban housing and related facilities deserves serious consideration.

RESOURCES FOR URBAN DEVELOPMENT

Type of Resources

Before discussing different methods to mobilize the resources needed for the creation of urban housing and related facilities, it may be appropriate to review briefly the types of resources required. Basically these are land, labor, skills, materials, tools, and products.

The basic means to make more land available for urban development and to prevent its market value from reaching prohibitive levels is the extension of transportation and utilities. The need for additional public policies to eliminate or curb land speculation and the advantages of public landownership have already been discussed. Whatever the form of landownership, the builder, whether homeowner or entrepreneur, will, in many cases, be able to pay for the land only over a number of years, and credit instruments for this purpose must be available.

Labor is the only resource which is in ample supply in the urban areas of developing countries. Some of the skills of rural migrants may be immediately applicable, but most require training. The development of skills on all levels is the most crucial precondition for the successful building and operation of housing and of cities. Decisive may be the availability of leaders who are able to apply and adapt creatively the scientific, technical, and managerial knowledge of the developed countries and to pass this modified knowledge on to a widening circle of their countrymen.

One of the most important tasks of technical leaders is the development of improved methods of using local materials and skills and of adapting traditional dwelling types to modern requirements. Equally important is the development of construction tools and machinery adapted to the specific needs of their country. Often a substantial increase in productivity can be achieved by the improvement of simple tools. Mass production and modular coordination of building parts and prefabrication of sections can substantially reduce the time and cost of building.

Work in these spheres of activity is most likely to develop successfully in the primate cities and then to spread gradually to smaller towns. However, creation of a first-class university may be one of the most effective means to build up other towns as countermagnets. It is questionable whether a large campus at the outskirts of the city is the best location for a university; a central location, even if it imposes restrictions in space, may better help to bring about mutual fructification of theory and practice.

Nonmonetary Resources

No country in the world, however developed and wealthy, has yet been able to mobilize sufficient resources to provide all its citizens with housing which, according to its own standards, is fit for habitation. It would be absurd to assume that developing countries can solve their far more difficult housing problem by using only "normal" ways of resource mobilization. In the normal way the consumer of housing transforms his or her labor force into monetary earnings and then buys, as purchaser or renter, the product of other people's labor. However, a large portion of the urban population in developing countries has no opportunity to transform all or much of its labor force into money. The only way these people can transform their labor into housing is by "bypassing" the monetary form, that is, by building their own houses. Evidently some materials and parts, as well as technical guidance, have to be supplied by others, and it is by supplying these missing elements that public financing can produce the greatest benefits.

Internal Monetary Resources

The emphasis placed throughout this discussion on maximizing the opportunities for self-help should not obscure the fact that a majority of the population, varying in size, will acquire housing by the "normal" way of paying for it in money. However, only a few persons will be able to accumulate sufficient savings to pay for the initial capital investment. But others can be induced to increase their savings if these can be applied directly to housing, by membership in cooperative building societies or other means.

External Monetary Resources

A few words may be said about the obviously highly desirable supplementation of insufficient domestic capital by monetary resources made available by wealthier countries. Broadly speaking, it is hard to see why it should be more advantageous, to either lender or borrower, to make resources available in the form of equity or mortgage investment rather than in the form of loans to national or municipal governments, enabling them to invest in housing in the form most effective under local conditions.

A somewhat different situation is represented by "package deals," in which a foreign organization supplies managerial and technical guidance together with construction machinery and building parts and materials. Sometimes this may be the only feasible way to supply adequate housing in short order. If and when such a project serves as a training school for local skills at all levels, and its product and methods of production are suitable for copying, it may make a valuable contribution. However, such projects can hardly supply a substantial portion of the total housing need without severe adverse effects on the balance of payments.

SUMMARY

1. Investment in urban housing and related services, while competing with industry for scarce resources, is indispensable as the producer of the kind of labor force without which industrial investment cannot produce the expected benefits.

2. Because the need for housing far exceeds the available financial resources, mobilization not only of the monetary savings, but also and primarily of the initiative and labor of the urban population is indispensable. Forms and methods of urban development must create favorable conditions for this mobilization.

3. Costs cannot be evaluated separately from the benefits which they produce. There are strong indications that benefits, measured in terms of productivity, are positively correlated with city size.

4. Costs of housing must be evaluated not in isolation, but in combination with those of the urban infrastructure, in particular of intraurban transportation.

5. Attention must be paid to the possibilities of mutual substitution of intra- and interurban transportation, and of migration and commuting.

Chapter 45

THE ROLE OF DESIGN

WHAT IS DESIGN?

In its broad sense the term "design" means the same as "planning"—the mental anticipation of a combination of means to achieve a goal, or a set of goals. In this discussion the goal will be defined more narrowly as a modification of the physical environment, and "design" as the creation of the form of city and country. Form is a container; it presupposes a content. The content of "environmental form" can only be the life of persons in the society which lives in the environment.

However, people modify this environment not only, and not primarily, by design. The men and women who overcropped and overgrazed the western plains did not "design" the dust bowl. The men and women who make, sell, and drive automobiles do not "design" traffic jams and air pollution. They just happen.

It is the planner's task to foresee what will happen as a consequence of human actions and to guide these actions in such a way that they help rather than hinder each other in achieving their goals. Patrick Geddes coined the term "synopsis"—together-seeing. He used it to denote the seeing together of the interaction of all the factors which determine the life of society, its content. But he used it also, and inseparably, as a seeing together of all the elements of the physical environment, as the perception and conception of form.

How far have American planners attempted and succeeded in designing form in the past? What may they do in the future?

PARADISE FOUND AND LOST

The American autochthons had an image of their environment as the sacred land of the tribe, and an image of their settlements, reflected in the forms created by the mound dwellers of Ohio or by the Navajos in the Southwest. The work of the mound dwellers had only an ephemeral continuation into later culture in the oddity of Centerville. The Navajo village community, antedating the distinction between public and private space, with the roofs of the family dwellings serving as the village streets, may regerminate in the concepts of "traffic architecture."

The European invaders brought a different concept from their shores. In Europe too the land had once been the sacred domain of the gods and their peoples, entrusted to

Source: Journal of the American Institute of Planners, September 1967.

the divinely sanctioned king. But the king had conveyed the land to his feudal retainers, and the lords had made their fiefs private property. The people who toiled on the land wanted themselves and the land to be free of them. The greatest minds of Europe shared that dream. Goethe's Faust found fulfillment of his lifelong search in "dwelling with free folk on free land," and his Wilhelm Meister ends his devious journey by organizing a group of men and women to settle in America.

America became the fulfillment of Europe's dream. It was "the land of the free" because the land was free. It was free to take—and to sell and buy. It was free to be subjected, appropriated by whoever had the power to buy. Land was no longer sacred; it was a commodity, "real estate." Divinity was exiled to the heavens, and had no business with the business of real estate: God in His heaven, and Mammon on this earth.

In order to be appropriated, the land had to be subdivided; and, just as Sesostris had done 5000 years before in Egypt, the young republic divided its territory by geometry into rectangular lots. America was not conceived of as a land of sacred mountains and streams, as ancient Greeks and Chinese had conceived their country, but as a subdivision of continental dimensions. Surveyors were its high priests; their lines went straight over hill and lake, regardless of natural form. As colonists have done at all times and places, the American colonists used their system of rural subdivision also to allocate lots in their towns. As the planners of Manhattan observed in 1810, "a city is to be composed of the habitations of men, and straight-sided and right-angled houses are most cheap to build, and the most convenient to live in." Rectangular lots added up to rectangular blocks, and the sum of rectangular blocks added up to a city. If more lots were needed, more blocks were added; the frontier of the city could expand to infinity. The grid of the streets, which gave access to the private properties and served for interchange between one private property and the other, was the only public element. The street plan was *the* city plan. What was built on the individual lots was the business of their owners alone.

True, the earliest settlers, both English and Spanish, had a concept of a community, centered around a commons or plaza with the church as symbol and dominant landmark. But with the expansion of the nineteenth century the res publica was drowned in a welter of contending res privatae, private businesses. *The* church was replaced by churches, whose founders, like everybody else, had to find the land they needed in the real estate market as best they could. With few exceptions the commons has become a subdivision, and the plaza a parking lot.

Even weaker was the influence of a younger tradition, the Renaissance ideal of the monumental building dominating the streets which fan out from it. It found a charming realization in Annapolis, and it inspired L'Enfant's plan for Washington—awkwardly superimposed on the ubiquitous grid. From these it was to surface again in the plans of "the city beautiful."

Basically the city of industrial capitalism—in Europe as well as in America, only less consistently—was an assembly of real estate for various purposes, served by various networks. The networks multiplied as the cities grew larger and more complex. To the expanding networks of streets were added other networks for water, sewer, gas, electricity, rail traffic, and telephones. They were designed as citywide systems by engineers. What was built on the lots served by the systems was the concern not of the city, but of the property owners. The dichotomy between the horizontal and vertical dimensions became complete. The concept of streets and squares as well-proportioned containers of the community's life, so highly developed in the eighteenth century, decayed in the Europe of the nineteenth century. In America it had hardly taken root.

The commercial industrial city came into being not as a place for living, but as a place for making a living, a place for "making money." Neither God nor man designed it; Mammon did.

BACK TO NATURE

Sensitive spirits rebelled against its inhumanity, on both sides of the Atlantic. "The intellectual versus the city" is by no means a purely American phenomenon. "God made the country, but man made the city" was a widely accepted belief.

If God made the country, He could be brought back to the city by bringing the country into the city or the city into the country. The latter was made possible by the development of the railroad and the resulting suburbs. But more important was the movement headed by Frederick Law Olmsted for the creation of large "natural" city parks. Olmsted's vision extended beyond the creation of parks to the entire city, but only the parks became a reality.

Both the parks and the railroad suburbs were designed by landscape architects. Both had their contemporary counterparts in Europe, but only in America did landscape architecture become the mother of city planning.

THE CITY BEAUTIFUL

Wealthy Americans traveling abroad were impressed by the magnificence of European capitals, and their pride stimulated them to rival and surpass these cities. The great example was the Paris of Haussmann, the creation of the Second Empire, which had replaced the revolutionary battle cry "liberté, égalité, fraternité" by the slogan "enrichissez vous." Its spirit certainly was not alien to the American business tycoons. However, the drive became popular through the example of the Chicago World's Fair and spread under the banner of "the city beautiful," under Daniel Burnham's leadership and vision and in his plans for Chicago and San Francisco. Its concerns extended well beyond civic centers and monumental avenues, but by and large only these were built. Every American city wanted to have its Roman forum, but in most cases the width of the streets and the exaggerated scale deprived them of spatial impact.

What was the content of this grand form? What went on in its centerpiece, the city hall? Just at this time, more than ever, it had become a marketplace for the sale of favors, which Lincoln Steffens branded as "the shame of the cities." Not accidentally the nadir of civic responsibility coincided with the zenith of the civic center. The sham of "the city beautiful" was to hide the shame of the cities.

THE REFORM MOVEMENT

Lincoln Steffens was not alone: he gave voice to a reform movement which had been rising throughout the land. Americans were determined to do something about the inhuman and degrading conditions in which millions of their fellow citizens lived.

The settlement house and the playground movement laid the foundation for the concept of the urban neighborhood. But the housing reform movement which led to the establishment of building and housing codes was to have the most lasting effect on the American city. For the first time the public hand reached beyond the property line to shape the environment of the occupants of private structures.

The housing codes attempted to protect the poor. However, the middle class also needed and wanted protection, protection of its property against incompatible uses. Zoning was established as a property-protection device. But the value of a residential property can be impaired not only by "incompatible uses," but also by disruption of its visual environment. Therefore prescriptions were made governing height, coverage, and setbacks, and sometimes other features as well. As the zoning ordinance had to conform to the basic concept of "equality before the law," it enforced monotonous conformity. More than any other public action, the zoning ordinance became—and still is—the main designer and form-giver of American cities.

As zoning banned certain uses from certain zones, it had to allot space to them in some other location. Thus zoning became "comprehensive," and the municipality, for the first time, was forced to look at and to decide on the distribution of the various land uses on its territory.

THE MASTER PLAN

Form the convergence of the landscape architects' work on residential suburbs and on parks, the architects' work on "the city beautiful," the reformers' work on housing and neighborhood facilities, and the lawyers' work on zoning, the modern American city planning profession was born. It had to find its place alongside the older professions, those of the surveyors and municipal engineers, who were firmly established within the municipal administration and who continued to make the day-to-day decisions. The main task of the city planner was the design of a "master plan," an image of the future city, picturing the future distribution of land uses and the public works to be carried out by the municipality.

The image which guided the master plans generally reflected the four elements, enumerated above, from which the planning profession had developed. Some aspects of the plans were carried out, at least partially, but practically nowhere was the comprehensive design realized. The master plan might envisage the complete three-dimensioned form of the city, but the instruments in the planner's hand could not shape it. These instruments were mainly negative. The zoning map, which was to carry out the land use plan, could prevent the undesirable, but it could not create the desirable. Moreover, it could not change what was already on the ground.

The positive stimulants were not in the planner's hand. The most powerful elements made their own plans. Railroads or other industries owned most of the harbor sites and determined the fate of the waterfront, a key element in most American cities. Transit, gas, and power companies and other public utilities, while more closely related to municipal governments, also made their own plans. Even the state highway departments and the city's own engineers did not necessarily follow the master plan.

The innumerable decisions concerning the development of the many thousands of properties out of which the city was composed were made by their owners—as they had always and everywhere been made. Inevitably, the owners were guided primarily by the desire to put their land to the most profitable use—its "highest and best use" in the terminology of real estate. With the real estate tax as the predominant source of income, municipal governments were dominated by the same motivation. Of necessity, they did (and still do) everything to "attract assessment." When the zoning ordinance or some other element of the master plan stood in the way, it was amended or bent out of existence.

The master plan had, of course, attempted to foresee and to accommodate these economic pressures. But in a highly dynamic economy they constantly outgrew its provisions. Quantitatively, the actual city expanded beyond the boundary of the legal city, and new demands and new techniques changed it qualitatively.

THE INVISIBLE HAND

Thus the contemporary American city has, in fact, been designed not by a master plan but by the forces of the real estate market—good old Adam Smith's "invisible hand," the hand of Mammon. The invisible hand, as Adam Smith discovered with delight, has its own logic and rationale. Its creation is not chaos, as is often charged, but an order which can be analyzed and understood.

Land economists and urban ecologists have explored the design of the invisible hand. It can be grasped intellectually, but it remains invisible to the eye—with one exception. Viewed from a plane at night, the American city presents an impressive image: from the profusion of lights at the center the intensity gradually fades toward the periphery. Colored lights represent commercial concentrations, and the stream of headlights delineates the traffic flows. Three technical achievements of the twentieth century—electric light, the airplane, and the automobile—have come together to create not only an impression of great sensuous charm, but a genuine form revealing a meaningful content.

From the ground, however, this content, the workings of the invisible hand of the market, remains invisible. To make it visible is a still unresolved task of the urban planner and designer. Such "cooperation with the inevitable" is sometimes referred to with contempt. However, only a fool refuses to cooperate with the inevitable; the question is to determine what is and what is not really inevitable.

The invisible hand is the hand of the market, of the transaction between two persons, buyer and seller. However, when the objects of these transactions are the physical elements of a closely interrelated spatial complex, a city, each transaction is bound to affect many other persons, singly and collectively. The buyer and seller, however, cannot and do not consider the resultant benefits and "malefits" to third persons. Thus the pursuit by all individuals of their own designs results in a total design of the city which frustrates the designs of every individual.

"NEW TOWNS"

This universal frustration has led many planners to regard existing big cities as being beyond redemption and to concentrate their efforts on the creation of "new towns," designed by the community so as to harmonize and fulfill all individual designs and desires.

Out of the new town movement have come some of the best achievements of urban design in twentieth century America: Chatham Village in Pittsburgh and Baldwin Hills in Los Angeles, the "greenbelt towns," and the "new towns" of Reston, Columbia, and Irvine. They have had a far-reaching influence, however diluted, on the design of "neighborhoods" and subdivisions throughout North America and beyond. Even the biggest of these, however, though larger in area and population than most older towns, are not self-contained new towns, but parts of a larger metropolis, on which they are completely dependent. In fact, they are glorified upper- and middle-class suburbs, whose inhabitants largely depend on jobs outside the area, and they are often combined with industrial estates, which largely draw on an outside work force.

THE NEW SCALE

The form of the historical town could be perceived in two ways: from the outside as a sculptured mass, and from the inside as a system of enclosed spaces, of streets and squares. The spaces and structures were on a human scale. They could be perceived and encompassed by viewing from a distance at which a person could be recognized. All distances could be covered by a human being walking on his own two feet. The structures were built by human muscle.

The scale varied from the intimate one of the domestic environment through an entire range up to the monumental one of the symbolic buildings of civic and religious life. But even the grand "superhuman" scale of gods and kings could be related back to the size of the human being.

The modern metropolis is far too extensive to be perceived from any point as a sculptured mass, or as a system of spaces by walking through its streets. Streets go on to infinity, and movement is primarily by mechanical means. The monuments of gods and kings do not dominate the secular city. There are other and more impressive structures which are neither on the human nor on the superhuman scale: the great bridges, piers, grain elevators, hangars, and, most pervasive, the freeways with their interchanges. They are used not by human beings, but by machines; they are built not by human muscle, but by machines; and they are seen primarily by human beings moving not at their own speeds, but rather at the speed of machines. Their scale is neither human nor superhuman. I have called it "extrahuman," because it is outside the human being, part of "outer" nature, like mountains or rivers. These structures are elements of a new metropolitan landscape.

Related to them, but not quite a member of the family, is the most characteristic creation of the American city, the skyscraper. It is not entirely extrahuman, because it shelters human beings and its floor heights and windows are determined by their size. It is therefore not surprising that in its early day it was regarded and treated as a new variant of the monumental building on a superhuman scale, as a "cathedral of commerce." But increasingly the elements relating it to the human scale, floors and windows, are hidden behind curtains of glass, metal, or marble, assimilating it into the purely technical structures of extrahuman scale.

In either form the concentration of skyscrapers in the center has created the characteristic silhouette of the American city. Only in a single case, on the tip of

Manhattan Island, have the skyscrapers grouped themselves into a sculptured mass. As this was possible only by complete disregard for leaving space open for light, air, and movement, it certainly will never be repeated. Typically, the skyscrapers are too far apart to form a group and too close together to dominate as individual structures, and outside of the central business core their distribution is entirely haphazard.

The vertical extension of the skyscraper—the product of mechanical means of vertical transportation—and the horizontal extension of the metropolis–the product of mechanical means of horizontal transportation—have obliterated the street as a defined space of interrelated proportions. It is not accidental that the utopian images of the two most creative designers of this century, Frank Lloyd Wright and Le Corbusier, both negate the street. In Wright's "Broadacre City" the buildings, most of them low and rambling with an occasional tower, are scattered broadly over the landscape. But in its apparent opposite, Le Corbusier's "Radiant City," the emphasis is also primarily on sun, sky, and green. "But where," you will ask, "are the buildings?" Le Corbusier wrote, "Up there, above the trees, those crystalline prisms."

The forces which those great architects attempted to express in their designs, have been given a less inspiring form by the "invisible hand." Instead of Broadacre City we have narrowacre suburbs. The houses are, indeed, scattered, too scattered to form a street or any other collective unit, and they are too close together to register as individual units. On the other hand, the "high-rise" apartment developments and redevelopments, on or off stilts, are not ethereal visions, but heavily oppressive.

DESIGN FOR A MOTORIZED WORLD

While both Broadacre City and Radiant City accepted—indeed, enthusiastically welcomed—the automobile, it was not architects or planners, but the "invisible hand" which derived from the automobile America's most significant contribution to urban design, the suburban shopping center. By the complete separation of pedestrian from vehicular movement, it created anew in its malls and plazas the street and square as well-defined outdoor living spaces, and pointed the way for the revival of the human scale in the urban environment. This pedestrian world, however, still exists only as an island in an ocean of parked cars.

When the shoppers get into their cars and drive off, they enter a different world on a vastly larger scale, which finds its most complete expression in the freeway. The freeway creates two design problems: the view *to* and the view *from* the freeway. In an urban environment the first is usually best solved by locating the freeway below grade, in a cut or even in a tunnel. But the view *from* the highway requires a location at or above grade. In the wider metropolitan landscape, outside the densely built-up core, such a location can often be found at an edge, where the freeway does not disrupt, but emphasizes the natural or man-made structure of the region. The driver's vision in motion can build up a composite memory image of the metropolis comparable to the composite image which was built up by walking through the streets of older and smaller towns. However, with the motor vehicle and other modern means of transportation and communication "urban" elements spread out further, destroying the traditional image of the countryside and bringing with them pollution of air, water, and soil.

THE REVENGE OF THE GODS

Not only the city is disrupting the ecological balance of nature. Practices of farming and logging have an equal share of responsibility. Typically the American farmer has not been a "husbandman," not married to the soil, but used to "mining" it. There is in Western thought no counterpart to the ancient wisdom of *feng-shui*—wind and water—which has governed Chinese city planning.

The ancient gods of the sacred soil will not tolerate forever the violation of their laws. Man may forget that he is part of nature and treat her merely as a source of "raw materials" to be utilized and then be thrown away as "waste," but the waste returns to haunt him. He can continue to live only if he preserves and restores the ecological balance.

This balance is not static. The American landscape is not just "Oh Wilderness!" It can be a man-made landscape, based on a new and different balance of all its elements, human beings and their works included.

THE NEXT FIFTY YEARS

The "design" of the continental landscape of America is perhaps the most challenging task confronting planners in the next half century. This includes the location of cities; the control of the flow of surface and subsurface waters; and the design of the shores of rivers, lakes, and oceans, from lonely beaches to the quays of city centers.

On the scale of the metropolis it means articulating its structure by a system of subcenters related to a main center, and making these relations visible by the concentration of tall structures at the focal points. It means giving form to the edges between districts of different character—land and water recreation spaces, various kinds of built-up districts—and unfolding the total image as a sequence of memorable images along the paths of vision in motion.

Within the centers there is the task of separating the realm of the pedestrian from that of the motor vehicle—vertically or horizontally—of shaping pedestrian islands on the human scale and of connecting them with each other. In an age of science the universities, as places for life-long education, may well become the most significant elements of urban centers.

In the vast residential areas the task is to overcome functional and structural sterile uniformity and, in particular, to develop new and richer forms for single-family houses and their groupings.

Technically the means at the disposal of the designer are almost unlimited, and they will become increasingly so economically as well in the decades to come. Will we, as a profession, together with the other design professions, have the creative imagination to use them? Will we, as a nation, have the will to use them?

A planner recently wrote: "The people of this nation expect to *provide* security for their capital, and *allow* for their community's physical development"[1] (emphasis mine). Will the people of the United States and of Canada reverse their priorities? Will they want, while *allowing* for security of their capital, to *provide* their community's physical development? That is the crucial design problem of the next 50 years.

[1] Roger Feinstein in a book review, *Journal of the American Institute of Planners.* Vol. XXXIII, p. 126, March 1967.

Appendix A
THE CAREER OF HANS BLUMENFELD

Hans Blumenfeld was born in Osnabrück, a city in northwest Germany, in 1892. His father was a lawyer in Hamburg, and his mother was from a prominent Hamburg banking family. An uncle and a cousin were art historians. He wanted to be an architect from an early age, but his family wanted him to study law. He registered as a law student at the University of Tubingen, but worked as a volunteer apprentice in an architect's office.

This experience confirmed his architectural avocation. He began his formal architectural studies at the Technische Hochschule in Munich, where he studied from 1911–1912, attending lectures by Heinrich Wolfflin, the noted and influential Swiss art historian and theorist. He continued his studies in Karlsruhe from 1912 to 1914, under Friedrich Ostendorf, a brilliant teacher of a methodical approach to complex problems, and A. E. Brinckman, a noted scholar of the history of city planning and design.

During World War I he served as a private in the German Army, from 1914 to 1918. His older brother, whom he much admired and who had studied law and political science at Cambridge, was killed in the war. His experiences at the front deepened his opposition to war; and, while still in the army, he joined political movements directed at the struggle for peace and social justice. He has maintained these interests throughout his life, as the philosophical and moral core from which his professional objectives derive.

After the war he resumed his studies in Munich under Theodor Fisher, architect and town planner. He earned his degree in 1921 from the Technische Hochschule in Darmstadt.

He worked in the United States from 1924 to 1927, in New York, Baltimore, and Los Angeles. In 1927 he returned to Hamburg, where he worked with Karl Schneider, a German architect of the modern movement. From 1928 to 1930 he worked in Vienna under Joseph Frank and Adolf Loos. He participated in Frank's project for the notable Berlin-Siemensstadt housing competition, which was won by Walter Gropius.

In 1930 he accepted an invitation to work in the Soviet Union, attracted like many others by an atmosphere of creativity and social purpose. From 1930 to 1933 he worked in the Russian State City Planning Institute in Moscow and Gorki, an experience that affirmed the main interest of his career, city and regional planning.

He worked on the plans of the towns of Vladimir and Vyatka (now Kirov). He became president of a German workers' club.

From 1933 to 1935 he did the planning for the nonindustrial portions of the city of Makeyevka in the Donyetz basin—site planning, housing, schools, recreation, cultural centers, sports, and so on. He returned to Moscow in 1935 to head the architectural division of the Moscow Provinces Project Trust. Meanwhile, political difficulties in Russia had intensified, and foreign experts came to be regarded with suspicion. Although Blumenfeld remained in Russia while many other non-Russian experts departed, he was finally compelled to leave in 1937.

Unable to return to Germany, because of Nazism and Jewish persecution, and having an expired German passport, he left Russia through Turkey and managed to reach France. He was unsuccessful in his attempt to enlist in the fight against Franco in Spain. He did manage to obtain a visa to the United States, where a sister and brother-in-law had been living since 1922.

Arriving in New York in 1938, he found work in the design of the General Motors model of a "future city" for the 1939 World's Fair. He became acquainted with the American planner, Melville Branch. During 1939–1940 he served as an architect and planner on public housing projects in New Jersey, and was active in the Citizens' Housing and Planning Council of New York, working with Henry Churchill, Charles Abrams, and other leaders of the American housing movement. He also worked with architect and planner Albert Mayer in 1940.

From 1941 to 1944 he directed research for the Philadelphia Housing Association, a private organization. He became an American citizen in 1944. From 1945 to 1948 he served as senior land planner with the City Planning Commission of Philadelphia. In both organizations he was associated with Edmond Bacon. From 1948 to 1952 he was chief of the Division of Planning Analysis.

He spent four months in 1949 in Germany at the invitation of planner and architect Samuel B. Zisman (uncle of the editor of this book). The purpose of the visit, sponsored by the U.S. Military Government, was to observe and comment on the state of urban planning and rebuilding in German cities. His German colleagues received him with great warmth.

In 1952 he was required to sign a "loyalty oath" occasioned by the Loyalty Act of the state of Pennsylvania. He did so, and then resigned in protest. After traveling for several months, he returned to Philadelphia, where he worked as a planning consultant until 1955. In 1953 the U.S. State Department had refused to renew his passport because of his previous political affiliations, making it impossible for him to travel abroad.

By now his work in North America had earned wide professional recognition. In 1955 he left the United States to become assistant director of the newly formed Metropolitan Toronto Planning Board, Toronto having become the first city in North America to adopt a metropolitan form of government. He served in this position until 1961.

Since then he has been teaching at the University of Toronto and has served as a consultant to the cities of Toronto, Montreal, and Vancouver, and to federal and provincial agencies of the Canadian government. He has been an advisor to the Grosvenor Estate in London and Hawaii, and to the United Nations and the Organization for Economic Corporation and Development. He has served as a consultant in several cities in Israel, and to the Israeli government.

He has also been a much sought after lecturer and teacher and has become a prolific writer. In 1967 *The Modern Metropolis,* a book of some 33 essays and book reviews, was published, written in the main over the previous 20 years. (For further information on this publication see Appendix B.)

His professional reputation and the esteem of his colleagues has been affirmed by the American Institute of Planners, which bestowed its Distinguished Service Award on him, and by honorary doctoral degrees from the Université de Montréal and the University of Waterloo.

In December 1977 the Toronto Association for Peace held a testimonial dinner in his honor. Charles A. Blessing, the eminent American city planner and past president of the American Institute of Planners, delivered an address in which he elucidated Dr. Blumenfeld's life-long dedication to world peace and human development has the moral foundation of his towering intellectual achievements in urbanism.

Dr. Blumenfeld lives in Toronto, where he maintains his professional activities as planning consultant, teacher, lecturer, and writer.[1]

---

[1] See also "Hans Blumenfeld: Humanist and Urban Planner," by Norman Pressman, published in *Plan Canada* (Journal of the Canadian Institute of Planners), March 1976.

Appendix B

CONTENTS OF "THE MODERN METROPOLIS"

An earlier selection of Hans Blumenfeld's essays was published as The Modern Metropolis: Its Origins, Growth, Characteristics, and Planning, Paul D. Spreiregen, Editor, M.I.T. Press, Cambridge, Mass., 1967 (paperback edition, 1971). Summaries of those earlier essays follow.

Section I The Modern Metropolis: Its Origins, Growth, and Form

Chapter 1 *Form and Function in Urban Communities*
A perspective on cities in history, their form, and the way planning operates.

Chapter 2 *Theory of City Form, Past and Present*
A discussion of form and its evolution, with the theories that grow therefrom.

Chapter 3 *Alternative Solutions for Metropolitan Development*
A discussion of possible and conjectural metropolitan forms.

Chapter 4 *The Urban Pattern*
Understanding urban form.

Chapter 5 *The Modern Metropolis*
The reasons for the formation of the metropolis, and what can be done to manage it.

Section II Metropolitan and Regional Planning

Chapter 6 *Metropolitan Area Planning*
A discussion based on Toronto.

Chapter 7 *Regional Planning*
The basis for a regional approach.

Chapter 8 *Some Lessons for Regional Planning from the Experience of the Metropolitan Toronto Planning Board*
Cogent lessons from experience.

Chapter 9 *A Hundred-Year Plan: The Example of Copenhagen*
An article written in response to C. A. Doxiadis' proposal for the metropolitan growth of Copenhagen. The 1947 "finger plan" and the 1960 "city section plan" are shown. A cogent discussion.

Section III   Transportation

Chapter 10   Experiments in Transportation–for What?
A common sense discussion of how urban transportation works. This article will disappoint "grantsmen."

Chapter 11   Transportation in the Modern Metropolis
A further discussion and clarification of urban transportation mechanics.

Chapter 12   Transportation in San Francisco
Observations.

Chapter 13   Montreal's Subway
The system, its design, its operations.

Chapter 14   Monorail for Toronto?
A clear debunking of an idea too long taken seriously. The first monorail, in Wuppertal, Germany, is described, as well as the unique reasons for its creation.

Chapter 15   Why Pay to Ride?
An old idea very clearly argued.

Section IV   Residential Areas

Chapter 16   Residential Densities
This article is a classic.

Chapter 17   Comments on the Neighborhood Concept
An old idea beautifully and wittily clarified.

Chapter 18   The "Good Neighborhood"
A discussion of Jane Jacob's neighborhood theories, again thoughtful, clarifying, and properly humorous.

Chapter 19   Urban Renewal
A no-holds-barred condemnation of a brutal system of American "slum clearance." A critique of attacking symptoms rather than correcting causes.

Chapter 20   Problems of Urban Renewal
More on the same theme.

Chapter 21   The Cité Ouvrière of Mulhouse, France
A description of a unique and model housing development enterprise from the mid-nineteenth century. A still applicable idea.

Section V   Urban Design

Chapter 22   Universal Dilettant
An unapologetic apologia for professional planners.

Chapter 23   Scale in Civic Design
A classic essay on the subject.

Chapter 24   Scale in the Metropolis
An extension of the principles of scale to a larger area.

Chapter 25   Design with the Automobile—The Metropolitan Region
An outstanding exposition on an often misunderstood subject.

Chapter 26   Continuity and Change of Urban Form
A penetrating and assuring insight into a fundamental urban phenomenon.

Chapter 27   A Visitor Looks at the Montreal Exhibition: "Expo 1967"

Section VI Methodology of Planning

Chapter 28 Science and Planning
A cogent essay on a cogent relationship.

Chapter 29 The Conceptual Framework of Land Use
A critique of normal practices, and a suggestion for alternatives.

Chapter 30 Projection and Planning of Transportation and Land Use
A discussion of methods.

Chapter 31 Limitations of Simulation of Future Behavior
Possibilities and limitations.

Chapter 32 Are Land-Use Patterns Predictable?
More on possibilities and limitations.

Chapter 33 The Economic Base of the Metropolis: Critical Remarks on the "Basic-Nonbasic" Concept
A detailed examination of a one-time focus of planning theorists.

Appendix C
ADDITIONAL ESSAYS

On The Metropolis

"On the Concentric-Circle Theory of Urban Growth," *Land Economics* (Madison, Wis.), May 1949, pp. 209–212.

> An analysis of data from the 1940 census for the city of Philadelphia, demonstrating the regular concentric distribution of significant qualitative as well as quantitative phenomena.

"The Dominance of the Metropolis," *Land Economics* (Madison, Wis.), May 1950, pp. 194–196.

> A discussion of the book *The Structure of the Metropolitan Community* by Don J. Bogue, indicating the possibility of a different interpretation of the data presented therein.

"The Tidal Wave of Metropolitan Expansion," *Journal of the American Institute of Planners,* Winter 1954, pp. 3–14.

> An analysis of the dynamics of population movement in the Philadelphia Metropolitan Area, 1900–1950, developing the new concept of the "crest of the wave of metropolitan expansion" as a tool for prediction of population distribution.

"The Exploding Metropolis," *Monthly Review* (New York), April 1959, pp. 476–486.

> A critical review of a book written by the editors of *Fortune* magazine, pointing out contradictions between the analysis of the problems and the remedies proposed.

"L'Habitation dans les Métropoles," *Architecture, Batiment, Construction,* Southam Ltd., Montreal, May 1966.

> An analysis of the changes in the characteristics and in the distribution of various housing types in response to economic, social, and technical changes, with some suggestions for modification of present practices.

"Metropolitan Area Planning," *Board of Trade Journal* (Toronto), 1956.

"Will Metro Continue to Grow?" Toronto Area Research Conference, March 1970.

"The Boundaries of Metropolitan Toronto," A Comment to the Royal Commission on Metropolitan Toronto, May 1975.

"The Meaning of the Inner City in the 20th Century," *Focus on Downtown,* Manitoba Division of the Community Planning Association and the University of Monitoba, Winnipeg, January 1966.

Editor's Note: The works listed here, together with those in *The Modern Metropolis* and the present volume, comprise all of Hans Blumenfeld's writings that have come to my attention. In addition, Dr. Blumenfeld has authored or contributed to a number of planning reports. These are not mentioned, since the essays here and in *The Modern Metropolis* cover their substance. There may also be some book reviews and other writings that evaded my search. I have tried, within reason, to be as complete as possible.

"**Regional Environment**" C.P.A. Symposium I: "Debunk: A Critical Review of Accepted Planning Principles," The Council for Planning Action, Boston, Littaver Center, Harvard, May 7, 1949.

> A brief comment.

On Planning Methodology

"**A Neglected Factor in Estimating Housing Demand,**" *Land Economics* (Madison, Wis.), August 1944, pp. 264–270.

> A study of the role of nonfamily households, predicting that high national income would lead to a vast expansion of housing demand from this source.

"**Correlation between the Value of Dwelling Units and Altitude,**" *Land Economics* (Madison, Wis.), November 1948, pp. 396–402.

> Demonstration of a consistent positive correlation between these two sets of data in Metropolitan Philadelphia in 1950, with an indication of its general validity in modern metropolitan areas.

"**The Planning of the Urban Structure,**" Xth Inter-American Planning Congress, Panama, 1974.

On Transportation

"**Transportation in the Modern Metropolis,**" *Queen's Quarterly* (Kingston, Ont.), Winter 1961, pp. 640–653.

> An earlier and shorter version of the article with the same title included in this volume.

"**A Factual Evaluation of Toronto's Investment in Mass Transit,**" *Proceedings of the Institute of Traffic Engineers,* 1963.

> An analysis of the experience of the Toronto transit system.

"**Criteria for Transportation Planning,**" *Proceedings of Symposium on Urban Transportation Research,* Organization for Economic Cooperation and Development, Paris, France, 1968.

On Design

"**The Integration of Natural and Artificial Light,**" *Architectural Record* (New York), December 1940-April 1941, pp. 49–56, 69–76.

> A study of the relation between light and seeing and of the characteristics of various means of natural and artificial lighting.

"**On a Peculiar Feature of the City Plan of Mohenjo-Daro,**" *Journal of the Society of Architectural Historians,* January 1942, pp. 24–26.

> An investigation of the relation of apparent irregularities of street lines to orientation as a possible indication of concepts and methods of pre-Aryan city planning in India.

"**The Toronto Civic Square,**" *Mosaic,* publication of the Architectural Society, School of Architecture, University of Toronto, 1957.

> A commentary on a major new civic plaza.

"**A New Theory of the Ventilation of the City**" (in Russian), *Sovietskaya Architekturn,* 1955.

"**Scale in the Metropolis,**" *Canadian Architect,* September 1957.

Additional Essays—Appendix C

On Russian Planning

"Regional and City Planning in the Soviet Union," *Task* (Cambridge, Mass.), Issue No. 3, 1942, pp. 33–52.

> A presentation of Soviet experience up to World War II.

"Russian City Planning of the 18th and Early 19th Centuries," *Journal of the Society of Architectural Historians,* January 1944, pp. 22–33.

> A presentation of the principles, methods, and achievements of Russian city planning during this period.

"Soviet City Planning," *American Review on the Soviet Union* (New York), November 1944, pp. 53–65.

> A presentation of the author's work on the replanning of the town of Vladimir.

"Municipal Reconstruction," *The U.S.S.R. in Reconstruction,* American Russian Institute, Inc., New York, 1944, pp. 72–82.

> Soviet activity in this field during the war.

"The Soviet Housing Problem," *The American Review on the Soviet Union* (New York), November 1945, pp. 12–25.

> Prewar and war experience and postwar plans

"Reconstruction U.S.S.R." *Task* (Cambridge, Mass.), Issues No. 7 and 8, 1948, pp. 25–33.

> A discussion of the principles, methods, and standards of Soviet city planning in the early postwar years.

Other Publications or Essays

"Mehico y Filadelfia," *Arquitectura* (Mexico), January 1949.

> A speech, originally, in which the two cities were compared.

Utopia, Ltd.: The Story of the English New Town of Stevenage, by Harold Orlans, Yale University Press, New Haven, Conn., 1953.

> A book review. Publication and date unavailable.

The City: The Urban Fact Throughout the World, by Pierre George (in French), Presses Universitaires de France, Paris, 1952.

> A book review. Publication and date unavailable.

"Residential Densities," *Task* (Cambridge, Mass.), 1957.

> This material is covered in other essays.

"Toronto and Hamilton," *Planning Opinion,* Central Ontario Chapter, Town Planning Institute of Canada, January 1959.

> A comparison of the two cities.

"Our Rivers, Today and Tomorrow," speech delivered in Arvida, Que., to the Community Planning Association of Canada, June 1962.

"Population: Another View," *Thoughts,* Science Council of Canada, 1972.

"New Urban Communities in Canada," *Contact* (University of Waterloo).

> Date unavailable.

SUBJECT INDEX

Agricultural land:
  land use controls, 192
  natural resource-commodity, 193
  rural non-farm adverse effects, 192
  urban absorption, 81-82, 189-194, 370
  urban adverse effects on, 192
  versus urban, cost-benefits, 193
Agriculture:
  limits to growth, 365-366
  water shortage, 366
Air pollution, 13, 42-43, 295
Airport:
  accident impact, 322
  air pollution, 322
  busses, 324, 326-328
  cargo terminals, 320, 328
  flight paths, 10, 319, 330
  land acquisition, 324, 329-330
  land requirements, 320, 324, 329-330
  limousine service, 326
  location, 324
    costs, 322, 324
  mail terminal, 328
  noise, 321
  passenger terminal:
    auxiliary, 325, 327
    building, 326, 327
    downtown, 323, 325
    location, 327
    scale and movement, 323
    transportation, 323-325
  rapid rail service to, 327
Alberti, Leone Batista, 9
Alpass, John, 69
Amortization:
  and real property tax, 259
Aristides, 153
Aristotle, 9, 332
Automobiles:
  accident, 7, 12-13, 40
  effect on urban density, 340, 342-345
  electric, 295
  and energy crisis, 351
  feeder systems, 298
  ownership in Canada, 296
  parking, *see* Parking
  social cost, 6-7, 294-296, 307-308

Barlow Report, 129
Beaubien, Charles:
  Perceptions 4: People and Agricultural Land
    (review), 189-194
Bicycles, 339, 343
  for developing countries, 384
Bloch, Ernst, 154
Blondin, Michel, 151
Blumenfeld, Hans:
  bibliography of works by, 407-409
  biography, 401-403
  Modern Metropolis, summaries, 404-406
Book review:
  Beaubien, Charles. *Perceptions 4: People and*
    Agricultural Land, 189-194
  Dennis, Michael. *Programs in Search of a*
    Policy, 227-230
  Grebler, Leo. *Europe's Reborn Cities*, 53-56
  Hall, Max. *Made in New York*, 61
  Housing and Employment, 207-208
  Lash, Harry. *Planning In a Human Way*, 110-115
  Maurizio, Julius. *Swiss Housing Estates,*
    1940-1950, 205-206
  Nader, George A. *Cities of Canada*, 62-64
  New York Metropolitan Region Study, 59-61
  Posokhin, M. V. *Cities to Live In*, 57-58
  Richardson, Boyce. *Future of Canadian Cities*,
    369-371
  Vernon, Raymond. *Anatomy of a Metropolis*,
    59-61
Boustedt, Dr. Olaf, 94, 96, 117
Buchanan Report, 11, 41, 286
Budget allotment for housing, 199, 217-218,
  234-235, 237-238
Burnham, Daniel, 395
Busses, 296, 298, 309
  for airports, 324, 326-328
  history, 306, 338

Caesar, Julius, 337
Canada:
  agricultural land, 191
  employment distribution, 148-149
  foreign investment, 241
  marriage statistics, 149
  National Housing Act, 145

natural resources, 159, 190
population distribution, 80-81, 90, 133, 139, 148, 291, 342
population size, 79, 291
urban future, 369-371, 400
urban history, 62-64, 141-142
urban versus agricultural land use, 191-194
Capitalism and urban problems, 369
Cars, see Automobiles
Central Business District (C.B.D.), 12, 28, 30-31, 59-60, 94, 297, 344-345
Central Mortgage and Housing Corporation (C.M.H.C.), 144, 147, 200, 223, 252-253, 330
report of, 227-230
"Central place" cities, 18-19, 62-63, 279, 289, 334
Chicago World's Fair, 395
Cicero, 34
Citizen:
 participation in planning, 88, 110-115
 roles in society, 367-368
City:
 centers, 5, 48-49, 54, 262-263, 280
 "central place," 18-19, 62-63, 279, 289, 334
 characteristics, 17-18, 332, 341
 countermagnet, 140, 375, 385
 definition and function, 16-18
 effect of internal transportation, 336
 effect of long distance transportation, 334-336, 340-342
 form, 82, 394
  bipolar, 21
  "city beautiful," 395
  determinants, 6-7, 9-11, 18-25, 337, 340
  radial, 21, 82
  growth ethic, 7, 114-115, 129-131
  growth forms, 82-83
  growth stages, 26-27
 harbor, 21, 279, 289, 302, 334
 life expectancy in, 373
 microclimate regulation, 44
 perception of structure, 279, 281, 286-287, 397
 planned versus organic, 17
 planner, see Planner
 primate, 375, 385
 productivity correlation, 381, 384
 space perception, 50-51, 398
Club of Rome, 361, 362
Codes, housing, 219
 in developing countries, 377
 history, 395-396
 and rehabilitation, 240-241, 254
 standards for setbacks, 270
 violation, 257
Communication, electronic:
 effect on settlements, 288-289, 339, 351
Commuting to work, 27-28, 37, 346
 centrifugal and crosstown trips, 298, 309, 313
 company vans, 350
 on expressways, 316
 future changes, 68
 Hamburg versus Toronto, 99
 type of transit used, 30
Conservation of buildings:
 definition, 233
Construction industry, 200, 214
Conurbation, 117
Corbusier:
 Unite complex, 274
 Ville Radieuse, 20, 399
Cost-benefit analysis:
 cost of foreign exchange, 379
 indirect costs, 378
 measuring benefits, 378, 380
 measuring costs, 377-378
 private versus public transit, 32, 83, 313-314, 349
Council housing, see Housing, projects
Countermagnet cities, 140, 375, 385
Crerar, Alistair, 192
Critical noise ratio, 321
Crown Corporation, 141, 147, 301

Decentralization of cities, 7, 34, 284
 Canada, 129-134, 140
 Eastern Europe, 187, 376
 Europe, 375
 planned economies, 376
 U.S. versus U.S.S.R., 187
 U.S.S.R., 376
Decentralization of industry, 261, 376
Dennis, Michael:
 Programs In Search of a Policy (review), 227-230
Dennis-Fish Report, 165, 227-230
Density, 339
 center versus periphery, 39-40, 39-40, 45, 290
 and community facilities, 269
 definition and measurement, 264-265
 European versus North American, 94
 need for limitation, 265-266
 need for variety, 47-48
 and open space requirements, 268
 and parking, 267-268
 and protection of light and air rights, 266-267
 underused housing, 257, 272
Developer, private:
 cost sharing of recreation facilities, 269-270
 land acquisition, 164-165, 172-173, 224, 232
 leasing land to, 166
 low income housing, 223
Developing countries:
 characteristics, 374
 community space, 383-384
 housing types needed, 381-382
 primate city, 375, 385
 resources for urban development, 390-392
 urbanization problems, 376-377
 utilities, 382
 work migration, 389-390
Development rights, 166-167, 170-171
Dial-a-bus, 309, 348, 350
Differential rent, 169-170, 212, 258

Subject Index

Disinvestment, 250-251
Downtown, see City, centers
Doxiadis, Constantine, 66, 116
Dumont, Rene, 366

Eesteren, C. van, 73
Ekistic logarithmic scale, 117
Energy crisis, 310, 365
Engel's law, 174, 212
Engine, internal combustion, 295, 307
Eutrophication of rivers, 43, 363
Expressway:
  accidents, 6-7, 40
  advantages, 315
  bypass, 31, 315
  for commutation, 316
  definition, 314
  design, 315
  elevated, 299, 317
  growth in America, 312
  views of and from, 51, 280-281, 299, 316, 399

Feng-shui, 400
Fertility rate:
  effect of urbanization, 362, 366, 368
Filtering process (housing), 222-223, 228
  accelerating, 245-248
Fish, Susan:
  Programs in Search of a Policy (review), 227-230
Floor area ratio, see Floor space index
Floor space index (F.S.I.), 265, 267, 269
  recommendation for establishing, 269-270
Fontana, Domenico, 21, 279
Foreign investment in Canada, 241
Freeways, see Expressway
Freidorf, Basel, Switzerland, 206
Fugger, Jacob, 256

Galbraith, Kenneth, 51-52
Geddes, Patrick, 46, 88, 117, 150, 390
Geography, effect on city sites, 18-25
Gertler, Leonard, 192
GO trains, 312-313
Goethe, J. W., 25, 394
Gottmann, Jean, 66, 116, 118, 124
Gourley, Robert, 4, 339
Government:
  coordination for planning, 301-302
  incentives for increasing housing, 248
  metropolitan regional, 301
  role in rehabilitation, 242
  as slum landlord, 254
Government, federal:
  agencies for urban affairs, 146
  local autonomy problems, 4, 142
  policies affecting urban areas, 133, 143-146
    242, 303-304
  research responsibility, 141, 304
  tax reform, 143
Government, municipal:

incentives to industry, 261
role in planning, 84-86, 135-138, 142-143, 219, 248
taxing capability, 143
Government, provincial:
  role in planning, 84-86, 134-135, 147, 160, 214,
    232, 248
Greber master plan, 73-78
Grebler, Leo:
  Europe's Reborn Cities (review), 53-56
Greenbelt, 13-14, 17, 21, 24, 34, 47, 57, 75-76, 78, 83,
  166
Grossman, Irving, 283
Gross national product:
  developing versus developed nations, 372
  rehabilitation effects, 241-242, 251
Growth, global:
  effect of urban concentration, 366
  ethics, 368
  limits, 362, 367
  technology needed, 363
Growth ethic, 7, 367
Growth rate of cities, 7, 114-115
  Canada, 139
  effect of transportation system on, 290, 332-352
  German Democratic Republic, 180-184
  hostility toward, 34, 370
  international comparisons, 129-131
  U.S.S.R., 184-186
Gustafson, Neil C.:
  study of megalopolis communications, 118-124

Hägerstrand, Thorsten, 154, 155
Hall, Max:
  Made In New York (review), 61
Harbor cities, 21, 279, 289, 302, 334
Haussmann, Eugene, 22, 395
Hegemann, Werner, 16, 340
Hellyer Report, 229
High rise buildings, 274-275, 398-399
Hire purchase agreement, 256
Hoegtorget project (Stockholm), 12
Household, size change, 272, 382
Houses:
  multifamily, 274
  single family, 273
Housing:
  building costs, 200, 243
  codes, 219, 240-241, 254, 257
  demand, 236-237
  and employment, 207-208
  filtering process, 222-223, 228
  hire purchase agreements, 256
  income allotment for, 199, 217-218, 234-235,
    237-238
  industry, 200, 214
  low income for Ontario, 209-225
  mortgage, 252-253
    interest rates, 201, 215, 253, 256
  for old people, 218, 221-222
  operating costs, 201, 215-216

ownership, encouraging, 256-257
policy, 227-230, 255
prefabricated, 200
price determinants, 5, 211-216
problems as function of poverty, 198, 236
projects, 202, 220
   access, 242
   limits discouraging investments, 246
   in Montreal, 202-203
quality versus quantity, price, 211
rehabilitation of old homes, 151-152, 202-204, 219, 221
   effect on gross national product, 241-242
   labor costs, 242
   by low income groups, 223-239
   versus new units, 202-204, 244
   by property owner, 240
   by public investment, 241-242
segregation, 5, 11, 15, 45-46
self-help, 214-215, 385-386, 391
standards, 211, 218-219, 229, 377
subletting, 215
subsidies, 145, 152, 201-202, 228
   versus direct subsidy, 218
   for ownership, 224
   for rehabilitation, 230
supply, 5, 47, 147, 202, 207-208, 209-211, 216-217
   determining need, 209
   in Ontario, 209-211
tax on excess rooms, 210
types:
   demand, 272, 381-382
   need for variety, 45-46, 224, 263, 275
underused, 257, 272
Howard, Ebenezer, 45, 60, 131
Hoyt, Homer, 137
Human scale, 50-51, 286, 398-399
   at airports, 323
   extrahuman scale, 398
   in skyscrapers, 398

Income redistribution, 198-199, 208, 217, 260, 369
Indians, American, 393
Islam, 83, 273, 337

Jacobs, Jane, 17, 50, 138
Jitneys, 350
Job choice, 11, 36-37, 39

Kropotkin, Peter, 34

Labor productivity, 364
   versus city size, 381, 384
   developing versus developed nations, 372
   in tertiary sector, 374
Land:
   acquisition by cities, 166, 248-249
   agricultural, see Agricultural land
   bank:
      acquisition of land, 166, 224

advantages of public ownership, 164-165, 172
allocation problems, 213
in Canada, 166
   for developed land, 167
as commodity, 175, 394
development costs, 213-214
monopoly, 165, 213, 229
public ownership, 5-6, 86-87, 137, 164-168, 172
   of development rights, 166-167, 171
speculators, 165, 171, 175
tax, 163-164
values:
   and allocative functions, 169-170, 213
   determinators, 162, 165, 169
   development rights, 166-167
   impact of planning, 170-172
   market price system, 162, 167, 169, 173
   in Montreal and Toronto, 165
Land planning:
   for decrease, 160
   in democracy, 153-156, 187
   effect on land values, 76, 170-172
   impact of transportation, 356-357
   and market economy, 187-188, 397
   master plans, 73, 112-113, 396-397
   projections, 353-354, 356
Lash, Harry:
   Planning In a Human Way (review), 110-115
Le Blond, 22
L'Enfant, 394
Limited dividend housing company, 245, 253, 256
Lithwick Report, 133, 137
Long range planning, 154-156, 171-172, 353-354
Lynch, Kevin, 279

Maisonnette, 273
Malthus, Thomas, 364
Manor, 16-17
Marx, Karl, 34, 110, 154, 170, 180, 219
Master plans, 73, 112-113, 396-397
Maurizio, Julius:
   Swiss Housing Estates, 1940-1950 (review), 205-206
Megalopolis:
   definition, 66, 116-117
   interaction in, 118
      measured by phone calls, 119-124
   validity of concept, 124-126, 290
Metropolis:
   concentric zone densities, 28
   definition, 4, 9, 27, 65
   future form, 65-70, 400
   role of economics in, 9, 27-28, 35-37
Metropolitan area, see Metropolis
Metropolitan Toronto and Area Transportation Study, 96, 133-134
Meyer, Hannes, 206
Mobile homes, 214, 224
Modern Metropolis, synopsis, 404-406
Monopoly on land holding, 165, 213, 229

Subject Index

Mortgage:
    insured, 252-253
    interest rates, 201, 215, 253, 256
Mound builders, 393
Multi-family houses, 274
Mumford, Lewis, 18, 116

Nader, George A.:
    Cities of Canada (review), 62-64
Natural resources:
    depletion, 362, 364-365
    recycling, 363
Neighborhoods:
    centers, 48-49
    density definition, 265
    growth cycle, 60
    harat, 83
    parking problems, 251
    as planning agencies, 84-85, 88, 154
    size, 47
New towns, 131-132, 320, 375
    in developing countries, 387
    land acquisition, 166
    in U.S., 397-398
    see also Satellite towns
New York Metropolitan Region Study (review), 59-61

Obsolescence:
    functional, 232, 250
    physical, 232
    rate, 232
Olmstead, Frederick Law, 4, 395
Ombudsman, 112
Ontario Planning Act, 142, 248

Papaicannou, F. G., 117
Parking, 13
    for commercial areas, 261
    and density limitations, 267-268
    needs in Toronto, Montreal, 294
    in rehabilitation areas, 251
    tax exemptions, 144, 297
Pascal, Blaise, 306, 338
Pedestrian:
    malls, 54, 262, 283
    traffic, 30, 40-42
        in Toronto, 262
    vehicular separation, 11-12, 41-42, 54, 263, 280, 283
Pennsylvania Redevelopment Law of 1945, 249
Philadelphia Housing Authority, 203, 243
Pipeline, underground goods movement, 292
Planner:
    role of, 87-88, 111-115, 155
Planning as profession, 87-88, 155
    history, 396-397
Plato, 17
Plazas, 394
Population:

concentration for development, 159, 292
distribution, 129-132
fertility rate, 362, 366, 368
global growth, 361-362, 368
migration:
    and city size, 291-292, 373
    from poor areas, 160
    into and out of cities, 67, 129-131, 139
    into and out of towns, 69
    research problems, 91
    rural farm decrease, 160
    rural farm versus rural non-farm, 139
    size, distribution in Canada, 79-81, 90, 132, 139
urban as percent of total, 187
Posokhin, M. V.:
    Cities to Live In (review), 57-58
Prefabricated housing, 200, 214
Primate city, 375, 385
Private developer, *see* Developer, private
Property tax, *see* Tax, real property
Public housing, *see* Housing, projects

Quality of life:
    physical environment influences, 35, 37-44, 45-52
    social influences, 35, 47-50, 88

Radburn Plan, 41, 283
Railroads, 3-4, 10
    as land planners, 396
    in prairie provinces, 160
    relocation, 76-77
Railroad suburbs, 4, 339, 395
Rapid transit, 280
    financing, 12, 32, 296-297, 308, 313-314, 348
    historical use, 6-7, 339
    individually controlled, 348
    requirements for efficient use, 30-31, 284-285
    STARR system, 348
Reconstruction:
    post W.W. II cities, 53-56
Recreational facilities, 44, 251, 395
    and building densities, 268
Redevelopment, *see* Urban renewal
Rehabilitation of older homes, 151-152, 202-204, 219, 221
    acquisition:
        costs, 244, 249, 251
        policy, 254
    costs, 244
    definition, 233
    and designation of urban renewal area, 249
    effect on gross national product, 241-242
    industrial-commercial sites, 260-262
    insured mortgages for, 252-253
    labor costs, 242
    by lower income groups, 233-239
    versus new units, 202-204, 244
    planning for, 255
    privately financed, 239, 255

by property owner, 240-241, 256
by public investment, 241-242
public services needed, 251-252
relocation costs of inhabitants, 239, 257
and social environment, 252
Reserved lane public transportation, 310
Richardson, Boyce:
Future of Canadian Cities (review), 369-371
Road system:
access versus through streets, 314
elimination of, 310
Roman, 335
see also Expressway
Row houses, 213, 224, 271, 273, 283
see also Zeilenbau

Satellite boroughs, 13, 82, 91, 131, 160-161, 386, 389
Secondary downtowns:
land acquisition, 300
as transportation centers, 300
see also Satellite boroughs
Segregation, housing, 5, 11, 15, 45-46
Setback standards, 270
Shopping centers, 41, 344, 399
Single family houses, 273
Skyscraper, see High rise buildings
Slum clearance, see Urban renewal
Slum landlords, 236, 254
Smith, Adam, 397
Smith Report on Taxation, Ontario, 136-137
Socialism and urban growth, 180
Solar energy, 364-365
Solar heating, 216
STARR transportation system, 299
Street:
block patterns, 20-21, 262, 394
obsolescence, 232
in pedestrian cities, 337
bridges, 55
historical vehicular use, 337-338
in modern architecture, 399
social use, 41, 47, 296
Streetcars, 310, 338
Subdivision approval and land values, 165, 172, 213
Subletting, 215
Subsidy, income, 218, 228
Subsidy housing, 145, 152, 201-202, 224-225, 228, 237
versus direct subsidy, 218, 247
for ownership, 224
for rehabilitation, 230
Subsidy means test, 224-225, 228
Suburb, history, 65
Subways, see Rapid transit
Sunlight and building density, 266-267

Tabacnik, Ruth:
Perceptions 4: People and Agricultural Land (review), 189-194
Tange, Kenzo, 286

Tax:
capital gains, on land sales, 173-174, 212, 387
central collection of, 303
on excess rooms, 210, 212
exemption of federal government, 143-144
improvements, 136
land, 163-164
real property, 4, 14, 86-87, 143, 163-164, 211-212
amortized-non-amortized investment, 259
dual nature, 174
effect on housing cost, 174-176, 212, 258
exemptions for rehabilitation, 216, 220
reform, 87, 136, 143
short term effects, 216, 259
site value, 5-6, 136, 143, 163-164, 212
Technocrats, 153-156
Telephone:
influence on urban development, 288
use as megalopolis interaction measure, 119-124
Teletrans, 299, 313
Television, closed circuit, 288, 351
Toronto:
building costs, 243
commutation number and type, 313
distribution of incomes, 234
distribution of workplaces, 99-108
employment:
density, 101-102, 298
type, 95
form determinants, 19, 95
growth plan, 134
housing costs, 201, 234-235, 243-244
housing type, 95, 101, 105-107
International Airport, 320, 323, 326
land use, 102
monopoly on land, 229
parking needs, 294
population density, 96-98, 100-101, 104
property tax, 258
rapid transit, 298
relocation of rail lines, 302
Transit Commission, 349
transportation statistics, 107-108, 282-283, 349
Traffic:
architecture, 299, 317, 393
congestion abolishment, 306
pedestrian, 30, 40-42
research, 354-355
separation of vehicles, pedestrians, 11-12, 41-42, 54, 263, 280, 283
vehicular:
within metropolis, 29
reasons for, 28, 39, 282
Transfer point city, 21, 279, 289
Transportation:
balance of public, private, 284-285, 308
centralizing effect, 289, 341
cost benefits, 37, 285-286, 293-296, 298, 305
for defining city structure, 279-281, 299
effect on city form, 6-7, 9-11, 26, 301, 311

Subject Index

effect on city growth rate, 290
elements of system, 333
feeder systems, 298
of goods, 292, 333
long distance, 301, 318
  conflicts with city, 319
  effect on city, 334, 341
long range planning, 355
myths, 305-310
policy, as planning tool, 141, 289
public:
  cost-benefits, 32, 83, 313-314, 349
  drawbacks, 298-299, 309, 348
  financing, 32, 296-297, 308, 313-314, 348
  history, 335-336, 340-341
  myths, 307-310
  short distance, 345
  type of use, 29-30, 284
reserved lanes for public transport, 310
surface, 285, 313, 349
terminals, 301, 318-319
  air, see Airport
  size, 323
traffic corridor, 300
views of and from roads, 280-281, 299, 316
water, 335-336
Travel-time budget, 343, 347
Truck movement of goods, 293

United States Department of Housing and Urban Development, 146
Urban Development Institute, 165
Urban environment, 50
Urbanization:
  characteristics, 36, 149
  cost-benefits, 92, 161
  future, 400
  growth point theory, 140
  research problems, 90-93
Urban renewal:
  in Canada, 145-146, 151-152
  causes of slums, 150
  definition, 150, 231
  designation of area, 249-250

in Hamilton, Ontario, 237-238
historically, 149-150
land acquisition for, 167
mistakes of, 46-47, 145-146, 151, 155-156
in Montreal, 202-203
neighborhood role, 88
and obsolescence, 231
paternalism, 238
in Philadelphia, 203, 243
rehabilitation of older homes, 151-152, 202-203, 219, 222
  versus new units, 202-204
relocation:
  costs, 239
  of dispossessed, 199
slum clearance, 235-236
subsidies, 145, 152
Urban shadow, 192

Vernon, Raymond:
  Anatomy of a Metropolis (review), 59-61
  on land planning, 155
Village, farming, 16-17

Waste disposal, 13, 42
Waste utilization, 13, 43, 363, 365
Water:
  pollution, 43, 141, 143, 363, 383
  shortage, 366
Women workers, 148-149, 346
  in eastern Europe, 178-179
World War II reconstruction, 53-56
Wright, Frank Lloyd, 399

Zahavi, Jacov, 343, 347
Zeilenbau, 205-206
Zoning:
  in flight paths, 330
  historical use, 4-5, 396
  and land values, 162
  large-lot, 293-294
  minimum frontage, 213
  as planning tool, 14, 49, 396

GEOGRAPHICAL INDEX

Aigmes Mortes, France, 17
Albertslund, Copenhagen, Denmark, 273
Alexandra Park, Toronto, Canada, 243, 244, 249
Alexandria, Egypt, 34, 337, 338
Alster River, 24-25
Amsterdam, Netherlands, 23, 335, 337
Annapolis, Maryland, 394
Ankara, Turkey, 384
Antwerp, Belgium, 335
Athens, Greece, 19, 26, 36, 153, 334
Atlantic City, New Jersey, 119
Augsburg, Germany, 256
Auschwitz, Poland, 368
Australia, 164, 175

Baldwin Hills, Los Angeles, California, 273, 398
Baltimore, Maryland, 118
Bangkok, Thailand, 337
Bath, England, 14, 36
Berlin, Germany, 16, 34, 181, 338-340
Birmingham, England, 129
Boston, Massachusetts, 25, 116, 118
Bruges, Belgium, 23, 337
Buffalo, New York, 115, 335

Calgary, Alberta, Canada, 229, 342
Canada, see Canada in Subject Index
Caracas, Venezuela, 384
Cassel, Germany, 283
Catal Huyuk, 17
Centerville, Ohio, 393
Charleston, South Carolina, 338
Chartres, France, 19, 334
Chatham Village, Pittsburgh, Pennsylvania, 273, 398
Chicago, Illinois, 11, 14, 117, 271, 320, 395
China, 13, 18, 20, 43, 44, 271, 362, 364, 365, 394, 400
Cité Ouvrière, Alsace, France, 256
Columbia, Maryland, 398
Concordia Project, Montreal, Canada, 370
Copenhagen, Denmark, 41, 262, 273, 283
Coventry, England, 54, 283

Décarie Freeway, Montreal, Canada, 317
Detroit, Michigan, 16, 21, 115
Dorval Airport, Montreal, Canada, 319-320, 323, 369
Dulles Airport, Washington, D.C., 320, 323

Edinburgh, Scotland, 338
Edmonton, Alberta, Canada, 166, 342
Egypt, 335
Erie Canal, 335
Expo '67, Montreal, Canada, 380

Flemingdon Park, Toronto, Canada, 283
Florence, Italy, 43, 272
Fort Worth, Texas, 30
Frankfort, Germany, 149

German Democratic Republic, 177-188
German Federal Republic, 178-179
Ghana, 387
Greece, 44, 273, 394

Hamburg, Germany, 23-25, 94-109, 290, 340, 344-345
Hamilton, Ontario, Canada, 217, 237-238
Hangchow, China, 338
Holte, Denmark, 69
Hongkong, 386

Iraq, 335
Irvine, California, 398
Israel, 188

James Bay Project, 370
Jericho, 26
Jerusalem, 26

Kanata, Ontario, Canada, 76
Kiev, U.S.S.R., 185-186
Kingston, Ontario, 336

Lachine Canal, 334
La Petite Bourgogne, Montreal, Canada, 202-203, 217, 238
Lawrence Park, Toronto, Canada, 242
Leningrad (Petrograd), 22-23, 180, 185-186, 188, 376
London, England, 14, 16, 18, 21, 26, 54, 129, 273, 284, 293, 323, 339, 345, 375
Los Angeles, California, 37, 78, 273, 289
Luebeck, Germany, 21

Manchester, England, 345
Marseilles, France, 274, 318
Miami, Florida, 119

Montreal, Quebec, Canada, 12, 20, 30, 42, 57, 66-67, 77, 80-81, 119, 132-133, 138, 146, 151, 165, 198, 202-203, 217, 238, 264-271, 280, 283, 298, 302, 316-317, 334, 346, 369-370
Moscow, U.S.S.R., 20-21, 57-58, 130, 180, 185-186, 188, 327, 334, 376
Mulhouse, France, 256

Netherlands, 13, 159, 188
Neubuehl, Zürich, Switzerland, 206, 273
Nevsky Prospect, Leningrad, U.S.S.R., 23
New York, New York, 20-21, 27, 33, 39, 46, 59-61, 66, 115, 124, 239, 280, 284, 293, 316, 318, 323, 324, 336, 339, 344, 399
New Zealand, 164, 175, 259
Norwich, England, 262
Novgorod, U.S.S.R., 20, 22

Ontario, Canada, 132, 209-225
Ottawa, Ontario, Canada, 30, 73-78, 115, 166, 262, 346

Paris, France, 22, 26, 34, 129-130, 140, 281, 284, 293-294, 306, 307, 327, 337-339, 345, 375, 395
Peking, China, 18
Philadelphia, Pennsylvania, 12, 20, 25, 26, 33, 42, 118, 151, 198, 203, 239, 244, 249, 258, 280, 283, 336
Pisa, Italy, 21
Pittsburgh, Pennsylvania, 273
Pont Neuf, Paris, France, 22, 281
Port Credit, Ontario, Canada, 163
Port Hope, Ontario, Canada, 336
Portland, Oregon, 19
Potsdam, Germany, 34
Pruitt-Igo Project, St. Louis, Missouri, 274

Quebec, Quebec, Canada, 342
Queen Elizabeth Expressway, Toronto, Canada, 287
Queensway, Ottawa, Canada, 78

Radburn, New Jersey, 41
Randstad, Holland, 130, 188, 375
Regent Park South, Toronto, Canada, 244
Reston, Virginia, 398
Rio de Janeiro, Brazil, 384
Rome, Italy, 12, 20, 21, 36, 41, 65, 271, 279, 283, 293, 335, 337, 395
Rotterdam, Netherlands, 54, 263, 283, 318
Ruhr, Germany, 130-131, 310

St. Lawrence Seaway, 334
St. Louis, Missouri, 21, 274
St. Petersburg, U.S.S.R., 22-23
San Francisco, California, 338, 395
Santiago de Compostella, Spain, 334
Saskatoon, Saskatchewan, Canada, 166
Siberia, 130
Singapore, 84, 349, 362
South Africa, 164
Spadina Expressway, Toronto, Canada, 135, 312
Sri Lanka, 362
Stockholm, Sweden, 12, 13, 30, 132, 133, 137, 161, 166, 200, 275, 300, 370
Stockton-on-Tees, England, 198, 217, 237
Switzerland, 205, 206

Tapiola, Finland, 275
Tel Aviv, Israel, 188, 375
Tenochititlan, Mexico, 337
Tokaido Railroad, 342
Tokyo, Japan, 19, 117, 317, 327
Toronto, Ontario, Canada, 12, 19, 21, 26, 28-30, 67-68, 77, 81, 94-109, 119, 132-135, 146, 149, 156, 165, 173, 199, 201, 211, 229, 236, 239, 262, 273, 282, 285, 287, 290, 298, 302, 310, 336, 344-346, 349, 370. See also Toronto in Subject Index
Trans Canada Highway, 297, 312
Trefann Court, Toronto, Canada, 199
Tyre, Lebanon, 338

Ulm, Germany, 166
Union of Soviet Socialists Republics, 179-180, 184-186, 187

Vallingby, Stockholm, 13, 132, 133, 137, 161, 275
Vancouver, British Columbia, 81, 110-115, 171, 274, 280, 320, 337, 368
Venice, Italy, 12, 23, 25, 272, 294, 337
Versailles, France, 34
Via Emilia, Italy, 116
Vienna, Austria, 21, 327

Washington, D.C., 116, 142, 161, 239, 320, 323, 394
Waterloo County, Ontario, 173
Westend, Vancouver, Canada, 274
Windsor, Ontario, 342

Zürich, Switzerland, 206, 273
Zuyder Zee, Netherlands, 335